D1261247

THE AGE OF ARTHUR

THE AGE OF ARTHUR

A History of
the British Isles from 350 to 650

JOHN MORRIS
Senior Lecturer in History
University College London

Charles Scribner's Sons
New York

3 5 7 9 11 13 15 17 19 V/C 20 18 16 14 12 10 8 6 4 2

Printed in the United States of America
Library of Congress Catalog Card Number 72-11121
SBN 684-13313-X

To

C.E. STEVENS

who inspired

CONTENTS

PART TWO ANALYSIS

MAPS

INTRODUCTION

This book surveys the history of the British Isles between the end of Roman Britain and the birth of England and Wales. Its aim is to make that history manageable, like the history of other periods.

In the 420s, the government of Roman Britain enlisted Saxon, or English barbarians from Germany to strengthen their defences; but in the 440s the English rebelled. Half a century of bitter fighting destroyed the Roman economy and technology of Britain, but the British won the war, under the leadership of Arthur, who restored the forms of Roman imperial government. The empire of Arthur lasted for some twenty years and on his death fragmented into a large number of small independent successor states. The English were contained within substantial defined reservations until they rebelled for a second time, at the end of the sixth century. In a generation they subdued most of what is now England; thenceforth the independent native British were confined to the west, and were called Welsh, a word that in old English meant 'foreigners'.

The personality of Arthur is unknown and unknowable. But he was as real as Alfred the Great or William the Conqueror; and his impact upon future ages mattered as much, or more so. Enough evidence survives from the hundred years after his death to show that reality was remembered for three generations, before legend engulfed his memory. More is known of his achievement, of the causes of his sovereignty and of its consequences than of the man himself. His triumph was the last victory of western Rome; his short lived empire created the future nations of the English and the Welsh; and it was during his reign and under his authority that the Scots first came to Scotland. His victory and his defeat turned Roman Britain into Great Britain. His name overshadows his age.

Two centuries of war and of separate co-existence moulded a political society unlike that of Europe, where Roman and barbarian experience merged more easily. These centuries are a historical period in their own right, more than a transition or interlude between Rome and the Middle Ages. To be understood, a well-defined period needs a name, as clear in meaning as Roman, Norman or

Tudor. The fifth and sixth centuries in Britain are properly termed the Age of Arthur, for modern historical convention normally labels periods according to their principal rulers. In early medieval Europe it distinguishes Merovingian and Carolingian periods, so called after dynasties who took their names from individuals. The Carolingian age extends from the grandfather of Charles the Great to his grandchildren's time; but the substance of history does not turn upon the personal ancestry of rulers. Though he had no royal father and founded no dynasty, Arthur was the heir of the emperors before him, and the kings who followed knew themselves to be 'heirs of great Arthur'. He straddles two centuries, and names them as fitly as Charles the Great names the eighth and ninth centuries in Europe.

The Arthurian age is the starting point of future British history. Thereafter, Britain has comprised England, Wales and Scotland; previously, these three countries did not exist. Their later history is harder to understand if their formative years are overlooked; for nations, like people, tend to form habits in infancy that their adult years harden and modify. But the early history must be seen in its own context; if its evidence is superficially raked over in a search for the origins of later institutions, then it is as uninformative as an archaeological site plundered by treasure hunters.

These centuries have often been termed the 'Dark Ages'. They are not dark for lack of evidence. The quantity of evidence is immense and unusually complex, hard to understand. Therefore it has been neglected, abandoned to a small number of specialists, who have often been obliged to limit their studies to their own particular patch. The specialist in pagan English pottery or brooches is rarely conversant with the literature of early Ireland, with late Roman administration, with Welsh or Germanic law, with Italian theology or old Welsh poems, with the techniques of the farmer and the shipbuilder, or with a dozen other disciplines that must be brought together, and related to the history of Europe, if the age is to be understood.

No one can be master of all these trades. The historian must be content to be the pupil and interpreter of many of them. But he must do his best to bring them together, for the evidence seems obscure only because its modern study is inadequate and fragmented. The significance of excavated objects cannot be perceived until they can be related to the written record of the people who used them. Yet most of the texts are made up of half truths, for they are abstracts derived from lost originals, distorted by the ignorance or interest of their compilers. They await the kind of critical scrutiny that centuries of scholarship have lavished upon the texts of other periods. Because that work has not yet been undertaken the historian of the fifth and sixth centuries has special problems. He has no main 'reliable' narrative witness, like Tacitus or Bede, to justify him in dismissing other evidence as 'unreliable' or 'forged'. He must borrow from the techniques of the archaeologist, and must uncover a mass of separate detail, most of it encrusted and corroded by the distortion of later ages. He must clean off as much of the distortion as he can, try to discover what the original sources said and then relate their statements to one another, and to the rest of the evidence.

The aim is modest, and has been well expressed by Professor Ludwig Bieler.

> according to a widely accepted view, it is the historian's task to find out 'what actually happened'. . . . This, I believe, is impossible. The historian cannot do more than collect, assess and interpret evidence.

He has to sum up like a judge, and decide like a jury. He may not blankly refuse to decide, but he cannot proclaim certainty. He must give an informed opinion on what is probable and improbable, and return an open verdict when the balance of evidence suggests no probability. He may not insinuate like an advocate, whose plea that evidence falls short of absolute proof covertly invites his hearers to disbelieve the evidence. It is irrelevant for him to assert his personal belief or disbelief. There is a reason for every statement in every text, and for the place where every archaeological object was found. His business is to ferret out the reasons. He may conclude that an author lied or misunderstood; but falsehood must be demonstrated as carefully as accuracy, and may not be casually implied by labelling a statement 'dubious', without argument. But, unlike the verdict of the jury, his conclusion is constantly subject to appeal, and he must therefore clearly distinguish between what his evidence says and what he deduces from it, that others may easily correct his inferences in the light of new evidence and deeper understanding. If he fails to offer clear conclusions from the evidence he knows, he infects his readers with false beliefs and woolly notions; if he leaves no conclusion to correct, the importance of new evidence is easily missed. He must acknowledge his own sympathies as openly as a Tacitus or a Bede, for the historian who rashly pretends to be free of bias unconsciously surrenders to the superficial assumptions of his own day; and is therefore always misleading, and usually dull.

The evidence must first be collected. Most of the main texts are printed, but many are to be found only in large or specialist libraries. They cannot be studied unless they are assembled for constant reference and comparison; and this book could not have been written without the exceptional facilities generously provided by librarians, especially of University College London, and of the London Library, who permitted rare volumes to be retained on loan for years at a time. The difficulty of getting at the sources is one of the main reasons why the period is so poorly understood; for any historical study is lamed if it can only be undertaken by a few experts, whose judgement their readers cannot easily criticise. If the Arthurian period is to be studied seriously in the future, the first need is to make the sources accessible, no longer the secret lore of the learned. The first steps have been taken. The most important single texts, *Gildas*, *Nennius* and *Patrick*, will shortly be easily available, in text and translation, with comment; the rest of the main evidence is collected in my *Arthurian Sources*

(Phillimore 1973), where the separate texts of Annals, Genealogies, Saints' Lives and other sources are collated, and the scattered information about people, places and problems is assembled and assessed in detail. The study of this collected evidence prompts the conclusions here expressed, some of which are bound to seem abrupt and dogmatic until these publications appear.

The Age of Arthur interprets this evidence. It places most weight on contemporary statements, for in any age the contemporary cannot outrageously falsify the knowledge that he shares with his readers; for the same reason, texts written within living oral memory of the events they relate command respect. A modern writer may distort the actions and motives of contemporary individuals or distant peoples, but he could not assert that modern Britain is immune from war or ignorant of electric power; he might bamboozle an illiterate audience with a story that Napoleon fought Marlborough at Minden, but he could not pretend that Gladstone lived in the eighteenth century, for many men are still alive who know that Gladstone lived in their fathers' time. So when Gildas told his readers that theirs was an age of civil war and external peace, and that Vortigern and Ambrosius Aurelanius had lived in their fathers' time, he could not have done so if these matters of public knowledge were wholly untrue. But once the threshold of living memory is passed, after about a hundred years, the antiquity of a text is of small moment; many that were written a thousand years later follow their sources more closely than others written two or three hundred years after the event.

Interpretation rests upon bringing the evidence together, once the superficial deposit of later fancy has been removed, for it is no use discussing the meaning of the sources, until we know what they do and do not say, as exactly as we can. The history is narrated and described by bringing their separate statements together. Not much faith can be placed on a single statement by a single source; confidence grows when a number of independent sources each tell something of the same story. The proof of the pudding is in the eating. The evidence hangs together, and tells its own story. Innumerable separate details combine into a plain and credible tale, more coherent than any that an ingenious later historian could devise.

The tale is plain. But any account that is built up from a mass of small items of evidence seems complex at first sight. It is doubly difficult to explain the age of Arthur simply, for most of the names are unfamiliar. The historians of later periods, whose kings are conveniently numbered, may assume that their readers know that Henry VII reigned before Henry VIII; and many well known tales make it clear that Elizabeth ruled after and not before the Henries. But in the fifth and sixth centuries even the names of persons of comparable importance are known only to specialists, and their relation to each other in time and place is often clouded, compelling examination of the evidence. In order that the unfamiliar names, dates and events may be more easily understood, a short Summary of Events and a Table of Dates is provided on pages 512 ff.

The story that the sources tell raised a difficulty that was not at first foreseen. It had been intended to start from the relatively firm ground of the late Roman Empire, and to end in the middle of the seventh century, whose events Bede recorded within living memory. But it soon became apparent that much that has been written in modern times about the seventh and eighth centuries jars awkwardly against the earlier evidence. The reason is evident. Many of those who studied the early English were well acquainted with later medieval history, and looked back from the standpoint of Norman or Plantagenet England. But the processes of history move forward in time; men are influenced by the experience of their forebears, but they know nothing of their descendants' problems; and history looks different when viewed the right way up. It has therefore been necessary to discuss some later problems, where misconceptions about the Arthurian period and its immediate sequel have caused misunderstanding. This discussion does not set out to contradict what others have written; rather, it deals with different questions, for much that looked puzzling from an eleventh-century standpoint seems no problem at all in the context of the sixth century, while some of the assumptions that seemed natural to historians of the middle ages prove alien to thinking of earlier ages. It has also been necessary to discuss some aspects of barbarian and medieval European history that have not been systematically explored; and therefore to disregard some modern notions entertained about them. Such differences of approach do not assert greater wisdom or understanding; they are the result of fortunate chances that have given me the opportunity to read and sift more varied sources than most other individuals.

It has only recently become possible to attempt an overall history of the Arthurian age, thanks to a number of important publications that have pulled together several sections of the evidence. They rest upon much detailed work, whose conclusions cannot always be discussed within the limits of this book. It has proved necessary to stick to the principle expressed by H.M. and N.K. Chadwick in the preface to their *Growth of Literature:*

> if we had read more widely, we would not have completed this book . . . which might have been the better course. The amount of time at our disposal is limited; we have preferred to give as much of it as possible to the primary authorities.

It is therefore necessary to apologise to the very many scholars whose work is not here acknowledged, and has often not been adequately assessed. It is also impossible to acknowledge the many scholars whose kind advice has been freely offered on many details; my expressed gratitude must be limited to those whose unfailing patience my many queries have most heartily exploited, notably Professor Kenneth Jackson and Professor Idris Foster; Mr J.M.Dodgson and Professor D.M.Wilson; and Professor Christopher Hawkes; to Michael Gullick, who drew the maps to my specification, with limitless patience; and to Dr John

Wilkes, Dr Ann Ward and Miss Vivienne Menkes, who have kindly read and commented upon the typescript. None of them of course bear any responsibility for the way in which their advice has been treated. I am also grateful to the indulgence of the publisher, since the mass of unfamiliar names and concepts has made it necessary to use capitals, figures and punctuation for clarity and emphasis, in disregard of convention; and I am particularly indebted to the advice and help of Julian Shuckburgh and Sue Phillpott.

The interpretation here given of the Arthurian Age can be no more than a preliminary attempt to open up questions, and to make it easier for future specialist studies to relate their conclusions to a wider context. The book is therefore published in the confident expectation that many of its conclusions will soon be modified or corrected. It will have served its purpose if it makes such correction possible. It would be kind if readers who detect figure mistakes or errors of fact, in the text or the notes, would notify the author, via the publisher.

John Morris

CHAPTER ONE

BRITAIN IN 350

In 350 Britain had been Roman for more than three hundred years. The lives and thoughts of her people were shaped and bounded by an economy common to the whole Roman empire; their public events were determined by imperial politics, their administration was controlled by men appointed in Italy. The empire still seemed eternal, an unquestioned guarantee of lasting peace. War was virtually confined to the frontiers, while behind them men knew of it only by hearsay. Within the Roman peace Britain had been particularly fortunate; barbarians might assault the northern forts or raid the coasts, but in the interior only one armed conflict is recorded in ten generations.

Much had changed in centuries of peace. Long ago, in the forgotten past, the British had been resentful natives ruled by foreign Romans. But for one hundred and forty years all freeborn provincials had been full Roman citizens, and five generations had made a reality of citizenship. Social difference divided the gentleman from the labourer, but each was as Roman as his counterpart in Italy or Africa or elsewhere. Apart from a handful of visitors, official or private, from other provinces, all the Romans in Britain were British, all the British Roman. The fourth-century Londoner was as much a Roman as the modern Londoner is English; to contrast 'Britons' with 'Romans' in the fourth century is as meaningless as to contrast modern Kentishmen with Englishmen.

Yet one immense difference distinguishes Roman and modern concepts of statehood. The Englishman confronts a German, a Frenchman, a Russian, who shares his civilisation, but obeys a separate national government. No comparable foreign state inflamed the patriotic sentiments of the Roman. Except in distant Persia, the frontier was the limit of civilisation, and the only foreigners were bloodthirsty savages whose law was the custom of their kin, or the command of warrior chiefs who drank deep in timber halls. The enemies of Britain, the Picts across the Forth and Clyde, the Scots of Ireland, the Franks and Saxons of the Low Countries, were barbarians like other foreigners, eager to burst upon the tempting wealth of Rome, plundering and killing poor and rich alike. In the face of the enemy, the common bond that linked Roman to Roman mattered more than the tensions which sundered one class or region from another. Half a century later, the poet Claudian sang of Rome who

Took the conquered to her bosom,
Made mankind a single family,
Mother, not mistress, of the nations,
Turning her subjects to citizens,
Conquering far-off lands a second time
By the bond of affection.

His orthodox enthusiasm was more than the propaganda of a government apologist. The event justified him, for, as the empire collapsed, none of its subject peoples took the opportunity to proclaim freedom from Rome; on the contrary, even the most radical rebels strove for a government better able to prolong its protective authority.

The common bond of Rome united unlike worlds, now separately ruled by two sons of the great Constantine. From his father's new city of Constantinople, Constantius reigned over the Greek-speaking provinces of the eastern mediterranean, whose magnates controlled three-quarters of the wealth of the empire and whose literate urban civilisation was older than Rome. The poorer western provinces obeyed his brother Constans. There, Roman conquest had first brought civilisation and towns, whose self-evident superiority had wiped out all but the haziest memories of the illiterate barbarian past.

In Britain and northern Gaul, urban civilisation had matured slowly. At first, government initiative had prompted the foundation of a few large towns, at once the symbol and the means of alien rule, each of them the capital of a native *civitas*, a people organised as a state. Each was the seat of a native administration, chosen by and from the native aristocracy, governing their fellow citizens under the remote but powerful supervision of the imperial governor. Recently, the word *civitas*, state, had shifted its meaning, to denote the physical city, the master and the natural head of all the urban and rural districts within its territory, termed *vici* and *pagi*. But the concentration of political authority matched a devolution of the economy. In the early empire, the roads between the towns had been furnished with small post-stations, each equipped with horses, carriages and waggons for the service of the government; but by the fourth century the majority of these stations had developed into thriving market towns, civil *vici* within their *civitas*.

In the early empire Britain had been polarised between a handful of imposing towns and a mass of farms and hamlets. Their pre-Roman economy was modified by the acquisition of commercial pottery, and presumably of more perishable manufactures; by a sprinkle of silver and copper coins, signs of produce sold on the market; and by corn-drying ovens, evidently constructed to service the same market. A few fortunate farmers, for the most part living within a mile or two of a town and a few hundred yards of a main road, prospered enough to build themselves solid, oblong stone-footed houses, with six or eight rooms on the ground floor; but they are rare exceptions beside the multitude of homesteads whose only archaeological trace is a trayful of potsherds, a few coins, or the post-holes of a timber cottage, often surrounded by tiny subdivided fields, the witness of peasant holdings still partitioned among the farmer's children.

In the fourth century, the solid farms are more numerous, the older ones enlarged and better appointed, save in a few coastal areas exposed to pirate raids, notably in Norfolk and the west Sussex plain. But the startling innovation is the sudden appearance, from about the beginning of the century, of great country mansions, normally enclosing three sides of a square some 150 feet to 200 feet long, containing anything from thirty to seventy ground-floor rooms, elaborately furnished with patterned mosaics, wall-paintings, heated rooms. Commonest in the Cotswold country, these houses are as commodious as their modern equivalents, Compton Wynyates, Hatfield House and the like, and one or two challenge comparison with Blenheim Palace. They are the homes of a nobility who lived more amply than any of their successors before the days of the Tudors, if not of the Georges.

Great men lived splendidly throughout the empire, but the scale and speed of recent prosperity was peculiar to Britain. Ninety years before, about the 260s, the continental frontiers had suddenly disintegrated, weakened by internal discord and assailed by barbarians grown more confident. Goths and Persians, Nubians and Moors had overrun the provinces they bordered, and the most terrible of all German invasions across the Rhine had destroyed the unwalled cities of Gaul. Only Italy and Britain escaped prolonged devastation. But the enemy were raiders who sought plunder to carry home; they were not yet invaders intent on settlement, and they therefore withdrew before a succession of strong military governments. The old frontiers were restored; but the wasted lands of northern Gaul recovered slowly, if at all. Henceforth the armies of the Rhine, whose needs they had hitherto supplied, were compelled to look to the cornlands and pastures of Britain for a substantial part of their supplies. The new-found prosperity of British agriculture is due, at least in part, to the sufferings of Gaul.

The fourth-century noblemen of Britain are voiceless and nameless. Whatever they wrote or did or said is unremembered. No document survives to illustrate their tastes and attitudes or to record their actions. Even their names are unknown. Nothing remains but the excavated ruins of their villas, set beside the archaeological traces of their peasants and their towns. Yet these material fragments describe a secure and comfortable aristocracy little different from their peers in Gaul. The nobility of Gaul lived in similar houses in the same economy, and something of their writing, their thinking and their action, described in their own words, has survived. The texture of their lives is plainly set forth in the easy verses of Ausonius, a fourth-century gentleman of Bordeaux upon whom chance thrust high office and great wealth. His favourite residence remained his ancestral estate of 1,000 acres, situated a few miles upstream from the city, whither

The clear river's tidal flow
Takes me by boat from home,
And brings me home again. . . .
Not far from town I live,
Yet not hard by. . . .
I change about,
And get the best of town
And country, turn by turn.

He was not only a landed gentleman, passing a part of the season in town; he was Professor of Latin in the University of Bordeaux, like his uncle before him. His father studied medicine and practised as a doctor, attending the poor without fee; he growled that though he sat on the local council, as befitted his rank, he never ran for public office, since he could not abide 'political agitation, party intrigue, lawsuits and scandal'. These were men whose code enjoined a paternal responsibility towards their social inferiors, and a duty of public service to the city of their birth and to the empire.

The rise of Ausonius and the proliferation of country mansions in Britain were symptoms of a general trend, the concentration of property in the hands of fewer and mightier magnates, at the expense of the poor and middling freeholders. Ausonius managed the numerous estates on which he did not live through his inefficient agent Philo,

The image of his class,
Grey, shockhaired, unkempt,
A blustering bully . . .
Visiting peasants, farms, towns and villages.

Increasingly, the great men passed the crippling burden of taxation on to the poor, and the Treasury found it cheaper to acquiesce. The law kept pace with economic change, reinforcing the authority of the *dominus*, master, over his dependents, distinguishing between *honestiores*, gentlemen, whom it condemned to fines, exile or execution by the sword, and *humiliores*, small freeholders, tenants, peasants, who expiated the same offences by torture, mutilation or burning at the stake. Starved by excessive taxation, bullied by blustering agents, denied justice in a landlord's court, the poor of farm, town and village were impelled to standing discontent and occasional rebellion.

The territorial magnates of the fourth century were powerful masters in their own districts, but they no longer dominated the central government. The old empire had been governed by the aristocracy of Italy, and of the Latin provinces of the western mediterranean coasts; and they had maintained a thinly spread frontier army on a shoestring budget. It was a necessary evil, but its costs were kept down because it was a static army largely financed by local supply. The new army was larger; the disasters of the mid-third century compelled it to maintain considerable mobile reserves, whose supply cost more. The new government was dominated by military men, who looked upon civilian landowners as the army's paymasters, and resented their selfish reluctance to pay for the army that protected their wealth. To constrain them to pay adequate taxes the government developed its bureaucracy, ill-paid, corrupt and ever-expanding. Its operations engulfed most of the finances and much of the jurisdiction that local landowners had once controlled through city councils. Fourth-century taxation assessed estates by the *caput*, head, and the *iugum*, yoke, that commonly measured the capacity of land; but the demands of revenue officials were more easily evaded by magnates than by modest landowners or town councillors.

The political administration was streamlined into an ordered hierarchy of small provinces, subject to four Praetorian Prefects, whose vice-prefects, or Vicars, each headed a *diocese* of several provinces. The four provinces of Britain, their capitals probably Cirencester, London, Lincoln and York, together constituted a single diocese within the prefecture of the Gauls. But the Vicars and the Provincial Governors were usually modest gentlemen whose tenure lasted one or two years; and they were exposed to the threats and bribes of provincial notables, who were often men of higher standing and greater political influence. Military commanders were as vulnerable. The *Magister Militum*, commander-in-chief, in control of a large field army and a variety of static frontier garrisons, was himself a man of might, high enough in rank to fear none but the emperor; but his subordinate officers were normally no more eminent than the civilian governors. In Britain, they were the Count of the Coast, later termed the Saxon Shore, who commanded a series of forts from Portsmouth to the Wash, and the *Dux Britanniarum*, responsible at York for the garrisons that held the northern frontier and policed the Pennines.

The geography of Britain gave the chance of somewhat greater independence to some of the governors and generals, for the towns, the great houses and the prosperous farms were virtually confined to the lowland south and east. Geologically, Britain is divided by a belt of limestone that snakes northwards from Lyme Regis by way of the Cotswolds, to the east of the Avon, the Trent and the Vale of York, to meet the sea again above Scarborough. It separates the fertile open lowland to the south and east from the heavier soils beyond. The north-west midlands are also low lying; and though all the lowland is interspersed with areas of heavy clay, that were often not broken to the plough before the later middle ages, it is free from natural obstacles, save for forests through which roads might easily be driven. It is therefore easily conquered, and as easily absorbs the civilisation of the conqueror. Beyond lie the rougher and poorer highland masses, the Pennines, the Welsh mountains, and the south-western moorlands of Exmoor, Dartmoor and Bodmin Moor. These three highland regions are separated from one another by the low-lying but less rewarding soils of Staffordshire and Cheshire, and by the rich lands of the Severn estuary.

These two gaps constitute the military keys to Britain in all ages. There the Roman armies constructed the fortresses of Chester and Wroxeter, of Gloucester and Caerleon; there were fought the decisive battles of the later English conquest, at Chester, and at Dyrham in Gloucestershire; there the Norman kings placed their marcher earldoms, and learnt from experience that the charge of Gloucester and Chester was most wisely entrusted to the king or his brother. Once these regions were secured, the sundered highlands found it hard to co-ordinate attack upon the lowlands, more natural to fight their battles on their own, easy to fight one another; for their hills enclose a multitude of valleys, whose population readily finds cause of dispute with its nearest neighbours. Control of the Severn and Dee estuaries has always secured the mastery of Britain. The Belgae and the Scandinavians failed to hold them or Britain; the armies of Parliament retained them in 1643 and 1644 and split the king's forces; and if Spanish, French or German armies had made good their landing, Chester and Gloucester would have become their necessary objectives, for the geography of Britain at all times concentrates political power in the lowlands, if the lowlands can hold their borders.

The geography of Britain also sharply separated the military from the civil power. Towns and villas, noblemen and their dependants were confined to the lowlands and the Severn shores. The backward conservative valleys of the Pennines, the Welsh mountains and the western moors supported no powerful landed nobility, and their only towns were those that grew around the army's forts. These differences also affected the social structure of Roman Britain. Throughout the empire the peasantry bore the double burden of rent and taxation that maintained the armies, the landowners and the administration. In the fourth century government and defence cost more, and the larger share of the burden fell upon the peasant. In many provinces much of the rural population was almost literally starved, paying up to five sixths of its produce in rent

---

Map 1

OLD ROCKS Palaeozoic and earlier

SANDSTONES Triassic

LIASSIC AND RHAETIC Jurassic

OOLITIC LIMESTONE Jurassic

OXFORD AND KIMMERIDGE CLAYS

WEALDEN BEDS

CHALK with greensand and gault

TERTIARY BEDS

SCATTERED DRIFT DEPOSITS ON CHALK

MAP I THE SHAPE AND SOILS OF BRITAIN

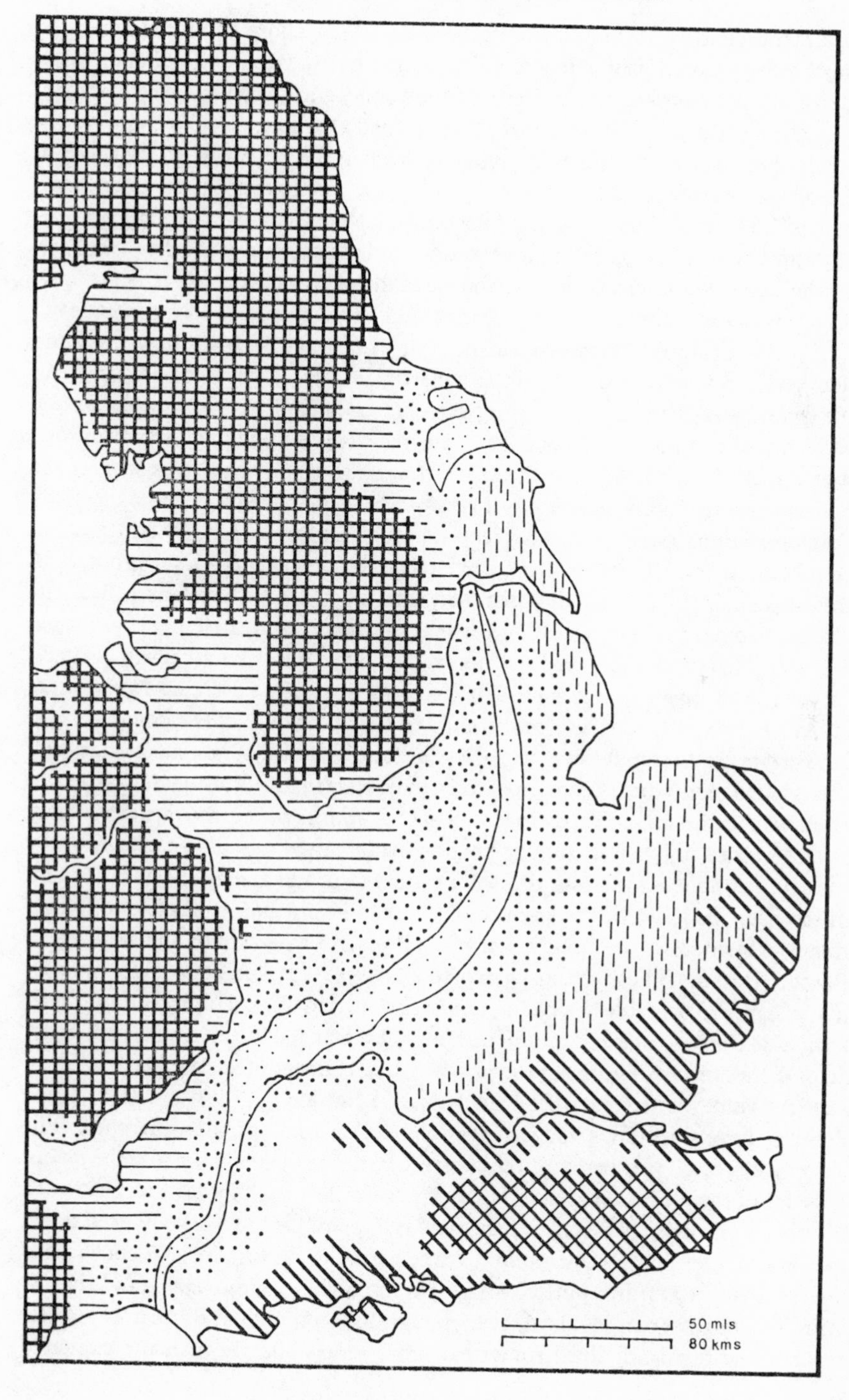

and tax, dwindling in numbers because it could not afford to rear children. In much of the empire it was too cowed to resist, but in parts of Gaul and Spain, above all in Armorica, the modern Brittany, peasant discontent was confident enough to break into the sustained revolt termed *Bacauda*.

The peasants of Britain may not have been quite so badly off as those of Europe. The evidence is not easy to assess, for the economy of the continent must be studied mainly through written documents, the economy of Britain principally through archaeological discovery, and unlike evidence is hard to compare. In the excavated towns of Britain the standard of physical comfort is not low; money was abundant and isolated farms could afford plenty of pottery. Some old farmsteads equipped themselves in the fourth century with window glass and doorkeys, evidence at least of property worth stealing. A two-roomed cottage in the grounds of the country house of Hambleden, near Henley, was plainly the residence of a quite poor dependant of the mansion, but one room was furnished with a tiled floor, the other with central heating. Several other sites suggest the homes of cultivators who lived well above subsistence level.

It also seems possible that society was more integrated in Britain than in Europe. The fourth century was an age of massive concentration of property in the ownership of a small number of great magnates. The Church and the Treasury, cities and individuals owned many different estates; one senator owned a dozen villas in Italy alone, another owned estates in various parts of Italy, Sicily, Africa, Spain and Britain. They were in the main sustained by the rents of tenants, whose labour also contributed to the cultivation of the home farm on each estate; agricultural slaves were few, but the pressure of famine and taxation constrained many small proprietors to become the tenants of magnates. When an estate changed hands, the rents of its tenants continued, but the owner of many estates needed only a few country houses; many lapsed into disrepair when they passed to absentee owners. A few were turned to productive use; but in Britain, in the great majority of the large rural houses, the splendidly appointed living-rooms remained in the occupation of well-to-do owners until the last age of Roman Britain. Those whose living-rooms were adapted to a more modest living standard, suitable to a bailiff, or were converted to agricultural or industrial use, as at Darenth in Kent or at Totternhoe by Dunstable, are a small minority. It is therefore possible that property was less concentrated, the proportion of resident landowners somewhat higher than in Europe.

Several considerations suggest possible explanations of the difference. The sharply increased prosperity of the fourth-century lowlands must to some extent have offset the pressure of rent and tax; there was less need for landowners to sell out to greater men, and some of the new riches are likely to have filtered down to some of the poorer cultivators. The geography of Britain also encouraged among them a sturdier outlook. The poorer highlands did not know the institutions of the great landlord, rich enough to build a villa. By reason of their poverty the highlands lived somewhat more independently than the exploited tenants of most of the empire. It is unlikely that their outlook was wholly bounded by the hills; possible that it enabled the lowlanders as well to withstand some of the grosser extortions that peasants elsewhere could not escape.

Fourth-century Britain differed from Europe and from its own past. In contrast to the polarised economy of the early empire, mid fourth-century Britain was an integrated community, graded from village and market town to local capital, from peasant croft through considerable farm to palatial mansion; it was dominated by a small aristocracy, based on the land, but still controlling the towns, its leaders the social equals or superiors of the governors and generals appointed by the imperial government. It was an orderly, secure society, where each man kept his place as clearly as in eighteenth-century England. The great men of Roman York or Cirencester would have been content to accept with little change the idealised panegyric that Ausonius of Bordeaux addressed to the citizens of Trier, the chief city of Belgic Gaul,

> Let me recall your peaceful farmers,
> Your skilful lawyers and your compelling orators,
> High champions of the accused.
>
> Let me recall the men your Council honoured,
> Your chief citizens, your own senators,
> The men your schools have trained in eloquence
> To match Quintilian himself;
>
> The men who rule their own towns,
> And keep the Bench unstained
> By the executioner's axe;
>
> The Vicars you have sent to govern Italy
> Or the British of the north,
> Or Rome itself, the world's capital,
> Its senate and its people.

CHAPTER TWO

THE ENDING OF THE WESTERN EMPIRE

Rebellion 350–353

In January 350, a military conspiracy in Gaul proclaimed Magnentius emperor. He was a senior officer, probably of British birth, son of a German settled in the empire by Constantine. Gaul, Italy, Africa, Spain and Britain quickly accepted his authority, and the high aristocracy welcomed him in Rome, where he married a daughter of one of the great senatorial families, Justina. Constans, the young emperor of the west, was soon killed, and his brother Constantius instigated the Germans of the Rhineland to attack and delay Magnentius while he assembled his own forces. The Germans were disastrously successful. For several years the Alamanni 'destroyed many wealthy cities and . . . overran the Gauls at will without serious opposition'; Strassburg, Wurms and Mainz fell, while enemy forces sporadically besieged Sens, Autun and other towns. Magnentius enlisted Frank and Saxon allies, but the main body of the Franks took the opportunity to seize Cologne and establish permanent homes on the left bank of the lower Rhine; Lyon itself, the chief town of central and northern Gaul, was attacked by *Laeti* and *Gentiles*, mixed German peoples who had been settled a generation or two earlier within the empire, in the double capacity of tied peasants and local militia. Constantius advanced slowly, carefully ensuring the loyalty of the Danube armies, and defeated Magnentius at Mursa, in the northern Balkans, by the Danube. The casualties were rated at something like a tenth of the whole Roman army. Constantius recovered Gaul in 353, but the whole of the Roman Rhineland was in the occupation of unsubdued barbarians for several years more.

The character of the new ruler of the west was depressing. Numerous contemporaries outline the same mournful portrait of a timorous bigot. Magnentius was a forceful commander, but Constantius at Mursa

> stayed away in a church outside the town. . . . The bishop, Valens . . . was the first to tell the frightened emperor that the enemy had fled. When Constantius enquired for the messenger, Valens replied that he was an angel. The credulous emperor believed him, attributing his victory to the merit of the bishop rather than to the valour of his troops.

The rational historian Sulpicius Severus despised the superstitious emperor;

but rationality was passing into eclipse, for Constantius' credulity foreshadowed the beliefs of the centuries ahead, to whom divine intervention was the natural explanation of human success and human failure.

Constantius' first concern was with precautionary vengeance, especially concentrated upon the nobility of Britain. Their sufferings are related by the contemporary historian Ammian, a serving army officer, whose disconsolate narrative is our principal source for the history of the next twenty-five years. The surviving portion of his work begins with the year 353, and his opening words on the west describe Constantius' inquisition, whose first named victim was a count Gerontius. The emperor's

> weak and narrow mind concluded that everything was directed against his safety.... The bloody flattery of courtiers enflamed the emperor's vain and angry suspicions....
>
> Chief among the flatterers was the Secretary Paul.... This viper ... was sent to Britain to arrest some officers who had dared to conspire with Magnentius. Arbitrarily extending his commission, he flooded over the fortunes of many men, ... framing accusations in contempt of truth.
>
> Martinus, then Vicar of the Britains ... repeatedly requested the release of the innocent ... When ... Paul ... threatened to arrest him and his staff ... Martinus, in alarm, drew his own sword on Paul, ... but failed to kill him, and therefore drove it into his own side. By that disgraceful death died a most just ruler.
>
> The bloody Paul returned to Constantius with a train of wretched filthy prisoners, for whom the racks, the hooks and other instruments of torture were made ready. Many lost their property, others were exiled, some executed. It is not easy to recollect an occasion under Constantius when a man was acquitted, though the accusation against him was but a whisper.

The punishment of Britain was exceptional; a convenient nursery of earlier and later rebellions, the island had doubtless sheltered the nucleus of the conspiracy. The victims have left some slight archaeological trace. An unusual number of coin hoards of this date are distributed all over the lowlands, often near villas. They look like the property of men deprived by the Secretary Paul of lands and liberty, who never came home to recover their money or disclose its whereabouts. Much of the confiscated property, whether retained by the crown, or sold, or granted to the favoured, passed to absentee owners. The revolt of Magnentius had decimated the Roman army and wasted Gaul; it also wounded the expanding aristocracy of Britain. The conspirators had intended to replace a weak and silly prince with an able general; their costly failure was a prelude to the disasters of the next half-century, that led public sentiment to a hopeless contempt for the enfeebled state.

Christian Dissent 350–361

As men began to lose respect for the state, they transferred their hopes to religion; and for the rest of the century, religious conflict mattered more and more in the political life of the Roman world. In the end, Christianity was to carry all before it, but its permanent triumph was by no means assured in 350. The Christian religion was rooted in the Greek east, and was strongest among the urban poor. Early experience left an imprint upon Christian thought that later theology was never able to eradicate; orthodox teaching long emphasised that salvation is the easy prerogative of the poor and lowly, that wealth and property are by definition evil, that the rich man is a prisoner of sin. Early in the second century, accepted apostolic teaching forbade the Christian to live like those who do not earn their sustenance 'by their own toil and sweat, but live by the unrighteous exploitation of other men's labour'; a generation later, a Christian leader in Rome, where rich converts were most numerous, pleaded that the rich man, though admittedly evil and unprofitable, might nonetheless be of some service to the virtuous Christian poor, just as the barren elm supports the useful vine. Even at the end of the century, Irenaeus, then the acknowledged spokesman of orthodoxy, asked '*Unde possessio*?' 'What is the origin of property?', and replied that it stemmed from the Mammon of Iniquity and was always the product of avarice and injustice.

From about the year 200 Christianity had begun to attract men of wealth and substance and to make its first impact upon natives of the Latin west, in Italy and Africa; but in Gaul and Britain, Christians remained few and insignificant. Government persecution, from 250 onward, failed to break the Christians, and its failure made them stronger in lands where they were already known; in a world demoralised by submission to authority, a faith that men held dearer than life commanded respect, and the Christians rightly claimed that every martyr made ten converts. Yet the Christians were ill-prepared for premature success. In 312 civil war made Constantine emperor of the west. As men realised that the new ruler was a devout Christian, bishops were bewildered by sudden promotion from the status of furtive sectaries to that of influential government advisers, and veteran confessors mistrusted the mass of new converts who embraced the emperor's religion. The body of simple Christians was confused, for the rival partisans of innumerable discords within the empire, social, regional and political, all learned to argue in a Christian idiom, and to discover that some older trend in Christian thought served their interest.

Confusion was worst in the east, where Christians were strongest. In the west, Christians were by now numerous in Africa and parts of Italy; the major cities of Provence had their bishops, as had the Rhineland towns, where government offices and field army units were plentiful. But in the rest of Gaul, no more than nine Christian communities are known to have existed before Constantine. The new faith first appeared in the west as a government religion, attractive to men of substance who sought government favour; but it was still weak in ordinary towns, non-existent in the countryside. It did not win the hearts of the people until later, when religious controversy united the Gauls against alien government and turned the church into a champion of the subject against unjust authority.

The controversy that overshadowed all others took its name from Arius, a priest of Alexandria who revived an ancient heresy in a new form. Plebeian Christians had for centuries clung to their faith in the God who died the death of a common criminal, the 'stumbling block to the Gentiles'. Arianism held that God the Father was of a similar, not the same, substance to God the Son, who died, and was by implication superior. The dispute deeply divided the churches when Constantine mastered the eastern provinces in 324. Like his predecessors, he believed that to escape the anger of heaven the Roman people must achieve unity in belief; unlike them, he sought unity under the Christian God. When the Christians divided, he strove for unity, and his first important initiative as emperor of the east, in 325, was to convene the first world conference of Christians at Nicaea, near the future Constantinople, where Europe and Asia meet.

In practice, the Arians proved somewhat more tractable than their orthodox opponents, and found a firm champion in the new eastern emperor, Constantius, in 337. His brother Constans therefore championed the orthodox, and when Constantius exiled the recalcitrant catholic leader Athanasius, Constans threatened war if he were not reinstated. Constantius yielded, but when he conquered the west in 353, he resolved to enforce unity behind the Arian creed. The weaker Latin Christians seemed to have little chance against the all-powerful emperor; but they withstood him, and thereby began to earn public sympathy, for their resistance voiced the resentment of the west against a Greek tyrant. At first, the emperor's energy won ground; the pliant were rewarded, and the obstinate were exiled, so that prudent men, though they might respect the integrity of the victims, learned to avoid their fate. In 359 the emperor was ready for a general assault.

The sequel is described by the contemporary Gallic historian Sulpicius Severus. The emperor summoned the western bishops to meet at Rimini, and promised the consulate to the prefect Taurus if he engineered unanimous agreement. Four hundred bishops assembled, and the emperor ordered that their expenses should be defrayed by the Treasury. The bishops of Gaul and Britain rejected the offer. But

> three of the British bishops, whose means were small, accepted the state allowance, rejecting the collections made for them, arguing that it was more Christian to be a burden upon the state than upon individuals. . . . Our bishop Gavidius called them pig-headed, but my own view is quite the opposite.

At first the Arians numbered no more than eighty, one-fifth of the whole. But the orthodox were induced to send a delegation to Constantinople, who brought back a statement 'couched in dubious wording, that expressed the catholic discipline with a heretical undertone'. The Congress was 'dismayed and confused', for 'protracted sessions had overcome their resolution'. The weaker gave in, and 'when the tide turned it became a torrent'. The prefect warned that they had been cooped up seven months in the city, and that once winter set in in earnest, they had no hope of getting home across the Alps. In the end, all but fifteen yielded, and the obstinate minority were exiled and deposed, so that formal unanimity was achieved. The minority seem to have included the bishop of London, Augurius.

Within a year, the resolution that had been secured by so much degrading government intrigue was a dead letter. Under the leadership of Bishop Hilary of Poitiers the Christian communities of Gaul refused to endorse it, and excommunicated the few determined Arians in their midst. Their temerity was vindicated when Constantius ceased to rule Gaul soon after. Non-Christians looked with distasteful wonder upon the obscure and sordid wrangles of the Christians; but the churches of Gaul for the first time appeared in a new light, as a force that was independent of government, and able to defy it with impunity. From its early years the church of Gaul and Britain was able to voice and organise the protest of the resentful subject.

Imperial Recovery 361–375

The strength of the Christians did not mature overnight. The wretched dispute of Rimini made few converts; but it brought no benefit to the government. An emperor who was at pains to manipulate conference votes in order to win the nominal approval of small conventicles of his humbler subjects earned the contempt of nobleman and plebeian, pagan and Christian; and seemed to mock the memory of bygone rulers, whose edicts men had accepted without question. Constantius' timid tyranny, the ferocity of his vengeance, and the upstart power of his low-born Greek administrators, aroused angry resentment. It soon found a leader. When he returned to the east, Constantius installed his young nephew Julian as ruler of Gaul. The inexperienced university student proved himself a brilliant and inspiring general; a couple of vigorous campaigns subdued the Franks and Alamanni, who had overrun the Roman Rhineland with the connivance of Constantius, and Julian restored the old frontier. At home, his drastic reform of the corrupt revenue departments delighted the commons and offended the bureaucracy.

Julian won golden opinions, but Constantius rightly saw his dazzling victories and soaring popularity as a threat, and sought to forestall it by posting his crack regiments to the east, early in 360. The troops feared to leave their homes exposed to German invaders, and proclaimed the unwilling Julian emperor. The armies of east and west again left their frontiers to fight each other, threatening a repetition of the disaster of Mursa. It was averted by the timely death of Constantius, which enabled his army to accept the rule of Julian.

The new emperor was an intellectual sickened by the sordid Arian dispute; he sought to rival both Christian factions with an esoteric pagan priesthood, hastily erected in pale imitation of the Christian hierarchy. In the west, and particularly in Britain, governors and loyal towns repaired derelict temples and founded new ones; but the sickness of the old Gods was mortal, and the revival, unconvincing even to its pagan supporters, disappeared on the death of its author, who was cut down by an unknown hand in Mesopotamia in 363. In his stead, the Army Council elevated a senior officer of unobtrusive Catholic orthodoxy, and on his speedy death replaced him with a like-minded colleague.

Valentinian let religion alone; resigning the theological east to his undistinguished brother Valens, he campaigned energetically in the west, and covered his European frontier with massive defences, reinforced by heavy fortifications of the interior towns. In the course of his operations, a serious incursion on the frontiers of Britain was reported; it was an irritant distraction, repeating similar raids in 360 and 364 when the emperor detached a senior general with four of the field army's crack regiments to spend some months in Britain. In 367

> a barbarian alliance brought Britain to her knees; Nectaridus, Count of the Coastal Defence, was killed, the general Fullofaudes ambushed . . . the Picts plundered at will, as did the warlike Attacotti and the Irish. . . . The Franks, and their Saxon neighbours, raided the Gallic coast, breaking in where they could.

Valentinian despatched Count Theodosius with a scratch force, soon reinforced, as in 360, with four crack regiments. He marched from Richborough to 'London, an old town later called Augusta', splitting his force into small detachments to round up bands of enemy plunderers. Next spring, he

> bravely and energetically set out from Augusta, anciently styled London, with an army raised by his skilful diligence, bringing maximum help to the beaten and discomfited British. Dispersing various peoples whom an insolence bred of impunity had emboldened to attack the Romans, he thoroughly restored the damaged towns and forts, founded long ago to keep the peace.

The invasion of 367 seems a problem; the considerable space that Ammian allots it would seem to argue an exceptionally heavy blow, that should have shown clear archaeological trace. Earlier and later disasters have left a grim trail of burnt buildings, unburied skeletons, unreclaimed coin hoards; but, though generations of excavators have tried to relate their discoveries to Ammian's story, there is very little evidence of any widespread destruction in lowland Britain in the 360s. One or two country houses seem to have been abandoned at about this time, but hundreds lived on intact, often for many years more; much of the London region declined in the later fourth century, but the cause is more likely to have been flood than fire, the work of nature rather than of barbarians. The prominence that Ammian gives to the exploits of Count Theodosius has a simpler explanation; Theodosius' son was emperor when Ammian wrote. The dead-pan flattery that monarchy commands in any age prompted the historian to devote many paragraphs to the triumph of the emperor's father, but the crisis that made Julian detach an equal force in 360 might be dismissed in a couple of lines, for its commander had less illustrious children.

Obligation to a patron might distort Ammian's emphasis, but not his facts; for he is a sober and scrupulous reporter, second only to Tacitus in the canon of Roman historians. The field army that Valentinian detached arrived in time to save the south; for, though the Count of the Coast was killed, the enemy broke in only 'where they could', in numbers few enough to be rounded up by 'small detachments'. Franks and Saxons were not mentioned in the invasion of 360, and their effort in Britain in 367 was modest, a minor enterprise when compared with the 'multitude of Saxons' whom Valentinian with difficulty repulsed on the lower Rhine in 370. The nature of their intervention is to be inferred from Ammian's incidental mention of a 'barbarian alliance'. The alliance is echoed in the historical tradition of the Irish, who held that about this time their High King married a Saxon wife, mother to the great Niall of the Nine Hostages, ancestress of almost all future High Kings. The condition of an alliance, sealed by a royal marriage, was evidently a diversionary raid; some Saxons undertook to pin down the armies of the south-east, while the Irish and Picts assailed the north and west.

The northern assault was far more serious; it was only after Count Theodosius marched out from London that he encountered 'various peoples' in arms, and it was in the north that he had work to do when they were beaten; for he

> protected the frontier with look-outs and garrisons, recovering a province that had yielded to enemy control, so restoring it that, as his report advised, it should have a legitimate governor, and be henceforth styled Valentia. Meanwhile, the *Areani*, instituted in times gone by . . . had gradually become corrupt; he disbanded them, for they were convicted of taking bribes to betray our army to the enemy. . . . Their duty was to penetrate deep into enemy territory and give our commanders warning of the movements of border peoples.

Archaeological discovery and native historical record make ample comment on Theodosius' northern settlement, in contrast to their reticence about his southern skirmishes. The 'look-outs' are evidently the signal-stations, wooden towers resting on four splayed feet, which lined the north Yorkshire coast from the estuary of the Tees to Bridlington Bay; they are served by roads that radiate from Malton, whither a coastal defence unit named the 'Anticipators' was transferred from Brough-on-Humber. New defences are commonly erected because experience has shown their need; the towers were a novel form of defence, upon a coast previously unfortified. Their siting indicates the danger they were meant to meet. They were able to warn the garrison at Malton of enemy vessels approaching the rich lands of the East Riding from the north; but their siting pays no attention to any threat from the Germanic raiders to the south-east. The Pictish fleet had evidently learnt to turn the flank of Hadrian's Wall.

Picts and Saxons were still raiders, whose object was to sail home speedily with plunder; but the Irish had larger ambitions. Substantial numbers settled in western Britain, and Irish tradition extends the authority of Crimthann, the mid fourth-century High King, over 'Britain as far as the Channel'. Irish colonies are abundantly attested in Wales and the south-west, but evidence is weaker for the north-west. The probable reason is the recovery of the territory that became the new province of Valentia; the Roman texts suggest that it lay in and about Lancashire.

On the northern frontier, Theodosius devised a new policy, whose impact was felt for a thousand years. Hitherto, Hadrian's Wall had been protected by a screen of forts, slanting the Cheviots from the neighbourhood of Carlisle towards Tweedmouth; they had served as the headquarters of the long-range reconnaissance patrol units, who were suspected of collusion with the enemy. Ammian reports that the units were then disbanded, and excavation has shown that the forts were then abandoned. The nature of the defence system that replaced them is outlined by the genealogists of the early middle ages. Their business was to trace the descent of the princes they served from well-known heroes of the late Roman period; as with most genealogists, the links in their chain are often dubious, but both ends are stronger, for living potentates seek connection with remembered rulers, not with invented names.

The northern lists concern four dynasties established north of Hadrian's Wall, a few generations before the emergence of the fifth-century kingdoms south of the Wall. The texts are obscured by their copyists' lack of understanding, but the originals appear to have recorded the establishment, about the period 370 to 380, of Quintilius Clemens on the Clyde, of Paternus, son of Tacitus, over the Votadini of the north-east coast, and of Antonius Donatus in south-west Scotland, and perhaps also in Selkirk. The fourth list is the most corrupt; it seems to mean that Catellius Decianus was imposed upon the northern Votadini, the Lothians beyond the Tweed, perhaps as far as the lower Forth about Stirling, in the territory that was later called the Manau of Gododdin. The date may also be about the 370s, or a little later.

The lists are independent of each other. But each says something of each ruler's origin; Clemens seems to have come from the mediterranean, Tacitus from Kent, Decianus from an island whose name is corrupted out of recognition. Donatus, but not the others, is said to have derived his authority from the emperor Maximus (381–388). All have Roman names. All the names are given in the old-fashioned form of *nomen* and *cognomen*, family and personal name, that in the later fourth century remained principally in vogue among the local nobility of the western *civitates*. Men so named were not native kings to whom Rome granted recognition, but Roman officers placed over border barbarians.

The policy that the medieval lists suggest is that which Theodosius is known to have devised. He applied it to the African frontier a few years later. There Ammian reports that in 371 he subdued border peoples 'by a mixture of intimidation and bribery', and then 'put reliable *praefecti* in charge of the peoples he encountered'. Subsequently the great African churchman, St Augustine of Hippo approved his policy, commenting that

> a few years ago a small number of barbarian peoples were pacified and attached to the Roman frontier, so that they no longer had their own kings, but were ruled by prefects appointed by the Roman Empire,

and adding that they soon after began to accept Christianity. It is evident that Theodosius applied to the British frontier in 368 the same policy that he carried through in Africa in 371, appointing Roman *praefecti gentium* as rulers of the border barbarians.

The installation of *praefecti* was one among several forms of government; circumstances decided the choice between alternatives. Valentia became a province, but Ammian's carefully chosen words stress that 'in his report' Theodosius advised that it be given a *legitimum rectorem*, a regular governor; the phrase implies that alternatives had been considered and rejected. The appointment of a prefect was one of several possibilities; Valentinian chose a different alternative a few years later. A deposed king of the Alamanni of the upper Rhine, named Fraomar, was transferred to Britain, his title changed to Tribune of a unit of Alamanni within the Roman army; though an army officer in law, his force was enough to make him the effective master of the district in which it was stationed; but its location is not known.

As the authority of the central government disintegrated in the next century, practice ironed out the differences, preferring to name the substance of power rather than its formal title. In northern Britain, as in Europe, officers clung to their authority, and bequeathed it to their sons, founding hereditary dynasties. Fraomar is not known to have left heirs, but the commanders appointed in a later age to Demetia, south-west Wales, also used officially the Roman military titles of Tribune and Protector, though contemporaries called them kings. The double usage lasted for several generations; when Patrick denounced the depradations of the Clydesiders under Clemens' grandson Coroticus, about the 450s, he protested that their behaviour made them

> not citizens of the holy Romans, but of the devil, living in the enemy ways of the barbarians.

The Damnonii of the Clyde had never themselves been Roman citizens; to Patrick, the prefect's grandson and his men were still Romans appointed to rule barbarians, but they had succumbed to his subjects' way of life. Coroticus was in practice a king; and the dynasties that Theodosius established in the name of Valentinian span the gulf between Rome and the middle ages. The dynasty of

Clemens of the Clyde endured until the Norman conquest; the dynasty of Paternus, transferred to Wales, expired in the thirteenth century, in the person of Llewellyn the Great, and its sovereign authority is perpetuated in the modern title of Prince of Wales.

Huns and Goths 375–400

Count Theodosius' expedition to Britain was an incident in Valentinian's western wars, soon to be eclipsed by portentous troubles that drew him to the Danube, where he died in 375. The western provinces and the Rhine armies acknowledged his adult son Gratian, but the Danubian officers proclaimed and controlled his infant son Valentinian II, child of Magnentius' turbulent widow, the aristocratic Justina, whom Valentinian had found it politic to marry. Gratian endured the rebuff, but broke with his father's military government. His tutor, the poet Ausonius of Bordeaux, became Prefect of Italy, guiding the administration of the west, while the influence of the empress Justina prevailed in the Balkan provinces. For the last time the high aristocracy of Rome had a government they liked; their spokesman Symmachus, patron of the conservative paganism now fashionable among them, sighed gratefully, 'Now the emperors do what the nobility want.'

Novel and more frightful dangers from beyond the Danube soon overshadowed domestic politics. Just before Valentinian's death, the Huns had crossed the Volga. Ferocious nomads, seen always on their tough desert ponies, like some fearful Scythian reincarnation of the ancient centaurs, their frightfulness fell little short of their reputation. A primitive people, ignorant of fields and farms, had no use for live prisoners, save as concubines; without fixed homes to defend, they could be defeated only by total annihilation. Their first onslaught destroyed the empire of the eastern Goths, and they remained the terrible masters of central Europe for eighty years. The western Visigoths sought safety on the Roman bank of the broad Danube. The government of Valens admitted the Visigothic refugees, but corruption let them keep their arms, and at the same time assured that they were fed only at outrageous famine prices. Life was intolerable for a people unprovided with coin, whose only marketable commodities were their children. When the scared Roman general tried to assassinate their leaders, and bungled his treachery, the starved and indignant Goths rebelled, destroying the army and the emperor of the east at Adrianople in 378.

In place of Valens, Gratian enthroned Theodosius, son of the general who had rescued Britain in 367. The energy of the emperor Theodosius in the long run preserved the eastern provinces; the Balkans were cleared by individual bands of Goths, hired to contain and subdue their fellow-countrymen. But this immediate solution begot new and bitter long term tensions. The sentiments of the Goths were divided; chieftains saw the prospect of power, wealth and the status within the superior civilisation of Rome with other eyes than the rank and file, whose continuing poverty perpetuated their patriotic hatred of the Roman name.

Roman opinion was equally torn; though Germans had long been frequent in the regular units of the Roman army, especially among the field officers, wholesale reliance on mercenary captains was suspect and unpopular. The federate allies were bound to the Roman society they guarded only by a personal contract with its sovereign, that dimly anticipated the patterns of medieval military rule. Federates were not admitted into the western provinces until the 5th century, but wherever they settled, landlord and peasant alike suffered from the boorish arrogance of the ubiquitous Germans; conservative opinion resented the indecent political prominence of their leaders, and sighed nostalgically for the days when Romans were masters of their own empire. Yet governments justly pleaded the compulsions of political realism, for they learnt that political and military success accrued to those with cash enough to hire the most barbarians, and tact enough to flatter the barbarian leaders' yearning for social and political acceptance.

The first crisis came quickly, and came in Britain. The miscellaneous grievances of Gratian's subjects found a focus in the army's dislike of his privileged barbarian bodyguard; for the young prince's gentle manners inspired no counterbalancing respect. One critic drily called him 'more pious than was good for the state', while his tutor Ausonius found but two virtues to praise; his excellence at running, wrestling and jumping; and his modest dress, daily church-going, abstemious table and chaste bed. The virtues of the athlete and the choirboy were fatal to the emperor, and a few years after Adrianople the diocese of Britain proclaimed Magnus Maximus, a Spaniard who had served under the elder Theodosius, and who now repelled a renewed Pict and Irish invasion. In 383 Gaul abandoned Gratian without a struggle, and soon after Spain, Africa and Italy acknowledged Maximus as emperor. Theodosius, heavily committed in his own territories, accepted the rebel for a while, but in 388 defeated and killed him in another bloody Balkan battle. Native tradition believed that the British units of his army settled in Armorica, the future Brittany.

The costly adventures of Magnentius and Julian were repeated, for the Franks again plundered Cologne, and extended their settlements about the lower Rhine. Yet Theodosius' success failed to tame the disaffected west; four years later the barbarian commander of the Rhine armies deposed young Valentinian, and Theodosius was again obliged to reconquer the west by force. Both armies engaged alien allies. Though Theodosius was reinforced by substantial forces of Arabs, Georgians and Goths, his victory was achieved only by the timely purchase of a considerable body of his rival's German allies. He died four months later, in January 395. He was the last sole ruler of the Roman world, the last to dominate his own government. Thereafter, the manner of political struggle changed. The docile sons and grandsons of Theodosius submitted to the direction of ambitious ministers, who learnt that power was more cheaply bought by palace intrigue and by assassination than by armed rebellion. Laymen and churchmen henceforth agreed to support the existing sovereign, however contemptible, in preference to the ablest rebel; for the victory or defeat of a rebel equally entailed disastrous civil war.

The principle of legitimacy triumphed too late to save the western provinces. The general Stilicho, son of a Roman officer of Vandal birth, controlled Honorius, the new emperor of the west, and sought a like authority over his brother Arcadius, emperor in Constantinople. The successive ministers of Arcadius, despite their mutual hostility, shared a common fear of Stilicho; and both courts were agitated by the struggle between those who sought to curtail the political power of German ministers and soldiers, and those who tried to assimilate and baptise the barbarians.

The multiple divisions of the Roman government emboldened the independent barbarians to renewed attacks. But at first Stilicho was brilliantly successful. Between 395 and 400 he won two resounding victories. An African border prince named Gildo, placed in command of the Roman armies, transferred his nominal allegiance to Arcadius, starving Rome of corn. But, with the support of magnates of the province, Stilicho swiftly subdued the rebel. Immediately thereafter he gained his second frontier victory, by the repulse of another concerted attack upon Britain by the Picts, the Irish and the Saxons. His victories demonstrated that a strong and able ruler could still hold the frontiers of the west.

The Fall of the West 400–410

In 400, the empire still seemed to be more than holding its own. Civil war was at a discount, separatism was checked, the frontiers were intact. Official policy and private judgment might reasonably anticipate the indefinite continuance of the familiar Roman world. Yet ten years later, western Rome had disintegrated beyond repair.

The decade of disaster opened with a crisis in the east. When a Gothic general seized Constantinople, his men were massacred in a fury of anti-German resentment. At the time, the recovery of Constantinople seemed a hopeful sign of reviving Roman strength, matching the western triumphs of Stilicho. Thenceforth, though individual Germans might hold high command, the eastern empire was permanently free of turbulent barbarian federate allies. It proved able to finance a native government and a native army; and when necessary to pay barbarians to go elsewhere.

But the salvation of the richer east proved to be the ruin of the impoverished west. The restless nation of the Visigoths, long quartered in the eastern Balkan provinces, deemed it easier to attack Italy. Stilicho twice held their able ruler Alaric, but in 403 he had to strip the western frontiers of

> the units that defended Rhaetia (Bavaria) . . . of the legion deployed in far-off Britain, that curbs the savage Irish and reads the marks tattooed upon the bodies of dying Picts, the regiments set against the blonde Sigambri (the Franks of the lower Rhine).

The legion was probably the Twentieth from Chester.

The temporary rescue of Italy entailed the permanent ruin of Gaul. A vast host of Vandals, Suebi and Alans, escaping from the central European dominion of the Huns, crossed the ill-defended Rhine, and fanned out across the interior provinces, threatening to invade Britain. Italy was powerless to help, and the British proclaimed a native emperor, Constantine III. He crossed to Gaul, and expelled the invaders; but they withdrew the wrong way, not back across the Rhine, but across the Pyrenees into Spain. There most of them stayed. The Suebi destroyed their Alan allies, and their descendants still inhabit north-western Spain; the Vandals passed on, to leave their name in Andalusia, and ultimately to found a stable kingdom in what had been Roman Africa.

The disaster cost Stilicho his life. He was arrested and executed in 408. The government of Honorius, insecure in Rome, had withdrawn to the shelter of the malarial marshes of Ravenna; and the anti-German party now sought to imitate Constantinople, by massacring the barbarian garrisons. But the aristocracy of Italy lacked the strength that had preserved the east. Without men or money or political resolution, the government of Ravenna was blown rudderless by changing winds. It attacked Constantine in Gaul, and killed his generals; their successors, 'Ediovinchus a Frank, and Gerontius a Briton', counter-attacked with vigour. Renewed civil war turned confusion into chaos. The *Bacauda*, the peasant rebels of the *maquis*, joined in against Ravenna; the Spanish relatives of the imperial family rose against Constantine's son, Constans, and Gerontius replaced him with an emperor of his own making. The armies of the Rhine elevated local emperors, and in Italy Alaric enthroned his own puppet emperor. While half a dozen feeble western governments disputed the majestic title of Roman emperor, Britain was subjected to continuing Irish assaults, and an exceptionally heavy Saxon raid. The failing Constantine was no longer able to help, and the states of Britain were impelled to restore their allegiance, too late, to the legitimate emperor in Italy.

The western empire reeled; its provinces had faced blows as heavy in the past, but never in such rapid succession. The end came on 24 August 410, when slaves or plebeian malcontents opened the gates of Rome to Alaric. He withdrew in less than a week, with a huge waggon train of loot and captives, including the emperor's sister, Galla Placidia, whom his successor married. A few years later, in 418, when the debris of rival emperors had been tidied away, the government of Honorius granted federate status to the unconquerable Visigoths. They were settled in Aquitaine, under the ordinary billeting laws, that had been designed long ago to provide temporary maintenance for troops on the move. They were allocated the use of a third of the lands and houses of their civilian hosts, exempted from the jurisdiction of magistrates, subjected only to the military discipline of their commanding officer. But old laws carry new meanings in a changed society. Since their settlement was permanent, and their commander was their national king, they in fact established the first medieval kingdom, owing only corporate and nominal allegiance to the emperor. Burgundians and others soon established comparable kingdoms, and these new nations smashed the fragile shell of imperial authority when they grew to maturity a few decades later.

The fall of the city shattered men's illusions, and a fearsome unknown future could no longer be denied. From Bethlehem, St. Jerome wept

> The Roman empire is beheaded; in the one City, the whole world dies. . . . All things born are doomed to die . . . every work of man is destroyed by age; . . . but who would have believed that Rome would crumble, at once the mother and the tomb of her children? She who enslaved the east . . . is herself a slave.

Old men mourned; but younger men were capable of looking to the future with confidence, even welcoming escape from a dead past. One young Briton wrote home from Sicily:

> you tell me that everyone is saying that the world is coming to an end. So what? It happened before. Remember Noah's time. . . . But after the Flood, men were holier.

The continuous history of a thousand years of Greek and Roman civilisation had suddenly snapped, leaving men nakedly aware, at the time, that the end had come. Those who could look beyond the deluge with assurance had already written off the headless corpse of the Roman empire. They were the conscious architects of Christendom, impatient to clear away the debris of the past that they might build upon its ruins a new society, that which in retrospect we call the 'middle ages'.

Christian Reform 361–400

Western Rome was mortally wounded in 410, though its death agonies were to last two generations more. As the state decayed, men looked elsewhere for protection and salvation. They found a Christian church, reformed and strengthened, that had learned from the disgrace of Rimini and the warning of Julian's abortive pagan revival. The leaders of western reform were three outstanding contemporaries, Damasus, Ambrose and Martin. They differed greatly in their work and outlook; but in a single generation, between 365 and 395, their combined endeavours transformed the structure, the morality and the composition of Latin Christianity.

Damasus secured the bishopric of Rome in 366, after bloody election riots. A masterful organiser, he induced the pious emperor Gratian to surrender to him the title of *Pontifex Maximus*, the ancient chief priesthood of the city of Rome, held by Julius Caesar and all the emperors after him. The title, and the magisterial authority it conveyed, make Damasus the first bishop of Rome to whom the modern term 'Pope' may fitly be applied. His contemporary Ammian was impressed by his novel and deliberate ostentation,

> riding in a carriage, wearing conspicuous clothes, keeping a table better than the emperor's;

and Ammian contrasted his magnificence with

> some of the provincial bishops, whose moderation in food and drink, whose plain apparel and downcast eyes commend their modest purity to the eternal deity.

The contrast between the splendour of a Roman prelate and the humility proper to a priest of Christ has provoked comment in most later ages. But Damasus took a political decision attuned to his times. Rome was still in men's minds the head and mistress of the civilised world, though it was no longer the residence of the emperor. The secular government was headed by the city prefect, but the Christian church needed a head whose authority extended over the empire. Praetextatus, the prefect of the City, the grand old man of aristocratic paganism, sensed the power of his rival, and protested with a jibe, 'Make me Bishop of Rome, and I will turn Christian'. The jest recognised reality, for Damasus had erected a Christian magistracy as powerful as the prefecture, and destined to outlive it for many centuries.

Damasus gave Latin Christendom a visible and efficient head. He also strengthened the sinews that bound it together. He commissioned the prolific scholar Jerome to prepare a single authoritative translation of the scriptures; and Jerome's Latin text, called the Vulgate, is still the canonical bible of the Latin church. Damasus also asserted the conscious independence of the Christian community by cleaning out the catacombs, and opening them as permanent exhibitions, in honour of Christians whose conscience had defied the unjust authority of secular government. The veneration of martyrs in small local shrines was not new; Damasus' innovation was to elevate the whole body of martyrs to a status in heaven and to make them a focus of worship on earth, whose observance emphasised that the Christian church was the independent equal of the political state.

The power of Damasus demonstrated the strength of the Christians; but it did not inspire personal affection. Ambrose of Milan combined the authority of the prelate with the humility of the priest. The son of a former praetorian prefect, he was himself governor of north-eastern Italy in 373, when a contested episcopal election threatened riots in Milan as violent as those in Rome in 366. A voice in the crowd, traditionally a child's, cried, 'Ambrose for Bishop!', and the crowd assented. Baptised, ordained and consecrated within a week, the former governor lived austerely with his brother and sister, dividing his considerable fortune between the church and the poor. To instil a like austerity into his clergy, he adapted to the urban Latin church the eastern phenomenon of the monk.

The solitary ascetic of the desert was older than Christianity; but monasticism did not become an important element in Christianity until the early fourth century, when tens of thousands of Egyptians migrated to the desert, during and after the persecution of Diocletian, rejecting the stresses of their civil society, to live in new communities, in direct personal relationship with God, without marriage or children. Though the example of Egypt spread to the deserts of Syria and Cappadocia, in western eyes the monks long remained another nasty oriental excess, slovenly drop-outs from decent society.

It was during the Arian controversy that Latin Christians observed that the monks were their steadfast allies against the heretics; and a number of wealthy nobles, men and women, adopted a personal monastic vow, living abstemiously in their own houses. Majority opinion in Rome condemned the novelty, and Jerome, the fiercest champion of the monks, withdrew to Bethlehem. But some provincial bishops responded to the new ideal. It was bishop Eusebius of Vercelli in northern Italy, who in the 350s

> first established monks who were also clergy, combining the abstinence of the monk with the discipline of the priest . . . though living in the town.

Ambrose praised, imitated and extended the practice of Eusebius, so that ordained monks, *in turba commorantes*, living among men, set a visible example of a more perfect life within ordinary society. In the next generation, numerous bishops induced all or part of their clergy to accept monastic vows, so that the cathedral monastery became a symbol of reform.

Damasus founded an independent Christian authority. Ambrose tested the strength of the church in conflict with the state. To the emperor Theodosius he stated the principle:

> In matters of finance you consult your departmental advisers; it is even more necessary that in matters of religion you should consult the priests of the Lord.

His warning to the usurper Maximus was sterner, that

> in the Old Testament, kingdoms were bestowed by priests, not usurped.

Words were put into practice when the empress Justina impounded one of the Milan churches for the use of Arian courtiers. Ambrose and his congregation occupied the church, cheering each other and intimidating the police cordon at the doors by singing songs, adapting the practice of the Greek east. Ambrose' defiant songs are the first Latin hymns; and the greatest of them, the *Te Deum*, belongs to this context and this generation, but not to this occasion. After three days, the police broke ranks and joined the besieged, thereby compelling the government to surrender.

The decisive conflict came in 390. When Theodosius massacred 3,000 citizens of Thessalonica, after a local rising, Ambrose refused to admit him to communion. After a few months of ineffectual resistance, the emperor yielded, performed penance, and consented to sign the ultimate decree, making non-Christian worship a civil crime. Theodosius' penance lies nearer to the experience of medieval princes who reigned a thousand years later than to the conduct of the emperors who had ruled in his own youth.

Italy learned that a well-loved bishop was stronger than the strongest emperor. Gaul learned a similar lesson from a very different man. Martin was a soldier, who won a discharge from Julian's army as a conscientious objector. He settled as a hermit near Poitiers, and an individual who practised in rural Gaul the fabulous asceticism of the east excited universal wonder, and was soon credited with the power to recall the dead to life. His biography was written in his lifetime by his friend and disciple, Sulpicius Severus. Against his will he was lured to Tours in 372, during another disputed election, and was acclaimed bishop by an 'incredibly large crowd of voters'. But he was opposed by

> a few . . . including several of the bishops summoned for the consecration . . . who . . . described him . . . as a lowborn person, of disgusting appearance, shabbily dressed, with untidy hair.

Martin resumed his hermit's life in a cave two miles from the city, gathering around him a monastic cathedral school of eighty pupils, including some sons of local notables, who shared his single wineless meal, and divided their time between prayer, the study of the classics, and the transcription of texts sacred and profane. The school, the *scriptorium* and the library were novelties, but they were an essential part of Martin's work, for

> many of his pupils became bishops; for what city or church was there, but longed for a bishop trained in the school of Martin?

The best-known of these pupils were Amator, later bishop of Auxerre, who is said to have ordained Patrick, and Victricius, later bishop of Rouen, who was to propagate Martin's teaching in Britain with considerable success.

Martin pioneered rural preaching, founding village churches in a land where Christianity was recent, hitherto virtually confined to the towns. His plebeian simplicity won the affection of peasants and of the urban poor, but it aroused opposition among his colleagues. His biographer Severus protested, 'It is the clergy alone, the bishops alone, who refuse to acknowledge him.' To Severus, they were men who 'degrade their dignity by subservience to royal hangers-on', whereas Martin compelled the choleric Valentinian to receive and heed him. He rebuked the usurper Maximus, intent on trying a case of heresy, in words as vigorous as those of Ambrose;

> for a lay judge to decide upon an ecclesiastical case would be a savage unheard-of crime;

and he long refused the emperor's invitation

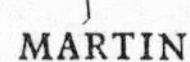

to sit at table with a man who has killed one emperor and expelled another.

Maximus swallowed the insult, and at last induced Martin to come to court where he had to endure the company he most detested of 'bishops and women'. He sat beside the emperor at a public banquet, and

the delighted king . . . ordered the cup to be offered first to the holy bishop, expecting and hoping that he would pass it back to him. . . . But, after drinking, Martin handed the cup to his own priest. . . . It made an impression . . . that Martin treated the emperor as no other bishop treated the minor officials.

Incidents like these made Martin a living legend; and made Sulpicius Severus' biography an immediate best seller, that became a model for an immense flood of 'Saints' Lives', popular literature published in Gaul and Britain during the next several centuries. The examples of Damasus, Ambrose and Martin showed that the Christians were champions of the underdog, strong enough to prevail. That example inspired millions outside their own sees, whose pressure impelled other bishops to respect the new morality. In one generation the success of the reformers turned the church of Gaul from a minority sect to a universal religion, so that by the end of the century 'the whole world became Christian', acquiescing without resistance in the new faith.

But conversion to Christianity did not mean that the convert ceased to be a pagan. As among many modern peoples, the same mind could accommodate several different religions at the same time; the church fathers might proclaim that 'the same mouth cannot praise Christ and Jupiter', but the poet Ausonius, consul and prefect, gave them the lie by composing hymns to Christ and also to Jupiter; and for centuries church councils found it necessary to disapprove of families who attended mass on Sunday morning, and sacrificed to their household gods on Sunday afternoon. What matters is that as late as 370, a majority of the population of the three Gauls still rejected the name of Christian, but that by 400 almost the entire population admitted Christianity. With Christianity, they accepted a new institution capable of binding their society together, as the old political fabric of the empire rotted away.

The triumph of Christianity came just in time, barely a decade before the capture of Rome, in 410, destroyed the emperor's hold upon the obedience of his subjects. Honorius lived thirteen years more, and his sister's son, Valentinian III, survived till 455. The prestige of the dynasty lent an authority that still mattered greatly in Gaul and Italy to those ministers who acted in its name; but Valentinian's successors, creatures of the successive German generals who dominated Italy, commanded little obedience beyond the Alps. Their feeble sovereignty persisted until Odovacer discontinued the nomination of western emperors, about 476, and transferred his nominal allegiance to Constantinople;

his administrative decision changed nothing of the realities of political power. Odovacer buried the western empire, but it had died twenty years before. The wistful comment of the chronicler Count Marcellinus accurately summarised its end:

> then fell the Empire of the West, nor had it ever strength to rise again.

CHAPTER THREE

INDEPENDENT BRITAIN: THE EVIDENCE

The loss of Britain was a detail in the dissolution of the Empire. In the year when Rome itself fell to the Goths, it passed almost unnoticed; one historian gave it half a sentence, reporting that

> Honorius dealt with the states of Britain by letter, telling them to look to their own defence . . . and remained inactive.

There was little else that he could do. In the catastrophe of 410, the imperial government could take no initiative in Britain; it turned down a British request, for it was then unable to spare men or money for the defence of the island.

The letter reveals something of events in Britain. It was plainly sent in answer to a letter from Britain that had asked for men and money to defend the frontiers and coasts. The diocese had proclaimed the rival emperor Constantine III; but in 410, Constantine was visibly failing, and the British returned their allegiance to Honorius. They could not have done so without first renouncing the authority of Constantine's prefects, vicars and governors. But they did not themselves appoint others in their place; that was the business of the emperor. The address of the letter is altogether unusual. Contrary to normal precedent, it is not directed to government officers in the province, but to the 'cities', the *civitates* or states; it was evidently sent to a provincial council of delegates from the separate states, who had decided to renounce Constantine and to turn to Honorius for help. In refusing help, the imperial government legalised in advance whatever administration the British chose to set up; but it thereby created a novel problem that proved insoluble. For four hundred years, the separate states had run their own internal affairs, supervised and controlled by governors appointed by the emperor, to whose universally acknowledged authority the army also owed obedience. Now they were obliged to choose an agreed sovereign on their own. The history of the next two centuries is the story of their failure to agree upon a stable central government, capable of enforcing general obedience.

The break with Rome in 410 was purely governmental and administrative. No one deliberately decided to abandon Britain for ever; the imperial government confessed its inability to help at the moment. There was no 'Roman evacuation of Britain', no 'withdrawal of the legions'. Such troops as could be induced to cross the Channel had already been withdrawn, by Maximus and Theodosius, by Stilicho and Constantine III; the letter did not and could not try to remove those who remained. They were doubtless under strength; Honorius' rescript meant that henceforth their numbers could be maintained and increased only by a British government acting on its own, without outside help. The internal machinery of government was not changed, and the Roman civilisation of Britain lasted some thirty years more, its towns and villas, its agriculture, trade and industry little affected by political independence.

The Sources: Archaeology

The break seems sharper than it was because one of its incidental consequences was a total change in our sources of information. The written record was transformed, and archaeological evidence lost its bearings; the sources must be assessed before they can be used, to see what can and cannot be expected of them.

The archaeological remains of the Romans and of their successors differ greatly. The Romans of Britain are chiefly known from their buildings, and from the things they used while alive. But the pagan English are known mainly from their graves, distinguished by the gear which their relatives buried with them for their use after death, for, as yet, their homes and halls are little known; and the Christian descendants of both peoples left little behind them that an archaeologist can yet recognise.

The contrast is sharp. The Romans built in brick and stone, and used many pots and coins that excavation easily discovers. The jewellery, the funeral vessels, and the rusted iron weapons of the pagan English also remain. But their Christian successors, British and English, buried bare bones. The materials that they used in life have rarely survived. The old craft skills died with the civilisation of Rome, and for many centuries men relied mainly upon perishable materials, wood, leather and other substances that have not withstood the corrosive action of the seasons. The archaeology of Rome and of pagan English burial shouts loud; but, from the 5th century onward, archaeology whispers. Even the evidence of pottery is scant. Some sections of society in some parts of the country used some vessels, for the most part in the larger towns, in monasteries and halls; but pottery did not return to plentiful use on ordinary open-country farming sites until the 12th century or later.

After the Romans, there is much less archaeological evidence; and what there is is harder to assess. All historical evidence speaks clearly only when it is well dated; and in literate ages, archaeology is ultimately dated by texts. Most of what we know of Roman Britain is learnt from the close study of a vast mass of excavated coins and pots that tell the date of the buildings in which they are found. We know the dates from Roman writers, who record the reigns of the emperors whose names are stamped upon the coins, report the dates when particular sites were built or destroyed, or identify the men honoured in inscriptions. But from the fifth century to the seventh, there are no coins and hardly any inscriptions to connect the people with the pots and give them dates, and it is rarely possible to discover when individual sites began and ended.

The familiar methods of the archaeologist fail. Until the last age of Roman Britain, his dating rests upon the contrast between what he finds and what is not there; a site that has plenty of first-century material, but nothing of the second century, is rightly deemed to have been deserted, because the second-century material is plentiful elsewhere, and must have been there if the site were then in use. But from the fifth century onwards such assumptions are no longer justified. The evidence of coins dries up, for the western mints issued very little small change after 403, and hardly any of it reached Britain. So long as men used money at all, the only coins that they could use were those that circulated about 400.

These coins, and the pots and other objects that are commonly found with them, have much to tell of how and where the latest Romans lived; but they say little of when their society ended. The meaning of the evidence has long been muddied by the rash guesses of earlier archaeologists, who pretended that sites were deserted soon after the minting of the latest coin found on them. Recent work teaches a more sober judgment. In the later 4th century the circulation of money was restricted, so that the latest coins are plentiful only on some kinds of sites in some areas; and among them most of the bronze pieces in use about 400 were already twenty or thirty years old, so that on many sites a bronze coin of Gratian is the latest that is likely to have been used in 400 or in 450.

Future research may give a more certain guide. But at present the discovery of the latest Roman material can only argue that the site was used after about 370. By itself, archaeological evidence cannot show when a site ceased to be inhabited. The end of Roman civilisation in Britain is dated by texts; they describe its violent overthrow in and after the 440s, but it is rarely possible to assign a particular date to a particular site. It can only be said that the latest Roman buildings were built and used between about 370 and about 450. The evidence cannot normally give a closer date; and to the vast mass of older archaeological reports which confidently assert the desertion or destruction of a site 'in the late fourth century' must be added the cautious warning 'or early fifth'. Within this period, the evidence of archaeology is competent to describe the manner of men's lives, but not to date them.

The archaeology of the British is a new study. After the disappearance of Roman technology, the descendants of the last Romans in Britain used few objects that excavation can recognise. The work of the last twenty years has just begun to learn to detect their traces; some imported mediterranean pottery reached the shores of the Irish Sea, including south-western Britain, and here and there in Britain home-made wares are observed; some Roman towns and farms remained long in use, outliving the fifth century; a few cemeteries and one or two fortifications and halls of the sixth or seventh centuries are known.

But the number of sites is still small and the quantity of objects found in them is minute. The researches of the next few decades are likely to disclose much more, but at present the evidence of archaeology is too weak to add more than a few random comments to the recorded history of the British heirs of Rome.

By contrast, the remains of the pagan English are abundant. Upwards of 50,000 burials are known, from some fifteen hundred burial grounds, with tens of thousands of grave goods; some scores of houses and one or two villages have also been excavated, though few have yet been adequately published. Much of this extensive material can be dated quite closely, for it is richly ornamented. The study of changing ornament and form is commonly termed typology. It gives dates that are valid if other evidence provides check-points to anchor the stages of its evolution, and thereby to show their pace and direction. The art of the early English has secure anchors, over a period of nearly five centuries. Its recognisable forms begin in Germany, in graves of the third century that contain numerous Roman coins, many of them perhaps looted in the great raids of the 250s. These forms steadily develop until they come to an abrupt end in Germany about the end of the fifth century; but in their last few generations, the grave goods of Germany are matched in Britain, brooch for brooch and pot for pot, and the steady evolution of their styles continued in Britain long after it ended in Germany. The basis of their dating is and always has been the written record of the English settlement of Britain, whose beginnings were rightly placed early in the fifth century by Plettke, the German scholar who grounded the scientific study of these grave goods in 1914. In principle, that which is found in both Germany and Britain belongs to the fifth century; objects found in Germany, but not in Britain, belong to the fourth century or earlier; those found in Britain, but not in Germany, to the sixth or seventh century.

Within this general framework, there are several intermediate checkpoints. Many late Roman graves in Gaul contain a mixture of Germanic and datable Roman objects. Frankish and English pots and ornaments are sometimes buried in the same grave, in Europe and in Britain; and the archaeology of the Franks is fixed by the known dates of their first arrival in northern and in south-western Gaul, and in Bohemia, as well as by the burial of a king who died in 481. Some of the latest burials in Britain contain 7th century coins, and one in Yorkshire bears the name of the thane Lilla, killed in 625.

These and other simple indications tie down two main stages in the evolution of pagan English grave goods, before and after the end of the 5th century. But within the main stages a mass of detail is intricately related, for an immense variety of objects were buried, and each has its own history. Their dates cannot easily be determined by the random study of particular objects on their own. The material remains of any society need to be surveyed as a whole, and they cannot be sensibly assessed until they are measured against a yardstick, a class of object found often over wide areas through a long period of time, whose changing forms are relatively easy to comprehend. In the earlier Roman centuries the red pottery called Samian provides such a yardstick; it is found in great quantities on sites dated by texts, coins and inscriptions, and it gives dates to the local pottery types and other objects found with it. In pagan English graves there are two such yardsticks, the brooches termed 'cruciform' and 'saucer'. Both are found in large numbers over a period of nearly two centuries; both evolve rapidly and recognisably from small brooches with simple designs to large brooches with complex ornament. The simplest forms of both are found in north-western Germany as well as Britain, and were therefore in use in the 5th century. Later forms are not. These brooches give dates to other grave goods commonly found with them, and they in turn date others.

The time when these brooches first came into fashion is clearly marked. The immediate models from which the earliest cruciforms evolved are securely dated in the mixed Roman and Germanic burials of Europe to the decades on either side of 400. In the Elbe lands the first cruciforms are often found in pots that are virtually indistinguishable from others that contained the latest examples of the Germanic brooch termed the *Armbrustfibel*, or 'crossbow'; no 'crossbow' brooch has yet been reported in Britain, though doubtless one or two may some day be discovered. The conclusion is clear. The prototypes of the cruciform brooches came into use about the 390s, the earliest of those commonly called cruciforms a decade or two after 400; they were first buried at about the time when the earliest English burial grounds in Britain were opened; and they indicate the approximate date of a wide range of grave goods, including pottery vessels, that in turn date other vessels, and objects found in those vessels.

The evidence of the saucer brooch is slightly different. On present evidence, it won widespread popularity a little later than the cruciform, though some individual brooches may be earlier. Its main 5th century forms derive from the chip-carved decoration of the late Roman army and represent either five running scrolls or an equal armed cross with scroll ends; and these alone are frequent in the German homeland of the English. Both forms of decoration extended to Scandinavia as well as to Britain; the cruciform brooch there evolved on diverging lines, and though the saucer brooch itself did not spread in Scandinavia, its ornamental motifs were reproduced on other objects, especially on early forms of the brooches termed 'squareheaded'. The evolution of Scandinavian ornament provides a useful check upon parallel developments in Germany and Britain, but in Scandinavia there is little independent means of dating grave goods; successive attempts to found a dating system upon typology have failed to find firm ground, since for practical purposes 5th century Scandinavian dates depend upon the evidence of Britain and Germany, and have no valid means of correcting or challenging them.

Fashions changed quite quickly in the three generations between the first burials in English cemeteries in Britain and the end of the main German cemeteries, about 500; and change is still faster in the 6th century, between the end of the German cemeteries and the last generations of the pagan cemeteries in

Britain. Changing fashion indicates half a dozen overlapping periods in the two centuries of pagan burial in Britain. At present they cannot be examined in depth, and only certain kinds of objects can be dated, for no comprehensive catalogue of the material exists, and no overall survey on the scale of Plettke's work in Germany has been undertaken. Understanding is therefore easily obscured by a maze of false trails and facile assumptions, about coins or weapons, unchecked typology or 'animal' ornament and much else, whose illusory conclusions are difficult to assess.

It is not easy to distinguish conclusions that rest upon a quantity of weighty evidence from those whose base is slighter; and the facile habit of citing a particular conclusion as though it were itself evidence, without indication of the argument behind it, is therefore difficult to avoid. Bewilderment spreads when piecemeal conclusions are found to contradict each other. The resulting confusion tends to deter students from exploring these uncharted and undermanned regions of study, and to divert their energies into easier areas whose need for basic work is less. Nevertheless a few recent wider studies have made it possible to investigate some of the more important evidence comprehensively.

When dating sticks closely to a few sure witnesses, notably to the presence or absence of objects in Germany, and to the evidence of the cruciform and saucer brooches and grave goods found with them, then it becomes possible to observe some regional characteristics and to establish approximate dates for their beginning, change and end. But it is rarely wise to date an object or a grave more closely than to within a generation, for a fashion commonly lasts through the working life of a craftsman, and through the adult years of his customers; and older fashions linger after the novelties that replace them have begun to be made.

The evidence never justifies an assertion that such and such an object dates to 'about 400', or 'about 525' or any other specific time. The height of each fashion may be placed within a date bracket of about 30 or 40 years, but no closer. Moreover, any individual object may have been buried when it was a novelty, or when it was already antique. It is therefore rarely wise to date a single object or a single grave. Historical conclusions must rest upon the survey of large numbers of burials and burial grounds. In practice, the several regions of Britain show common characteristics, and marked differences, with grave goods that are found time and again in some districts in some periods, but are absent elsewhere; it is the regional study of all the evidence, not the study of particular objects or particular graveyards, that outlines the history of English expansion in Britain. That study permits some objects to be placed in overlapping generations of 30 or 40 years; within the half dozen periods so determined, it is possible to note the kind of objects that are present or absent, frequent or rare, and to learn from them something of the changing nature of early English society. The evidence is unevenly balanced; living Romans and dead Englishmen left ample material remains with few texts to explain them; the archaeology of the British is negligible, but many documents describe important aspects of their lives in some periods.

Texts

Written evidence is also uneven. The Romans of Britain are mute and anonymous. Not a word survives of their own literature. Mediterranean writers mentioned Britain when an important personage crossed the Channel, but most such visitors were soldiers, so that these notices outline the frontier wars, and say little of civilian life; and very few such persons came to Britain after 410. But in the last years of the western empire, the British found their own voice. The extant works written by British authors of the early fifth century fill a fair-sized bookshelf. Most, but not all of them wrote abroad, and most wrote theology. But theology was in their day the stuff of social and political controversy, so that these writings have much to say of the manner of life of the British, of their disputes, and of the ideas that moved them. Most of these writers were educated gentlemen, brought up in comfortable mansions; their books trace their cultivated Roman society down to about the year 440, but no further.

Its annihilation is described by their descendants, men barbarised in speech and understanding by the force of the explosion. Many of them try to report what happened; but the Roman past had been so savagely uprooted that they misconceived its nature, misunderstood the events they described, and the context in which they happened. Other writers were story-tellers, who were no more expected to conform to historical truth than a modern novelist. Their business was to edify and to entertain. In successive generations, new editions left out what offended the taste of their own day, or had no meaning, and added stories taken from other times and places, combining and distorting different originals.

Most of these texts are full of half-truths, seen out of focus. They cannot be interpreted until the date and purpose of each has been determined, the original separated from the additions, the contemporary report distinguished from the recollections of the next century, when living memory was still green, and both from the imagination of later ages. Even then, a single statement in a single text carries little weight; confidence comes only when independent texts from different peoples and different standpoints combine to record the same event or to outline the same situation. Their evidence is scantiest in the late fifth century; but from the beginning of the sixth century, its volume and its detail continually increase.

Gildas' Narrative

Only one work outlines a connected narrative of fifth-century British history. About 540, the priest Gildas published a forthright attack on the princes and bishops of his day, and began with a historical preface, tracing the origins of the evils he denounced. One statement, first set down within his own lifetime, and copied by a much later writer, reports that he was born beyond the Roman frontier, in the kingdom of the Clyde; but he was brought south in childhood, to be schooled in a fully Roman educational tradition by the shores of the Severn Sea. He was a man in his middle years when he wrote. His theme is that the disasters of the fifth century had been God's punishment of the sins of past generations; and that if their children, in his own day, do not quickly cease from evil, then God will destroy them, like the Israelites of old. His historical introduction refers to events broadly familiar to his readers, and selects those that prove his argument, illustrating the inborn wickedness of the British nation, the awfulness of divine vengeance, and God's favour to the endeavours of the virtuous and valiant few. The book is a sermon, not a history. Gildas set down so much of the past as he thought fit for his purpose, and left out what he held to be irrelevant thereto.

Gildas knew his Bible thoroughly; he also knew some classical authors, and the ecclesiastical literature of the late Empire; but he had almost no written sources for the history of Britain. He was dependent upon the memories of men who were old when he was young, and was grotesquely ignorant of earlier generations. From 'the time of the Roman emperors', he cites only two events, the rebellion of the 'unclean lioness', Boudicca, in 60, and of Maximus in 388, and uses them to show that the British had always been stubborn rebels against the laws of God and man. He knew nothing of the three hundred years between these revolts, and nothing of what followed. He knew the visible defences of the Roman frontier, the northern walls and the Saxon Shore forts of the south-east, but explained them as constructions of the early fifth century, due to two Roman expeditions, sent in response to appeals by the feckless British for help against the barbarians. Wholly ignorant of the events of 410, he supposed that the

> Romans told our country that they could not go on being worried by such troublesome expeditions, and that the Roman standards, her great and splendid army, could not be worn out for the sake of such unwarlike wandering thieves.

So they taught the British how to defend themselves, advising them to build the northern wall and southern coastal forts, and then

> said farewell, intending never to return.

When the British made a third appeal, further help was refused.

Gildas, like his readers, knew little and understood less of the Roman past. He had no conception that there had ever been a standing Roman army in Britain. His expeditions returned 'to Rome' or 'to Italy' when their work was done; the British were held down

> by whips rather than by military force . . . so that the island was regarded as Romania rather than Britannia.

He took Maximus for a native Briton, and when he went to Gaul, Britain lost her

> armed forces, her governors, brutal as they were, and the bulk of her youth

who went away, 'never to return'. He knew nothing of Theodosius, Stilicho or Constantine III; the 'Roman name' ended with Maximus; thenceforth Britain was Britannia, and 'Romania' meant the continent of Europe.

Gildas' narrative does not become real until he reaches the threshold of living memory, about a hundred years before his own time. The raids and expeditions were followed by a long period of peace and prosperity, so rich that 'no earlier age remembered the like'. Prosperity bred luxury and vice, manifested in repeated rebellion against legitimate rulers. Then came a rumour that the Picts threatened renewed invasion, this time aimed at settlement. The foolish councillors and the 'proud tyrant', the government of Britain, invited three shiploads of the 'unspeakable Saxons' to defend them against the Picts, and settled them in the east of the island. The Saxons thereafter increased their numbers, rebelled, and physically destroyed the civilisation of the island, so that a large part of the survivors emigrated overseas, taking with them such written records as remained. But in Britain a 'miserable remnant' rallied under the leadership of Ambrosius Aurelianus, son of an emperor who had been killed in the troubles, whose degenerate descendants survived in Gildas' own time. Ambrosius initiated a long war of alternating victory and defeat, that ended soon after a decisive British victory at Badon Hill, fought more than 43 years before Gildas wrote.

Nennius

Gildas' outline narrative is amplified by a mass of later documents. The fullest and earliest of them are contained in a collection of historical records first put together in the 8th century, known by the name of Nennius. The compiler did not try to write a history from his sources; he says with truth, 'I have made a heap of all I found,' and his editorship is confined to arranging his texts in what he considered to be their historical order. These documents are independent of each other, and need to be assessed individually. Some are fanciful legends, some concern the sixth and later centuries, but two are of major importance for the history of the fifth century; a *Kentish Chronicle* concerned with events between 425 and 460, and the work of a *Chronographer*, who strove to find exact dates for early fifth-century British events. Both documents were probably first written not much later than the sixth century. They are supplemented by a great quantity of later British and Irish material, and a little contemporary evidence.

Dates

None of these documents touches more than a part of the story that Gildas outlines. They have no context and their meaning is obscure until that story is dated. Just enough is recorded to outline the context. For more than a century after the break with Rome in 410, no event can be dated to a precise year; but three of the main events in Gildas' narrative are dated to within a year or two by contemporaries, two of them by European writers, who relate them to the known chronology of Europe. These three dates give a time scale to Gildas' story, and a context for the rest of the evidence.

The revolt of the English, or Saxons, is reported by a Gaulish chronicler who wrote in 452; he placed it ten years earlier, in or about the year 442, when

> Britain, which had hitherto suffered a variety of disasters, passed into the control of the Saxons.

The statement is terse, but it is clear, definite and decisive; it explains another vaguer contemporary allusion. It is the chronicler's only reference to Britain in his own day, and is therefore an event that seemed to him of first importance. Writing ten years after the event, he understood it to mean that the Saxons had mastered Britain, as Visigoths and Burgundians had mastered parts of Gaul; and that their rule had come to stay. In 452, it could not be known that Germanic supremacy was to be overthrown in Britain, that its ultimate victory was to be postponed for more than a hundred years.

The English came to Britain some time before they rebelled. Both Gildas and the Nennius texts say that a small force was first recruited, and later swelled its numbers until it was strong enough to revolt. The length of that period can hardly have been less than ten years. But it cannot have been much longer, for contemporaries had remarked upon resounding British victories in the first years of independence, about 411 or 412; thereafter followed a long period of peace, and several rulers rose and fell before the English came. The renewed danger that prompted the British government to invite their aid cannot have occurred much before 420 or 425; the first English arrived somewhere in or about the 420s, probably nearer to 430 than to 420. Very many texts call their leader Hengest, and give the name Vortigern to the British ruler who invited them, Gildas' 'proud tyrant'. The *Kentish Chronicle* and Nennius' Chronographer calculate exact dates by a variety of reckonings, putting Vortigern's accession to power in 425, the arrival of the English in his fourth year, 428. The date cannot be pressed to the exact year; but it cannot be more than a year or two wrong.

The second date is the migration. Several contemporary Gauls give reports of the British immigrants, whose fighting force they reckoned at 12,000; with wives and children, old folk and servants, the total must have been four or five times as large. The migration was complete before 461, when a 'Bishop of the British' took his place beside the territorial bishops of the northern Gallic cities in a church council; the British were then recently arrived, for a few years later they had been absorbed into the settled sees of Gaul, and no longer had their separate bishop. The migration dates to the end of the 450s, fifteen or more years after the English rebellion.

Gildas himself supplies the third date. Writing about 540, or a year or two earlier, he complained that orderly government survived during the lifetime of those who had witnessed the wars, but

> when they died, and their place was taken by a generation that had not experienced the troubles, and knew only our present security, all the controls of truth and justice were shaken and overthrown.

The men he denounced were not rebellious youth, but the rulers of his own time, men mature in years; the wars had ended before their time. This is the kind of statement that a man cannot make about his own lifetime unless it is substantially true; if it were not, all his readers would know that he was lying. The troubles ended with Badon, and they ended a generation or more before Gildas wrote. He adds a more precise date. The battle had been fought forty-three years and one month before. The date is not far from 495.

Three dates in a century are not many; but they are enough to tie down Gildas' timeless narrative, and to relate it to the rest of the evidence. But though they are clear, they have been obscured by an unhappy mistake of Gildas. His narrative rests on the oral tradition of living memory that knew no dates, and was hazy about the interval between events. He knew a single dated document, an appeal for help against unnamed barbarians, sent by 'the British' to the Roman commander in Gaul, 'Aëtius, consul for the third time'. The date is between 446 and 454, but Gildas did not know it. He had to guess the place at which he should insert the letter in his narrative, and he guessed wrong. He knew only a tradition of appeals to Rome for help against the Picts, in the years after 410, and so he cited the letter in connection with these appeals. But the date of Aëtius makes it clear that the enemy were Saxons, the cause of the appeal the revolt of about 442.

Bede

The earliest and best-known edition of Gildas' introductory chapters was published by the English historian Bede in 731. Bede's *History of the English Church* begins with the landing of St Augustine in Kent in 597. It is prefaced by a historical introduction surveying the Roman and pre-Roman past, taken chiefly from continental writers; and when they failed him, after 410, his account of the fifth century is a word-for-word transcript of Gildas, leaving out some of his more exuberant language, with a little added from other sources; and when Gildas failed him, at the end of the fifth century, he jumped straight into his main narrative at 597, with no account at all of the sixth century.

Before 597, Bede is a secondary writer; all the sources that he knew are extant, known to us independently; and many other texts are known which were not available to Bede. Though his readers may admire the skill with which he used his sources, they can learn nothing from his introductory chapters that they could not also learn elsewhere. But Bede, and his readers, were bedevilled by Gildas' mistake. Bede's problem was to link Gildas' dateless story with datable continental events; he did not know the Chronicle of 452, and the only date he had was the Aëtius letter. He wrestled with it in vain. In his own Chronicle, published in 725, he placed the letter among the events of the 430s. Six years later, in the History, he had discovered its date, and entered it at 446; but he had no evidence that could help him to correct Gildas' mistake; he had to preserve Gildas' order of events, although the intervals were plainly wrong, giving a very few years where Gildas had written 'a long time', and placing many years between events that Gildas made consecutive. Bede therefore allowed as much time as he could for Gildas' long interval between the letter and the coming of the Saxons, and dated their arrival to the reign of the emperors Marcian and Valentinian, in his reckoning, which was one year out, between 449 and 456; later still, the 9th century editors of the Saxon Chronicle, to suit the form of their annals, left out Bede's date bracket, and entered the arrival of Hengest under the year 449.

Bede's error was unavoidable; he inherited Gildas' mistake, and had no means of righting it. But it entailed lasting confusion. Bede is one of the world's great historians, widely read by millions of men over the centuries; but Gildas is a little-known preacher, read only by a few scholars. The date 449 or 450, that Bede gave as an approximation, was repeated as an exact year by the Saxon Chronicle, and was universally accepted by English historians for centuries; it has only recently succumbed to the pressure of contrary evidence. It has hamstrung the study of pagan English archaeology; for it was long maintained, on the supposed authority of Bede, that the cemeteries in Britain could not be earlier than 450. But German scholars paid no attention to Bede; relying upon the Chronicle of 452, they placed the first Saxon pots and brooches in Britain in the early fifth century, almost 50 years earlier than the date assigned to the same objects by their English colleagues. Few archaeologists now maintain the date of 450, but the litter of mistaken judgments founded upon that error is by no means yet cleared up. Students of the Saxon Chronicle have been similarly handicapped; its text began with a list of events, and a note of the approximate interval between them, to which later editors added years in AD dates. The sequence of these inserted dates begins with 449; it is approximately 20 years too late, so that all the events to which the early editors assigned AD dates in the fifth century, or the first years of the sixth century, are misdated; twenty years needs to be subtracted from each date, in order to recover the time scale of the earliest version. But printed texts still give only the dates inserted in the manuscripts, without editorial correction.

This long-lived confusion is an instance of the problems that have caused the Arthurian centuries to be regarded as dark, obscure and difficult. Darkness is not deeply embedded in the evidence itself; mistakes like Gildas' misunderstanding of the Aëtius letter are common to most early writers, in Europe as in Britain. They are the ordinary stuff of historical criticism; and over the centuries modern scholarship has sorted out most such confusions in European texts. Obscurity is not to be blamed upon the sources, but upon modern scholarship; it is the fault of the workmen, not of their tools. Yet the fault does not lie in the quality of the workmanship; it arises simply because the work has not been done; the labourers are too few.

Words

Confusion is made worse because the words that describe peoples and nations altered their meaning in an age of rapid change. The stable society of the Roman British before 410 is easily recognised, altogether different from the barbarians in Ireland and beyond the Forth and Clyde. From the seventh century onward the political geography of the British Isles is also readily intelligible; four main nations, the English, the Welsh, the Irish and the peoples of the future Scotland, shared the same religion and a similar culture, though each was still divided into a number of small states. But in the centuries between, new names and old jostle each other. The British were no longer Roman, but were still British. They coined an additional name for themselves, the 'fellow-countrymen', *cives* in Latin, *combrogi* in their own language, whose modern forms are *Cymry* in Welsh, *Cumber* in English. The English knew them by both names, and added a third, calling them 'foreigners', *wealh* or *wylisc* in Old English, *Welsh* in modern English. All these words are alternative descriptions of the same people.

The various names of the Welsh are real and ancient, but made-up modern names still obscure the identity of the English. The newcomers from Germany were drawn from many different nations, but in Britain they adopted a general collective name, 'Engle', or 'Englisc', which Latin writers wrote as *Angli*, and evidently did so before the middle of the 6th century. The form 'Angle' is an invention of recent antiquarians, a simple transliteration of the ordinary Latin word for 'English'. It was not restricted to the territories of the East, Middle and Northern 'Angles', but also comprehended the West, East, South and Middle 'Saxons'; for in their oldest written record, the laws of the 7th century, king Ine styled himself 'king of the West Saxons', but described his subjects as 'Englishmen' or 'Welshmen', not as 'Saxons'. Saxon became a collective national term, but no individual in Britain is known to have been called a 'Saxon' in his own language. 'Saxon' was the term which foreigners applied to the entire nation, and still do; *Saesnaeg* and *Sasanach* are the modern Welsh and Irish words for 'English', and in the elegant Latin of the 7th and 8th centuries *Saxonia* was used as freely of the Northumbrian 'Angles' as of the 'Saxons' of Wessex. Frisians and Jutes, 'Angles' and Saxons, Alamanni and Scandinavians all called themselves English when they settled in Britain, and were all described as 'Saxons' by their British neighbours. In time, custom fixed upon their southern territories the national name used of them by their British neighbours, Saxons, western and southern, eastern and middle, and restricted their own national name, English, 'Angle', to their northern and midland territories. The words do not mean that the south country was settled by immigrants from lower Saxony, the north and midlands by men from Angel in Schleswig. Saxon and Angle are valid terms for regions of Britain, but not for the continental origin of their inhabitants.

Later accident increased the confusion. Eighth-century continental writers devised the term *Angli Saxones*, English Saxons, to distinguish the Saxons of Britain from those of Germany. Early in the ninth century, when the Wessex kings mastered all the English, they took over the term to demonstrate that they were as English as their Mercian predecessors; and sometimes varied it to 'Angul-' or 'Anglo-Saxones', or distinguished the West Saxons with the more honourable title of 'West Angli', and encouraged new words like 'Angligena' or 'Angelcyn'. The usage was short-lived, and was confined to official documents, chiefly in Latin. It was occasionally employed thereafter by those who copied such Latin documents, but it was not revived in the English language until the 18th century, and was employed to link the English colonists in America with their cousins at home, as well as to denote their remote ancestors. Its usage spread slowly, and the terms 'Old English' or 'Saxon' long remained in use; it was not until the 20th century that the unhappy hybrid 'Anglo-Saxon' altogether prevailed, under the influence of historians who pretended that English history begins with the Norman Conquest, and welcomed a word that divorced the pre-Conquest English from their descendants. It is already beginning to pass from use, for many archaeologists are discovering that the terms pagan, middle and late Saxon convey a clearer meaning.

Other peoples were known by different names in different languages, but their usage is simpler. 'Scot' is the Latin name for the Irish, and 'Pict', painted, is the Latin name for the British beyond the Forth, whom Rome never subdued; the Irish called them 'Cruithni', British, and knew their country as Alba, or Albania, Albany, from Albion, the earliest name of Britain, that was known to the ancient Greek travellers. It was not until the 9th century that an Irish Scot dynasty secured the throne of Pictland, and ultimately gave their dynastic name to all northern Britain, thenceforth called Scotland. These terms confuse the unwary, but none are in conflict; British and Welsh, English and Saxon, Scot and Irish are interchangeable terms, naming the same nations in different languages.

Personal names also have their problems. It is not always obvious whether the same name refers to different people, or the same person. As in all ages, common sense is the only guide. Some names are rare, others frequent; some are restricted to particular times, regions or social levels. Some, like Caswallon, Edward or Caradog remain in use, others, like Edbert or Fernvael, passed from fashion; others again, like Hengest or Maelgwn, were used by one person only, and were rarely given to others, if at all. But sometimes a great man's eminence prompted parents to name their children after him; as in modern times, Florence Nightingale, named uniquely after the city in which she was born, made her strange name so common for three generations in southern England that it became almost a synonym for servant-girl; and therefore passed from use. In recognising persons, it is obvious that a common name like Ceredic does not by itself help to identify the people who bore it, unless further detail links them; but to suppose that two separate persons of the same date and status bore the unique names of Hengest or Maelgwn would be as idle as to suggest that two different persons called Marlborough commanded the armies of early 18th century England.

The roots of confusion are names hazily understood and dates apparently contradictory. Gildas' narrative, and the contemporary evidence that dates it, divide the history of fifth-century Britain into three main periods. The generation from the break with Rome in 410 to the outbreak of the first Saxon revolt about 442 is the last age of Roman Britain. Then followed nearly twenty years of conflict between the Roman British and the Saxons, or English, that ended when the bulk of the organised southern British forces accepted defeat and sent their emigrants to Gaul, shortly before 461. The third period, a generation of about 35 years, from about 460 to 495, witnessed the successful resistance of the British. That resistance was begun by Ambrosius; some time before the final victory of Badon, its captaincy passed to Arthur.

The outline of the next century is simpler. British and English traditions both prolong the peace of Badon for three-quarters of a century. A second Saxon revolt won decisive victories in the 570s, and by the early 7th century had permanently mastered most of what is now England. Gildas' narrative is supplemented by a good deal of detail until about 460; from then until the 530s, evidence is meagre; thereafter, information rapidly becomes fuller, and increasing contemporary and continental evidence gives growing confirmation and precision.

CHAPTER FOUR
INDEPENDENT BRITAIN: VORTIGERN

Civil Government

Britain was still Roman in 410, and remained Roman for a generation. Political independence did not disrupt the settled Roman economy. In 429 Germanus of Auxerre encountered opulent bishops and normal civil life, and at about the same date Patrick found his family secure in their property; in the 440s Patrick was concerned with cultured bishops who still exercised normal ecclesiastical authority, while Germanus met a civil government that still ruled its region effectively in southern Britain. But since the imperial government no longer gave protection, the British had to fight to keep their civilisation. Roman writers were impressed when

> the British people took up arms, bore the brunt of the attack, and freed their cities from the barbarian threat.

Various sources name their enemies. The Gallic Chronicle of 452 reports a dreadful Saxon raid upon the Channel coasts in 411. The Irish Annals put the death of the high king Niall in the Channel a few years earlier, and Gildas recounts victories in colourful detail, that may repeat a story told in his native north-west.

> Hordes of Picts and Irish . . . swarmed from their coracles . . . and seized the whole of the far north, as far as the Wall. . . . Our countrymen abandoned their cities and high walls . . . and the disasters from abroad were aggravated by internal disorders, for repeated incursions had emptied the whole land of food.

However, when the Romans refused to help, the British rallied and

> went on fighting back, basing themselves on hills and caves, moorland and woods, . . . trusting not in man, but in God; they then defeated the enemy raiders for the first time. . . . The enemy withdrew.

A bare Irish record of a battle, or a ravaging, of the Clyde, in the time of Niall's successor, Nath-I, may remember the same attack.

Gildas and the continental contemporaries agree on the essential fact of British success against the barbarians. The Gallic writer names Saxon enemies,

Gildas names the Irish and the Picts; the Irish allege their own presence in the Channel and in the far north, and have left scattered traces of a considerable settlement in western Britain.

Military victory was achieved by the armies of Britain. Raising and maintaining armies requires a political government, and one contemporary says something of how it came to power. A homily addressed to a young widow, published in or about the year 411, bears the name of a British bishop named Fastidius. One passage concerns contemporary political events. The author consoled the widow for the seeming injustice of God, who had taken her virtuous husband, though so many evil-doers were left alive, and referred her to what was happening in the world about them at the time, when

> we see before us many instances of wicked men, the sum of their sins complete, who are being judged at this present moment, and denied this present life no less than the life to come. This is not hard to understand, for in changing times we expect the deaths of magistrates who have lived criminally; for the greater their power, the bolder their sins. . . . Those who have freely shed the blood of others are now forced to shed their own. . . . Some lie unburied, food for the beasts and birds of the air. Others have been individually torn limb from limb. Their judgements killed many husbands, widowed many women, orphaned many children, leaving them bare and beggared . . . for they plundered the property of the men they killed. But now it is their wives who are widowed, their sons who are orphans, begging their daily bread from strangers.

A government had recently been overthrown by violence; rough justice killed some and lynched some, but others received a formal trial. It was not simply a peasant or plebeian rising, for victors and vanquished were both men of property. But the language is remarkable. Governments in plenty were overthrown in the fourth and fifth centuries. But they were personal governments; their enemies uniformly abuse the 'satellites' of an 'unspeakable tyrant' or 'wicked minister'. Fastidius' account is unique because the fallen rulers are not described as the agents of any tyrant or minister; they are magistrates, treated as equals of each other. His language suits the exceptional situation in Britain in 410 or 411. It may be that the government which had seized power in order to secure help from Italy was itself overthrown when that help was not forthcoming. If it had tried and executed Constantine's leading supporters as rebels against Honorius, it could not expect mercy from their friends when its promise came to nothing.

The political events of the next dozen years are not recorded. But the political forces, the pressures and the institutions which decided them are known. In Britain, as in Gaul and Italy, there were two main native political forces, the landed nobility and the army. In Europe, there was a third force that had as yet no equivalent in Britain, the power of large barbarian peoples headed by their kings. But Britain may have had one political pressure that was negligible in Europe. In and about the year 410 British writers abroad, notably the unnamed author known as the Sicilian Briton, developed an astonishingly advanced egalitarian political philosophy, exalting the Christian virtues of the poor against the sin of riches, and urging the abolition of the rich. Their views had a brief influence, sufficient to provoke popular disturbances in Rome and alarm the imperial government for a few months in 418. Their tracts refer to individual outspoken plebeians who dared to lift their voices and argue politics with men of substance, demanding social justice. One at least of their writings still circulated in Britain more than a century later, and is cited by Gildas. An egalitarian peasant commune subsisted for a short while in Armorica, but there is little sign of such peasant rebellion in Britain, and the writings of the Sicilian Briton and his fellows agitated the urban rather than rural poor in Italy. In Britain, Fastidius condemns the old government and approves the new, and urges with unusual force the view that in a stable society governments and men of property must use their wealth to care for the poor.

> Do you think yourself Christian if you oppress the poor? . . . If you enrich yourself by making many others poor? If you wring your food from others' tears? . . . If, when you are bidden to distribute your own property, you seize other people's . . . ?
> A Christian is a man who . . . never allows a poor man to be oppressed when he is by . . . whose doors are open to all, whose table every poor man knows, whose food is offered to all.

The sentiments of Christian charity are not novel, but such insistence in the fifth century is exceptional; so is its context, related to a government which Fastidius regards, or pretends to regard, as committed to practise them. These writings do not suggest that the urban or rural poor constituted an independent organised political movement with a social programme of its own. They do suggest that the pressure of the poor for social justice was somewhat more effective in Britain than in Europe.

Europe resolved these conflicting pressures by continuing the government in

---

Peoples and Places **Map 2**

● Capitals of *Civitates*

■ Coloniae; legionary fortresses; and London

○ Other major military centres

MAP 2 ROMAN BRITAIN

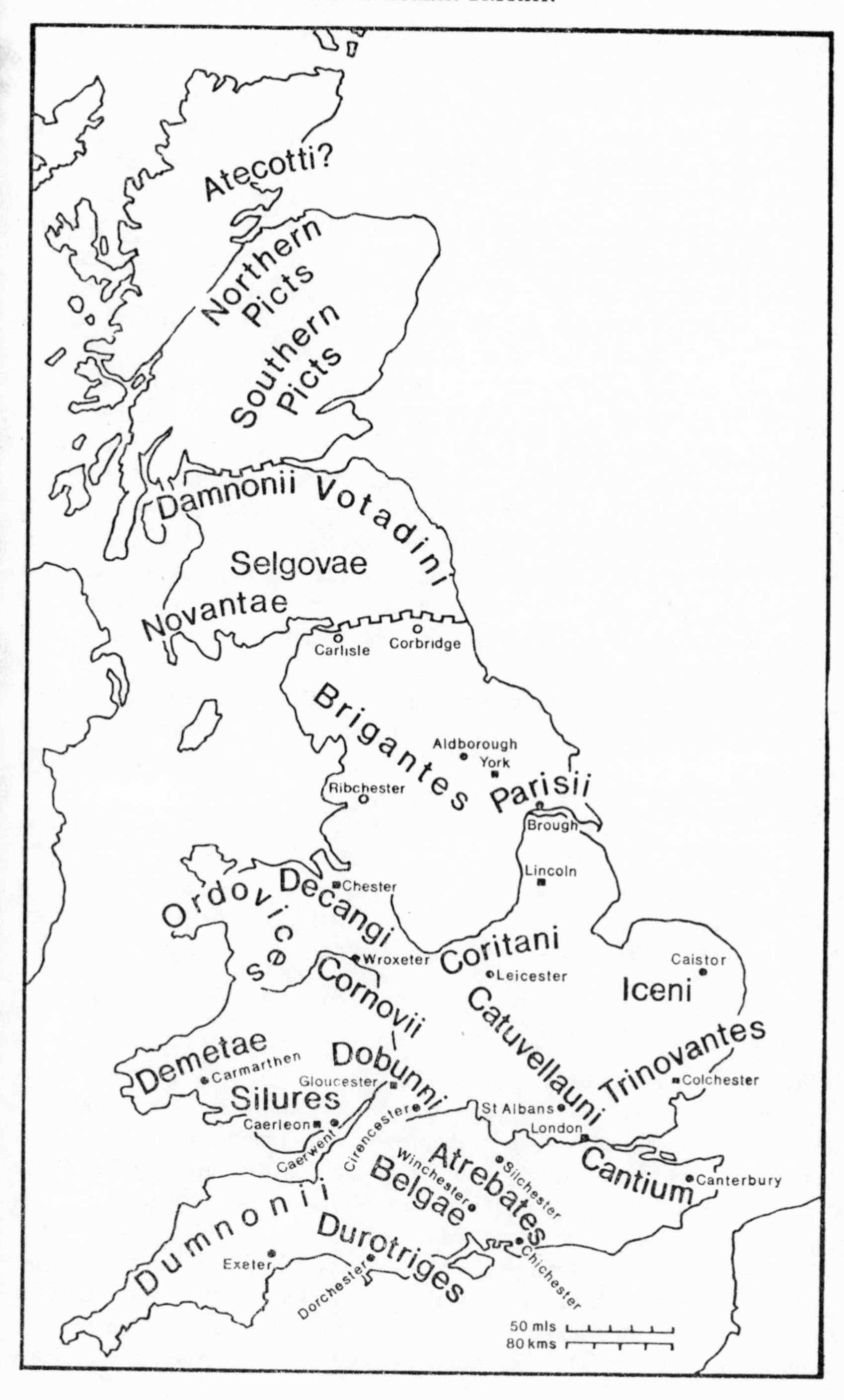

the name of the infant and feeble heirs of legitimate emperors. Britain had no such legitimate heirs. Yet the long-established constitution of the Empire was the only possible form of government. An emperor ruled through civilian prefects, military *magistri*, and lesser departmental heads, appointed consuls to name the year and to discharge the ancient formal functions of the Roman state. Aristocratic tradition had in the past tried to run the empire by a council of appointed noblemen, and had failed. It was impossible to revive such governmental forms in the fifth century, in Europe or in Britain; the army, and the plebs, had for centuries rejected aristocratic government in favour of a monarchy able to curb senators and to reduce the risk of civil war. The governments of 410 and 411 were necessarily created by the *civitates* meeting in council to get rid of the emperor Constantine and to find a successor. When their natural choice, Honorius, failed them, they had to seek another. They could not themselves endure, without an emperor. But it was not easy to agree upon an emperor whose government all would accept. Any stable ruler must command the obedience both of the aristocracy and of the army; and must prove tolerable to the plebs. An emperor, whatever his origin, must heed the whole of the pressures within the empire; but his subjects pressed chiefly the interests of their own group and class. Noblemen naturally distrusted a military emperor, generals distrusted a civilian. Any magnate appointed to rule must encounter the resistance of his fellow noblemen, who knew that his origins and claims were no better than theirs, so soon as other pressures forced him into policies they resented. An army officer crowned emperor risked both the jealousy of his colleagues and their resentment at concessions to the civilian taxpayer. Civil conflict was as inevitable in Britain as in Europe, when once there was no clear succession.

A few notices assert the obvious, that such emperors were appointed, and faced civil war. Procopius, writing in Constantinople in about 550, says that after the end of Roman rule, Britain was governed by 'tyrants', illegitimate emperors. Gildas, writing ten years earlier in Britain, says that in the early fifth century, after the repulse of the barbarians and during the period of prosperity,

> kings were anointed . . . and soon after slain . . . by those who had anointed them.

From the late 4th century on, the word 'king', *rex*, was used colloquially of emperors, though never officially; and the letter of Honorius legitimised emperors who ruled in Britain alone. One of them is known. The parents of Ambrosius Aurelianus, who headed the resistance of the 460s, had 'worn the purple'; the words mean that his father was emperor, for no subject 'wore the purple'. He is perhaps the Ambrosius who is reported to have been Vortigern's rival in the 430s.

The government of an emperor required imperial officers and institutions, prefects, masters of the soldiers, consuls, senators. One of them is attested; the Sicilian Briton, writing home to a wealthy relative who sat in judgement on a tribunal, and therefore held office, politely wished him an 'everlasting consulate'.

The probable meaning is that he was a consul, recognised in Britain alone. But the institution that looms largest in the narratives of Gildas and Nennius is the Council. The Council of the province or diocese, composed of magnates from the separate *civitates*, was a normal institution. It was usually weak in the face of the imperial government; but when the magnates of Britain could make and unmake their own emperors, the Council clearly mattered more, and may well have taken the place of the Senate.

The Army

Vortigern is said to have come to power about 425. He is described as king or tyrant; as such, he held the power, and probably the title, of an emperor. Nothing is reported of the persons or the circumstances that brought him to power, but the principal political interests that pressed upon his government are known. They were rooted in different regions. Throughout the lowlands, territorial magnates were still powerful, especially rich and numerous in the Cotswold country. Beyond them lay the poorer states of Dumnonia, Devon and Cornwall, of Demetia, Pembroke and Carmarthen, and of central and northern Wales; there landowners were humbler men, nearer to their tenants in interest and outlook, in language and culture, with less Latinity in their speech and thought; and it is probable that more of the land was farmed directly by its owners.

The third main region of Roman Britain, the north, was the domain of the army; and the army had the means to make and unmake governments. There is plenty of archaeological evidence for the late Roman army in Britain, and a precise contemporary description survives. But the evidence is difficult to assess and interpret. The *Notitia Dignitatum*, or List of Offices, is a comprehensive schedule of all senior civilian departments, and of the army units, throughout the Roman Empire; its western lists were kept up to date until the early 420s, about the time of Vortigern's accession. They were maintained by the imperial government in Italy; but it had not ruled Britain since the enthronement of Constantine III in 406, and it is unlikely that the British lists had been revised thereafter. They were retained because the separation of Britain from the rest of the empire was the result of an emergency, and might be ended.

Three distinct commands are recorded in Britain. A small mobile field army force, of three infantry and six cavalry units, under a *comes*, or count, had no fixed stations; and might have followed Constantine to Gaul. The names and stations of two static frontier commands are also entered, the coastal garrisons of the Saxon Shore, under their own *comes*, from Southampton Water to the Wash, and the army of the north, under its *dux*, or general, whose headquarters were at York. The static units were hard to move, for their wives and children were exposed to enemy attack if they were absent. Stilicho managed to withdraw a legion in 403, and perhaps some Saxon Shore forces, and Constantine III may have persuaded some at least of the younger men to follow him abroad; but it is unlikely that the bulk of the garrisons could have been induced to leave.

Elsewhere in the empire, most garrisons stayed where they were until they were overwhelmed.

In most of the empire, garrison units of the 'major schedule', normally those raised in the fourth century, and the legions, are listed first in the *Notitia*, followed by the 'lesser schedule' of the auxiliary units that survived from the early Roman army, the *alae* and *cohortes*, wings or squadrons of cavalry and regiments or battalions of infantry; where a military command extends over more than one civil province, the units in each province are listed separately. The northern British list follows the normal pattern. After the legion at York, and fourth-century units in the Pennine forts, follows the 'lesser schedule', with a cross heading 'Also on the Line of the Wall', naming the auxiliaries from Wallsend to Westmorland. It is followed by a new list, of one unit of the major schedule and two of the lesser, in Lancashire and the West Riding; the second list clearly relates to a different province, perhaps Valentia.

Throughout the empire, the units of the major schedule were still effective fighting units, wherever evidence is available to show their history; but those of the lesser schedule were not. Some were wholly absorbed in civil administration; some existed only in name; and ultimately many of their personnel spent much of their time earning a civilian livelihood. At best they could defend their homes against attack; for they were armed. A commander might commonly deploy his major units, or move their station, at least within their own region; but he would be fortunate if he could persuade the lesser units to operate beyond the next neighbouring fort. So long as he retained the allegiance of his men, the *dux* at York might rely upon his major units to secure the Pennines against a lowland government, in case of dispute; and might in times of crisis induce detachments to aid the south against an enemy, or to challenge its authority. But essentially his armies, and those of the *comes* on the south-eastern coast, were regional forces, not readily available for the defence of the rest of the country, or for interference in its government.

No adequate commentary on the *Notitia* has yet been published; its absence has permitted strange speculations, based chiefly on considerations of the British lists on their own. In particular, it is often asserted that the Wall list was fifty or a hundred years out of date by the 420s, and that the units named had long ceased to exist, chiefly because the Wall was badly battered in the disaster of 367, and was restored by makeshift repairs, to which labourers from the civilian south contributed. The text does not justify such inferences; nowhere else does it preserve lists so long obsolete, and in Britain it notes the changes introduced in 368, omitting the forts north of the Wall that were then abandoned; it places upon the Wall lesser schedule units whose engineering standards are likely to have been as poor as those that excavation has revealed. It is likely that, as in Egypt and on the Danube, units maimed by invasion were left under strength, perhaps paid in kind rather than in cash, and allowed to dwindle to the calibre of an ineffectual local militia.

The names of the units are however of secondary importance. Though late coins are rare upon the Wall, late pottery abounds, and lasts as long as Roman pottery was manufactured in Britain. Some of it was made locally, but the bulk of it was imported from far away, chiefly from the kilns of the East Riding; and these imports argue that the Wall forts were still supplied by the army command at York. The date when these kilns ceased production is not known, but it is unlikely to have been much later than the Saxon revolt of the 440s. The disappearance of the pottery is evidence of the closure of the kilns, but has no bearing on the ultimate fate of the Wall forts; when their population could no longer import, it had to do without imports. No evidence is available for most forts; but some rebuilding is very late, and burials of the later 5th century, and of the 6th, some of them British, some Germanic, have been reported from a dozen forts; and some elaborate rebuilding looks as late. The burials are evidence that some men continued to live in some of the forts, whether or not they constituted the fading relics of the units named in the *Notitia*.

One section of the northern command seems to have perished early. The watch towers of the Yorkshire coast, unlike the forts of the Saxon Shore, the Pennines and the Wall, were violently destroyed; the skeletons of armed men and dogs, who rotted where they fell, are lurid witness of a final disaster. The skeletons give no date; but at one poor farming site near the Scarborough tower, the British population was replaced by an English settlement as poor, probably during the fifth century. It may be that the population fled when the tower was stormed, and that thereafter the English were installed in their place.

Excavation has shown other fortifications, not named in the *Notitia*. The four corners of Wales, Chester and Caernarvon, Cardiff and Carmarthen, are left out of the lists, perhaps because much of the Welsh coast was in the hands of Irish settlers. No fortifications are known in Dumnonia; but a few late Roman coins on coastal sites from Barnstaple to Plymouth, in regions where coins of all periods are rare, may be the consequence of government payments to local militia, in districts also open to the Irish. In the interior, there is no record of military forces, other than the small field army that may or may not have remained. But the massive fortifications of late Roman towns point to a huge gap in our knowledge; there is nothing to show who manned their walls and bastions, though the walls were built for armed men to hold. Their defence necessarily fell to the local population, ill-equipped, ill-trained and inexperienced, perhaps sometimes reinforced by army units. Excavation hints at local officers; the ceremonial symbol of military rank was the belt, *cingulum*, worn by military and civil officers, splendidly adorned for higher ranks. Many such belts have been discovered; the more elaborate are decorated in the style termed *Kerbschnitt*, or 'chip-carving'. The ornament imitates in bronze the technique of wood-carving, and is probably of Germanic inspiration, though it was the fashion for officers of any nationality all along the western frontiers from about 380 to about 430.

These belts are sometimes found in graves, and a man who was buried with military equipment was usually a barbarian, who followed barbarian burial customs. There were many German officers in the late Roman army; most of them commanded native Romans, and were themselves assimilated to Roman and Christian ways, but there were also a few units of Germans, officered by Germans. Few remained permanently German, for many of those that were maintained for more than twenty or thirty years commonly drew their recruits from the frontier where they were stationed, and became Roman, retaining only the name of their original nationality. But two or three newly raised barbarian units are known to have served in Britain, and there were doubtless others that have left no trace.

There were also humbler German forces in the western empire, termed *gentiles*, perhaps also in Britain. The *Notitia* lists among them *Laeti*, mostly Frankish, in Gaul, and *Sarmatae* in Gaul and Italy. The Gallic *Laeti* were the descendants of prisoners surrendered by treaty at the end of the third century, who were settled in or near the towns of the interior, with the double purpose of agricultural labour on landlords' estates and of local defence. The last page of the list is missing; it may have included *gentiles* settled in Britain, though they may not have been called either *Laeti* or *Sarmatae*. Recent archaeological observation suggests that such communities existed. Some men were buried in Roman cemeteries, with ordinary 4th-century pots, but also with Germanic spears, as at Colchester. But from the end of the third century onward, a number of commercial Roman potteries in Britain manufactured for sale a variety of wheel-made wares, whose shapes and decoration imitated the hand-made vessels of the Saxons and English of the lower Elbe lands of Germany. They are found chiefly in the eastern and midland counties, between the Bedfordshire Ouse and the Thames estuary, most of them in or near Roman towns and country houses, occasionally also in Saxon Shore forts. They were made for customers who liked and bought Saxon styles; and it is likely that such customers were of Saxon origin, *gentiles* settled in Britain, at much the same time, and on much the same terms, as the *Laeti* of Gaul. They have nothing to do with the later pagan English immigrants of the fifth century; they used normal Roman cemeteries and their wares were not buried in pagan English graves. By the time of Hengest, four or five generations after their settlement in Britain, they can have had no common cause with their distant kinsmen; for Germans beyond the frontier had little love for those among them who took service with the empire. The interest and affection of the *gentiles* tied them to the economy of Britain, and numbered them among the allies and defenders of Rome.

The military forces of the south are likely to have consisted of local residents, prepared to defend only their own walls; of a few German army units; of *gentiles*; and of such field army units as Constantine III and his successors had been able to raise and maintain in Britain. Unless the armed forces of the north and south agreed to obey a British emperor, each must follow its own fate. What little is known of the disintegration of the Roman army elsewhere indicates the possibilities that lay before them. In northern Gaul, the last Roman commander-in-chief, Aegidius, refused allegiance to the puppet emperors of later fifth-century Italy. His independent command became a kingdom, that he bequeathed to his son Syagrius, who maintained it until he was overwhelmed by the Franks in 486. Another general established a similar kingdom in Dalmatia, and left it to his nephew.

Similar possibilities were open to the *dux* at York, whose major units still provided combatant units. Detailed information on the fate of auxiliary army units of the lesser schedule comes from the Danube. In the province of *Noricum Ripense*, roughly the territory of modern Austria, a monk named Severinus stiffened the resistance of the still Roman towns again the barbarians, who dominated the countryside. His biographer, writing in 511, about events forty or fifty years earlier, naively remarked

> While the Roman Empire still existed, they used to maintain soldiers in many towns at the public expense. . . . When this custom lapsed, . . . the unit at Passau continued it. Some soldiers from this unit were sent to Italy to fetch the last pay due to their comrades. . . .

They were murdered by barbarians. But if they had reached Rome, the *Notitia* proved their entitlement. It names their unit, the 9th Batavians, which had been stationed for 400 years at Passau, on the Inn, now the frontier between Austria and Germany, and had given the place its Roman name, *Batavis*. Here, one unit long outlived the collapse of the frontier. The defence of different towns along that frontier greatly varied. In one of them, 'the tribune Mamertinus, later a bishop' commanded a few frightened soldiers who dared take the field only when Severinus inspired them with a rousing speech and a blessing. Another town was burdened with a barbarian garrison, apparently of federate allies of Rome; another, once the fortress of a legion, was now packed with refugees from abandoned towns, but there is no sign of troops; the citizens themselves mounted guard on the walls.

Lesser units were as feeble, and as long-lived, in Egypt, where no barbarians overawed the countryside. Some of the units named in the *Notitia* continued to raise local recruits in the 580s; and their grandchildren served in the same units when the Moslems overran Egypt in 640. But though the recruits became regular soldiers, they were part-timers, boatmen, bakers, basket-makers, who worked at their trade in the morning, and paraded for drill in the afternoon.

These reports from the Danube and the Nile match the evidence excavated in Britain. When civilians and soldiers sheltered together inside the walls of forts, the distinction between them was blurred, as in Egypt. The northern British frontier was not stormed, like the Danube; but in much of the south, during and after the Saxon revolt, conditions were similar. Barbarians roamed at will in the open country. Some towns were abandoned, others were not; the uneven scatter of military equipment suggests that some towns were defended by military units, of Roman or barbarian origin, whose morale and discipline is likely to have been as varied as on the Danube. It is unwise to look for a definite time when the male population of a town or fort ceased to be a military unit, or to suppose that each place was abandoned at the same date. The frontier garrisons dwindled and disintegrated, the fate of each of them separately determined by local accidents. In Britain, as elsewhere, the Roman army did not die; like the proverbial old soldier, it faded away.

In Britain, there is no sign that the frontier was ever stormed or evacuated. On the contrary, it held, and barred the Picts from attacking south by land. Its central authority remained, to develop like that of Aegidius in Gaul. The future political organisation of the north is outlined in the genealogies, whose later names are celebrated in the old Welsh poems, at the end of the sixth century. The several dynasties of the Pennines and the Wall trace their common origin to Coel Hen, whom they place early in the fifth century. One of the greater dynasties ends with Eleuther of the Great Army, and his son Peredur of York. The kings named might all have been actual descendants of Coel; but the genealogy would take the same form, and treat them as descendants, if they were subordinate commanders who rejected the sovereignty of York, but founded their authority thereon. The early tradition is that Coel ruled the whole of the north, south of the Wall, the territory that the *Notitia* assigned to the *dux*; but that in later generations it split into a number of independent kingdoms. It suggests that, like Aegidius, he was the last Roman commander, who turned his command to a kingdom. But his kingdom lasted longer than that of Aegidius. So did his name; for medieval fantasy turned him into Old King Cole, and on the strength of the name transferred him to Colchester.

In the early fifth century, the *dux* was not yet a king; but his army made him an independent ruler who need not bow to a government he did not respect. His power was limited by the difficulty of moving his forces out of their own territory, and by the sudden cessation of his normal resources. His predecessors had looked to Italy for men and money. He could look only to Britain, and the wealth that must maintain the army was concentrated in the hands of wealthy southern magnates. Therein lay the basis of agreement between the military and the civil power; or of disagreement. In the years immediately after 410, there was evidently concord. The British repelled their enemies with outstanding success; and could hardly have done so unless the *dux*, the *comes* and the civil government worked together; and unless some effective forces were recruited and maintained in the south.

Concord did not endure. Gildas complained that

> the island grew affluent. The abundance of commodities outstripped the memory of any earlier age. But with prosperity grew luxury . . . and all the vices natural to man . . . hatred of truth . . . and love of lies. . . . Kings were anointed . . . and soon after slain.

Throughout the late empire, landowners had no love of armies; the imperia, government found continuing difficulty in raising recruits, for landowners pulled every excuse to avoid surrendering their tenants and labourers, and to avoid payment of taxation. The magnates of Italy and Gaul resisted the demands of a legitimate long-established government for men and money, even when danger was acute; their peers in Britain are unlikely to have met their obligations willingly in times of peace and prosperity. Britain cannot have escaped the consequences that followed in Europe; the government was forced to walk the tightrope between the needs of the army and the interest of the landowners; its officers, in search of money, squeezed the peasant and the poorer landowner, who lacked the strength to defy or cheat the tax-collector. The root conflicts between the rich and the poor, the army and the civilians, were sharpened by personal antagonisms between individual generals, individual magnates and individual states. Secular conflict inflamed religious dispute, and rival theological ideologies surfaced into bitter clashes in times of political crisis. In Europe, the universal fear of civil war attached public opinion to the legitimate dynasty, so that conflict might be resolved by the intrigues of ministers, who ruled in the name of inoffensive nonentities. But Britain had no legitimate dynasty; a change of government still required the overthrow of an emperor, and therefore 'kings were anointed and soon after slain'.

Vortigern

Out of these conflicts came Vortigern. The genealogists make him a notable of Gloucester, one of the four known *coloniae* of Britain, the only one of them situated among the great mansions of the Cotswolds. Tradition sets him among the wealthiest of the landed aristocracy. Other rulers are credited with a like origin; Ambrosius Aurelianus was a 'gentleman', a *vir modestus*; and his father had been emperor before him. It is not easy to see that persons elevated by the *civitates* of Britain could have had any other origin, unless it were military.

Vortigern excelled among his fellows, for he managed to preserve his authority for a generation, despite disastrous reverses, where his predecessors had been quickly overthrown. His success betokens a wide support, and his name suggests its origin. It cannot have been his normal and original name. The other known notables of early fifth-century Britain all bore ordinary Roman names, even if they also had British names. Several did. Patrick, of a fifth-century landed family, was also called 'Maun'; the Cornovian Marcus in the sixth century was also named Conomorus; and the original text of the genealogies may have read 'Vortigern, that is Vitalis' (or Vitalinus), later misinterpreted as 'Vortigern, son of Vitalinus'.

But Vortigern is not a name. It is a description. It means 'Overking'. It was not a title, and did not become so; but it is a description that fitted one person only, as surely as in the 1940s 'the Old Man' meant Churchill and no one else, or as a century before 'the Duke' meant Wellington and no other duke. The widespread use of the word implies that it was popularised by people who spoke British rather than Latin; and that they liked him. He seems to have appealed to their affections, for two of his three sons were known by their native names, and are among the earliest late Roman notables known to have used such rustic native names in preference to polished Roman names. It is therefore possible that one of the reasons that enabled him to maintain a longer and stronger authority is that he was able to call upon support from the poorer areas of Wales and the south-west, as well as from the Cotswold magnates; and that he may have appeared as the champion of the peasant, the urban poor and the underdog, echoing the radical sentiments of Fastidius. Such support, and such sentiments, must have offended some amongst his fellow magnates; but it was a support that gave strength, as popular support had once strengthened Caesar against Pompey, and was in a later age to strengthen the Tudor kings against the great lords. Vortigern's name was perhaps Vitalinus; his formal title is not known. It was quite possibly emperor, 'Imperator Caesar Augustus'; and he would have followed precedent if he named Hengest his *Magister Militum*, commander-in-chief.

Picts and Saxons

Whatever the forces that brought him to power, Vortigern faced a serious external crisis on his accession.

> The feathered flight of a not unfamiliar rumour reached the keen ears of everyone, that their old enemies were come again, bent as was their wont on destruction and on inhabiting the country from end to end. Yet they took no profit from the news . . . but rather . . . rushed down the broad way that leads to death . . . until . . . a deadly plague struck down so many many in a short space, with no sword, that the living could not bury all the dead.

The danger was new and severe. The enemies were not merely raiders; they now aimed at conquest and settlement. Goth, Burgundian and Vandal had shown that barbarians might settle within the empire, and had warned Romans of the consequence. The faint native traditions of the Picts emphasise their own rising ambition; after a list of bare unmeaning names, the first of their kings to whom their records give a date or ascribe an action was Drust son of Erp, who 'fought a hundred battles' and is said to have reigned from 414 to 458, in Vortigern's time. Gildas' 'old enemies' were the northerners. The Picts, as well as the Irish, were to him, *transmarini*, from overseas; both sailed to Britain 'in their coracles' and both had carried their booty home 'across the sea'. Gildas is not composing an academic study of British geography; he describes the means by which the enemy reached the Roman diocese. The Irish came by sea because they lived in an island; the Picts came by sea because the northern frontier armies withstood them by land, and because even without armies, many hundreds of miles of poor country separated them from the riches of the south. These riches were vulnerable. The Cotswolds lay open to Irish landings by the Severn Sea, and were also less than a week's march down the Icknield Way from the flat beaches of the east coast.

The 'rumour' reached the British well in advance of the invasion. Evidently some fresh initiative had advertised the enemy intention before their armada was ready. This event may have been the destruction of the Yorkshire signal towers, a necessary preliminary to any Pictish offensive. Their end was sudden and final. All that can be said of its date is that it was probably before the first English settlement in the East Riding, in the earlier 5th century. One scrap of evidence suggests the possibility that Pictish raiders may have penetrated as far as Norfolk.

The British took no immediate action. But events moved fast.

> The time drew nigh, when the iniquities of Britain should be fulfilled, as with the Amorites of old. A Council was convened, to decide upon the best and soundest means of withstanding the frequent brutal invasions and raids of the aforesaid peoples.
> All the members of the council, and the proud tyrant, were struck blind. . . . To hold back the northern peoples, they introduced into the island the vile unspeakable Saxons, hated of God and man alike. . . . Nothing more frightful had ever happened to this island, nothing more bitter. The utter blindness of their wits! What raw hopeless stupidity! Of their own free will, they invited in under the same roof the enemy they feared worse than death. . . . So the brood of cubs burst from the lair of the barbarian lioness, in three 'keels', as they call warships in their language. . . . At the orders of the ill-fated tyrant, they first fixed their fearful claws upon the eastern part of the island, as though to defend it. . . . Their dam, learning of the success of the first contingent, sent over a larger draft of satellite dogs. . . . Thus were the barbarians introduced . . . in the guise of soldiers running great risk for their kind 'hosts', as the liars asserted. They demanded 'supplies' which were granted and for a long time 'shut the dog's mouth'.

Nennius' Kentish Chronicle is shorter, but more detailed.

> Then came three 'keels', driven into exile from Germany. In them were the brothers Hors and Hengest. . . . Vortigern welcomed them then, and handed over to them the island that in their language is called Thanet, in ours Ruoihm.

The Nennius Chronographer dates their coming to the year 428, the fourth year of Vortigern.

Gildas' retrospective fury is understandable; but, at the time, the Council's decision was not so silly. Governments before and after successfully set a thief to catch a thief, and it was plain sense to hire Saxons, the greatest seamen of the age, against seaborne invaders. Hengest was an outstanding freebooter, a Dane allied with Jutes in Frisia, whose fame in German saga outlived his contemporaries. The Saxons were settled, like the Goths of Gaul and other barbarians, under the normal billeting laws, whose technical terms, 'hosts' (*hospites*) and 'supplies' (*annona*), Gildas accurately repeats.

Such federate settlement was a novelty in the western empire, first permitted some ten years before, when the Visigoths were established in Aquitaine in 418. The Visigoths were a large and dangerous people, united by powerful national kings. Hengest's men were few, a scratch force recruited by an adventurer for the occasion. The first small contingent is said to have been conveyed in three 'keels', that could have carried no more than a few hundred men; even if tradition exaggerated, it amounted to no more than the addition of one barbarian unit to the army of Britain; the newcomers did not amount to an independent power, capable of acting on their own initiative, until later events had much increased their numbers. In the 420s they were innocently few, tucked away on a remote offshore island, no threat to the security of Britain.

Vortigern's councillors would have found it hard to make a rational case against the employment of a tiny force under a capable captain, though men already knew the dangers of barbarian allies, and were soon to learn the almost limitless opportunities open to a resolute commander. In a society that had relied for centuries upon professional soldiers, a few armed men might terrify thousands

---

Map 3

	Inhumation alone	Inhumation with a little Cremation	Cremation alone	Cremation with a little Inhumation	Mixed rite	Uncertain rite
Large cemeteries						
Cemeteries						
A few burials	‖		=			//
Single or family burials	|		—			/

House or houses	△
Uncertain date	?
Roman roads	---

MAP 3 PAGAN ENGLISH SETTLEMENT I
THE EARLIER 5th CENTURY

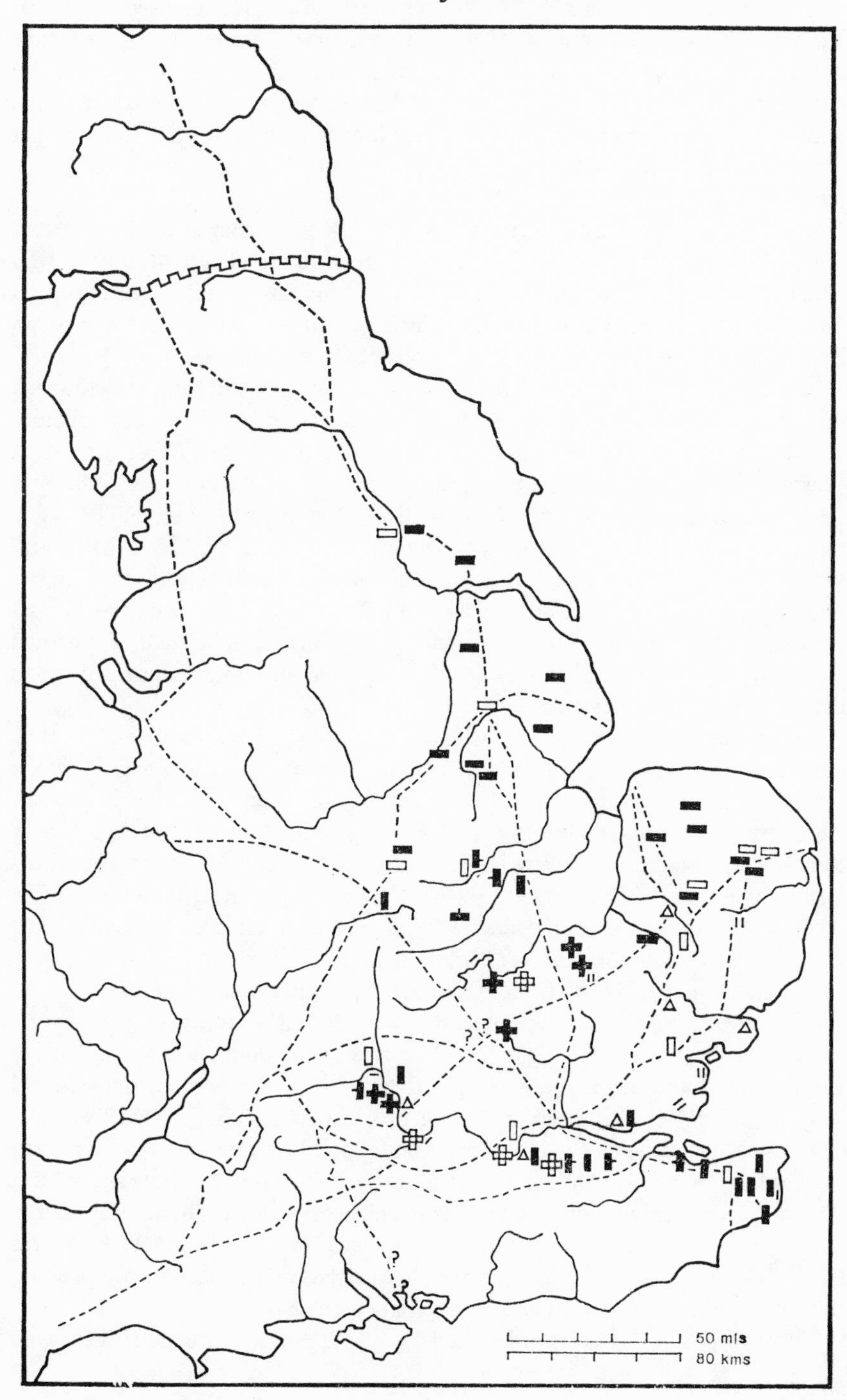

of civilians, whose instinct was to fly from weapons, unless town walls offered shelter. Yet the enlistment of so small a contingent seemed to offer effective defence at low cost. Roman landlords who grudged recruits found it more convenient to contribute the cost of a soldier than to surrender a farmworker; and, since cash payments might be deferred, each member of the Council that authorised the hiring of the English might reasonably hope to dodge at least a part of the imposts he voted.

But a single small force on Thanet was no adequate answer to the expected invasion. It was speedily reinforced by 'a larger draft of satellite dogs', who 'fixed their fearful claws upon the eastern part of the island'. Excavation has pinpointed the places where the claws fastened. Map 3 distinguishes the pagan English cemeteries that contain grave goods of the earliest period.

The excavated evidence does not permit close dating; and cannot distinguish the first comers from the larger drafts who followed, up to the middle decades of the century; save that an unusually large number of the earliest urns from Caistor-by-Norwich suggests that the city may be included among the first settlement areas; and very early brooches from Luton and Abingdon also argue that their owners were among the first comers. But throughout the fifth century, each group of new immigrants tended to settle near their fellows, and even the cemeteries whose earliest burials date from the end of the century are located around and between earlier burial grounds. The map cannot locate the individual sites to which Vortigern's first federates were posted, but it indicates the districts that they protected against the Pictish threat.

These forces were stationed far from the enemy, near to the lands they defended. It is an axiom of military science that a commander's dispositions reveal the nature of the attack he anticipates, or intends to launch himself. Vortigern's allies lined the north road from York to Stamford, with outposts near the Lincolnshire coast, but were most numerous in Norfolk. A few sites in north-east Kent and in the Colchester area closed the estuary of the Thames, and a few guarded the southern approaches to London. Inland, forces by Cambridge, Dunstable and Dorchester-on-Thames, with northward protection at Sandy and Kempston by Bedford, secured the major intersections of the Icknield Way. These dispositions are an intelligible answer to a seaborne invasion threatened from the north, aimed at the riches of the Cotswolds, whose most likely landfall was foreseen on the north Norfolk coast, at the head of the Icknield Way. Relatively strong forces also took precautions against the most obvious alternative, a landing on the Humber, to be followed by a march down the north road or the Fosse Way. A much lighter force forestalled the less likely alternative, that the enemy might by-pass the main defences and sail all the way to the Thames; and Portsmouth harbour was perhaps also protected. The reserves by the Icknield Way formed a last resort, in case the enemy succeeded in piercing the coastal screen. Vortigern and Hengest knew their business.

These dispositions also reveal something of the political situation; their wide distribution demonstrates that the greater part of the lowlands acknowledged the authority of Vortigern and the Council, while the presence of federates at York and the East Riding shows that the northern armies concurred. It is also evident that the northern armies were still regarded as an effective force. No foreigners were yet established north of York; since they were not needed, the army clearly felt able to hold the land frontier on its own. In the east and south, Germanic troops were accepted almost everywhere. Within the area of their settlement, most of the major towns and many smaller places have fifth-century Saxon cemeteries just outside their walls, positioned like the Roman burial grounds. They are clearly the cemeteries of forces billeted in or near the towns. The outstanding exception is Verulamium, where extensive excavation has so far shown no sign of English burials earlier than the 7th century. The government of the Catuvellauni evidently declined to receive a garrison in their capital; they might reasonably have regarded the forces stationed in their territory about Dunstable, thirteen miles to the north, as sufficient protection.

Either the Picts attempted invasion and suffered defeat, or they abandoned the project in face of the massive defences. No invasion succeeded, and the sequel was a British counter-attack. The initial plan showed a boldness of conception foreign to the static defence that had dogged Roman military thought in the fourth century; it provided not only an elastic net to trap an invader, but a means of going out to meet him. The core of the heavy concentration in Norfolk was a group of sites close to the navigable waters of the Yare; and Yarmouth offers the most northerly adequate base whence a large flotilla of beached vessels might quickly reach the open sea. The Saxons were above all seamen, the Picts landsmen who travelled by sea; experienced sailors needed no manual of strategy to teach them that enemy transports were best sunk at sea, or attacked in a night-time anchorage. But whether or not these convenient opportunities were then used, the Saxon seamen are said to have counter-attacked a few years later. The Kentish Chronicle reports that

> Hengest said to Vortigern . . . 'Take my advice, and you will never fear conquest by any man or any people, for my people are strong. I will invite my son and his cousin, fine warriors, to fight against the Irish. Give them the lands of the north, next to the Wall. . . . He invited Octha and Ebissa with forty keels; when they had sailed round against the Picts and plundered the Orkneys, they came and occupied several districts beyond the 'Frenessican Sea', as far as the borders of the Picts.

Gildas records recent enemy penetration as far as the Wall, and though the original purpose of the northern expedition is said to have been to restrain the Irish, Octha was established upon the Pictish border, after attacking their coasts and the islands beyond. He and his men may well be those who first used a group of dateless cemeteries in northern Northumberland, whose dead were interred with no grave goods, save an occasional Saxon knife to prove their nationality; and who left a few place names in south-western Scotland, notably Dumfries, the fortress of the Frisians.

Vortigern's decision brought notable and immediate success. The menace of the highlanders, which for centuries had bogged down upon the British frontier the largest army of the Roman empire, was for ever stilled. Not until 1745 did the south country again have cause to fear invasion from the lands beyond the Forth. Though in the long run the invitation to the barbarians of the lower Elbe was to turn southern Britain into England, immediately it saved Britain from becoming Pictland. Two of the three ancient enemies had been quieted, by pitting one against the other.

The Irish

The danger from the Irish was met by other and subtler means. Though Hengest is said to have offered to fight the Irish, Gildas and the Kentish Chronicler emphasise that the main weight of the English forces was directed against the Picts. The archaeological evidence concurs. Saxon cemeteries are found in the east, not in the west. Their distribution is a result of the decision of Vortigern and his council; if they had decided to use the English against the Irish, the cemeteries would be found in Cumberland, Wales and the south-west. They did not so decide. Nevertheless, the Irish were ancient enemies of the British, repeatedly and recently allies of the Picts, and already had numerous colonies in western Britain. The Picts might reasonably expect their Irish allies to join them against the British.

One incident shows that there was danger in the west. In 429 the bishops of Gaul, with papal approval, sent bishop Germanus of Auxerre to combat the Pelagian heresy in Britain; the date is given by Prosper of Aquitaine, a well-informed contemporary. But since the date given for Hengest's arrival, 428, is much less precise, it cannot be known whether Germanus came before or after Hengest. During the bishop's visit, 'the Saxons and the Picts made a joint campaign against the British', at Easter time. Germanus, who had commanded armies before he took orders,

> offered himself as commander. His light troops thoroughly explored the country through which the enemy's advance was expected; choosing a valley set among high hills, he drew up his army . . . in ambush. As the enemy approached, he ordered the whole force to respond with a great shout when he cried out. The bishops cried out thrice together 'Alleluia'; the whole army replied with a single voice, and the great cry rebounded, shut in by the surrounding hills. The enemy column was terrified; the very frame of heaven and the rocks around seemed to threaten them. . . . They fled in all directions . . . many drowning in the river they had to cross. . . . The bishops won a bloodless victory, gained by faith, not by the might of men.

The biographer who tells the tale, Constantius, was probably well acquainted with Bishop Lupus, who was with Germanus at the battle, and it is his first-hand account that he reproduces. The rocky valley and the broad river are real features of the British countryside, most obviously to be sought in Wales; there, in and near the Vale of Llangollen, a number of early traditions honour Germanus. At first sight, Picts and Saxons seem out of place in Wales, where the normal enemies were Irish. It may be that Lupus' memory muddled the names, but there is no evidence and no reason to suppose that he did. Pict, Irish and Saxon were old allies, and Hengest's small Saxon force was not the only one of its kind that tried its luck in western waters in these years. But whoever the enemies were, there was a real danger that the triple alliance of the past might be renewed, this time in support of a Pictish attempt to conquer all Britain. Vortigern forestalled the alliance, detaching the Saxons by purchase, the Irish by a blend of diplomacy and force.

Germanus' campaign was fought when Vortigern's strategy was beginning to take shape. It formed part of that strategy; for so important a decision, the despatch of an eminent continental bishop to bless a British expeditionary force and advise its commanders cannot have been taken without the goodwill of the British government. The political consequence of the victory is related in another life of Germanus, transcribed among Nennius' documents after it had been lavishly embroidered by the story-tellers. In this account, Germanus, on his first visit to Britain, destroyed the stronghold of a wicked king named Benli, and replaced him with one of his subjects, Catel, 'from whose seed the whole country of Powys is still ruled to-day'. Vortigern is not named in the text, but an inscription set up by the king of Powys about the year 800, termed the 'Pillar of Eliseg', claims Vortigern as the political authority who established the kingdom. The origin of the dynasty was traced to Brittu, who is made a 'son' of Vortigern, 'whom Germanus blessed'; and Vortigern's own legitimate authority is asserted by making him son-in-law to the emperor Maximus, who 'killed the king of the Romans'.

Native tradition placed Germanus' military activity in a countryside that fits the eye-witness description of mountain and river that Constantius learnt from Lupus; though tradition did not know that account. The names of places and persons add detail. The term 'Powys' is a Welsh spelling of the Latin *pagenses*, the 'people of the rural districts'; it implies a separation of the upland rural territory of the Cornovii from the city of Wroxeter, set in the flat lands of the Severn valley. It also implies that the separation took place when Roman administrative terminology was still in use. The names of the first rulers, Catellius and Bruttius, are ordinary Roman family names, appropriate to the landed families of the *civitates*. By contrast, the dynasty of the Cornovii themselves favoured somewhat different names, above all the two personal names Constantine and Gerontius, used by many men for many centuries. These two names may have owed their popularity to the emperor Constantine III and his general Gerontius;

they are recorded among the Cornovii alone, until later accident made Constantine popular among the northern British and the Scots. One medieval Welsh poem appears to echo a tradition that a commander who fought with Germanus was named Gerontius.

The personal and district names associate Germanus with the notables of the Cornovii in a campaign, fought in 429, that recovered their hill territory from the rule of aliens, presumably Irish; and thereafter made it a separate political state, under the rule of men with Roman names. The native tradition concentrates upon the reduction of the principal enemy stronghold. Constantius describes a battle, evidently fought before the siege of the stronghold, against a mobile force of Picts and Saxons; since they also fought the Romans and British, they were necessarily *de facto* allies of the entrenched foreigners, the Irish, very possibly their formal allies.

Local place names add topographical detail. The hill fort of Moel Fenli in Ruthin in northern Powys preserves the name of Benli, or else inspired it. An exceptionally large late Roman coin hoard there buried argues that it was in the fourth or fifth century the residence of a powerful ruler. Twenty miles to the south, on Deeside by Llangollen, Moel-y-Geraint bears the name of Gerontius. Places and churches named after Germanus abound in Powys, but are rare elsewhere in Wales, though they occur in three or four scattered groups in England.

All this diverse evidence hangs together. Each of the several items, considered on its own out of context, bristles with obscurities and tempts the unwary modern critic to speculate without evidence that its statements are 'untrue', or to replace them with others that occur in no source at all. But in context they tell a plain tale. Hostile Irish had settled in numbers in northern Wales; when a force of Picts and Saxons appeared in the area, they threatened to renew the alliance of the barbarians and to establish a firm operational base for continuing attacks upon lowland Britain. A British force was sent to prevent the establishment of that base, to deal with the Picts and Saxons before they reinforced the Irish. Germanus' neat stratagem brought them victory, and Vortigern's political solution prevented a repetition of the threat. The enemy kingdom of the upper Dee was overthrown. A Roman British authority was established in the hilly rural districts of the Cornovian state; though its first commanders doubtless held the rank of Roman military officers, protectors and rulers of the *pagenses*, their command endured, and became the kingdom of Powys.

The establishment of the new kingdom was the first step towards the reduction of the Irish settlements of western Britain. Success required the neutrality of the mainland Irish. In 431, two years after Germanus' visit, the pope sent a Roman priest, Palladius, to fortify the orthodox of Britain and to convert the Irish. He was ill-received in Ireland, and returned after a few months, to die in Britain; in the following year he was replaced by Patrick, a British monk trained in Germanus' cathedral monastery. The young High King Loegaire received him without enthusiasm, but gave him licence to preach. The next event recorded in the Irish Annals, in the same year or the year after, is 'the first Saxon raid on Ireland'. It does not say whence the Saxons came. But the Irish coast is far from the Elbe, and British harbours are nearer. Vortigern may well have let his allies loose against the Irish, to warn Loegaire that it was henceforth dangerous to aid Pictish adventures or to succour colonists in Britain. Vortigern profited, whether or not he was responsible for the attack. No Irish aid to Picts or to colonists is recorded, in British or Irish texts; as far as the evidence goes, the Irish stood idly by while the British mopped up their kinsmen. Two generations later, at the end of the century, Irish attacks were resumed for a few years, and failed. No more are mentioned, and the ancient threat from Ireland ended as abruptly as the Pictish danger.

The sudden end to hostilities is said to have been accompanied by the marriage of Vortigern's daughter to the son of the Irish king, and by the conversion of a number of Irish notables and plebeians to the religion of Britain and Rome, preached by Patrick. The lasting peace, the dynastic marriage, and the admission of the Roman religion of Britain suggest the conclusion of a formal treaty. Such agreement could not have been reached unless a significant body of Irish opinion was ready for it. Recent experience had prepared them. Many of the Irish had seen something of the Roman world and of the Christian religion; some had served with the previous king, who was killed 'in the Alps' in 428, presumably in Roman employ, and a few individual Irishmen had already adopted Christianity. But agreement was reached only by the active diplomacy of lay and clerical leaders. Patrick's biographers assert that his mission was undertaken with the approval of the Gallic bishops and of the Pope; and Patrick himself recalls the prior approval of the British bishops. Such approval was necessary; Patrick would not have been heeded as a private visitor, without the backing of the British church and of the Head of Christendom. But the mission could not have been undertaken without the consent of the Irish government; and the political agreement required the interested participation of the British government, for its secular consequences were plainly considerable. The despatch of Germanus' pupil to Ireland, three years after Germanus had intervened among the Irish settlers in western Britain, indicates some negotiation, discussion and agreement between the governments of Britain and Ireland and the churchmen of Britain, Gaul and Italy.

The basis of agreement lay in identity of interest. The Gallic bishops' main purpose was to confound heretics. They made little headway among the churchmen, and needed what help the government could give them. Vortigern had cause to avoid dispute with the orthodox catholics of Gaul, for he had enemies at home who might seek their aid. Native British tradition is quite clear that relations were friendly during Germanus' first visit, when the bishop blessed the king, and were hostile only during the second visit; the contemporary record agrees, for the army could not have taken the bishop's advice unless secular authority approved. Their interests also coincided in the Irish problem; Patrick is said to have been Germanus' pupil, whom he proposed to send even before the Pope sent Palladius; and the British government required catholic approval for a mission to win the Irish to the religion of Britain. The timely understanding with the Irish was hardly reached without the exercise of considerable diplomatic skill; and the advice of the shrewd experienced bishop is likely to have guided the diplomacy. Constantius credits the bishops with a bloodless victory in Wales; it may also be due to them, at least in part, that Ireland was pacified without bloodshed.

Cunedda

Once the neutrality of mainland Ireland was assured, Vortigern was free to subjugate the Irish colonists of western Britain. They were reduced, not by the conventional Roman method of sending campaigning armies who returned to base after victory, but by the drafting of settlers from other parts of Britain, who made their permanent homes in the territory they regained. A document in Nennius' collection specifically describes the reconquest of Wales

> Cunedag, ancestor of Mailcunus, came with his eight sons from the north, from the district called Manau Guotodin, CXLVI years before Mailcunus reigned, and expelled the Irish . . . with enormous slaughter, so that they never came back to live there again.

The genealogies have much to say of Cunedda. He was the great-grandfather of Mailcunus, or Maelgwn, and his alleged descendants ruled north Wales for eight centuries. The later kings of Cardigan and Merioneth also claim descent from him, and he is said to have recovered Cetgueli, Kidwelly, the eastern Carmarthenshire coastal region. The figure of 146 years is given in Roman figures, that are easily corrupted in copying. It conflicts with the evidence of the genealogies that place Cunedda in the 430s. Since the figure occurs once in a single text, whereas the genealogies are repeated by many writers, and in this instance date both the descendants and the ancestors of Cunedda, their evidence is stronger. It is probable that the figure was miscopied, and that Cunedda was a contemporary of Vortigern.

Cunedda was a portent. Posterity has popularised his name, nowadays spelt Kenneth. His origin, his career, and his name link the Roman past with the medieval future. He was a grandson of the Paternus who had been appointed, probably by Valentinian, to rule the Votadini of the north-east coast, between Tyne and Forth. Like Vortigern's sons, he is one of the first persons in authority in Britain who were known only by a native personal name. His father, grandfather, and great-grandfather had all borne normal Roman names, and are given an origin among the cultured Romans of the south. His own 'sons' and 'grandsons' divide equally between those with Roman names and those with native British or Welsh names; but their later descendants almost all used Welsh names. The memory of Rome was fading.

Cunedda's northern territory had been incorporated within the empire for a short while, centuries before his time; and had thereafter remained a border state dependent on Rome. The lands of the Votadini are naturally divided by the Tweed, and each portion contains a large prehistoric hill fort, evidently the centre of government until the English conquest. Traprain Law in the north, in the Lothians, has been excavated; it contained quantities of Roman coins and other objects, and a remarkable early fifth-century treasure, of silver vessels smashed ready for smelting, looted by someone from Gaul, and presumably received as a gift by the Votadini. Traprain Law was plainly the residence of rulers long in contact with Rome, and northern tradition makes it the residence of a sixth-century Lothian king. The southern fort, Yeavering Bell, by Wooler, in north Northumberland, has not been excavated. But when the English subdued the region, they established a royal centre at its foot, on a hideously uncomfortable windy site that was abandoned a few decades later; their choice of so unsuitable a site cannot easily be explained, unless it was a dynastic centre similar to Traprain Law before they arrived. Cunedda's movement, and later northern tradition, suggest that he ruled at least over the southern Votadini. He may have ruled the north as well, for the Nennius text gives his home as the Manau of the Gododdin, or Votadini, the northernmost of their territories, about Stirling. If the text is literally accurate, he ruled there, but since the Manau was the last portion of Votadinian territory to remain in British hands after the English conquest, an eighth-century writer may well have used it as synonymous with the whole Votadinian country.

Only a portion of the Votadini are said to have accompanied Cunedda; his eldest son is reported to have remained behind, but his heirs followed in the next generation. One group of inscriptions seems to concern a Votadinian family who moved to north Wales; and implies that the immigrants also brought settlers from the Clyde, as well as from more southerly territories in Liddelwater. The inscriptions also show something of the nature of the reconquest of Wales, for some were found in and near Roman forts. Reconquest was evidently the work of several decades, not of a short campaign; Cardigan takes its name from Cunedda's sons, Merioneth from his grandson; Irishmen remained in the north to renew the war at the end of the century, and Cunedda contained Demetia in the south-west, but did not subdue its Irish dynasty. The inscriptions show that some Roman forts were occupied in the fifth century, during or just after the reconquest, though excavation cannot yet recognise their occupants. Other forts were doubtless held, whose defenders have left no inscriptions, and Caer Rhun on the Conway bears the name of one of Cunedda's descendants. Cunedda's strategy and his military organisation were necessarily geared upon the Roman roads and forts; and it is hard to suppose that any such war, fought to regain control of north Wales, can have had any other main base than Chester.

Cunedda's arrival changed the history of Wales. His departure brought consequences scarcely less important to the north. At home, he may well have been as much an enemy as a friend. His ancestors had been installed to protect the Roman army against the Picts, replacing the unreliable *Areani.* The single written reference to Cunedda in the north suggests that the new guardians may have become as unreliable as their predecessors. A late poem incorporates and adapts verses whose meaning was forgotten, and uses the place names current in its own day. They tell of Cunedda's wars in the north, singing

> Splendid he was in battle, with his nine hundred horse, Cunedda
> . . . the Lion . . . , the son of Aeternus,

and two obscure corrupt lines appear to say that he fought against the inhabitants of the north east, the future Bernicia, and that 'the forts will tremble', thanks to him, 'in Durham and Carlisle'. Whatever lies behind these lines, they imply that Cunedda attacked the lands south of Hadrian's Wall. He can only have done so before he moved to Wales. The story is not improbable. Gildas' report of enemy settlement between the walls early in the century convicts the Votadini either of collusion or of inability to resist. The Traprain treasure has similar implications. Either the Votadini accepted gifts from the enemy; or they required expensive presents from the British to ensure their loyalty and alliance. Cunedda's removal may well have relieved the north as much as it benefited Wales.

Cunedda's migration implies an authority accepted by the whole of the Roman diocese. The movement cannot have been accomplished without agreement between Vortigern and the army command of York. It left a gap in the defence of the north that required filling; and separate accounts indicate the measures taken both by Vortigern and by the northern army to fill it. Vortigern sent Octha north with English federates; they left traces in and about Dumfries, slight enough to suggest a short-lived settlement, but established permanent homes on the north Northumbrian coast, in the southern Votadinian lands south of the Tweed. The genealogies place at about the same date an offshoot of the dynasty of York, that appears to be located in or about the Lothians, headed by Germanianus, 'son' of Coel. There is nothing to show whether both movements were simultaneous, or were separated by an interval of years; nor whether they were agreed between Vortigern and the northern army, or were separate settlements undertaken in rivalry. But they are linked by geography; Octha and Germanianus both moved into lands that the Votadini left.

The Cornovii

Cunedda's migration was matched by another, equally vaguely dated to about the time of Vortigern. The territory of Roman Dumnonia had also been settled by Irish colonists. It comprised the modern counties of Devon and Cornwall, with much of Somerset. It retained its name, but accepted rulers called Cornovii, whose homeland lay on the upper Severn, with their capital at Wroxeter, near Shrewsbury; and centuries later, when the English conquered its eastern portion, the ancient name of Dumnonia, pronounced Dyfneint in Welsh, and Devon in English, was restricted to English territory, while the still unconquered west became known by the dynastic name of Cornovia, Cornwall, the land of the Cornovian Welsh.

The date of the Cornovian migration is given in no text. But Docco, said to have died in old age about 473, and Gerontius, killed about 480 in youth, are both represented as sons of Dumnonian Cornovii. The date should therefore lie in the first half of the fifth century, not far removed in time from Cunedda's migration. The two movements were similar in aim and nature. The purpose of both was to expel or subdue Irish settlers. Both involved military peoples who bordered on the highlands.

The Cornovii were the only *civitas* of Roman Britain with a military commitment. The *Notitia Dignitatum* lists a unit called the *cohors I Cornoviorum* at Newcastle-upon-Tyne. It was not there in the early empire; it is the only unit in the Roman army that took its name from a British *civitas*; and it is the only British unit known to have served in Britain at any time. The origin of the unit is readily explained. The territory of the Cornovii included a number of forts in Wales, whose likely Roman garrison was not regular units, but the *iuventus* of the Cornovii, their men of military age. It was probably some of them who were raised to the status of a cohort and posted to Newcastle, in the late third century or the fourth. It is likely that the Newcastle cohort continued to recruit among its own people, and that with their *iuventus* and their cohort, the Cornovii had a long military tradition not shared by other *civitates.*

Though the date of the move to Dumnonia is uncertain, this military tradition suggests its context. The changes on the northern frontier are likely to have ended the connection of the Cornovii with the cohort at Newcastle, if it had not earlier ceased; and the establishment of the new state of the *Pagenses*, Powys, ended whatever military responsibilities the Cornovii may have retained in their own territory. The creation of the new state is likely to have meant that some Cornovian notables lost lands and lordships, that some troops experienced in fighting Irishmen in hill and moorland lacked employment. The opportunity to seize and settle lands occupied by enemy aliens in the south-west compensated their loss, and profited the government.

The Dumnonian end of the migration suggests the same context as the movement of the Votadini, for it also presupposes a strong central government. Though it was legal to billet native armies upon the same terms as foreign federates, the existing civil authorities of Dumnonia could hardly be expected to undertake the permanent maintenance of such a force, unless constrained thereto by a superior government able to enforce its will. No evidence suggests that either the predecessors or the immediate successors of Vortigern enjoyed such authority, and it was therefore probably he who organised the migration of the Cornovii, as of the Votadini.

Vortigern's Success

The precise date and sequence of these important events cannot be determined, but the crowded energy of Vortigern's first ten years fills the sources. Later ages vituperate him as the unhappy author of the English occupation of Britain, but in the early 430s disaster had not yet come. Judged by his early achievement, Vortigern assumes the stature of a major statesman, whose enterprise came near to salvaging a powerful and enduring state from the wreckage of the western Roman empire. The British frontiers were intact, more securely held than at any time in the previous two hundred years, and past losses were in process of recovery. The problems that had outwitted the generals of the empire were permanently solved. Mediterranean opinion might wonder that

> the British had freed their states from the barbarian threat . . . and set up a native constitution on their own,

for no other region of the west could claim as much. The orderly household of bishop Fastidius' widowed correspondent, the quiet estate of Patrick's father, betokened a security then rare in Europe, so that the last years of the Roman British seemed to their nostalgic grandchildren a legendary time,

> affluent . . . with abundance beyond the memory of any earlier age.

CHAPTER FIVE

THE OVERTHROW OF BRITAIN

Civil War

It was civil war, not foreign invasion, that destroyed Vortigern and opened Britain to the English. A Nennius text pinpoints the three main dangers that he faced on his accession. He was threatened by

> the Picts and the Irish, by a Roman invasion, and, not least, by fear of Ambrosius.

The Picts and the Irish were successfully contained. The other two dangers were linked. Ambrosius, who was Vortigern's enemy in the 430s, was too old to be identical with Ambrosius Aurelianus, the resistance leader of the 460s; but the elder Ambrosius may well have been father of the younger, and the father of Ambrosius Aurelianus ruled for a while as emperor, either in Vortigern's time, as his rival, or before him. Nennius' Chronographer reports that the elder Ambrosius made war on Vortigern in or about 437, and one late tradition exiles him to Gaul and brings him back with an army from Europe. Whether or not he managed to persuade the Roman government to invade Britain, Vortigern had good grounds to fear that he might. Any dispossessed British emperor must necessarily look for aid to Roman Europe, though his chances of arousing sufficient interest in a distracted Gaul were doubtless slim. There, army commanders had their hands full at home; barbarians and peasant rebels made more urgent demands than the domestic affairs of the British. But the church had a greater interest, for unorthodox opinion might cross the Channel. If the government of Britain were shown to be heretical, its enemies might count upon the support of the bishops.

From the standpoint of Europe, the church of Britain was no longer orthodox. After 410, the trenchant theology of Augustine prevailed in the western empire, but it had not penetrated Britain, where the milder philosophy defended by Pelagius escaped challenge. The imperial government had proscribed the Pelagians in 418, but its writ no longer ran in Britain; there, laws enacted in Italy had no validity, unless the British government chose to enforce them. It is unlikely that it did, for there is no sign that the controversy bit deep in Britain. Fastidius was shocked and amazed to discover that there were churchmen abroad who discounted the efficacy of good works; but he treated them as eccentric rather than as dangerous, and for the next several centuries there is almost nothing to show that Christians in the British Isles were aware of Augustine. Augustine's triumph was decisive for the Christianity of Europe, but in Britain it made no change.

The indifference of the British was matched in parts of northern Gaul. There, the Chronicler who wrote in 452 casually observed that 418 was the year in which

> Augustine is said to have invented the heresy of Predestination.

He chronicled a remote event that for him had little immediate local consequence. But the vigorous churchmen of southern and central Gaul could not so easily dismiss the new philosophy of the mediterranean; whatever their personal estimate of Augustine, their concern was to preserve the unity of the church against schism. They could ignore Britain so long as the British church left Gaul alone. But latent conflict became acute soon after Vortigern's accession. According to Prosper, the reason why Germanus came to Britain in 429 was that the British bishop Agricola had 'revived' Pelagianism. Prosper was a staunch Augustinian, in close touch with senior ecclesiastical opinion. The bishops of Gaul could not ignore Agricola; he had evidently restated the views of Pelagius, forcefully enough to bring aid and comfort to the critics of Augustine in Europe.

The dispute gave the British government an embarrassing choice. If Vortigern championed the Pelagians, he offended catholic Europe, and heightened the risk that his enemies might find foreign support; but if he opposed the Pelagians, he offended an influential section of his own people. What is reported of the sequel indicates a judicious compromise. Germanus came, and failed to win the churchmen. Vortigern welcomed him and gave him licence, but used no coercive secular authority to aid him against the heretics; instead, he diverted the bishop's energies into help and advice on secular problems.

Judicious compromise might soothe and postpone impending conflict; it could not remove its causes, and the relatively mild antagonisms of religion were soon overshadowed by the political and financial consequences of the government's defence policy. While the foreign danger remained acute, men acquiesced in the mounting cost of federates, and in the drastic demands of the central government upon each individual state. But, so soon as the crisis was past, the states protested. The Kentish Chronicle tells the story plainly.

> The king undertook to supply the Saxons with food and clothing without fail; and they agreed to fight bravely against his enemies. But the barbarians multiplied their numbers, and the British could not feed them. When they demanded the promised food and clothing, the British said, 'We cannot feed and clothe you, for your numbers are grown. Go away, for we do not need help.'

The Chronicler accurately distinguishes between the 'king', and the 'British'. An assembly of the states of Britain had endorsed the original invitation to

Hengest's three keels; whether it had been consulted about their heavy reinforcement is doubtful. At all events, a Council now determined to end the agreement, evidently after Vortigern had found that the taxation necessary to maintain the federates was no longer forthcoming. Compared with the real wealth of the province, the cost was probably not excessive. The barbarians cannot yet have numbered more than a few thousand, nor could their upkeep have cost much more than the annual income of the owner of the North Leigh or Woodchester villa. But to Roman noblemen costs on such a scale seemed insupportable; twenty years before, the ransom that Alaric exacted from the defenceless Roman Senate appeared enormous, yet the sum he demanded was little more than one year's income of a rich senator. But paying an adequate army would have cost even more. Rome fell because its great men would not pay for its defence. So did Britain.

Indignation at the cost of barbarians was inflamed in Gaul by resentment at their uncouth manners and simple arrogance. The same causes operated in Britain; and there, if the magnates of some regions declined to deliver the subsidies due, an added burden fell upon the areas least able to bear it. For Vortigern's authority rested upon the willingness of individual states to obey his government. In the east, where the federates lived, their presence gave him the physical power to enforce payment, but it was less easy to coerce the states of the south and west, the Belgae, the Durotriges and the Dobunni, if their magnates induced their state councils to discontinue supplies, or if numerous wealthy individuals decided to withhold or diminish their contributions. These states comprised the richest areas of Britain, and if they defaulted, the full cost fell upon their poorer eastern neighbours, who could not so easily avoid payment.

The Council's decision to dismiss the Saxons was understandable; but it presented an insoluble problem. The barbarians were the main military force in the areas where they lived. If their promised supplies failed, they at once became a danger; the only alternatives were to feed them, to pay them to go away, or to expel them by force. The only force strong enough to oust them was the northern army; but even if its commander was able or willing to lead his men to the Thames, it is unlikely that he was asked, for his victory might depose both Vortigern and the Council in favour of a military monarchy. Yet some such military intervention must have seemed for the moment possible, for the cautious Hengest, though he 'took counsel with his elders to break the peace', held his hand for several years more.

The open breach between Vortigern and the Council gave Ambrosius an opportunity. Nennius' Chronographer baldly reports the event.

> From the beginning of Vortigern's reign to the quarrel between Vitalinus and Ambrosius are twelve years; which is Guoloppum, that is the battle of Guoloph.

His date is 437. The place is perhaps Wallop, in Hampshire. The genealogists knew Vitalinus as ruler of Gloucester, closely connected with Vortigern; he was perhaps identical with him. The struggle was between the adherents of Vortigern and those of Ambrosius; Vortigern's opponents now included a majority of the magnates who composed the council and had voted to expel the barbarians; many of them doubtless rallied to Ambrosius.

We do not know who won the battle, but the ultimate victor was the Saxon. Vortigern, rejected by a powerful section of his subjects, had no choice but to lean upon his federates. The Saxons were not a well-knit people, but they had a leader.

> Hengest was a man experienced, shrewd and skilful. Sizing up the king's weakness, and the military inexperience of his people . . . he said to the British king, 'We are few; if you wish, we can send home for more men, to raise a larger number to fight for you and your people.' Envoys were sent across the sea, and returned with nineteen keels full of picked men.

This was a force to be numbered in thousands rather than in hundreds. The first modest contingent had been enlisted to repel foreign invaders; civil war compelled Vortigern to bring over larger reinforcements to fight his British enemies. He was now irrevocably committed to his federates, a tyrant holding down his own people with their aid. He had to pay dearly for their support.

> In one of the keels was Hengest's daughter, a very beautiful girl. . . . Hengest arranged a banquet for Vortigern, his soldiers and his interpreter, named Ceretic. . . . They got very drunk . . . and the devil entered into Vortigern's heart, making him fall in love with the girl. Through his interpreter, he asked her father for her hand, saying, 'Ask of me what you will, even to the half of my kingdom'.

The romantic morality is sensational journalism; marriage alliances between emperors and barbarian generals had august recent precedents; the emperor Arcadius' cousin married the Vandal Stilicho; and on the strength of another sister's romantic promise, Attila the Hun demanded half the empire. The husbands may or may not have loved their brides, but the motive of their marriages was political.

Marriage demanded a gift to the bride's father.

> Hengest took counsel with the elders who came from the island of Angel; they agreed . . . to ask for the district that their language calls Canturguoralen, ours Kent. Vortigern granted it, though the then ruler of Kent, Gwyrangon, was unaware that his kingdom was being made over to the heathen, and he himself abandoned to their control. So the girl was married to Vortigern and he slept with her and loved her deeply. . . . So Hengest gradually brought over more and more keels, till the islands whence they came were left uninhabited, and his people grew in strength and numbers, established in Canterbury.

Canterbury is the only city in Britain that the Saxons are said to have acquired by treaty, rather than by conquest; it is also the only city where Saxon pottery of the earliest period has yet been excavated from dwellings, set side by side with the homes of the latest Romans. Its new inhabitants were presumably billeted as federates in the normal manner, but in numbers sufficient to make them masters of east Kent, in control of its native ruler.

It is at this point that the Kentish Chronicler inserts the expedition of Octha and Ebissa to the lands about the Wall. His date may be right. If so, their settlement may have had an additional purpose. Placed on the flank of the northern armies, it may have helped to deter any possibility of their intervention in the affairs of the south on behalf of Vortigern's enemies; other local leaders might fear to be overridden as rudely as Gwyrangon of Kent, and might be dismayed at the extent of Vortigern's dependence on his federates.

The First Saxon Revolt

Tension increased. Hengest, confident in his swollen numbers, now openly threatened both parties. The federates

> complained that their monthly deliveries were inadequately paid; deliberately exaggerating individual incidents, they threatened to break the treaty and waste the whole island, unless ampler payments were heaped upon them.

The formal complaint was doubtless accurate, for it is doubtful if Vortigern commanded sufficient revenue to pay the growing number of immigrants. Hengest must have valued him less as a paymaster than as a legal cover for the increase of his own following; but as his numbers grew the legal sanction of a weakening government mattered less. In or about 442, Hengest was ready to strike; Britain 'passed into the control of the Saxons'.

The disaster was final and all-consuming; a century later Gildas still shuddered at the horror.

> The barbarians . . . were not slow to put their threats into action. The fire of righteous vengeance, kindled by the sins of the past, blazed from sea to sea, its fuel prepared by the arms of the impious in the east. Once lit, it did not die down. When it had wasted town and country in that area, it burnt up almost the whole surface of the island, until its red and savage tongue licked the western ocean. . . .
>
> All the greater towns fell to the enemy's battering rams; all their inhabitants, bishops, priests and people, were mown down together, while swords flashed and flames crackled. Horrible it was to see the foundation stones of towers and high walls thrown down bottom upward in the squares, mixing with holy altars and fragments of human bodies, as though they were covered with a purple crust of clotted blood, as in some fantastic wine-press. There was no burial

> save in the ruins of the houses, or in the bellies of the beasts and birds.

The rhetoric leaves little to the imagination. The drama is heightened. Some excavated towns ended in scenes of horror; thirty-six bodies lay unburied in one burnt building at Caistor-by-Norwich, but other houses were undamaged; several bodies were buried beneath the charred remains of a gate at Colchester, but the interior of the town seems to have escaped destruction. Lincoln itself was little damaged, but the east gate was forced by an enemy, who burnt down the wooden gate and the timbers in the stone guard chamber.

Excavation can uncover the traces of such disasters, but it cannot date them. The revolt of the 440s is the probable occasion of the final destruction of Caistor, in the centre of the strongest English kingdom, where nothing suggests that the British ever regained control; but Colchester recovered, for the same gate was stormed on two widely separate occasions, and was therefore rebuilt after the first disaster. But not all towns suffered. There is nothing to suggest that Wroxeter, far from the English districts, was then attacked, and the city is said to have remained in British hands for two hundred years thereafter. Lincoln might have fallen in the revolt; but the occasion might as easily have been the campaigns of Arthur in Lindsey; or the English conquest at the end of the sixth century, or even the later wars between Northumbria and Mercia. Yet it is likely that in some places civilised Roman life ended abruptly and permanently in the 440s, for where 'there is no burial save in the ruins, or in the bellies of beast and bird' men have ceased to dwell; if life had been resumed before grass concealed the ruins, the bodies would have been swept away. But the sensational discoveries of lurid archaeology are rare. More characteristic are some hundreds of hoards of the latest Roman coins, buried by men who never came back to reclaim them. They are the memorials of those who fled before the sudden onslaught, taking their valuables or hiding them, leaving empty undefended homes that were not worth the burning. In town and country, the majority of excavated buildings were destroyed by time and weather, not by human violence; most were abandoned in their prime, their painted plaster walls not disfigured, their floors intact, occasionally scorched by ashes from an overturned brazier. No evidence dates the desertion of these houses. Common sense suggests that many among them were left empty when the Saxons rebelled in the 440s.

Men fled because raiders came; they failed to return because the raiders destroyed the economy upon which town and villa rested. The surest index to that economy is its ceramic industry, for fragments of broken pottery are virtually indestructible, and are numerous enough to warrant well-based conclusions. For more than three hundred years, the homes of Roman Britain had relied upon the marketed manufactures of professional potters. Their output was suddenly cut off; save in a few areas, there is no sign of a slow decline, of clumsier workmanship, of any growing mixture of home-made substitutes found side by side with commercial products; a prosperous and sophisticated industry was pulled up short in full production. With their customers gone, the shops closed, the roads unsafe for pedlars, the kilns ceased to work. The extinction of the potteries is a symptom of the whole economy, for the same causes cost the villas their market and their income, deprived the towns of food, and ended the manifold trades their craftsmen served. In much of the lowlands, the ferocity and the long duration of the revolt snapped the customary compulsions which held society together; for no peasant freely offered rent, or grew a surplus for the townsman, unless constrained; and those who survived the catastrophe had enough to do to feed themselves and their families.

Gildas' horror and the sharp epitome of the Gallic Chronicler at first sight suggest that the fury of destruction burnt itself out in a matter of months or days; but the wording of Gildas, the narrative of the Kentish Chronicler, and a quantity of other evidence describe a long uneven struggle that followed the uprising. The first blow was enough to shatter the economy and the political cohesion of Britain, but it did not give Hengest a kingdom like that of the Goths in Gaul, or of the Germans of the next generation in Italy. Hengest already held Canterbury and East Kent. The destruction at Colchester and at Caistor-by-Norwich, probably during the revolt, suggests that in East Anglia the federate rebellion was successful. In Yorkshire, an English tradition held that in the mid fifth century Soemil 'separated Deur from Bernicia'. 'Deur', Deira, is the East Riding, Bernicia the rest of the north-east. The tradition implies a revolt whose context and meaning the genealogist did not comprehend; all that Deira could be 'separated' from at that date was the authority of the British of York.

It does not follow that the rising was successful everywhere. The archaeology of Saxon cemeteries is the principal guide. In Yorkshire, the early English settlement about Sancton and Goodmanham, by Market Weighton, continued unbroken; but there was very little expansion until the end of the sixth century, and at York itself there were two extensive cemeteries; only a few grave goods are preserved, but they are all early, with virtually nothing of the sixth century, and little that need be late in the fifth. At Elmswell, by Driffield, and perhaps elsewhere, British and English seem to have lived peacefully together. It looks as though the rising was soon suppressed; the federate settlement was permitted to continue in the Market Weighton and Driffield areas, but not at York itself. In Lincolnshire, open country sites are more numerous, and most continue; but at Lincoln itself, very few burials are known, and these few may be as early as at York. There may be undiscovered cemeteries whose grave goods would tell a different tale; but the present evidence does not suggest that Lincoln or York became English in the mid fifth century, like Caistor and Canterbury. Elsewhere, however, the great majority of the earliest cemeteries remained in use, and it is likely that the English at once mastered many of the districts where they lived.

The immediate reaction of the British is known. They sought help from Gaul, in or soon after 446, pleading with Aëtius that,

> the barbarians push us to the sea, the sea pushes us to the barbarians; between the two kinds of death, we are either slain or drowned.

There is ample evidence for a drastic change in the sea level of Europe and the mediterranean towards the end of the Roman empire; its severity affected the coast and rivers of southern and eastern Britain. It has not yet been comprehensively studied; its date is uncertain, and it is not yet known how much of it was sudden, how much gradual. The letter to Aëtius means that in parts of Britain the flooding was extensive, sudden, and recent in the 440s. But, since the British put the danger from floods and the danger from the barbarians on the same level, the letter also implies that, after the initial rising, the extent of the enemy menace was not disproportionately greater than the threat from flooding. The rebels of the mid fifth century destroyed the economy of Roman Britain; they controlled the districts where they themselves lived, and made the open country unsafe for many miles around. But they were too few to exploit their success, for the

> fire of their vengeance licked the western ocean . . . but . . . after some time the savage plunderers went home again.

The rebels raided the west, but did not conquer it; and they raided westward only after they had 'wasted town and country' in the 'east of the island'. The magnates were not all consumed at once in a single dramatic holocaust; they perished more slowly, as the economy that had made them rich withered away. It was mortally wounded in the 440s, when it lost the communications that had sustained its elaborate distributive trade. But it died piecemeal; in much of the west, fragments of the disintegrating Roman society lasted for generations, but in much of the east, decline was plainly sharper and sooner.

The experience of Severinus in Noricum, Austria, in the same years, shows something of how Roman towns, as well as the Roman army, ceased to be. There, the barbarians controlled the open country, but Roman urban life long struggled on, and ultimately ended on a definite occasion; but only because Italy was near enough for the whole remaining population to walk there, with an armed escort provided by the government of Italy. Previously, several towns had been abandoned, one by one, on separate occasions, their shrunken population often doubling up with the inhabitants of another town. When each town was evacuated, opinions often divided; some left home, and some decided to remain; sometimes those who stayed were too few to man their walls, and soon succumbed to barbarian attack. Once, an unexpected raid carried off 'the men and the cattle who were outside the walls at the time', and one lively tale focuses the chances that threatened dying towns.

> The citizens and refugees from the upriver towns sent scouts to explore the places that looked suspicious, to guard themselves

> against the enemy as far as human precautions could. The Servant of God . . . arranged . . . for them to bring inside the walls their poor property . . . that the enemy might be starved. . . . Towards evening he said . . . 'Post proper sentries on the walls tonight, but keep a sharper watch, and be on the look-out for a sudden . . . enemy attack.' They replied that the scouts had seen no sign at all of the enemy. . . . 'If I prove a liar, stone me,' he replied; so they were constrained to post sentries.
>
> They went on guard. But a nearby haystack was accidentally set on fire by a torch, and lit the city up, though it did not burn it down. Everyone began shouting and screaming. The enemy, who were lurking in the woods, thought that the sudden light and shouting meant that they had been observed, and so stayed quiet. In the morning, the enemy surrounded the town, and ran around everywhere; they failed to find food, except that they seized a herd of cattle whose owner had obstinately despised the saint's prophetic warning to make his property safe.
>
> The enemy withdrew . . . and the citizens went outside. They found ladders near the walls, which the barbarians had prepared for their attack on the city, but had abandoned when they were disturbed by the shouting during the night.

These are the realities of a Roman population, sheltered by town walls against barbarians who mastered the open country but were not yet strong enough to break inside. The citizens lived within the walls, cultivating as best they could the lands immediately nearby, bringing the cattle and agricultural gear within the town when they had reason to suppose that raiders were near; though it is evident that such raids were relatively infrequent, since the citizens clung to a false security. Occasionally excavation suggests similar conditions in parts of Britain. At some time in the fifth century, a large corn-drying oven was constructed in the centre of Verulamium. Such ovens are a normal feature of open country farms, though they are rarely so large, but they are not elsewhere reported inside towns. It is evident that corn was grown outside the walls, conceivably also on deserted sites within the town, and processed within the walls as soon as it was harvested. The reason was presumably fear that the countryside was no longer safe after 441; the presence of considerable numbers of English near Dunstable, thirteen miles away, is sufficient explanation of the fear. But Verulamium survived, and undertook further skilled Roman building work, long after the oven had gone out of use. It is clear that the conditions of each town varied, that the history of the Roman British fragmented into a number of separate local histories. Just as Severinus negotiated with the barbarian king, so the inhabitants of Verulamium might reach an understanding with the English of Dunstable; guaranteed immunity from raids might be bought for a price. Such risks, however, varied greatly. Verulamium, very close to English villages, was exposed to frequent attack. Cirencester or Bath, farther from the fifth-century English, had less to fear, but doubtless risked occasional danger from larger and bolder expeditions that roamed further.

The British asked help of Aëtius in Gaul. He could not help, for he was heavily committed to the defence of Gaul against the Huns. But Germanus paid a second visit, a few years after the outbreak of the revolt. Germanus was on this occasion more successful against the heretics. Accompanied by the Bishop of Trier, he was received by 'Elafius, the chief man of the district', and

> the whole province followed Elafius.... The bishops sought out the authors of heresy, found and condemned them.... They were expelled from the island, handed over to the bishops... who returned home.

As before, there is no sign that any churchmen or any synod rejected Pelagianism; but on his second visit Germanus found a secular government, willing and able to arrest and deport heretics, in some part of Britain. The locality can only be guessed. Common sense suggests the south coast, Selsey or Southampton the probable landing area, since Kent was in enemy hands. Elafius may have been the chief citizen of the Belgae of Winchester. He may or may not have still acknowledged the authority of Vortigern; in the British tradition reported by Nennius, Germanus on his second visit attacked and condemned Vortigern, 'with all the clergy of Britain'. After the catastrophe, it is likely that many of the British states ceased to obey Vortigern; but there is no tradition of an alternative government, or of any other force yet able to focus resistance against the enemy. Elafius may have been among the British who asked help of Aëtius. He gave Germanus greater aid than Vortigern had done in 429, and doubtless urged the bishop to use his influence to gain help. Perhaps he did so. But if so, it was unavailing. Germanus shortly after went to Italy, and there died. He is said to have urged the imperial government to pardon the defeated Armorican rebels, but is not said to have carried or furthered any plea from the British.

Counter-attack

After the immediate shock of the revolt, Vortigern and the British fought back. The chronicles of the British and the English independently record a protracted campaign. At first, the British were successful; Hengest tried and failed to capture London, and was expelled from Kent; but he returned. The Kentish Chronicler sets down two parallel versions, the first a general summary of the fifth century, the second a fuller account of part of the earlier fighting.

> Vortigern's son Vortimer fought vigorously against Hengest and Hors and their people, and expelled them as far as the island called Thanet, and there three times shut them up and besieged them, attacking, threatening and terrifying them, and drove them out for five years. But they sent envoys overseas, to summon keels full of

> vast numbers of warriors; and later they fought against the kings of our people, sometimes victoriously advancing their frontiers, sometimes being defeated and expelled.

This first account distinguishes two stages, a war in the east, in the course of which Vortimer drove Hengest back to Thanet, and a later campaign when the heavily reinforced enemy fought, not the single Vortimer, but the 'kings of our people' over a wide area with shifting frontiers, evidently against Ambrosius Aurelianus and his captains. The second account gives details of the first stage, of Vortimer's wars. He fought on the river Darenth; also at the ford called *Rithergabail*, 'Horseford' in British, or 'Episford' in English, where Hengest's brother, Hors or Horsa, and Vortimer's brother Categirn both fell; and won a third battle at the 'Inscribed Stone by the Gallic Sea'. The place was evidently Richborough, whose most prominent monument was a massive arch of marble, fragments of whose dedicatory inscription still survive. Then

> the barbarians were beaten and put to flight, drowned as they clambered aboard their keels like women.

The Saxon Chronicle also lists three battles, with the same results, in the same areas, but gives them different names, and reverses the order of the first two. In the English story, Horsa was killed at Aylesford. Neither version claims a victory; the two fords might not be identical, but the word limits the choice to places where a road crossed a river, as at Aylesford, and is likely to mean a major road and a major river. It was then that 'Hengest took the kingdom'. At Crayford the English claim a victory, when the 'British forsook Kent and fled to London'; the place is two miles from the junction of the Cray with the Darenth, where the British name a battle but claim no victory. The third battle was at 'Wippedsfleot', the estuary of 'Wipped', where the English record the death of twelve British leaders and of the 'thane' Wipped, but claim no victory. The third battle was a decisive British victory that expelled the English from Kent. The estuary or inlet of 'Wipped' must lie in east Kent, and is likely to be the Wansum channel at Richborough, between Thanet and the mainland.

The two versions correspond too closely for coincidence. Each names its own dead, reports its own victories, uses the place names of its own language. Neither is likely to have borrowed from the other, and their common origin is plainly events differently remembered, rather than invention by either side. The Kentish Chronicle gives no dates. The Saxon Chronicle spreads the events over ten years. Its dates are late additions, but its wording shows the time that its compiler intended. The first battle is placed in the year in which Hengest 'took the kingdom'; the words regularly mark the beginning of an independent reign, and are also used of the foundation of later kingdoms after the second revolt in the late 6th century. Here, the first assertion of independence indicates the outbreak of the first revolt, in or about 442. The intervening ten years date the British victory at Richborough to about 452.

The strategy of the campaign is implicit in the places. Hengest's base was in east Kent, beyond the Medway. His first two battles were fought outside his territory, between the Medway and London. He needed London, for he was not only the leader of the Jutes of Kent. He was the captain and the main architect of the migration of all the English. Outside Kent, the strongest of the early settlers were the East Angles, between Yarmouth and Cambridge. Their location compelled Hengest to reach for London, and compelled the East Angles to push southward to join him there. But though the British fell back on London after their defeat by Crayford and Dartford, English tradition does not claim that Hengest was able to pursue them and take the city. His effort failed.

No account survives of the fighting north of the Thames; nor does any report of what Vortigern was doing himself while his son was fighting in Kent. His principal concern was necessarily to hold London, and to prevent the junction of the main enemy forces. It is probable that the East Angles tried and failed to reach London; and that Vortigern fought them off.

In the south-east, the British held their own. To the north, in Lincolnshire and Yorkshire, tenuous evidence suggests that the revolt was locally contained. The few small inland pockets of English, about Dunstable and about Abingdon, maintained their existence, but did not expand; both were too small to send useful forces to other areas without leaving their own wives and children unprotected.

In ten years' fighting Vortigern and his son had defeated the federate rebellion. Kent was cleared, the East Angles were contained, and the rest of the English were subjugated or overawed. A strong government might have been able to restore an economy and a civilisation that was severely damaged, but not yet destroyed, if the government had been accepted and financed by the effort of the whole of Britain. But there is no sign that the wealthy west and south contributed to Vortigern's victories, or continued to admit his authority. Many of his enemies must have been tempted to see his troubles as a well-deserved retribution. Shrewd men might sanely calculate that the distant English were too few to menace the west, and might thank them for weakening the tyrant's power. They might equally fear that if Vortigern wholly subdued the English, or struck a bargain with them, he would be able to turn his arms westward or northward.

The Kentish Chronicler's closing chapters hint at the divisions that followed the defeat of the Saxons, and gave the enemy a second chance. Vortimer died soon after his victorious campaign, and told his 'warband' to bury him on the coast in the port whence the enemy had fled, prophesying that then the enemy

> will never again settle in this land, whatever other British port they may hold.

But his men ignored his request, and buried him elsewhere.

The mystique of protection by the tomb of a dead leader veils the content of his injunction, that the enemy could not everywhere be expelled, but must remain held in some areas in subjection; and that the strategy essential to continuing British supremacy turned upon the control of London and of Richborough. Kent had been recovered. This was the land that the English could not subdue, so long as the British held its key fortresses. But to be held, they must be manned. Yet the maintenance of an adequate force on the Thames estuary was a heavy charge that could not be met without the financial backing of the whole country, willingly and regularly contributing money and men to the central government, an expense that fell heaviest upon the magnates of the still undamaged west.

Vortimer's dying charge was not heeded, for Vortigern lacked the means to enforce contributions. He was obliged to make an ally of his vanquished enemy, presumably to defend himself against Ambrosius the elder, or other aristocratic dissidents. The Kentish Chronicler reports that

> the barbarians returned in force, for Vortigern was their friend, because of his wife, and none was resolute to drive them out again. Britain was occupied not because of the enemies' strength, but because it was the will of God.

Vortigern's affection for his wife is an inadequate motive; it had not availed to limit the bitter fighting of the last decade. The Kentish Chronicler explains how the Council was obliged to accept harsh realities. The barbarians

> sent envoys to ask for peace and to make a permanent treaty. Vortigern called a council of his elders to examine what they should do. Ultimately one opinion prevailed with all, that they should make peace. The envoys went back, and a conference was summoned, where the two sides, British and Saxon, should meet, unarmed, to confirm the treaty.

The advocates of partition recognised that the existing English settlements were too strong to evict, at least for the present. Their critics objected, but were ultimately persuaded to agree. The policy reflected the common attitude of Roman realists, ready to absorb barbarians they despaired of expelling. In Britain, as in Europe, it aroused opposition, but its opponents could offer no viable alternative, for they could not or would not raise and maintain an adequate native army. There therefore seemed no prospect of decisive victory for either side, for the enemy were still too weak to conquer Britain. They had failed to take London; they had been chased from Kent, and might be chased again; but the obstacle to a total British victory was the powerful force entrenched in Norfolk, behind natural and man-made defences of river, dyke and forest. Moreover, renewal of the war threatened a double danger to the British; defeat risked opening all Britain to the enemy, but the success of an army raised and officered either from the west or from the north was likely to eclipse the power of Vortigern; or if Vortigern broke with Hengest and led a united Britain to victory against the Saxons, then the west and north must permanently submit to his authority.

Massacre and Migration

A stable treaty might have given Britain a chance to recover her strength; but the 'shrewd and skilful' Hengest did not afford that chance. At the conference, he

> told his men to hide their daggers under their feet in their shoes, adding, 'When I call out, "Saxons, draw your knives", take your daggers from your shoes and fall on them. . . . But do not kill the king; keep him alive, for the sake of my daughter, . . . and because it is better for us that he be ransomed.' The conference met, and the Saxons, friendly in their words, but wolfish in heart and deed, sat down to celebrate, each man next his British neighbour. Hengest cried out as he had said, and all Vortigern's three hundred elders were killed; the king alone was taken alive and held prisoner. To save his life, he ceded several districts, namely, Essex and Sussex.

The catastrophe was final; the three hundred 'elders', deputed by the Council of the Diocese to sign and celebrate a momentous treaty, must have comprised most of the great men of the island, the natural political leaders of both parties, many of them born in the distant age of the great Theodosius, school-fellows of Fastidius and of Faustus of Riez. Their death, at the moment when their fellows anticipated a permanent peace at the close of a long war, left the battered states of Britain leaderless and unready, open to Saxon assault. The old king survived, a disgraced and impotent wreck; hated by all men of his own nation,

> mighty or humble, slave or free, monk or layman, wandering from place to place, till his heart broke and he died without honour.

Vortigern's tragedy was not the failure of one man, but the tragedy of Britain, and of the empire which had schooled her people and shaped her institutions. His early mastery of the 'old enemies' from Ireland and the north, and the early checking of the Saxon revolt, owed nothing to good fortune; these successes were the achievement of a more than ordinary ability and courage, then rare in Europe. Lasting victory was twice snatched from him at the moment of triumph, because he was left dangerously dependent upon an enemy as able as himself. He was exposed to the barbarians by the same feckless infirmity that had opened Italy and Gaul to the Goths of Alaric forty years before, and 'none was resolute to drive them out again'; a leaderless nobility too proud to condone a government that hired Germans, but too tight-fisted to free it from the need, too divided and inept to construct an alternative, drifted to disaster, and stood amazed when catastrophe destroyed them, blaming their own futility upon the will of God.

The Great Raid

Retribution came swiftly to the British; 'the fire of righteous vengeance . . .

burnt up almost the whole surface of the island'. When Hengest was hard pressed in Thanet he had sent urgent appeals to Germany for more keels; they did not arrive in sufficient numbers to give him victory over Vortimer, when his prospects offered a greater chance of heroic death than of British plunder. But, 'later', when the island lay open at his feet, 'huge number of warriors' crossed the sea to 'fight against the kings of our people'. It was this second stage of the war that left the midland, the south and the west defenceless against raiders who inspired panic flight from town and villa, and destroyed the economy that nourished them. Gildas recalled how

> some of the wretched survivors were caught in the hills and slaughtered in heaps; others surrendered themselves to perpetual slavery in enemy hands . . . ; others emigrated overseas, loudly wailing and singing beneath their swelling sails no shanty but the Psalm (*44, 11*):
>
> 'Thou hast given us like sheep appointed for the eating.
> And among the Gentiles hast thou scattered us.'
>
> Others entrusted their lives . . . to the rugged hills, the thick forests and the cliffs of the sea, staying in their homeland afraid, until, after some time, the savage plunderers went home again.

This is a familiar account of raiders who came to plunder and destroy, but not to settle. Excavation confirms Gildas' accuracy, for except in ceded Sussex, there is little sign of settlement in new areas in the middle of the century, though graves and cemeteries in the older areas are more numerous. Hengest's return re-established the kingdom of Kent, but the strongest concentration of the English was in Norfolk and in the Cambridge-Newmarket region, a secure base conveniently sited at the head of the Icknield Way, the highroad to the west. Yet the English did not take London. Modern building operations have repeatedly uncovered extensive Roman cemeteries outside the walls, but have found no pagan English burial ground, though much less intensive disturbance of the soil has revealed such cemeteries in large numbers in the districts that the English held.

The two main groups of English settlers, in Kent and in East Anglia, were still separated by the inhospitable clay lands of the Thames basin. They were no longer rootless federates, whose only security lay in the political success of their captain; many of their villages had been established for twenty years and more, and many of their men had been born in Britain, and now fought to defend and enrich their native land. The Jutes of Kent had been expelled and recently restored, but in his old age Hengest no longer retained the supremacy that had been his in his prime. Though he is said to have survived another fifteen years, his descendants credited no more victories to him and his men. Primacy among the English had passed to the better established East Angles, whose early traditions are not preserved; while the British were left without a rallying point.

These calamities are quite closely dated by the memory of the English, and the firm witness of contemporary Gaul dates the emigration of the British in the late 450s. Some five or eight years after Wippedsfleot, therefore in the late 450s, the Saxon Chronicle noted Hengest's part in the great raid, when he

> fought against the Welsh and captured countless plunder, and the Welsh fled before the English as from fire.

This is the last Kentish annal for a century, apart from the record of Hengest's death. It is immediately followed by the first Sussex annal, setting down the consequences of its cession, the arrival of its first Saxon inhabitants, seven leap years, over a quarter of a century, after the coming of Hengest to Thanet; a date also about the late 450s. These dates are fallible, rough approximations when they were first written down by English Christians many generations later, probably in the margins of an Easter Table; and they were easily liable to corruption by later copyists. But they coincide with the Gallic record of the migration. The massacre of the elders of Britain is dated not long after 455; the chaos and the fearsome raid that followed are sufficient motive for the mass migration.

The common ruin of Vortigern and his British opponents ended the half century of independent Britain, still Roman in its civilisation but governing itself. Its early success contrasted with the lethargy of the European provinces that remained nominally subject to the Emperor Valentinian III, but its fearful overthrow seemed to commend the cautious common sense of European magnates; for timely surrender had preserved the bulk of their property and many of their institutions. Yet it was this independent resistance to the barbarians that for the first time distinguished Britain from Europe, whose civilisation had hitherto dominated her history and her economy. Even its failure snapped the old compulsions that had constrained the British to imitate and adapt the changing fashions of the mainland; and set her people free to begin to evolve their own society.

CHAPTER SIX

THE WAR

The years of Arthur's lifetime are the worst recorded in the history of Britain. Some two generations, a little over half a century, separate the age of Vortigern from the Britain that Gildas described. Gildas' world and Vortigern's differed greatly, and there is just enough evidence to distinguish their chief differences; Vortigern ruled in the last age of Roman Britain, but when Gildas preached the future nations of the British Isles were beginning to learn their identity. Yet almost all that happened in between is misty, its detail forgotten. When Gildas was young, most elderly men had been born and schooled in a world still Roman, and had witnessed its destruction. Their names are not remembered, and their successors preserved only hazy notions of what they did and how they did it. Later centuries knew only one outstanding name, Arthur, the last emperor of Britain. They portrayed him as an all-conquering military commander, a paladin who ranked with Caesar and Alexander; and as a mighty ruler, a just and admirable protector of humble men. The portrait is stylised; in each version, its features are those of the age in which it was painted. The authentic features have all but vanished, because later men had no use for them. The power of Arthur crumbled soon, and when it was gone, men dwelt upon the single fact that that benevolent power had once ruled all Britain. How it had been achieved and what it meant in its own day mattered little. The future needed a legend, not a history. Men yearn for the gleam of a golden age, not for an analysis of its metal.

To modern men, the gap in the evidence is tantalising and frustrating. The change that turned Roman Britain into England and Wales is the sharpest snap in British history, and the enquirer is irritated that so little can be known of its crucial central years. Yet the seeming blank is natural to the historical record of quick and drastic change in distant times. The history of the Roman empire itself suffers from a similar baffling vacuum of knowledge in its crucial transformation in the third century; for the story of the early empire, when Rome was unchallenged mistress of the known world, was eagerly remembered; the church remembered Christian Rome, but the age of change between is reported only in stark and jarring outline, so that the middle decades of the third century constitute the dark age of Roman history. Sixth-century Britons, like fourth-century

Romans, preferred to remember that their world had once been stable, and to forget the mournful story of its disintegration.

The sources that describe the overthrow of Roman Britain have little to say of the immediate sequel. The Kentish Chronicle ends with the death of Vortigern, and Gildas gives no more than a couple of sentences to the next several decades. Their silence cannot be mended by guesses. The evidence is not there, save for a few scattered random details. But what can be known is the circumstances in which these details are set, the limits which men's ideas and their physical resources set upon their possible action. We cannot grasp the personality of Arthur. We can only understand the man and his achievement by inference from what is known of the age in which he lived, the circumstances that explain the few incidents that later writers report. These inferences and incidents become intelligible only when they are seen in the context of the Europe of their own day.

Britain and Europe in the 460s

The ruin of Britain was sudden. Her Roman noblemen perished or fled abroad at almost the same time as the death of the last legitimate emperor of the west. Valentinian III was murdered in 455, and thereafter 'the western empire fell, and had no strength to rise again'. His short-lived successors commanded little respect in Italy, and what was left of the provinces slipped from Italian control. Valentinian's widow rashly invoked the aid of the Vandal king of Africa; Rome fell for a second time, and Gaul proclaimed its army commander, an elderly nobleman named Avitus, as emperor. He appointed Aegidius, a fellow-nobleman, to take over the armies of Gaul, and himself hastened to Italy, where he was acknowledged by the senate; but he was soon deposed by Ricimer, captain of the German federates. Ricimer thereby attained in Italy the factual sovereignty that had eluded Hengest in Britain. But his authority was confined to Italy; the general Marcellinus in Dalmatia and Aegidius in northern Gaul withheld obedience to the nominal emperors he enthroned.

Aegidius was a provincial noble, who owed his military command to a transient

---

Map 4

B Places named *Bretteville*

\+ Dedications and place names of British Saints

Inset

Area of sites shown on main map

MAP 4 THE BRITISH IN GAUL

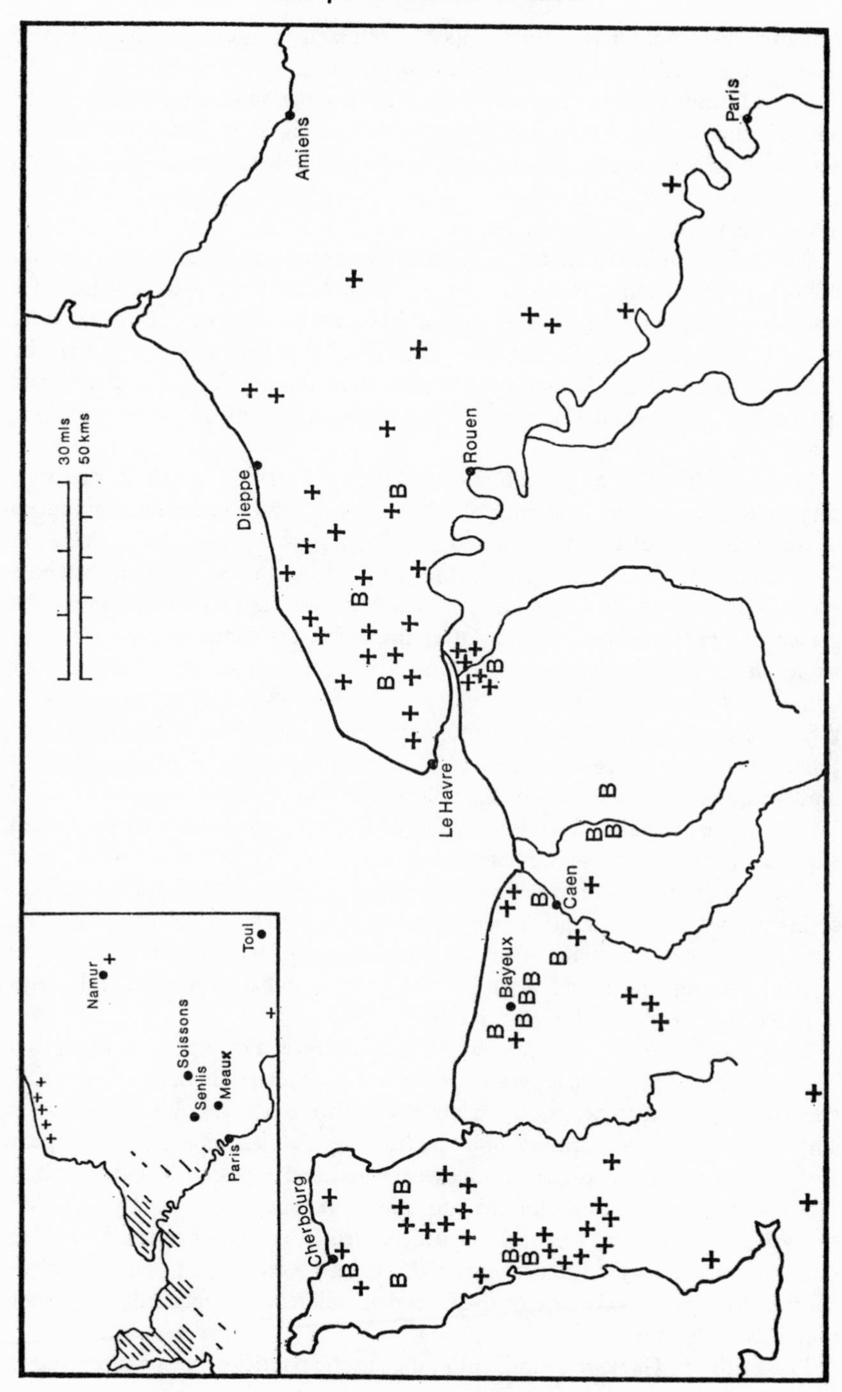

emperor. He could not impress upon Goth and Burgundian the inherited majesty that had surrounded the feeble grandson of the great Theodosius. Western Europe dissolved into a series of separate kingdoms, equal in sovereignty, and Aegidius found himself transformed into the 'king of the Romans', ruler of a state with defined frontiers, bordered by the comparable kingdoms of the Franks, the Goths, and the Burgundians, whose own further frontiers faced other sovereigns in Italy, Africa and Spain.

When German rulers mastered the mediterranean and the Rhine, the Romans of northern Gaul and of Britain looked to one another. The kingdom of Aegidius was established too late to aid Vortigern, almost at the same time as the massacre of the nobility of Roman Britain; and its own stability was gravely threatened by the destruction of the Roman power in Britain, for the Saxons acquired safe harbours in Sussex and Hampshire, whence they freely plundered the Atlantic coasts of Gaul.

It was the British who brought aid to Gaul. The survivors of the catastrophe despaired of their homeland, and sought security in the still Roman dominions of Aegidius. He welcomed them, and gave them estates 'north of the Loire', in the 'Armorican Tract', that the *Notitia* extends from the Seine to the Atlantic. It was probably already sprinkled with British settlers, descendants of army units placed there seventy years earlier, after the defeat of Maximus; and the place name Bretteville, widespread in Normandy, probably locates some of their homes.

The British immigrants were Roman provincials, who moved from one province to another, from Britain to Gaul, with no more of a wrench than a modern Englishman who moves from Yorkshire to Somerset. They were headed by the well-educated and well-born, for Gildas complains that they had taken with them the books that were no longer available; and in Gaul, Sidonius of Clermont-Ferrand wrote to their leader, Riothamus, to seek redress for a friend of his against a substantial British landowner. These were the men who had owned the Roman mansions of the British countryside, whose rents and markets Hengest had destroyed; and all the adults among them had been born in the days of peace and prosperity, before the English rebelled.

The immigrants did not come empty-handed, receiving their new lands as a charitable gift. They were a fighting force of 12,000 men, whom Aegidius badly needed. The German armies upon his borders were not the only threat to his authority; much of the Armorican Tract had long been exposed to the insurgent *Bacaudae*, who had dispossessed landowners, and had repeatedly resumed their rebellion after punitive expeditions had come and gone, most recently some ten or twelve years earlier, when Germanus carried to the government a plea for their pardon. It may be that some of the British were settled upon lands recovered from the rebels, where their resident military strength might prevent uprisings in the future.

The British in Gaul are prominent in the chaotic politics of the next ten years;

and so are the Saxons, hitherto rarely named in the history of Gaul. In or about 468, the Gothic king, 'observing the frequent changes of Roman emperors, decided to master Gaul in his own right'. Anthemius, a nobleman of Constantinople temporarily enthroned as emperor in Italy, enlisted the British, who sailed up the Loire to Bourges; they were beaten before the Romans could arrive, and driven into Burgundian territory, but the Goths failed to master Gaul. Yet the struggle was not a clear-cut division between Goth and Roman; each leader played his own hand, and the last Roman Prefect of the Gauls, nominally the viceroy of Anthemius, urged the Gothic king

> not to make peace with the Greek emperor, but to attack the British beyond the Loire instead, asserting that the Law of Nations partitioned Gaul between Visigoths and Burgundians.

The last imperial act of the Roman senate, obedient to Anthemius, was to impeach the Prefect for the treasonable incitement of Goths against the loyal British; but the charge was framed in terms that had lost their meaning, for many Romans of Gaul already preferred the firm rule of a resident Goth to the intrigues of a remote Greek manipulated by a German in Italy.

A fragment of a local history of the lower Loire, preserved by chance, gives a jumbled list of events in these years, whose complexity must have dazed contemporaries almost as much as the modern reader. The Franks had for a while chosen Aegidius as their king, when their own young king Childeric had suffered exile to Thuringia for his too great freedom with his subjects' wives. But Childeric's friends secured his recall, and after his return he fought at

> Orleans, while Odovacer and the Saxons came to Angers. There was a great plague, and Aegidius died, leaving a son, Syagrius. Then Odovacer took hostages from Angers and other towns. The Goths drove the British from Bourges, killing many of them at the village of Dol.
>
> The Romans and Franks under Count Paul attacked the Goths and took booty, but when Odovacer reached Angers, king Childeric arrived the next day, killed Count Paul, and took the city, burning its church in a great fire.
>
> The Saxons and Romans then fought each other. The Saxons turned tail; many of them fell to the Roman pursuit, and the Franks seized and overthrew their islands, killing many of their people. There was an earthquake in the September of that year. Odovacer and Childeric made a treaty, and conquered the Alamanni, who had overrun part of Italy.

Most of the dates and places and people are known. Aegidius died in 464; the Goths took Bourges about 468, and Dol is perhaps Déols, its border village, thirty or forty miles south-west of the city. Paul is otherwise unknown, but was apparently Syagrius' general. The events are confusing, because four or five different armies changed alliances rapidly; and the account is unclear, because it is no more than a local report of what the armies did in one district, and does not say why or whence they came to Angers. But the context makes its meaning plainer. Syagrius or his father had evidently stationed the British on the frontier where the main Gothic attack was expected, well south of the Loire. The survivors of the British army evidently withdrew towards their homes north of the Loire, and were thenceforth numbered among 'the Romans'. The Romans enlisted other allies. The Franks had been subjects of Aegidius until Childeric's return; and, whether Childeric had fought against Goths or against Romans at Orleans, he fought with Romans against Goths after the British defeat. On the Roman western borders, the Saxons had sailed up the Loire, either as enemies or as invited allies; they were evidently enlisted by Aegidius against the Goths, and were stationed on islands to hold the river against the Goths from Angers downstream. But both allies rebelled. First, the Franks killed the Roman general; but when the Saxons also rebelled, the Franks helped the Romans against them. In the end, Syagrius held the Loire; the Gothic bid to master Gaul was checked; and the Saxons and Franks went off together to Italy.

This isolated flash of detail warns of the intricacies that lie behind the summaries of the history of fifth-century Gaul and Britain given by short chronicles. It is true that in the end Gaul passed from the control of Rome into the control of Goths and Franks, but the detail is not simple; in Britain, as in Gaul, engagements when all the Romans fought on one side, and all the barbarians on the other, are likely to have been the exception rather than the rule; and both countries felt the impact of far-off decisions taken in Italy or Constantinople.

Though the narrative concerns only incidents in the local history of a small district, the campaign it reports was decisive. The Goths were held, so that Gaul did not become Gothia, and was able to become Francia, or France, in the next generation. The campaign also involved both British and Saxons in the wars of Europe. Continental British tradition preserved its own memories of the campaign. It knew the Saxons of the Loire, and recalled the

> devastation of the Frisians, and of their leader Corsoldus

which took place just before south-western Brittany was permanently mastered by the British, whose commander 'John Reith', also called 'Regula' and 'Riatham', is evidently identical with Riothamus. A later poet celebrated Gradlon, the local British leader who controlled Quimper in the mid fifth century, who,

> when the enemy race was laid low after the barbarian wars, defeated the 'keels' of five chiefs, and cut off their heads . . . Let my witness be the river Loire, by whose fair banks so many battles were then so keenly fought.

Bitter memories of the massacre and of the great raid at home gave the British immigrants a keener hatred of the barbarians than continentals could experience or understand; and preserved their pride in permanently denying the Loire to Saxon keels. But they had not saved the coasts of Britain itself, and Saxon ships were for a period free to distress the people of the Atlantic coasts. The Irish Annals place the 'second Saxon raid on Ireland' in 471, and in 478 Sidonius, poet, senator and bishop of the Auvergne, called them 'masters of the sea', whose raids on the Biscay coast were deterred by a Gothic admiral's

> half-naval, half-military duty of coasting the western shores, on the look out for the curved ships of the Saxons.

The notices of these far-ranging raids are limited to the twenty years or so after the fall of Vortigern, while the unconquered Saxons of Britain controlled the south-coast harbours, their seamanship not yet obliterated by the habits of settled farming. These were dangerous years, for while they kept their sea power, the Saxons might still carve themselves a kingdom in Europe. If the settlers on the Loire had managed to retain their foothold, they might have done so, for in Odovacer they had a commander as capable and as ambitious as Hengest had been. In the end, he won himself a kingdom, but he led no nation and he left no heir. He was the son of a general of Attila the Hun, and was probably Saxon by birth. When he was defeated on the Loire, he led the surviving Saxons to Italy to fight the Alamanni, in alliance with the Franks; and he may also have enlisted some of his British enemies, for the later British entertained the otherwise surprising belief that in the late fifth century a son of one of their emigrant leaders became king of the Alamanni. What happened to the allies when they reached Italy is not reported; the alliance may well have broken and reformed as rapidly as it had in the campaign of the Loire. The one known result is that Odovacer did not immediately prosper; he is next reported on the Danube a few years later, a leader without a following. He soon found one, and led a mixed German force to conquer Italy, where he ended the appointment of puppet western emperors, acknowledged the nominal suzerainty of the emperor in Constantinople, and ruled as the first German king in Italy.

Britain in the 460s

In such an age, the simpler ties of nation, tongue and kinship melted into a world of warlords, whose miscellaneous following obeyed whichever paymaster offered a more promising reward. National cohesion was somewhat more easily preserved in Britain, for geography shielded the British lands from most of the rival armies whose wanderings disturbed the loyalties of Europe; moreover recent memories united the British in fear and hatred of the Saxons, and obliged the Saxons to stand together against the superior numbers of a nation whose government and state they had destroyed, but whose will to resist was not yet crushed.

Organised resistance did not everywhere collapse as absolutely as Gildas' dramatic picture would suggest. In the occupation of Sussex the Saxon Chronicle reports that

> Aelle and his three sons, Cymen, Wlencing and Cissa, came to Britain in three keels, at the place called *Cymenes Ora*, and there slew many Welsh, driving some of them in flight to the wood called Andredsleag.

The landing place was near Selsey Bill, close to Chichester. The Kentish Chronicler understood that Vortigern had formally ceded Sussex to the English; and Aelle may have hoped that Chichester would respect the remnant of his authority, and submit. Instead, he was opposed. His force is said to have been small, and he did not take the city. Part, but not all of the British army withdrew to the Weald, behind Anderida, Pevensey. Aelle followed, but his men were confined to the coast of east Sussex. There, pagan burial grounds are numerous, with plenty of fifth century grave goods, but none that proclaim a date in the first half of the century. But in west Sussex, the first English graves are more than a hundred years later. Chichester is not called Elchester from Aelle, but bears the later name of Cissa, one of his three 'sons'; the earliest English object in the area is a brooch found in the Roman cemetery of St. Pancras, that dates to the time of Aelle's grandchildren. Its isolation suggests a Saxon woman who lived and died in a British community rather than a Saxon settlement. The absence of pagan burial grounds in west Sussex argues that the English did not reach Chichester until more than a hundred years after Aelle's time; Cissa was more probably his remote heir than his son.

Aelle was hard put to maintain his tiny kingdom. Eight years after his arrival, he had to fight the Welsh at 'Mearc Redes Burna', the agreed frontier river, and he did not take Pevensey till six years later. British and English tradition, and the excavated evidence, agree upon the date and nature of the origin of Sussex. The Kentish Chronicle puts Vortigern's cession of the territory immediately after the massacre of the Council, at about the same time as the migration to Gaul, at the end of the 450s; the Saxon Chronicle enters Aelle's landing nearly thirty years after Hengest's, also in the late 450s. The name of the river where Aelle fought argues that within a few years he made a formal treaty with the British of Chichester, defining a frontier; the pagan English sites reach near to the Arun, but no further west, and suggest that the Arun was the frontier. Their northern limit is the crest of the Downs to Beachy Head; and even after the fall of Pevensey, early in the 470s, Aelle's men ventured no further eastward. But they had won good harbours, and might raid by sea more safely than by land.

In ceded Sussex, settlement was limited and opposed. Vortigern is also said to have surrendered Essex, but there further evidence is wanting. No written tradition has survived, and the pots and brooches from the few known sites seem earlier, nearer to Hengest's first years. In Middlesex and Hertfordshire sites are even rarer, and none are known to the south or west of London, save in districts where the first federates had settled. The London clays are unfriendly soils for primitive farmers, and the city has prospered only when safe communications have made it the centre of trade and government. But it remained a strategic stronghold, keeping the main English regions apart; if the men of Kent or the East Angles tried to reduce it, they did not succeed. A few seals, stamped with the name of Syagrius, who reigned at Soissons from 464 to 468, show that some merchantmen might still trade between Gaul and the port of London, in spite of Franks and Saxons.

Ambrosius

London and Chichester were held; Verulamium and some other cities still did not admit English settlement near their walls. Though evidence survives only from Sussex, it is likely that the men of other cities had to fight as stoutly as those of Chichester. But the enemy could not be contained by local defence alone. A well-organised offensive was needed. In the panic of the great raid, 12,000 men who might have undertaken it had gone to Gaul. Those who stayed at home took time to recover from the shock. When the enemy returned to their homes after the great raid,

> God strengthened the survivors, and our unhappy countrymen gathered round them from all parts, as eagerly as bees rush to the hive when a storm threatens . . . 'burdening the air with prayers unnumbered' (Vergil, *Aeneid*, 9, 24). . . . To avoid total destruction, they challenged their conquerers to battle, under the leadership of Ambrosius Aurelianus, perhaps the last of the Romans to survive, whose parents had worn the purple before they were killed in the fury of the storm; though his present-day descendants have greatly degenerated from their ancestor's excellence. . . .
>
> To them the Lord granted victory; for, from then on, sometimes our countrymen won victories, sometimes the enemy, that the Lord in his accustomed manner might test in this people a modern Israel, to see whether they loved him or no. This continued until the year of the siege of Badon Hill, almost the last defeat of the bandits.

The alternating struggle corresponds to the later stage of the war, summarised in a Nennius text, when 'vast numbers' of fresh arrivals from Germany fought against the 'kings of our country', 'sometimes victoriously advancing their frontiers, sometimes being defeated and expelled'.

The resistance evidently began at some time in the 460s. It lasted some 30 or 35 years. It was conducted by the 'kings' of the country, leaders military and civil thrown up in the several states of Britain. 'To avoid total destruction', they took the offensive, leading their forces out of their own territory, and accepting the overall command of Ambrosius. Ambrosius headed the early years of the resistance, but by the time of the final victory Arthur was the 'commander of the kings of the British in the war'. Whether Ambrosius was killed, died, or was superseded by a younger general we do not know. His successor was a man of similar background. Artorius is a Roman family name, like Catellius of Powys, or Calpurnius the father of Patrick; in the fifth century it places his birth and origin among the owners of villas, from whose ranks came the leaders of the separate states, the members of the council, the 'elders of Britain'.

The nature of the war compelled an unusual strategy. The early poetry of the Welsh consistently sings of mounted warriors wearing scarlet plumes and using swords, riding well-fed horses, who fought an infantry enemy equipped with spears. Their picture of the English is accurate; Germans nearer to the mediterranean used cavalry, but further north among the Franks, the kings and their bodyguards alone had horses, while the English had none, and were said not even to know what a horse looked like. Horse gear does not begin to appear among their grave goods until the late 6th century, and then only in the occasional possession of a leader who rode to battle while his men marched.

The evidence for the fifth-century British is slighter. Most early Welsh poems concern the sixth century. Then, though men fought on foot in mountainous Wales, the heroes of the Pennine kingdoms and of the west midlands were almost all mounted men; and cavalry was the outstanding arm of the Armorican British. Only one surviving poem sings of a battle of Arthur's. It describes a defeat of his horsemen by English infantry. Otherwise, there is no direct evidence that Arthur's men fought like their children and grandchildren; but no evidence at all suggests that they fought differently, for there is no contemporary account of how the Romans struck back at the barbarians in Britain. But in Gaul, there is first-hand evidence. There, fifth-century success was entirely due to the use of cavalry alone against an infantry enemy. About 471, Ecdicius routed thousands of Goths at Clermont-Ferrand with only 18 mounted men, for the Goths, like most German forces, were poorly armed. Sidonius describes the consequence.

> You were welcomed with an ovation. The courtyards . . . were crowded with people, some kissing the dust of battle from your person, other unharnessing bridles slimy with blood and foam . . . and sweat-soaked saddles. . . . The crowds danced for joy. . . . You had to put up with the most fatuous congratulations.

Thereafter Ecdicius, from his private resources,

> raised what was in practice a public force . . . that curbed . . . the audacity of the barbarian raiders. . . . Surprise attacks wiped out entire regiments. . . . To the enemy these unforeseen onslaughts proved disastrous.

Ecdicius' horse 'never lost a moment in following up the rout' so that the enemy had no time for the proper burial of their dead; sometimes 'bodies piled on dripping carts' had to be hastily shovelled into cottages that were then fired over the corpses 'till the debris of blazing roofs formed their funeral pyre'.

Ecdicius in Gaul was a lone hero, whose single campaign had no sequel. He received 'small help from the magnates'. They lived in a relatively stable Gaul, side by side with barbarians whom they did not fear. Their homes and estates were normally secure; and would become the first casualties in any attempt to extend the adventure of Ecdicius into a national effort. In Gaul, such resistance was unthinkable. The Goths were too firmly rooted, and the Gauls had too long acquiesced in their rule. Ecdicius' campaign was soon over, and three years later, when Sidonius wrote, he had abandoned the struggle.

Ambrosius' resistance had begun in Britain some ten years before Ecdicius attacked; and it is not improbable that Ecdicius had himself been fired by stories of Ambrosius. His strategy was the only effective way in which Romans could fight back with hope of success, and was as valid for lowland Britain as for Gaul. Sixth-century British and late fifth-century Gauls relied on cavalry alone, unencumbered by slow-moving infantry; tradition held that the late fifth-century British fought in the same manner, and is plainly right.

The most brilliant strategy fails unless it has the supplies it needs. Ecdicius was a magnate who raised a force from his own resources. Those resources were lands where horses might be bred and pastured, and corn grown for their fodder, peopled by dependants able and willing to tend the horses and to ride them. Any well-stocked estate might send a few bold raiders on a single expedition, but a war that lasted for a generation required ample lands secure from enemy counter-attack. In Britain such resources were to hand in the Cotswold country from Dorset to Gloucester, in Salisbury Plain and in Hampshire. There, if the remaining magnates and their dependants had the will, cavalry forces could be raised and trained, sheltered between campaigns, their losses replaced. No central government could any longer extract the taxes to maintain a professional army or pay mercenaries; but landlords could still raise forces among their tenants.

The Cymry

Gildas says that during the great raid those who did not emigrate fled to the rough country, some of them to hill forts. When the raid was over, 'a remnant' took up arms, and were thereafter joined by great numbers of their fellow countrymen, *cives*. In distinguishing a 'remnant' from the mass of the population, and in describing their leader as the 'last of the Romans', he means that the initiative was taken by what was left of the political and military leadership of Roman Britain. The first authors of the resistance were men of standing, Roman landowners who, like Ecdicius in Gaul, could raise forces from their own estates. Some still remained; and in the west country, though raiders had come and gone, the enemy were not near, and the old social relationships were not yet wholly overthrown.

But resistance was not long confined to those who began it. In Gaul, the first successes of small mounted units had inspired wild enthusiasm among humbler citizens, who 'danced for joy'. In Gaul, bold young men infected with that enthusiasm had no opportunity to join and spread the movement, for one campaign opened and closed the resistance. But in Britain, opportunity increased for more than thirty years. The counter-offensive was begun by the remnant of the Roman nobility of Britain, raising forces to defend their own lands against raiders and robbers; it became a national war of liberation, and its successes created a nation with a new identity.

As that identity was born, the forces of Ambrosius and Arthur adopted an enduring name, that distinguished them not only from the English, but also from Romans abroad. For Gildas' *cives* is the Latin equivalent of the British word *Combrogi*, fellow-countrymen, whose modern form is *Cymry* or *Cumbri*, still the national name of the Welsh and of the north-western British. The name is shared between them, and therefore originated before they were separated by English conquest. It existed in or before the sixth century, and was adopted throughout the former Roman territories of Britain; for when the English gave names to villages whose population was still Welsh, they called a number of them Comberton, Cumberlow, or the like, in the London region and the south-east, as well as in the west and north. They did so because their inhabitants called themselves *Cumbri* at the time of the English conquest.

The new name was born when Roman Britain died. The armies of Ambrosius recruited men who had lost respect for the fallen majesty of Rome; and it registered a change in the outlook and structure of their society. The values of Roman civilisation were enshrined in Latin literature; and, though most men in all classes knew something of both languages, Latin alone was written. Roman values died sooner among men who could not read, or read but rarely; and when the material civilisation of Rome was gone, the need to know Latin disappeared among laymen. The word Britain meant the whole island. *Cymry* was the name adopted by the native population in the former Roman diocese, after Britain ceased to be Roman. Their descendants were called Welshmen by the English.

The armies of the *Combrogi* were mainly cavalry, acting alone; those of the English were infantry alone, without any mounted men. Such warfare imposed strict and unusual demands upon both sides. The tactical success of the British depended upon surprise, that put the enemy to flight and killed him as he ran. But since the stirrup was not yet known, the horsemen could not strike hard; to attack spearmen who held their ground invited the loss of horses that could not be replaced without return to base, and left unseated riders unprotected. Even if the enemy were overridden, the winning of a battle might lose a campaign if losses were too heavy. But disciplined cavalry wisely led had little need to engage an enemy who did not flee. Their tactical success required them to concentrate stronger numbers against weaker enemy forces; free of footmen, able to move four or five times as fast as the English, their scouts were in a position to locate the enemy quickly, and to make such concentrations possible.

The existence of such mounted units was clearly able to deter the English from raiding in small parties and to hinder the assembly of larger armies; for men drawn together in numbers from scattered small villages left their homes weakly defended, and the British cavalry was free to ignore the ordered army and attack its villages. Immediately, such warfare enabled relatively small numbers of British to curtail the English raids; but cavalry was less well equipped to conquer, destroy or expel its enemies. To overrun even a small stockaded village, held by the men whose wives and children it sheltered, required more than a single charge. Though the smaller English settlements about Dunstable and Abingdon might be exposed to unexpected assaults, whence the British might speedily withdraw into friendly territory, no such cavalry army could hope to reduce the denser populations of Kent or East Anglia. The nature of the fighting invited a stalemate, with little hope of decisive victory by either side.

Cavalry skilfully led might easily escape attack in the open; but they were weak and defenceless when dismounted, and men must sleep at night. An infantry army may carry spades and palisade posts like the Roman legion, to throw up speedy defences when it bivouacs, but cavalry so encumbered loses speed. If infantrymen are attacked without warning, they have only to jump and seize their weapons; dismounted cavalry taken by surprise may find their horses hamstrung or dispersed before they can mount. Tactical needs therefore required the British to seek out enclosures with defined ready-made defences. There they risked only siege by a force much larger than their own, surrounding them tightly enough on all sides to prevent them breaking through in a concentrated charge. In much of the lowlands, small walled Roman towns, eight to twelve miles apart along the main roads, offered such protection; elsewhere, ancient Iron Age forts, often on sharp-sided hills, provided comparable security; excavation has shown that many western forts were refurbished in the Arthurian centuries, particularly where Roman roads are farther from each other, and towns correspondingly fewer. The excavation of these forts suggests that some, like South Cadbury Castle, became permanent strongholds, especially in districts far removed from English settlement, while others may have protected forces that stayed for a few days or a few weeks in the course of a campaign.

Inferences from the circumstances of the war show only the problems that the fighting thrust upon a prudent commander. They do not show whether commanders were prudent, nor how much or how soon they learnt from experience. But oral and written tradition has preserved something of Ambrosius. His name passed into Welsh legend as Emrys, and spread thence into modern usage. One or two sites in Wales, and perhaps in Cornwall, bear his name. Features of the landscape named after heroes, like Dinas Emrys or 'Arthur's seat', are never by themselves evidence that the hero had anything to do with the place. What they show is that when they were so named the local population knew and loved stories told about those heroes, and liked to imagine that their exploits were performed in their own familiar countryside. The urge to localise a national hero is strong in every generation, in the twentieth century as in the middle ages; antiquarian fancy buries Boudicca and king Arthur in half a dozen different parts of the country, and it does the same for Oliver Cromwell.

Places named after stories of Ambrosius are fewer than those inspired by the

Arthur legend, and are evidence of when and where the stories were told. The Arthur names derive almost entirely from the Norman romances of the 12th and later centuries; but they are fewer in Wales than in England, and in Wales the legend of Ambrosius was well established by the eighth century, though it was not long-lived. It may be that during the sixth and seventh centuries the name of Ambrosius was as well loved as that of Arthur.

It is also possible that Ambrosius' name survives in England for reasons that owe nothing to legend. 'Ambros' or 'Ambres' is considerably commoner in English place names than is Emrys in Welsh. Strenuous efforts to find an English origin for these names have failed; since they are not English, they are names that were used before the English came. The syllables have no meaning in any relevant language; the early spellings suggest that they usually represent the name of a person, and probably always do so.

In late Roman usage, cities often bore the names of emperors, but lesser places were rarely so distinguished, save in one particular context. Army units often named the places that they garrisoned, and in the late empire army units commonly bore the names of the emperors who raised them; the 'Theodosiani' and the 'Honoriaci' were regiments raised by the emperors Theodosius and Honorius. It is likely that any units raised by Ambrosius were known as 'Ambrosiaci', and possible that they named the places where they were garrisoned, in lands they had recovered and pacified. The English towns and villages called Ambrosden, Amberley, Amesbury and the like are found only in one part of the country, in the south and south midlands, between the Severn and East Anglia, on the edges of the war zone between the Cotswold heartlands of the *Combrogi* and the powerful English kingdoms of the east. Half of these places are suitably sited to defend Colchester and London against Kent and the East Angles, and three more border on South Saxon territory. Several of them are the names of earthworks. If garrisons were there stationed, they were established when the Thames basin was securely held, and they stayed long enough to leave their names behind, into and beyond the time of Arthur.

The conclusion is no more than an inference from a puzzling group of place-names. The solution to such puzzles must be sought by strict logical deduction from what is known of the late Roman Empire and early English Britain. These problems may not be evaded by the feeble and self-evident assertion that we do not know the answer, or that the conclusion might be different if we had more evidence. In this instance, the conclusion is the most probable inference from the available evidence. It may be overset by other evidence or by sharper logic; until it is, it suggests that Ambrosius raised numerous units during the war, and that when the British regained secure control of the Thames basin Arthur stationed them in permanent garrison upon its borders.

The War Zone

The archaeology of the war is as inferential as its place names. Excavation has

MAP 5 THE WAR ZONE

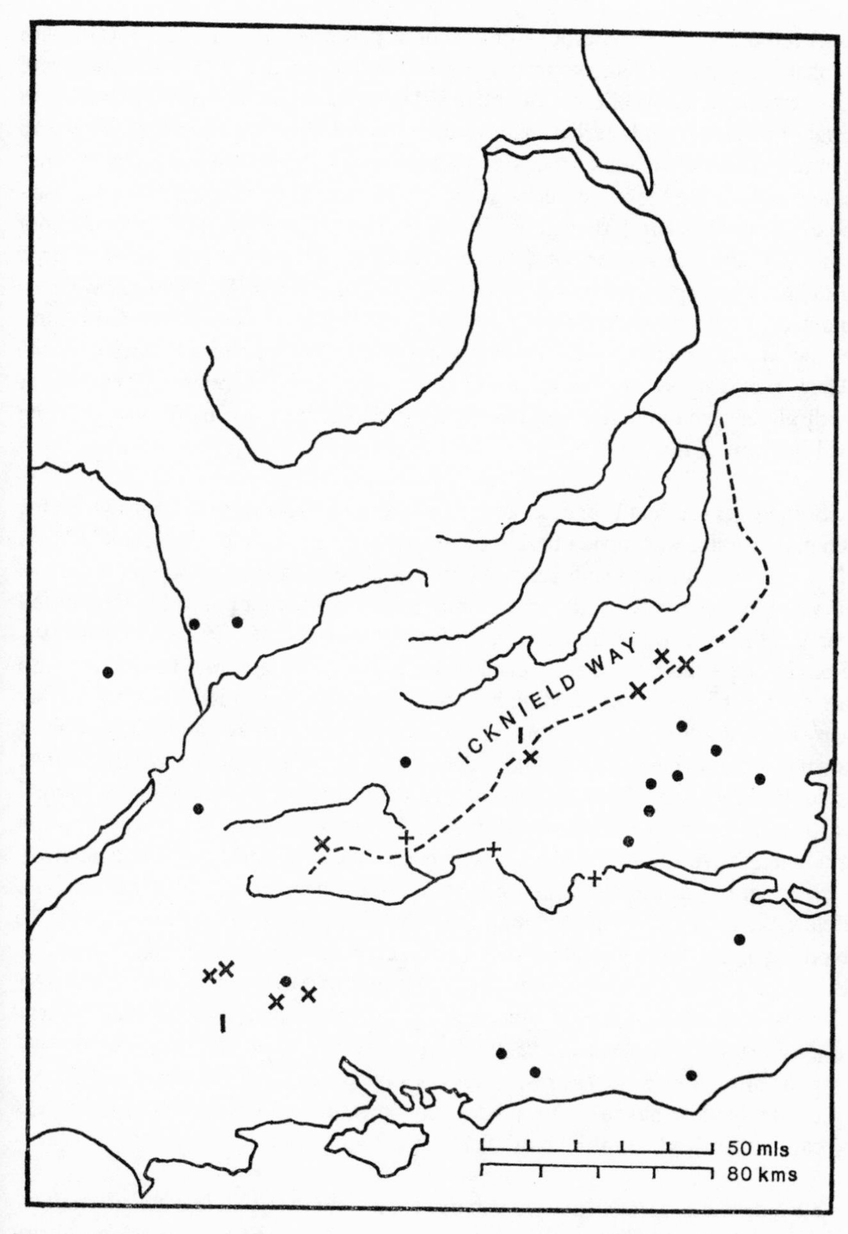

× 'Massacres'
+ Concentrations of weapons in the Thames
| Burials with fatal bone wounds
● Ambros- Place Names

uncovered a number of groups of executed prisoners, of warriors buried with broken weapons and fatal wounds, of swords and spears dredged in quantity from river crossings. None of them can be dated within a hundred years; most of them might be relics of raids earlier than Ambrosius, or of the campaigns of the late sixth century, or of incidental struggles in between. Common sense suggests that some at least are the material traces of battles fought during the main British–Saxon war of the late fifth century. Their distribution is precise; they reach from Wiltshire and the borders of Gloucestershire to the Cambridge region. Large numbers of weapons have been found in the Thames by Wallingford, where a main route of the Icknield Way crossed the Thames, others near Cookham, below Marlow, perhaps the crossing point of the Verulamium–Silchester road. They were dropped by Saxons who had no opportunity to retrieve them, for at both places a competent swimmer could have recovered a valuable weapon if he had had time.

Sometimes the detail suggests an incident. On a Roman farmstead at Dunstable a Saxon warrior was buried beside the upper summer track of the Icknield Way. The underside of his skull was stove in, smashed by a blunt instrument before he was buried; and with him was a broken spear without a point. He was buried hardly later than the fifth century, for by the second half of the sixth century a Saxon village and its cemetery occupied the site, and these later burials cut into his grave; it was therefore already forgotten and unrecognisable. A mile away across the Watling Street a spur of the Chilterns rises sharp above the Roman town to a flat defensible top. Half-way down the hillside, a ditch of unknown date is cut into the chalk. It was dug in an unusual place, unlike the ditches of normal earthworks, at the point where the slope suddenly ceases to be sharp and becomes gradual. Above the ditch, the descent is too sharp for horses to be ridden on slippery grass; at the ditch men might mount to charge down the gentle incline. Below the ditch, men on foot might run uphill; above it they could only walk. Nothing dates the ditch; but the site suggests the possibility that a force of British cavalry encamped upon the hill-top, intending to attack the Saxon villages grouped about Dunstable, and took precautions against counter-attack. The injuries to the dead man's skull are those that a horse's hoof could have caused. But if it were so, the result was not a decisive British victory. The villages of the Dunstable Saxons continued uninterrupted, and the survivors were able to carry their dead from the battlefield for decent burial.

Such dramatic reconstructions can never be more than possible interpretations of the evidence; and interpretation is possible only on the rare occasions where precise detail has been carefully recorded, at the time of excavation. Most accounts are looser and vaguer reports, of skeletons with their hands behind their backs as though tied, or with their heads cut off, published without detailed study of the bones or examination of the surrounding countryside, usually with even weaker evidence of date. Guesses about the possible occasion of each tragedy remain guesses. But the geographical limits of the area where such discoveries have been noted are more important than speculation about individual sites; and, as with most distributions, the blanks upon the map are as informative as the symbols. Map 5 shows the sites that might concern the wars; where none are shown, there is not even suggestive evidence. These sites do not intrude into English Norfolk or Kent, and penetrate only the borders of the British west. Neither side could overwhelm the other. The hesitant witness of the archaeology and the place names concurs with the generalities of the British writers, that the war was a long struggle of alternating victory and defeat.

Arthur

The battles and campaigns of Ambrosius are unremembered; it may be that he was still in command about 470, when Pevensey fell to the enemy; and it may be that he used the fort as the base for an unsuccessful attempt to recover the Sussex harbours at the mouths of the Cuckmere and the Ouse; for if he could deprive the Saxon ships of their mastery of the Channel, there was some chance that some of the British of Normandy might be induced to sail home to reinforce their countrymen. The strategic importance of the place is obvious; but the only evidence is a brief English report, that for reasons unstated Aelle besieged the formidable walls of a fortress beyond his borders. But whatever the occasion, the Sussex campaign is the only incident that any source reports from the earlier years of the resistance war that Ambrosius began.

There is no indication of when Ambrosius died or retired. Since he earned a place in legend, he is likely to have lived for several years after the beginning of the resistance, in the early 460s; and since his successor was probably in command by about 480, a date in the 470s is probable. Ambrosius was replaced by Arthur as the supreme commander of the British. The change roughly coincides with a change in the character of the war. When the resistance began, it was a simple patriotic struggle between all the British on one side, and all the English on the other. But the notices that concern Arthur and the second stage of the fighting point to a more complex situation. The early West Saxon entries in the Saxon Chronicle are exceptionally confused, duplicated under different dates and, at first sight, contradictory. The confusion has a special cause. The easier ambiguities of the Kent and Sussex annals are the consequences of fading memory and of tradition ill-understood; but the Wessex entries are the deliberate contrivance of ninth-century scholars, devised to serve the political needs of their own day. Their story is that the kingdom of Wessex owed its origin to Cerdic, who was in command of a number of separate Saxon forces under named leaders, at a date that was originally set at about 480. Cerdic is the only founder of an English kingdom who has an unequivocably British name. His pedigrees alone are patent inventions, for his 'ancestors' are lifted from the straightforward traditions of other English dynasties, and later Wessex kings are represented as his descendants by improbable and contradictory links, that credit some of them with two or three different fathers. A ruler with a British name, with no ancient tradition of English forebears or English descendants, is plainly British. Though he was the earliest ruler of the future Wessex whom the later English knew, the claim of ninth-century Wessex kings to suzerainty over all the English could not be built upon the authority of a British king. He had to be treated as an Englishman. The relationships are invented; but the substance of the tradition that had to be disguised is itself ancient.

Cerdic was regarded as the ruler of the Winchester–Southampton area in the late fifth century; as the commander of the Saxons who landed in that area; and as a king who consistently fought with the English against the British armies. This is a tradition of a British ruler of the *civitas* of the Belgae who rebelled against the authority of Ambrosius and of Arthur, and hired English federates to hold his territory against them. Excavation locates and dates the homes of his federates, and suggests where he raised them. The earliest English of Hampshire were stationed at and near Portchester, perhaps by Vortigern. But towards the end of the fifth century they were reinforced by people who used grave goods akin to those of Kent and Sussex; and Bede includes them, with the men of Kent, among the Jutes. At the same time, the newcomers began to bury their dead outside the city of Winchester. It is also the time at which Cerdic is said to have ruled in the same territory.

Two accounts explain how the English came. The entries of the Saxon Chronicle land one force in Southampton Water and another on the Isle of Wight. A third contingent came to Portsmouth harbour.

> Port and his two sons, Bieda and Maegla, came to Britain at the place called Portsmouth, and slew a young Welshman, a very noble man.

The name of Port is plainly invented to explain the name of Portsmouth. Of his two 'sons', Maegla is the British Maglos, Bieda straightforward English. The local British and the English were allies. They beat off the attack of a British army, which had evidently been sent to suppress Cerdic's rebellion.

The battle of Portsmouth harbour inspired the only detailed tradition of the war that the British remembered. One Welsh poem, the 'Elegy for Geraint', describes a battle of Arthur's.

> Before Geraint, the enemy's scourge,
> I saw white horses, tensed, red.
> After the war cry, bitter the grave. . . .
>
> In Llongborth, I saw the clash of swords,
> Men in terror, bloody heads,
> Before Geraint the Great, his father's son.

In Llongborth I saw spurs
And men who did not flinch from spears,
Who drank their wine from glass that glinted....

In Llongborth I saw Arthur's
Heroes who cut with steel.
The Emperor, ruler of our labour.

In Llongborth Geraint was slain.
Heroes of the land of Dyfneint,
Before they were slain, they slew.

Under the thigh of Geraint swift chargers,
Long their legs, wheat their fodder,
Red, swooping like milk-white eagles....

When Geraint was born, Heaven's gate stood open;
Christ granted all our prayer;
Lovely to behold, the glory of Britain.

The poem is not early; its language is not that of the earliest Welsh poems, and no Welsh poem could be anywhere near as old as Arthur's time, for the profound changes that turned the British language into Welsh did not take full effect until about a century after the death of Geraint. Any elegy composed in or near the time of Arthur would have been in British, not Welsh. But the poem has nothing in common with the twisted concepts of Arthur current in the eighth and ninth centuries. It is fresh and vigorous, shot through with a sense of personal loss, as close to its hero as are the laments for the late sixth-century heroes of Gododdin and of Reged. It vividly describes a battle, fought as battles were fought in the fifth and sixth centuries, before the final English conquest, not in the manner of Welsh battles thereafter. The genealogies record its hero Geraint, prince of Dumnonia, now called Dyfneint in Welsh, Devon in English. The poem reads like a late written version of an older Dumnonian poem, originally composed while the memory of its hero was still green, its language modernised and translated from British into Welsh as the original wording became difficult and archaic.

The English tradition dates the battle to about 480. The Welsh poem puts it in the later stages of the war, after Arthur had replaced Ambrosius, but before the war ended at Badon, somewhere between the 470s and the 490s. Llongborth is the 'ship port'. 'Llong' in Welsh carries the general meaning of ships of all sorts; but when the word was first taken into British from Latin it had the more precise meaning of warship, *longa navis*. A port of warships, a naval base where a prince from Devon fought and died in the fifth century, can hardly be other than Portchester, the westernmost of the Saxon Shore forts listed in the *Notitia*, at the head of Portsmouth harbour. The poet describes the same event as the prosaic entry in the chronicle. It would be absurd to suppose that the native poet learnt English, read, interpreted and elaborated the pedestrian language of the chronicler; or that the chronicler learnt Welsh and condensed a poem. The common source of the two accounts is an event, differently remembered.

Neither poet nor chronicler says who won the battle. The Dumnonian leader was killed, and the Saxons retained Portchester fort; at best the battle was a strategic defeat for the British. Wessex tradition names two other battles in southern Hampshire, and the Saxons were also settled at Winchester. But they did not reach the Salisbury area until the second Saxon revolt seventy years later. Cerdic lived to fight again; his rebellion was contained, and his authority was perhaps limited to the Winchester–Southampton area, but it was not crushed. The south coast was not recovered, and the independent Saxons held Portsmouth and Southampton Water as well as their Sussex harbours.

The English as well as the British found new leaders in the later stages of the war. Hengest's death is put in the 460s, not long after Ambrosius began the resistance. Later kings of Kent claim descent from the Bernicians of the far north, whose leader Oesc returned to rule Kent, either immediately after Hengest's death or some time later. Reinforcements arrived from Germany.

> The Saxons increased their number and grew in Britain. . . . But when they were defeated in all their campaigns, they sought help from Germany, and continually and considerably increased, and they brought over the kings from Germany to rule over them in Britain.

All evidence agrees that the flow of immigrants in the later fifth century much increased. Bede and Nennius' text both say that the homeland of Angel by Schleswig was left empty, and the archaeological evidence on both sides of the North Sea assents. In Britain recognisable burials of the later fifth century much outnumber those of the earlier fifth century, while in Germany burials virtually cease before the end of the century. As with other migrations, the movement of the dynasty was decisive; kings tend to move when the bulk of their subjects have gone before; the remnant left leaderless and undefended at home is likely to succumb. In Britain, older settlement areas on the east coast acquired a denser population, and the dynasty from Germany appears to have established itself at first among the East Angles; but few new regions were settled. In the north Midlands, about Leicestershire and Northamptonshire, there was some extension of territory as far as the evidence goes, though it is possible that further study may show that the earlier fifth century settlement was more extensive than the record at present reveals. In the south-east the evidence is somewhat clearer; a small group of newcomers with a strong Scandinavian background

MAP 6 PAGAN ENGLISH SETTLEMENT 2
THE LATER FIFTH CENTURY

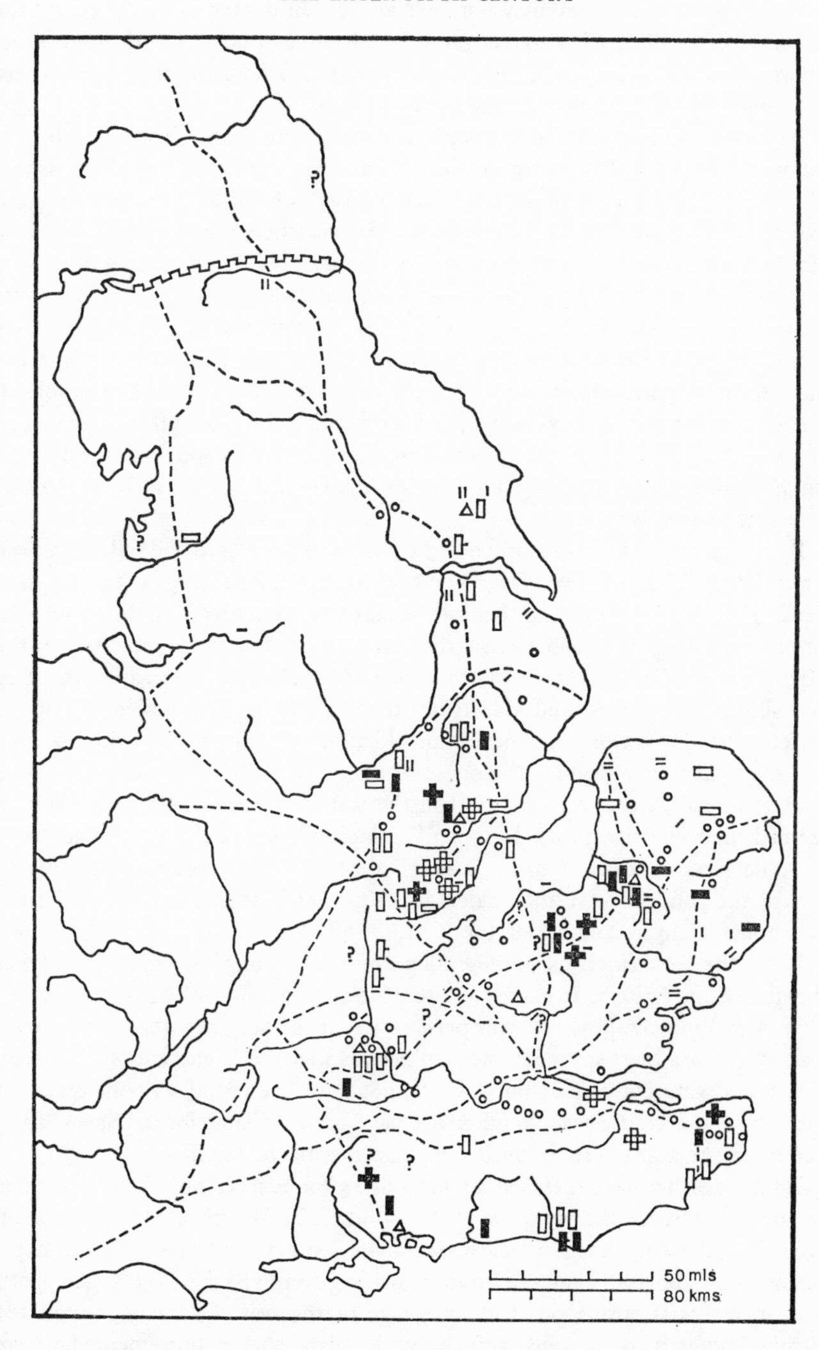

o Sites shown on Map 3, p. 59. Other symbols as for Map 3.

reached Ipswich, but they may not have arrived until later, after the end of the wars. Danish influence is also recognisable in Kent, at much about the same time. Newcomers were many, but the areas newly settled few; the majority of these later immigrants lived near to their predecessors.

The aims and hopes of the new settlers differed from those of the men who had followed Hengest half a century before. In his time, the western empire was still in being. He was an ambitious Dane, who raised a band of Jutes and Frisians, and then recruited English adventurers. His ambition might reach towards a kingdom like Odovacer's, or to the power that a *magister militum* might exercise under a weak emperor, as Stilicho had governed in Rome. His prime need was for armed men, preferably maintained by the Roman taxpayers in Britain; they looked for land when other means of support was lacking. But in his lifetime, the bulk of the English stayed in Europe; and when he failed, for lack of numbers, further recruits were not extensively forthcoming, for he could offer no guarantee of security. Moreover, much of northern and central Europe was still open to English immigrants, who might expect less dangerous enemies in Pomerania or Bohemia than in Britain.

By the 480s the shape of Europe had changed. The empire had fallen, and the barbarians in Europe moved faster and grew stronger. At home, the expansion of the English was blocked, and their old homes were squeezed and threatened. In Britain, the long war had shown that away from the main battle-zones the English lived secure. They had not conquered the British, but their young men had shown themselves well able to ward off attack and to ensure a peaceful agricultural life for women, children and older men. Emigration to Britain was no longer an exciting appeal to warriors in search of glory and adventure; there was land to be had, easier and richer than the soil of the homeland, and life now seemed safer in Britain than Europe. The main wave of new immigrants came as settlers rather than soldiers. Though there was still plenty of fighting to occupy the younger men, their elders had a greater interest in maintaining their new homes than in conquering the British.

None the less, extensive immigration and the coming of the English kings threatened the British. It made the prospect of reconquest of the main English territories almost impossible. Nor perhaps was it the only new threat. The Irish wars were for a brief space renewed, in north and south Wales and in Cornwall. The Irish were contained; but they cannot have been held without diverting men and resources that would otherwise have been available for the Saxon wars; and it may be that the Irish invaded in concert with the English.

Both sides had lost their earlier incentives, for neither now had reasonable grounds to foresee the conquest of the other. The British could not overrun Norfolk and Kent, but they held most of the country, and most of its strategic strongholds, above all London. London, holding Kent and the East Angles apart, was an essential strong-point at any stage of the war. Ordinary unmounted citizens might man its walls, and the walls might shelter horsemen who were able to enforce the submission of the nearby countryside. It was not only a fortress that could stand a siege; it was able to secure a wide surrounding territory. There is some evidence of the nature of that control. Eight miles south of London lies the small cluster of fifth-century English villages about Mitcham and Croydon. They are too few to have constituted a threat to the city; their grave goods are not found in or around the walls, and when they did expand, they spread southward on to the arable downs, not northward towards the river. But the city threatened them. Their agriculture was quite impossible if it was exposed to raids from nearby enemy horse. The villages continued, and can only have done so by the consent and agreement of London. The nature of their grave goods emphasises their dependence. In Surrey, and in the West Kent sites in the Darenth valley, their ornament is wholly different from that of Kent, beyond the Medway, closer to that of the middle Thames Saxons. The differing ornament means that they had little or no contact with the kingdom of Kent across the Medway, but had contact with Saxons on the other side of London. It had been the long experience of Roman governments that barbarian settlers in Roman territory, if securely controlled, might both cultivate the soil for the benefit of Roman townsmen and landlords, and at the same time defend the lands Rome gave them against other barbarians. That was the function of the *Laeti* of Gaul; it was the necessary function of Saxon villages that remained in contact with the lands across the Thames beyond London, but were denied intercourse with Kent.

Between London and the Medway there are no such dramatic signs of war as in the south midlands, and though there was doubtless some unrecorded fighting, there is no evidence that the men of Kent made serious attempts to break out of their Medway frontiers towards London before 568; and then it was Saxons who opposed them and defeated them. In the fifth century, the successors of Hengest are not known to have revived his earlier wars against the British of London. Their frontiers were secure, their lands were fertile, military ambition was dangerous and unprofitable. The trade of London implies that at least for some periods the English agreed to live in peace with their British neighbours; for vessels could not have risked the long voyage round the Kentish coast if Kent had been at war, its longships intent to seize merchantmen that used the port of London.

Similar considerations indicate the defence of London north of the Thames. The nearest formidable enemy were East Angles many miles away. It is not likely that they were held without heavy fighting, and perhaps one or other of the Cambridge dykes constructed in the years after the Romans may constitute a frontier, erected in defence, accepted by agreement. But, as in Surrey, the differences of ornament among the English command attention and require explanation. The fifth-century ornament of the East Angles is abundant in and around the town of Cambridge. But nearby were a different people. Five miles south-west of Cambridge, the Roman road from Wimpole and Sandy climbs a slow but sharp ridge just after the village of Orwell. Behind that ridge, stretching southward to the Royston–London road, is a small group of large cemeteries, one of which, Haslingfield, 'the open land of the Eslingas', records the name of the people who used them. There, the 5th-century ornament is matched on the middle Thames; only in the 6th century did these people acquire Anglian jewellery from Cambridge as well. They were at first as sundered from Cambridge as were the men of Surrey from Kent. But they were nearer the town, in sight from the top of the ridge, and their difference argues a firm unfriendly frontier that admitted no intermarriage and no exchange.

Such frontiers seem puzzling only if it is assumed that all the British fought all the time on the same side, all the English on the other. It had always been a main principle of Roman diplomacy to subsidise nearer groups of barbarians against the potential attacks of their farther neighbours, and to guarantee them protection when necessary and possible. The Eslinga Saxons lived on the edge of the large Anglian complex, but no sizeable English settlement lay between them and London. If they were enemies of the British, there was nothing to prevent British horsemen raiding and burning their homes, and riding off towards Essex or London long before help could come from nearby Cambridge. It may be that some such raid had taught them that alliance with the British was safer. But there is a more probable explanation. Present evidence suggests that the cemeteries differ in kind from those of Cambridge, and also began somewhat later, after rather than before the middle of the century. If it be so, the people may well have been placed there by the British. Throughout the history of the empire, terms dictated to conquered barbarians frequently exacted the surrender of fighting men or family groups, to be settled where the Romans needed them. Such had been the origin of the Sarmatian units in the army of second-century Britain, and of the family groups of the *Laeti* in third-century Gaul. The fifth-century British had ample precedents to follow if they subdued the Saxons about Oxford and obliged them to send a part of their population to curb the aggression of the Angles of Cambridge.

All such inferences derive from what is now understood of the grave goods. New discovery may suggest different conclusions. But until it does, the implications of the evidence now to hand is that the war began with an alliance between the English and Vortigern's party among the British against another British faction; that for a short period in Hengest's later years, his success turned it into a clear conflict between the English and the British; but that it ended with a more complicated pattern of local variation. The little evidence that shows Saxon sundered from Saxon, British at odds with British, warns that such divisions are likely to have been more numerous than we know.

The English held

The scattered evidence suggests that the British cavalry units gradually ended the threat from raiders, and confined the English behind recognised frontiers. The East Angles, the men of Kent and the men of Sussex were each checked, perhaps before the dynasty of the English moved to Britain. Outposts drawn from the peoples who accepted the name of Saxons were placed upon the borders of the Angles and the Jutes, and behind them the places that bear the name of Ambrosius may locate some of the permanent garrisons established to consolidate territory regained and secured by the British in the middle years of the war.

The whole of the known operations of the British–Saxon war are located in the south and the south midlands. Nothing suggests that the northern armies and the Pennine kingdoms intervened; and some considerations hint that they did not. Within their territory, English settlement remained extremely small, and did not extend beyond small regions of the East Riding and the poor sparse settlements in the 'region about the Wall'. There are a few English burials outside the walls of some of the Pennine Roman forts; but they are too few to be the cemeteries of communities, as in the East Riding. They show the presence of some English men and women among the defenders of the forts, rather than the advance of enemies. The Saxon rebellion was contained in the north; some English settlements were suffered to continue, and the fort burials imply that some of their young men were enlisted in fort garrisons, perhaps that some of their women married British husbands.

The southern border of the Pennine kingdoms was the river Trent. English settlements stretched along its right bank in considerable quantity, in Lincolnshire and Nottinghamshire. But no cemetery of the 5th or 6th century has yet been reported from the opposite bank. The Trent became a clear-cut frontier between the British and the English. There may have been unrecorded fighting, but whether there was or no, the lasting frontier demonstrates that agreement was reached, either in formal compact or informally in practice. The northern British forebore to attack the English, but forbade them to cross the river, so that the English were enabled to live safely by the river bank, not confined to lands more safely withdrawn.

The principal casualty was the *civitas* of the Coritani, centred upon Lincoln and Leicester. Its countryside was settled by the English in numbers large enough to argue that they were in political control, or at least were strong enough to coerce whatever British government remained. But English expansion halted on the west at the Watling Street, and did not penetrate westward into the territory of the Cornovii. The Cornovii had a military tradition that gave them easier possibilities of raising their own defences than the Coritani.

Apart from the struggle at Portsmouth, the only direct statement about the wars of Arthur is a document in Nennius that lists twelve of his battles, evidently victories, the last of them at Badon. The list looks like a prose summary in Latin of a lost Welsh poem. Most of the sites named cannot be located with any confidence; but a few can. Celidon Wood is located in the north, and one or two other sites may also be northern. The City of the Legion is either Chester or Caerleon. It is unlikely that such battles had anything to do with wars against the English. If the text accurately reports the poem, and if the poem was close to reality, these were campaigns fought in later years by Arthur to subdue the highlands after he had beaten the English and recovered the lowlands.

But one identifiable site is the river Dubglas in the district of Linnuis, made the scene of four battles. Linnuis translates *Lindenses*, the men of Lindsey about Lincoln; the only significant river of Lindsey is the Witham, whose ancient name is not known, but might have been Douglas. A campaign may have entailed four nearby battles, but the more likely explanation is that this battle received four stanzas in the poem, the others one each. On any interpretation, it was evidently regarded as the most important of the battles, apart from Badon. It is the only other identifiable site where the enemy is likely to have been English, and its special importance may be that it was a major campaign against the national enemy. The effort was needed. The British had contained the older settlements, but in the later 5th century almost all the remaining Angles crossed to Britain with their king. If he would unite the East and Middle Angles with the men of the East Riding, he must hold Lincoln.

The text implies a British victory and an English failure; and the consequence of victory was more than local. The rescue or recovery of Lincoln meant that the British army must first march through and reduce the numerous settlements of the Middle Angles in Coritanian territory in the north-east midlands. Victory in Lindsey made the British masters of the island; London and Lincoln held the main enemy concentrations apart, and the inland groups about Dunstable and Oxford lay isolated, deep in British territory, too small to be more than a local menace. It is more likely than otherwise that the Lindsey campaign, remembered only in a paraphrase of a forgotten poem, is a real event, and belongs to the later years of the war, giving the decisive check to English expansion. But whatever the details, English expansion was halted.

Both sides had fought themselves to a standstill. Hitherto the English had been able to summon new reserves from Germany. Now there were no more left to come. The reinforced English were far too strong, far too long established for the British to expel them. But their interests and character changed. They were no longer raiders, and there was no longer a wealthy lowland economy to raid. They were settled farmers and there is no reason to suppose that they were yet gravely short of land, or under any compelling need to attempt a conquest that experience had shown to be difficult, dangerous and unprofitable. Though some might urge a desperate renewal of the struggle, prudence constrained the kings of the Angles to heed the sentiments of all their subjects, and to discourage rash enthusiasm. Both sides were ready for agreement and peace.

Badon

The southern English made a last effort at total victory. Badon was in the west country; one direct statement, and several early English spellings, identify Bath with Badon. An English army that could penetrate so far to the west must have been exceptionally large, the joint force of a number of kingdoms. Only one

English king is directly stated to have fought at Badon, Oesc of Kent. Little is known of the man, save the name he chose for his son, Eormenric, who was apparently born and named at about the time of the battle. The great Eormenric, dead more than a hundred years before, had been the mightiest of the kings of the Ostrogoths, conquering a vast empire in eastern Europe from the Baltic to the Black Sea. The king who revived his name and gave it to his heir at the end of a long war was a man who dreamt of empire.

A few texts indirectly suggest Oesc's probable allies. Wessex tradition places the death of Cerdic at the same time as the death of Oesc and the battle of Badon; and Aelle, of the small obscure kingdom of Sussex, is the first of those whom Bede believed to have exercised superior authority over other English kings. There is no possibility that the south Saxons fought or conquered the West Saxons, the men of Kent or any other English kingdom; Aelle's authority can only have been voluntarily bestowed. At the end of the fifth century, Sussex was the smallest of the southern English kingdoms, but Aelle was the eldest of their kings. These notices suggest that the English force comprised the armies of Kent, and of the south and west Saxons, under the overall command of Aelle. There is no hint that the Angles took part. Had they done so, it is unlikely that the high claims of their kings could have admitted the supremacy of Aelle, however senior his age. Moreover, if East Anglian expansion had been checked by Arthur's victory in Lincolnshire, recent defeat is likely to have deterred them from further adventure.

The aim of a large infantry army advancing deep into British territory must have been to overwhelm the main force of the British cavalry by weight of numbers, and to destroy the bases whence it drew remounts and fodder. Gildas calls Badon a siege. Though he does not say who besieged whom, it is probable that the infantry besieged the cavalry. He describes the site as *Mons Badonicus*, a distinct and separate hill at or near Badon. Hard-pressed cavalry required the shelter of a steep sided hill not too large for their dismounted men to hold against superior odds. There are many hills and hill forts in the neighbourhood of Bath. Most are defended spurs, easily attacked from the rear, or forts placed on the flat tops of large hills. One hill only is a separate *Mons*, sharply escarped on all sides, small enough to be defended with ease by a body of dismounted cavalry, Solsbury Hill by Batheaston. Though there are endless possibilities, this site best fits both Gildas' choice of words and the nature of the campaign.

Whatever the precise site, the circumstances are the same. The size of the forces engaged cannot be known, but there is no reason to suppose that the British cavalry numbered above a thousand men, if so many. To entertain hope of success the English required an army several times as large as the British. A siege of cavalry on a steep hill demanded more of logistics and supplies than of tactics; if the siege had been in English territory, only time was needed before starvation forced the besieged to try to break out whatever the odds. But in British territory, time favoured the defenders. An exceptionally large infantry army must needs live on the country; and any supplies available in the immediate neighbourhood of the siege must quickly have been consumed. In British territory, small foraging parties of the English risked encountering larger forces of armed men on foot, for men without horses might fight in their homelands near the shelter of their walls. The despatch of larger parties in search of food also risked weakening the encirclement. Nennius' poem allots the siege three days. The figure might be chosen to suit the metre, but it is not unreasonable. Competently organised cavalry with well-stocked saddle-bags might last three days with greater ease than a larger infantry force hungry in an alien land. At the end of the three days, the poem makes Arthur charge, slaughtering 960 of the enemy. Few of the English can have had hope of escape. Unless the survivors were very numerous, able to withdraw in good order, those who escaped the first charge were at the mercy of the pursuit, in enemy country where none would give them shelter.

Badon was the 'final victory of the fatherland'. It ended a war whose issue had already been decided. The British had beaten back the barbarians. They stood alone in Europe, the only remaining corner of the western Roman world where a native power withstood the all-conquering Germans. Yet the price of victory was the loss of almost everything the victors had taken arms to defend. Ambrosius and Arthur had fought to restore the Roman civilisation into which they had been born. But in most of Britain, the society of their fathers was ruined beyond repair. What emerged was a new world, startling not only because it differed from the past, but because it differed from the rest of Europe.

The war had begun when the emperor Valentinian was newly dead, while his successors still claimed an authority over Gaul, that men did not yet know was soon to die. Throughout the greater part of the war, the territory of Aegidius and Syagrius was still Roman, and the British might hope for aid from Gaul if they could regain control of the sea coast. But permanent change came to Gaul as well as to Britain. In 486 Clovis, the new king of the Franks, killed Syagrius and took his kingdom. Ten years later he overran the Alamanni of south-west Germany, and the Franks occupied Bohemia; he accepted catholic baptism, and in 507 he acquired the kingdom of the Visigoths in Aquitaine, chasing their survivors over the Pyrenees into Spain. The Burgundian kingdom acknowledged his authority, and was annexed by his sons. Gaul had become France, the land of the Franks; and the Franks dominated central Europe. Italy changed no less. Odovacer had discontinued the appointment of western emperors. He was a military captain grown great, but in 489 the Ostrogoths destroyed him and set Theodoric the Great upon the throne of Italy, the heir of an ancient national dynasty. What had been the western Roman empire in the childhood of the victors of Badon was now wholly comprised within the powerful Germanic kingdom of Gaul, Italy and Vandal Africa, with the smaller states of Spain. In Europe, German notables merged with the Roman nobility, and, in the words of a shrewd observer

> the poor Roman copies the Goth, but the rich Goth copies the Roman.

In Britain alone no such fusion was possible. The English were left to build their society in their own territories, almost wholly free of direct Roman influence. The British were faced with the challenge of rebuilding a successor state in half an island, all that remained of western Rome.

CHAPTER SEVEN

THE PEACE OF ARTHUR

The Reign of Arthur

Arthur is celebrated as the supreme commander who defeated the English; and as a just and powerful ruler who long maintained in years of peace the empire of Britain, that his arms had recovered and restored. Arthur the ruler is as elusive as Arthur the conqueror. Contemporary and later writers honour and respect the government he headed. A few notices describe events and incidents that happened while he ruled. None describe the man himself, his character or his policy, his aims or his personal achievement. He remains a mighty shadow, a figure looming large behind every record of his time, yet never clearly seen.

Arthur's name and fame were honoured by men who lived soon after, and had known his contemporaries, before legend had had time to obscure reality. The oldest mention of his name is in a tribute to a warrior who died about 80 years after his time; the poet praises the warrior's prowess but adds 'still, he was no Arthur'. A little later, the last lowland British armies, destroyed in the middle of the 7th century, were remembered as 'the heirs of great Arthur'. The name of Arthur meant a famous commander of the past, greater than any in the poet's time. The name itself says something of his origin, and of his reputation, for Artorius is a normal Roman name. It is not previously reported in Britain, but in the half century after his death, half a dozen rulers gave their children the name of Arthur. Thereafter, the name altogether dropped from use, and is not known to have been used by anyone anywhere for some six hundred years, until the Norman romances gave it lasting popularity. But in the sixth century Arthur was a great name, held much in honour.

The sixth century is silent. No text at all that could have named Arthur survives, except Gildas; for the memory of later ages dwelt upon the monks who lived after Arthur, and the kings who helped or hindered them. Gildas praises Arthur's government, but does not name him, for he names no one at all in the 80 years before his own day, save only Ambrosius; and his name is invoked in order to reproach his degenerate living descendants. No other 6th-century texts survive before the old Welsh poems; but traces of lost texts are many. Nennius in the 8th century epitomised a poem that was already old; the Llongborth poem probably translates a lost original. Later Welsh verse is rich in allusions to lost poems about Arthur. Catalogues of old tales, and chance incidents, assert that during the 8th and 9th centuries tales of Arthur were commonly told in Britain, in Brittany and in Ireland. Arthur's exploits did not go unrecorded; but the record perished early, because from the 9th century onwards it ceased to interest the British and the Irish, who remembered only his name. Yet though the older stories are not now preserved, they lingered long enough, at least in oral tradition, for the Norman poets to found upon them their romances. Why the Normans chose Arthur as their central hero is a problem that concerns the history of France and England in the 12th and later centuries; it does not concern the history of 6th-century Britain, or of Arthur himself. That history must derive from the notices that concern Arthur's lifetime.

The Cambrian Annals place twenty-one years between Badon and the death of Arthur. These were the years in which Gildas grew to manhood. He looked back upon them with nostalgia as years of good stable government, when

> rulers, public persons and private, bishops and clergy, each kept their proper station;

when the 'restraints of truth and justice' were still observed, not yet 'shattered and overthrown'. Gildas was a contemporary, a subject of the state Arthur ruled, and his statement of what his readers well knew is the starting-point of any attempt to understand and interpret the reign of Arthur. Gildas' outlook was conservative, and other men of his day, with less respect for the institutions of the past, may have disliked the government that he admired. His value judgement is personal. But his statement is not to be disputed, that a stable government persisted for a generation, so long as the men who had known Badon and the wars still lived. He distinguishes political rulers from public servants and private persons, and these laymen from an established episcopalian church. These institutions existed. They are not the institutions of a society that had entirely disintegrated, but of a society whose rulers were at least trying to rebuild the administrative order of the past. Arthur's government had only one possible and practicable aim, to restore and revive the Roman Empire in Britain.

The Legend of Arthur

Gildas' historical Arthur headed a strong orderly government that upheld the 'restraints of truth and justice'. It did not endure. But in its failure it won everlasting fame, so that millions of unlettered men who have never heard the names of Roman emperors and medieval kings know at least the name of Arthur. The stories of Arthur's knights have retained their popularity for so many ages that anything that may ever be learnt of the historical Arthur must always be overshadowed by the power of the legend. From all the past heroes that it might have chosen, western Europe selected the short reign of Arthur as the pattern of a golden age of good government.

The legend developed late, several hundred years after the event; but it is one of the great tales of Europe, told again and again in all lands that speak a Latin or Germanic language, still loved today. In the twelfth century, the spoof history of Geoffrey of Monmouth made Arthur a conqueror who subdued not only the Saxons, but most of Europe as well; Geoffrey's Arthur served the ambition of Plantagenet kings, but their subjects welcomed and perpetuated a different Arthur, the hero of the Norman poets, gentle, wise and courteous, whose chivalrous knights, just champions of the afflicted, were all that medieval lords should be, but were not. Their legend first appeared in the twelfth century, its source vaguely described as *Matière de Bretagne*, or *Leis des Bretons*, a story taken from the British of Normandy, or from Brittany. Soon, king Arthur's court became a central tale that drew to itself stories of other heroes, whose tragic loves and brave quests made them worthy knights of the Table Round. Some of them had origins in other lands, and some brought with them stories from the repertoire of international folk-tales. But many were British. Peredur of York, killed in 580, grew into Sir Perceval. Chance has preserved the prosaic historical basis of one among them, Tristan, in legend nephew to king Mark of Cornwall and lover of Iseult, who lived in Castle Dore, by Fowey in Cornwall. The real Tristan was an ordinary mid sixth-century British kinglet. He lived at Castle Dore, but he was son, not nephew, of king Mark, and lived three generations after Arthur. Many of the other legendary heroes are likely to have a similar origin that chance has not preserved. They were real people. They had little to do with Arthur; but the story-tellers depicted them as his companions, because his was the best loved name of all.

Tales of king Arthur existed in Wales as well as in Brittany well before the Norman romances seized upon them; but it is from the Norman stories that the legend grew, retold in succeeding ages in words and sentiment adapted to changing taste. The classic English version is Malory's, written in the later fifteenth century; the taste of his day, as of Shakespeare's, required that the heroes of romance and drama should wear modern dress, so Malory's knights wear fifteenth-century armour, as fitly as Hamlet the Dane wears an Elizabethan doublet. In English literature, the story was for a while obscured by Tennyson's misty Pre-Raphaelite version, with its banal explicit comparison of Arthur with the Prince Consort, 'Albert the Good'; and such vulgarity invited mockery, in the American cinema, or in English musical comedy. But the straightforward retelling of the tale in this century has rescued its essentials from their temporary degradation, and proved by commercial success that the legend has not yet lost its popularity. Its appeal remains extraordinarily potent. Even today it is possible to raise large sums of money for the excavation of archaeological sites that later tradition associates with Arthur, though no such sums are offered by the public for the exploration of sites connected with Julius Caesar or Claudius, Edward I or Henry VIII. The response is not simply due to the mystery that surrounds Arthur; Vortigern and Old King Cole are as mysterious, but their names do not inspire the public to finance the solution of the mystery. Arthur remains popular because of the content of his story, even when it is only dimly remembered by adults who read the tales in childhood.

The core of the story has always been melancholy regret for a strong and just ruler who protected his people against barbarism without and oppression within, but was in the end defeated by treachery and disunity. The moral varies in each age. Malory wrote towards the end of the Wars of the Roses. He made his king Arthur rescue Britain for a short space from 'great jeopardy', at a time when 'every lord that was mighty of men made him strong, and many weened to be king', so that at the final catastrophe his knights exclaim

> in this realm will now be no quiet, but ever strife and debate. . . . For by the noble fellowship of the Round Table was king Arthur upborne, and by their noblesse the king and all his realm was in quiet and rest.

Tennyson's Sir Bors was

> a square-set man and honest; and his eyes,
> An outdoor sign of all the warmth within,
> Smiled with his lips . . . a smile beneath a cloud.

He is the pattern of a Victorian hero, just, benevolent, protective to his inferiors of any class or colour, so long as they keep their station; and the twentieth-century version sees in Arthur's kingdom

> the model of chivalry and right, striving against the barbarism and evil which surrounded and at length engulfed it.

Each retelling of the tale clothed Arthur in the ideas of its own day. Malory wrote for readers weighed down by the licence of the barons. Tennyson's readers had been taught to admire benevolent and chivalrous empire-builders. In the 1950s, men believed in the defence of western civilisation against evil eastern barbarism.

It is this timeless universality which gave the legend its power over men's minds; it spread wherever Norman poets sang or were imitated, and even the sad destruction of the golden age gave men hope for its future restoration. Many peoples in many lands dreamt of a distant hero who is not dead but asleep, who will one day awaken to rescue his people from conquest and oppression; and in Europe king Arthur sleeps beneath Mount Etna in the legend of Sicily, as well as in Scottish rocks or English hill-forts, his second coming a commonplace of country fancy.

This central feature of the legend, the portrait of the strong just ruler whose good government was overthrown by the jealous ambition of lesser lords, is fully historical. It is the contemporary picture painted by Gildas, who was probably over twenty years old when Arthur fell. But all the rest is the painted fancy of later centuries; some of the legendary companions of the Round Table may have lived at other times and places, and the origin of many is unexplained. The idealised picture of the courtly king attended by heroes delighted the poets of early medieval Wales and their princely patrons, and is told most fully in the story *Culhwch and Olwen*, which is older than the Norman tales, and independent of them.

Ecclesiastical tradition preserves a more rugged attitude to Arthur, plebeian and nationalist, portraying a foreign lowland enemy, cruel, lascivious, and fearful, and is found in all three highland zones. In central Wales, at Llanbadarn Fawr, near Aberystwyth,

> a certain tyrant came from foreign parts. . . . He cast eyes on bishop Paternus' tunic and greedily demanded it. Paternus answered: 'This tunic is not for wicked men to wear, but for priests.' Arthur left the monastery, raving furiously, and came back in a rage, trying to take the tunic by force . . . cursing and swearing and stamping the ground. Paternus said: 'Let the earth swallow him up.' The earth straightaway opened and swallowed Arthur up to the chin. . . . He begged forgiveness; the earth spewed him up . . . the saint forgave him.

In south Wales, St Cadoc's father Gwynlliw abducted the king of Brecon's daughter, escaping across the frontier with the girl on the back of his horse, closely pursued by the angry father.

> But lo, three noble heroes, Arthur and his two knights, Cai and Bedwyr, were sitting on top of a hill, playing dice. When they saw the king and the girl, Arthur's heart was fired with lust. . . . Full of evil thoughts, he said to his knights: 'I am on fire with desire for the girl that that warrior is carrying on his horse.' But they replied: 'You must not do anything so criminal; we are supposed to help the needy and distressed. Let us go and help these people who are hard pressed.' Arthur answered: 'All right; if you would rather help him than grab the girl for me, go and ask whose land they are fighting on.'

Since the land was Gwynlliw's Arthur helped him, and he 'came to his palace under Arthur's protection'. The old tale was too strong for the author who copied it; his readers knew the character that Arthur ought to assume, and so he awkwardly made Cai and Bedwyr remind him of the role in which he was cast. The story is told in the Prologue to a Life written about 1100, preserved in a manuscript of about 1200; the author's emendation is one of the earliest traces of the chivalrous Arthur, and if the prologue is of the same date as the Life, it is earlier than the time of Geoffrey or of the Norman poets.

Another tale from the same Life, certainly written down in about 1100 from an earlier original, shows no such compunction.

> A great general of the British, Ligessauc Longhand son of Eliman, killed three knights of Arthur, the illustrious king of Britain.

> Arthur pursued him everywhere, and no man dared shelter him, for fear of the king, until . . . he found sanctuary with Saint Cadoc . . . who feared Arthur not at all. . . . He stayed seven years. . . . Then he was betrayed to the king, and Arthur came with a great army to the river Usk.

Arthur demanded compensation, and arbitrators awarded him a 'fine of 100 cows', since 'from ancient times among the British this kind of judgement and price had been laid down by the lawmen of kings and chiefs'. Arthur 'arrogantly rejected cows of one colour, but after much wrangling accepted cows coloured red before and white behind'. The saint's magic however tricked him by turning the cows into bundles of ferns, and restoring the animals to their owners' stalls.

The tradition of Wales is matched in Dumnonia and in Scotland; in north-western Somerset, in Dumnonia,

> Cato and Arthur ruled, living in Din Draithov. . . . Arthur tried to use the altar as a table,

but was constrained to repent and to grant estates to the church of Carantoc. In the far north, Arthur encountered the 'sons of Caw', who ruled 'beyond Bannauc', north of the Clyde, probably by the upper Forth. The eldest, Cuill (Hueil), represented as blood brother of Gildas,

> was a vigorous warrior and famous soldier, who submitted to no king, not even Arthur. He would often come down from Scotland, burning and raiding with victory and honour. The king of all Britain, hearing what the high-minded youth was doing, persecuted the victorious and admirable young man although the people used to hope and avow that one day he would become king. He killed the young robber . . . and after the murder, Arthur went home, very pleased to have killed his strongest enemy.

When he is not hated and feared, Arthur is still a remote suzerain, commanding a power and prestige far beyond the local prince's. The young Illtud, allegedly an Armorican,

> hearing of the magnificence of . . . king Arthur, longed to visit the court of so great a conqueror. . . . When he arrived, he saw an abundance of soldiers . . . and received an appointment suitable to his military ambition. When he had earned the honours he wanted, he withdrew from the court in high favour . . . and came to Poulentus, king of Glamorgan, who retained him because he was a royal soldier . . . preferring him to all his own military companions . . . and appointed him as his *magister militum* (commander-in-chief).

These stories are not historical; Arthur was dead before most of these saints preached. But they record an attitude that was certainly taken by some people.

They describe a ruler of the lowlands who succeeded in imposing his authority on all Britain, on Wales, the south-west and the north, and even beyond the borders of Britain, north of the Clyde and Forth. The tyrant came from 'foreign parts', from 'beyond the Usk', but he is not resisted by the kings within Britain; rather, he is the patron of Gwynlliw, the respected overlord of Poulentus, sovereign of king Cato's Dumnonia. He ruled over them, but not among them. The centre of his power lay east of Wales, in the lowlands that are now England.

His army was much larger than the regional warbands; it attracted the ambitious, even from overseas, rewarding their loyalty with a standing that of itself earned honour in the separate states, mastering rebels so effectively that 'none dared shelter' them. The Arthur thus portrayed is the same great sovereign whom the literature of the kings held in honour; but he is seen from a different angle, through the eyes of humbler men, whose children and grandchildren revered the saints and first composed their praises. They suffered and resented the depredations of the subordinate kings, and fastened their greatest resentment upon the person of their author, patron and supreme head of all predatory warbands, the alien emperor in the lowlands.

The stories are the fancies of a later age. But their viewpoint is not. Some of the places named are mentioned because they serve a medieval interest, but other places, and the regions defined, derive from earlier traditions. When the medieval author brought Arthur to the monasteries of Paternus and Carantoc, he did so for the benefit of their medieval inmates. But the monk who wrote a life of Gildas in southern Brittany had no such interest in reporting Arthur's campaigns beyond the Clyde; and he wrote out his northern proper names in the spelling of the 6th century, revealing that he copied from an early original. Cadoc's biographer had no interest in locating Arthur's captains and armies upon a barren mountain moor, or at a particular crossing of the Usk. His interest and invention was to link his patron Cadoc with stories set in a generation earlier than Cadoc's.

These places belong to an older tradition, secular and local. That tradition preserves the highland view of Arthur, a tyrant who came to conquer, and came from foreign parts, east of the Usk, outside Wales and the west. The tradition of an alien Arthur, an enemy who ruled the lands that became England, is not a medieval invention. It conflicts with the legend of the hero Arthur, but it is not the product of a different age; it stems from a different social class. The concept of the warrior Arthur was popular with princes. It was already old in the 8th century or earlier, repeated in the translation of a Dumnonian poem and in the verses epitomised by Nennius; it was an established legend by the time of Aneirin's *Gododdin*, early in the 7th century, and was widely accepted in the middle of the 6th century, a generation after Arthur's death, when kings named their sons after him. It was already yielding to the notion of the gentle and courteous Arthur when the author of the Cadoc prologue doctored his rough original to fit it.

The stories of the detestable Arthur, the national enemy, reflect the outlook of humbler folk, who had no love for kings and lords, warriors and rulers. They are preserved only in the Saints' Lives, for the early monastic leaders also quarrelled with kings, and many of the monks themselves came from humble homes, in later centuries as in the 6th century. Their stories preserved the outlook of the subject in the kingdoms of the Welsh. They are not part of monastic experience, for Arthur died before the monastic movement developed. The monastic tradition picked up and perpetuated a viewpoint that it found in the world around it, a plebeian tradition of deep-rooted local resentment against the suzerainty that Arthur powerfully and successfully asserted over the peoples of the highlands of Britain.

Arthur's Frontier Wars

Arthur's authority, and the campaigns that enforced it, were the inescapable consequence of the victory of Badon. The war had been won principally by the effort of the lowlands. Once it had been won, the necessary business of a government that sought to restore the past was to recover and reunite the whole of the former diocese of Roman Britain, and to restore its ancient frontiers. A number of separate stories, one of them preserved in considerable detail, describe campaigns fought to re-establish the Roman frontiers, near to the year 500. A few of them name Arthur as the victorious commander, but all of them fall within the early years of Arthur's empire, soon after Badon, and all the British commanders named lived within or on the borders of Roman Britain, and therefore owed allegiance and obedience to a restored Roman government. Some are said to have been chastised as rebels; those who did not rebel prudently accepted the new government, and fought their wars as Arthur's generals, the military *duces* of the revived empire.

In the south-west, the Dumnonian poem accepts Arthur as emperor and superior ruler over its own hero Gerontius during the wars; after the war the Life of Carantoc accepts Arthur as well as the local king, Gerontius' son Cato, as rulers over Dumnonia. The tradition of the Cornovian forces in Dumnonia makes them steadfast allies and main supporters of Arthur's rule; and their loyalty appears to have been rewarded by a large eastward expansion of their dominion, into Hampshire, that was to make them for the next several centuries the rulers of the most considerable British state; their preponderance is obscured because few of their records have been preserved.

In the north, the Nennius poem gives Arthur several battles in the Cheviot region north of Hadrian's Wall. There his enemies were certainly not the English, and the date is therefore probably after Badon. The story of Cuil carries his northern campaign farther, to the line of the Antonine Wall, between Edinburgh and Glasgow. The campaign reasserted imperial authority on the furthest borders that Rome had reached, and effectively reunited the Clyde kingdom with the rest of Britain. The genealogies name its king, at about 500, as Dyfnwal, whom they honour more prominently than any of his northern contemporaries. The extent of his power is not reported, but the independent traditions of the Lothians also acknowledge a king Dyfnwal at the same time; he was a mighty ruler, whom early medieval Wales regarded as the legendary lawgiver of the nation, who took a census of his dominions to establish the financial and taxation system of the future. That system was in practice heavily indebted to the conventions of Roman administration, and it may well be that Dyfnwal of the Clyde was Arthur's ally, rewarded with a larger territory as a trustworthy guardian of the northern frontier, who there undertook a census that Arthur enforced throughout Britain.

The faint memories of Dyfnwal are one part of a major reorganisation of the northern frontier, attributed in several stories to these years. When Britain had last obeyed a single government, seventy years before, Vortigern had solved the frontier problems by a double-sided movement of military forces. The troublesome Cunedda of the Votadini was moved away from the north to be employed against the Irish in north Wales. The government of Arthur exploited the connection between north Wales and the north-east, and repeated Vortigern's policy. The Votadini of the north-east received Dyfnwal; and Marianus, grandson of Cunedda, head of that branch of the dynasty which had stayed in Votadinian lands in Vortigern's time, was now moved south to Wales, to name the territory still called Merioneth. He did not move alone. A few inscriptions of southern Scotland name others who migrated at about the same time; and Cauuus, or Caw, the father of Gildas, was also transported to Powys, in his son's early childhood, about 500.

The settlement of the north removed commanders of doubtful loyalty and imposed trusted local rulers. It also involved the enlistment of Irish allies. Fergus of Dal Riada ruled a tiny north-eastern people whose home was squeezed by powerful neighbours, and was immediately threatened by Mac Erca's alliance with the Ulaid. He moved the seat of his dynasty to safety overseas. The date given by the Irish Annals is 503. Fergus settled in Kintyre, the long peninsula that commands the estuary of the Clyde, and stretches southward to within a dozen miles of the coast of Dal Riada in Ireland. It is probable that he settled among colonists who had long preceded him, perhaps by several centuries, but the movement of the dynasty entailed a considerable increase of Irish strength on the Clyde. For many years there is no record of conflict between Dal Riada and the Clyde, but ample record of wars between Dal Riada and the Picts. The Clyde kings could not have tolerated the establishment of a hostile dynasty in command of their seaways; and were powerful enough to reduce enemy invaders. Fergus' peaceful migration is likely to have been undertaken with the goodwill of the Clyde kings, who had cause to welcome allies against the Picts; and in the context of Arthur's northern campaign it required the approval of Arthur, and was perhaps due to the initiative of the central government of Britain.

The Irish were a problem, for in Britain they were ready to fight on either side.

Arthur's British had enlisted Irish allies before, during the war; two surviving inscriptions name Irishmen, Cunorix at Wroxeter and Ebicatos at Silchester, who probably commanded hired Irish troops; and a generation after Arthur's death Cynric of Winchester bore the same name as Cunorix of Wroxeter, and perhaps was also Irish. But considerable numbers of Irish colonists remained unsubdued in western Wales and in Dumnonia, after the first force of the fifth-century campaigns of Cunedda and of the Cornovii was spent. Several British stories report successful campaigns by British generals in Arthur's time to reduce the pockets of independent Irish in Britain, and a number of Irish traditions report the support that the Irish in Britain were able to secure from Ireland.

In north Wales Cunedda's grandson Catwallaun Longhand is said to have expelled the Irish from Anglesey about 500, at the close of a long campaign; their commander is given a Leinster name, and the Caernarvonshire peninsula of Lleyn bears the name of the men of Leinster, evidently because they had there settled in considerable numbers. Early Leinster tradition independently remembers that king Illan, who reigned from 495 to 512, fought eight or nine campaigns in Britain; but it knows nothing of any other wars by Leinster kings in Britain at any other time. Catwallaun's victory was final. Thereafter, Irish place names remain, and there are a few traces of Irish monks, but there is no further record of independent Irishmen in arms in north Wales. Nennius' poem records a battle of Arthur at Urbs Legionis, either Chester or Carleon. If it were Chester, either Illan's armies struck deep, or else Arthur had to fight to impose his authority upon Catwallaun.

But the strongest Irish colony in Britain was in south-west Wales. In the earlier fifth century, Cunedda's forces had recovered Kidwelly, eastern Carmarthenshire, but not Demetia, Pembrokeshire and western Carmarthenshire. There, a branch of the Ui Liathain of Munster had ruled an Irish kingdom for a century or more. Both the Irish and British have preserved quite independently the list of the succession of Demetian kings; in both versions the kings have Irish names until about 500, when suddenly they are replaced by kings with British names. The names of the first new rulers are not merely British. They are Roman; and in contemporary record as well as in later genealogies, they use the titles of senior officers of the imperial army of the late empire. They begin with Agricola, son of Tribunus. It may be that the genealogist has turned two names of one person into two persons, and that in his original he found Agricola the Tribune; but it is also possible that Agricola was the son of an officer whose personal name has been forgotten, and who is remembered only by his title 'the Tribune', just as Vortigern before him is remembered by a title rather than a name. Agricola is well dated to about 500, for he was father of Vortipor, who was old and grey when Gildas wrote about 540. Vortipor bore a British personal name, but his tombstone survives, and on it he is styled, not king, but Protector. The term is a Roman military rank, and meant in origin an officer who protected the emperor, much as in later armies a guards officer guards a king; and the genealogists use the same term, for the rulers of Demetia and of Demetia alone, though their uncomprehending transcripts turn the title into the personal name of an ancestor of the dynasty.

Chance has recorded a large number of fragments of the story of Arthur's recovery of south Wales, and of the generals to whom the armies were entrusted. Many of them are embedded in nonsense even wilder than is usual in medieval story, but the separate items are independently preserved in the accounts of Wales, Cornwall, Brittany and Ireland; and when they have been extracted from the fantasies of their context, they combine to tell an intelligible tale. Their story begins with an Irish invasion of Wales towards the end of the fifth century. The crazily perverted documents of Brecon derive the name of the town and region from Brychan, the son of an Irish chief, who is also dated to the beginning of the sixth century. The traditions of south Cardigan make Brychan's father land on their coasts, accompanied by the Irish king of Demetia and by captains with Munster names, at a date that seems to mean the 490s. An isolated line of Irish place names leads inland from their alleged landing-place to the Roman fort at Llandovery, whose site commands the approaches to Demetia from the west.

These movements make strategic sense, if the Demetian Irish took the offensive, renewing the alliances of the past and intending to help the last effort of the English at Badon; or if they stood on the defensive after Badon, anticipating attack from beyond the Severn. Other stories report such attacks. One of the Glamorgan tales brings Arthur to the Usk, and if his battle at Urbs Legionis were not at Chester, then it was also on the Usk, at Caerleon. Another Glamorgan tale takes him farther, and makes him fight against Brychan, and check his advance, at a strategic point on the Roman road from Cardiff to Brecon, half-way between the forts of Gelligaer and Merthyr Tydfil; it puts him in alliance with the local forces of the Cardiff region. The tales are in themselves jejune miracles; their purpose is to claim the authority of Arthur for privileges granted to monasteries that did not exist until after his death. The connection between the saint and Arthur is invented; but the localities are not. The monks of Llancarfan served their interest and honoured their founder by associating him with Arthur; but no such interest was served by placing one incident upon the Usk, and another upon a remote and windy hilltop above Merthyr Tydfil. In detailing one particular spot upon a Roman road in deserted country, the monastic writer transcribed a statement that he found in a tale told before he wrote; which he annexed to his patron and turned to his own purpose.

Theodoric

The Brecon narrative extends the geography of the fighting, with new names. A general named Theodoric advanced down the Roman road that runs from Gloucester to Brecon through Hay, and reached Brecon. He then despatched a force under Marcellus, which drove on down the Roman road through Llandovery and Carmarthen to Porth Mawr, Whitesands Bay by St. David's, and lost a hundred men at each of two named places on the way, staged 25 to 30 miles apart. The visible ruins of Porth Mawr stand above a little estuary harbour, that the recession of the sea has now dried up; but in other texts it is named as a principal port for voyages to and from Ireland, whence Patrick was held to have sailed. Four miles inland, directly on the line that links Porth Mawr with the nearest known stretch of Roman road, lies Caer Farchell, the 'fortress of Marcellus'; and Llan Marchell lies 5 miles west of Hay.

The Brecon texts make strange fancies of their story, reading Marcellus as Marcella, and turning 'Marchel' into a woman, whom they represent as the daughter of Theodoric and the mother of Brychan. But what they describe is a military expedition, for armies are commanded by men, and when they lose men by the hundred, the cause is battle with an enemy. The texts name six places in all. They are not medieval inventions, for after the starting-point, they serve no recognisable Brecon interest. They relate to a military campaign, for they are all sited on or close to the Roman road, at staged intervals and strategic points, though the texts do not remark the fact. The names and tales of the people are also not the creation of fancy, nor are they invented for the benefit of later ages. Agricola and Marcellus, *Tribune* and *Protector*, reek of the Roman past that Arthur tried to revive, and have some contemporary confirmation; Vortipor's stone gives his rank, and his father is the only sixth-century king whom Gildas praised. The places and the people belong to the time in which the tale is set, and owe nothing to the world of the medieval author who preserved its fragments.

The name of Theodoric, son of Theudebald, also belongs to the 5th century rather than the 12th. It is remarkable because it is German, neither British nor Roman; and not only German, but, at this date, specifically Gothic, not yet adopted by Frankish kings. The employment of a Goth in Britain fits the date and context, for Arthur, like other late Roman rulers, had elsewhere engaged foreign captains. The appearance of a Goth in Britain suggests a date and context, for such commanders are commonly enlisted with their men, not empty-handed. Theodoric's later career implies that he had ships at his disposal, and argues that a Gothic admiral who lacked employment was available to aid the British. The troubles of Gaul suggest that such an officer was driven out in the middle years of Arthur's reign, and at no other time. The kingdom of the Visigoths had maintained a Biscay fleet in the later fifth century, but in 507 the kingdom was destroyed by Clovis the Frank, and the Goths were expelled over the Pyrenees into mediterranean Spain. Their fleet lost its Atlantic harbours. No writer reports what happened to the ships and crews; but it is evident that a commander who had lost his homeland and his base might find it prudent to transfer all or part of his fleet to the service of the British; and Arthur's campaigns had a use for a naval force.

Theodoric was a Goth by name. That he brought the Gothic navy to Britain is no more than a possibility; but it is a natural and normal possibility, not an improbable oddity. Nor was he the only German to find employment in Demetia.

MAP 7 THE DEMETIAN CAMPAIGN

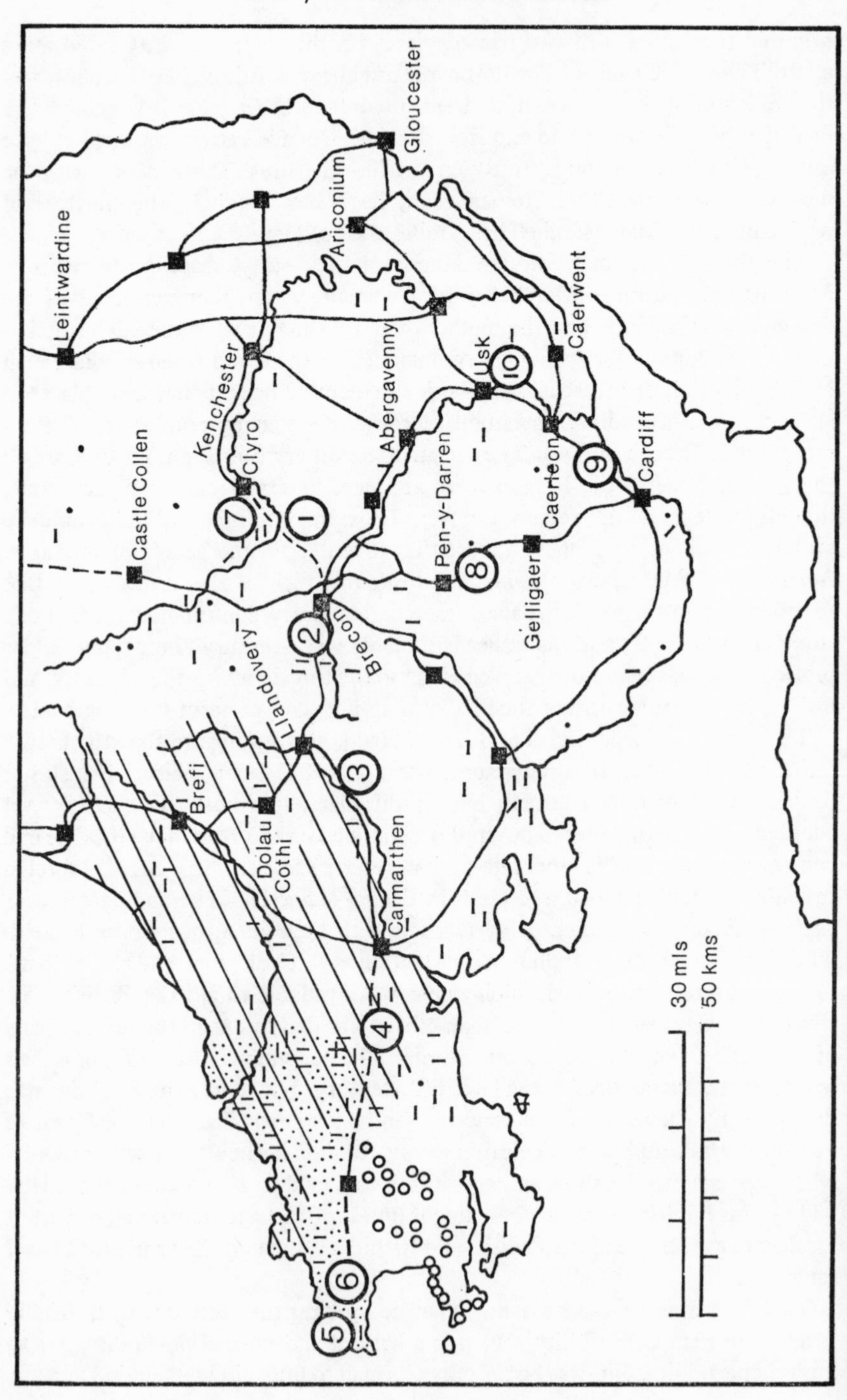

The Life of David reports in the next generation a ruler named Boia, also commanding a fleet, who was established within a few miles of Porth Mawr and of Caer Farchell, where a fortified hill and a cove still conserve his name. He annoyed the saint by parading naked women before his monks. Later writers guessed that he was Irish or Pictish, but his name is Germanic, and Germanic only. He or his father may well have been a subordinate of Theodoric's, rewarded with a permanent lordship in the lands he helped to recover.

The Demetian campaign was successful. The Irish dynasty was expelled, and Agricola was installed as the new ruler; his heirs founded a new, British, dynasty. Irish rule was ended, but the Irish were not expelled or exterminated. Demetia long remained a bilingual state. There, and there alone, the Irish word 'rath' became the normal description of small defended earthworks, whatever their date; and the use of the Irish language was officially admitted, on the memorial of the king, as well as on many private monuments, inscribed in both Irish and Latin.

Map 7

IRISH

I	Inscriptions with Irish Ogam characters or Irish personal names
///	Place names in *-cnwc* and variants, densely concentrated
	Names in *Moydir* and variants
•	single sites
⁘	concentrations
—	Names in *Cil-*
\	Names of Irish saints (excluding Patrick and Brigit)
+	Names incorporating *Gwyddel*
o	Earthworks termed *raths*

ROMAN

——	Roads
- - -	Roads, course uncertain
■	Forts and roadside towns
O	SITES NAMED in texts connected with the military forces of Theodoric, Marchel and Arthur.

see Notes to the Maps

Brecon also remained in the possession of the heirs of Brychan. Language as well as geography henceforth made Demetia a principal bridge between Britain and Ireland, a region where in the next generation the experience of civilised Roman and of barbarian Ireland was fruitfully mixed. David, the most forceful of the British monastic reformers, placed his chief monastery close to Porth Mawr; the bishop who baptised him, and his outstanding pupil and successor, were both Irishmen, and his stern but popular plebeian rule was most eagerly welcomed in and about Demetia and Brecon, where Irish settlers were most numerous.

Memories of Theodoric's wars against the Irish extend to Cornwall and Brittany. Tradition names the Cornish parishes of Trigg, north of the Padstow estuary, after the 'daughters' of Brychan; and is confirmed by an inscription dated to the decades on either side of 500, that commemorates Brocagnus son of Nadottus. The name is identical with Brychan, but it is common all over Ireland, and the Cornish Brychan, with a different father from his Welsh namesake, is probably a different person. But he was one part of the same substantial Irish migration, noted in many sources at the turn of the century, in Arthur's time. Theodoric is reported to have contained another invasion further south. After an unsuccessful attempt to land in Brittany, an Irishman named Fingar disembarked an army of 770 men, with an Irish king, at Hayle Bay, near St. Ives, where he fought in alliance with a second army, commanded by Guiner, whose name is British. They were met by Theodoric, who anticipated their attack, patrolled his coasts, and caught them as they landed, defeating both armies separately. In Cornish tradition, the survivors were absorbed into the native population. They included Findbar of Fowey, Breaca, and other followers of the early monks of the Shannon, Ciaran of Saigir and Senan of Inis Cathy; between them they name many south Cornish parishes. Irish tradition preserves independent echoes of the migration; it knew nothing of the battle, but, though it rarely remembers Irishmen abroad, it stresses the activity of the Shannon saints in Cornwall.

Cornish tradition thereafter gives Theodoric a permanent lordship south of the Padstow estuary, where he was remembered as the subordinate associate of the Dumnonian king. His principal residences are located near St. Ives and near Falmouth; the ruins of both are visible, but neither has yet been excavated. He is also reported to have sailed across the Channel to fight in Brittany; for Guiner, the ally of Fingar, whom he killed at Hayle Bay, is said to have been on his way to help his 'uncle Maxentius', whom Theodoric had previously 'deprived of part of his territory'. The name of Maxentius is as startling and as unusual as Theodoric's. Even in Gaul it is rare, reported only once in these centuries among laymen; that report is placed at the same date and in the same region, and is also linked with Theodoric. The brothers Budic and Maxentius, heirs to the British kingdom of Quimper in south-western Brittany, are said in Breton tradition to have returned from abroad at the beginning of the sixth century, and to have recovered their patrimony from a ruler named Marcellus. The name Marcellus, though common enough in earlier Roman centuries, is also very rare in Gaul, unique among the British. These relationships concur, for the Marcellus of Demetia and of Brittany were both allies of Theodoric, and may well have been the same person.

The quite independent traditions of south-east Wales connect the dynasty of Brittany with Theodoric's Demetian allies. Maxentius' brother Budic was subsequently expelled, and found refuge in Demetia; the story does not name his enemy, but, in Brittany, as in Wales, a common cause of a king's expulsion was the superior strength of a brother or near relative. Budic was restored to his territory with the help of a powerful fleet provided by Agricola of Demetia. The probable sequence of the events told in separate stories is that after killing Marcellus, the brothers divided the kingdom of Quimper; that Maxentius expelled Budic and seized his portion of the kingdom; and that thereafter Theodoric, commanding Agricola's Demetian fleet, restored Budic, thereby 'depriving' Maxentius of 'part of his kingdom'.

The substance of the story is preserved only in disjointed morsels of medieval tradition. But Budic, and his connection with Theodoric, were known to the contemporary historian Gregory of Tours, who wrote at the end of the 6th century. He reports that Budic died about 557, and gave the name of Theodoric to his own son, who was born about the year 510 to 530. At that date, it was a quite exceptional choice for a British father; among the thousands of British persons known, no other is reported to have given a Gothic, or any German name to his child. The exceptional choice implies that the father was beholden to a friend who bore that name and earned his gratitude. Theodoric had fought to enthrone Agricola. He sailed the seas, and perhaps commanded the fleet that Agricola sent to restore Budic to his inheritance.

In yet another local Cornish tradition, Theodoric is said to have lived long as the local lord in the Falmouth region, and to have died in a hunting accident between 530 and 550. His career is not in itself exceptional; it is less remarkable than the history of Odovacer, or of many another bold adventurer dispossessed by a quick change of fortune, and lifted up again. It is unusual only because chance has preserved so much vivid detail, in so many different records. Portions of his story are remembered in medieval texts that are wholly independent of each other, in Ireland, in south-west Wales, in two distinct traditions of south-east Wales, in three separate regions of Cornwall, in Brittany and in Ireland; in two contemporary inscriptions, and in the contemporary witness of Gregory in Gaul. The diversity of these notices, and the chance that three among the people involved in the tale bore exceptional names, while two more used Roman titles, rule out the possibility that the story derives from a late legend. Most of the detail is presented in a grotesque context concerning a particular saint in one locality. These accounts have no common written origin; each ultimately derives from an original that was first set down when the memory of Theodoric was green in the district that each story concerns, and reported only local events, knowing nothing of the wider story.

Theodoric came to Britain in the maturity of Arthur's empire, and outlived him, to die about the time that Gildas wrote. He was a wartime captain who became the peacetime ruler of a small territory, far from the land of his birth. He was a relatively unimportant officer of Arthur's armies, and became a subordinate local lord. His story matters because chance reports more of him than of other men. It outlines the unromantic portrait of one of Arthur's lesser 'knights'; and explains the origin of one among the 'generals' and 'tyrants' of whose upstart independence Gildas complains. His career typifies the experience of hundreds of his contemporaries, who are nameless, or known by name alone, who lived like him with their retainers in small defended halls, local replicas of the greater commanders, whose heirs Gildas was to denounce as 'ill-starred generals', the curse of Britain when Arthur was dead.

Arthur's Civil Government

These several stories of Arthur's frontier wars describe the restoration of the territorial integrity of Roman Britain. The Irish were finally subdued or expelled wherever they had survived, in the south-west, in south Wales and in north Wales. The northern frontier was recovered to its farthest limits. Some stories of the frontier wars survive because it was in these western and northern regions that the language of the British remained in use long enough for medieval writers to salvage a few scraps of their history. In the lowlands, the language died out much sooner, and no such incidents were remembered even in twisted forms; for in the lowlands no one transcribed the lives of British ecclesiastics or copied out the genealogies of lay rulers. But the traditions of the highlands are emphatic, and are agreed upon one chief essential of Arthur's rule. He was the emperor, the all-powerful ruler of the whole of Britain, and the seat of his power was in the lowlands; in the western and northern highlands he was a foreigner whose authority was accepted resentfully, and asserted by superior force.

The government of a lowland emperor is an earlier and more credible tradition than medieval folk-tales told of a western king in Wales and Cornwall. The men who followed Ambrosius and Arthur had fought to preserve and restore the Roman civilisation of their fathers; when they won the war, they could not do any other than try to restore its political institutions, and 'emperor' is the natural title for the head of those institutions. Gildas' description of Britain a generation after the fall of Arthur frequently mentions institutional titles, and Gildas is a writer who consistently and carefully uses technical terms precisely and accurately; *foederati*, *annona*, *hospites*, *praepositi*, *consilium*, and *consiliarii* are late-Roman terms correctly used, as is *cuneus* for a military formation; *cyulae* and *curucae* are exact terms for the ships of the Saxons and of the Picts and Irish, *naves* for Roman ships; and each term is used rightly for the people concerned. In his preface, Gildas mentions the titles of his own day. He apologises for speaking out; others should be more competent than he to redress the evil, for

> Britain has *rectores*, she has *speculatores*.

These also are technical terms. *Rector* means a provincial governor. Gildas elsewhere uses the word several times for governor, once for the Deity; he never applies it to any of the rulers whom he calls *reges, tyranni, duces*, for these words also have a defined meaning and describe other offices. *Speculator* also has an exact meaning; it is the normal term for the executive officers who served the *rectores*, their watchmen or police.

Gildas means what he says. Though sixth-century provincial governors in Britain seem startling to modern notions, there was less cause for surprise at the time of Badon. Their revival was a necessary part of restoring the administration that a Roman emperor must re-establish. Imperial government also required the appointment of a praetorian prefect, and of a *magister militum*, with *duces* and *comites* to command the armies. Gildas makes no mention of prefect or *magister*, for these were the officers of the central government, and could not have survived its collapse, on Arthur's death, years before Gildas wrote. But he has much to say of the *duces*, the regional and local army commanders. On the rare occasions when he names them without reproach, he accords them their formal title, *duces patriae*, 'the generals of our country'. But when he abuses them, he attacks their factual authority, and denounces them as *reges* and *tyranni*, 'kings' and 'tyrants'. He follows the usage of Europe in his own day. In Europe, the Roman generals Aegidius and Marcellinus had become kings in Gaul and Dalmatia; in Africa, a Moroccan inscription of the year 508 honours

Masuna, king of the Moorish peoples and of the Romans

and records the official Roman titles of his subordinates, 'prefect' and 'procurator'. Among the British of Armorica, Gildas' younger contemporary Gregory of Tours remarks that their rulers had in the 5th century called themselves kings, but that when they admitted the nominal suzerainty of the Frankish kings, after 511, they consented to adopt the more modest title of *comites*; and the Lives of the Armorican saints accurately observe the change of usage that Gregory reports, naming 5th-century kings and 6th-century *comites*.

In Britain, as elsewhere, men used the appropriate term in its right context. Later Welsh usage in Britain called Arthur *ameraudur*, emperor. Gildas includes Vortipor of Demetia among the *reges* he abuses, and calls him *tyrannus*. But on his official public monument, Vortipor is described by his official title of *Protector*, and is not called *rex*. Vortipor and his father had owed their title to Roman imperial authority. When Vortipor died and Gildas wrote, that authority had ceased to be. The military rulers were still officially *duces*, generals, but they had in practice become *reges*, kings.

For civilian officials Gildas uses the generic term *publici*; those who administer the law he terms *iudices*, judges, and one of them is named on his tombstone in north Wales, not far from 500, with the formal title of *magistratus*. The numerous technical terms of late Roman administration, correctly used, are the debris of an apparatus of government restored or revived by the victors of Badon, though it did not long survive them. It was the government of a Roman emperor, equipped with a hierarchy of civil and military officers, on the model of that which had existed in the earlier fifth century in the western provinces, and in Britain in the childhood of the men who were old when the war was won.

These institutions endured for at least thirty years after Badon. Gildas had noted the growth of the 'crimes' he denounced over 'many years', but the total subversion of the old standards of good government was comparatively recent, for it was only over a period of 'ten years or more' that he had been moved to action, previously hesitating to speak out. The heart of his complaint is one familiar enough to late Roman experience; the excessive power of the military, overawing the civil administrators. Of his *rectores* and *speculators* Gildas says that

> they certainly exist, and they are not short of the proper number, even if they do not exceed it. But they are under such immense pressure that they have no room to breathe.

Throughout his invective, Gildas consistently distinguishes between the *tyrannus* and the *iudex*; the *tyrannus* usurps the functions of the *iudex*, overshadows him and makes him his creature; both show a brutal disregard of established law. Gildas' *regula recti iudicii*, the rule of correct judgement, can only mean the written law of Roman Britain.

Gildas' complaint is that the *publici* of his day were corrupt, whereas those of Arthur's time were not. These 'judges' and 'magistrates' are the proper terms for the civil heads of the separate *civitates*. When Gildas wrote, they were overborne by the tyrants, generals who had become kings, but submitted to no sovereign who could compel their obedience or control their licence. His praise of the good old days, in the lifetime of Arthur, when military commanders, like civil officials and private persons, each kept to their proper station, is praise of the government established and headed by Arthur after the war. Gildas names no names, but he confidently asserts the stability of Arthur's government in the face of readers who had been his subjects and had known how he ruled.

Partition

The greater part of Roman Britain had been recovered, but a number of eastern areas remained in enemy hands. It is probable that their independent existence

---

Map 8

IIII English Areas. III Areas probably English. Areas with 5th-century and later 6th-century burials, without clear evidence of earlier 6th-century burials, stippled.

MAP 8 PARTITION

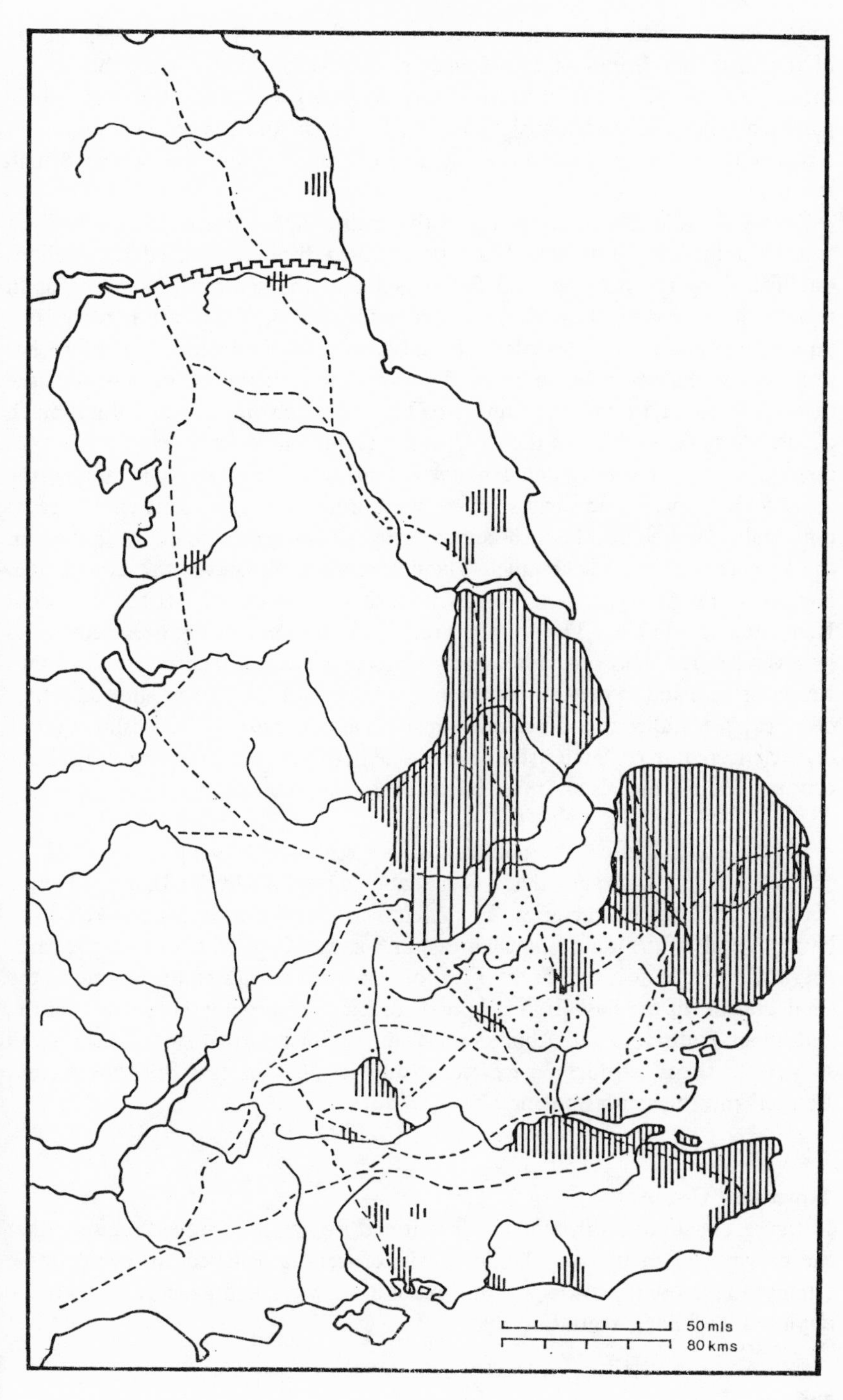

and precise frontiers were determined by formal treaty. In regretting that many of the martyrs' shrines of the Roman past were no longer accessible to the British, Gildas gives the reason, *lugubri divortio barbarorum*, the 'melancholy partition with the barbarians'. The word *divortio* implies formal cession of territory to aliens, not merely the tolerated existence of federates within British territory.

Plainly these ceded lands included the main English areas in Sussex, Kent and Norfolk. The frontiers of the peace must have recognised the realities established by the fighting, and the evidence of the cemeteries shows that in many other areas the English continued undisturbed. There are however important exceptions. The very large burial-ground of Kempston by Bedford has produced more Saxon grave goods than any site in Britain; but, among those that can be dated, there is a striking gap. There is much of the fifth century, much of the late sixth, nothing of the early sixth. Though in theory some of the ornament that cannot yet be dated might belong to the missing generations, the absence of recognisable early sixth-century ornaments, abundant elsewhere, is remarkable; moreover, the fifth-century grave goods are Anglian, while those of the late sixth century bear much Saxon ornament. Whatever the explanation, Kempston received different treatment during the peace of Arthur. Nor does Kempston stand alone. The scattered record of more poorly reported cemeteries in several other areas is similar. Early sixth-century ornament is rare in south Leicestershire and in most of Northamptonshire; and in Hertfordshire and most of Essex, in Middlesex and Buckinghamshire, and in most of Oxfordshire. These districts have one particular setting; they lie between regions where early sixth-century English burials are more plentiful.

On present evidence, the population of these areas was either removed, or subjected to such restraints that it was unable to bury its dead with normal grave goods or in normal cemeteries. The effect was to clear wide bands of territory between each of the main English areas, in Sussex, Kent, Norfolk, and the Mid-Anglian counties near the Trent. Elsewhere normal burials continue only in the small clusters of the East Riding, in parts of Lincolnshire, by the lower Thames, and about Dunstable and Abingdon. Whatever their formal status, their small size made them harmless, necessarily subject allies of the British of York, London and the south midlands.

Town and Country

In the rest of southern Britain, a reconstituted Roman government required that the province of each *rector* should consist of *civitates* centred on towns. Some attempt to restore the towns was made, but it was weak and unsuccessful. Gildas deplored its failure, regretting that

> the cities of our country are still not inhabited as they were; even to-day they are squalid deserted ruins.

St. Jerome used similar words of fourth-century Italy, meaning that cities were shrunken, decayed, dying, but not that they were grassgrown archaeological sites without human inhabitants. Gildas' complaint is that the cities were not peopled 'as they used to be'; some men lived in some cities, but they failed to make them more than 'squalid ruins'. Excavation illustrates some detail. At Wroxeter and Silchester, late fifth-century inscriptions name Irish chiefs. They were neither saints nor passing strangers, but men in authority, who left behind them followers numerous and permanent enough to erect memorials in their honour. The most probable explanation is that they had headed forces raised by the British during the wars. Later, not earlier than the sixth century, when the Silchester stone had long weathered, someone threw it down a well, together with much late Roman pottery and other rubbish. Either the well was a convenient rubbish dump, or it was a danger to the children. In either case, someone still lived at Silchester, and tidied up the debris; and in the centre of Wroxeter, men lived in solid timber houses, built over vanished Roman ruins.

Inscriptions are few. Elsewhere, evidence is less precise. Some of the excavated buildings of Verulamium lasted far into the fifth century, if not later; the latest construction on one site, a well engineered water main, is likely to have been built nearer to Arthur's time than to Vortigern's; and occasionally other evidence suggests a date as late in other towns. British cemeteries of the period are beginning to be recognised, at Verulamium and at Magiovinium near Bletchley, near Swindon, in Scotland and Somerset, and in other places. In Colchester, a substantial building was constructed over a late Roman street, but it lies beneath the medieval street; and an elegant chapel by the castle is later than the Romans, earlier than the Normans. York and London were still inhabited, but in many towns there is little direct evidence, one way or the other.

The little evidence is matched against much legend. The name of Arthur is attached to many hills, earthworks, and natural features, often named Arthur's Seat, Arthur's Leap, and the like. He sleeps till the trumpet shall arouse him to succour his people in many places, on Hadrian's Wall, in Richmond Castle and at Cadbury Castle, near Yeovil in Somerset, near Manchester, under Mount Etna, in Savoy and in Arabia, and elsewhere; but not in Wales, where tradition firmly asserts that his grave is not known. These names and local legends show where the Arthurian romances became popular in the middle ages, but they have nothing to do with early tradition. They are made-up names, invented by medieval men who read or heard the romances.

By contrast, some of the places named in the Norman romances themselves are real. They come from earlier sources; and the geographical knowledge of the Norman poets is greater than their historical understanding. King Mark's castle by Fowey is accurately named and precisely located. The misty land of Lyonesse across the sea, *pagus Leonensis* in north-western Brittany, is still called Leon. Many of the city names, London, Carlisle, Caerleon, remain in use and give no problems. The romantic Avallon is a common Roman Celtic place name; it is still the name of one small town in central France, that was known as Aballo in the Roman period. The letters 'Avallon' painted upon a dusty board on the railway station are a healthy reminder of its prosaic reality, for it means no more than 'Appleton'. A dozen modern English villages bear this ordinary name, and some of the many hundreds of small places in Roman Britain are also likely to have been called Aballo; Glastonbury may or may not have been among them.

These are places that preserve in recognisable form the names they bore in Roman times. A similar origin must be sought for Camelot, represented as among the most important of several cities where Arthur held court. Nearly all the others were large towns of Roman Britain, Chester, York, Gloucester and others, set down in their medieval spelling. Camalot, the more usual early form of the name, is therefore plainly a medieval spelling of the Latin name of a large Roman town in Britain. The only town with such a name is Camulodunum, Colchester.

Colchester had obvious advantages as a political centre in reconquered Britain. It was well sited to observe and to intimidate the two most formidable English territories, East Anglia and Kent. Easy roads linked it with the British north and west; and shipping from its harbours might reach Europe without approaching too closely the coast of English Kent. Contact with Europe mattered at the time of Badon, for then the struggle of Goth, Roman and Frank had not yet finally decided the fate of Gaul. But before the death of Arthur, the victories of Clovis the Frank had permanently turned Gaul into France. Thenceforth, there was nothing Roman left in northern Europe to comfort the British; and the collapse of a central authority in Britain ended the need for a political centre. Colchester lost its brief advantage.

Colchester was able to serve a new government for a short time because London was in decline. Throughout its history, London has prospered when commerce is busy and government secure and active. When the fifth century wars ended commerce and destroyed the government, London became a fortress, for the accidental reason that the main enemy forces were based on Kent and Norfolk. When the wars ended, London could have no health unless prosperity and strong government were successfully and permanently restored. They were not so restored.

Colchester might have been a frequent residence, but Arthur's was not a government that could rule from a single capital. It could only try to restore what had been smashed, but victory came too late for men to look back, too soon for them to start anew. The memories of the victors reached back to their own childhood, before the slaughter of the elders and the emigration of the survivors had throttled the Roman economy and the Roman institutions of Britain; and because these memories remained, men could not ignore them and devise a society that matched the actual conditions of their own day. Memory forced them to look at the past. They might recreate its outward political forms, but its economy could not be restored. Soldiers and civil servants might be placed within the walls of the decayed towns, but there is no evidence to suggest that any countryside villa was restored. Except in the west, the landlord economy was gone. So was the industry, the technology and the market economy. All that was left was subsistence agriculture, poor farmers producing food for their families, unable to procure what they could not make at home. Such an economy could not grow enough food to maintain a substantial urban population, or a numerous army and administration.

A shrunken town might feed itself from fields outside the walls, like Verulamium in wartime. But when the war was over, farmers might live more conveniently among their fields, no longer needing the shelter of walls. Government, and townsmen who did not farm, must depend upon what they could wring from small farmers; in Wales, the *duces* exacted tribute in cattle and corn, honey and beer, from reluctant peasants. In the west, tenants still paid rent. But in much of the lowlands, landlords had emigrated, joined the army, or perished and left no heirs. The old compulsions had been broken too long, and the grandson of a former landlord could not easily coerce the grandson of a former tenant into resuming a rent that had lapsed for half a century. Subsistence economy condemned each town and each warband to live on what it could get from its own area. No central government could hope to collect taxes and distribute them to its agents; its income was what it could persuade or force each local ruler to contribute. If Arthur's central army and administration were of any considerable size, no single area could afford to maintain them for long periods, save perhaps in parts of the west. East of the Cotswolds, Arthur can only have progressed from centre to centre, eating his way through his country like a medieval king. His personal prestige maintained his empire while he lived. When he fell, the empire ended. No new emperor was or could be proclaimed; actual power passed to the generals.

The Economy

The economy was not strong enough to bear a central government. Only a long period of peaceful recovery could have restored its strength, and then only if the armies were disbanded, their leadership and manpower directed to the slow reconstruction of agriculture, industry and towns. But after a generation of war the armies were made up of men who knew no trade but fighting. With no foreign enemy to fight, they fought each other. The restraints that Arthur's rule imposed checked their discords for a decade or more, but Gildas' protest that civil war was the ruin of Britain was amply justified; and it was unavoidable. Older men might dream of restoring the past, but younger men knew only the present. The realities of political power could not tolerate a strong government.

The power of Arthur's captains had rested on their ability to levy horses, men and food, much of it drawn from the peasants of the areas they protected. But aid given willingly in wartime tends to become a grievance, resented in peacetime. Yet actual power resided in the military commanders, not in the failing towns and vanished magnates; and Arthur's rule depended on the willingness of his captains to obey, and upon their ability to supply his needs. A few armed horsemen among unarmed civilians were in a position to enforce their orders; but they were not instruments for the restoration of justice, and a government that sought to restore ancient ways clearly had frequent cause to quarrel with the commanders upon whom it depended. The decisions of Arthur and his officers must heed both the temper of the *duces* and the protests of civilians, and must seek to reconcile the conflicts of one general and one area with another. Only years of quiet without conflict could renew the old habits of obedience and respect for government. But recurring conflict was built into the structure of postwar Britain, and quiet did not endure.

The victors of Badon faced an all but impossible task. They could act only according to their notions of their past, but they were subject to the pressures of their chaotic present. The most emphatic witness to the stature of the historical Arthur is that they succeeded for as long as they did. Gildas observed that evil tendencies had been growing for a long time, but dates the definitive collapse of good government ten years or so before he wrote. It had lasted well into the 520s, nearly thirty years after Badon, throughout Arthur's lifetime and some few years beyond. The twenty years allotted to the rule of Arthur after Badon are pictured as years of internal peace, the civil wars as an evil that followed them.

Camlann

A bald notice in the Cambrian Annals is the only record of Arthur's end:

> the Battle of Camlann, where Arthur and Medraut fell.

The entry is placed 21 years after Badon, and should indicate a date a year or two either side of 515. Later legend insists that Medraut was the enemy and not the ally of Arthur, but the earlier Welsh bardic tradition makes him a hero who served Arthur. The Annal could bear either meaning, and the only other record of a fifth or sixth century Medraut makes him the heir of a southern dynasty, and perhaps locates his son in Suffolk. Nothing else is known of the battle or its cause, or even of its whereabouts. Camlann means 'crooked glen', and the Roman fort at Birdoswald on Hadrian's Wall has that name. But so did other places; one in Merionethshire is still so called, and there are many crooked glens in England whose former British name has perished.

But whatever the place and cause of the battle, the result was catastrophe. With Arthur died the unity of Britain, and all hope of reviving it under British rule. In the next generation, Gildas denounced the anarchy that followed; but it did not occur to him that a strong central government could or should be established to check it. He admitted Roman law and magistrates; he endorsed the fourth-century criticism of the emperor Maximus, a rebel against a legitimate emperor; and he praised the government of his own youth, that Arthur had headed. The rule of Arthur had been an age of order, truth and justice, to be praised in retrospect; but Arthur was also the author and the patron of the *duces* whom Gildas denounced. When his empire fell, it could have been restored only by the predominance of the brutal Maelgwn, or of some other general, over his rivals, a tyranny that neither Gildas nor any other civilian could have welcomed. In retrospect the institution of the emperor was ranged on the side of the generals against the judges. No one wished its return; civilian and conservative opinion saw no future in the emergence of a supreme tyrant, and the local tyrants had no wish for a master. The emperor and his restored Roman government were dead and best forgotten, no longer practical politics.

Arthur dominates and unites the history of two centuries; his victory was the climax and consummation of the fifth-century struggles; and his undoing shaped the history of the sixth century, the mould wherein the future of the British Isles was formed. He was at once the last Roman emperor in the west, and the first medieval king of the country now called England. He left behind him the memory of a splendid failure. The story-tellers who sang of a strong, just and chivalrous king might have chosen for their hero Edwin of Northumbria, or Maximus, or Cormac of Ireland, or Theodoric of Ravenna or another famous name. They chose Arthur, and preserved his essential story. Yet even the barest outline of who he was and what he did must be inferred from dubious uncertain hints. There is just enough to show that Arthur existed, and was honoured in the next few generations as the greatest general and ruler of the recent past; just enough to show that in Britain he subdued the Germans who elsewhere mastered Europe, that the prestige of his victory and the force of his character maintained for two decades a strong government against impossible odds among the ruins of Roman Britain. He left a golden legend, and he rescued a corner of the Roman world from barbarian rule for a short space. Posterity may echo the judgement of the Norman historian William of Malmesbury,

> this is that Arthur of whom modern Welsh fancy raves. Yet he plainly deserves to be remembered in genuine history rather than in the oblivion of silly fairy tales; for he long preserved his dying country.

THE SUCCESSOR STATES

CHAPTER EIGHT

PAGAN IRELAND

The history of the fifth century is the story of the destruction of Roman Britain, and of Arthur's unavailing efforts to rebuild its ruins. Men who lived within the former frontiers could still regard themselves as fellow-citizens of a single state, distinct from Irishmen and Picts beyond; when Patrick determined to go to Ireland, the natural reaction among the British was to wonder that he should risk his life 'among the enemy'. The war ended the ancient division between Roman and barbarian, but it also killed the ancient unity of the Roman diocese. The southerners fought as *Cumbrogi*, and won their victory with little help from the north, while Wales fought its own Irish wars. The victors restored something of the old unified administration, and forced the highlands to acknowledge its suzerainty. So long as its authority endured, contemporaries could still see Britain as a political unit, and describe its history in a single narrative. But after the death of Arthur and the end of his empire, the several nations of the British Isles have their separate histories; neither the ancient nor the modern historian can blend these accounts into one comprehensive narrative. From the early sixth century onward, the histories of the Irish and the Picts, the British and the English, must be told separately.

The four nations deeply influenced each other; their military and political strength set the limits within which each might develop. The balance of power changed decisively and permanently during the sixth century. The peace of Badon lasted for more than two generations, and when the second Saxon revolt broke out, no one was left alive who could remember clearly the earlier troubles. The revolt began soon after the fearful bubonic plague, that wasted Europe in the middle of the century. In the south, it led to crushing victories in the 570s. In the north, it gathered strength more slowly, but in the thirty years after 580 the English armies ended British rule forever. England, Wales and the future Scotland had taken shape, though none yet had a central government of its own. The British Isles were divided between a number of separate kingdoms. They differed in their speech and in their memories, but henceforth they shared a comparable economy and political structure.

The bond that reinforced similar customs among each people was the monastic church, common to all of them. It was created and shaped by the British during the peace of Badon; the Irish welcomed it with enthusiasm, and carried it to the Picts and the English, and thereafter to Europe. Through the church, the example of Ireland deeply influenced the secular development of the other British peoples. Though the Christian religion reached Ireland in the fifth century, it first seized hold of Irish society in the decades immediately after the death of Arthur. Its impact on barbarian Ireland was explosive, for Ireland was changing rapidly, ready to pour its national traditions and morality into a Christian mould.

Irish Christianity was a major influence in the formation of the new society in Britain. Christian clerks and statesmen who had been trained in Ireland or by Irishmen were prominent among its builders; and they are chiefly responsible for the manner in which its history was preserved. The records of Britain cannot be interpreted intelligibly without an understanding of their Irish background; and that Irish background leans heavily upon the long traditional history of pagan Ireland. The story of pagan Ireland is full of fancies, its reality hard to determine; yet what mattered to the future was not the reality, but the beliefs that men of the sixth and seventh centuries held about the past; and those beliefs are more easily discovered.

The Sources

The early historians of the British, the English and the Picts learned much of their trade from the Irish. They imitated the forms in which they recorded events and shared their fundamental assumptions. Unlike most of their contemporaries in Europe, they took it for granted that both the distant and the recent past of their regions and peoples ought to be remembered and explained, and ought to be cited as a guide to present conduct.

These records took many forms. Unlike the peoples of Europe, the nations of the British Isles preserved long pedigrees of royal and notable families; they did so because they believed that a man who could claim a notable ancestor deserved honour in the present. Though some of the continental Germans had once had oral genealogical traditions, their descendants did not prize them, and most of them perished without written record; but the English genealogies reach back to the ancestral gods, and name human kings who were held to have reigned in the third or fourth centuries, long before their descendants approached Roman territory. Their form, particularly in Northumbria, follows an Irish model, and some of the kings they list were also remembered in heroic tales, that were written down in England, though their counterparts in Europe were not transcribed, and were forgotten when they ceased to be sung. The British pedigrees are more numerous than the English. Their ancestral tradition rarely extends back beyond the fifth century; but its form and content are also heavily indebted to the enormous corpus of Irish genealogy, vastly older, richer and more developed than its British or English counterparts.

The study of Irish genealogy has also become easier since the publication of the first volume of O'Brien's *Corpus Genealogiarum Hiberniae* (1962), whose index names 15,000 to 20,000 persons who were held to have lived before the tenth century, with many more thereafter. The scattered texts of the Welsh and English pedigrees are also nearly all in print. Like all genealogists, their authors sought to connect living patrons with heroes of the past, so that, apart from remote and fanciful origins, the beginning and the end of each line normally copy original record, but the links between are often corrupt. The principal difficulty in their study is superficial; most of the important lines are preserved in a number of different versions, many of which leave out, insert, or duplicate an entry or miscopy their original, so that no single text preserves the whole of the tradition it reports. That tradition can be discovered only by critical comparison of the several manuscripts. All the English and Welsh early texts, and the more important Irish lines, are therefore collated in *Arthurian Sources*.

The British and the English owe a still greater debt to the Irish Annals. The Christian Irish set down a detailed account of their pagan past, and to do so they adapted the form of Roman Christian annals. Their Roman model had been shaped by Eusebius of Caesarea in the early fourth century. When the Christian Constantine conquered Rome, Eusebius set himself the task of synchronising the historical tradition of Rome with the legends of Greece, of the Near East, and of the Old Testament; and thereafter his chronicle of world history was continued by many other writers. The Irish set themselves a comparable task, of synchronising the stories of their own pagan past with the world chronicles of Eusebius and of his successors. The earlier surviving versions preserve many of the European entries that were used to fix the dates of native events, but later recensions omit them, copying only the native entries.

The Irish Annals survive in half a dozen main versions, drawn up between the 11th and the 17th century, and published in good, bad and indifferent modern editions. All the surviving texts are collations of earlier lost texts, and each makes its own selection, so that some entries occur in all, some in several, some in one only. They list events under years, but the AD dates printed in the margins are all the work of late editors, from the 14th century to the 20th. The later editors, and their lost sources, used different dating systems, so that reference to the separate texts gives a bewildering superficial impression of discordant and uncertain alternatives; and confusion is increased because the editors of all extant texts themselves faced conflicting dating systems in their originals, and therefore often enter the same event two or three times, under different years, either naming their source, or commenting 'as others say'.

These are technical problems, awkward only because they have not yet been sorted out. The manuscripts of the European chronicles abound with comparable difficulties, that have been resolved by the labours of nineteenth-century editors. The study of Irish dating has been made much easier by Mac Airt's exact and critical edition of the *Annals of Inisfallen* (1951), which has made it possible to collate the several versions in *Arthurian Sources*, permitting each event to be referred to a single year, according to its position within the Inisfallen series of dates. Collation does not resolve all problems; but it makes them manageable, by distinguishing the real historical problems from unreal apparent difficulties, that are created only by a faulty manuscript tradition.

The study of the Irish Annals does not concern Ireland alone. The English and the Welsh Chronicles derive both their form and their earlier entries directly from their Irish exemplars. The 'Cambrian Annals' are, for the fifth and sixth centuries, a transcript of the Irish Annals; of the first 22 entries, 18 are copied from the Irish, and only four British notices are inserted among them; and Irish entries still form a majority of the seventh-century notices. The Saxon Chronicle also follows the Irish form; in its earlier entries, concerning the first century, it makes the same selection as the Irish make from Bede, or from his source, and shares with the Irish half a dozen items not found in Bede. But from the 5th century on, it copies only native entries, as in the later texts of the Irish Annals; for it is preserved in a relatively late version, edited in Wessex in the 9th century.

The Irish Annals are also a direct source for the history of Britain. They preserve some hundred and fifty notices of events in the British and English kingdoms in the 6th and 7th centuries, many of them not recorded elsewhere. But the influence of the Irish historians bites deeper than its form, its example and its additional information. It also underlies the interpretation of its imitators, sometimes implanting in their texts an arbitrary date, that deeply influences later historical thinking, but cannot be explained until its Irish origin is examined; for example, the Irish plague entry of 551, wrongly interpreted as 547 in the Welsh text, was there used to date the death of Maelgwn of Gwynedd, and the Saxon Chronicle in turn used the Welsh notice of Maelgwn to give a date to Ida of Northumbria, whom it therefore entered at 547. Nor is the influence confined to dates. It extends to the Chronicler's judgement of what he should enter, how he should record it, and how the moral should be pointed, often by the Irish technique of inserting a long vivid tale into the bald list of events, in a manner alien to European practice.

The English and Welsh derivatives have fewer textual difficulties. The Welsh or 'Cambrian' Annals are preserved in two main versions, that do not substantially disagree, save that one of them leaves out about one-tenth of the entries. Half a dozen versions of the Saxon Chronicle survive, but they have been many times published, with critical commentaries, and have long since been collated. The narrative of the Chronicle however preserves three serious confusions; as in the Irish texts, the marginal AD dates are inserted by later editors into earlier notices, and, since their starting-point is too late, all events earlier than 550 are placed some twenty years later than the original version intended; the notices of the origins of Wessex are entered three times over, in the manner of the duplicate entries in the Irish Annals; but, unlike the Irish, the 9th century West Saxon authors of the Chronicle thoroughly misconceived the early history of the north.

The Lives of the Saints constitute the third main source for early Irish history. They chiefly concern the 5th, 6th and later centuries, and are an important source for the history of the British and the English as well as of the Irish. Their information about places and regions is supplemented by the evidence of so-called ancient dedications. The modern word has occasioned some confusion; a peculiar 'Celtic' custom of 'dedication' has been alleged, and refuted. The arguments exist only on word play. There were no 'dedications'. The Christians of the British Isles continued to name churches after the fashion of 4th century Europe, long after Europe had changed its practice. Churches were 'dedicated' to God alone; but they were distinguished from one another by the name of their founder, or of a teacher whom he honoured. In Rome the Basilica of Liberius was so-called because it was built by pope Liberius; it did not receive its lasting name of S. Maria Maggiore, in honour of the Virgin, until the 430s, a quarter of a century after political separation from Italy had hindered the spread of religious and political novelty to Britain. The first church in Tours was known as the Church of Litorius, after the bishop who built it; when Martin died in 398, his pupil and successor built a new Church of Martin above his tomb. At the same time in Britain another admirer of Martin, Ninian, gave Martin's name rather than his own to his church at Whithorn. Thereafter the churches, chapels and monasteries of the British Isles were regularly known by the name of their founder or of the teacher he admired, or by their geographical location.

From the later 7th century the English, but not the Irish or the Welsh, began to adopt the new European custom of naming churches after long dead Christian leaders, notably Saints Peter, Paul and Martin. The Normans introduced the more recent names of Michael, All Saints and others, and energetically imposed them, together with the name of Mary, upon churches known by older names. Sometimes local and national tradition re-asserted itself, especially in Scotland during and after the time of David I, and prompted new dedications to ancient saints; but such dedications are recorded only in regions where the old saint was already widely honoured, and are confined to a few major national saints, Ninian and Kentigern, Patrick and Brigit, David, Samson and Arthmael. No instance has yet been observed of the importation of a local saint in Norman or later times into a region where he was not previously honoured. The study of the names of churches, wells and other holy places is therefore a useful guide to the expansion of the monastic movement in 6th century Ireland, as in Britain.

Most of the main sources are to some extent affected by the art of the story-teller. In any land and in any age, the story-teller is not supposed to submit to historical accuracy. The early Irish scholars strove to keep history and story-telling apart; they could not wholly succeed, especially in their account of pagan Ireland, when other record was weak. The Annalists transcribe the substance of some ancient stories, often with expressed distaste and apology, and the genealogists traced their patrons to a few of the shadowy heroes of early story. But because the effort was made, the influence of romance is easily discerned, and often acknowledged. These main sources are supplemented by others, notably King Lists, that give the length of each reign; in the Irish, though not in the Pictish lists, the figures are usually wildly corrupt, contradicting each other and other evidence.

The evidence clings together. Annals and Genealogies, Lives and Lists name the same people over and over again, nearly always in the same regions at the same times, without serious disagreement; and from the middle of the sixth century, their story receives increasing confirmation from the history of Bede and from continental authors. Inferences are seldom wisely drawn from a single statement in a single source; they are founded upon a combination of scattered notices from different sources. The records of each people commonly note their own nationals; but the church linked them. Sixth-century Irishmen are prominent in Welsh accounts, Welshmen in Irish tradition; in the seventh century, Englishmen are frequently remembered by the Irish, Irishmen by the English, and both begin to attract the notice of Europeans. The collapse of Roman Britain and the expansion of monastic Christianity brought barbarian Ireland fully into the company of the peoples of the British Isles, and the Irish contributed as freely as the Welsh and English to the moulding of their new society. The history of the British and the Welsh is therefore lamed if Irish experience is ignored; for, in a trite truism, the Irish Sea became a bridge, not a barrier, and a bridge that was much in use, by traffic in both directions.

Prehistory

The story of Ireland's impact upon Britain and Europe cannot begin with Christian Ireland; for the monks who made that impact were soaked in the learning, the customs, the social outlook of their own historical tradition. It extended back to the Creation, to the Flood, and to the first arrival of mankind in Ireland. It began with the legends classified among the Mythological and Heroic Cycles by the story-tellers, which the Annalists tried to link with Roman dates for Hebrew, Greek and Roman history. The legends are woven around the names of imaginary kings and wondrous battles, that the early Irish historians thoroughly distrusted. One ancient Irish verse protests

> Though antiquaries record it
> The Just Canon does not;

and subsequent writers plead

> I like not to have the labour of writing this section imposed upon me; wherefore I beseech you . . . not to reproach me for it,

warning that what they record is not 'genuine history' but what they 'found written in old books'.

Nevertheless the nonsense conceals an underlay of 'genuine' tradition, whose reality could not be discerned until modern archaeology established something of the main outlines of Irish pre-history. The legends preserved by the early Christian Irish writers discuss and reject the notion that men lived in Ireland before the Flood; and there is as yet no proven palaeolithic, or Old Stone Age habitation in Ireland. The artefacts of mesolithic food gatherers have been observed, and tradition remembers the first inhabitants as men who 'lived on fishing and fowling till the coming of Partholon'. Partholon's people were the first agriculturalists; at about the time of Abraham, reckoned at 2016 BC in the chronology of Jerome, they came to Ireland from Sicily and southern Italy, bringing with them the first ploughs and oxen, dairy farming, husbandry and houses, and they buried their dead in 'long graves' in 'stone heaps'. The first farmers in Ireland arrived in the neolithic, or New Stone Age, in the third millennium BC, or some centuries before; they buried their dead in long stone chambered graves in long barrows, ultimately derived from the rock-cut tombs of Sicily and southern Italy. The legends recall later colonists of the same economy, who included Nemed, 'the holy man', whose children also peopled Britain, and others whose names are paralleled in Gaul, who also established themselves on the coasts and islands of western Scotland and in the Hebrides.

Several centuries later came quite different peoples, who used metal, including the bronze cauldron, the sword and the spear, and brought with them the smith and the wright, the carpenter and the doctor, and also druidry, learning and the gods, including Nuada Silverhand, or Nodens, Lug, Ogma and Dagda, the Good God. They buried their dead 'not in stone heaps' but 'in the *sid* mounds', round barrows; some of them are called a 'people of ships' who 'drank from beakers'. These particulars closely correspond to the excavated remains of middle Bronze Age peoples in Ireland, in the second millennium BC; even the improbable route assigned to them, from Greece to Ireland by way of Scandinavia, is matched by the distribution of some types of Bronze Age cauldrons.

Some 200 years later a more important metal-using people followed. The sons of Mil, ancestors of the later Gael, migrated up the Danube and down the Rhine, sailing thence to Spain through the Channel, plundering the coasts of Britain on their way. From Spain their descendants came to Ireland, adding riding horses, royal forts and tombs to the arts and crafts of their predecessors. Their fourth king first smelted gold in Ireland, and introduced brooches of precious metals. A century or so later king Muinmon, the 'Neck-decorated', caused kings and chiefs to wear collars or chains of gold about their necks, and his successor added rings and bracelet arm bands of gold. The gold *lunulae* of Ireland, crescent shaped collars of gold, sometimes solid, sometimes composed of separate chains, were not clearly recognised until modern times, more than a thousand years after this tradition was first committed to writing.

The next decisive immigration is dated to the 'time of Darius', around 600 BC, or later, early in the Atlantic Iron Age. Labraid the Exile regained Leinster with the aid of the 'Black Gauls', armed with the terrible new broad green spear. The adventures of Labraid anticipated the fatal opportunism of another Leinster king who reigned 2000 years later, the exiled Diarmait mac Murchada, who recovered his throne with the aid of Strongbow's Normans and the terrible new weapon of heavy Flemish horses, and thereby opened Ireland to lasting foreign rule.

Labraid's allies help to explain a linguistic puzzle posed by the earliest Roman accounts of Ireland. Irish is distinguished from other known Celtic languages by a number of peculiarities, of which the most striking is the general use of a K sound, designated in the vocabulary of modern philologists by the letter Q, where British, Pictish, Gallic and related speech used a P sound; so that the word for children, *plant* in Welsh, is *clanna* in Irish, and the name of Patrick was heard by 5th-century Irish ears as *Cotriche*. Throughout Ireland, and wherever the Irish settled in northern Britain, Irish place names are almost without exception preserved in a Q Celtic form; and there is virtually no trace of any P Celtic names. But when the Roman geographer Ptolemy listed the names of Irish peoples and of their principal forts in the 2nd century AD, most of the names are in P Celtic, the language of Britain and Gaul. Ptolemy's source probably dates to the beginning of the 1st century AD. But its informants were not academic philologists who troubled to transliterate Irish names into their appropriate British forms; they gave the names as they were then pronounced.

At that date, a number of the ruling peoples of Ireland were known by British or Gallic names. The background of some of them is precisely indicated; the Cauci and the Manapii, whose name the modern Irish transliterate in Fermanagh and Monaghan, were offshoots of peoples who dwelt upon the coasts of Flanders, while the portions of the Brigantes, the Gangani and others also lived in Britain. Irish tradition remembered something of these British and Gallic peoples, who were in later times treated as subject aliens. They include the *Galioin* or *Gailenga*, originally settled in Leinster, and the numerous peoples known as *Cruithne*, whose name is a simple transliteration into Irish Q Celtic of *Pritani*, the oldest P Celtic spelling of the *Britanni*, the British. The Irish used the word to describe the Picts, the northern British who had never been conquered by Rome; in north-eastern Ireland one large and important group of Cruithne retained their name and identity, though not perhaps their language, into the 7th or 8th century AD, and several other groups elsewhere, who were earlier absorbed, have left ample traces of their existence. Irish tradition was acquainted with a legend of conquering foreigners, armed with powerful weapons previously unknown, who were introduced by an exiled prince some centuries before the Romans conquered Britain; and also of peoples who lived on in Ireland, and were still known as British, throughout the Roman period and for some centuries thereafter. The Roman record confirms that peoples with British or Gallic names were dominant in parts of Ireland at about the time of the Roman conquest.

From the remotest prehistoric times to the threshold of the historical period, Irish tradition records a number of basic details that coincide with the discoveries of modern archaeology, and with contemporary Roman observation. These coincidences are too many and too marked to be the result of chance. They are real details remembered. Story-tellers richly clothed them with legends of insubstantial people and dramatic events, as the story-tellers of later Britain clothed the meagre memories of Arthur in imaginary glories; but a solid tradition remains when the gaudy clothing is removed. Its substance has the same significance that Kenneth Jackson detected beneath the stories of the Heroic Cycle:

> The characters . . . and the events . . . are . . . unhistorical. But this does *not* mean that the traditional background, the setting . . . is bogus. . . . In the same way, Agamemnon and Helen are doubtless not historical, . . . but the Mycenean world dimly depicted in Homer was a real one.

Modern prejudice tends to impose an arbitrary limit of three or four centuries upon folk memory, without argument or evidence; for the narrow experience of literate Europe is unacquainted with the long memory of illiterate societies, and easily condemns uncritically what it does not understand. But the few faint details of their past that the Irish remembered through several thousand years are neither unusual nor remarkable. The oral Homeric tradition itself preserved accurate background detail for the best part of a thousand years; and Tacitus reports that the Silures of Roman Britain still remembered that their remote ancestors had come from Spain, though four centuries of literate Roman civilisation soon obliterated their oral recollections. Similar traditions have lasted far longer in Asian countries where widespread literacy developed later. The precise syllables of Vedic verse accurately report that the worship of the phallus and the humped bull belonged to the indigenous religion of pre-Aryan India in the second millennium BC; and despite centuries of Brahminical insistence on Hindu teetotal and vegetarian observance, tradition remembers that the early Hindu gods drank deep and feasted on roast beef. There the background setting has persisted in oral tradition for something over 3,000 years; the furthest recollections of Irish legend claim no greater antiquity. They are remarkable only because they were written down before they were forgotten.

The tales told in the Mythological Cycle help to show what is real and what is unreal in the legendary history of pagan Ireland; modern excavation and a Roman description demonstrate that the background setting, the main stages in the evolution of Irish society, were accurately remembered in broad and general outline; they do not confirm the reality of the people and events. The stories that concern the Roman centuries must be assessed upon the principles revealed by the earlier tales, for no later Roman descriptions survive, and the archaeological evidence is not closely enough dated to offer useful comment, except in rare individual particulars. These later tales depict an Iron Age society that had inherited powerful living influences from the Bronze Age past, and say something of its relations with the Roman power established across the Irish Sea in Britain. As the narrative draws nearer to the time when it was committed to writing, the possibility that some of the events were accurately remembered grows stronger. Many cannot sensibly be confirmed or denied; but the reality or falsity of the events and names is not important. What matters is the evolution of Irish society, and the impact upon it of the Roman government in Britain in successive generations.

The stories of the Heroic Cycle are set shortly before the coming of the Romans to Britain. Thereafter the Annalists and Genealogists are increasingly emancipated from the influence of the story-tellers, and concentrate upon attempts to relate Irish people and events to the history of Rome. The principal warriors of the Heroic Tales were the Ulaid of the north, who name modern Ulster. They were aristocrats, akin to Homer's heroes, with their chief centre at Emain, Navan, near Armagh. Their enemies were the northern *Cruithne*, and also the southern *Erainn*, the 'men of Erin', from whose name the Greeks and Romans called the island 'Ierne'. Tradition does not allot to the southerners chieftains comparable with the northern heroes. It celebrates the triumph of the northern heroes, who reduced their enemies to subjection.

Tuathal

Legend ends the old order with a successful rising of the *Aitheach Tuatha*, the subject peoples, dated to the reign of Domitian (81–96). Exiles found refuge in Britain, and early in the reign of Hadrian (122–138), one of them, Tuathal, returned from Britain 'with a great army'. He destroyed the Dumnonii of Ireland, the *Fir Domnann*, mastered the Ulaid and then the rest of Ireland. The nobility of all Ireland agreed to 'accept him as their king, since he delivered them from slavery to the serfs and subject people'. He created the central province of Meath out of pieces detached from Ulster, Connacht, Leinster and Munster, and established a fortress in each part of Meath; and he imposed upon Leinster the *Boruma*, the cattle tribute.

Tuathal is treated as the restorer of a monarchy immemorially old. But its earlier traditions are nominal and sketchy. In relating full and precise detail of Tuathal, the story makes him the effective founder of the central monarchy of Ireland, the ancestor of the future dynasty of High Kings. The initial basis of its power is said to have been a military force raised by an exile in Britain and employed to destroy the political structure of an older Ireland, that had been divided between numerous independent peoples, in the manner of Britain before the Romans. Tradition thenceforth regarded these older peoples as subjects; in treating their former independence as the short-lived result of a recent rebellion, it asserted an immense and misty antiquity for the institutions of its own day, and reduced the significance of the intervention of the army from Britain to a casual detail.

The colourful native legend must always be compared with the scanty prosaic notices that Roman writers give of Ireland. In 81 AD Domitian's legate Agricola entertained an Irish prince, exiled *seditione domestica*, by internal conflict, and thought of sending a Roman army to restore him. The Roman date coincides with the date Irish legend gives for the exile of Tuathal's family. It does not confirm the detail of the legend, for there were doubtless numerous other exiles then and later who found shelter with the Romans in Britain; and successive Roman legates must, like Agricola, have considered whether Roman interests were served by helping them. When Hadrian built the Wall from Tyne to Solway in the 120s he continued the fortified line down the Cumberland coast. He feared attack by seaborne enemies, and those enemies clearly included the men of north-eastern Ireland. The record of his reign is not full enough to say whether or not his legates adopted the proposal that Agricola rejected, and used their armies to install in Ireland a native ruler, bound to Rome by treaty, charged to restrain his subjects from raids on Roman territory. He might have done so, for the early empire frequently imposed such kings, and tried to keep them strong enough to control their subjects, yet not so strong that they could threaten Rome. The evidence of Roman fortifications shows that it would have suited Hadrian to intervene if opportunity arose; but it does not show whether he did so. Irish tradition believed that he did. The legend is not confirmed, but the story it tells is far from improbable.

The story precisely formulates the social basis of Tuathal's rule. He was the ally of a warrior nobility, whose main strength lay in the north, against their social inferiors, and also against the older peoples of Ireland, some of whom were held to be of British origin. The gist of the story is that Tuathal imposed a

---

Map 9

-·-·- Approximate boundaries of the main kingdoms
..... of internal divisions

≡ Northern Ui Neill territories

|||| Southern Ui Neill territories

Districts contested by the Ui Neill are shown by broken lines

■ Royal centres

+ Episcopal centres

• Monasteries

Inset and border
the Irish National Grid

The royal centres shown were not all inhabited in the 5th century

MAP 9 5th CENTURY IRELAND

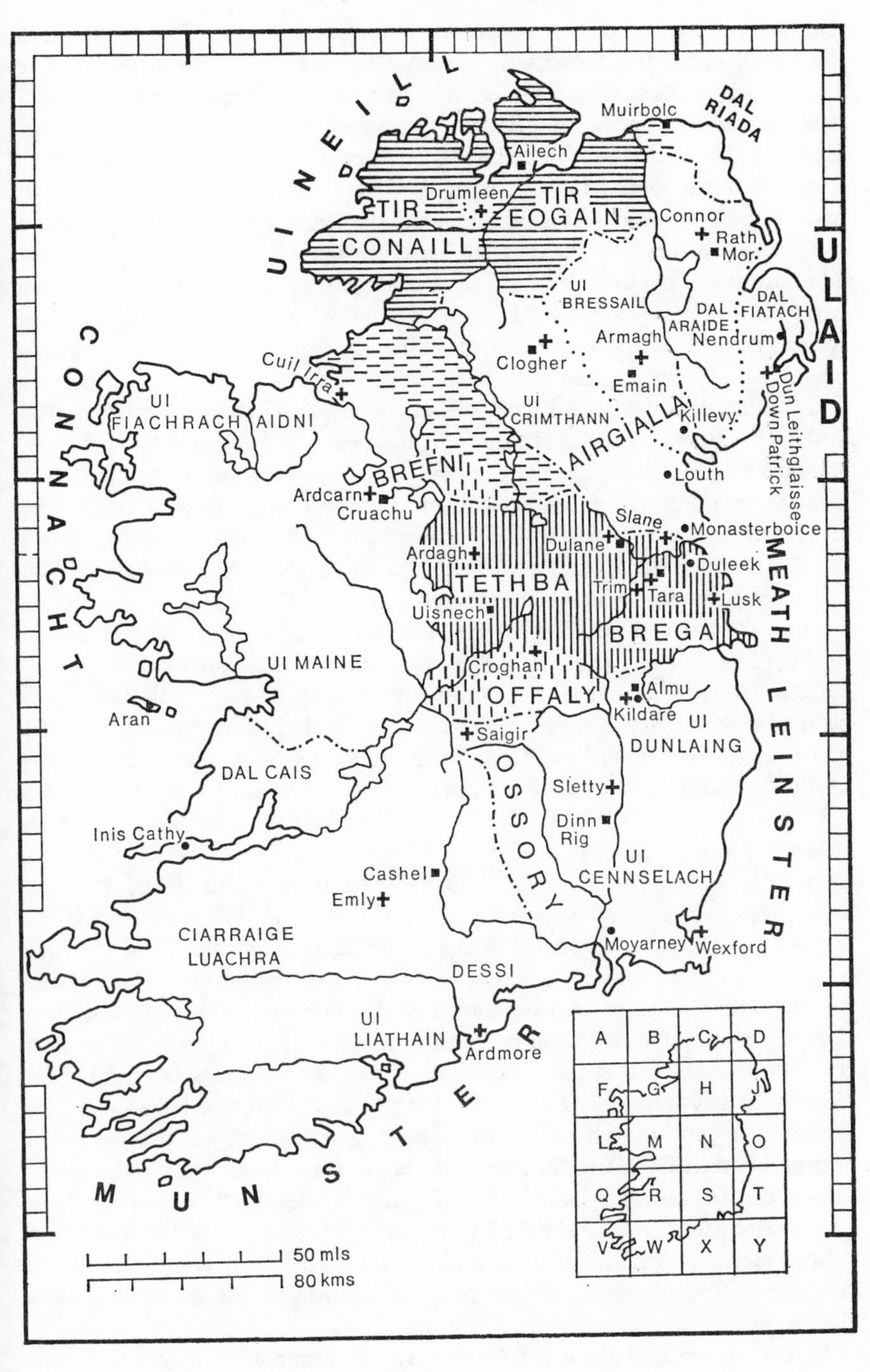

temporary unity, and tradition is precise about how he did it. He is described as the author of the five 'provinces' of early Christian and modern Ireland. The Irish word for these provinces, *coiced*, 'a fifth', itself implies that they are a deliberate administrative sub-division. The names of three of them, the Ulaid of Ulster in the north-east, the Laigin of Leinster in the south-east, and Mumu, Munster, in the south and west, argue that these regions had an older identity, and so do the traditions of Connacht, in the north and west, though the name itself is said to have originated after Tuathal's time. But regional identity and administrative definition are different things. All Gaul was divided into three parts before Caesar campaigned; but it was the Roman conquest that gave the regions defined and lasting frontiers. Irish tradition asserts that it was Tuathal who gave a similar permanence to the regions of Ireland.

Tradition does not regard Tuathal's monarchy as a lasting sovereign central authority. His successors are made to fight repeated wars against the unbroken strength of the Ulaid for two centuries, until decisive defeat reduced their territory to the modern counties of Antrim and Down; and wars against the Leinstermen lasted longer, without comparable success, while fighting against the Munstermen was sporadic and even less decisive. The story-tellers knew many tales of mighty kings who ruled these regions from the first century AD to the fifth; but the Annalists and Genealogists were unable to relate them in time to the story of Tuathal's dynasty, and different versions make discordant connections.

Connacht was treated as the peculiar patrimony of the High Kings who claimed descent from Tuathal, and there they rarely had to fight. It bears the name of Tuathal's grandson, 'Conn of the Hundred Battles', sovereign of the north. One early tradition divides Ireland into two. The north is termed 'Conn's half', but the south is the half of Mog Nuadat, the 'servant of Nodens', a god who is also honoured in Britain. The heirs of Mog, whom the genealogists treat as his grandsons, were called Eogan and Cian. Their names were assumed by the *Eoganachta*, who ultimately made themselves rulers of all Munster, and the less successful *Cianachta*, originally of central Ireland. These three are the only names that end in *-achta*; they describe not peoples or territories, but ruling families who claimed descent from a common ancestor. They are the first Irish dynastic names. This tradition portrays a significant political change, which it dates towards the end of the second century; and in restricting the territory of Conn's dynasty to Connaught, the land of the *Connachta*, it acknowledged the factual independence of the Ulaid in the north-east. The story of the division of Ireland between Conn and Mog asserted the formal independence of the south. It also proclaimed the establishment of dynastic rule over the older southern peoples, for Mog 'expelled the *Earna* (Erainn) from Munster, such as would not submit to him'. Their social order differed, for their leader was no dynast; he was named Nemidh, 'holy', and his principal companion was known as Dadera the Druid.

Irish tradition outlines a pattern of struggle common to numerous Indo-

European and other peoples. The society of Gaul before the Romans, as of early Aryan India, also recognised distinct classes of priests, warrior nobles, simple cultivators, and craftsmen and traders. Centralised monarchy grew strong when the interest of one class, or allied classes, demanded united leadership against the rest of society, or against a foreign enemy; monarchy weakened when priests or nobles ruled without threat of challenge, separately or in combination.

In Ireland the stature of the monarchy grew when the Irish began to attack Britain. Roman evidence clearly indicates the date. In the first years of the third century the emperor Severus found it necessary to rebuild the fort of Caernarvon on the Irish sea. Irish tradition held that about 200 AD Art the son of Conn, and Eogan the grandson of Mog, were driven into an alliance of north and south in the time of Severus' son, and were destroyed by 'Benne Brit, king of Britain', who was supported by the Erainn, and installed one of their leaders as king of Ireland. The name Benne is not British or Irish, but Roman, Bennius, or perhaps Benignus. As under Hadrian, the Roman record is too thin to indicate whether or not there was such an expedition, or whether a legionary legate was so named.

Cormac

Thereafter Irish tradition fastens upon the splendid portrait of Art's son Cormac, dated from 218 to 256, who expelled the intruder. The Annals give him far more space than any other king. Though he is the hero of many romances, his portrait in the Annals and the Genealogies is clear and consistent, unembarrassed by the conflicts of time and place that surround his predecessors. In the pleasant idiom of the Clonmacnoise Annalist, he was

> obsolutely the best king that ever Raigned in Ireland before himselfe.

His first dozen years were spent in subduing the north, and, unlike his predecessors, he is made to conquer Connacht as well as the Ulaid. Then, in the 230s, his 'great fleet was overseas for three years', and he became 'sovereign in Alba', Britain. In entries dated before the middle of the sixth century, the Annalists and Genealogists normally apply the word 'Alba' to the whole of Britain, 'as far as the Muir nIcht', the 'sea of Wight', the English Channel, but thereafter Alba is restricted to Pictland, beyond Edinburgh and Glasgow. The monarchy of Cormac is represented as insecure; while the fleet was away, the men of Leinster seized Tara; Cormac was 'dethroned by the Ulaid', and enlisted the aid of the Eoganachta and the Cianachta to subdue them. In his last years he faced a revolt of the Dessi, the subject peoples of Meath; when he reduced them, the greater part migrated to their permanent home in Eoganacht territory, in Waterford of Munster.

Thus far the dry notices of the Annalists. Their Cormac was a king of Meath who mastered the north, made Leinster tributary and Munster an ally, and led the first recorded Irish attacks on Roman Britain. The tradition reported by the

Clonmacnoise Annals and by the seventeenth-century Keating gives an enthusiastic rationalised account of his civil administration; and the story-tellers built a cycle of romances thereon. He was the first lawgiver, the inventor of written record. From his great new rath, or fortress, at Tara he maintained a central administration with a hundred and fifty governors, *rectores* or *reachtaire*, and a standing army, the *Fiana*, commanded by Finn Mac Cumail, the 'slave girl's son'. Recruits, 'of very huge and tall bigness', were required to graduate in the learning of the *filid*, the professional scholars, and also to undergo a strenuous commando training and to accept a quite un-Irish discipline. They were organised in sections of nine men, brigaded by fives and tens into divisions, termed *tricha cet*, or thirty hundred, three of them in peacetime, seven in time of foreign war. The Fiana took a personal oath to their supreme commander, *Ri Feinnidh*, equivalent to the Roman *sacramentum*, and their kin were obliged to forswear claims for compensation on their death. They were paid, and were forbidden to plunder civilians; they were the 'hired warriors of the king of Ireland', their business to 'uphold justice and prevent injustice', to guard the country from foreigners, their ordinary task 'putting a stop to robbery, exacting the payment of tribute, putting down malefactors'. Abroad, Cormac was a greater conqueror; at home he was

> wise, Learned, valiant and mild, not Given causelesly to be bloody as many of his auncestors were; hee Raigned magestically and magnifitiently.

The legends of Cormac and Finn are told more amply than any other tales of Ireland in the Roman centuries. The essence of the story is familiar enough in Roman experience; the might of the imperial army impelled border barbarians to try to unite under a single centralised state, able to organise a large disciplined army under a single commander, strong enough to meet the Romans in the field. The aim and achievement that legend ascribes to Cormac is the same that Roman writers describe in the persons of the historical Maroboduus in Bohemia and of the Dacian Decebalus. Its claim, that the united Irish became strong enough to assault Roman Britain in force, is well proven; inscriptions and coin hoards show when and where the attacks fell.

Before the accession of Severus in 193, not more than 3 or 4 in a hundred of the military inscriptions of Britain were set up in the west coast forts; over the fifty years thereafter, the proportion rises sharply to one quarter; and in the next twenty years, from 244 to 264, all datable military inscriptions in Britain come from the forts of Lancashire and western Cumberland, or from Caerleon, all but one of them within the years that the Annalists assign to the reign of Cormac. The stones do not record the reasons why they were set up, but in these years it is only on the west coast that military units are known to have had reason to undertake reconstruction or to inscribe dedications.

The known west-coast coin hoards increase as rapidly as the inscriptions, but somewhat later. Those buried in the years between 222 and 260 are twice as many as in the previous forty years, but those buried between 260 and 300 are seven times as many. In Cormac's time, none are known from the rich villa lands of the Severn estuary, but nearly 50 are recorded from these lands in the next forty years. The implication of the Roman evidence is that in the years before 260 the Irish were engaged in breaking down the Roman defences of western Britain; and that in the years thereafter, assigned in Irish tradition to Cormac's successors, they were able to plunder the rich estates by the Severn Sea.

The Roman evidence does not prove that Cormac and Finn existed. It does imply that in the middle decades of the third century some power in Ireland achieved the successes that Irish tradition credits to them; the Irish were able to concentrate an effective military force against Britain on an unprecedented scale. The importance of the story in Ireland was that it was believed, and influenced the thinking of the early Christian centuries. One of the main sources that later writers cite for their account of Cormac is Amargein, who is said to have been the principal *file*, historian and adviser, to king Diarmait mac Cerbaill. Diarmait was the most powerful of the sixth-century kings of Ireland, and came nearest to realising in historical times the strong monarchy that legend ascribed to Cormac. Diarmait's adherents may have coloured the story of Cormac, but tales of Cormac are also likely to have strengthened Diarmait.

No tradition claims that Cormac's stable central government endured. His grandsons disputed the succession. Muiredach dispossessed his three cousins, named Colla, who compensated themselves by the final destruction of the ancient Ulaid power and annexed its western territories, including the old royal centre of Emain. The Annalists' date is 330, and the evidence of recent excavation tends to agree. The conquered territory was henceforth known as *Airgialla*, 'Oriel', and thence descendants of the Collas are said to have sailed overseas, to become Lords of the Isles, and of medieval Argyle.

Muiredach's son Eochaid, dated 358–365, is accorded the rare distinction of a peaceful death at Tara, and is chiefly celebrated for his wives and children; from his first wife, Mongfind of Munster, descended the future kings of Connacht, and his second wife, Cairenn, 'daughter of the king of the Saxon foreigners', was mother of Niall of the Nine Hostages, who was an infant when his father died. The second marriage rubs shoulders with reality. The contemporary Roman historian Ammian stressed that the invasion of Britain by Picts, Scots and Saxons in 367 was a *conspiratio barbarorum*, a barbarian alliance; in the late fourth century, dynastic marriage commonly sealed alliance.

Crimthann and Niall

Eochaid's adult son succeeded him as king of Connacht, but not of Ireland. Crimthann of Munster is the only southerner whom all traditions accept as king of Ireland before the 11th century. He is represented as ruler of the Cruithne of the coastlands, as the brother-in-law and ally of Eochaid against the growing power of the Eoganacht. Victory abroad secured his power at home. He was remembered as the first of the conquering kings who subdued and colonised western Britain. The Annals, austerely uninterested in Irishmen abroad, knew nothing of his wars in Britain, but other sources make much of them. He, and Niall after him, is styled king of Ireland and of Britain in the genealogies. He visited Britain and built there the royal fort of Din Tradui. Several other notices assert migration from Munster to Britain in the late fourth and early fifth centuries. Cairpre of Kerry is named as founder of the 'Eoganacht Maigi Dergind i nAlbae', the 'Eoganacht of the Plain of Derwent in Britain'; and as father of Aengus, 'ri Alban', king in Britain. Dergind is a place name wholly alien to Ireland, but Derguind or Derguenid may denote any river or place that the Roman British called Derventio, any now named Derwent, Darenth, Dart or the like. Most such places lie in hill country. But the plain of the Devonshire Dart is the likely location of a Roman *Statio Derventio*, and all its 5th and 6th century inscriptions are Irish. It may have been a short-lived Irish kingdom until the Cornovii reduced the Irish of Dumnonia in Vortigern's time.

Several sources record settlements in Britain of the *Ui Liathain*, from southern Munster. A British document preserved by Nennius reports their conquest of Demetia; they were driven out of its eastern borders, about Kidwelly, by Cunedda, in the middle of the fifth century, but both British and Irish texts prolong their rule in the rest of Demetia for another two generations, until Agricola's campaign ended their independence and their dynasty, in Arthur's time. Theirs was the longest-lived and most stable of the Irish kingdoms in southern Britain, notable enough for a late Irish tale to pirate their tradition and annex it to their neighbours, the Dessi. Nor was Demetia their only settlement, for the ninth-century Irish scholar Cormac, king and bishop of Munster, located a principal fort of theirs 'in the land of the Cornish Britons', in the same part of the country as Glastonbury. They were the best-remembered colonists, but even in Demetia they were not the only immigrants. A relative of Crimthann is said to have founded there 'the Cenel Crimthann in Britain'; and his mid fifth century grandson bore the name Eogan Albanach, Eogan of Britain. In north Wales also there are hints of settlement from Munster and from Leinster.

The armies of Cormac are portrayed as raiders, who took their booty home, but the subjects of Crimthann are described as settlers. No Irish tradition states the contrast, or even observes it. It reports settlement without comment, for the notices of the overseas exploits of both kings are few and casual. The Irish record is insular throughout, without interest in Britain. The several notices that survive are not stressed, but are minimised; what is noted is a few comments from much older records, that had ceased to be interesting long before they were copied into the manuscripts that survive. Yet these chance reports trace among the Irish the same evolution that Romans observed among other continental barbarians. All along the frontiers, the third-century enemies of Rome were raiders who went home again, however deeply their raids penetrated; but in the later fourth century and the fifth Rome everywhere faced bolder enemies, migrating peoples on the move, eager to settle within Roman territory.

Stories of Irish settlement in Britain begin with the reign of Crimthann; they extend into the time of his successor Niall, the late born son of Eochaid, whose reign is dated from 379 to 405. He was the best known of the fighting kings of Ireland, and is said to have invaded Gaul and to have been killed in the English Channel. His successor, Nath-I of Connacht, was the last of the raiding kings, and is said to have been killed in the Alps in 428. But the stories of raiders and settlers end with Nath-I. The next king was Loegaire, son of Niall, and Saint Patrick's arrival is placed in his fourth year. The coming of Patrick makes a sharp break in the historical tradition, separating Christian from pagan Ireland.

Irish Monarchy

The emphasis on religion masks profound changes in Irish secular society. From the beginning of the fifth century, the ancient peoples of Ireland submitted to the authority of an immense number of petty local princes, whose trivial and bloody feuds were to impoverish their subjects for centuries to come, and to dispose them to welcome the security of Christian monastic life.

The speed and the nature of the change are obscured because the writers of early Christian Ireland were unaware of it. They took it for granted that the institutions of their own day had existed from the remote past. The evidence lies in the detail they report, not in the interpretation that they placed upon it. Yet it was in the turmoil of a rapidly changing society that Irish Christianity was moulded; its assumptions and practices were already hardened before the Irish monks journeyed to Britain and Europe; so that the conflicts within Irish society became an important influence on the peoples who responded to the preaching of the Irish, and underlay much that they found startling in the Irish outlook.

The changes that matured in the fifth century were the climax of processes that had been at work since Rome conquered Britain. The earliest account of the political geography of Ireland is the work of the Roman Ptolemy, whose sources probably date from the early first century AD. His description of Ireland differs only in detail from his account of Britain. But thereafter the histories of Ireland and Britain diverged, for Rome conquered Britain, but not Ireland. In Britain, Roman conquest froze the political boundaries of the first century by fixing the frontiers of permanent states. But in Ireland, the struggles that caused one people to wax great and another to decline went on unchecked, so that the political geography had changed out of recognition by the fifth century. In addition, the impact of the Roman power across the sea had modified the internal structure of Irish political society, and altered the relations between her several peoples.

The Rise of the Dynasties

The traditions of Ireland during the centuries of Roman Britain stress still greater differences. They mainly concern attempts to establish large centralised monarchies. One single tradition, agreed by all sources, traces the history of the ancestors of Niall. He was heir to the dynasty that Tuathal had established with the aid of armies from Britain, later consolidated in Connacht. But the traditions of other regions are not agreed. A few great names are reported from the rest of Ireland, but different Annalists and different Genealogists relate them differently in time to one another and to the Connacht dynasty. They agree that the Eoganachta and Cianachta tried without success to establish similar large kingdoms in the west and south towards the end of the second century, and were thwarted by intervention from Britain. The Cianachta never succeeded, and the Eoganacht mastery of Munster, ruled from Cashel, was not consolidated until the beginning of the fifth century, when Corcc 'discovered' Cashel, hitherto a previously uninhabited hill, situated on the borders of two ancient peoples; for the shadowy notices of Corcc's predecessors chiefly concern indecisive efforts to subdue the older populations of Munster. The traditions of other regions are even more uncertain. The several sources agree upon the succession of early Ulaid kings, but disagree chaotically about the relationship in time between these kings and later Ulaid rulers, and about their connections with the Connacht dynasty, and the traditions of the few great rulers placed in early Leinster are as confused, until the establishment of its future dynasties during the fifth century.

These are stories about attempts to establish the direct rule of regional monarchs over large numbers of separate nations, with little sign of intermediate lordships. They are matched by the parallel account of the rise of the monarchy of all Ireland, under Cormac, Crimthann and Niall, equally pictured as supreme sovereigns. These stories resemble Roman accounts of other western barbarians, who united behind military kings when they fought Rome, but rarely obeyed stable dynasties in time of peace. But the tenor of the narrative changes in the fifth century. When Niall died, Connacht and the kingship of Ireland passed to his nephew; but his sons carved out for themselves lasting small kingdoms in northern and central Ireland, and their initiative was soon followed by men great and small throughout Ireland. The mightier kings mastered the lesser, and graded them into a hierarchy of rulers.

The new departure brought with it a new system of names, of persons and of territories, that survives to the present. Tyrone and Tirconnel mean 'the land, *tir*, of Eogan' and the 'land of Conall', who were sons of Niall's sons. Collectively his descendants were known as the *avi* or *Ui* Neill, in modern spelling O'Neill. Their separate branches were styled *Cenel Eogain, Cenel Conaill*, and other dynastic families used indifferently 'Ui', 'Cenel', 'Sil', 'Clanna' (children of) and other terms to denote their members. By the middle of the fifth century, the dynasts were already numerous, for Patrick's converts included several 'sons and daughters of *reguli*, under-kings'; and by the middle of the sixth century the greater part of the Irish were ruled by such kinglets. Most of them began as lords of a particular territory, and mobilised its strength to subdue their neighbours.

Their immediate territories were treated and taxed as 'free', those they subdued as 'subject', and the favoured status of the 'free' helped to hinder their subjects from concerted resistance.

Some dynasts grew greater and mastered many lesser lords and peoples; but they were content with a tributary supremacy, and did not normally annex conquered lands into large consolidated kingdoms ruled directly, in the manner of the earlier dynasties. By the end of the fifth century, the hierarchy of kings was adapted to the older structure of the Irish regions or 'provinces', so that in Ulster, Connacht, Munster and Leinster at least two major dynasties competed and alternated in the use of the title and the revenues of the provincial king. They claimed supremacy and tribute from lesser kings within their territory, but often had to fight to enforce their claim; though they admitted the formal supremacy of the High King of Ireland, their armies commonly resisted his authority. None the less, seventh-century Ireland accorded to the High King a sovereignty to which they gave a title that they had learnt from the Roman government of Britain. Muirchu, the biographer of Patrick, writing soon after 650, described one High King as *Imperator*, and a generation later Adomnan used for another the almost equally sonorous title of *totius Scotiae regnator*, sovereign of all Ireland. These high concepts of the kingship long outlived its practical authority, so that in the 11th century the last of the great High Kings, Brian Boru, himself used the title *Imperator Scottorum*, emperor of the Irish.

The dynasties jealously guarded and limited their identity. The dynastic name was strictly confined to those who were accepted as actual descendants of the founder, while the mass of the subject population were described by their national origin. Writers of the seventh and eighth centuries self-consciously set down the social origin of nearly everyone they name, translating *Ui* by the Latin *nepotes*, grandchildren, descendants, and using *gens*, nation, for the Irish *moccu*, or giving the Irish word untranslated. Adomnan, writing about 690, himself a member of the Ui Neill, meticulously distinguishes noblemen born, like Columba 'e nepotibus Neill' or 'Cormac nepos Leathain', of the Ui Liathain, from plebeians like 'Comgellus mocu Aridi' or 'Columbanus episcopus mocu Loigse'. The main monastic tradition, principally preserved in later texts, preferred to ignore social origins and distinguish individuals by giving their fathers' names, in place of their dynasty or nation; but among laymen the use of a *Ui* name became a badge of gentility, as highly prized as a *de* or a *von* among later Frenchmen and Germans, and was one of the main reasons for the preservation of the immense body of Irish genealogy. It is not surprising that one conscientious twelfth-century genealogist complained that his documentation was corrupted by the massive intrusion of plebeian families who falsely claimed dynastic descent.

The usage of the genealogists dates the rise of the dynasties to the beginning of the fifth century; for in the main genealogical tradition no dynasties are named from persons held to have lived earlier than the time of Niall or Crimthann, and only a very few late glosses loosely apply dynastic terms to the supposed ancestors of older peoples. The date suggests why and how the dynasties arose, during and after the wars against Britain. After each expedition, some Irish captains settled in Britain, but many more came home, accompanied by young warriors enriched by slaves and other booty. The Irish word for slave-girl, *cumal*, became the normal standard of value, equivalent to three cows. War brought social difference. Men who were rich in slaves and strong in armed retainers made themselves lords; and when the overseas expeditions ended, early in the 5th century, the energy that had been directed against Britain was for the future absorbed by domestic warfare, as the dynasts fought against each other and against rebellious subjects. Though Irish writers assumed that lordship had always existed, they preserve a few stories of prolonged resistance to dynastic rule. Conall of Tirconnel was killed by 'the old peoples' in 469; in the sixth century

> the prophet Bec me De . . . prophisied that lords would loose their Chiefries and seignories,

but his radical prophecy echoed a wish that was not fulfilled. Similar sentiments were attributed to Brigit in the late 5th century, who is said to have proclaimed that

> all subjects (*plebei*) serve the Lord . . . but the children of kings are serpents, children of blood and death, save for a few of whom God hath chosen.

Christian protest did not prevent the increase of dynastic power. Though some of the older peoples, notably the Luigne, long fought to rid themselves of their sovereigns, most submitted; and many discovered that the best way to withstand the assault of neighbouring kings was to establish their own dynasties. By the middle of the seventh century, when a changing economy brought famine and crisis, Ireland was sharply divided between nobles and plebeians; the struggles of 'old peoples' against the institutions of 'chiefries and seignories' fade from record.

Dislike of dynastic violence was a principal incentive to the sixth-century Irish. It disposed them to welcome the Christian religion of Britain and Rome, and to find in the monasteries a refuge from a disordered world. The acceptance of the new religion also joined Ireland to Britain. From the beginning of the sixth century, the history and the historical record of the peoples of the British Isles are inseparable. They hang closely together, because they were jointly exploring a new dimension in European civilisation. The Irish, the Welsh and the English were the first European peoples, since the mediterranean authors of Greek and Roman antiquity, to write in the vernacular spoken language of the people; for centuries to come, European literature used only Latin, alien to German-speakers and far removed from the spoken Romance languages. Within this common enterprise, Irish initiative was foremost; the poets and story-tellers who popularised the legendary history of pagan Ireland deeply impressed early Welsh romance and verse, and exercised a notable influence on the earliest English literature; and the impact of Irish historical and political experience worked powerfully among the British and English peoples, especially upon the notables who took political decisions; the decisions became precedents, and the men who took them shaped their still raw and malleable political institutions, often consciously. Throughout the 7th century and the early 8th, the English and the Welsh retained a warm affection for the Irish, and gladly acknowledged the inspiration that had come from Ireland.

CHAPTER NINE
CHRISTIAN IRELAND

The Sources

Christian Ireland begins with the landing of Patrick; thenceforth the older sources are reinforced by histories of churchmen. Most numerous among them are the Lives of the Saints, termed 'hagiography' by modern writers. Each author's purpose is simple, to display the wonderful virtues of his hero, and his usual method is to recite jejune miracles. He was a story-teller rather than a historian, and his business was to edify, to exhort and to entertain. But the first author of each Life told of a real person, who lived in particular places at a particular time, and most later versions preserve something of the detail, sometimes much. Serious assessment of these misty texts must start from the shrewd assessment of the French historian, Fustel de Coulanges:

> Saints' lives are also history . . . their aim was . . . to demonstrate the sanctity of their hero . . . in the interest of the church or abbey that had taken him for patron. . . . The life of each saint was written by one of his disciples, or by a man who knew him, or at least on the evidence of his acquaintances. But this primitive version has hardly ever come down to us. . . . Each century recopied it, making changes and additions. . . . It is very difficult to distinguish what . . . has been added. . . . Though there are often errors of date, transposition of proper names, facts distorted . . . that is unimportant. What we need to look for are the . . . facts that the hagiographer had no incentive to change.

The incentive is the key to the study of the Lives. In principle, that which serves the morality and the practical interest of the copyist in each age is likely to be his addition; detail that serves no such interest is normally what he found in his original. The detection of interest is not a matter of guesswork, for numerous texts show its conventions; a number of Lives survive in successive editions, and the differences between them disclose the ways in which later editors corrupted their originals. Some boast that they have suppressed dubious morality and doctrine, or abbreviated the tedious 'British garrulity' of their predecessors leaving out the 'uncouth and barbarous British names' of people and places no longer of interest to the later reader. Such names are rarely added; when they remain, they nearly always derive from a contemporary original, and sometimes preserve its spelling. Often the authors of surviving Lives omitted them. In their place a few great names, notably Patrick, David and Arthur, are dragged into many Lives, out of time and place; saints are made to visit places where later ages revered their relics, and any saint who visits Rome at any date meets Gregory the Great, and at Tours meets Martin. But when other popes are named, or when stories are told of obscure places and persons, they are transcribed from earlier versions, whose 'barbarous garrulity' the copyist retained. Many monks met long-dead saints in visions, and were at the time convinced of their reality; Jonas, the 7th century biographer of Columban, was personally present in the room when St. Peter visited his abbot, though, to his regret, the abbot did not wake him. Later versions of such visions leave out the dream, and make the living and the dead meet in the flesh. Many authors purloin striking miracles from other popular Lives and sometimes transfer people and places with the story. Late custom gave many saints royal fathers. These and many other conventions are the normal practice of the hagiographer, and are not hard to recognise when the texts are submitted to the ordinary processes of historical criticism.

A few surviving works, like Adomnan's Columba or the first Life of Samson, were written within living memory; but most are copies of copies. They vary greatly. Most of the Irish Lives in Latin are preserved in two main collections. Their medieval editors gave them a standard form, so that the biographies are much alike, preserving an immensity of detail, but coating the saints with a uniform sickly sweet piety. The Irish-language Lives are mainly derived from Latin originals, and are brightly coloured to suit the taste of listeners accustomed to the rugged imagination of the story-teller. But few of the Latin versions are as distorted as the 12th-century British Lives, though few are as close to their originals as the early Armorican texts.

The Lives are amplified by other evidence, by martyrologies, or calendars, that list saints according to the anniversary of their death, and by the places and churches that bear their names. The early British and Irish Christians continued the practice of 4th-century Rome, that dedicated churches to God alone, but described them by their situation, or by the name of a living or dead patron whom they honoured. Later ages dedicated churches to long-dead humans, to apostles and martyrs, to the Virgin, to All Saints or to Archangels, and these later dedications often effaced the older name. Later Irishmen and Welshmen dedicated churches to Patrick, Brigit and David; and Martin of Tours was admitted to the canon of dedication. But lesser men were not, and a church that retains the name of a local native saint or of a European ecclesiastic is usually located in an area where he was honoured in his lifetime, save on rare occasions when the name stems from the transfer of relics in later generations. This evidence, together with the statements of the Lives and Martyrologies, is summarised in *Arthurian Sources*.

Loegaire

Fifth-century Irishmen were ready to welcome protection against the growing violence of their lords. Tradition looked back with nostalgia to the golden age of Cormac, a prince 'not given causelessly to be bloody', whose royal police preserved quiet and good order for the private individual. But Loegaire and his fifth-century successors exercised no such authority. From Patrick's time onwards, some Christians were able to curb some of the violence. Soon after his death, the virgin Faencha upbraided the young chief Enda for leading his men to avenge his father's death. Enda was as startled as any honest soldier who is told that his trade is immoral; but he was converted, and thereafter Faencha took pains to send him abroad to Britain to be schooled, lest he relapse into the violence of the society whence he came. Another chief rejected conversion with a straight answer, 'I am a soldier, so I cannot be religious.'

The Christian leaders withstood wars. Ciaran of Saigir and others are said to have succeeded in preventing some fifth-century battles. They also withstood civil violence. They forced kings to release prisoners, hostages, and persons unjustly enslaved; they rebuked royal cruelty, denounced war, opposed the execution of political opponents and of ordinary criminals; and the tradition of the church makes Irish Christians play a large part in preserving the laws and the learning that were older than the princes. In the early fifth century, dynastic power was only beginning to spread. The changes that it heralded were taking shape, and the coming of Patrick was a part of those changes. He is said to have landed in 432, four or five years after the death of Nath-I. Simultaneously, the political relations between Britain and Ireland were transformed. After two hundred years, Irish raids on Britain suddenly ceased, and were never resumed, save for a brief space, in different circumstances, about the 490s. The evident reason is the superior force of Vortigern. Irish tradition reported a raid in or about 434 by Saxons, who are likely to have been his federates, and implies that his daughter married a son of Loegaire, the new High King.

These were political events. Vortigern's concern was to subdue the Irish colonists in Britain. His was the first British Government to control an adequate naval force, able to deter Irish intervention; and the report of a dynastic marriage suggests that he exacted a formal treaty. Patrick's mission was a part of this political situation. It was long discussed, approved by the Pope, by the bishops of Gaul, and by the bishops of Britain, some of whom were aghast at the risk of sending a bishop 'among the enemy'. The proposal to send Patrick could not have been realised without the agreement of both governments.

It was plainly to Vortigern's interest that as many as possible of Loegaire's subjects should embrace the religion of Britain and of Rome. The texts suggest that Loegaire was constrained to agree, and Patrick's own writings demonstrate that he was given licence to preach, but that he received little positive encouragement from Irish authorities. The earlier traditions of his life set his headquarters at Saul by Downpatrick, and put the area of his missionary work in the north-east. After his death, about 460, four or five bishops ministered to the Christians of the north and centre, but southern tradition points to the separate creation of its own sees by the papacy, in or about the 460s, at first under the guidance of the church of Britain. All early sources assert that throughout the fifth century, and in the early years of the sixth, Christians were still a relatively small minority in most of Ireland. The massive conversion of the bulk of the population is presented as the achievement of the monastic reformers, centred on the 530s and 540s.

Meanwhile, the political structure of Ireland was changing. Loegaire was restrained from attacking Britain. Leaders whose fathers had found wealth and power in plundering Britain were forced to confine their ambition to Ireland. Loegaire himself is depicted as a powerful monarch, who had no need of force to levy the tribute of Leinster, until his last years. The dynastic struggles that faced him and his successors were of two kinds. The heirs of Niall's sons and brothers were all-powerful in the north and centre, strong enough to contain the kingdoms that they did not directly rule, of the Airgialla and the Ulaid. But Leinster paid tribute only under compulsion, and none was claimed from Munster, whose kings acknowledged no more than precedence to the northern dynasty. The kings of Ireland were northerners who needed force to maintain even nominal authority in the south; but the dynasty itself comprised several branches, and each strove to secure to itself the title of king of Ireland.

Loegaire, late-born son of the great Niall, met no opposition from within his own dynasty. His wars were southern. Leinster submitted in 455, and he invaded Munster. He withdrew without a battle, but without being attacked, presumably because the Munster king formally acknowledged his suzerainty. But he did not consolidate permanent power in the south. The men of north Leinster threw up a national dynasty of their own, whose king decisively defeated Loegaire, just before his death in 461. The new High King, Aillel of Connacht, thereafter fought the Leinstermen with varying success for twenty years.

Mac Erca

Aillel was the last High King for five centuries who was not of the Ui Neill, the dynasty of Niall. He was brought down at the battle of Ocha, in Meath, in 482, by a grand alliance. The leader of the northern Ui Neill, Muirchetach mac Erca, king of Ailech, near Londonderry, united the several branches of Niall's heirs, bought the support of the Ulaid by the cession of border territory, and was joined by the king of Leinster. The battle became a landmark in Irish history, for it ensured that thenceforth all High Kings were drawn from one or other branch of the Ui Neill.

Mac Erca dominated Irish politics for half a century, and is said to have leaned heavily upon the advice of a British ecclesiastic. He was very young in 482, and the High Kingship went to Loegaire's son, Lugid. But it was Mac Erca who led the struggle to subdue the south. In Leinster he allied with a new southern dynasty, who overthrew their northern rivals, and joined him to destroy the king of Munster, in 492. In 500 the alliance ended, and Mac Erca subdued Leinster; and in 502 he replaced the king of Connacht with a nominee of his own. In the next year he succeeded Lugid as king of Ireland, and reigned in peace for nearly thirty years, with no reports of opposition in the subject provinces.

Mac Erca was the contemporary of Arthur. It is in the years of his triumph that Irish and English tradition both record renewed Irish intervention in Britain, though none is reported in the previous 75 years, since Nath-I's death, or again in the future. In the extreme north, Mac Erca's relative and ally, Fergus of Dal Riada, found his tiny state surrounded when Mac Erca ceded his borders about Coleraine to the Ulaid; many of Fergus' subjects had already crossed the seas to settle in Kintyre, on the flank of the Clyde estuary, and about 500 Fergus transferred his royal residence to his colonial territories. There his heirs fought the Picts, but long remained at peace with the British of the Clyde.

Further south in Britain the Irish were enemies, not allies. King Illan, whom Mac Erca's victories had enthroned in Leinster, is said to have fought eight or nine battles in Britain. The Laigin of Leinster named Lleyn, the tip of Caernarvonshire, and the British remembered the fierce campaigns of Catwallaun Longhand, father of the Maelgwn whom Gildas denounced. They culminated in the expulsion of 'Serigi the Irishman' from Anglesey, in the years between about 490 and about 510. The name is rare in Ireland, but Irish tradition knew a Serach as the son-in-law of a Leinster king.

It is in the same years that the Demetian Irish received considerable reinforcements, under leaders whose names were used only in south-west Munster. At a date that seems to indicate 493, their forces are said to have pushed inland to Brecon, and to have attacked towards Cardiff. It may be that they came to help their old allies the Saxons in their last effort at Badon; but they succumbed to Arthur's counter-attack, when the forces of Agricola ended Irish rule in Demetia, perhaps some ten to fifteen years later. It was also in the same years that Theodoric repelled a formidable Munster invasion of Cornwall. The last Irish assault on Britain failed when the empire of Arthur was still strong.

These armies had reason to leave Ireland. The growing power of the dynasts threatened small men, and Mac Erca's victories threatened local dynasts. When he subdued Munster, the men of the west coast sought lands and adventure overseas; and Leinstermen too weak to fight the king of Ireland also turned to foreign war. But theirs were local enterprises. There is no sign that Mac Erca backed them or dreamt of reviving the overseas ambitions of Crimthann, Niall and Nath-I. He respected the power of Arthur, and lived at peace with Britain, content to consolidate his sovereignty in Ireland. The Ui Neill ruled unchallenged. Their security was disturbed only by an internal rift, when Ardgal, of the southern Ui Neill of East Meath, rebelled in 518. The rebellion was repressed, but it was a portent, the first recorded conflict between members of the dynasty. It became a precedent, for Mac Erca was succeeded by Tuathal

Maelgarbh, of the West Meath line. He began his reign by exiling Ardgal's nephew and heir, Diarmait mac Cerbaill, and thenceforth the throne of Ireland was in dispute between the several branches of the Ui Neill dynasty.

Diarmait

Ireland was dramatically transformed when Mac Erca died, in 532. For a hundred years, since Patrick's coming, there had been a Christian church in Ireland, governed by bishops; but it had not yet seized hold of Irish society. It is in the reign of Tuathal that ecclesiastical tradition placed the mass conversion of the Irish to monastic Christianity. An important section of the early monks maintained the earlier Christian antagonism to the princes. One of the greatest of them, Ciaran of Clonmacnoise, whose plebeian origin is deliberately emphasised by his constant description as the 'artisan's son', confronted and confounded Tuathal. He is also said to have sheltered the exiled Diarmait, who used Clonmacnoise as a base while he organised the assassination of Tuathal, whom he succeeded in 548.

A year or two later the great plague devastated Ireland, and Ciaran died. Monastic tradition did not endorse support for Diarmait. Brigit is made to foretell that he would be 'bloody, cursed by his birth', and to many monks one new tyrant was no better than an old one dead. But the movement was none the less sucked into the struggles of the dynasties. The most forceful among the younger monks who survived the plague years was Columba. He was a royal prince, of the Tirconel branch of the Ui Neill, now Diarmait's principal dynastic rivals. His father was second cousin to Mac Erca, and two of his own first cousins became High Kings. His powerful personality made as deep an imprint on the history of mankind as any man of his century in Europe, and he overshadows all Irishmen of his day. There is little doubt that if he had not been a monk, he rather than his cousins would have been chosen king. His birth and his outlook sharply contrasted with Ciaran's and later tradition expressed the realities of his time when it made an angel warn Ciaran that

> what you have surrendered for the love of God is nothing but the tools of your father's trade; what Columba has forgone is the sceptre of Ireland, his by ancestral right.

Columba was a prince and a monk. Both his career and Ciaran's served to fulfil the judgement of the doyen of the older monks, Lasrian of Devenish, that 'in the end the saints must prove stronger than the kings of Ireland'. Both men were pupils of Finnian of Clonard, but when they left him, at much the same time, about 545, their ways parted. Ciaran withdrew to the seclusion of the Lough Ree area, where the borders of the great provinces meet, as far as possible from the courts of great kings; but Columba established his first major monastery at Derry, in his own family territory, on land given to him by his cousin Ainmere, then king of the northern Ui Neill. The saints who opposed the dynasts and their wars cannot have looked kindly upon Ainmere, who in the same year killed the aged king of Connacht, and began a career of military aggrandisement, on the model of Mac Erca, that was ultimately to win him the throne of Ireland, and must from the outset have been seen to have had that end in view.

Diarmait stands out as one of the great kings of Irish tradition, as memorable as Cormac, Niall and Mac Erca before him, not again equalled in stature before Brian Boru in the eleventh century. He is Adomnan's sovereign *regnator*. With an almost Thucydidean insight, the Irish historians select two dramatic events, his quarrels with Ruadan and with Columba, to illuminate the critical conflicts of his reign. The Life of Ruadan and the Annals of Clonmacnoise recount at length the dispute over the punishment of Aed Guaire, dated to the year 558. The Ruadan account is sympathetic to Diarmait, despite the saint's hostility, and calls him a 'powerful peaceful king' who 'upheld the peace so strongly in his realm that no man dare even strike another's face in anger'. Other traditions agree; an Ulaid poet, allegedly his contemporary, is made to sing of 'Diarmait the Good, a ruler without slackness; no robber can escape the speed of his death sentence'. His stern justice executed his own son, convicted of stealing a nun's cow; he overawed the provincial kings; he married a Munster princess; the army of Leinster withdrew before him without daring to fight; and the king of Connacht gave his son as hostage.

Diarmait's efforts to enforce the king's peace embroiled him with Ruadan. He ordered that the gates of the raths, or castles, of all the local lords throughout Ireland should be no narrower than a spear's length, and sent his officers to inspect them and to destroy those that were not wide enough. As the royal officer made his rounds among the Ui Maine of Connacht, 'boasting of the king's authority in lands not his own', he reached the rath of Aed Guaire when its lord was absent. Aed's men obeyed the royal order, broke down the gate, and entertained the king's officer to dinner. During the meal, Aed returned. Enraged at the broken gate, he killed the officer, and then, 'for fear of the king', fled for protection to a relative who was a bishop in Munster. But the Munster bishop, 'not strong enough to shelter a man guilty of killing a royal officer', directed him to Ruadan at Lothra, in the monastic enclave near Clonmacnoise. Diarmait sent men to arrest him, but Ruadan smuggled him out of the country. He sought refuge with a British king, but Diarmait's arm was long, and his envoys demanded the criminal's extradition, under threat of invasion. 'Not daring to stay in Britain', Aed returned to Ruadan, who hid him in a cellar. Informers told the king, whose men arrested him in the monastery, took him prisoner to Tara, and condemned him to death.

Ruadan was outraged at the violation of the sanctuary, and resisted the death penalty. With his near neighbour, Brendan of Birr, and a company of monks, he went to Tara. The saints rang their bells in the streets, calling for a fast, or hunger strike, against the king. The king 'refused to relax the law of the land', and met the saints' fast by fasting himself. 'The saints could achieve nothing, while the king fasted and prayed', for the king was a 'peace-loving defender of his country, who helped the churches and the poor, was truthful, just in judgement and absolutely trustworthy'. So the saints tricked him, by pretending to break their fast. The king was deceived, and ate. That night he dreamed that he saw a great tree, whose shadow overspread all Ireland, felled by the sharp axes of a hundred and fifty clerics; the fall of the tree portended the end of his life, and the handing over of the kingdom to the saints of God. The king went out to upbraid the saints who were keeping vigil, protesting

> I have made the country secure. I have established the rule of law in all places, so that the churches and peoples live securely in peace everywhere. I defend the right according to Christ's law, but you do ill to defend a murderer. Much may follow from small beginnings.
>
> Turning to Ruadan, the king said, 'Ruadan, for what you have done, the Holy Trinity will punish you. Your monasteries shall fail in Ireland'. . . . Ruadan replied, 'Your kingdom shall fail, and none of your seed shall ever reign. . . . This your royal town of Tara, whence the kingdom of Ireland has been ruled these many years, shall be left empty.'

After a considerable further exchange of prophetic curses, the king turned to the other saints and addressed them.

> You, Fathers, are protecting evil. But I am defending the truth in Christ's name. You may kill me, and you may ruin my kingdom; God may love you for your merits more than me, but I place my hope in the loving kindness of my God. So go. Take the man away free. But you will render a price to the kingdom for this man.

The tale is unique in Irish historical record, utterly out of keeping with the unctuous uncritical praise that normally reduces every incident to the background of a routine miracle. It is cast in the rational narrative form of an earlier age, skilfully narrated to illustrate a major crisis through the detail of a single incident. But the Ruadan story excels in one rare gift, the ability to communicate intelligibly the motives of both contestants, to depict a conflict of two rights, rather than the victory of right over wrong.

Ruadan fought for a principle, and found himself the champion of an unruly local dynast against the central monarchy. He campaigned in the streets in full publicity, and his victory humbled the king. Diarmait's troubles multiplied. The Cruithne overthrew the dynasty of Dal Araide, and Diarmait intervened in vain. In 560 he summoned the Royal Feast of Tara, the last recorded, and began his conflict with Columba. The story is told in full in short versions and long, and its details recur in a great number of documents, Annals, Saints' Lives, tales and verses. The clash centred on two distinct issues, but rests on a deeper antagonism. Columba was not only abbot of Derry. The enormous vitality of the royal abbot attracted disciples in numbers far greater than the followers of other monks, and

Columba is credited with the foundation in Ireland of some twenty to forty houses, who looked to him as their chief and ruler. He was as mighty as a king. Religion and the world combined to make him Diarmait's enemy, for he inherited the resentment of the monks against the great king, the head and protector of the whole body of lesser rulers, and also the antagonism of the northern Ui Neill to the kings of Meath, Diarmait's own territory.

The first quarrel arose over a book. The monk Finnian of Moville visited Pope Pelagius, who reigned from 555 to 560, and on his return 'first brought the whole Gospel to Ireland', evidently a Vulgate text. Columba borrowed it and transcribed it, 'working day and night, remote from the noise and sight of other men who might have hindered him'. Finnian was 'furious that the book was copied secretly without his permission', and claimed the copy as his of right. The dispute was referred to Diarmait, and Finnian argued that it was as though Columba had cut his corn without permission. Columba replied

> I admit I copied the book, but it was with my own labour and in my own time. Finnian's book is none the worse for being copied.... Whatever I find in any book, I have the right to copy and to place at the disposal of other men, for the glory of God.

But Diarmait decided for Finnian, 'either because he wrongly weighed the arguments, or because he was influenced by private interests'. He delivered his judgement

> in a phrase still famous in Ireland, 'As a calf is to the cow, so is the copy to the book.'

Private interest there was. The monks were the king's enemies, and Columba was Diarmait's dynastic opponent; Finnian was bishop of the Ulaid of Dal Fiatach, who were hereditary enemies of the northern Ui Neill, but were Diarmait's allies against the Cruithne. But it is a tribute to the reputation of Diarmait that even the Columban tradition admits that his mistake might have been honest. Columba himself denounced the decision as 'irrational, manifestly wrong, and untenable'.

Finnian's visit to Rome is dated to the years just before the Tara Feast of 560. A still graver conflict came in the year of the Feast, evidently during it. The king of Connacht's son, Curnan, a hostage with Diarmait, killed the son of a royal steward in a quarrel at the games. The offence was worse than Aed Guaire's; homicide in the royal household, on the occasion of a rare and solemn festival, was unforgivable. For a less offence, the king had executed his own son. The young man fled to Columba for protection; the king overrode his right of sanctuary, enforced royal justice, and had the boy executed.

The breach was beyond healing. Columba was outraged. He went home to Tir Connel, raised his cousins of the northern Ui Neill, king Ainmere and the sons of Mac Erca. The king of Connacht, father of the dead boy, joined him in 561.

> They gave battle to Diarmait and his army at Cuil Dremhni. Columba was present with his forces . . . and besought God by prayer and fasts to grant victory over the insolent king without loss to his own men. . . . At the king's request, saint Finnian . . . prayed for the royal army. . . . But the royal army was dispersed in flight, losing 3,000 men, their opponents losing one man only. . . . Columba made peace with the defeated king . . . and kept the book.

Diarmait survived for three years more, but his strength was gone. The issue decided at Cuil Dremhni was weightier than those that had occasioned earlier battles. They had merely determined which individual should rule. But if Diarmait had routed the combined armies of the north and west, and with them the greatest of the monks, then the authority of the king of all Ireland would have been firmly vindicated, the independence of provincial kings and lesser dynasts curbed, the political power of the monks broken. When he failed, it was not one king who fell, but the monarchy itself. In an age when all Europe saw the hand of God in each earthly decision, victory could not be ascribed to the superior generalship of king Ainmere. Columba and Finnian had both invoked God with conflicting prayers, and God had made a clear decision. Columba had gone to war to vindicate the independence of the church, upholding the right of sanctuary against royal justice, denying the right of the king's law to forbid the free circulation of the word of God. Finnian was a bishop who served his king. God had decided that the church was stronger than the king.

The great tree had fallen, and Ireland was changed. The quite different western traditions of Brendan of Clonfert, remote from the central conflict, echo the same view. The king's wise men, interpreting a different dream, are made to tell him:

> Your kingdom is taken away, and is to be given to holy churchmen.

The judgement was sound. No later king attained anything near to the authority that is credited to Diarmait. He was succeeded in 564 by Mac Erca's two elderly sons, who reigned jointly. When they were killed, a year later, division increased. Several simultaneous rulers are accorded the title of High King, but only Columba's cousin Ainmere and his son Aed earned record, beyond their name and date, in the memory of later ages.

Their successors are better documented. From Columba's time onward Irish local political history is remembered in considerably greater detail than that of England, Wales or Scotland. Its meaning cannot be disentangled until the extensive documentation is scrutinised, for the record of the Annals is a dreary tale of mounting slaughter, with battles ten times as numerous as before, fought for no greater cause than the aggrandisement of individual families. The combatants are increasingly lesser kings, fighting each other on their own account in disregard of the High King, and the High Kings' wars are principally fought in defence of their own individual dynastic territories. The High Kings continue to receive some tribute and to give gifts, to preside over conferences and to settle ecclesiastical disputes; but they are no longer credited with the power or the will to discipline provincial or lesser kings. Those bold enough to claim the cattle tribute of Leinster perished in the attempt, and their successors ultimately remitted the impost. The title remained with the descendants of Niall, but their effective power was limited to their own dominions, scarcely noticeable in the south, weak in Connacht.

The Church Triumphant

The squalid secular violence of seventh-century Ireland is matched by the splendid vigour of its church. Columba's war had been as much a crisis for the monks as for the king. The military victory of an all-powerful royal abbot brought with it the danger of a divine monarch. The threat was real. In contemporary Britain Cadoc was held to have ruled as both abbot and king, and several later rulers of Munster were to combine the offices of king and bishop; in Italy, the disastrous invasion of the Lombards was thrusting local temporal responsibilities upon the head of Christendom, and the phenomenon of the prince-bishop was to appear in several parts of Europe. In Ireland, there is little doubt that if Columba had been free to wear a crown he would have been the obvious successor to Diarmait. One late tale asserts that he was actually offered the throne. Whether it were so or not, the story expresses a situation. The danger was conceivable, for the autocratic abbot who ruled far more monks than any other cleric might have imposed upon Ireland an authority stronger than Diarmait's. There is no sign that Columba was tempted by such ambition, or that the monks or laity of Ireland were disposed to submit to it. But the possibility warned that the monastic church, designed as a withdrawal from political force, might find itself transformed into the instrument of an all-powerful clerical state.

The monks of Ireland faced the danger. A synod condemned Columba's intervention in the wars, and excommunicated him. The sentence was stayed, on the proposal of Brendan of Birr, and gentle Lasrian, most senior of the monks, advised Columba to leave Ireland for ever, in voluntary exile, that he might 'win as many souls for Christ as he had caused to die in battle'. Columba accepted the sentence and sailed away to Iona. He too was transformed by the fearful shock of the crisis. In Britain, he steadfastly refrained from becoming the national saint of his Irish fellow-countrymen, and made it his business to convert their Pictish enemies. He remained the spiritual adviser of their king, Bridei, as well as of the Irish, and his stern authority earned him the reputation of the 'dove of peace'. So long as he lived, Irish Dal Riada remained at peace with Bridei, and also with its British neighbours.

The future history of Ireland was to be the history of its church. The crisis that had sent Columba to Iona compelled the Irish monasteries to seek and find a new direction. The traditions of Ireland, Britain and Brittany agree that they summoned the aged Gildas to visit them and advise upon the ordering of their future. They were already strong. Victory over the secular government had given them unchallenged independence, and a considerable moral authority. They used it to restrain the violence of kings. They failed to stop it, but in the end they curbed it. In 697 a conference of the principal bishops and abbots endorsed a code of war. The principal initiative was attributed to abbot Adomnan, the biographer of Columba, who named the law, known as the *Cain Adomnan*, and to his English friend, Egbert of Iona; their notable southern allies included Muirchu, the biographer of Patrick, and his patron, bishop Aed of Sletty. War crimes were defined, and severe ecclesiastical penalties were enacted for offences against non-combatants, especially for the killing of women, children and students. Governments were not consulted. Adomnan's law was imposed upon them, and fear of the monks' spiritual authority commonly deterred soldiers from perpetrating atrocities against civilians until the coming of the Scandinavians.

The power of the monks put bounds upon the licence of rulers, but they did not reform Irish political society. They withdrew from it, and built an enduring alternative society. Lay violence continued, but the learning and the art of Irish monasteries won the admiration of Europe and of future ages. The continuing disorder of secular politics attracted new recruits in each successive generation, men who welcomed escape from the conflicts of kings. Some sought new lands beyond the Atlantic, but many more carried their piety and learning to known peoples. They converted the northern English, and spread their monastic life throughout England; thereafter, the English and Irish inspired the Franks and Germans with their monastic fervour. At home, they wrote down the traditions of their forefathers while they were still remembered, and gave a Christian blessing to the legends of the pagan past; in so doing they preserved a unique record of the manners of barbarian society in western Europe, that remains essential to the understanding of the excavated remains of illiterate peoples elsewhere.

The Ireland that the scholars describe evolved with few sharp and sudden breaks, but in definite stages. From the second century to the middle of the fifth, its history is the story of a single dynasty, of the Ui Neill and their ancestors, told consistently and with coherent dates; to it the scholars attached fragments from the debris of other traditions, though their valiant attempts to 'synchronise and harmonise' these outside stories were unsuccessful, for the unchecked imagination of the story-tellers contradicted each other, and confused the sources of the annalists and genealogists. But from the middle of the fifth century, annalists and genealogists agree and record settled traditions from the different regions of Ireland, that concur with each other. The history of the sixth century is told in increasing detail, and is supplemented by the Lives of the earlier saints. Few contemporary documents survive, but the quantity of information preserved in medieval texts is immense, complex, and consistent. A full account of the sixth and seventh centuries, whose local conflicts are reported more profusely than in any other European land, would fill a large volume on its own.

Until the monastic upsurge of the mid sixth century, Ireland was still barbarian, its customs little affected by the impact of Christian and Roman ideas. The accounts of its last generations, in the years between 480 and 560, describe in detail a still unmodified Iron Age society. The records of the next century describe the struggle of the Roman religion to transform barbarian Ireland. At first, the monks were in conflict with still powerful Druids, and deeply distrusted those baptised Druids who sought to marry alien worlds. But later the abbot and the bishop replaced the Druid, whose title devolved upon lowly intellectual craftsmen. On the initiative of Columba, the arts over which the Druids had formerly presided were accommodated within the structure of Christian Ireland. It was that compromise which enabled the scholars to write down the records, laws and customs of the past, adapting them to the outlook of Rome and Christendom. The monasteries were also enabled to perpetuate in durable materials the artistic skills of their ancestors, and to apply their uninhibited energy to the learning and theology they found in Europe.

Early Christian Ireland, like the Hellenistic Age and the Italian Renaissance, is numbered among those societies which combined enormous intellectual and artistic vitality with the extremes of irresponsible violence, cruelty and insecurity. Its faith stemmed from Britain, and its strongest impact was returned upon the peoples of Britain. Its political direction was determined by the new-found strength of fifth-century Britain, which ended the earlier raids and defeated the renewed attempts at expansion in Mac Erca's time. The Irish Christians were themselves convinced that they owed their inspiration to Britain, their initial conversion to Patrick, their mass monastic movement to the reformers who grew to manhood in Arthur's lifetime and in the generation thereafter. Monasticism brought Ireland into a common polity with Britain. No longer aliens, the Irish also were included among the heirs and successors of Arthur, who shaped the common future of the British Isles. A monk of Columba's Iona moulded the church of Northumbria; Bede grew to manhood in a monastery fostered and protected by a king born and bred among the Irish, who was honoured in both countries as the most learned Irishman and most learned Englishman of his day.

The great age of Ireland lasted some three centuries. The victory of the monks equipped the Irish to become the intellectual inspiration of Europe. But the cost was heavy. The monasteries absorbed the energies of the ablest Irishmen, and spent them in the service of all lands. Emigration remained the natural outlet of the liveliest minds; for in breaking and rejecting the structure of secular society the monks left it unreformed and robbed of reformers. Lay society was left leaderless, with no tradition of secular national strength, never able to rally round a native equivalent of a Hereward, a Llewellyn or a Wallace, in time to become the easy victims of an invader. Eight centuries of bitter national humiliation were endured without rational hope of liberation until our own day. In the idiom of the story-teller, the monks who destroyed the early national monarchy entailed upon their successors a great price to be paid for the freedom of a lawless chieftain.

CHAPTER TEN

THE DAL RIADA SCOTS

Geography

Modern Scotland owes its name to immigrants from Ireland. But they were only one among the many peoples whom the medieval and modern kingdom united. The present-day border lies virtually upon the same line as the frontier of the Roman empire. It is a frontier dictated by geography and by the convenience of armies. The high unpeopled moors of the Cheviots run north-eastward from the rivers that water Carlisle to the richer lands of the Till and Tweed. They are the feasible limits of a northern power, based on York, that controls Tyne and Solway, but cannot subdue the enormous open spaces beyond. Yet the border did not last continuously from Roman times, for it is only a military and geographical line. It was not and is not a clear national boundary that separates one language and one culture from another. When the centralised power of Rome disintegrated, it was eclipsed by the political frontiers of smaller peoples, and the old line was not permanently reasserted for more than six hundred years, after the Norman conquest of England.

The frontier, and with it the identity of Scotland, took long to establish because the population beyond it was mixed. The English, the Irish and the Welsh were each a coherent people, bound together by language and tradition. Northern Britain was peopled by portions of these nations, and also by the Picts, the Atecotti and the peoples of the islands, to whom later centuries added Scandinavian settlers. The medieval kingdom was not united by language or by a common culture, but by the compelling demands of geography, the seas that enclose it on three sides and the military frontier of the Cheviots on the south.

Scotland comprises three large regions, the lowlands, the highlands, and the north-west. Each of them is sub-divided by nature. The southern lowland is a rectangle, marked by the two Roman walls, from Forth to Clyde, and from Tyne to Solway; and was in the fifth century British in speech, culture and political allegiance, bound by its past to the Roman south. It is cut diagonally by the Cheviot frontier, that is most easily controlled by the rulers of Northumbria and the lower Tyne. Beyond the Cheviots, the Pentland Hills divide the Lothians from the western lands that lie open to the rulers of the Clyde. In the centuries after Arthur, the English proved able to conquer and absorb the British of the Lothians, but they never overran the Clyde.

Beyond the Forth and Clyde the main mass of Pictish territory is bounded by the Great Glen, from Inverness to the Firth of Lorn. It includes the Grampian mountains, the highlands that reach the sea just south of Aberdeen. They separate two fertile regions, the coastal plain of the northern Picts from Aberdeen to Inverness, with its extension to the nearer firths of Beauly, Cromarty and Dornoch; and the southern Pictish country about the long valley of Strathmore, from Perth to Kincardine and Stonehaven, south of Aberdeen.

The long narrow triangle of the north-west is a wilder and emptier country. Its internal communications distinguish its northern and southern portions. In the north, half a dozen narrow roads radiate from Inverness like the fingers of a hand, with no cross routes between them, except the winding coast road. To the south, communications are poorer still. There is no coast road, and only two roads run from the coast to the Great Glen, their outlets dominated by Forts

---

Map 10

ROADS

The modern roads follow and indicate the ancient and natural routes. The roads are shown as classified by the Ministry of Transport (MoT) and by the Automobile Association (AA).

SOUTH OF THE CLYDE AND FORTH ESTUARIES the map shows only

= Trunk Roads (A 1, 7, 8, 9; 68, 70, 74)

NORTH OF THE CLYDE AND FORTH ESTUARIES the map shows

= Trunk Roads (A 9; 80, 94, 96)

▬ Main Roads (all other roads classified by the MoT with two figures)

NORTH AND WEST OF THE GREAT GLEN AND DORNOCH FORTH

all roads and vehicle tracks are shown

— Roads over 12′ wide

--- Roads classified by the AA as 'narrow or rough surface, with passing places', by the MoT as A

··· Classified by the MoT as B, or unclassified

HILL AND MOUNTAIN RANGES

1 The North West Highlands
2 The Grampian Mountains
3 The Sidlaw Hills
4 The Ochil Hills
5 The Campsie Fells, and Lennox and Kilsyth Hills
6 The Pentland Hills
7 The Southern Uplands
8 The Cheviot Hills

THE TWO ROMAN WALLS are shown

MAP 10 SCOTLAND, COMMUNICATIONS

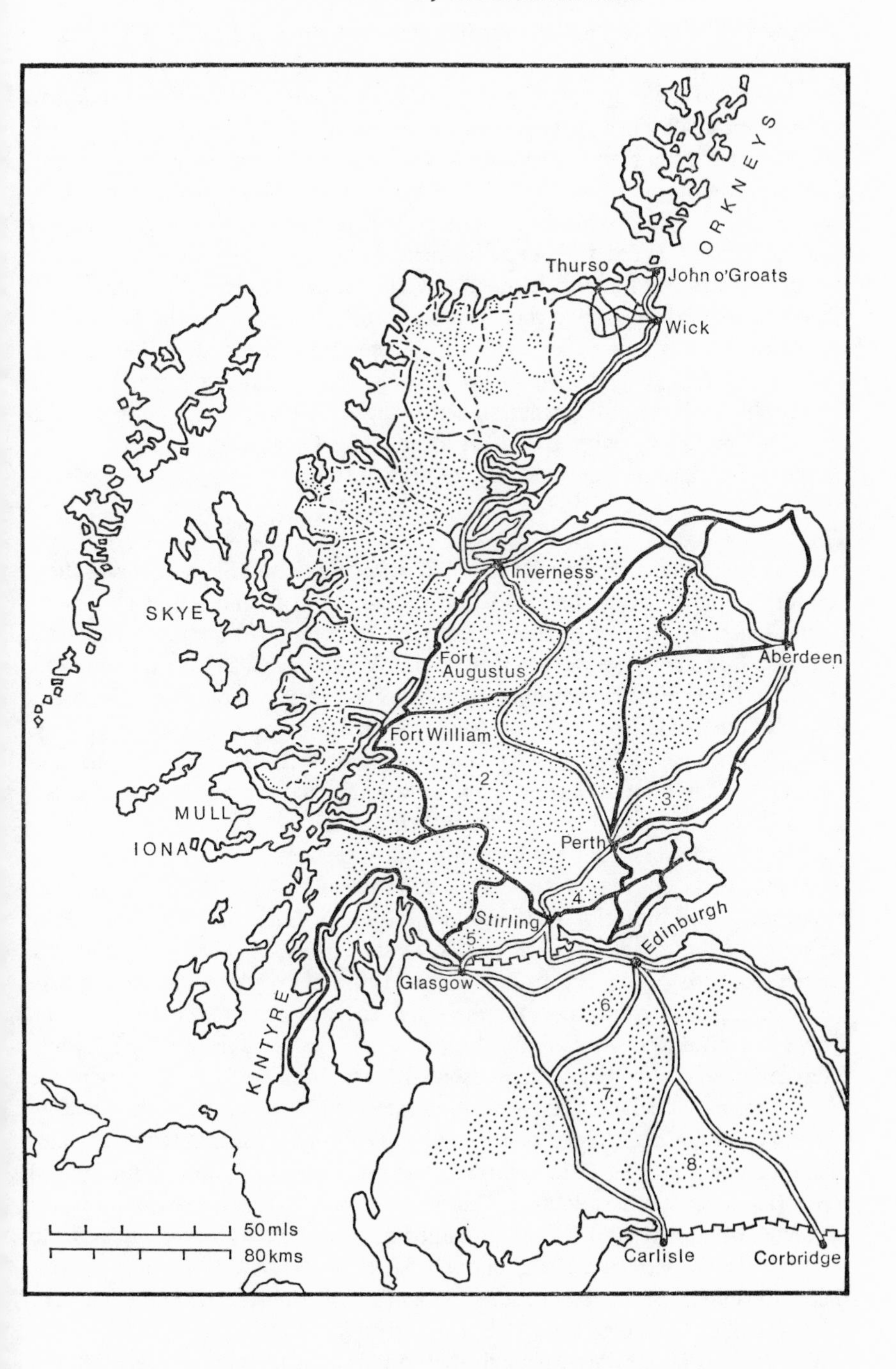

William and Augustus, and the fortifications that preceded them. This precise and exacting geography made the early inhabitants of the north and west aliens and enemies to the richer peoples across the Great Glen. Their natural political centres were at all times the larger and nearer islands that dominate the scattered harbours of the mainland coast. The people of the Orkneys may easily control Caithness, the fertile tip of Britain, unless the power of Inverness is unusually strong. The peoples of Skye are masters of the mainland they face, and may raid the Great Glen at will, to retire behind the safety of the sea if they are pursued by stronger forces. Whenever a warlike seafaring people controlled both Skye and the Orkneys, they constituted a formidable threat to the south. The richest and nearest prizes open to Orkney seamen lay in the lands of the northern Picts. But a ruler of Skye might sail his coracles unhindered to north-eastern Ireland, or might reach Dumbarton across the Argyle lochs with no more than five miles marching, with coracles carried. The Great Glen afforded to the northern Picts a route almost as easy towards the Clyde.

The Scot Kings

Islands and headlands screen the Clyde from Inverness and Skye. It was in them that the Irish, or Scots, of Dal Riada settled. Irish legend, known to Bede, recalled extensive settlement long before the 5th century. But the Dal Riadans became a formidable people when their king Fergus forsook Ireland about 500, and made Kintyre the centre of his kingdom. He evidently came as the ally of the British of the Clyde, and the Clyde king was well-disposed to Ireland, giving his son an Irish name and marrying him to an Irish wife. His interest was well served if the ambition of the new kingdom was directed against the Picts and the men of Skye, shielding the Clyde from their attacks.

Fergus' successors built a powerful military monarchy, and turned its arms against the Picts. It grew slowly at first; and there is no sign that all the colonists submitted to the authority of the dynasty in Fergus' time. Two texts, originally set down in the middle and the later seventh century, trace its evolution; the district dynasties (*ceneil*) are made to derive their authority from Fergus, and are neatly arranged in pairs, their founders artificially represented as his brothers. Only the central territories are firmly attached to royal line from the beginning. They are named after Fergus' grandsons. Kintyre itself was the territory of the *Cenel Gabrain*, and its nearest westward extension, Cowall, bears the name of Gabran's brother and predecessor, Comgall. Gabran is remembered as the first of the conquering kings. He is termed 'king of the Forth', and in the central territories of the southern Picts, in Strathmore, north of Perth, Gowrie preserves his name, while beyond it Brechin is named from another Irishman, unknown to the genealogies, perhaps the ally or subordinate of Gabran. The names suggest that in the middle of the sixth century Gabran's Irish armies overran the southern Picts and planted lasting colonies on their territory.

The records of the Picts, though they preserve little more than names and dates, also suggest that their kingdom was in disarray in Gabran's time. But they recovered their strength. About 556, they took the novel decision to choose a foreigner for their king, and selected Bridei, brother of the most powerful ruler in Britain. Bridei restored their fortunes. He defeated and killed Gabran in 560, and recovered some territory from the Irish, perhaps much; for when Columba reached Britain in 563, Iona is said to have been granted to him not only by Conall, the new Dal Riada king, but also by Bridei.

Columba

Columba was foremost among a number of Irish monks who brought their religion to northern Britain. Conversion was slow, but it opened new possibilities. Iona was centrally placed to reach the Picts, the Irish of Dal Riada, the men of the north-west and of the Isles, and to influence the British of the Clyde. It served them all, and became the burial-place of the Pict as well as the Scot kings. It retained its pre-eminence. Though Ninian, Kentigern and very many Irish monks were honoured locally and regionally, only Columba was honoured in all parts of the future Scotland.

Columba's pre-eminence gave the northerners a common ecclesiastical centre, in an age when kings heeded clerics. But his principal impact was upon his fellow-countrymen in Dal Riada. When he arrived, neither they nor their monarchy were yet consolidated, and they had proved unable to withstand the Picts. Dal Riada grew strong in Columba's lifetime and under his guidance; but not until he had lived many years in Iona.

Wars against the Picts were not renewed, but in 568 Conall and the king of Meath undertook a joint expedition to the Western Isles. In striking up the coast, Conall of Kintyre necessarily assumed the leadership of the Irish settlers on his northern borders. They may not have welcomed his intervention, for he was killed in 574, and with him 'many of the allies of the sons of Gabran'. When the enemy is not named, and when the casualties are described as the allies of a dynasty, the language suggests that the battle was fought between different groups of Irish colonists. But its outcome taught them to unite. Their tradition asserts that it was the next ruler, Aedan, son of Gabran, who became 'king of the separate portions of Dal Riada'. The sovereignty of the dynasty was thenceforth accepted by all the Irish colonists, and the genealogies drawn up half a century after his time contrive to represent all the local lords as heirs of cadet branches of the royal house. The contrivance implies a conviction that all Dal Riadans ought to unite behind a single monarch.

Aedan

Conall had failed to unite the Irish, but Aedan succeeded. No tradition suggests that Conall received or listened to advice from Columba; since the stories of Columba abound with the names of kings who heeded him, their silence about Conall suggests that he did not. But it was Columba who selected and appointed the new king. He is said to have preferred Aedan's brother Eogan, but he was visited three nights running by an angel with a 'glass book of the ordination of kings', who ordered him to consecrate Aedan, lashing at him with a whip until he obeyed. The curious story comes from abbot Cummene, who wrote within sixty years of Aedan's death, and adds the saint's promise of continuing political success so long as the king remained faithful to Iona, and refrained from war against the Ui Neill dynasty of Ireland. Aedan came to Iona, and was consecrated by Columba.

Whatever the reasons for Columba's preference, whatever the pressures brought upon him, the central assertion of the story is that the choice of a successor in practice required his consent, and the story was believed while men who had known Aedan were still alive. It was a quite extraordinary power in an ecclesiastic; no abbots in Ireland and no bishops in Europe commanded such authority. In Europe, Ambrose of Milan had sternly reminded the emperor Maximus that the Old Testament priests had appointed kings, but no Roman emperor had owed his throne to bishops. The authority of Columba was exercised in the name of heaven, but it was accepted in deference to his own strength. His imperious personal force was inseparable from his birth; and it prevailed with his cousin, the High King of Ireland.

Columba took Aedan to Ireland. King Aed m Ainmere had summoned a Convention at Drum Ceat, 15 miles east of Derry, probably in 588, and the tradition of Columba records those decisions wherein his views prevailed. Disputes between north and south were assuaged when he interceded for a son of the king of Ossory, then Ainmere's prisoner; he achieved a concordat between the church, the state, and the secular scholars of Ireland, thereby legitimising and baptising the preservation of ancient legend in Christian Ireland; and he negotiated a lasting agreement between Dal Riada and the Irish monarchy. The colonists in Britain were exempted from normal tribute, but agreed to contribute their quota to the High King's army, and to send no aid to his enemies.

Columba's authority prevented war between the Dal Riada Scots and the Picts of Inverness, the men of the Isles and the king of Ireland. It also preserved the long-standing peace with the British of the Clyde. At almost the same time as Aedan's accession, Kentigern returned to the Clyde from long exile in Europe. He is the only major monastic reformer of the British north, credited with an authority in his own land as eminent as Columba's in Dal Riada. He is said to have met and worked with him, but whether or not they were ever able to meet personally, their outlook was similar, and they had common concerns. Adomnan reports that King Riderch of the Clyde sent a secret mission to secure peace through one of Columba's most trusted and experienced diplomats, and obtained his request. Columba's emissary to Dumbarton must have been accredited to Kentigern the bishop rather than to the king, and Kentigern was plainly as concerned as Columba to negotiate agreement. Their efforts succeeded, and Aedan remained at peace with the British, at least until after Columba's death in 597.

Aedan's power grew. In 581 he attacked the Orkneys; their king had earlier submitted to Bridei, giving hostages, and Aedan's attack is more likely to have been made on Bridei's behalf than against him, perhaps after an Orkney rebellion. No wars against the Picts are recorded until the last year of Bridei, who was killed in 584 by southern Pictish rebels. In 583 Aedan won the battle of Manaan, probably on the borders of the southern Picts and the Lothian British; at that date, the southern Picts, apparently already in rebellion under a separate king, were Bridei's enemies as well as Aedan's. After Bridei's death they ultimately asserted their supremacy, for future Pictish kings whose territory is recorded ruled from Fortrenn, about Stirling and Perth, not from Inverness.

Aedan fought to recover the conquests won and lost by his father Gabran. All his recorded wars were fought eastward. Leithrig, fought in 593, was perhaps near Stirling. About 591 he is reported to have joined with the Ulaid from Ireland, to help the British against the English at Bamburgh. In 599 his army suffered heavy losses at the hands of the southern Picts in Strathmore, but the enemy fled. In 603, reinforced by the King of Ireland's brother, he was able to lead a large force to help the British for a second time against the English, at 'Degsa's Stone'. The place has not been identified. The allies went down in crushing and decisive defeat. Thenceforth 'no king of the Scots ever dared to meet the English in the field' for centuries to come. The British dynasty of the Lothians foundered without trace, and their territory was opened to unimpeded English settlement. But Aedan's kingdom survived, and so did some of his annexations in Pictish lands. His son was styled 'king of the Picts' as well as of the Scots, and the Scots retained the upper Forth; they were still able to penetrate the main territories of the southern Picts, until the disastrous reign of Aedan's grandson, Domnall Brecc.

Aedan's heirs

Domnall fought his neighbours in turn, and earned the reputation of a splendid warrior. One Dal Riada tradition credits him with establishing colonies under his sons in Fife, deep in Pictish territory. But enemies unnamed, presumably Picts, defeated him in 636, probably very near to his royal fortress of Dunadd. He then directed his energy and his armies towards Ireland, in support of an exile, and was defeated by the High King at Mag Roth in Ulster in 639. The battle was celebrated in splendid tales, but Domnall earned the enmity of Iona, for he had defied the precept of Columba and broken the agreement between Dal Riada and the Irish monarchy, that the colonists should never make war upon the kin of Columba; for the king he attacked was the grandson of Columba's cousin. His contemporary Cummene, subsequently Abbot of Iona, ascribed his death soon after to divine vengeance, exacted for his disobedience to Columba.

Domnall was no more fortunate in Britain. He was again defeated in 640, at Glenn Mureson, perhaps Mureston, a few miles south-west of Edinburgh, and the next entry in the Annals records a siege of Eitin, Edinburgh. Who besieged whom, and who beat Domnall, is not stated; but the locality suggests his ambition. Lothian wars were a dangerous gamble for high stakes. The English power was recent and not yet secure. Pict, Scot and Clydeside British might still hope for rich prizes. Their opportunity came when Penda of Mercia killed Oswald of Northumbria in 642 and advanced as far as Bamburgh. The Annals enter two battles under the next year, 643. The British killed Domnall Brecc; and they also attacked Oswy, the new king of Northumbria. Whether their attack succeeded or failed is not reported; but their intention was evidently to recover the Lothians. Domnall may well have had the same aim. But both failed. The Lothians were not recovered; and Domnall's ambition ended in disaster.

Domnall's repeated defeats cost many lives, and wasted the limited fighting strength of a small kingdom. His failure ended the power of his people and the authority of his dynasty. The Picts passed from defence to attack. It was some twenty years later that abbot Cummene recalled Columba's warning; if Aedan's heirs attacked the sovereign dynasty of Ireland, they would 'lose the sceptre of their kingdom from their hands', for 'the hearts of men would be taken from them'. He saw its fulfilment in the misfortune of the Dal Riada Irish, for

> from that day till this they are in subjection to foreigners; which fills the heart with sad sighs.

The monarchy of Dal Riada disintegrated. When it was restored, at the end of the seventh century, the new king of the 'separate portions' was not a descendant of Aedan. He was Ferchar the Tall (680–696), chief of the Cinel Loarn about Loch Linnhe, to the north, who were further and safely removed from the Pictish armies of Fortrenn, but were also ill-placed to challenge them. Although the Cenel Gabrain ultimately returned to power, it was to be almost two hundred years before Pictish military supremacy was overcome; and victory was not clear-cut. In 844 a Scot king with a British name, Kenneth mac Alpine, established a dual monarchy wherein the king of the Scots was also king of the Picts; but though the dynasty and its language were Irish, its seat was established in Pictland. Along with the neighbouring nations that they subdued, its inhabitants ultimately consented to be known by the national name of their Irish monarchs; but when they did so, they submitted, not to Irish military conquest, but to the cultural superiority of the Irish Christian religion and of the literate Irish language.

These were the ultimate consequences of the faith that Columba preached, and of the political conduct he imposed upon the Irish immigrants. He died in 597. As a monk he had founded a potent church rooted not on organisation, but on a particular concept of Christianity, that was to hold 'the hearts of men' for centuries, uniting the kingdoms of northern Britain, and also most of England. But his eminence also made him a political leader, his policy grounded on the knowledge that kingdoms, like churches, are maintained by the hearts of men. Apostle to the diverse peoples of northern Britain, spiritual counsellor of the

Picts, of the men of the Isles, and of his fellow Irishmen, friend and ally of the British, he was the first architect of the later Scotland. So long as he lived, he held the four nations together at peace, and his own Irish king was accepted as their joint leader when they had to face a common English enemy. The time for permanent political unity was not yet. But the processes that were to combine these several peoples into the Scottish nation were already at work.

CHAPTER ELEVEN
THE PICTS AND THE NORTHERNERS

The Picts

Half a dozen different peoples inhabited northern Britain in and before the fifth and sixth centuries. They are easily confused with one another, because Roman and Irish writers used the same words with different meanings. Earlier Roman writers regarded them all as British, because they lived in the island of Britain. Late Roman writers distinguished the British, who lived south of the Antonine Wall, between the estuaries of the Clyde and the Forth, from the barbarians beyond. They described the barbarians as they saw them, as the *Picti*, the 'painted people', because they tattooed their bodies, but they had no distinct word for the distant peoples of the north and west, whom they rarely saw.

The Irish were better informed and used more exact words. They restricted the Latin word *Picti* to the nearer neighbours of Rome, who called themselves *Albani*, inhabitants of Alba or Albion, the oldest name of Britain; and in Irish called them British, *Cruithne*. Their language, known only from the names of people and places, was akin to British and Gallic. Their ancestors had reached Britain long before the Roman period, and their principal archaeological relics are some thousands of forts, very numerous in their territory, and also south of the Antonine Wall. A scatter of forts beyond their borders, many of them destroyed by fire, witness their failure to subdue the far north-west. They were simply the British peoples whom Rome never conquered, who therefore remained barbarian.

Their language preserved a few Gallic words that are not known to have survived among the Roman British. But it was never written. The scanty records of the Picts are set down in Latin or Irish, and form no more than a small subsection within the immense body of Irish documentation. The most informative of their texts is a King List, that survives in several versions. It begins with made-up names. 'Cruidne, Father of the Picts' is 'Briton', transliterated into Irish, and his 'sons', Fib, Cat, Circin, Fortrenn, and others are the names of districts, Fife, Caithness and the rest of Pictland. Real names begin in the Roman centuries, when one king, vaguely dated to about the 3rd century, is given a name that is attested in a Roman inscription of the early 3rd century. Real people begin early in the 5th century. The first king of whom anything but the name is reported is Drust, son of Erp, who 'reigned 100 years and fought 100

MAP 11 THE PICTS

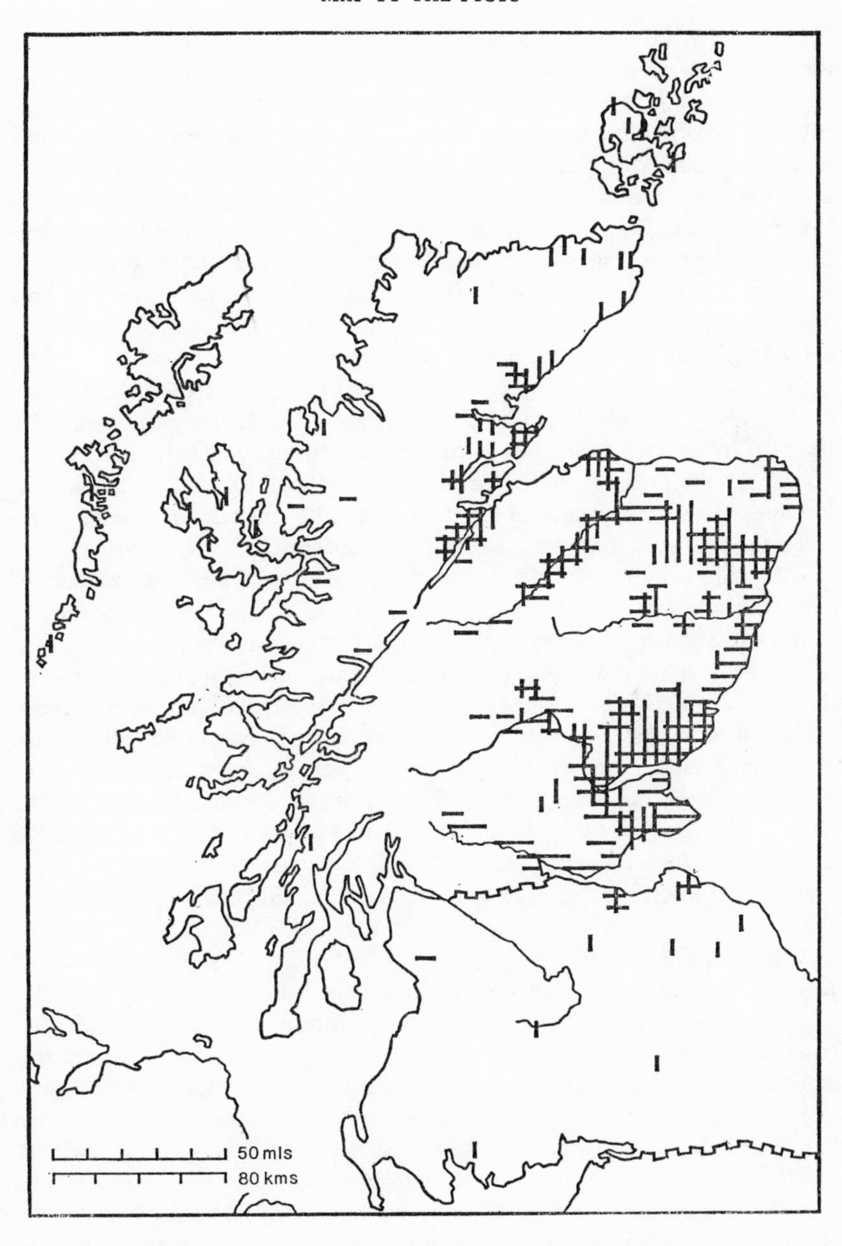

— Pictish Place Names | Memorial Stones

battles; in the 19th year of his reign St. Patrick came to Ireland'. The Irish date for Patrick places his accession in 414, and the Irish Annals also name him, putting his death at 458, after a reign of more credible length. The 'hundred battles', as in Irish usage, mean that he was regarded as a great warrior. These dates make him Vortigern's contemporary; and Gildas reports the audacious intention of the Picts to conquer and settle the rich lands of southern Britain in Vortigern's time. The name and precise dates of Drust are not elsewhere confirmed; but in his time some Pictish leaders organised a large and daring expedition on an unprecedented scale. Had it succeeded, Britain might have become Pictland. It failed; but it was the enterprise of the Picts that caused Vortigern to enlist English aid, so that in time southern Britain became England.

The territories of the Picts are well defined. They were the people of the eastern coasts and glens, not of the north and west. Their place names are confined to the lands that their ancestors had fortified and held, between the Forth and the firths about Inverness; their archaeology and their pictorial inscriptions are concentrated in the same region. But they did not form a single political unit. Their own tradition names seven principal provinces, but these provinces are a late simplification, listing the regions over which the later kings of Albany claimed suzerainty, from the ninth century onward. First-century Romans loosely described the whole of the barbarian north as Caledonia; but the Roman geographer Ptolemy recognised their dominant nation, the *Caledones*, as the people who dwelt by the Great Glen and Inverness, one among several named peoples. Later writers, from the 3rd century to the 8th, distinguish between the northerners, whose capital lay in or near Inverness, and the southern *Meatae* in Fortrenn, about Stirling, in Circinn, or Strathmore, and in Fife. Though the stronger rulers were able to command the obedience of both, the separate identities of north and south long outlived the name of Pict, and remained a powerful political force in the medieval kingdom of Scotland.

Brochs and Duns

Beyond the Picts lived several other peoples. Long before the Romans came, the western coasts and islands were inhabited by a people whose small defended strongholds are nowadays called *duns*. They may have been Irish in their speech and their remote ancestry, but they were alien to the peoples of Ireland, who knew their country by the simple geographical name of *Iardomnan*, the western lands; and they were perhaps the unnamed raiders who savaged the northern coasts of Christian Ireland in the years from 617 to 619. But the people who mastered the Orkneys built more formidable castles, called *brochs*. They are tall round towers, swelling at the base, with their habitable rooms within the thickness of the wall, that encloses open space. They were the castles of conquerors, for, on a few sites where excavated evidence outlines their history, their inhabitants moved out after a few generations, to live beside their ruins in more convenient houses that no longer needed such defences.

MAP 12 BROCHS AND DUNS

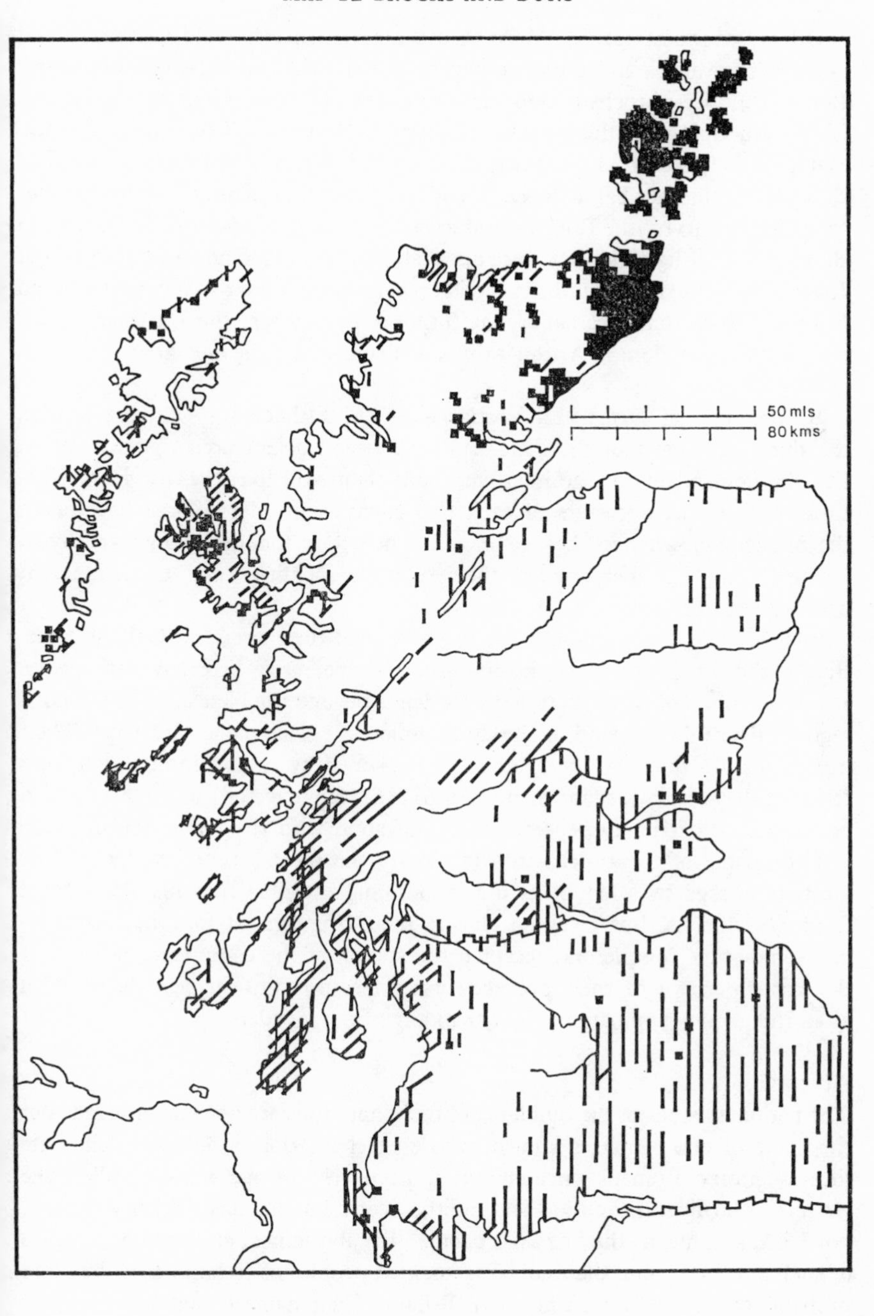

■ Brochs / Duns | Forts

Orkney conquest spread. More than a hundred brochs held Caithness, and guarded the valleys and estuaries beyond, on the west and south. In the early Roman centuries, brochs in numbers controlled Skye and the nearby coasts and islands, subduing the duns of the northern *Iardomnan*. A few reached further. Half a dozen penetrated southern Pictish lands on the upper Forth and the Tay estuary, and another half a dozen extended into the Lothians and Galloway. But they did not survive the Roman conquest of the lowlands, to Forth and Clyde, in the second century; and they were never able to invade the northern kingdom of Inverness, or the main southern Pictish regions. Nor were they ever established in the south-western headlands, the future Argyle, where the Dal Riada Scots erected their kingdom in Arthur's time, in a land where the *duns* are many.

By the time of Drust and Vortigern, in the fifth century AD, the brochs, the duns, and most of the forts had long been ancient archaeological ruins. But the descendants of the men who built them still lived beside them. Centuries before, the ancestors of each had come as invaders. Time had dulled the memory of whence they came and when, but the divisive geography of north Britain had perpetuated their separate identities and their different national languages.

In the fertile east and south the Picts retained their ancestral Gallic tongue. But in the north and west, burnt forts and the rarity of their place names attest the failure of the Picts to settle the lands beyond the Ness and the Dornoch region. There, in the land of the duns, almost all place names are Irish. Their numbers and extent are too great to be explained by recent immigration from Ireland; they imply that for many centuries the language of the north-west had been Irish, a barrier to peaceful communication with the Gallo-British Picts.

The people of the brochs were evidently the most recent invaders. Their location, backed by a few other indications, suggests that they may have come from Scandinavia, but gives no clue to their language. It may be that they, like some other conquerors, accepted the speech of the conquered, perhaps of the Irish, perhaps of their predecessors; for some signs suggest the survival of an indigenous population, older than any of the invaders.

Atecotti

The national names of the builders of brochs and duns are not remembered. But the name of one people is known, whose exact location is not recorded. Late fourth-century Romans encountered a peculiarly savage nation, called the *Atecotti*, who lived near the Picts and the Scots. The word is British or Pictish, not Irish, and means the 'very old people', the aborigines; and there is no trace of such a name among the richly documented peoples of Ireland. It is therefore probable that they lived in northern Britain. Their name is matched by a few traces of an aboriginal language. Columba met one old man who came to Skye and spoke a tongue that was neither Irish nor Pictish. Speakers of an older language also seem to have survived in Pictish territory. The Picts themselves carved many memorial stones; and incised them with pictures or symbols, not with letters. But in and near their borders are also a small number of stones inscribed in Irish Ogam characters. Yet when they are transliterated, most of their wording is gibberish, apart from a few personal names. If the characters had the same sound values as in Irish, the language is neither Irish nor Pictish nor any form of Celtic. It is an unknown language, still undeciphered, whose speakers made a brief unsuccessful attempt to express its sound in Irish characters. It is unlikely to concern the peoples of the brochs or duns, who left little trace of settlement where the stones are found. It may be the language of the aboriginal peoples who dwelt in northern Britain, before the coming of the British, and before the builders of brochs and duns, who found a brief separate identity when the barbarian nations combined to assault the Roman frontiers in the 360s, and inscribed a little of their language centuries later, when they were familiar with Pictish memorials and the Irish alphabet.

Christianity

The records of the Picts and Scots alone are preserved. They are easily misinterpreted if the existence of their neighbours is overlooked. To Roman historians, the Picts were an undifferentiated mass of northern barbarians, to be fought and feared. But the attitude of the army was not the outlook of all Romans; a significant trend in late Roman Christianity advocated that barbarians be tamed, absorbed and assimilated by baptism. Not many missionaries preached beyond the frontiers, but some worked among the Picts. Patrick, writing in the 440s, denounced Picts who were apostate from Christianity. Someone, some time before, had converted a considerable number of Picts, but in the intervening years Christianity had died out or been suppressed. The date of the mission cannot have been less than a generation before Patrick's time, not later than the first years of the fifth century.

Native tradition adds detail to Patrick's generalised statement. Bede reported that Ninian of Whithorn in Galloway had converted the southern Picts, under the inspiration of Martin of Tours. Local legends date the beginning of Ninian's preaching to Martin's last years, in the late 390s; and the places where his name was venerated extend into southern Pictland. Ninian's work was undone when Patrick wrote, in the time of Vortigern and Drust; for when the Picts combined in a national effort against the Roman south, those of them who had embraced the Roman religion are likely to have been submerged. But Christianity regained its hold. Bede knew nothing of the apostasy, and remembered only that the southern Picts, unlike the northerners, had become a Christian people well before 560. Pictish tradition gives detail. Nothing is known of Drust's short-lived successor, but the next king, Nectan Morbet, who reigned from 462 to 486, is held to have revived Christianity, receiving the missionary Boecius from Italy, and entrusting Abernethy on the Tay to Brigit of Leinster.

Nectan was a southerner, but he is styled 'king of all the provinces of the Picts'. Throughout the fifth century the King Lists acknowledge only one ruler at a time. But early in the sixth century, after the establishment of the Scot monarchy in Dal Riada, their record is troubled. It suggests that the kingdom was divided about 528; and the evidence of district names argues that the southern kingdom was overrun and colonised by Gabran of Dal Riada, between 540 and 560. Four kings are said to have died in the years 553 to 556, when Gabran's power was great.

Bridei

It was then that the Picts took an extraordinary decision. They preserved an ancient custom, long since extinct in Europe, that passed the inheritance of property and of political sovereignty through the mother rather than the father, so that no Pictish king was ever succeeded by his son. Hitherto, all their recorded kings had been sons of Pictish fathers, but about 554 they chose a foreigner, Bridei, son of Maelgwn, the mighty king of north Wales, whom Gildas had attacked. He was evidently eligible, for Welsh tradition gives Maelgwn a Pictish grandmother.

When the Picts chose Bridei, they knew who he was. His father, recently dead, had been the strongest king in Britain, 'dragon of the island'; they could reasonably hope that the son of such a foreigner might unite their own strength and draw upon outside resources to mend their fortunes. Bridei justified their choice, and proved himself the greatest of their kings. But he was not at first universally accepted. He ruled in the north, and for the first two years of his reign he is said to have shared power with another king. Welsh legend suggests what happened. At about the time of his accession, his brother Rhun, the new king of north Wales, is said to have marched a vast army to the Forth and beyond. The Welsh remembered the expedition for its unprecedented size and duration, and though they knew nothing of why it marched its context makes plain its purpose and achievement. Rhun's campaign avenged his own wrongs; but when the armies of Bridei's brother crossed the Forth, they entered the southern Pictish lands, that the Dal Riada Scots had recently invaded and colonised. Bridei was doubly strengthened; the rival Pictish king disappeared; Bridei was acknowledged for a generation as sole ruler; and in 560 his armies decisively defeated the Dal Riada Scots.

Bridei's reign brought deeper changes than reunification and the recovery of lost lands. For nearly a hundred years, religion had divided the Pictish kingdoms. The southerners were Christian, the northerners still pagan. Bridei was a prince from a Christian kingdom, and many among the northerners who invited him were disposed to accept the new king's religion. Christianity came, but later ages simplified the manner of its coming. The brief entries of the Pictish lists telescope the conversion into a headline, that

> Bridei was baptised by St. Columba in the 8th year of his reign,

and northern legend envisaged the speedy conversion of the king's subjects by wholesale baptisms in Loch Ness, much as the pagan English were converted in later times. As early as Bede's day, in the 8th century, tradition had hardened into the simple belief that 'Columba converted the Picts', and had come from Ireland to Britain for that express purpose. But the stories told by Columba's biographer, Adomnan, in the 7th century, give a more exact account. Columba spent his life among his fellow Irishmen; in thirty years, he made three or perhaps four missionary expeditions to the Picts. Nothing is said of the baptism of the king, who was already Christian. Columba received the king's support, and needed it. On his first visit to the royal fortress by Inverness, he was denied entrance; when the outer gates were opened by a miracle, the king and his 'senate' came forth from the 'house' within the fort, to meet the saint with respect. A powerful faction in the Council of the Picts was clearly reluctant to admit the emissary and the faith of their Irish enemies; and acceptance was a personal triumph for the king over the conservative elements among his subjects. But for the rest of his life, on each visit, Columba faced bitter resistance from the *magi*, the established pagan priests. He engaged with them in wonder-working contests, like St. Paul in Cyprus, or St. Patrick in Tara; he confounded the heathen by sailing against the winds, and magnified the God of the Christians in the eyes of 'pagan barbarians', when his curse repelled a monster that dwelt in Loch Ness and had overturned a boat.

The conversion of the Picts was achieved over many years by many men. Even in his old age, Columba laboured to convert individual lords, while their fellows remained pagan. He could not speak the Pictish language, and he was but one among many Irish monks whose labours among the Picts and their neighbours are reported. But he towers among his fellows by reason of his personal eminence, of the lasting vigour of his central monastery at Iona, and of his spiritual and political guidance, which the Picts and the Scots heeded, and the Clydeside British respected. In keeping the peace in the North for thirty years, he gave a new generation time to grow up free from the scars of former hatreds, able to accept the new religion, even though it was the faith of their enemies.

Bede calls Bridei an 'exceptionally powerful king'. He had no need to fight wars after the victories of his first years. The king of Orkney was his tributary, and gave him hostages. The once formidable power of the islanders was curbed, and was not again reasserted until the Norse invasions. A few Pictish monuments, in Orkney, Skye, and their adjacent coasts, with a few Pictish place names on the mainland opposite Skye, suggest that the Pictish kings installed some colonists, prefects or advisers when they subdued the islands.

Art

Secure sovereignty and the spread of Christianity gave a new stability to Pictish society, that found expression in their art. The imagination of their craftsmen devised memorial stones, depicting bold and splendid designs of abstract mathematical figures and vividly impressionistic animals. The designs plainly convey a meaning, and amount to an attempt to develop from scratch a form of pictographic writing. The attempt is itself a considerable intellectual enterprise. The artistic concepts are as original as the idea, and their execution is precise and beautifully ordered; some of the designs are also found in Irish and Northumbrian manuscripts, from the 7th century onward; and though some are imitated from Irish originals, others are more likely to be Pictish innovations that the Irish manuscripts copied. Though their beauty is shrouded by the unexciting modern description of 'symbol stones', they rank among the notable achievements of Celtic art in any age or land. The stones are difficult to date. The earliest might possibly be as old as Bridei's time, but it was under his successors that they became fashionable and frequent. They indicate the emergence of a class of notables, eminent and rich enough to acquire permanent memorials; they derive from the stability that his government engendered, and emphasise secular change. But they coincide in time with the establishment of numerous monasteries, both among the Picts and among their subject neighbours. The monasteries gave new cohesion to a people who had previously known no centres but the residence of a chief or king; they soon recruited native converts, and with the Irish language they brought literacy to a people who had hitherto known nothing of writing. The more convenient symbols of an alphabet based on Latin limited the pictorial script to the memorials of great men, but in imposing a single written language upon diverse peoples who spoke different tongues, it brought into being another powerful force that was to unify the north.

Bridei's heirs

Bridei's wide sovereignty did not endure unchallenged. In 581, twenty-five years after his accession, the Irish Annals record both the brief reign of 'Cennaleth, king of the Picts', evidently a rebellious rival among the southern Picts, and also 'Aedan's expedition to the Orkneys'. More than 200 miles of Pictish territory and Pictish waters separated Aedan from the Orkneys; if he had fought against Bridei, he could not have assaulted the Orkneys without first defeating the Picts, in a war that the full record of the Irish Annals could not have ignored. It is more probable that Aedan helped Bridei to suppress an Orkney rebellion. But the troubles in the south persisted. In 583, Aedan won a battle in 'Manaan', probably the Stirling area; his enemy may have been British, or southern Pictish, and he is again likely to have fought as Bridei's ally, for in 584 Bridei was himself killed by the southern Picts. Thenceforth, the Pictish kingdom was more loosely organised. The King Lists of the next half-century recognise only a single succession of kings, all of them sons of Picts. But the Irish Annals also record a series of notable Picts, whom they do not describe as kings; they may well have been independent lords of Inverness.

These are the years in which the Northumbrian English grew from a tiny people clinging to their coastal strongholds into the most powerful kingdom in Britain. The British, the Dal Riada Scots, and the mainland Irish combined in vain efforts to check them, but no account involves the Picts in their alliances. They appear to have made short-term gains when the English weakened their southern neighbours. The British kingdom of the Forth is not again recorded after the English victory of 603; and English settlement began to spread English place names all over the Lothians. But when the English reached Edinburgh, they knew its nearby hills by the name of 'Pictland', or 'Pehtland', now Pentland; and Bede believed that the native name of Abercorn, at the eastern end of the Roman Wall on the Forth, was its name 'in the Pictish language'. The Picts had evidently subdued the lands on both banks of the upper Forth, and annexed the former British kingdom of the Manau of Goddodin.

For fifty years more, the Picts were little troubled. The power of the Dal Riada Scots was dispersed by the incompetent ambition of Domnall Brecc, and the main effort of the English was directed against their own fellow-countrymen in the south. In 617 the Picts and the Irish received the numerous refugee sons of Aethelferth of Bernicia, exiled by the victory of Edwin of Deira, and taught them Christianity. When the British and the Mercians killed Edwin in 633, one of the sons, Eanfrith, returned for a brief inglorious reign, perhaps with Pictish help. His brothers Oswald and Oswy soon restored their dynasty, but for 20 years their authority was circumscribed by the power of the Mercians and the British on their southern borders.

The ambition of the Picts revived. In 648 they fought the chiefs of the Kintyre Scots, heirs of Aedan and Domnall; and in 652 they chose an English king, the son of Eanfrith. Their choice was a challenge, for their new king had a better ancestral claim to the throne of Northumbria than Oswy himself. But Oswy soon triumphed. In 655 he overthrew the Mercians, and in the next year the English king of the Picts died or was killed. Then Oswy overran southern Pictland. Bede reports that he

> conquered the greater part of the Picts and Scots, who hold the northern parts of Britain, and made them tributary.

The impositions of the conqueror were not limited to tribute. The Northumbrians installed an English underking, and the main territories of the southern Picts in Strathmore are thick with English place names, witnesses of heavy colonisation; the place names have not yet been studied, but their most probable origin begins with Oswy's conquest.

Beyond the conquered territory, the Picts chose an Irish king. But when Oswy died in 670, they attacked his son Egferth, and also expelled their Irish king, choosing another Bridei. The second Bridei was the son of a British king of the Clyde, and was first cousin to Egferth. A contemporary Northumbrian complained of

> the bestial nations of the Picts, who despised subjection to the Saxons, and gathered innumerable peoples from the cavities of the north.

Egferth surprised them and overwhelmed them, but Bridei survived, and strengthened his kingdom, recovering control of the Orkneys in 681. When his power grew Egferth again attacked, and in 685 set out to 'waste the provinces of the Picts'. This time, he was defeated and killed at Nechtansmere, near to the southern Pictish capital. The Northumbrians, influenced by their clergy, who were well-disposed towards their fellow monks among the Irish and the Picts, chose Aldfrith as his successor, a pacific prince, trained at Iona to esteem both Scots and Picts, who shared the clergy's dislike of Egferth's military aggression. Bridei restored an ancient kingdom. He also created the core of a larger state. He and his successors were known as 'kings of Fortrenn', and the Stirling region remained the centre of government for centuries. For, though the monarchy of Dal Riada was also reconstituted, Fortrenn long remained the dominant northern power. Unlike the kingdom of the first Bridei, it was a multilingual state, for though the English government was expelled, the English colonists and their language remained; but the continuing expansion of the literate Irish church also taught men to read Latin and speak Irish.

By the middle of the seventh century, the other nations of the British Isles were set upon their future courses, within borders that have not greatly changed thereafter. But there was as yet no likeness of the future Scotland. Both Pictish territories obeyed a single king, who held their northern and western neighbours in subjection. But the name 'Scot' was still restricted to a weak and alien Irish kingdom, and the British and the English still ruled south of the Forth and Clyde.

Yet the pressures that were to create Scotland were already felt, and the origin of the nation seems obscure unless their growth in the succeeding centuries is outlined. The Picts long retained their military supremacy, containing the Scots and breaking their armies. They were reduced, not by military conquest, but by their own archaic institutions. They did not learn to write their own language; their monumental pictographs delight the eye, but were unsuited to ordinary communications. A stronger state had greater need of written paper, and the Irish and Latin languages of its clerks and court overlaid the native speech. The new monarchy was more than a national institution of the Picts; it ruled subjects who spoke half a dozen tongues, and was increasingly tied to an Irish church that also served its neighbours.

The alienation of the monarchy from the Pictish people was accelerated by their antique inheritance custom. Powerful kings married their daughters to foreign princes; and since inheritance passed through the woman, more and more kings were sons of British and Irish fathers, born and bred abroad. The old tradition snapped in 843, when victory in civil war enthroned Kenneth Mac Alpine, by the right of female descent. Through his father, he was king of the Dal Riada Scots, and he determined that his brother and son should succeed him in both kingdoms. Though for a few generations the patrilinear dynasty of the Scots was challenged by the heirs of the daughters or sisters of past kings, it maintained its hold.

Albany

The dual monarchy permanently united the Scot and Pict kingdoms. The dynasty retained the name of Scot, but made its principal seat in Fortrenn. Its ancient home of Dal Riada became a province, known in later times as Argyle. But to Fortrenn itself, the Irish kings brought Irish political concepts and Irish notables. The king became a high king, suzerain over regional dynasts termed *mormaers*; the provinces of the northern Picts obeyed a dynasty that named its founder Morgan, and placed his lifetime soon after the foundation of the dual monarchy. His name proclaims his origin, for it is British, at home south of Forth and Clyde, whence it had passed by marriage into the usage of the Dal Riada Scots. The tradition is that Kenneth or his son installed an Irish Scot dynasty in Inverness; but continuing northern wars bound the dynasty to its subjects, and later rulers asserted the title of king of Moray, ruling the lands west of the Spey in virtual independence.

In the south, the name of the Picts passed from use. It had always been a Latin term, alien to native speech; and Latin henceforth elegantly adapted the ancient name of Britain, Albion, turning it to Albania, or Albany. The descendants of the southern Picts long declined to be known by the name of their foreign Irish dynasty; and as late as the 12th century, their battle cry was 'Alban!', not 'Scot!'. But pressures from abroad tied them to their dynasty. From the outset the dual monarchy faced fearful enemies. Six years after Kenneth's death the Norse of Dublin overran Albany; Orkney and Skye were also lost, and the Great Glen again became a frontier. Beyond, the half-Irish, half-Norse kingdom of the Isles was not securely reunited to the mainland crown until the later middle ages.

The conquests of the Norsemen revived the divisions of the Pictish past; geography imposed upon the *mormaers* of Inverness the obligation to defend Albany against the foreigner, and it compelled them to rely principally upon their own resources. But it also damped down the occasions of conflict between Inverness and Stirling. The northerners were too busy to attack the south, and the ambition of the Albany kings saw easier opportunities to the south. The Scandinavian inroads upon the English enabled the Clydeside British to extend their borders deep into the Northumbrian Pennines and also permitted the Scot kings of Albany to push far beyond the Forth into English lands. They acquired Edinburgh about 960, and the Lothians in 1018. In the same year the last British king of the Clyde died or was killed; and the grandsons of the Scot king succeeded to the government of the British and the English south of Forth and Clyde.

Scotland

The medieval kingdom of Scotland was in being; King Malcolm II of Albany was suzerain of Inverness, Glasgow and Edinburgh, and ruled well to the south of the later border. But the new kingdom was insecure, and its dynasty was destroyed by the intemperate ambition of Malcolm's grandson and successor, the young Duncan of Cumbria. He assembled the forces of his vast dominions, and asserted his authority over the king of Inverness, but was disastrously defeated by the Orkney Norse. He marched south to besiege Durham, but the English dispersed his army in an even greater disaster. The victorious Northmen invaded and wasted Albany itself, where their arms had not been seen for two centuries. The triple catastrophe drove Duncan's subjects to rebellion, and he was killed 'in youth by his own people' in 1040, six years after his accession. His infant sons went into exile, leaving none of his dynasty to succeed him. His notables offered the vacant throne to the able king of Inverness, Macbeth, whose arms had driven back the Norse invaders.

After nearly twenty years of strong and peaceful rule Macbeth was overthrown in 1058 by an English invasion. The conquerers installed the exiled son of Duncan, Malcolm III, termed Canmore, 'Big Head'. He owed his throne to foreigners, and kept it with their help; and their obsequious historians transformed Macbeth into the villain whom Shakespeare immortalised. Malcolm married Margaret, an English princess reared in Hungary, who could not stomach native manners and highland custom. Her English companions received lands and authority; the king's residence was transferred to English Edinburgh, and the Queen's English became the language of court and government. When the Normans destroyed the English monarchy in 1066, Malcolm revived his father's ambition, and sought to extend his borders by repeated unprofitable invasions of England. But he was no match for the Norman kings, and he lost his ancestors' southern conquests. In 1092 William Rufus fortified Carlisle and colonised Cumberland; when Malcolm lost his life next year in another ill-organised invasion of Northumbria, the eastern border was permanently fixed upon the Tweed, and the old Roman frontier of the Cheviots was at length re-established.

The Normans gained more than a serviceable frontier. Malcolm's subjects expelled his heirs, but they were again restored by English arms. The kings of England were now Normans, who had learnt how the castles of foreign lords might subjugate a hostile nation. Numerous Norman freebooters arrived to bolster the king they had imposed, and were rewarded with lordships that permanently fringed the lowlands, and overawed the highlands. Notable among them was Walter of Oswestry, grandson of an Armorican British adventurer who had accompanied William the Conquerer. Walter's brother William was the ancestor of the Fitzalans and Howards of Arundel and Norfolk, and Walter himself became Steward of the Scottish kingdom in or about 1136. In office for forty years, through four reigns, he moulded the form and practice of the Norman English monarchy of medieval Scotland. He was succeeded by his son. The office became hereditary, and its title became a surname, until his 14th-century descendant, the Steward Robert, acquired the throne as the first of the Stewart kings.

The monarchy was transformed into an instrument of English supremacy. Its efficiency was limited, for the conventions of Norman government encouraged vassals to defy their lords when they had the strength; and the narrow bounds of the sea and the Cheviots bred a national sentiment that warmed to kings who renounced English suzerainty. But their independence was half hearted, for they ruled by English methods and by English consent. Native lowland lords resented the new Norman nobility, but their strength was curtailed by the spread of the English language, already deeply rooted in the lowlands. English clergy were thrust upon the church, and the Irish language, once the vehicle of a superior culture, became the uncouth speech of highland barbarians. When highlands and lowlands were sundered by language, lowlanders were easily taught to fear and hate highland ferocity; and within the highlands earlier identities dissolved when the peoples of each district were subjected to the rule of foreign dynasts, and were encouraged to massacre each other in the name of artificial local loyalties. The English suborned the allegiance of king and noble by generous grants of estates, that were easily forfeit by rebellion.

But though successive kings dampened the growing national cohesion of their subjects, they could not destroy it, and could not permanently withstand its power. In spite of the kings and nobles, the peoples of the north persisted in building a common Scottish nationality, that the modern world accepts as on a par with English, Welsh and Irish nationhood. The medieval historians of Scotland ignored or denied popular feeling, save when it served the interest of authority; and have successfully kept the modern Scots indifferently aware of their own early history, still prone to clothe it with legendary romantic nonsense. But though the nation took longer to create, and has been denied a proud clear record of its origins, its unity none the less derives from the men of the sixth and seventh centuries, above all from Columba of Iona, who first taught Picts and Scots to live at peace, and fired the imagination of ordinary men, who dimly perceived a future nobler and kinder than the wars of local dynasts.

CHAPTER TWELVE

BRITISH SUPREMACY

British tradition is preserved in the same kind of sources as Irish tradition, especially in Annals, Genealogies and Saints' Lives. But the texts are fewer. The Cambrian Annals insert no more than a dozen entries of the 5th and 6th centuries, into a short transcript of the Irish Annals. The Genealogies list some scores of names from these centuries, instead of thousands. The Saints' Lives are in worse shape. Those that are preserved in Armorica conserve much 6th-century material, but most of the mainland British texts are reconstructions of the 11th and 12th or later centuries, put together after long oblivion, in which no one had cared to read or copy ancient lives. Several of their authors complain that they have had to research among illegible decayed manuscripts, and others boast that they have drawn upon sources written barbarously, of unsound morality and doctrine, and have replaced them with new works adapted to modern standards, phrased in elegant Latin. Some reproduce recognisable sections of their originals, but others modernise or omit the names of people and places.

British tradition is weak, and archaeological evidence is still slight, but contemporary evidence is strong. Gildas' invective is directed against authorities whom he and his readers knew at first hand. His judgement and his interpretation are his own, but the reality of the men, the institutions and the events is not to be gainsayed. His notions of the past are full of misunderstandings, and similar incomprehension pervades many of the texts that Nennius assembles. But they aim, in the Roman manner, to give a factual record. They too apologise for faulty sources; but they do not replace them with polished moral tales. The sixth- and seventh-century British also have a great deal of poetry. It is great literature, much of it heroic verse. Some of it is contemporary with the events it concerns, some composed not long after; some of the later poems are modernised versions of older tales, and others are rich in oblique allusion to lost poems. These principal sources are supplemented by a number of specialised documents, notably the charter memoranda of Llandaff and Llancarfan, that illuminate disconnected incidents, and have much to say of the structure of their society. The record of the early history of Britain is more uneven than that of Ireland, a torch that lights isolated patches amid the surrounding obscurity.

Gildas' Kings

Gildas first attacks the secular authorities, thereafter the churchmen. His carefully ordered paragraphs balance the enormities of kings and judges in alternating sentences, whose force is clearer when his reproaches are set forth in pairs.

> Kings Britain has, but they are tyrants; judges, but wicked ones. They terrorize and plunder the innocent; they protect and defend criminals, and robbers.
>
> They have wives, but they are whores; they swear, and perjure themselves. . . .
>
> They make war, but wars civil and unjust; they zealously chase thieves throughout the country,
>
> yet they love and reward the thieves who sit at their table; they sit on the seat of judgement, but they rarely seek the rule of right justice.
>
> They despise the humble and the harmless, but they praise to the stars . . . their military companions, bloody arrogant murderers and adulterers, enemies of God, who should . . . have been altogether rooted out, together with their very name; they keep many prisoners in their jails . . . more often the victims of intrigue than of their just deserts.
>
> They hang about the altars, taking solemn oaths, and soon after scorn them as though they were dirty stones.

The alternation contrasts the function of the king and of the judge; Gildas is outraged because the king has usurped the function of the judge, or made him his passive instrument.

The invective is a bold frontal assault upon a system of military government, maintained by *duces*, generals, who have become *reges* and *tyranni*, kings and tyrants. Critics of Gildas, then and now, might protest that he exaggerates; but they could not deny the existence of the generals and the judges, the companions and their wives, the wars, the jails and the altars. Gildas' tirade establishes beyond question the general form of the government in the generation after Arthur's death, for no man complains that the wrong people are in prison, unless there are prisons and prisoners inside them. The armies that had won the war had not been demobilised thereafter; on Arthur's death, they had become independent warbands. They, the *commanipulares*, the fellow-soldiers or military companions of the generals, were in Gildas' eyes the main cause of political disorder; and they ought to have been abolished. But the warbands persisted. Their evil conduct looms large in the tradition of the Saints' Lives, several of which categorise the notables of early sixth-century Britain as 'the kings, their companions, and the nobles'. Later, nobles and 'companions' fused into a single class; but in Gildas' day, as in the late Roman empire, they were distinct and antagonistic. Military tyrants and their retainers overbore the civil authorities.

Not all tyrants were of military origin. There is no reason to suppose that the dynasties of Honorius of Gwent, Constantine of Wroxeter, Vitalinus of Gloucester owed their origin to military commands. When central government is weak, hard-pressed cities easily accept the rule of one overmighty citizen in place of an aristocratic senate; many Italian cities did so before Rome regulated their government, and did so again in the Renaissance. Other Roman cities submitted to tyrants as the power of the imperial government weakened in the fifth century. One incident is typical. In the summer of 444, the imperial chancery was shocked at recent events in Emesa in Syria: its edict reads

> it would not have been necessary to issue this ruling, if the effrontery of miscreants were restrained by fear of the laws or respect for the imperial authority.... Valerianus, a councillor of the city of Emesa ... invaded the offices of the governor of the province, with a large force of barbarians, and had the audacity to claim the foremost place for himself, sitting at the right hand of the man in whom we have invested jurisdiction, and to whom we have entrusted the fortunes of the provincials.... Being as rich as he is criminal, he summoned the other councillors to his own house, and, to defraud the public revenue, imposed a servile garrison of his own on the revenue officials, causing great loss to the Treasury of Our Serenity.... Wherefore we sentence him to be deprived of the military belt and of the rank of *Inlustris* (Most Honourable).

In fifth-century Britain, several of the magnates who lived in Cotswold mansions were great enough to bear Most Honourable rank, and to wear the *cingulum*, the richly ornamented belt that marked high military and civil office. Their wealth and eminence made them the social superiors of the governors and gave them enormous local influence. As in Syria, some may well have openly usurped political power. In Syria, the imperial government was still strong enough to prevent a Valerianus from founding a hereditary dynasty, and Gildas attributes a like authority to the government of Arthur. But when 'all the controls' of good order were swept away, many generals and some civilian potentates openly asserted the sovereignty latent in their actual power. In Gildas' time, the local despots were a recent evil, a serious menace only in the last ten years or so. He spoke out because the governors of Britain and their staff were as hopelessly overwhelmed as the constituted civil authorities of fifth century Syria.

Gildas follows his general invective with a denunciation of five named kings, who between them ruled the west country from Chester to the Channel. Their criminal violence is not unparalleled, for it recalls the licentious brutality of the sixth-century Frank kings in Gaul, that Gregory of Tours chronicles with no less horror. Political violence was no novelty in Britain, for some of the kings are rebuked for crimes committed 'many years ago'; what was shocking was that these outrages had recently become the normal practice of governments who ruled large regions.

The kings had met resistance and beaten it down. Constantine of Dumnonia, while 'clad in the garb of a holy abbot', had recently murdered 'two royal youths', in a church and in the presence of their mother. 'Many years before' he had put away his wife; he had sworn 'never to harm our countrymen', and Gildas urges him to 'come back from your far-off haunts of sin', for 'I know full well that you are still alive'. Gildas refers to recent events well known to his readers; his allusions are not clear enough to reveal the details, but they suggest their outline. When Gildas wrote Constantine was no longer a reigning king; his whereabouts were unknown, and men might doubt whether he still lived. He had reigned years before, but had lost his throne, entered a monastery, and sworn to abstain from violence. He broke his oath; and the murder of the princes and renunciation of his wife explain the context of his offences, the bitterness of dynastic conflict.

Gildas names next Aurelius Caninus (Conan), perhaps of Gloucester, whose 'hatred of the country's peace' and 'thirst for civil war, and unjust and repeated booty' has shut the doors of heaven to his soul. He is left alone 'like a withering tree in the midst of the field', forgetful of the 'vain ambition of your father and brothers, of their death in the immaturity of youth', and hell awaits him. The third king is the greying Vortipor, tyrant of Demetia, whose life's end is now near; the evil son of a good king (Agricola Longhand), he too was 'sunk in murder and adultery', and now, after his wife's virtuous death, he had 'violated' his daughter. The charge may mean that he had married his step-daughter; other kings married heiresses, and, if his wife had a daughter by an earlier marriage, a motive is clear for so sharp an affront to the laws of the church.

Cuneglassus of north Wales had fought against man and God. Like Constantine he had put away his wife, and now he sought to marry her 'pestilential sister', though she had promised to God the 'everlasting chastity of widowhood'. Again dynastic marriage with an heiress is likely. Cuneglassus was first cousin to Maelgwn, the

> last in my list, but the first in evil, mightier than many, and mightier still in malice, profuse in gifts and in sin, strong in arms, but stronger still in what kills the soul . . . greater than almost all the generals of the British in the size of your kingdom, as of your physical stature.

Maelgwn was the 'dragon of the island', who had 'deprived many tyrants . . . of their kingdoms and their lives'. His story is told more fully.

> In the first years of your youth, you crushed the king your uncle and his bravest troops with fire and spear and sword. . . . When your dream of violent rule was realised, your longing for the right road pulled you back, perhaps because your sins then bit your conscience;

> day and night you pondered . . . the life of the monks, and then publicly proclaimed that you would vow yourself a monk for ever, before God Almighty, in the sight of the angels and of men with no thought of going back on your promise.
>
> You seemed suddenly to have broken through the vast nets that normally entangle fat bulls of your kind, the chains of royal power, of gold and silver, and, what matters more, of your own overweening will . . . when you came to the caves of the saints. How great the joy of the church our mother, if the Enemy of all mankind . . . had not snatched you from the Lord's fold, . . . with no very vigorous resistance on your part . . . to make you a wolf like himself. . . . For the rejoicing at . . . your conversion to the good fruit was as great as the grief . . . at your reversion to . . . your frightful vomit. . . . Your excited ears heard no more the praises of God, sung by the gentle voices of Christ's soldiers, nor the melodious chanting of the church, but your own empty praises, shouted by lying thieves . . . shrieking in frenzy.

Maelgwn killed a kinsman, left his throne to turn monk, and later returned to the world. The earlier events of his reign recall those of Constantine's in Dumnonia; and they happened for similar reasons. It was the custom of many British kingdoms, as of the Franks in Gaul, to partition a dead king's territory among his sons; the genealogists explain that on Cunedda's death his son Ceretic and his grandson Marianus inherited and named Cardigan and Merioneth; the north passed to another son, Einiaun, and on his death it was subdivided between his sons, Maelgwn's father, Catwallaun Longhand, and Cuneglassus' father, Ewein Whitetooth, whom Maelgwn killed. Where such partition prevailed, each strong ruler was constrained to hack his way to power through numerous uncles, brothers and cousins, before he could found any considerable state; and if he succeeded, the kingdom built on dynastic violence must again be partitioned when he died, inviting a renewal of the fratricidal wars. This fatal practice prevented any one among the generals or kings of the British from mastering his fellows and uniting his people, and was to split Wales for centuries into impotent and quarrelsome lordships, rarely able to combine against the English until one among them had first subdued his neighbours; so that success itself destroyed the loyalties to which a national leader must appeal.

The evil was new in Gildas' time. He foresaw its consequence, and repeatedly warned that the anger of the Lord would raise up the heathen against kings whose civil wars and dynastic murders sinned against man and God. The heathen English were not raised up until the year of Gildas' death, but the fatal violence of the British kings already filled their subjects with foreboding. Gildas deplores the familiar evils, repeated in Maelgwn's second reign.

> Like a lively foal, to whom any unknown place seems inviting, your boundless fury carried you over wide plains of crime, adding new

> sins to old. You renounced the proper wife of your first so-called marriage . . . and sought not a widow, but the beloved wife of a living man, not even a stranger, but your own brother's son. This uttermost limit of sacrilege bent your stiff neck . . . from the lowest crimes to crimes still lower, by an audacious double murder, the killing of the husband and of the wife you had once held yours. Then you publicly married the woman whose collusion and encouragement had swelled your crimes . . . and the lying tongues of your parasites cry . . . that the marriage is legal, because she is a widow!

Gildas spends more words on Maelgwn than on the other four kings put together; and these words express a more intimate personal feeling, the bitterness of hope deceived that reveals some trace of former affection. There is no doubt that he had been genuinely moved when the great king seemed to have put aside his earthly power and his overweening will, and the simile of the young animal roaming wide plains touches a note of sympathetic understanding. His conclusion is also personal. The other kings are formally exhorted to repentance; not so Maelgwn, for his redemption is a possibility that might have been, a chance now lost beyond recovery. To Gildas, the hope of the British people, their moral and spiritual salvation, their religious and political strength and unity, lay in their acceptance of the new teaching of the holy men, the saints or monks. The genuine conversion of the greatest prince of the age, the example of his high station and the energy of his powerful personality, could have helped that movement to transform society, to create a Britain of a new substance, strong and confident in itself, an example to the world. These were not idle hopes, for, a few years after Gildas wrote the conversion of an Irish prince, Columba, no less eminent or able than Maelgwn, was to become a principal influence in the transformation of his society. Maelgwn's defection was a bitter sorrow; Gildas continues:

> Is there a saint whose bowels do not weep at such a tale? . . . Nor had you any lack of counsel, for as your mentor you had the finest teacher of almost the whole of Britain.

The greatest teacher of the age, remembered in the accounts of several of his pupils, was Illtud; and the best remembered pupil of Illtud was Gildas himself. Gildas was much the same age as Maelgwn, and might have been his fellow pupil. Past personal friendship may well underlie his words. But Gildas had now abandoned hope of salvation through the conversion of kings, and reluctantly appealed to the people over their heads, after long hesitation,

> constrained by the religious prayers of the brethren

among whom he evidently already had some standing. He called his work

> the history of the evils of this age, written in protest and with tears.

His readers found heart and courage in an attack fearlessly directed against the 'proud and stubborn princes of this age', that concentrated upon the greatest of them all, the leader who had first inspired the reformers and then betrayed them. The book was a formal renunciation of obedience to the authority of established kings and bishops, a denial of their right to rule, delivered on behalf of the reformers. It made Gildas their leading thinker, and he retained their respect; he became the arbiter of their disputes, the architect and apologist of the theory behind their practice.

Gildas ends his attack on Maelgwn, not with a vain appeal to repentance, but in sorrow at his fate. Repentance of course is urged upon the people.

> Despise not the unspeakable mercy of God, who said 'I shall speak to the nation and the kingdom, to . . . destroy and ruin it . . . but if the nation repent . . . I too will repent of the evil that I said I would do unto it.' (*Jer.* 18, 7–8)

But Maelgwn himself is almost beyond hope. Gildas thunders

> if you listen with deaf ears, you despise the prophets, spurn Christ, and spurn me too. I am a man of little standing, and you may count me of no weight, but at least I keep the word of the prophets with a sincere heart. . . . But you have set your course, and that dark flood of hell shall roll its bitter waves fatally around you, always torturing and never consuming, for it will be too late and useless when your eyes recognise the punishment, and repent of evil.

Maelgwn was not only the greatest of Gildas' kings. Wherever the traditions of the British are remembered, he dominates his age. Lawyers credit him with judicial reforms, and the stories of the monks abuse his government. Poets who knew nothing of Gildas report the fear that his arm inspired; and his heirs prolonged his power. His son Bridei created the strongest kingdom of the north, and his other son, Rhun, who succeeded him in Wales, was able to march his national army unopposed throughout the Pennines; and a century later, the national army destroyed Edwin of Northumbria. Medieval poets called it the 'host of Maelgwn' and complimented later heroes who seemed 'of the calibre of Maelgwn'. The middle ages knew him as the *Gwledic*, the supreme 'ruler of the land', before the Welsh forever lost 'England and the crown and sceptre of London'. In his own day, he came nearer than any other of the successor kings to achieving primacy over his fellows; he failed, because his society could not revive the institution of a sovereign emperor, or even evolve a high kingship on the Irish model.

Gildas lived in the west, and named only western kings. But he mentioned others, who did not share their vices, and constituted a pious threat to evil kings.

> What are these ill-starred generals now to do? Those few among them who have left the broad way and are finding the narrow are

> forbidden by God to pour out their prayers for you, so long as you persist in evil. But if, on the contrary, you had sought God again with your hearts, it would have been impossible for them to punish you, for . . . even the prophet Jonah could not punish the Ninevites, though he greatly desired to do so.

The threat is plain, real and political. The few good rulers who cannot pray for bad kings will not punish them if they repent. The converse is implied, that they will punish unrepentant wrongdoers. With God's blessing, good kings might dethrone the wicked. The good kings are not named, but since they were not to be found among the westerners, they are to be numbered among the rulers of the north and east.

The threat did not mature. Men listened to the second part of Gildas' denunciation, directed against the clergy, and in fact reformed the church. But the praiseworthy *duces*, heirs of the last generation when men had kept their station, did not overthrow the arrogant highland tyrants. In the event, the dynasties of the western kings lasted for centuries, but the states of the rest of the country were destroyed soon after Gildas' death. The language of the British kingdoms survived in Wales and the north-west, and therefore something remains of their tradition. Elsewhere, their language died with them, and almost nothing is recorded of the sixth-century rulers of lowland Britain.

The Lowlands and the West

The political frontiers of sixth-century Britain emerged from the *civitas* states of the Roman past, sometimes swollen and sometimes dismembered by the impact of the wars and of the break-up of Arthur's empire. Most of what is known concerns the west, and its evidence must help the interpretation of the few hints that suggest the political organisation of the lands that in the end became England.

South Wales

The culture of the Roman lowlands extended into south Wales. There, two major Roman states are known, the Silures, whose capital was Caerwent in Monmouthshire, and the Demetae of Carmarthen and Pembroke. The boundary between them is not known, but it is commonly assumed, probably rightly, that the fertile vale of Glamorgan was Silurian. The name and identity of the Demetae survived; their country is still called Dyfed in modern Welsh. The state was colonised and ruled by the southern Irish while Rome still governed Britain; in Vortigern's time, Cunedda recovered Kidwelly, south-eastern Carmarthenshire, but the rest of Demetia was not subdued until Arthur's time; thenceforth the dynasty of Agricola and Vortipor ruled the kingdom for centuries.

But the name of the Silures died with Rome. During the fifth century the dominion of Caerwent, known as Gwent, was reduced to a strip of land between the Usk and the Wye. Its ruler was named Honorius, Ynyr, and the city is the only *civitas* capital of Roman Britain where the ordinary incidents of urban life are reported in texts that concern the sixth century. The future Glamorgan was known as Glevissig, and at the end of the fifth century was partitioned between several local lords, whom tradition collectively named the 'sons of Glivis'. Most of them are figments, coined from the district names of later times, but a few have tangible human names, and are named in other texts. Marcianus ruled westward from the Thaw, at the southernmost point of Wales, perhaps as far as Gower. On his east, Paulinus ruled Penychen to the neighbourhood of Cardiff, whence Gwynlliw's small territory extended towards Newport, with Etelic established in the Usk valley. These tiny lordships were detached from Gwent, and from the early sixth century they appear to have acknowledged the suzerainty of Demetia, perhaps after Agricola's conquest; for a late sixth-century writer who knew the country well gave Demetia and Gwent a common border, on or near the Usk, and a hundred years later the Englishman Aldhelm of Malmesbury equated all south Wales with Demetia. Ecclesiastical tradition concurs, for in the first years of the century bishop Dubricius ministered in both Gwent and Glevissig, but a generation later Teilo of Carmarthenshire is reported as both bishop in Demetia and in Glevissig.

These small territories amalgamated during the sixth century. Gwynlliauc and Penychen combined under the rule of the abbot-king Cadoc, and formed the nucleus of a powerful military monarchy that emerged at the end of the century, in the course of resistance to English conquest. In its later history it was several times split among heirs, reunited by strong kings who slew their uncles and brothers, and again divided; it threw off Demetian sovereignty, perhaps in 645, but it was not until the 10th century that Glevissig took its modern name of Gwlad Morgan, the land of Morgan, or Glamorgan, from an exceptionally powerful ruler.

Military monarchy developed late in Glevissig, after Gildas' time, for it was a land where Roman gentility lingered long. Medieval texts record many Roman names, and contemporary inscriptions confirm them; some old-fashioned family names persisted, like Pompeius, and Turpilius, a distinguished Italian name, rare in the provinces. Illtud inherited a mansion on a Cotswold scale, its buildings decayed, but its estates intact. The owner of another estate, near Chepstow, kept the baths of his villa in repair, and used them 'usually on Saturdays'. The stories of the monks know more of learning and letters than elsewhere in Wales, and treat of men who wined and dined in civilised comfort; Gildas' later letters defend abbots who travelled in a carriage and pair, 'because it is the custom of the country'.

North Wales

The Llandaff texts preserve the traditions of south Wales in some detail; but the history of the north rests on genealogies, supplemented by scattered

MAP 13 BRITAIN ABOUT 550
KINGDOMS, DISTRICTS AND CENTRES

British, as BATH. English, as Luton.

notices elsewhere of some of the kings they name. Only two Roman *civitates* are known, the Ordovices and the Decangi, or Deceangli, perhaps separated by the Conway. The kingdom of Powys was detached from the Cornovii of Shropshire and Staffordshire early in the fifth century, and soon the conquests of Cunedda overlaid older boundaries. Tradition also gives Cunedda many sons, some with Roman and some with native names. Other tales suggest that though Ceretic, Marianus and Einiaun may literally have been his descendants, some or all of the others are as likely to have been his subordinate district rulers. Gildas' contemporary account describes the same kind of dynastic warfare in the north as the Llandaff texts report among the kings of Glevissig. The furniture of well-to-do Roman life is much less evident than in the south, but some traces survive of civil government. One inscription, west of the Conway, roughly contemporary with Gildas, records a civil 'magistrate', and gives the country its native name of 'Venedotia', Gwynedd.

Dumnonia

South of the Severn estuary, fainter traditions outline a similar history. The *civitas* of Dumnonia is prominent in all records, but its eastern neighbours disappear, the Durotriges and Belgae of Dorset, Wiltshire and Hampshire. One remarkable earthwork suggests their history. The Wansdyke was thrown up after the late Roman period; and the name the English gave it, Woden's Dyke, implies that they did not know who made it, and found it there before they came. It runs eastward for some sixty miles from the hills opposite Bristol, south of the Avon, till it turns south to point towards Portsmouth, roughly on the former border between the Roman Belgae and the Atrebates. It defends as one unit what had been the territory of three Roman states. The stories of the wars suggest a context for their union. The late fifth-century ruler of the Belgae had enlisted barbarians, fought against Arthur and killed his ally, Gerontius of Dumnonia; and had perhaps also fought and fallen in alliance with the English at Badon. Gerontius' successor Cato is remembered in the tradition of the monks among the most prominent and loyal subjects of Arthur; it may well be that his loyalty was rewarded by the addition of the Belgae and Durotriges to his kingdom, and that the Wansdyke marks the frontier of an enlarged Dumnonia.

The South

The kings of Dumnonia were Cornovii. Their genealogies are scantily preserved, but they indicate that the kingdom was divided among heirs, as in Wales. Only the rulers of the west, where the language persisted, are distinctly remembered. But the genealogies and the Saints' Lives also name a few great kings whom they cannot locate in any part of Wales or the west. Somewhere between the middle Thames and the south coast lay the kingdom of Caradoc

Vreichvras, 'Strong Arm', who is said to have ruled on both sides of the Channel in the mid sixth century. He may have inherited some of the western territories of Cato's Dumnonia. Away from the coast, a little archaeological evidence demonstrates that in the early or mid sixth century, somebody still inhabited Silchester, the capital of the Atrebates; and dykes were dug north-west of the city, facing towards the small English territory about Abingdon.

North of the Thames, English texts record British states. In 577, the English killed three kings and took three 'chesters', Bath, Gloucester and Cirencester. The spelling of the entry is very nearly contemporary with the event. The Chronicler reports victories, and by 'chesters' he meant inhabited walled cities, not empty archaeological ruins. His words imply that the three towns were the capitals of the three kings; they may well have been heirs who partitioned a kingdom that had once been larger, including Gloucester and the Roman *civitas* of the Dobunni.

The Midlands

Further east, the English remembered that they destroyed a British army near Bedford in 571, and followed their victory by marching down the Vale of Aylesbury to the Thames. A south midland state and army existed. The Welsh poets knew a king Catraut, whose kingdom Calchvynydd, the 'hill(s) of limestone or chalk', lay to the south of Powys; one dubious text locates it between Trent and Thames; and late medieval Welshmen believed that it included the towns that in their time were called Dunstable and Northampton. Both of these towns lie within the Roman *civitas* of the Catuvellauni, whose civil capital, Verulamium, prolonged sophisticated Roman building techniques to the end of the fifth century or later; Verulamium is one of the few major Roman towns of the south-east where extensive excavation has noted no sign of fifth or sixth century English settlement; the nearest English were established around Luton and Dunstable, where the apparent signs of British military and royal power have been uncovered. If further discoveries confirm the implications of present evidence, the likely inference is that the armed forces were strategically sited near to the English villages and far from the Roman city; the magistrates of the Catuvellauni were perhaps less overawed by the power of the army than their fellows further west.

London and Colchester also show no trace of permanent English settlement before the end of the sixth century. The British of London imported a few mediterranean wares, and traded with Roman Gaul, until the Franks annexed it; and tradition gives the Roman name of Colchester to a principal residence of Arthur. Present evidence argues that both remained British. The tradition of Arthur's campaign in Lindsey implies a belief that he recovered most of Lincolnshire, and the Welsh poems prolong the independence of the Cornovii in Shropshire and Staffordshire to the middle of the seventh century. The poets sing only of their last military hero, and his warband, but recent excavation at

Wroxeter has uncovered well-built timber houses constructed in the Roman architectural tradition over the ruins of the Roman town centre, the homes of civilian British who lived in the city.

The evidence now available does little more than signal where the British lived in Gildas' time. Most of the archaeological discoveries are quite new, their meaning still uncertain; but many are the result of new methods of enquiry, that may soon show something of how the successor states were organised, and how far those in the lowlands differed from their better-known western neighbours. Already the new evidence suggests that in the lowlands men lived more comfortably than the texts make known; though Roman technology was forgotten, the men who worked in perishable materials were craftsmen of considerable skill. Their kings made war, as in the west; and the rulers of the Cornovii and of Cirencester at least seem to have garrisoned their frontiers with English federates. But, whatever the difference, all these states grew from the same political context, the final disappearance of a central imperial government and of the economy on which it had rested. Though urban life might be stronger in some towns than in others, all towns were feeble echoes of their past, full of ruins that men could not or would not repair. Though the authority of civil magistrates lasted longer in some states than in others, the power of the military was everywhere growing. Roman society was dead. The controls of ordered government were gone, and force was the only law.

The empire of Arthur had recovered and reunited almost all of Roman Britain. Though its governors, magistrates and other officials persisted into the middle decades of the sixth century, political power devolved upon military successor states, each of them small and independent, each liable to fragment by partition among heirs, each unsure of its legality and permanence, each exposed to the intemperate ambition of its neighbours. The power of each ruler depended upon his armed retinue, and upon his ability to feed his men and supply them with arms and horses. He could secure the necessary income only by extracting it from his own impoverished subjects, or by plundering other kingdoms. Since the business of an armed force is fighting, the logic of each king's immediate needs impelled him to attack his fellows. The new dynasts of Britain were as grave a threat to the peace of their countrymen as were the dynasts in Ireland. The peasant cultivator risked either the requisition of his crop and stock by his own ruler, or its seizure or destruction by the invading army of a neighbour state. Noblemen who retained some property faced the same risks, and were exposed to insult and injustice at the hands of needy rulers. Conservative opinion looked back with envy on the ancient stability of the empire, and its more recent revival by the victors of Badon. Gildas voiced their protest, calling for the overthrow of the new rulers, pleading for a change of heart among his countrymen, warning of the vengeance that the Lord would otherwise raise against them.

The North

North of the Trent, the conflicts of the late sixth century are the theme of contemporary poets, and are remembered in later English tradition. But events before the 570s are chiefly known from the genealogies. The poems identify the districts where many of the later kings ruled; the genealogies trace and date their evolution from a single Pennine sovereign, Coel Hen, Coel the Old, dated to the early fifth century. His name did not pass into living oral usage; it was transmitted in writing, and its origin is Latin, deriving from Coelius, or perhaps Coelestius. The lands ruled by his heirs comprise the whole of the region garrisoned in Roman times by the troops of the *Dux Britanniarum*; and it is possible that Coel was the last regularly appointed *dux*.

Nearly all the other people listed have ordinary personal names, and most of them are mentioned in other texts. A few are manufactured from places, but even they say something of their tradition. Coel's 'wife', Stradwawl (Wall Road) and his 'daughter' Gwawl (The Wall), named as the wife of Cunedda, confirm his date, and show that his authority was held to have extended to Hadrian's Wall.

These traditions make Coel the elder contemporary of Vortigern, ruler of the north when the English first came. Early English settlements were few in the north, confined to parts of the East Riding, to York itself, and to the forces of Octha and Ebissa, that Vortigern despatched to the 'regions about the Wall' when Cunedda moved south to Wales. One English tradition echoes a belief that the rebellion of the 440s extended to the north, and asserts that about the middle of the fifth century the Deirans, the English of the East Riding, 'separated' themselves from the rest of the north, whose only effective authority was then the British ruler of York.

The rebellion was contained, and its impact in the north was less catastrophic than in the south; the English were fewer, the wealth to be plundered was less, and the British were better armed. But it permanently disrupted one vital region. The principal English forces were stationed in the East Riding, in place of its former garrison, the 'Anticipators' of Malton, with their coastal watch-towers. They were put there because those were the rich lands that invited raiders and needed defence, the only part of the north where the comfortable landlord economy of the villas flourished. When the English rebelled, they destroyed that economy. It included almost all the known northern pottery kilns, whose products had supplied the northern forts, and Hadrian's Wall. Their production ceased, and such local wares as may have replaced them have not yet been recognised.

The rebels evidently held out for a considerable time. They were eventually subdued, for their cemeteries at York seem to have gone out of use well before the end of the fifth century, and for more than a century there is no more sign of an independent English power. The English of the East Riding stayed within the borders of two tiny regions, and the little evidence of farms and villages within them suggests that there the English and the British lived side by side, at peace after the revolt.

The first dynasty to branch off from the line of Coel is dated to the years of the revolt itself, about the 440s. The descendants of Germanianus ruled a kingdom that was probably located between Tyne and Tweed, the territory that the British knew as Bryneich, the English as Bernicia. Its Roman garrison had been overwhelmed long before, in 367, and not restored. It was replaced by a *praefectus*, commanding native forces, whose heir was Cunedda; and about the time of Cunedda's departure, English garrisons were installed. No source says whether they rebelled or not; but the appointment of Germanianus sufficed to prevent or suppress rebellion. Little more is heard of the Bernician English until the later sixth century, and their cemeteries altogether lack the grave goods of the south; no more than an occasional knife identifies a few of their graves as English, and suggests that some other similar burials and burial grounds, with no knife to prove their nationality, may also be English. Further west, not even cemeteries are known; the only traces of the early English are a few place names, several of them described as the homes of Frisians.

Germanianus seems to have been installed in the lands Cunedda left, among the southern Votadini. Their probable headquarters was the great prehistoric hill-fort of Yeavering Bell, by Wooler, inland from Bamburgh, south of the Tweed; for at its foot the English kings later established a royal centre, and the choice of so windy and uncomfortable a site is not easily explained unless it were already a centre of government. Germanianus owed his authority to Coel; and whether or not he was a blood relative, the idiom of the genealogists made him a son, because in their day authority passed from father to son. He is as likely to have been an officer commanding a force permanently detached by Coel or his successor to hold the north-west coast.

The territories of the *dux* remained intact till the end of the fifth century. Then the lands west of the Pennines became a separate kingdom, called Reged, and in the next generation it split into a northern and southern portion, roughly corresponding to the future Lancashire, and to Cumberland with Westmorland. Lancaster, or Ribchester, and Carlisle were their principal fortified towns, and southern Reged may have approximately coincided with the Roman province of Valentia. At about the same time as the division of Reged, somewhere about the 530s or 540s, the remainder of Coel's inheritance was partitioned into three kingdoms. Eleutherius of the Great Army was father of Peredur 'Steel Arm' of York; tradition characterises their armies as 'spearmen', and thereby suggests that they included a larger force of infantry than other rulers. Keidyaw was father of Gwendoleu, who ruled by the western end of the Wall, north of Carlisle, and of two other sons. Keidyaw was perhaps master of the whole line of the Wall, and divided his inheritance between his sons. The third region passed to Pabo, Pillar of Britain; one of his sons, Donatus or Dunawt, named Dent, in northernmost Yorkshire, and another, Samuel, apparently reigned in the southern Pennines. Pabo probably ruled all or most of the Pennines, and also divided his kingdom between his sons.

The authority of Coel prompted other rulers, far beyond the Roman frontier, to claim descent from him. Kynvelyn, or Cunobelinus, of Edinburgh, and Guallauc of Lennox, whose name perhaps means the 'man of the Wall region', denoting the Antonine Wall from Forth to Clyde, are both intruded into the Ceol pedigrees; but the intrusion is awkward, for in both cases the generations are misplaced, and the names of districts and peoples are transformed into persons. But the intrusions may echo early tradition, for neither of these rulers derives from the dynasties established beyond the frontier, and they may have acquired their kingdoms as allies, perhaps as dependants, of the heirs of Coel. Tradition firmly groups the three armies of York, of Reged and of Kynvelyn of Edinburgh as natural allies, who ought to fight together, and were invincible when they did; it gives their armies distinct names that may translate the titles of late Roman army units. The tradition implies a belief that Kynvelyn brought an army from York to seize and hold Edinburgh.

The intervention of the Pennine powers beyond the Roman frontier has a context in local tradition. Bishop Jocelyn's unctuous medieval Life of Saint Kentigern of Glasgow claims to be an edifying modernised portrait, strained from crude originals that the author despised and could not understand. The meaning of some of its particulars is explained by other texts, in Gaul and Britain, that treat of Kentigern and his times. It preserves a story of important change about the 540s. North of the Tweed, Votadinian territory extended to *Manau Gododdin*, the 'Manau of the Votadini', whose name is preserved in Clackmannan, below Stirling, by the lowest crossing-place of the Forth, and in a few other place names. South of the Forth, the Lothians take their name from Leudonus, who was held to have reigned in the late fifth century in the northern Votadinian capital of Traprain Law, a fortress as large as Yeavering Bell; and his descent is traced from a prefect installed by the emperor Valentinian. On the Clyde Dyfnwal, the successor of king Ceretic, the contemporary of Patrick, was the heir of another of Valentinian's prefects. Wisps of memory indicate that he was a mightier king than most, and the genealogists make him succeed Germanianus as ruler of the southern Votadini, in or about Arthur's time. A Clyde king who ruled by the Tweed as well must also have made the Lothians tributary.

Dyfnwal's enlarged kingdom did not endure. In the 540s, his grandson ruled on the Clyde, and bishop Jocelyn's sources told him that the country, which he knew by the medieval name of 'Cambria', extending 'from sea to sea, like the Wall built long ago by the emperor Severus' was seized by a king called 'Morken', aided by his arrogant subordinate, 'Cathen'. Both names are listed by the genealogists; about the middle of the sixth century, Caten was the reigning descendant of Leudonus, and Morcant Bulc was the heir of Germanianus. Both names are altogether exceptional; Caten is almost unique, and though Morgan later became and remains a much-used name, Morcant Bulc is the earliest individual known to have borne it. The tradition of the genealogies hints at what happened. Dyfnwal of the Clyde had mastered both Votadinian kingdoms; in the 540s, both Votadinian kings rebelled as allies and overran the Clyde, expelled Dyfnwal's heirs and occupied his kingdom.

Morcant's conquests were also short-lived. By about 560 Riderch Hael, heir of the expelled Clyde kings, had recovered his throne; his neighbours and allies included Mordaf, uncle of Caten, and Nud, perhaps ruler of Dumfries and Peebles, on his southern border. He is also given a fourth ally, Clytno, son of Kynvelyn of Edinburgh, the ally of York. It was plainly the interest of the rulers of York and of Hadrian's Wall to prevent the consolidation of a large Votadinian state on their northern border; and Riderch evidently profited from rivalries within the Lothian dynasty, that echo conflicts between uncle and nephew, akin to those that Gildas deplored in north Wales and Dumnonia and that the Llandaff texts report in south Wales.

The story of Riderch's restoration is reported in scattered fragments, that make no sense until they are placed side by side. The story of his wars thereafter is reported in a precise, coherent Welsh account. Elidyr, a king of the Reged dynasty, probably of Lancashire, son-in-law of the great Maelgwn of Gwynedd, sought to wrest Gwynedd from Maelgwn's son Rhun, probably about 560. He came by sea to the Menai Straits, but was killed by his landing place, near Caernarvon. He is not reported to have been aided by the York or Pennine kings, but Riderch and his northern allies sailed to Gwynedd to avenge him. They had a direct motive, for Rhun's brother Bridei had become king of the Picts; the combination of the power of Gwynedd with the hereditary enemies of the British of the Clyde and Forth was a threat to the whole north. In invading Gwynedd the northern kings might hope to forestall the danger. But the allies did not succeed. They burnt Arvon and withdrew. They had shown their striking power, and it was doubtless wise not to stay until Rhun was able to concentrate his forces.

Rhun's reply was his march to the Forth. It brought aid and comfort to his brother and the Picts. It was also a powerful and decisive demonstration of strength, a threat far stronger than a naval raid. The army of Gwynedd was an infantry force accustomed to fight in the narrow space of their native hills. Their long march became a legend among their own people, for they are said to have stayed away so long that their wives 'slept with their bondservants'. A king who could raise a levy of his subjects and keep them under arms for a long time in distant lands was beyond the reach of the smaller retinues of the northern princes. His army must have marched either by York or, more probably, by Carlisle. He is not said to have met resistance and one report argues that he did not. His route necessarily passed through Lancashire. Elidyr's son and successor was Llywarch Hen, then very young. He is widely famed as a poet, greatest of the 'amateur' bards of early Wales, but is nowhere honoured as a great warrior. Instead, he is numbered among the 'passive princes', who did not assert their fathers' inheritance. He died in extreme old age, a refugee in Powys, after the English had overrun his kingdom; but the time when his father's inheritance needed to be asserted was in his youth, when Rhun marched through his kingdom. He or his advisers evidently deemed it wiser to allow Rhun free passage than to attempt vain resistance, inviting the enemy to waste their lands.

The kings of York and the Pennines are also not reported to have intervened. They perhaps reached agreement, for Rhun is said to have married the king of York's cousin. Agreement was prudent, for Rhun's march proved him to be as powerful as his father, perhaps more so. He was military master of northern Britain from the Trent to the borders of his brother's Pictish kingdom. He left a great name. The tradition of the northern poems remembered the hosts of Gwynedd and of Maelgwn as the pre-eminent military power of the past; but in his own land, the foremost of the medieval Welsh poets, Cynddelw, described Gwynedd not as 'the land of Maelgwn', but as 'the land of Rhun'; and the Roman fort that commands the two halves of Gwynedd, Caer Rhun on the Conway, bears his name and not his father's.

Rhun appears to have withdrawn undefeated, satisfied to have shown his strength. His withdrawal floodlights the political weakness of the British. Though he was militarily supreme, he did not and could not consolidate his gains into a large kingdom, like his Irish contemporary Diarmait, or like the English kings of the next century. His army was composed of his subjects in Gwynedd, and it caused wonder that they stayed away from home as long as they did. They were not professional soldiers who could be imposed as standing garrisons upon conquered territory. Nor was there any body of opinion in the lands through which Rhun marched that could constitute a government to rule for him. The dislike of kings that Gildas voiced extended at least as much to the all-powerful stranger as to the local ruler, perhaps more so, and Rhun was heir to the hatreds that Maelgwn had aroused as well as to the armies he had trained. The British had no obvious need to unite behind a powerful monarch, for there was as yet no hint of danger from the English. The tiny impoverished Bernician population of the north Northumbrian coast, and the few small Deiran communities about Market Weighton and Driffield in the East Riding, were in the 560s still insignificant, politically and militarily. No external threat prompted a sense of national unity among the cultivators who tilled the soil of the northern kingdoms. Each of them was ruled by the 'military companions' of 'ill-starred generals'. The northern poems vividly express the outlook of faithful warriors, each devoted to the personal triumphs of their own lord, their highest duty to support him against his neighbours, their deepest disgrace to desert him. No sentiment urged them to join one another in the service of a greater captain; to do so, most warbands must first betray their chief.

The new monarchies were to become the nucleus of medieval kingdoms; but in the sixth century they were recognisably rooted in the Roman past. Arthur had restored the familiar institution of a sovereign emperor, who appointed generals and maintained a centralised civilian administration. The generals remained, but the remnants of the administration were fast fading, and the centralised authority was gone for ever. Yet the kingdoms of the generals were still bunched into groups marked off from each other by the political frontiers they had inherited from Rome. Between the Walls, the descendants of the fourth-century Roman prefects knew that they were British, alien to the barbarian Picts and Scots. The Pennine kingdoms were still grouped as descendants of Coel, joint heirs of the Roman army of the north. The political boundaries of Wales, and of the south and south-west, had been chopped and changed by Irish conquest and then by reconquest, under the new dynasties of Cunedda and the Cornovii; but the chopping and changing left some of the older boundaries intact, amalgamated some states, fragmented others, and the process of fission and fusion continued. In the lowlands, frontiers were less disturbed. Even where English settlement was dense, the borders of Kent and of the East Angles, of Lincolnshire and of the Middle Angles, did not greatly differ from the frontiers of Roman Cantium, of the Iceni, and of the Coritani of Lincoln and Leicester. Further east, the midland Cornovii and the Dobunni, the Atrebates and the Catuvellauni maintained their capitals and their identity, though most of their old names passed from memory. But the lowland states now formed a compact and distinct group. The government of Arthur had cleared the independent English from many regions, but suffered them to remain, in numbers, all along the right bank of the Trent, from Derbyshire to the Humber. But no English crossed the river. The Trent became a frontier, and its English garrison in practice shielded both their own kinsmen and the British of the lowlands from the armies of the British north.

In all the British states, the military power was dominant. Theirs was the system of government that Gildas attacked. The inbuilt pressures of the new kingdoms drove them to wars against each other, and to internal dynastic struggle. The best that could be done was to limit the frequency and ferocity of their wars. In some regions they were limited. Columba stilled the far north, and after Rhun's triumphant march, there is little to record of warfare in most of Wales and the southern Pennines. But in the north-west, the Annals and the poems report successive battles. The most celebrated was fought in 573, at Arderydd, now Arthuret, ten miles north of Carlisle, near to the Roman fort of Netherby. It was the subject of an extensive group of poems, now lost, known only through obscure allusions in much later mystic verses. Though the verses are principally concerned with the consequences of the battle, the identity of the two forces is clear. It was a battle between different branches of the Coel dynasty. The kings of York combined with Dunaut of the Pennines to destroy their cousin Gwendoleu, who ruled in the Carlisle region.

Gwendoleu was defeated and killed, but it was not the victors who benefited. The armies that marched from York to Carlisle were no more able to exploit their success than those which Rhun had led to the Forth. But when they withdrew, they left a vacuum, and nearer neighbours filled it. The principal burden of the surviving poems is the sorrow of Gwendoleu's bard Myrddin, who hid in Celidon forest, in these verses apparently the upland between Dumfries and Peebles, fearing and hating a king who favoured monks and frowned on bards. But the king he feared was not Dunaut or Peredur of York, who had fought the battle, but Riderch of the Clyde. The leader of the monks whom Riderch favoured was Kentigern, who had returned from long exile abroad and now established an important monastery at Hoddam, by Ecclefechan near Dumfries. Riderch had extended his frontiers to annex the greater part of south-western Scotland. It was the first such annexation of territory that proved permanent, for Riderch's gains laid the foundation of the large kingdom that was in the future to be known as Strathclyde. Unlike most British kingdoms, it was not subdivided on the deaths of kings, and later rulers much enlarged its dominion, maintaining its independent power until it was merged with the Scot kingdom of Albany in the 11th century.

Riderch's conquests endured, but in 573 the greatest gainer was Urien of northern Reged, whose royal residence lay close to the borders of Cumberland and Westmorland. He became lord of Carlisle, and probably also secured control of much of the northern coast of the Solway Firth. Urien was immortalised by his bard Taliesin, the earliest of the Welsh poets whose works survive. His adventurous daring won successive victories over his neighbours and made him chief among the kings of the British in the few years that remained before the outbreak of the second Saxon revolt in the north, in and after 580.

British Political Society

About 540, Gildas protested at a new and growing evil; upstart generals had usurped the functions of civil government, and they and their retainers ought to be abolished. By the time he died, thirty years later, the military kingdoms had taken root, and civil government was dead. Though some sections of the old administration were to prove adaptable, the fledgling kings of Britain had no native example to teach them kingship, for the institutions of their past embodied obedience to imperial sovereignty, and failed them when the sovereign was no more. The only available model of independent kingship was Irish, for Rome had obliterated all memory of earlier British kings. The embryo courts of sixth-century Britain reproduced something of the manners of the Irish kingdoms. Ceretic of the Clyde in the fifth century, and Maelgwn of Gwynedd in the sixth, maintained court musicians, as Irish kings kept poets and harpists, to celebrate their deeds and to embroider legends of the mythological past; and the mythology that survived into medieval Welsh tales is chiefly Irish, for little of the Celtic legends of Britain had outlived Roman civilisation. The kings housed their warriors in halls and in Roman and pre-Roman forts in the highlands; but in much of the lowlands Roman town walls afforded the equivalent of the great raths of Ireland. In south Wales and parts of Dumnonia small defended homesteads match the accounts of the little lordships of Glevissig; and one small stronghold, near Dinas Powys, by Cardiff, still bears the name of one sixth-century local lord; its thorough excavation, clearly reported, offers the best evidence yet available of how the smaller *duces* lived.

The structure of Irish kingship was hierarchical. Some of the greater British kings seem to have achieved a short-lived overkingship; Maelgwn and Rhun in Wales and the north-west, Dyfnwal and Riderch between the Walls, the Demetian kings in south Wales exercised a kind of supremacy, for which the later Welsh coined the word *Gwledic*, ruler of the country; such authority might have matured into a superior kingship, if successive generations had had time to consolidate it; and it may be that some of the kings of Dumnonia and of York exercised a similar regional supremacy. But its growth was hindered by the custom of divided inheritance. The Irish royal hierarchy turned upon their practice, similar to that of the Goths in Europe, of passing an undivided territory to one member of the dynasty; and some of the Irish kingdoms passed from father to son in many successive generations. British practice varied. Some of the greater kingdoms most open to Irish influence, Demetia, the Clyde, and Gwynedd after Maelgwn, adopted the Irish model, but in most of the smaller kingdoms British heirs, like the Franks in Gaul, divided their inheritance, and with the same result; a king who tried to bequeath or to inherit an undivided realm was liable to be challenged to battle by outraged relatives, whose claims were approved by public opinion. The consequent repeated changes in the size and power of lesser states prevented the formation of any regular hierarchy below the greater rulers; though some came near to the status of Irish provincial kings, they could acknowledge no sovereign superior, and could not organise the local kings below them.

But the British kings did not acquire their revenues in the manner of the Irish. The Roman past offered a better model. Like the Irish kings, Maelgwn and other British rulers levied a tribute of cattle, corn and other dues. In Ireland each lesser king was required to deliver dues to his superior, and to receive gifts in return. Payment depended on continuing loyalty, and loyalty was enforced by obliging the lesser king to deposit one or more of his sons as hostages at the court of his superior. The British kings found more efficient means of levying tribute; the stories of the Welsh monks are stuffed with dramatic miracles whose occasion is the visit of royal officers demanding tribute and maintenance for their men.

The laws of medieval Wales detail the functions of such officers, and some of them are recognisably Roman. Late Roman military commanders were entitled to receive fixed quantities of *annona*, supplies and maintenance, whose collection was supervised by *erogatores*, armed with warrants authorising the requisition of stated commodities from named villages. In fifth-century Gaul the Goths were billeted on landowners by Roman law, and received *annona* also collected by *erogatores*. In Gaul and Italy, the title and the function of the *erogator militaris annona* long outlasted the days of the emperors; and in fifth-century Britain

Gildas describes the supplies due to the English federates by the technical term *annona*. There is little doubt that in Britain too they were collected through *erogatores*.

In medieval Welsh law the revenue officers were termed *Cais*. The word is formed from *ceisio*, to ask, seek, search for, and is the linguistic equivalent of the Latin *erogator*, 'a person who asks' for revenue on behalf of the state. Like the *erogator*, the *cais* visited each district in turn to collect its stated tribute, in a circuit called *cylch*. The tributes were those which the Saints' Lives condemn, a 'cornage' of miscellaneous foodstuffs, with a cow payment, and *dofraeth*, billeting and maintenance. But the Welsh system is not confined to Wales; it persisted until the 12th century throughout northern England from Cheshire to Northumberland and Durham, and in the Clyde kingdom, and was accompanied by much Welsh land tenure. The term *cais* was commonly Englished as *Keys*, or was translated by 'serjeant'; and the serjeant made similar circuits, collecting cornage, cowgeld and maintenance.

The elements of the system are simple, and might naturally arise in a simple society. But they differ radically from the practice of the rest of England; and when identical customs and identical terms are found in Wales, northern England and southern Scotland, then it is evident that their origin dates back to a time before these territories were separated from each other by English conquest, in the late sixth century. They already existed within a hundred years of the days when *erogatores* collected *annona* for the army that Coel commanded in northern Britain. It is probable that Coel and his heirs continued the fiscal system of the late Roman army, and thereby provided a model for other British kings to imitate.

The pale image of a Roman financial administration was no new burden to the north, for the north had always fed an army. But in the rich lands about the lower Severn something of the sophisticated life of Roman country gentlemen had escaped the furnace of the wars; there the imposition of tribute by an arrogant military tyrant from the mountains of Snowdonia seemed outrageous. Gildas spoke for civilised men who were disgusted by the theatrical violence of unrestrained military rulers. Protest was keener in south-east Wales, and across the estuary in north Somerset and beyond, areas where Roman practice lingered, and where the new monarchy was still weak and undeveloped. Demands for tribute turned a generalised resentment into a personal grievance. The stark brutality of the kings destroyed even the remnant of ancient virtue that Arthur's victory had salvaged from the wars. Royal exactions hit landowner and tenant alike; royal corruption of justice threatened the liberty of both, and royal control of venal bishops degraded their church.

Protest grew quickly stronger during the 530s. Its pressure impelled Gildas to write; and he explains his hesitation.

> I deplore the general dissipation of the good, and the mounting force of evil. . . . I have kept silent for ten years or more, aware of

> my own inadequacy. . . . Can I tell myself that it is my business to withstand the violent assault of the torrent, the all-pervading rope of crimes tautened over so many years? But 'there is a time to keep silence, and a time to speak', . . . and I have yielded to the pious entreaties of my brethren.

Gildas' manifesto focused the grievances of many men, and resentment exploded into a mass movement. Gildas denounced the evils of society in the hope that men might be stirred to remedy them. But his readers did not share his optimism. In Britain, as elsewhere, there had long been a few who admired and imitated the principle and practice of the monks of Egypt, and withdrew from a corrupt society to seek personal communion in the desert with their God. In the years immediately after the publication of Gildas' book tens of thousands followed their example. Men left their homes to settle elsewhere, away from the dominion of the tyrants, either overseas, or nearer home, under the protection of holy monks; and the weight of public opinion compelled tyrants to respect those whom the monks received. The movement matured soonest and strongest in the lower Severn lands. It was not confined to those who took monastic vows. They were its centre and its impetus, but numerically they were few; the monks who moved were accompanied by men of property and standing, and by large numbers of harassed cultivators. Gildas expressed the contempt and anger that men already entertained for governments shown to be criminally irresponsible. His readers did not undertake its reform. They wrote it off as sick beyond hope of recovery, and abandoned it to its fate.

The Plague

The enfeebled economy of Britain was wasted by the great plague. The pestilence killed Maelgwn about 550, and many monks and kings in Britain and Ireland are reported to have died of the infection at the same time. It was bubonic plague and was the central disaster of mid sixth-century Europe and the mediterranean. It began in Egypt in 541 or 542, and reached Constantinople in 543, whence it ravaged 'the whole Roman empire'. Gregory of Tours, then a child in the Auvergne, narrowly escaped infection in November, probably of 544; he records its sweep through central and southern Gaul in 544 and 545, naming places that lie along the trade routes to the upper and middle Rhine, but neither he nor any other writer extends it to the lower Rhine, or to northern or north western Gaul. The Irish Annals put the first outbreak in Ireland in 544, but assign the heaviest mortality to its backlash, the relapsing fever called the 'Yellow Plague', at its worst in 550 and 551. The traditions of Brittany report it as much less severe in their land, for they have several stories of plague refugees who came to Brittany for safety, and others of earlier British immigrants who hurried home to help their distressed countrymen in Wales and Cornwall.

The geography of the plague in Europe shows the way in which it reached Britain. Contemporary notices tell incidental stories of sea-borne trade between western Britain and Europe and the eastern mediterranean in the sixth century. An Egyptian Saint's Life concerns the voyage of a merchantman that imported lead from Britain, presumably from Cornwall or the Severn estuary; central Ireland imported wine, and a ship of Gaul brought news of Italy to Kintyre; vessels of Nantes were regularly 'engaged in the Irish trade'; though many of the saints who sailed abroad are made to float on leaves and stones, others are prosaically recorded to have paid their fares to commercial shipowners. The archaeological evidence matches the texts. Several details of the style and wording of British inscriptions argue influence from central Gaul and the Bordeaux area. A number of excavated monasteries and royal residences in south-western Britain, Ireland and south-western Scotland contained pottery imported from Egypt and southern Gaul. It is evident that the ships which brought the pottery and the wine also brought the rats that spread the plague.

The plague hit the Irish and the British, but not the English. Texts and archaeology explain their immunity. Gildas emphasises that the British were altogether unable to visit the shrines of martyrs 'because of the unhappy partition' of Britain; the British did not journey into English areas. The silence of the Saints' Lives concurs. A couple of Irish stories record Irishmen who preached to pagan Saxons, both of them before the outbreak of the plague; there is little record of British monks among the English except for a single journey, placed in the 590s; and thereafter several continental writers record their astonishment, at the extravagant refusal of the British to have any dealings with the English, refusing even to dine or lodge with them in Rome, or when they met in Britain. Gildas shared their attitude; it never occurred to him that the British should attempt to convert the heathen; instead, he sighed for a Gideon to exterminate them.

The English escaped from infection from the British, because the British refused to have contact with them. They escaped infection from Europe because they did not import from plague-infected areas. What trade they had is indicated by their grave goods; their imports were the ornaments and weapons of northern and north-eastern Gaul, and of the Franks of the lower Rhine. These are the regions which Gregory omits from his account of when and where the plague was rampant. The lack of contact cannot of course have been absolute, but there is no reason to suppose that the disease ever took hold upon the main body of the English. Their simpler life offered greater immunity, for, as an acute contemporary observed of 6th-century Africa,

> plague favours war and does not harm the rough races.

There it spared the Moors and devastated the Roman population. In Britain and Ireland its impact burnt itself into the memory of later ages. It was plainly as crippling and weakening as it was in southern Gaul and in the mediterranean, and there it wasted the population on a scale that compares with the plague of 1348. In Britain it infected a people who were already enfeebled and dispirited by the decay of their political government. It was the prelude to the second rebellion of the English. But it was not the cause of the British collapse, for other societies survived fearful pestilence, then and at other times. At most, the plague hastened the dissolution of states that were already dying of a deadlier disease, the rotting of their own society.

CHAPTER THIRTEEN
BRITISH COLLAPSE

The South

The second Saxon revolt did not mature until the 570s, but its first stirrings began immediately after the plague. The Saxon Chronicle reports that Cynric put the British to flight at Salisbury in 552; in 556 he fought them again at Barbury, thirty miles to the north, near Swindon, but no victory is reported, and he is not said to have advanced further. English tradition is sharp, and sure of its names and dates, for the entries in the Saxon Chronicle begin to be confirmed by other evidence from the middle of the sixth century. The dates, though still approximate, are reckoned backwards from the living memory of a literate age and are no longer dependent upon a mistaken date for the landing of Hengest and Horsa. But tradition still had no clear idea of the meaning and context of the events it chronicled.

The Saxon Chronicle naturally took Cynric for an Englishman, and was substantially right, for his men were English. But his own name is Irish, and so is his successor's; for the same two names occur together on an Irish inscription from Wroxeter, that was probably erected a generation or two earlier in honour of other people of the same name. Cynric may or may not have been a son or grandson of his Irish namesake, but the men who served under him were not Irish. A small English population had lived in eastern Hampshire since the fifth century, and the ornaments in their graves indicate that many or most of them had come from Sussex. A few of their cemeteries came into use in the immediate neighbourhood of Salisbury towards the middle of the sixth century, perhaps some decades earlier than 550; and their ornament soon spread to East Shefford in the Berkshire Downs, 15 miles to the east of Barbury. But it did not yet reach north of the Downs to the English of the middle Thames.

The circumstances that caused an Irish general to lead the English to victory over the British are not known. But they pose no problem. The fifth-century English who had settled near Winchester were suffered to remain in Arthur's time, probably within an enlarged Dumnonia; and the British ruler of Winchester was free to entrust the command of his armies, Germanic and native, to a commander of Irish or any other nationality, and to use them against his neighbour at Salisbury when the Dumnonian kingdom fragmented like other British states in the earlier sixth century. Cynric's victory may have been gained on behalf of one

British ruler against another; or he may have overthrown and replaced his British king, as generals before and since have overturned the governments they served.

At the time, Cynric's campaign may well have seemed no more than another incident in the civil wars that Gildas lamented. But when the victorious army was English, the state soon ceased to be British; and in 560 the command passed to Ceawlin. He is remembered as the first conquering overking of the southern English, but at first he did not attack the British. In 568, he fought in alliance with Cuthwulf, or Cutha, whom the evidence of genealogies and of archaeology seems to locate as leader of the Eslingas of south-western Cambridgeshire. The allies drove back Aethelbert, the young king of Kent, who had tried to break out from his ancestral borders beyond the Medway. His objective is not stated, but it was plainly London. They defended the city against the armies of Kent, but their victory made them military masters of the London region. Yet they did not exploit the victory to establish English colonies in or near the city; for English burial-grounds of the middle and later sixth century are plainly recognisable, but none have been found amid the enormous mass of archaeological material discovered in London and its vicinity. Half a dozen chance finds suggest that a few individual Saxons from Mitcham and Croydon visited the city in the 5th and 6th centuries, some of them perhaps admitted as residents. But their territory is marked by the cemeteries placed near to their homes, and when they expanded their new homes reached south into the Downs, not northwards to the city, for they sought easy agricultural land, not to be found in the London clays and gravels. They too were numbered among the allies of Ceawlin and Cutha, for the ornamental styles favoured in their territories are common in Surrey, whose people were still strangers to the fashions of Kent. London came within the control of English rulers and English armies, but it was not yet peopled with English-speaking inhabitants.

English ambition was directed elsewhere. The Chronicle records that in 571 Cuthwulf routed the British of the midlands, at or near Bedford. His victory mattered more than Cynric's local gains in Wiltshire twenty years before, for he destroyed a once-powerful kingdom, and opened the whole of the midlands to the free movement of the English. He immediately marched down the Vale of Aylesbury to the Thames, where the English of Abingdon had lived for almost 150 years, a small isolated people, surrounded by large territories in which no English had hitherto been able to make their homes. Cuthwulf's arrival liberated the Abingdon English, but he did not become their king. The Thames-side towns that he is reported to have taken, Eynsham and Benson, lie outside their borders, on the opposite bank of the river, as does north Oxford, where he appears to have been buried. He died in the same year, 571, and was succeeded by Cuthwine, also called Cutha for short, who continued in alliance with Ceawlin, and with the Abingdon English. They were known as the *Gewissae*, 'federates' or 'confederates', but they ultimately accepted the national description of Saxon, probably because it was the word used of them by their British neighbours.

The allies marched west, and in 577, at Dyrham, seven miles north of Bath, they killed the British kings of the lower Severn, and took Bath, Gloucester and Cirencester. Badon was avenged, not far from the old battlefield. A second major British territory, formerly the *civitas* of the Dobunni and the *colonia* of Gloucester, was destroyed for ever. Cirencester became English. It had been ringed by English villages for a generation or more; but there was no longer a British king for their inhabitants to defend or threaten. Before the end of the century, not long after the battle, an English warrior was buried within the city, and a few other scraps of archaeology attest the advent of an English population. But beyond the Cotswold escarpment there are no signs of English settlement, in Gloucester or Bath or in between, for another half-century. If any government replaced the kings who fell at Dyrham, they left no trace; and it may be that there was a long interregnum between the end of British rule and the establishment of English authority. The cities are not heard of again for nearly a hundred years; then, when English kings founded monasteries within their walls, Gloucester had a population of 300 families, about 1,000 persons. Nothing is said of their language, but there is little reason to suppose that many of them yet spoke much English.

Ceawlin's campaigns did not stop at the Severn. In 584 he fought the British at 'a place named Fethanlea', and his ally Cuthwine was killed. He is said to have taken many places and much booty, but to have come home 'in anger'. There was a field called Fethanlea near Banbury, but other sites are possible, and include Hereford. But wherever the battle, a strong British and Irish tradition remembers a vigorous English campaign beyond the Severn in the years about 580; and no tradition, British, Irish or English, knows anything of English armies in that region at any earlier time, or for many years thereafter.

A number of independent stories describe the English invasion. In Leinster, in south-eastern Ireland, the Life of Maedoc of Ferns relates that when he was a pupil of David in Demetia

> the English raised a great army and came to Britain. . . . The British assembled quickly against them, and sent to David, to ask him to send them Maedoc. . . . Maedoc came . . . and, since the British were engaging battle ill prepared, Maedoc . . . prayed to God for the British against the English; the English were forthwith put to flight, and the British pursuit lasted for seven days, with great slaughter.

David's death is placed at 589; Maedoc was his pupil for some years, between about 575 and 585.

Another Irish Life recounts the active help of Finnian, a life-long companion of Cadoc at Llancarfan, in the vale of Glamorgan.

> The Saxons invaded and wasted the land of the British. When they were encamped in a valley between high hills, the British besought

> Finnian to pray to the God of Heaven against their enemies. The man of God . . . went to the Saxons and urged them to return home without attacking other peoples. When they refused, the man of God returned to his own side, and said to the British, 'Let us go round the hill tops that surround the enemy with my staff'. . . . The sequel was marvellous, for the high hills are said to have poured down upon the enemy, so that none of them escaped.

The English, unused to the terrain of Wales, were evidently not yet alerted to the danger of falling boulders prised loose by British staffs. The story carries no close date, save that Finnian was not greatly younger than Cadoc, who died about 580, and did not long survive him.

Cadoc was the principal saint of Glevissig, roughly identical with the later Glamorgan; and is also said to have been the secular ruler of its eastern portion. It had been a land of small lordships, too weak to withstand invasion, and found itself defenceless before the armies of Maelgwn, and hard-pressed by the kings of Brecon. In his last years Cadoc is said to have found the secular government too much for him. He

> prayed the Lord to grant him a king, who should rule his people for him, and Mouric, son of Enhinti, was granted him.

Mouric is exceptionally well recorded, in the Llandaff and Llancarfan texts, and in the genealogies. Enhinti was sister to Urien of Reged, who was then at the height of his power, conqueror of Powys, his armies dominant from the Cheviots to the borders of Gwent. Southern Welsh tradition links the new kingdom with the dynasty of Budic of Quimper, in Armorica, and names Mouric's father, Theodoric. Theodoric, son of Budic, bore the name of Arthur's naval commander, who was perhaps his grandfather. The younger Theodoric was a contemporary of Gregory of Tours, who reports that after spending most of his adult life in exile in Britain, he briefly regained his throne in advanced years in 577. In selecting Theodoric's son, Cadoc chose wisely. The new king was heir to a name already famous on both sides of the Severn Sea, and was also nephew to the most powerful king in Britain; but he was not a native of his new kingdom, and was free of the jealousies that must hamper any local lord elevated above his fellows.

Mouric was installed because Glevissig was threatened by British neighbours, but he soon faced a deadlier enemy from the east. The Llandaff texts tell the story.

> King Theodoric . . . commended the kingdom to his son Mouric, and undertook a hermit's life among the rocks of Tintern. While he was living that life, the Saxons began to invade his country, against his son Mouric.

An angel bade him leave his cell to aid his people, and promised a victory, after which the enemy will not dare to attack this country again for 30 years, during your son's time.

Theodoric was mortally wounded at Tintern Ford, by Brockweir on the Wye, while Mouric pursued the defeated army. When it is freed from its turgid 12th century presentation, the story fits the age; Bede tells a similar tale of king Sigbert of the East Angles, who commended his kingdom to his son half a century later, and was recalled from his cell to aid his people against pagan Mercian invaders.

The Irish and Welsh tales describe the repulse of an English invasion that reached at least as far as the Wye in the early 580s. The English report a westward invasion that began with the battle of Dyrham in 577 and ended with a withdrawal 'in anger' in 584. It is likely that the two versions report the same invasion, that it was Mouric who defeated Ceawlin by Tintern; the various stories do not necessarily all concern the same battle, and there were doubtless several engagements during the course of the war. But the British victory was decisive. The Wye remained and remains the frontier, save for the administrative eccentricity that has treated Monmouthshire as part of England for several centuries. Both the English and the Welsh report no wars for a generation after 584. The Welsh prophecy, made after the event, implies a belief that there were no more attacks for 30 years. The next English report of a battle against the Welsh is dated to 614, exactly 30 years later; that battle was fought against Dumnonians, near Axminster on the Devon–Dorset border, but the Dumnonians and the south Welsh were evidently both attacked together, for the next Welsh report of English wars is an account of an English defeat between Monmouth and Abergavenny, at the hands of king Idon of Gwent, probably in the first years of the seventh century.

Ceawlin's power soon crumbled, and though the 7th-century West Saxon kings overran eastern Dumnonia, they made no inroads into Wales, and were overshadowed in England by the Mercians. But Mouric's kingdom grew great. He began as the local ruler of eastern Glamorgan, probably accepting the status of an under-king within the dominion of Demetia, whence he summoned help against the English; for when the monks sent Maedoc, their king is likely to have sent troops. The Llandaff grants trace the expansion of Mouric's power after his victory. He married the daughter of the king of Gower, and inherited her father's kingdom; towards the end of his reign, the dynasty of southern Gwent disappeared, and his son became king of Gwent, evidently under his father. Though Mouric's kingdom was partitioned on his death, it was speedily reunited by his able and ruthless grandson Morcant. In his time the dynasty of northern Gwent, known as Ercig or Archenfeld, also disappeared, and so did Demetian supremacy; the entries in the Cambrian Annals that record the 'overthrow of Demetia' in 645, and the 'slaughter in Gwent' in 647, perhaps record his victories.

In Morcant's time, control of the lower Severn passed from the West Saxons to the Mercians. Like other Welsh kings, Morcant seems to have been the ally of Mercia, and the enemy of the West Saxons, attempting when he could to recover the lost southern chalklands. In 652 the West Saxon king fought at Bradford-on-Avon, near Bath, against the Mercians or the Welsh. The Dumnonians long held much of Somerset, and when Mercian power was briefly broken in 655, they are said to have been reinforced by British refugees from Lichfield. When the Mercians regained their independence in 658, the British attacked the West Saxons, and probably reached Selwood, barely 25 miles from Salisbury, before they were driven back. The British army may have come from Dumnonia or Glevissig or both; but in 665 the Cambrian Annals record the second battle of Badon and the death of Morcant. They do not say who fought or won the battle, and do not explicitly assert that Morcant fell there. But the record of the half-century from 614 to 655, with two battles near Bath and a British advance towards Salisbury, implies a determined effort by Morcant and the Dumnonian kings to join forces and regain control of the south-west, whenever such attacks did not involve war with Mercia.

Attempts at reconquest failed, and are not reported under Morcant's successors. But the British checked the English advance. Western Dumnonia, modern Cornwall, retained its independence until the Scandinavians came. Morcant's kingdom lasted longer, and lived at peace. His son ruled it for many years without division, and without record of foreign war; though his grandsons partitioned their inheritance, they are not reported to have fought each other, and the last of them lived on until 775. Their long peaceful rule gave their territory an enduring unity. Gwent survives, under the modern name of Monmouthshire, and Glevissig received from a later Morcant its permanent name of Glamorgan. The dynasty of Mouric and Morcant retained for their people one part of the fertile lowland of Britain, the land where Roman letters and Roman manners lingered longest, where Gildas and the reformers had been bred; and their heirs preserved it from annexation by the conquering English.

The North

The story of the south is pieced together from a few perfunctory English annals, supplemented by fragments scavenged from the luxurious legends of Llandaff. The conquered vanished silently, for Ceawlin and his allies permanently destroyed the southern British states within a decade. The capture of Gloucester separated Wales from Dumnonia, and both were effectively contained from the end of the sixth century. The British of the lowlands accepted defeat sooner and more completely than their northern neighbours. Over the next few centuries they abandoned their ancestral language, and absorbed the culture and the speech of the conquerors. The memory of their defeat died with their native speech. But the northerners long retained their language, and clung proudly to their memories, crying their disaster to the heavens in the earliest and noblest vernacular verses of medieval Europe. The lands where civilised Roman life had been most deeply rooted more readily forgot that it had ever been; but the poorer hills, where the rough new monarchies grew strongest, made their defeat the proud foundation of their future nationhood.

The ruin of the northern British and the triumph of the Northumbrians in the late sixth century are described in sources of a quite different kind. The kingdoms of north Wales and of the Clyde received refugees from the Pennine states, who brought with them their poets; posterity preserved their verses in the lands that sheltered them. It is therefore the record of the British that is full, much of it written quite soon after the event, the record of the English that is twisted, broken and distorted, set down long afterwards by men who did not understand what they reported. But the Welsh poems are hard to interpret, precisely because they are contemporary, for the poets took for granted the knowledge that they shared with their readers, without explanation.

The old Welsh poems are of three main kinds. Some, notably the *Canu Taliesin* and the *Canu Aneirin*, are probably of the late 6th and early 7th centuries, and much of the surviving texts are quite possibly the work of the poets to whom they are ascribed; others, particularly the *Canu Llywarch Hen*, are in their present form not earlier than about the 8th century, but include poems that may be modernised versions of older originals; the third and largest group consists of much later poems, full of mystic prophecies, which allude obscurely to older poems that have not been preserved.

Good modern critical editions have been published of the Taliesin, Aneirin and Llywarch poems, and of a very few others, but the text and introduction, notes and commentary are usually available only in modern Welsh, not yet translated into English. Most of the other poems have been published, but only in facsimile or diplomatic form, without critical discussion. Translations of varying quality are available for a few scattered verses from some of the main texts, but none of the longer poems has yet appeared in any but a literal translation. Consequently, a number of the important problems of the texts have not yet been resolved; for a translation with adequate commentary must face historical problems that a literal rendering or a linguistic commentary in Welsh can afford to overlook.

It is therefore not yet possible to make full use of the abundant information about the last age of independent Britain that is embedded in these poems. They deserve and urgently require full study and proper publication, not only as sources of historical information, but because they are the earliest literature written in a living European language, apart from Greek. They constitute one of the chief glories of Wales; but they remain a private and neglected glory until they can be understood and appreciated by men of other speech.

The Saxon rebellion in the north begins with Ida, king of the Bernicians, who lived by the northern coasts of Northumberland. A text preserved by Nennius brackets him with Maelgwn, allots him a twelve year reign, and states that he 'joined *Din Guayrdi*, Bamburgh, to Bernicia', and was opposed by

Outigirn, who is otherwise not known. The Saxon Chronicle therefore enters him at the date the British assigned to Maelgwn, 547, and later versions explain that Bamburgh was built by him, fortified at first by a stockade, thereafter by a rampart. Revolt began with the seizure or construction of a coastal fort, probably between 550 and 570.

Urien

The praises of Outigern, and doubtless of his wars with Ida, appear to have been sung by the poet Talhearn, whose works do not survive. Late verses preserve allusions to poems that described the battle of Arthuret in 573, but the oldest extant poems honour Urien of Reged, who emerged immediately thereafter as the most powerful of the northern princes. In verse, and in the brief entries of Nennius, Urien stands out as the greatest and best-loved prince of his age, chief of the thirteen kings of the north. He is said to have fought on the Clyde, and also to have captured Solomon of Powys, who lived on to die at Chester in 613; his cousin Llywarch is represented as his constant ally, and his arms threatened Calchvynydd 'in the south'. These notices make Urien supreme in the west from Galloway to Shropshire; and his nephew Mouricus was installed as king in Glevissig, on the Severn Sea.

Urien was more than a king who overawed his fellows; he is celebrated as the one British king who organised his neighbours against the English and beat them soundly. He is well remembered because his bard was Taliesin; and Taliesin acclaims him

Urien of Echwyd — most liberal of Christianmen
Much do you give — to men in this world
As you gather, — so you dispense
Happy the Christian bards — so long as you live. . . .
Sovereign supreme — ruler all highest
The strangers' refuge — strong champion in battle.
This the English know — when they tell tales.
Death was theirs — rage and grief are theirs
Burnt are their homes — bare are their bodies.

The poem, like most that Taliesin addressed to Urien, ends with a signature:

Till I am old and failing
In the grim doom of death
I shall have no delight
If my lips praise not Urien.

These words were probably written while Urien was still alive, and are the oldest living European literature. The idiom is impressionistic, altogether alien to the imagery of English, or of Greek and Latin poetry. It appeals to the ear and the emotions rather than to the eye and the understanding. A line of two or three long words outlines a figure that a Latin or Germanic poet describes in a stanza;

and the resonance of the individual syllables observes a musical notation as strict as the harpist's. The structure of the English language admits no comparable use of words; and translation cannot therefore do more than hint at the force of the original.

Taliesin's poem was written late in Urien's life, when the English had become his main enemy. But in the early 570s, when Urien grew great, the British were still preoccupied with wars against each other, and Urien's rapid victories earned him enemies. The northern English were not yet seen as a greater menace, for they were still confined to their small settlements, tucked away on the north-east coast between Tyne and Tweed, remote from the main centres of British power. Their earlier history is obscured, because the southern editors of the Saxon Chronicle thoroughly misconceived northern history. They treated the two widely separated regions of Deira and Bernicia, the East Riding and the north-east coast, as though they were already the single united Northumbria of later times. They therefore tidied up the distinct records of the two peoples into a neatly dated scheme, that made Aelle of Deira the successor of Ida of Bernicia and the predecessor of Ida's sons. Its confusions persist because the Saxon Chronicle is easy reading, and tempts the uncritical historian to brush aside the evidence that contradicts it.

But the northern evidence is strong enough not only to show that the Chronicle is wrong, but to outline the history it distorted; for other records give the context in which the Welsh poems are set. The Cambrian Annals were better informed than the Saxon Chronicle; so were Bede and his contemporaries, and among them were the authors of the northern genealogies and king lists, who equipped their texts with brief notes and commentaries, some of them probably set down in the 7th century, just within living memory of the events they describe.

All records agree that the English conquest of the north was the work of the Bernicians, not of the stronger and more numerous Deirans. The revolt began when Ida fortified Bamburgh, and thereby proclaimed independence. The date and scope of his wars is uncertain, but it seems probable that he died shortly before the rise of Urien. He is said to have united the Bernicians under a single command, but their unity was not permanent; on his death, their tiny territories were split between several separate leaders. But they are not reported to have fought each other, and one of them, Adda, is said to have destroyed Gurci and Peredur, joint kings of York, at Caer Greu, in 580. The site is not known; but since it was the Bernicians who killed the York kings, not the Deirans, it is probable that the kings had marched north to destroy the growing power of Bernicia, and were killed in Bernicia. Their defeat was as decisive for the north as Cutha's victory had been for the south nine years before. The British kingdom ended with its last kings; and York was necessarily the most important of the British northern states. Peredur's son Gwgaun is remembered in British tradition among the 'passive' chiefs who failed to recover their inheritance, bracketed with Llywarch Hen. With his father's army dispersed, York was undefended.

Hitherto there had been no sign of rebellion by the English of Deira in the East Riding. But their king Aelle is described as an independent sovereign in the pleasant tale of Gregory the Great's encounter with Deiran boys in Rome, dated between 585 and 590, and also by Bede in 597. It is likely that he, or his father, occupied the city when Peredur's army was routed in 580.

The sudden and total destruction of the greatest of the northern British kingdoms compelled its neighbours to unite; and Taliesin's poems describe their response. Urien mastered Catterick, the northern bastion of the lost kingdom. Catterick is the strategic nerve-centre of northern warfare, for it commands Scots Corner, where the road from York branches north-west over Stainmore by the Bowes Pass to Urien's Carlisle, and northward to the Tyne and Bernicia. Its seizure kept the two English kingdoms apart, and defended Urien's Reged against invasion from Deira. English record lists the Bernician rulers of these years, apparently lords of small districts, contemporaries of Adda. Urien fought one of them, who was named Theodoric, after the kings of the Goths and Franks, and killed another, called 'Ulph' by the Welsh, who was perhaps either the Theodulf or the Freothulf of the English lists; but the battleground, 'at the Ford', is not identified. The Bernicians united in face of Urien's assault, and 'Fflamddwyn', the Firebrand, probably the Welsh name for Aethelric, invaded Reged in command of four Bernician armies combined under his sole command. He demanded hostages, but Urien and his son Owain beat him 'on a Saturday morning' in 'Argoed Llwyfein', Leven Forest. The year is not known, and neither is the site. Leven names survive near Bewcastle, near the Roman fort of Netherby, north-east of Carlisle, and also in Furness; Bewcastle is geographically more probable, but other northern rivers, that now have English or Scandinavian names, may have been called Leven in Urien's time.

Urien's elegy calls him the 'Pillar of Britain' and rejoices that he 'overcame Bernicia'. One of Nennius' documents brings him nearer to the stature of a national British leader than any other northern king; and gives detail of his effort to expel the English altogether, of his near success, and of the cause of his failure.

> Hussa reigned 7 years. Four kings fought against him, Urien and Riderch Hen, and Gaullauc and Morcant. Theodoric fought bravely against the famous Urien and his sons. During that time, sometimes the enemy, sometimes our countrymen were victorious, and Urien blockaded them for three days and three nights on the island of Metcaud (Lindisfarne).

The allies were Urien's northern neighbours. Riderch of the Clyde and Guallauc of the upper Forth had been his enemies before; Morcant, whose territory probably included Lindisfarne, was a hereditary enemy of Riderch. Necessity compelled the kings to forget former enmities; but it did not rally all the British north, for the list leaves out the princes of Edinburgh, Dunaut of the northern Pennines, Rhun map Neithon, probably of Selkirk and Peebles, and others. The list is limited to British kings, but other texts add other allies. One Irish story recalls that Aedan of the Dal Riada Scots and king Fiachna of Ulster, who reigned from 589 to 628, fought together against the English; and another Irish story relates that Fiachna took Bamburgh, received hostages, and apparently installed an Irish garrison. The stories cannot concern Aedan's later campaign against the English, when he had different Irish allies. They imply that Urien enlisted Irish as well as British armies, and that the allies took Bamburgh and drove the English from the mainland, to stand siege on Lindisfarne, the offshore island opposite Bamburgh. These stories also indicate the date; it was some time before 593, the year in which Bede begins the reign of Aethelric's successor, for Aethelric outlived Urien; but not earlier than 589, when Fiachna's reign began. The time is therefore very near to 590.

The Bernicians were on the verge of annihilation. They were saved by the discord of the British. The Nennius text continues

> But while he was on the expedition, Urien was assassinated, on the initiative of Morcant, from jealousy, because his military skill and generalship surpassed that of all the other kings.

Tradition names his murderer, Lovan; a variant blames the princes of Edinburgh, whose names the Nennius text markedly omits. But the tales suggest that Morcant's jealousy had an immediate occasion. Bamburgh lay within his territory; it was from him that the English rebels had seized the fort and to him it should return. But when the Irish took the fort and held it as the prize of victory, Urien's consent ceded Morcant's territory over his head.

These are the motives of discord that the surviving evidence implies. If there were more evidence, it would doubtless modify or amplify the causes of the quarrel. But whatever the causes, the murder was fatal to the alliance. The besieging British army disintegrated, the English were saved from extinction, and Taliesin lived to lament the fate of Urien's sons, who were now bound to avenge their father's murder in war against his former allies, and were therefore exposed to the assaults of British enemies as well as of the English. They fought alone, but not in vain. The English recovered from their near disaster, rallied behind Aethelric, and attacked Urien's son Owain. They were heavily defeated, and one of Taliesin's finest poems celebrates the last northern British victory

> When Owain slew Fflamddwyn
> It was no more than sleeping.
> Sleeps now the wide host of England
> With the light upon their eyes
> And those who fled not far
> Were braver than was need. . . .
>
> Splendid he was, in his many coloured armour,
> Horses he gave to all who asked

Gathering wealth like a miser
Freely he shared it for his soul's sake
The soul of Owain son of Urien
May the Lord look upon its need.

If Fflamddwyn was Aethelric, as is probable, the date is 593. But his death and defeat did not quell the English, for Owain's cavalry might win a battle, but could not on their own expel or exterminate the homes where their young men were born and trained to arms. After the defeat, Aethelric's son Aethelferth permanently united the separate portions of the Bernicians, and soon overwhelmed the north.

Owain died or was killed soon after, for Taliesin's poem is an elegy upon his death, and knows of no later wars or victories. The kingdom of Reged died with him. Its military glory was short-lived, for barely 20 years passed between Urien's early victories and the death of Owain. But Urien's wider vision of British unity and Taliesin's verses have made it the most famed of the British kingdoms. Its fame was earned in their day, and perpetuated by their immediate successors, for Urien's death is the central tragedy of many of the poems attributed to his cousin Llywarch, that were set down in their present form something over a century later. The elegy on Urien's death is vivid.

The head I carry at my side,
The head of Urien, the open-handed captain.
On his pale breast black carrion. . . .

Urien's sister grieves that he was slain by the assassin Lovan at Aber Lleu, the estuary of the Low, that enters the sea opposite Lindisfarne. The Christian armies are now 'a swarm without hive'. Urien's enemies are listed; Dunaut the fierce rider bears down upon his sons, Owain and Pascent, and Guallauc upon his other son, Elphin; Morcant and Bran attack, and the speedy end of Reged is depicted.

This hearth, wild flowers cover it.
When Owain and Elphin lived
Plunder boiled in its cauldron. . . .

This hearth, tall brambles cover it.
Easy were its ways.
Reged was used to giving.

This hearth, dockleaves cover it.
More usual upon its floor
Mead, and the claims of men who drank. . . .

This pillar and that pillar there.
More usual around it
Shouts of victory, and giving of gifts.

The later poet laments a vanished age, the society of the warrior states of the north, that had perished in the relatively recent past. He mourns the death of a kingdom and a stronghold, not the death of an individual king. He does not say who killed Owain or destroyed Reged, but he blames its destruction upon the enmity of its British neighbours. He had no need to point the moral of their folly, for men knew that the fall of Reged had brought them all to ruin. When Owain died, the halls and hearths of Reged died with him, and so did its military force. Aethelferth's strongest enemy was gone, and the defence of the northern Pennines and of Catterick, the strong-point that severed the Bernicians from Deira, necessarily fell to Dunaut. But Dunaut was killed in 597, presumably by the Bernicians.

Catraeth

In the next year, 598, the Annals enter the battle of Catraeth. The powers of the far north made a last attempt to rescue the Pennines. Mynydawc and Cynan of Edinburgh led a northern army to confront the English near Catterick, perhaps within the earthworks of the ancient pre-Roman fortress of Stanwick, in the angle of the strategic road fork at Scots Corner. The gain that victory would have brought is obvious. The army of Edinburgh took the Bernicians in the rear, evidently approaching through Carlisle and down the Bowes pass. At that date Aethelferth had not yet annexed York; Aelle was still king in Deira. His attitude is not known, but he had as much cause as the British kings to fear the power of Bernicians. Victory would have made a British–Deiran alliance possible, with a reasonable hope that the British might prove the stronger partners, and that the allies might again drive the Bernicians into the sea, as Urien had done a few years before. It is possible that the alliance had already been agreed, and that the circuitous march of the Edinburgh armies was designed to make contact with the Deirans, for the British complained of Deiran treachery. But these prospects were not realised. The expeditionary force was annihilated. Its defeat is the theme of the longest and best-known of the early poems, the *Gododdin* of Aneirin, the 'sovereign bard'; the core of the poem was probably composed not long after the battle, and it quickly became a widely loved epic, recited in all surviving British courts, for verses were added during the seventh century that brought into the story the heroes of very many dynasties, some of whom died long before the battle, and some of whom lived many years later.

Aneirin's solemn lines contrast the confident enterprise of the Edinburgh British with the fearful emptiness that followed.

> Men went to Catraeth
> Shouting for battle,
> A squadron of horse.
>
> Blue their armour and their shields,
> Lances uplifted and sharp,
> Mail and sword glinting. . . .
>
> Though they were slain, they slew.
> None to his home returned. . . .

Short their lives,
Long the grief
Among their kin.

Seven times their number,
The English they slew.
Many the women they widowed
Many the mothers who wept. . . .

After the wine and after the mead
They left us, armoured in mail.
I know the sorrow of their death.

They were slain, they never grew grey. . . .
From the army of Mynydawc, grief unbounded,
Of three hundred men, but one returned.

Aneirin describes a single small cavalry force from one kingdom. It may have been accompanied by allies from other states, but the wide popularity of the poems in other kingdoms, while the expedition was still remembered, guarantees that it formed the core of the expedition. The force was totally destroyed; the army of Edinburgh was eliminated, like the armies of the Pennines. Aethelferth's English were numbered by the thousand; their losses were heavy, but the survivors might march at will to the Forth, to face the kingdoms beyond. The prudent rulers of the Clyde are not reported to have challenged them, but Aedan of Dal Riada prepared to halt the English advance. He sought help from the Irish of the mainland, and Mael Uma, brother of the High-King, brought a task force of shock troops to aid him against the Northumbrians. In 603, at Degsastan, whose site has not been determined, Mael Uma's men overwhelmed and killed Aethelferth's brother, but Aedan was driven from the field, decisively and permanently beaten. Northern resistance was crushed. 'From that time forth', wrote Bede 'no king of the Scots dared face the English in the field.'

Chester

Aethelferth was free to turn south, and in 604 he occupied York and annexed Deira. The children of its royal house escaped; Aelle's son, Edwin, is said to have found refuge with the king of Gwynedd, his relative Heric among the British of Elmet, about Leeds. For ten years, no further wars are reported; but in or soon after 614 Aethelferth attacked north Wales, perhaps in fear that the British might endeavour to restore Edwin. The Northumbrian army marched to Chester and defeated the combined forces of Gwynedd, Powys and the lowland Cornovii. Over a thousand of the monks of Bangor-on-Dee accompanied the British army to battle, praying for its victory. The pagan Aethelferth protested

> if these men invoke their God against us, they fight against us, even if they have no arms,

and launched his first attack upon them.

The loss of Chester severed Wales from the Pennines, as the loss of Gloucester 25 years before had sundered it from Dumnonia. The Welsh were confined to Wales, and Cadfan, the new king of Gwynedd, is the first of its rulers who is known to have resided in Anglesey, as far removed as possible from the English border. He fought no wars, and his tombstone styles him the 'wisest of kings'. He was a realist, accepting defeat, and turned his wisdom to the consolidation of his kingdom. But, as on the lower Severn, though the British kingdoms were destroyed, the English were still too few to people the lands they had subdued. Aethelferth may have plundered captured territory and may have placed garrisons in Chester and nearby, but his limited manpower was needed for his army rather than for colonisation, for wars against the other English drew him south. While he had conquered the north, Aethelbert of Kent had mastered the southern English. All Britain south of the Clyde was overshadowed by two great English kings, and each might hope to win the sovereignty of the whole island. One strand in Kentish thinking seems to have contemplated the conquest of Northumbria, but Aethelbert died in 616. The southern English rejected the authority of his son, and southern supremacy passed to Redwald of East Anglia. He sheltered the exiled Edwin of Deira, and Aethelferth marched against him. He was defeated and killed. But the power of the Northumbrian armies was unbroken. Edwin was accepted as king by both the Bernicians and the Deirans, and Aethelferth's sons went into exile among the Picts and Scots. The last British Pennine king, Cerdic of Elmet, was speedily removed. Edwin overran north Wales, reduced the Isle of Man, and asserted a supremacy over the southern English that they did not challenge.

All that remained of the British north consolidated around the kingdom of the Clyde. When the line of Riderch failed, early in the 7th century, the throne passed to nearby lords, apparently the kings of the Lothians. But they moved to the old centre of government, the impregnable fortress of Dumbarton, downriver from Glasgow, a base as fit for a navy as for an army. The centre remained, and even when quieter times made the more comfortable situation of Glasgow a safe royal residence, the kingdom changed only its name, from 'Alclud', the Rock of Clyde, to 'Strathclyde', the Vale of Clyde. Its fortunes and its frontiers varied. On its southern borders the people of Urien's northern Reged kept, and still keep, the national name of the fifth-century British, the 'countrymen', *cives* or *Cumbrogi*, that the English called Cumber Land; and when Northumbria later weakened, the Clydesiders quietly regained control of what had been Reged, and in the 10th century extended their borders as far as Leeds, briefly regaining most of the Pennines. But the Clydesiders never seriously challenged English Northumbria; they were not a British power intent on evicting the English, but a northern kingdom on a par with its neighbours. Its kings were content to hold what they had, to acquire only what fell to them without risk. Their business was to keep their kingdom intact, free from English conquest. They succeeded, and were spared not only invasion, but also the dynastic warfare that emaciated medieval

Wales. Throughout their long history, there is no hint of division between heirs; son succeeded father as king of an undivided inheritance for five or six centuries. Too late the British heeded Gildas' warning that civil war would bring upon them the wrath of God, and deprive them of their patrimony.

Catwallaun

Elsewhere, the armies of the northern British were dispersed before the death of Aethelferth. But English rule was not yet secure. Speedy conquest risked reconquest, and a still small English population ruled vastly greater numbers of subject British. On the south-west, the power of Gwynedd was still unbroken. For long, it offered no threat. King Cadfan ruled quietly, while his people recovered from the disaster of Chester. But his son Catwallaun revived the ancient military reputation of his forbears. His early history is obscure, for the vestiges of poems that honoured him can only be discerned in fragments embedded in a distorted 18th-century paraphrase. Bede reports that Edwin invaded Gwynedd, and subdued the 'Mevanian Islands', Anglesey and Man; but he gives no date. In the Welsh tradition, Catwallaun was at some time besieged on Puffin Island, Priestholm, off Anglesey, and spent seven years in exile in Ireland; in Gwynedd, Edwin's armies were opposed by the local king of Lleyn, opposite Anglesey.

But Edwin withdrew. Catwallaun returned, rallied his countrymen, enlisted the support of other north Welsh kings, and found an ally in Penda, king of the Mercians, who 'separated the kingdom of the Mercians from the kingdom of the Northerners'. The allies killed Edwin in 633, and Catwallaun marched his army to the north, repeating the exploit of his ancestor Rhun, ninety years before. For a year he ruled as a high king from the Thames to the Forth, supreme over British and English underkings. Had his rule endured, he might have recovered London and the south, and restored the empire of Arthur. But reconquest came too late. The northern British had accepted English rule for nearly half a century, and only the very old remembered the days of independence. Catwallaun's plundering armies came as aliens, and Penda's pagan English were worse. Hungry armies far from home were a threat to farmsteads that Edwin's settled rule had protected. Catwallaun aroused no national movement, and found no welcome as a liberator. His empire quickly collapsed, destroyed in a single battle, when Oswald, the exiled son of Aethelferth, returned from Ireland and caught him off his guard, on Hadrian's Wall.

Oswald immediately succeeded to the overkingship of Catwallaun, and extended it to include the English south of the Thames. He permanently destroyed the fighting power of the British. The Irish Annals report the burning of Bangor in 634. The king of Merioneth was killed on the Severn in 635; Oswald was then in Wessex and was presumably his victorious enemy. The dynasty of Gwynedd was deposed, and so was the king of the Clyde, who had in that year perhaps supported Catwallaun. Both thrones passed to 'plebeian' kings; though it may be that the subjects of both kingdoms organised rebellion against kings and nobles who had suffered defeat, it is more probable that the words describe nominees intruded by Oswald, who had no royal ancestry, for both were removed when he died. But the restored dynasties ventured no more counter-attacks. The Clyde kings held their frontiers, and in Gwynedd Catwallaun's son earned a reputation like his grandfather's, honoured as a saint rather than as a warrior. Almost nothing is known of his successors save their names, until a new dynasty revived the power of Gwynedd in the 9th century.

Cynddylan

Oswald's supremacy lasted for eight years. He was killed in 642 at Maes Cogwy, or Maeserfelth, that was thereafter renamed Oswestry. His enemies were the old allies, Penda and the Welsh; but with the power of Gwynedd broken, Penda of Mercia, and not a Welsh ruler, was the supreme king. Oswald's wide supremacy passed to Penda, and the Mercian kings maintained it for a century and a half. It was interrupted for three years, when Oswald's brother Oswy rebelled in 655, killed Penda at 'Gaius Field' on the river 'Winwaed' near Leeds, and regained supremacy. Penda's son, Peada, ruled a reduced Mercia as Oswy's tributary, but in 658 the Mercians rebelled, killed Peada, and enthroned his brother Wulfhere; he and his successors reasserted Mercian supremacy over all the English except the Northumbrians, and retained it until the coming of the Scandinavians and the rise of the West Saxon dynasty in the 9th century.

On the north-western borders of Mercia, in the modern counties of Shropshire and Staffordshire, the *civitas* of the Cornovii held the remnants of the Roman British lowland, and maintained its independence under its own kings throughout Penda's lifetime. They are known from poems preserved in Powys, in the collection that bears the name of Llywarch Hen. Their territory had been divided, probably by partition among heirs, and in the early 7th century the borders of king Constantine reached southward to the Wye near Hereford, while Cyndrwyn the Stubborn ruled Wroxeter, whose armies fought against Aethelferth at Chester. The poems immortalise his son Cynddylan,

> Whose heart was like the ice in winter . . .
> Whose heart is as the fire of spring. . . .

He ruled Pengwern, the Shrewsbury region, and Wroxeter, the

> White Town by the woods . . . twixt Tren and Trodwydd . . .
> twixt Tren and Traval,

that was his father's home. To survey his heritage, the poet looked down from the top of Dinlle Wrecon, the Wrekin, the pre-Roman fort that preserves the old name of Wroxeter, Vriconium. The army may have reconditioned the ancient fort, but recent excavation suggests that a significant urban population remained in the centre of Wroxeter, living in well-built timber houses, when

Roman building technology in masonry had been forgotten; no close date can be put upon them, but the royal hall of Cynddylan or his forbears may well lie among them.

The first dated notice of Cynddylan's wars concerns the year 642.

> I saw the Field of Maes Cogwy
> Armies, and the cry of men hard pressed.
> Cynddylan brought them aid.

The next verse names his ally, a prince of Powys. Cynddylan fought with Penda against Oswald at Oswestry. Two separate elegies upon his death survive. One, partially rewritten by a later poet, describes a different campaign. Each stanza ends with a signature, like Taliesin's.

> Till I am in my oaken coffin
> I shall grieve for the death
> Of Cynddylan in his glory
>
> Glory in battle, great was the fortune
> Cynddylan won, who led the attack.
> Seven hundred was the army in his court.
>
> When the son of Pyd commanded
> For him there was no marrying, he was not wed.
> By God, whence came his tribute?
>
> Till I rest beneath the mound
> I shall grieve for the death
> Of Cynddylan, honest in his fame.

Pyd is the Welsh word for danger; but it also transliterates Peada, and the word-play fits the idiom of Welsh verse, that commonly gave Welsh epithets to English kings, as Flamddwyn for Aethelric. The statement that 'he was not wed' might refer to a proposal for dynastic marriage that was rejected; but similar usage elsewhere means the death of a very young man, not yet old enough to be married. The probable meaning of the verse is that some English king, probably Peada or his son, demanded tribute from Cynddylan, and was killed when he tried to exact it, or died before he was able to. The date is therefore probably 655 or soon after, the context that Cynddylan refused to pay tribute to an English overlord.

Other verses describe a victory won at much the same time. Detail is precise, but the context is enigmatic.

> My heart is aflame, like a firebrand. . . .
> Brothers I had, better it was when they were alive,
> Heirs of great Arthur, our strong fortress.
>
> Before Caer Luitcoet they triumphed;
> There was blood beneath the ravens, and fierce attack;
> They shattered shields, the sons of Cyndrwyn.

Till I am in my resting place
I shall grieve for the death
Of Cynddylan, the full famed lord.

Glory in battle, great plunder,
Before Caer Luitcoet, Morfael took it.

Fifteen hundred cattle, and five (stewards?)
Four score horses, and splendid armour.
Each bishop rushing to the four corners,
Hugging their books saved not the monks.

Caer Luitcoet is Wall-by-Lichfield. Only one other medieval text names a prince called Morfael; the genealogy of a local lord in south Wales claims descent from Morfael, who moved from Luitcoet to Glastonbury in the 7th century. Two contemporaries both with the same unique name, both from the same town, are clearly the same person. The exact list of booty suggests the enemy. They were settlers with many cattle, but their army had few horses; their eighty contrast with Cynddylan's seven hundred; and bishops and monks are numbered among the enemy.

These particulars hint at the context. Morfael of the Lichfield region reigned on Peada's borders, for pagan Saxon burials, that last into the early 7th century, stop short at Tamworth, the future Mercian capital, seven miles east of Lichfield, and also at Yoxall and Wichnor, the same distance to the north, where the Trent formed the frontier. Morfael and Cynddylan fought in alliance at Wall. Their infantry enemy was English; and the enemy were accompanied by clergy, who cannot have been present with the English earlier than 653, when Peada first received Christian priests from Oswy. The context argues that the battle was a consequence of the British refusal to continue tribute to the conquerors of Penda, and was fought about 655. The terse notice of the Cambrian Annals that Oswy 'came and raided' in or about 656 perhaps refers to the same campaign. It was the last lowland British victory, and was soon after avenged. Morfael fled to Dumnonia, and Cynddylan was killed by the English; his son withdrew to Powys, and Wroxeter was in Mercian hands a few years later, for its people are entered as the *Wrocensaetna* in the census of Mercian territories termed the 'Tribal Hidage', that was probably drawn up in or about 661; and a ford over the Severn, in the neighbourhood of Melverley, ten miles west of Shrewsbury, received the name of 'Wulfhere's Ford'. The Severn there remains today the border between England and Wales; and the ford may be the place where Wulfhere and the king of Powys met to demarcate their permanent frontier.

The English who killed Cynddylan might have been Wulfhere's Mercians, soon after 658; but were more probably the Northumbrians of Oswy, whose raid in 656 avenged the British victory at Wall. But whoever killed him, Cynddylan and his kingdom were brought down. The stateliest of all the old Welsh poems mourns their destruction, praising Cynddylan, who 'defended Tren as long as he lives', and turns to his fatal end.

> Cynddylan, hold thou the hillside
> Where the English come today. . . .
>
> Cynddylan, hold thou the ford
> Where the English come through Tren. . . .

The English came, and the poet looks upon the ruin that they left.

> Cynddylan's hall is dark to-night.
> There burns no fire, no bed is made.
> I weep awhile, and then am quiet.
>
> Cynddylan's hall is dark to-night.
> No fire is lit, no candle burns.
> God will keep me sane.
>
> Cynddylan's hall. It pierces me
> To see it roofless, fireless.
> Dead is my lord, and I am yet alive.
>
> Cynddylan's hall is desolate to-night
> Where once I sat in honour.
> Gone are the men who held it, gone the women.
>
> Cynddylan's hall. Dark is its roof
> Since the English destroyed
> Cynddylan, and Elvan of Powys.

In the empty hall, now there is 'no warband, no bright fire, no singing, no lord and no company'. Then the poet turns to the future of Cynddylan's heirs.

> High may the mountain be.
> I care not that I herd my cattle there.
> Thin, thin seems my cloak.
>
> Hard is my goatskin bed.
> Yet once I was drunk
> On the mead of Brynn.

He contrasts the vanished past.

> Gone are my brethren from the lands of the Severn
> Around the banks of Dwyryw.
> Sad am I, my God, that I am yet alive.
>
> No more the well trained horses, no more the scarlet cloaks,
> No more great golden plumes.
> Thin my legs, bare, uncovered. . . .

Brothers I had who never lost heart,
Brothers who grew like hazel saplings.
All are gone, one by one. . . .

The dykes endure. He who dug them
Is no more.

The Loss of Britain

The dignity of Cynddylan's requiem accepts final irrevocable defeat without self pity. The northern poets each mourned the loss of one leader or one kingdom; Cynddylan's poet wrote the epitaph of a nation. His sentiments are those of a later generation, but of one that was near enough to its heroes to know the full worth of all that was lost. The poet who looked from the top of the Wrekin across the wide and pleasant midland plain had lost more than mountain peoples could know or understand. When he contrasted past glories with the mountain cattle and the goatskin beds, he accepted perpetual exile to the bleak unlovely hills. His words are an explicit recognition that the British had lost the fairer part of Britain, and were to be Welshmen for the rest of time. His fellows accepted their lot, and made ready to shape the future of the Cymry.

The end had come with appalling speed, compressed within the compass of a single adult lifetime. It was a melancholy commentary upon the warnings of Gildas. Kings and people had not ceased from evil, and God had delivered their inheritance into the hands of the heathen. Gildas had looked to the reform of political society; but the young men whom his words inspired withdrew from it, to pattern a new and better way of life, in monasteries that were in time to matter more for Britain and for Europe than any patching of a dying society. They withdrew because their world was utterly rotted. It fell to pieces, for none could heal its manifold divisions. The English triumphed because the British could not unite. The immediate causes of disunity varied; in much of Wales and the south, close relatives slaughtered each other in dynastic dispute, but in the north wars between kinsmen are less in evidence. There, the Pennine kingdoms fought against neighbours in the farther north, and in Wales and the South.

The occasions of war, and their consequence, have deeper origins. The men of the fifth century had fought to defend and restore Roman Britain. Their arms were in the end victorious, but the tragedy of Arthurian Britain was that victory came too late. The Roman society it championed was already dead, and the forgotten forms of government that it sought to revive could not be rooted in a poisoned soil. The failure of Arthur denied any chance of success to those who came after; the military units that had won the war could not be demobilised, and since their business was warfare, they fought each other when there was no foreigner to fight. Though the personal prestige of the victor of Badon held his empire together while he lived, it could not be inherited. Its military forces dissolved into warbands, who bled each other and their country to death.

The warbands ceased to protect their people, and became a grievous burden, a more real and present threat to the working farmer than the unseen danger of distant Saxons. The poems praised the open-handed munificence of kings called *hael*, 'generous', who 'gathered wealth like misers' and freely gave horses and other gifts to their fighting men. But the poets say little of whence the wealth came; for the corn that the 'well-fed horses' ate, the barley for their riders' food and drink, and much else beside, had to be extorted from impoverished farmsteads. Though a successful raid might sometimes seize the cattle of a nearby kingdom, the arrogant soldiers whose honourable virtues were bloodshed and deep drinking were poorly equipped to protect the cattle of their own subjects; the monumental scale of the Wansdyke, and the numerous lesser ditches that line the borders of the successor states, proclaim the constant need for such protection, but their great length far exceeds their kings' capacity to garrison them, and the dreary routine of a frontier patrol does not rank among the glories that the poets honour. Cynddylan's poet proudly acclaims the warrior's ideal, longing for the excitement of byegone wars, when

> Commoner was the broken shield
> Come home from battle, than the returning ox. . . .
>
> Commoner was the blood upon the grass
> Than the plough in fallow land.

He sang of an adventurous world that might stir young heroes, but could only offer a hateful and fearful insecurity to their inferiors who ploughed the land.

Warbands so weakly rooted could endure reverses, but could not survive defeat. Once they were dispersed, their power of compulsion was gone. No survivor could requisition new horses, constrain peasants to deliver grain or meat, or raise fresh recruits, unless there was a will among the population to recreate the warband. There are no signs of such will. When each king lost his men and his horses, political government ceased. His subjects were eased of a burden, and waited passively until the English came, a week later or half a century later; and when the foreign English came, they imposed a less costly government that gave a surer defence against cattle robbers and armed strangers. But the English infantry were less vulnerable than the British warbands. Their national armies had infinite resources, for unless an entire population was literally exterminated, even the total destruction of an army could be made good in a few years, as children grew to manhood. The English won England because they were a nation in arms; the British lost their inheritance because their 'ill-starred generals' enfeebled and disgusted their own countrymen.

When the British lost the greater part of Britain, they ceased to be British, and became Welshmen, confined to the western extremities of the island. But though their kings failed them, the independent energy of the British people determined the future history of the British Isles. Their churchmen brought the Irish and the northern barbarians into a common polity with the former Roman province. In two centuries of resistance, the subjects of Arthur and of the successor states set abiding limits to English conquest, and delayed the hardening of English society until the English had forgotten much of their Germanic past, and were ready to accept the religion and the political conventions of their new homeland. In taming the English, the British pioneered a civil society that greatly differed from that of Europe. There, the quick and easy victory of the Germanic invaders led to speedy fusion. The rich barbarian became Roman, and the poor Roman was barbarised. Institutions useful to authority survived, to cripple early medieval Europe. The heavy hand of the Roman landlord was not removed, and it acquired the added strength of a barbarian sword, that long overawed submissive peasants. In Britain the institutions of authority were smashed, but much of the peasants' culture survived; for in Britain, alone among the former provinces of Rome, men still speak modernised versions of the indigenous languages that their ancestors spoke in Roman times. The country was divided between natives and newcomers, who interacted, but did not fuse. Yet from the empire of Arthur and from the church that his successors built, both inherited a conviction that Britain was or should be a unity. The long resistance of the British imposed upon the future a fruitful diversity within unity, greater local responsibility, and a stronger sense of the rights and freedom of the individual; it enabled concepts of national identity, rooted in popular beliefs of what was fitting, to mature sooner in Britain than in Europe.

In the sixth or seventh centuries no one intended or foresaw these remoter consequences. But it was the last generations of the independent British who created Wales, who brought a monastic church into being, and who inspired the universal legend of a just and powerful sovereign, enshrined in the name of their own emperor. The last age of the British was clear-sighted. More clearly than most others, it diagnosed its own disease, though it could not cure it; Gildas' analysis moved men's hearts because they knew it to be true. Though they could not act upon it, they bequeathed to their successors a passionate belief that sooner or later arbitrary authority must yield to the rule of law. They knew the past for what it was, but they recognised the present and the future. Cynddylan's poet knew that his people were the 'heirs of great Arthur', the last of the successor states of Roman Britain, and when he addressed 'Cynddylan, vested in purple', he echoed the last devolution of imperial Roman authority. But he also knew that the empire of Arthur was a fading memory, failed and finished, severed from the bleak future.

Sixth-century Britain died because its people no longer wished it to live. It was not destroyed by the rebellion of the English. Their blow fell upon a ruin already rotted. Yet it died in honour. The passing of the warlords redeemed their sordid history; though their triumphs were futile and petty, they turned disaster to a greater glory. Urien and Cynddylan were men who inspired the affection and enthusiasm of great poets. When the last battles were lost, leaders who were left alive without followers accepted their fate without pretence, leaving fevered prophecies of the ultimate reconquest of England to the fretful boasting of a meaner age. The calm dignity of Cynddylan's poet looked the future in the face, without hope, without fear, and without illusion.

CHAPTER FOURTEEN

BRITTANY

The Armorican British have no early annals and few pedigrees. But their Saints' Lives are earlier, fuller and better preserved than those of the British; for in Britain interest in the stories of the early monks was revived by the discords of the 11th and 12th centuries, when most of the original texts had perished, and much of what remained seemed rugged and offensive to elegant ecclesiastics. But in Brittany interest in the origins of the nation and its church was revived by the victories of kings Nominoe and Salomon in the 9th century, when many old texts still survived, and were held in high esteem.

One Life, Samson's, is preserved entire as it was written, about 600 AD or perhaps a few years before, thirty or forty years after its hero died. Ninth-century texts are numerous, and many of them drew upon manuscripts not yet decayed, for they reproduce names of people and places in old-fashioned spellings that hardly outlived the sixth century. In addition to the texts that survive, many disappeared in the French Revolution. Some were rescued by odd chance; one, brought to England by a refugee, and then lost, was tracked down in 1881 by the pertinacious enquiry of a French scholar, who ultimately recovered it from a pile of magazines in the drawing-room of a Yorkshire country house. But the industry of a 17th-century priest salvaged something of many that did not survive the Revolution. Father Albert Le Grand of Morlaix read and epitomised a vast number of texts and translated his own versions into French. His volatile imagination commonly rendered 'Britain' by 'Angleterre', and turned the British *duces* into Earls of Oxford or the like, leaving out the names of greater kings, but making them wear their crowns in London. Many of the places and people he so disguises cannot be recognised, and his text is sprinkled with Roman emperors and startling Roman dates, selected by himself from such printed histories of the late empire as he knew. But when this bizarre ornament is removed, what remains is a collection of medieval Lives, in varying stages of devolution, that share the normal difficulties of such texts, heightened by Le Grand's translation and imagination, but made easier because many of the sources that he used were early and well-informed. In addition, three collections of medieval charters include corrupted lists of kings and bishops, with a few doctored grants that adapt fifth-century names.

The main political events of 6th-century Brittany are well dated, for the Armorican peninsular formed part of the Roman province of *Lugdunensis III*, whose ecclesiastical head was the bishop of its metropolis, Tours. Gregory, the historian of 6th-century Gaul, was bishop of Tours from 573 to 594. He knew the recent history of his own territories; his statements about the Armorican British are not numerous, for their churchmen gave small respect to his nominal diocesan authority, but most of the people he names were his contemporaries, and many of them are prominent in the Lives of the Saints, and they include rulers whose careers also concerned mainland Britain. Gregory's stories are also an important illustration of how the sixth-century monks and kings behaved, and of the beliefs and assumptions that moved them. He himself received at Tours a penniless ill-kempt British ascetic, who had set off in a provocative goat-skin dress to walk to Jerusalem; though this pilgrim halted at Tours, he undertook a journey that many of the British saints are said by their later biographers to have completed. Gregory's plain tale of the dramatic adventures of Macliavus of Vannes, murderously pursued by his brother, tonsured, consecrated bishop, and then made lay ruler, recalls Gildas' account of Maelgwn and Constantine in Britain, and is also matched by the colourful stories of the murders of Melor and Meliau and others in the Saints' Lives. Their many tales of distant pilgrimage and lurid violence might easily be dismissed as pious fancy, if Gregory's sober record did not show that such things actually happened.

Insular British texts also have much to say of Brittany, and distinguish three main migrations from Britain to Gaul. Their belief is firm and clear that the armies which Maximus took to Gaul in 383 never returned 'to Britain to their wives and children and property', but were settled in

> many regions from the lake on the top of Mount Jove to the city called Cant Guic, and as far as the western mound, that is the West Ridge; and they are the Armorican British.

'Cant Guic' is Quentovic, a lost port near Etaples and Le Touquet, and the territory defined, covering the whole of modern Normandy and Brittany, includes nearly all of the fourth-century Roman coastal command known as the *Tractus Armoricanus*. The leader of these settlers is consistently called Cynan Meriadauc, whose residence was Nantes, and whose name is still preserved by several places in the Vannetais, the Roman *Civitas Venetorum*, in south-eastern Brittany. The story is unconfirmed, but is not silly, for the emperor Theodosius, who subdued Maximus, is praised by contemporaries for his clemency towards the rebel's followers. He had a use for troops in Gaul, as well as an incentive to deprive the turbulent army of Britain of recent rebels; for it had enthroned four usurpers in Gaul in the past hundred years. Some of the place names of northern Brittany are military. Leon is the *pagus Legionensis*, the legionary district, and Plou Dalmezeau, probably *plebs Dalmatarum*, bears one of the commonest of the names of fourth-century army units. Such place names suggest that some army units were settled in Armorica at some time in the 4th century.

The second migration, about 458–460, after the first Saxon revolt in Britain, is abundantly attested by Roman writers. It was located in the same wide region, for contemporaries place the British 'north of the Loire', in the territories of Aegidius of Soissons, and a scatter of place names, especially 'Bretteville', extend throughout Normandy. The emigrants also settled in Brittany, for the Roman writer Sidonius, bishop of Clermont-Ferrand, corresponded with their leader Riothamus, who is remembered in the legends of Brittany, along with Gradlon and other local leaders of the mid fifth century.

The British of Normandy were absorbed into the empire of the Franks and the diocesan structure of the Gallic church, but the Franks failed to conquer Brittany, and the Armorican sees disappear from the records of the church councils. Actual independence was secured by token submission; the tactful rulers of the British were content to relinquish the title of king and accept the status of counts, but they admitted no Frank armies, and continued to dispute possession of Rennes and Nantes with their nominal suzerains. When the Franks mastered western Gaul in 507, the British were still weak, and might in time have been absorbed, in Brittany as in Normandy. But within thirty years they received the powerful reinforcement of the third migration, sparked off by the movement of the monks, but strengthened by the participation of numerous armed laymen.

Riwal and Fracan

Emigration was on a considerable scale, organized, led and encouraged by governments. Contemporary notices locate Conomorus as a strong king who ruled in both Britain and Brittany, and later Lives say the same of Caradoc Vreichvras. Riwal, who in his own day was apparently known by the Roman name of Pompeius Regalis, was a 'chief of Dumnonia', and is therefore linked with its dynasty, and made a descendant of Arthur's Gerontius and Cato. He

> came from the overseas British with a multitude of ships, and took possession of Lesser Britain;

he was 'chief of the British on both sides of the sea', the 'first of the overseas British to come' to Brittany, in the sixth century. From Britain the central and eastern coasts of northern Brittany took the name Dumnonia, and retained it in French, as Domnonie. Riwal is said to have had his headquarters at St. Brieuc, in western Dumnonie. His followers included Fracan, who is also made a relative of Cato. Fracan

> discovered an estate of moderate size, just about right for a single *plebs*, surrounded by woodland and brambles, that is now known by its founder's name, and is enriched by the waters of the river Gouet.

Modern Plou-Fragan, *Plebs Fracani*, near St. Brieuc, retains his name and lies two miles south of the banks of the Gouet.

Very many miracles relate to the colonists' preoccupation with the clearance of new land, and with the care of corn and stock. A few concern new forms of recreation devised by the pioneers, and one of the most striking describes a novel sport conceived by Fracan. He challenged his powerful neighbour Riwal, who lived six or seven miles away, to a contest

> about the speed of their horses . . . over a measured course. . . . Highborn and lowborn attended the meeting in numbers; the lightest boys, specially trained for the race, were mounted . . . Fracan's horse was leading, but his rider, Maglos son of Cunomaglos, . . . could not hold him, and was thrown among sharp stones. . . . His people took up his dead body. His parents were in tears, and so was Fracan, who was held responsible for the unhappy outcome.

It was decided to bury the body, but Fracan's son Winwaloe asked the crowd to draw back, insisting that the boy 'is not dead, but very ill'; and restored him to health.

The story is contemporary, for Cunomaglos and Maglos are spellings of the 6th century. Fracan was blamed for a dangerous innovation, for earlier race-horses had been harnessed to a car or chariot, controlled by a standing driver. Light jockeys galloping over a measured course were new. Winwaloe saved the reputation of his father's experiment, and ensured that flat-racing should spread beyond its birthplace, Plou-Fragan.

Paul Aurelian

Other settlers also took over abandoned Roman estates. Paul Aurelian, on the west, in Leon, landed with a dozen priests, and as many nobly born lay relatives, with 'sufficient slaves'. He too found an 'estate', known as the 'Villa Petri', equipped with an ample spring or fountain, and also protected by 'thick woodland and a great marsh', which constituted one of the 'tribus' in the 'Plebs Telmedoviae'. It also took his name, and is now Lampaul in Plou Dalmezeau. But at another estate of Paul's, the 'Villa Wormavi', there was no visible water supply; the saint, who evidently knew that Roman villas must have had water, dug his staff several times into the ground until he located the fountains. Many other immigrants must have found similar estates, not yet wholly reverted to nature; and Paul Aurelian's Life includes a vivid description of a ruined Roman town. Paul travelled

> along the public road . . . to the town which now bears his name. He entered through the town gate, on the western side, that is now nobly constructed, and immediately found a bright spring of moderate size. . . . The town was then surrounded by earthen walls

> built in antiquity, wonderfully high, but much of it is nowadays fortified with stone walls built higher still. The place is like an island on all sides but the south . . . stretched . . . like a fully drawn bow on the British sea . . . facing south and looking to every aspect of the sun from east to west.
>
> It will not be absurd to describe the inhabitants that saint Paul found in this town, . . . a forest sow; . . . in the hollow of a tree, a hive, full of bees and honey; . . . a bear . . . that fled in fear at the sight of the saint; . . . and a wild bull, which he expelled. . . .

The biographer, Wrmonoc, is clearly describing a place that he knew in the ninth century, a substantial Roman town with both an earth bank and a stone wall, though he is probably mistaken in supposing that the stone wall was built after the Roman period. The description, however, better fits Roscoff, a few miles to the north, where pottery from an ancient site has been found in the sandhills, than modern St. Pol-de-Leon.

These stories describe the settlement of immigrants in a land of ghosts, far emptier than Britain. A deserted city, a countryside full of abandoned farms, had decayed far enough for trees to grow within the ruins, and for beasts to make their dens within. But the decay was relatively recent. Some town buildings still stood, for Paul was able to restore the city when he chased the animals away; and in the countryside the boundaries of the neglected estates were still clearly recognisable, the cleared land still distinct from the surrounding woodland and waste. It was a little less than a hundred years since the peasant republics of the *Bacaudae* had overset the political economy of Roman Armorica. Estates and towns had not recovered.

The second migration of the British, about 460, had left fewer traces in northern than in southern Brittany, and was evidently not numerous enough to revive the failing economy. When Paul came to the city, he was seeking the local *comes*, named Victor, to obtain permission to settle. Victor is described as

> a pious Christian who ruled by authority of the Lord emperor Philibert.

'Philibert' is Childebert of Paris, who reigned from 511 to 558; and Victor turned out to be Paul's cousin. He lived in the offshore island of Batz and his dominion was evidently small. But permission to settle was needed. It was eagerly sought and easily obtained. Very many are said to have crossed, with clerical companions ranging from a dozen to a hundred, often with laymen and servants in addition. The modern place names preserve ample traces of the settlers; there are over 150 lay *plebes*, now spelt Pleu-, Plou-, with similar variants, together with almost as many ecclesiastical centres, *Llan*, *Locus* and others, and many more that bear the names of individual saints. Wherever the origin of these names can be checked, the great majority belong to the sixth century. The migration plainly involved some tens of thousands of persons; though some came from Ireland, a few from Dumnonia and a few from north Wales, the great majority of the monks whose origin is given are said to have been born or educated in Gwent or Glevissig, the southern Welsh lands where Roman manners lingered. But the tradition of the secular immigrants is different. The greater part of their leaders claimed descent from the Cornovian princes of Dumnonia, and their district names proclaim the same origin. In the north-east the name Dumnonia probably prevailed from the 6th century onward, since it is common in the Saints' Lives; the south-western kingdom of Quimper was known as Cornouailles, but the name did not come into use until the 8th century or later, at much the same time as Cornwall became the usual name of the south-western tip of Britain.

The Armorican peninsula is naturally divided into clear-cut regions. A hilly wooded upland runs eastwards from the bay of Brest, dividing the northern from the southern coastlands, fertile regions of nearly equal extent; and rivers running north and south from the hill subdivide both coastal territories. Achm and Léon in the north-west are separated from Dumnonia by the Morlaix river, and the Gouet separates eastern from western Dumnonia; south of the hills, the Blavet is the natural frontier between the territory of Quimper, or Cornouailles, and the Vannetais. The size and fertility of the eastern states made them stronger than their western neighbours, and the constant need to hold their frontiers against the Franks forced them to maintain powerful armies, so that Dumnonian rule easily extended over Léon and Achm, and Vannes might as easily subdue Quimper. But in the west, the hills interpose a compact region between the northern and southern powers; they fork like a claw to enclose the territory of Carhaix. Its surrounding hills make it a natural fortress, that might serve a strong ruler as a base whence he could strike in all directions to subdue the rest of Brittany; but when its natural defences were breached, it became a prize to be disputed between Léon and Cornouailles.

The whole peninsula became permanently British from the time of the third migration, in the 540s and 550s, and was already known to Gregory, about twenty years later, as 'Lesser Britain', *Britannia minor*. The speech and identity of the former population was altogether obliterated and forgotten, though on the ill-defined eastern border the bishops and civic authorities of Vannes, Nantes and Rennes regarded the townsmen as Latin and Roman, isolated among the dangerous and unwelcome British of the surrounding countryside.

Budic

The immigrants brought with them the political conventions of their homeland, and their counts fought each other as readily as the kings of Britain. Little is remembered of the men of the first migration save the name of their leader,

MAP 14 BRITTANY

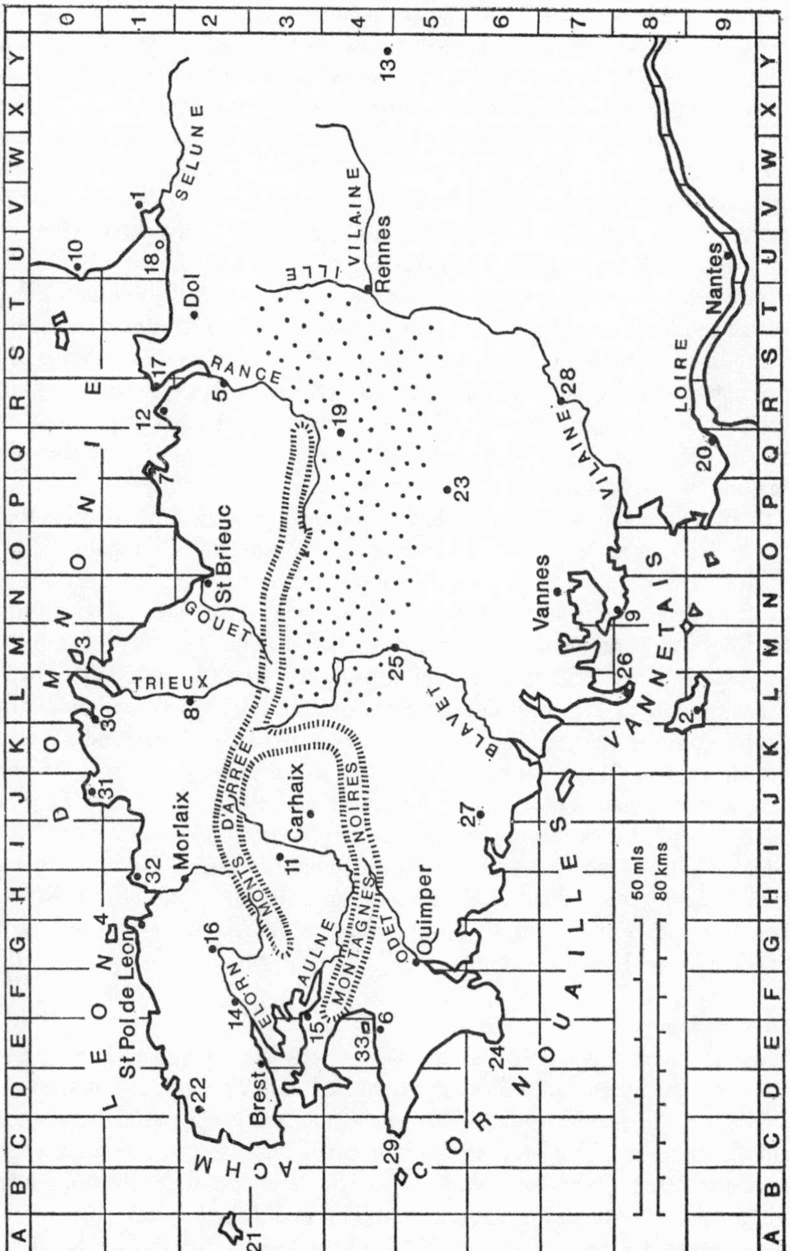

For numbered places and reference grid see Notes to the Maps

Cynan Meriadauc. Places that bear his name are commonest in the Vannetais, and Conan became a much-used name in later Brittany; Gregory knew of a ruler of this name, in early 6th-century Vannes, who may or may not have been the heir of Meriadauc. Riothamus, leader of the second migration, was regarded as the founder of the dynasties of eastern Domnonie, and the later rulers of Quimper also claimed descent from his 'son' Daniel Dremrud, who left Gaul to become 'king of the Alamanni'. The strange assertion served no later writer's interest, and is unlikely to be deliberate invention. It might derive from some unexplained misreading of a lost manuscript, but it may be that a British force accompanied the Frank and Saxon expedition that Childeric and Odovacer led against the Alamanni of northern Italy in the late 460s. Tradition is anchored to reality in the early 6th century, with Budic, whose old age and death are known to Gregory. In youth, he and his brother Maxentius, sons or heirs of Daniel, returned to Brittany to 'kill Marchell and recover their patrimony'. Budic was later exiled to Britain, probably by his brother, and reinstated with the help of Agricola of Demetia and the elder Theodoric, in Arthur's time.

Budic died about 556, after a reign of nearly forty years. The sequel is told in two unlike halves, part in the brief contemporary notice of Gregory, part in a much distorted Life. The stories complement each other. Gregory relates that Budic made an agreement with Macliavus of Vannes that when either was dead, the other would protect his son; but when Budic died Macliavus drove his son, the younger Theodoric, into exile in Britain, and seized his territory. The Life of Melor extends the story and gives its context. Melor's father, Meliau, was another son of Budic, established by his father as king in Léon, and married to the daughter of Riwal of Domnonie. Budic had evidently mastered the north-west, and overshadowed Carhaix. But Riwal invaded and conquered Léon, and killed Meliau; Melor, the infant heir, took refuge with Conomorus of Carhaix, who tried and failed to protect him from Riwal's assassins. His adherents also seem to have taken refuge in Britain, for the little-known boy saint is patron of Amesbury in Wiltshire, one of the very few British saints whose cult was localised in the English lowlands.

Conomorus

Budic had built a powerful western realm, that was dismembered on his death. The next four years decided the future of Brittany. Three rulers contended for supremacy, Macliavus, now master of the south, Riwal, master of the north, and Conomorus of Carhaix, enclosed between the western mountains. Their origins differed. Riwal was overlord of the recent immigrants from British Dumnonia, but Macliavus' subjects had been established in Armorica for more than a century. Gregory recounts his troubled past. A little before 550, Canao, or Conon of Vannes had made away with three of his brothers; the fourth, Macliavus, was sheltered by Conomorus. Canao was too strong for Conomorus to defy, and sought his brother; Conomorus hid him in a tomb, pretending that he was a corpse. Macliavus then had himself tonsured, and consecrated as bishop of his brother's kingdom; and when Canao died a few years later, he exchanged his crook for a sword, to become the new ruler. Conomorus was a Dumnonian king who still ruled in Britain, but in Brittany he was at first a lesser Lord. In Britain Paul Aurelian had visited his court at 'Villa Banhedos', Castle Dore by Fowey, and knew him as 'Conomorus, also called Marcus'. His name may still be read on the memorial stone of his son Drustanus, that stands on the cross-roads near Castle Dore, at Tywardreath. He quickly became the greatest of the three, in the accounts of Gregory as in the Lives, and he lives on in legend as King Mark of Cornwall; but until after Budic's death, he was still weak, unable to withstand either Riwal of Domnonie or Canao of Vannes.

Conomorus grew great by diplomacy and swift action. Monastic writers condemned his many marriages. He had been married to Budic's daughter. He had sheltered Macliavus in his adversity, and married his sister when he ruled Vannes, making him his enduring ally. Free from danger in the south, he annexed eastern Dumnonia, killing its ruler, whose son Iudual found refuge at the court of Childebert of Paris, in or before 557. When Riwal of western Dumnonia died, probably in 558, Conomorus occupied his kingdom, that included the recent conquests of Achm or Léon, and is said to have married his widow also. Conomorus was now more powerful than his ally Macliavus of Vannes, and controlled all the rest of Brittany. The northerners protested, and a deputation of clerics, headed by Samson, Paul Aurelian, and bishop Albinus of Angers, journeyed to Paris, to induce Childebert to restore Iudual. But Conomorus thwarted them by himself accepting the status of Prefect of the king of the Franks.

Conomorus overreached himself in a greater gamble that failed. He made a friend of Chramn, son of Childebert's brother Clothair, who had quarrelled with his father and found shelter with his uncle. But when Childebert died in 558, Clothair acquired his kingdom, and his rebel son fled. Conomorus received him in Brittany. The stakes were high. If Chramn had prevailed against his father and his brothers, he would have mastered the whole of the Frankish dominions from the Atlantic to the Elbe, with a fair hope of retaining them undivided; Conomorus might expect high influence at Paris, with his title to all Brittany secured, Rennes and Nantes added to his dominion.

The gamble failed. Clothair's army killed Chramn and Conomorus, in December 560. The hard fought campaign is told in dramatic detail by Gregory and in the Lives, which saw only the victory of Iudual, backed by Frank allies. Samson's biographer, writing 30 to 40 years after the event, describes his return from Paris with Iudual, by the way of the Channel Islands, where he distributed 'little gold coins', evidently Frankish *trientes*. The fullest story is told in Le Grand's version of a lost life of Samson. Iudual's landing inspired a general rising, that enabled his army to strike westward, pushing Conomorus back into his inland territory of Carhaix in two battles, and thereby winning control of the north coast. Conomorus brought over reinforcements from Britain, who included 'Danes, Northmen and Frisians'; though Danes and Northmen are words often used loosely of north German barbarians, Frisians have no such connotation. The word suggests a source written near to the time when Frisians were still a distinct entity among the Saxons of Britain, hardly later than the 6th century.

The German forces landed at Ile Tristan in the bay of Douarnenez, on the west coast. The name is arresting, for neither Le Grand nor his source knew that Conomorus was king Mark, or connected him or the island with the legend of Tristan; the name of the island implies an early association, perhaps a belief that Conomorus' son commanded the reinforcements landed there. Thus strengthened, Conomorus marched north to meet Iudual and Clothair at Ploueneur Menez, a dozen miles south of Morlaix. At first the Frisians overwhelmed the enemy infantry, but after two days they were broken by a charge of Iudual's formidable British horse. Conomorus was wounded in flight, fell from his horse, and was trampled to death in the press of the rout; his body was recovered and buried at Castle Dore. Chramn escaped to the ships, but returned to rescue his wife and children; he and they were caught, locked in a cottage, and burnt. The Germanic troops hastened to their vessels, but found them burnt by peasants, who wisely sided with the victors.

The battle was decisive for the future of the Franks as well as the British. Clothair died at Tours in December 561, a year and a day after the death of Chramn. As he died, the old king protested

> Wa! Wa! How great is the king of Heaven, who can kill kings as great as I am.

He was the last of the great Merovingian kings. His surviving sons divided his kingdom, but none of his descendants revived the united power of the vast empire that he had held, and that Chramn had sought to inherit. In Brittany, Iudual and the son of Riwal recovered their inheritance, and Macliavus retained or regained Vannes; one tradition asserts that Caradoc Vreichvras, a king in southern Britain, ruled Vannes for a time about the middle of the sixth century, and it may be that he ousted Macliavus in 560, either as the ally of Conomorus or of Clothair.

Waroc and Iudicael

Pre-eminence in Brittany soon passed to Vannes. Macliavus was himself killed in 577, by Theodoric the younger, who returned from Britain with an army that regained his father's kingdom of Quimper. Gregory gives the date and the event; the genealogists of Britain held that he married the sister of Urien of Reged, then all-powerful in the north, and the marriage suggests that at least a part of his army also came from Reged. But in Vannes itself Macliavus was succeeded by his son Waroc, who soon made himself the most powerful prince in Brittany.

The Vannetais was thenceforth known as Bro-Guerech, the land of Waroc; Gregory's last chapters report Waroc's stubborn campaigns, fought to win Rennes and Nantes. They were prolonged for more than 200 years, and seem to have succeeded soon after Gregory's death, when a British ruler is said to have been installed in Rennes.

Waroc evidently avenged his father's death, for the traditions of south Wales held that Theodoric returned to Britain to die on the Wye, where his son Mouric founded the dynasty of Glevissig. Thereafter Waroc united the Armorican British against the Franks; a second Budic ruled Quimper; a son of Conomorus campaigned as Waroc's ally; in the north, Iudual's son Iuthael was the ruler of Rennes, evidently also as Waroc's ally. His long reign shifted the centre of power to the north, for he married the heiress of western Dumnonia, and his son Haeloc ruled the united territory. His sole rule was maintained by a ruthless uncle and a forceful cleric. Haeloc's uncle ensured that his brothers were either murdered or tonsured, lest their claim divide the kingdom, and ecclesiastical pre-eminence passed not to the successors of Samson at Dol, but to the formidable and tempestuous Malo, whose biographer praised his aristocratic contempt for the rabble, and emphasised the widespread hostility that his vast monastic estates aroused. But in the end an 'impious generation arose', expelled Malo, overthrew Haeloc, and fetched his brother Iudicael from his monastery to replace him, early in the 7th century.

Iudicael was a man of religion. He reigned in the generation when Irish and English monks were spreading the ideal of ascetic simplicity through northern and eastern Gaul. His own monastic allegiance was to Samson's pupil Meven, wholly alien to the prelatical ambition of Malo. He concluded a lasting peace with king Dagobert of the Franks in 637, and his close personal friends included Dagobert's ministers Eligius and Dado, better known as St. Eloi and St. Ouen. In 640, all three abdicated secular authority; Eligius and Dado became bishops; and Iudicael returned to the monastery of his friend Meven. His faith was shared by his family, for his brother Iudoc, St. Josse, founded numerous monasteries in eastern Brittany, as well as in Picardy and Flanders, and his son Winnoc of Wormhoult became, and remains, the patron saint of the Belgian littoral.

Almost nothing is recorded of the history of Brittany for two hundred years after the abdication of Iudicael. Its ninth-century kings made large gains in Normandy, but though they were driven back, Rennes remained British. Its dynasty had an illustrious future. Count Alan of Brittany brought a large contingent to the army with which William of Normandy conquered England; many were rewarded with lordships and lands on the Welsh border, where they understood the speech of the natives; one of them was the ancestor of Geoffrey of Monmouth, whose alleged 'little book' from Brittany made him the most influential writer on British history for centuries to come, and another was ancestor of the Fitzalans of England and of the Stuart kings of Scotland.

Brittany was named and created by the British in the first generation of

Arthur's successors. Theirs was the largest migration. The descendants of the earlier immigrants were ultimately absorbed into the native population, leaving nothing behind them but a few place names. Without the reinforcement of the sixth-century migration, the earlier settlers in Armorica might also have been absorbed; and could not have withstood Frankish conquest and colonisation. The best-remembered immigrants were monks. But the laymen who named tens of thousands of farms and hamlets and towns far outnumbered them. They left Britain to escape the society of the tyrants whom Gildas denounced. Armorica became Lesser Britain because the tyrants seized power and gave men cause to emigrate. The existence of Brittany is to be reckoned among the consequences of Arthur's victory and Arthur's failure.

CHAPTER FIFTEEN
ENGLISH IMMIGRANTS

The Homeland

The homeland of the English was the sandy coast of north-western Germany, between the Zuyder Zee and the northern tip of Denmark. Very many of the pots and ornaments there buried are exactly matched in fifth-century graves in eastern England, and a number of identical names for peoples, regions and persons were and are in use on both sides of the sea. The grave goods of the coastal peoples distinguish them from their neighbours; from the Danes, who then lived in southern Sweden, and from the Frisians, the Franks and the Suebian Germans to the south. They also mark their internal differences.

Roman writers and Germanic legend mention a number of Ocean peoples, Jutes, Varni, Angles, Myrgingas, Langobards, Saxons and others. Many of their names are long forgotten, but some endure. Jutland is still the name of northern Denmark, Angel of a district in north-eastern Schleswig, and Lower Saxony still describes much of north-western Germany; other names survive where emigrants took them, for the English, called *Angli* in Latin, now live in Britain, and the Langobards have given their name to northern Italy, Lombardy.

Peoples were on the move, and took their fashions with them. In the 4th and 5th centuries, the ornament north of the Elbe differed from that used to the west of the estuary. There styles began to mingle from the early or middle 4th century, several generations before the migration to Britain. Peoples originally distinct were combining to form a single nation. Late Roman writers knew that nation as Saxon, and extended their name to all the northern Germans immediately beyond the Frisians and the Franks; they neither knew nor cared to remark its internal divisions. Germanic tradition knew the Saxons as one among the constituent peoples, but does not clearly indicate their territory; it is commonly assumed to have lain west of the Elbe.

The emigrants moved for specific purposes, that stem from the history of the Roman empire and of barbarian Europe. The central fact of that history in the fourth and fifth centuries is the Migration of the Peoples, known to modern German writers as the *Völkerwanderung*; the voyages of the Saxon peoples were one relatively late part of that general movement. Migration had two aims; those who moved wished to leave where they were; and they also wished to settle where they arrived. But these aims were not equally easy to realise; for men could leave home freely, but they could only settle where they conquered or found a welcome; so that many peoples wandered far, and often fast, in an unsuccessful search for secure lands. The evidence is often oversimplified, for most of it comes from Roman writers, who observed the arrival of barbarians upon their borders, but were rarely interested in their origins. Sometimes powerful peoples, like the Ostrogoths and the Huns, subdued many other barbarian nations, and grouped them into large empires. Sometimes an entire population moved, or was absorbed by greater neighbours. More often, sections of a population, large or small, left home, sometimes with their women and children, sometimes as groups of adventurous young men. Several different detachments might leave the same homeland in different generations; some might settle in their new homes for a few years, some for centuries, and sections might move further on. It was therefore quite normal for several distinct groups of the same nation, like the Heruli or the Rugii, to live at the same time on or near different Roman frontiers, while others of their kinsmen remained in their old homeland; and in the conquered lands groups drawn from numerous distinct origins might combine into a single people in their new homes.

These complexities make it difficult to relate the archaeology to the statements of Roman writers. Often there is no archaeology, for small peoples, or those who moved on after a few years, left little behind them. Peoples who stayed permanently in their new homes, like the Saxons in Britain, left ample trace, but bands of footloose warriors, or of groups too small to take with them skilled jewellers and potters, could at most carry to their graves the ornaments they brought with them; their children must use the ornament available in their new homes, or none at all, as in Britain the Bernicians have virtually no ornament in the 5th and earlier 6th centuries. Moreover, ornamental styles do not always correspond with political groupings. When a Roman writer called the Chamavi of the eastern Netherlands a 'part of the Saxons' he was politically right, for he meant that they were allies or subjects of the Saxons; but they did not use Saxon ornament. Conversely, many writers carefully distinguish the Angles from the Varni, and some characteristic place names also help to tell the one from the

---

Map 15

Modern national frontiers ------

In GERMANY and the NETHERLANDS

o 5th century saucer brooches

+ 5th century cruciform brooches

In DENMARK

Inhumation burials, probably 4th century

probably 5th century

Cremation burials, probably 5th or 6th century

MAP 15 THE HOMELAND OF THE ENGLISH

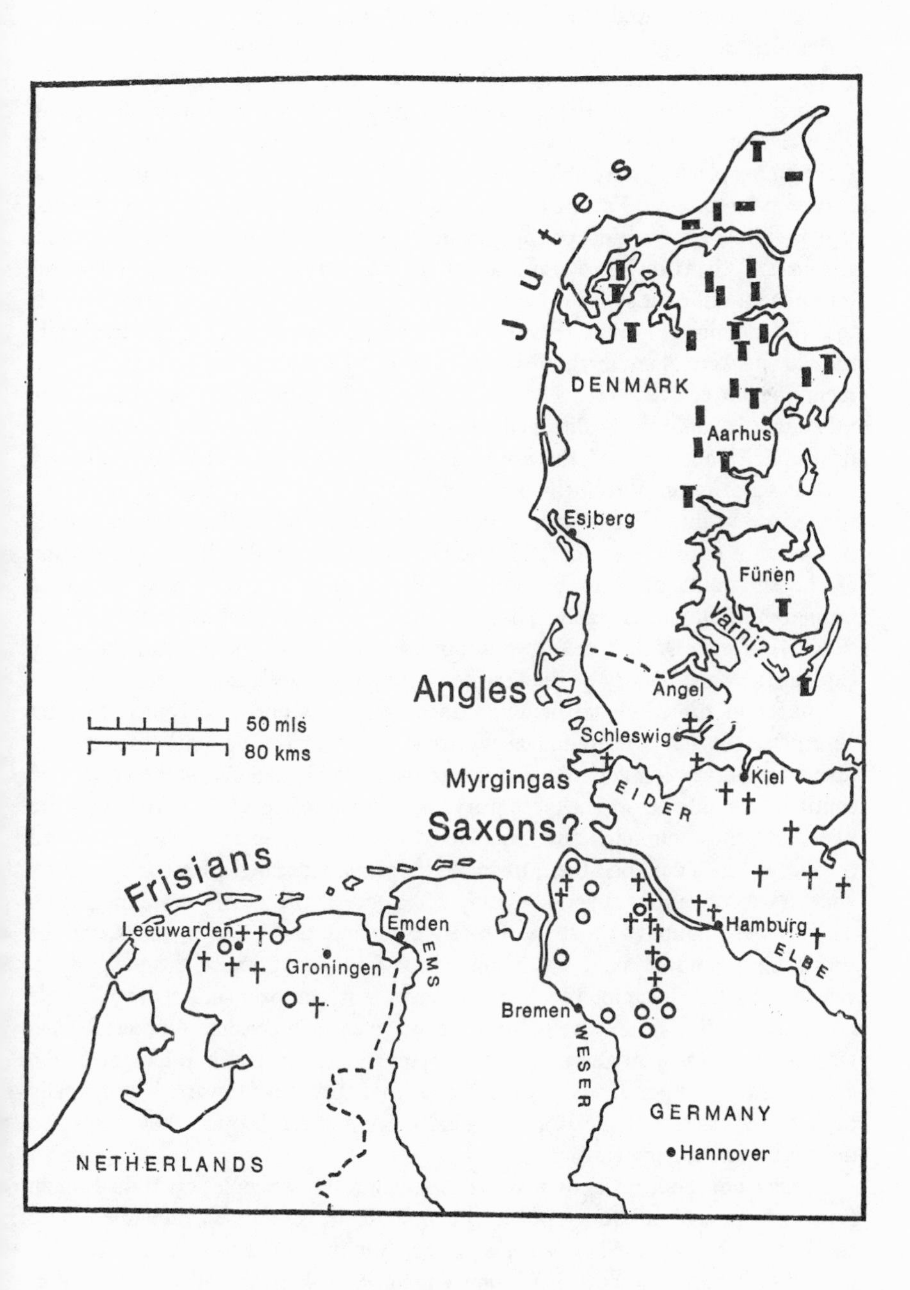

other; but they shared the same ornament, and cannot yet be distinguished archaeologically.

The Saxon peoples were buffeted by the same stresses as the rest of the Germanic migrants; but their history is somewhat better evidenced than most. They learnt to write their own language much earlier than any European German people, and were able to remember some traditions of a distant past that had been forgotten in Europe before men bothered to seek it out. Their archaeology is simpler, for in Europe the repeated fission and fusion of separate peoples encouraged them to borrow and adapt their neighbours' fashions, so that the interplay of different styles is hard to decipher, and tends to limit modern study to a few dominant groups, Frankish, Langobardic and the like. But in Britain the Saxons were alone in an alien land, cut off by the sea, and their main ornamental styles evolved relatively simply, so that the impact of particular foreign influences is more easily detected, in the districts and at the time when each developed. None the less, the impulses that brought the Saxons to Britain are part of a European movement. Emigrants left home because a large population was squeezed into a small area of poor soil, and left when they saw reasonable prospects of finding more comfortable homes elsewhere. At first, only a portion of the emigrants came to Britain, and Britain also received some Germanic immigrants from other regions. The reasons that caused the bulk of the population to move to Britain, and to outnumber other Germanic peoples there, are explained by the history of the Germanic migrations in Europe.

The main direction of the migrations was from north to south; to later chroniclers in Italy, Scandinavia was the 'womb of the nations', the original home of Goths, Langobards and others. Germanic nations were established south of the Baltic before the 1st century AD, evenly spread over the north European plain, but the mountains and woodlands of southern Germany, Bohemia and the Carpathians confined them to smaller regions, separated from each other by wide tracts of empty upland, thickly forested. In the north-west, the Saxon peoples were limited to a strip of sandy coastland, and to river banks, for the rough hinterland of bog, heath and moor forbade agriculture and pasture. Except in east Holstein, the habitable area was compact and narrow, rarely more than a few hours' walk from sea or river to moorland. Earlier Roman writers give occasional glimpses of the attempts of the Angles and Langobardi to expand into the open lands beyond the heaths; they were thwarted, principally because the barrier of the Roman Rhine prevented the peoples they wished to dislodge from moving further.

It was from the Elbe lands that the assault of interior peoples upon the Roman frontier began. About 165, a portion of the Langobardi crossed Bohemia to raid the Roman Danube. They were repulsed, but the emperor Marcus Aurelius replied with an invasion of what is now Czecho-Slovakia, that failed. The frontier broke, the northern Balkans were overrun, and fifteen years of bitter warfare left the frontier where it had been. The war brought to the surface latent social, political and regional conflicts within the empire, and also taught the barbarians that Rome was not invincible. Within a generation, the small peoples of the upper and lower Rhine grouped themselves into the large federations of the Alamanni, the 'All Men' and the Franci, the 'Free Men'; the Goths and Heruli moved south towards the Ukraine, while other peoples of central and northern Germany pressed upon the Danube. In the middle of the 3rd century the combined assaults of these peoples smashed the European frontiers of Rome, while Persians and African barbarians overwhelmed the eastern and southern mediterranean. The frontiers were restored, but remained under constant attack; and the barbarians, hitherto raiders in quest of plunder to take home, began to aim at conquest and settlement.

The fourth century was an age of consolidation upon the Roman frontiers, of turbulence in central Germany. Constant warfare encouraged the coherence of larger political units, and stimulated the growth of military monarchy. Eormenric the Goth established a vast empire from the Baltic to the Black Sea, that included Slavs and Ests as well as Germans and Sarmatians. Roman writers begin to notice warrior kings among the Franks and Alamanni, who were now also pressed in the rear by Burgundians and Vandals from the Baltic; and also to distinguish the Saxons from the Franks, and to deplore their frequent raids upon the coast of Gaul and Britain, though at first only the Jutes seem to have contributed to the southward migrations, leaving Jutland considerably depopulated.

Native tradition differentiates between the constituent peoples. It emphasises that the Saxons themselves did not create a national monarchy until the 9th century, but it believed that among the northerners, the Jutes, the Angles and the Varni, the institution of monarchy was already established by about the end of the third century. The triumphs of Offa of Angel were remembered in two old English poems, in legends that the medieval monks of St. Albans adapted without understanding, in two Danish chronicles, and in the dynastic tradition of the Mercian kings. Offa's grandfather Wiglaet is said to have defeated and killed the Jutish king Amlethus, the original of Shakespeare's Hamlet; Offa's father was hard-pressed, losing the stronghold of Schleswig to his northern enemies, but young Offa secured the southern border of the Angles upon the Eider, and went on to greater conquests in his mature years.

The tradition is matched by the archaeological evidence. In the time assigned to Offa, in the later 4th century, Anglian brooches and pots spread eastward through east Holstein to Mecklenberg, in large cemeteries, in lands not peopled by their ancestors; in the 5th century they extended through Pomerania to the borders of Poland, mainly in scattered burials in lands that were formerly Burgundian or Vandal or Rugian. In the south, Anglian cemeteries became numerous in Thuringia, and stretched eastward to the Elbe about Dresden, whence smaller groups crossed the mountains to join the Germanic peoples of Bohemia, about Prague, and to mingle with Quadi on the Danube, about

Bratislava. In the west, Saxon cremation burials invaded Frisian territory in the northern Netherlands, where previously an exceptionally dense concentration of Roman objects argue that the power of the empire had long prevailed; and after the late fourth century, Saxon inhumation burials with Jutish brooches suggest an additional northern migration, early in the 5th century.

The reign of Offa approximately coincided with the Gothic empire of Eormenric, that was overturned by the Huns in or about 375. Their terrifying invasion pushed the German barbarians against the Roman Danube and beyond it, and in 378 the Goths destroyed the armies of the eastern empire. Their children pressed upon Italy, opening the passes to other Germans behind them. The imperial government stripped its frontiers to defend Italy, but in vain. Vandals, Alans and Suebi swept across the Rhine, and the Goths took Rome in 410. The Goths soon settled permanently in Aquitaine, and were followed by Burgundians and others. The rivers that had dammed the expansion of the Germans for centuries ceased to be frontiers; and one of the consequences of the fall of western Rome was the creation of an independent Roman government in Britain, whose needs drove Vortigern to enlist the followers of Hengest to defend his coasts.

Hengest

The early fifth century is the time in which the saga of Hengest is set. Its outline is preserved by two documents. The old English epic poem *Beowulf*, written down in Christian England, probably in the eighth century, concerns wars between the Danes and their neighbours early in the sixth century. In the poem Beowulf's warriors are entertained by tales of still earlier heroes, in a past that was already remote to them, and one of these tales is the 'Saga of Hengest'. The poem gives a summary of the story, and a small fragment of the full saga also survived in another manuscript, termed the 'Fight at Finn's Burg', evidence that at one time the story was well known in literate Christian England.

Much is obscure, but the essence of the tale is clear. The Danish king Hnaef, with a small retinue, visited his brother-in-law, Finn Focwalding, king of the Frisians, whose forces included a body of Jutes, apparently independent, relatively recent settlers accepted into his service. Fighting broke out in Finn's hall, and many heroes fell, including Hnaef; but the hall remained in the possession of the Danes, whose leadership was taken over by Hengest, a 'royal thane'. The Danes eventually agreed to enter Finn's service and to evacuate the hall; they were given another in exchange, which they held on the same terms as the Jutes, who lived nearby. Hengest himself passed the winter with Finn, probably as a hostage; but he plotted revenge, and in the spring, with the help of reinforcements summoned from home, he surprised and killed Finn. The inhumation burials indicate that a small number of Jutes had settled in Frisian territory about the years 400 to 430; they date the incident, and locate it to the Leeuwarden area.

The texts and the burial-grounds of Britain tell the sequel. Hengest was a successful adventurer, whom chance brought to the Jutes of Frisia. Vortigern's need gave him greater opportunity. He brought a small force to Thanet in three ships, that can hardly have carried more than a couple of hundred men; but Vortigern's continuing troubles demanded ever more men and Hengest's initial success attracted willing recruits. When their number grew, he risked rebellion, in the early 440s; but the revolt misfired, and fifty years of warfare left the Saxons in possession only of limited and defined territories.

Their extent and the origins of their population are chiefly known from their burial-grounds. The evidence is full and consistent; though undiscovered sites may well be 20 or 30 times as many as those that are known, what is known is a fair sample of the whole. A map of the sites and objects known in 1920 would have far fewer symbols than one drawn in 1970, but the regional variants it shows would not greatly differ. Modern understanding of the evidence has greatly increased, and is likely to increase much more in the next half-century, but the character of the evidence is unlikely to alter significantly.

The main guides to regional difference are the manner of burial and the type of grave goods. Close study of burial rites will doubtless reveal important variation, but so far only the obvious differences between cremation and inhumation have been generally noticed. The ornamental styles of pots and brooches show more difference in detail; urns are the principal evidence for cremation burials, brooches and buckles for inhumations. Their differences and similarities help to distinguish local communities, for fashions spread easily when brides are free to meet and marry men of other districts, and when peddlars may move freely; but when adjacent areas use quite different styles, political and ethnic frontiers intervene.

Grave goods of the 5th century are easily recognised, for they are paralleled in Germany. They cannot often be as closely dated as modern studies sometimes claim, for fashions last a lifetime and overlap; but it is possible to distinguish many that were most popular early in the century, and others that came into favour later. Their evidence is consistent, for though graves often contain objects normal in different successive generations, very few contain any that are farther apart in time; it was not uncommon for a woman to take to her grave the brooches she wore as a bride and those she acquired as a grandmother, but antiques and heirlooms are rare. Inference does not however rest upon individual objects or particular graves; when several graves in the same cemetery contain similar ornament of the same date, and when the cemeteries of a region repeat common characteristics, they show whence and when the population came.

Map 3 sets down the sites where objects of the early fifth century have been recognized, and Map 6 gives those of the later fifth century. The first map indicates where the first English communities settled, within the approximate date limits of 420 and 460. Of all their many grave goods some three or four brooches and a few urns were already old-fashioned by the 420s, in vogue a generation earlier; but they are a small percentage of the total, and cannot argue that the cemeteries came into use earlier, for any immigrant population brings with it a small proportion of old-fashioned gear. The evidence cannot distinguish sites where burials began before the revolt of the early 440s from those that came into use soon after; but the revolt did not expand the territories occupied, for each region and each kind of cemetery has something of the earliest grave goods, and Gildas and the Kentish Chronicle report that after the first fury of the revolt, the Saxons returned to their previous homes in Britain, and were obliged to fight hard for the best part of twenty years to retain them. The population was still too small to fill and hold its lands, not yet able to acquire new territories; those who immediately followed the first contingents settled near their predecessors. The map therefore signals the regions of the earliest settlement, in the 420s and 430s.

The Saxons were stationed where Vortigern wanted them, from the Thames Valley to the Humber waters, to guard the east coast. If Vortigern and his Council had decided to use them against the Irish, they would have been distributed between the Dee and the Severn estuaries. Their location has nothing to do with mythical 'routes' of 'invaders' who 'penetrated' up valleys; it is the simple consequence of a decision taken by a British government at a particular time. In detail, many cemeteries are located, like Roman cemeteries, outside the walls of Roman towns, large and small, indicating that the Saxons were billeted within the walls. Others are placed on or beside Roman estates; some guard river crossings, and most of the open country sites are located by river banks, on alluvial soils easy to till. It is very possible that those which are strategically located are the earliest, billeted by government decision, and that some of the rural sites in the same regions were established by kinsmen who crossed five or ten years later; but archaeological evidence cannot deny or confirm dates so close.

The burial rite distinguishes three sharply differentiated regions. From Norfolk to York, all the dead were cremated, with the exception of a small pocket of inhumation cemeteries in and about Rutland. By the Thames estuary all the dead were inhumed unburnt. But from Cambridge to Oxford and Abingdon, down the Icknield Way and the Ouse, in the area conveniently termed the Icknield region, both rites were practised side by side in most cemeteries, from the earliest burials onwards; and in all three regions the original burial rites were maintained in the earliest cemeteries for nearly two hundred years, until pagan burial ceased, without admixture of other rites. Other customs were observed at sites that did not come into use until later, but the original cremation cemeteries admitted no pagan inhumations of any period, nor did the original inhumation cemeteries admit cremation, save that occasionally one or two cremations, usually of children, are found in large inhumation cemeteries.

These well-marked differences are linked with the origin of the settlers. Cremation prevailed through most of the Germanic homeland, except among the Jutes. But the early inhumations cannot be attributed to Jutes alone, for the burial custom of late Roman Britain was inhumation, and many of the Thames and Icknield burials are the graves of men who lived in the richest centres of Roman civilisation and most readily adopted Roman ways; moreover different rites do not always bespeak different peoples, for some simple societies develop different rites for different kinds of people, sometimes, for example, inhuming bachelors and cremating married persons.

The difference of rite is no more than a general indication. Its meaning is explained by the grave goods. The cremation cemeteries cannot be examined in detail until a comprehensive catalogue of urns is available for study; but preliminary work suggests some important conclusions. Vessels paralleled in Jutland are also found in Europe in Frisia, but not in the lands between. In Britain they are commonest in Kent and Surrey, but elsewhere they have been observed only in the cremating regions, nearly all of them in the earliest cemeteries. Frisian urns of continental Anglian or Saxon inspiration are very numerous in earlier 5th-century graves, also commonest in the cremating areas. Anglian and Saxon traditions were already mixed to the west of the Elbe before the migration began, and are as mixed in Britain, though Anglian influence is somewhat more evident in many of the cremating cemeteries, Saxon influence in the mixed cemeteries of the Icknield region.

The indications of the pottery will remain faint and tentative until the whole assemblage can be surveyed; they suggest that in the early 5th century many of the immigrants did not move in compact bodies from one Germanic to one British region. Jutes, Angles, Saxons, Frisians and others were not each confined to one region of Britain; but though each region drew some settlers from several German districts, each had its majority element. Jutes were most prominent in the Thames estuary, Angles and Frisians in the cremation areas, Saxons somewhat more noticeable in the Icknield region. These indications are matched by the evidence of brooches. The newcomers used many kinds of brooch, but only those called 'cruciform' and 'saucer' are numerous and datable, and evolve continuously throughout the pagan period. Both evolve from small, simple and delicate early 5th-century forms to large ornate later versions. The early cruciform is a slender graceful brooch, its foot suggesting a horse's eyes and nostrils, its head decorated with three small knobs at top and sides, which give it its name; the saucer brooch is so termed because it is a concave disc, its common 5th-century decoration five running scrolls neatly rendered in chip carving. The earliest cruciform brooches are few, found in Kent and Essex, in and near Cambridge, by Bedford and on the northern borders of Northamptonshire; the smallest and simplest saucer brooches are found in the Oxford region, at Luton and in Surrey. In Europe both are found in Frisia and on the west bank of the Elbe; but between the Elbe and the Baltic, in Holstein and Mecklenburg, where 5th-century Anglian colonists were numerous, cruciforms brooches are plentiful, saucer brooches unknown. The cruciform brooch is in principle Anglian and Jutish, the saucer brooch proper to the mixed Anglian and Saxon culture west of

the Elbe. In Britain each had its zones, the cruciform brooch most popular wher
Jutish, Anglian and Frisian urns are most used, the saucer brooch predominan
at the southern end of the Icknield region; but these zones are not exclusive, fo
one of the early saucers was buried at Norwich, and in the fifth century crucifor
brooches were buried by the middle Thames as often as saucer brooches. In th
earlier sixth century, partition was to restrict each area to its own fashion
confining the cruciform brooch to the Anglian north and midlands, but as yet n
frontiers barred the free movement of ornamental styles, and free movement wa
regained after the English victories of the late sixth century.

The mixed settlement of the fifth century was not remembered, and late
national names implied a simpler link between the regions of Britain and of th
homeland, so that in the 8th century Bede inferred that

> The nation of the English, or Saxons . . . came from three of the mightier peoples of Germany, the Saxons, the Angles and the Jutes. The men of Kent and Wight descend from the Jutes. . . . From the Saxons . . . come the East, South and West Saxons. From the Angles, of the country called *Angulus*, between the districts of the Jutes and the Saxons, which is said to have remained empty thereafter until the present day, came the East and Middle Angles, the Mercians and all the stocks of the Northumbrians. Their first leaders are said to have been two brothers, Hengest and Horsa.

Bede made a natural deduction from the names in use in his own day, when th
Jutish origin of Kent was still remembered, to the names he knew in Europ
His summary says nothing of Frisians, or other smaller peoples, and he knew n
details of the fifth-century migrations. But he knew that many other nation
participated in them; in his day, Egbert intended to evangelise pagan German
for

> he knew that there are many nations in Germany, from whom the English, or Saxons, who now live in Britain, are known to have originated. . . . There are Frisians and Rugii, Danes and Huns, Old Saxons and Boructuari, and many others, who still observe pagan religious practices.

Bede lists the pagans whom Egbert meant to visit, not the ancestors of the Britis
for the Jutes and Angles are missing; but the context shows that in Bede's vie
these pagan peoples were or might have been among those whose ancestors se
emigrants to Britain.

Burial rites, urns and brooches hint at the origins of future kingdoms. Th
core of Hengest's first followers were Jutes and Frisians, widely distributed fro
Thames to Humber. But the recruits who followed in the next few decades we
more compactly grouped, and included larger numbers from the Elbe lands,
well as more Frisians and Jutes. Many Angles settled in the territories that lat
took their name, and many Saxons settled in the Icknield region. These a
conclusions inferred from the limited studies that have yet been undertaken. Th

of course leave many unanswered questions. The Bernicians are said to have followed Hengest's lieutenant, Octha, regarded as his son. They inhumed their dead without grave goods, and therefore they can only be shown on a distribution map by a question-mark, based on the written report, not on their archaeology. Elsewhere several of the cremation cemeteries are not known to have contained urns of the earlier 5th century, and can therefore be shown only on a later map; yet many are poorly recorded sites, only a few of whose urns survive; and it is likely that some of them belong to the earliest settlement. Some individual objects also raise queries. One brooch 'found in a tunnel' at Hornton near Banbury cannot people an otherwise empty region. In Hampshire, a few fifth-century objects have been found at Portchester and Droxford; but these few objects are more than a generation earlier than any others south of the Thames valley, within a distance of scores of miles, and until they are confirmed by future discoveries they cannot by themselves demonstrate isolated settlement at so early a date. But these queries are marginal, and do not contradict the clear pattern set by the majority of sites.

Icel

The second map shows what changed in the later 5th century, to about the time of Badon. Added territories are few. The most important are east Sussex, whose earliest grave goods contain plenty of the mid fifth century, but nothing that seems earlier; and Worthy Park by Winchester, whose first settlers brought Kentish and Sussex grave goods, towards the end of the 5th century. Both have a context. Sussex and Essex are said to have been ceded by Vortigern in the late 450s, and the Saxon Chronicle reports the landing of Aelle at much the same date. In Hampshire, the English who served Cerdic are said to have arrived about 480. But in older areas there is noticeable change, especially in the Cambridge region. On the northern border of the Icknield region of mixed cemeteries, an inhuming people settled near the River Lark. A single outpost cremation cemetery of the early 5th century, at Lackford, south of the river, was ringed by eight or nine inhumation cemeteries, all of which have 5th-century objects, none of them of the earliest period; and a few similar sites extend southward. One or two inhuming settlements were also established on and beyond the frontiers of the earlier Norfolk territory, in the north-west by the Fens and the Wash, and in eastern Suffolk. Such sites are also numerous, but more widely spaced, among the Middle Angles, between Northampton and Lincoln, and on both sides of the Humber; and a few were established near Banbury, and on the borders of the original middle Thames territory.

Though they buried their dead unburnt, the principal ornament of these newcomers was the Anglian cruciform brooch. The population of the Anglian regions grew, for in addition to the newcomers, burials in the older cemeteries were more numerous. Many more men and women had crossed the sea. One early record preserved by Nennius explains their coming. The earlier settlers throughout

Britain had all accepted the overall command of Hengest, but when he died, about 470, his hopes of conquest had faded, and the armies of Ambrosius and Arthur were winning important victories. So the English,

> when they were defeated in all their campaigns, sought help from Germany . . . and brought over the kings from Germany to reign over them.

The kings came when many of their people had gone before; and when the kings abandoned their homeland, the remainder of their population followed. The east Roman historian Procopius reported that early in the next century, a large empty land lay between the Slavs and the nearest Germans, the Varni, who were the northern neighbours of the Angles, on the modern border between Denmark and Germany. It had been the home of the Angles; and Bede was told that Angel was still unpopulated in the 8th century.

The only kings whom the English could bring were the kings of Angel, the successors of Offa. The later kings of Mercia claimed to descend from them, and knew the dynasty as the *Iclingas*, named from Icel, whose date is placed in the mid or late 5th century; and the Scandinavian epic *Beowulf*, preserved in England, recited the names of the kings who ruled in continental Angel down to Icel's father, but no further. These traditions imply a belief that king Icel moved his royal centre and the remainder of his subjects from Angel to Britain in the later fifth century. He came when the superior authority of Hengest failed. He inherited sovereignty over all the Angles, but not over Jutes, Frisians or Saxons; and in Kent, Hengest was replaced by Oesc, son of Hengest's captain in Bernicia, who came south to found the Kentish royal house, thenceforth known as the Oescingas.

The Iclingas were a dynasty, a royal family, and not a people. In their name later Mercian kings claimed sovereignty; the heir of a cadet branch, father of St. Guthlac of Crowland, ruled a substantial territory among the Middle Angles in the 7th century; and a village named Hickling lies near to Nottingham. But the places that bear the name of Icel and his dynasty concentrate in East Anglia. Hickling near Norwich lies in the heart of the old cremation area, but Icklingham lies among the new settlements on the Lark, and was in later times a royal residence, where a king's daughter was born; and Ickleton lies half a mile from one of the largest of the new cemeteries, outside the Roman town of Great Chesterford in Essex, south of Cambridge. Its contents, excavated nearly 20 years ago, are not yet published and cannot be examined, but it is known that of 200 or so burials no more than about 30 were cremations, doubtless of immigrants from the nearby Cambridge settlements.

It is therefore probable that Icel reinforced the Angles and established a royal centre among the East Angles of Norfolk and the lower Ouse. The new cemeteries reached northward to Kesteven, south of Lincoln, and occupied the south bank of the Humber, but did not reach Lincoln itself or the greater part of Lindsey;

and it is there that British tradition remembered the greatest of Arthur's battles before Badon. Icel, like Hengest before him, failed to win Britain; and when the southern English kings, who were not his subjects, made their last effort at Badon, the dynasty of Icel is not reported to have joined them; it may well be that his power had already been broken and contained.

The tiny territory of the Eslingas suggests how the power of Icel was curbed. Their homes were shielded from nearby Cambridge by a steep escarpment that serves as a natural dyke, but they also straddled the roads that lead from Cambridge towards London and the west. Their grave goods begin in the later 5th century, and are at first altogether alien from those of Cambridge, but resemble those used by the Saxons of the middle Thames, opposite Oxford. These differences suggest that they are likely to have been the enemies rather than the friends of the English of Cambridge. They came at a time when the political control of the region changed. Earlier in the 5th century, Cambridge had been the furthest outpost of the mixed cemeteries of the Icknield region, its burial customs distinct from those of East Anglia and the Lark; but in the later 5th century Icel and the new inhuming peoples engulfed Cambridge on the south and east. The Eslingas, with their Thames-side ornament, were settled there when Arthur was defeating Anglian armies, probably some years before Badon. Earlier Roman emperors had often enough levied men and families from vanquished barbarians, known as *Gentiles*, *Laeti* or by other names, and used them to guard Roman frontiers. It may well be that the Eslingas originated as subjects of Arthur's British, employed to watch the borders of the independent East Angles of Icel's kingdom.

Elsewhere movements of peoples are less noticeable. The kingdom of Kent was contained behind the Medway, and the grave goods of what is now west Kent are also akin to those of Surrey and of the Thames people. The Kentish kingdom itself was open to foreigners. Frankish influence began to be noticeable; Anglian cruciform brooches were numerous in Kent in and after the middle of the 5th century, but they ended within the century; and before they disappeared, saucer brooches began to appear in numbers. A little cremation spread in Kent and Surrey, but there, as among the Middle Angles, the history of the mixed cemeteries differs. In the Icknield region cremation and inhumation began early in the 5th century at the same time, and continued side by side; but among the Middle Angles late 5th-century inhuming immigrants appear to have joined earlier cremating communities, while in Kent colonies of cremating peoples seem to have joined earlier inhuming settlers. More exact study of the grave goods may in the future give a clearer idea of what happened, but at present the evidence gives no hint of why these people moved or upon whose authority.

The English in Europe

Grave goods in Britain show something of when and where the English came, but nothing of why they came. The burial-grounds of Europe suggest reasons. In the earlier 5th century many young men followed Hengest and brought their families; but many stayed at home, and many others moved elsewhere, eastwards towards the Oder, and southwards to Thuringia and Bohemia. The manner and the motive of the movement of the several peoples differed; the Angles, and their northern neighbours, the Varni, were ruled by kings, and had little or no Atlantic seaboard. Their earliest movement was in disciplined contingents, and at first by land. But the Saxons and the Frisians moved by sea, and the Saxons obeyed no kings. A fifth-century Gaul remarked with surprise that among the Saxons

> every oarsman is a pirate chief, so that all of them both rule and obey.

They plundered on both sides of the Channel, attracting most notice in the thirty years or so after 460, when they controlled the Sussex and Hampshire havens, raiding the Atlantic coasts of Gaul and Ireland as well. They moved fast in small mobile groups under temporary leaders, leaving little archaeological trace. In the middle of the 5th century 'Corsoldus' savaged Armorica, and Odovacer's Saxons settled briefly on the lower Loire; they followed him to Italy, and are no more heard of. A few remained, for there were some Saxons near Nantes a century later, and many more lived in northern Gaul; but there is as yet no way of telling whether these men were descended from Odovacer's people, or from later immigrants. Other substantial bodies of Saxons, with or without their families, are recorded on particular occasions in different parts of Europe in the 5th and 6th centuries, but few stayed long enough to leave recognisable burial-grounds, and the texts do not often distinguish Atlantic Saxons from the Angles.

English Expansion in the Earlier Fifth Century

In the middle of the century the Angles and the Saxons and their allies were the most extended and the most vigorous of the northern Germans, in arms from Pomerania and Bohemia to the Atlantic. But by the end of the century they had all but disappeared from Europe. The fundamental reason is plain; they were too dispersed to resist the pressures that bore upon them. Had the whole nation migrated together to Britain in Hengest's time, they might have won the island quickly, and held it as firmly as the Goths held Aquitaine, or as the Vandals held Africa; or if they had all moved south together, they rather than the Franks might have mastered central Europe north of the Alps. But they were not yet a compact nation; Angles and Varni under their kings, Saxons and Frisians in separate bands, each went their own way. Yet theirs was an age when other barbarians were forming into large nations, and they succumbed to stronger peoples who pressed upon them from the south, the north and the east.

MAP 16 THE ENGLISH IN EUROPE

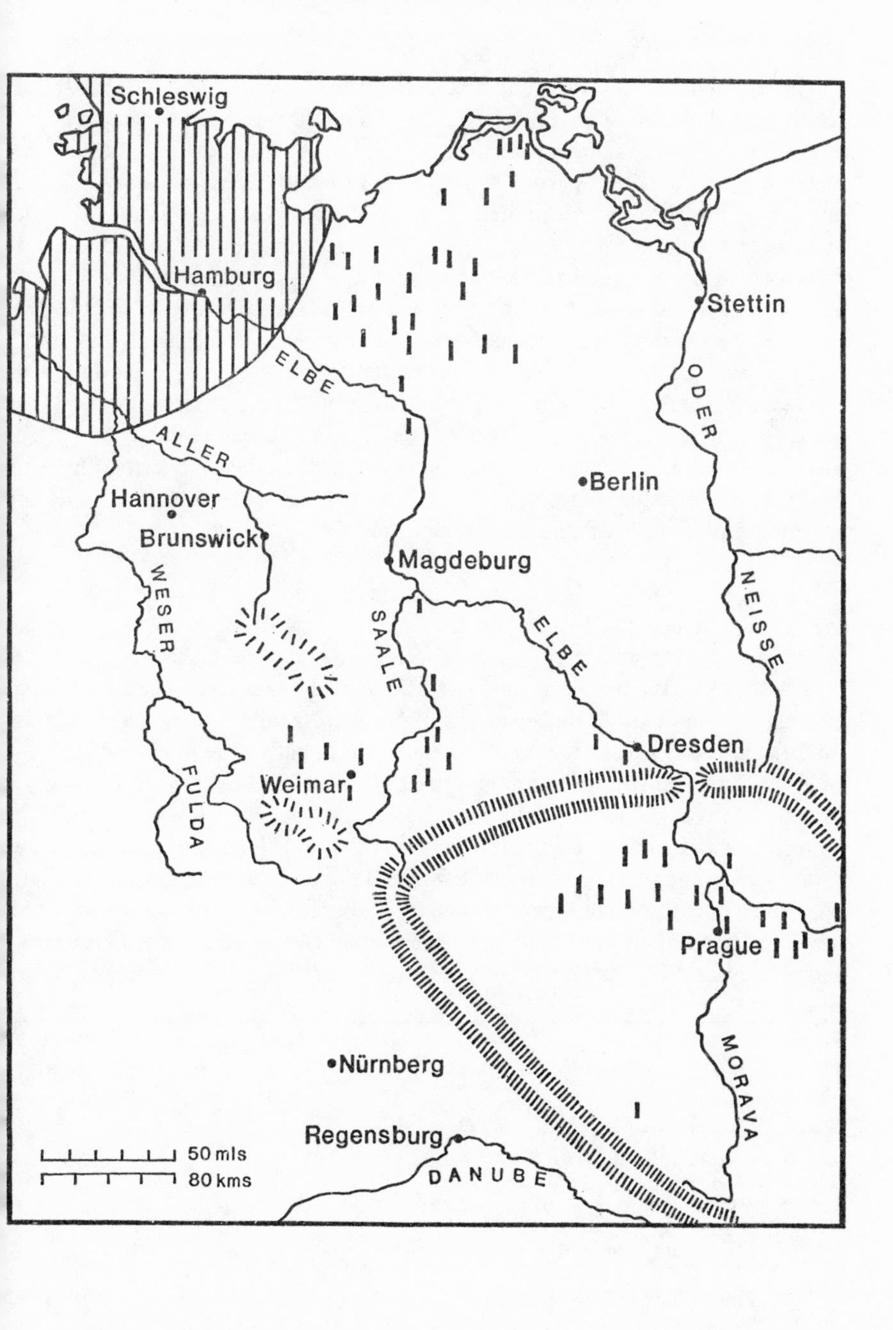

| | | The Homeland (see Map 15) | English grave goods elsewhere

Pressures on the English

These pressures are not easy to assess, for peoples on the move are harder to study than those who stay in one region; and enquiry is further hampered by modern political divisions. Government budgets oblige scholars to survey the material available within particular states, and to seek the early history of their present populations. These limitations are not easy to avoid, but they do not help understanding, for the peoples of the migration age were not contained within these borders, and the ancestors of many modern nations had not yet occupied their future lands. The study of Britain is relatively easy, for the sea marks a frontier that time has not changed; but even in Britain it has until quite recently been fashionable to concentrate upon the origins of the English, disregarding the bulk of population as an irrelevant fringe of Celtic twilight, to be treated as though the natives were exterminated or driven into Wales, where their history should properly belong, without impact on the conquering English. In Europe, confusion is worse, for modern frontiers cut across the lands of ancient peoples, and remain sensitive and unstable.

The peoples nearest to the Roman frontiers are best recorded, and it was they who circumscribed the English on the south. Political power changed out of recognition during the later 5th century. In the middle of the century the Franks were still the people of the lower Rhine, and had not yet penetrated deep into the interior of Gaul. But in a reign of 30 years, from 481 to 511, king Clovis subdued all Gaul except the mediterranean south, and made it France. In 496 he also subjugated the Alamanni and mastered southern and central Germany; Frankish grave goods intruded into Thuringia, and in Bohemia Frankish cemeteries suddenly and completely replaced those of the north Germans. The break is sharp enough to mean that the former Langobard and Anglian population was driven out; the Angles merged with the Langobards, who established themselves on the frontiers of Pannonia, on the Roman Danube, in modern Hungary, before they crossed the Alps to occupy and name northern Italy in 568. The

---

Map 17

—— Western frontier of the Slavs, and of place names in *-itz*

–·–·– Approximate limit of place names in *-in*

– Place names in *-büttl* or variants

I Place names in *-lev* or *-leben*

······ Western border of the Thuringians

MAP 17 PRESSURES ON THE CONTINENTAL ENGLISH

Franks also mastered the Frisians, and subsequently helped them to repel a Danish invasion, in about 525. The Frisians later spread westward to the Weser, into lands that had formerly been Saxon; but the wide dominion of the Franks already blocked southward movement from the English homeland.

Pressure from the north was gentler but nearer. During the later 5th century the Danes migrated from southern Sweden into the Baltic islands and the thinly peopled peninsula of Jutland; an occasional grave that contains both Jutish and Danish ornament suggests that they were accepted with little resistance, but their conquest was complete; they gave their new homes the permanent name of Denmark, and bore upon the territories of the Varni and the Angles.

Pressure from the east was stronger, but it is harder to define and to date. The archaeology of the northern Slavs is indifferently studied, for in countries that remain Slavonic to the east and south, interest concentrates upon their own territories, while in the lands that medieval immigrants conquered in the north, the study of early Germans is more popular than the study of Slavs. By the end of the 8th century ample evidence indicates a stable frontier. Slavonic territory reached near to Kiel and Hamburg, and the border ran southward on a line not greatly different from that which today divides eastern from western Germany. The Slavs expanded west of the middle Elbe, to include much of Hanover, which is now in west Germany; but Thuringia, now east German, centred upon Weimar and Erfurt, remained a German land.

The evidence is poorly studied, chiefly because of an easy modern view, which tends to assume without argument the Slavs 'filtered' late into lands that Germans had earlier abandoned voluntarily. But the place names and the archaeology are not easily reconciled with such romantic notions. The pottery of the Slavs is simple and conservative. The characteristic decoration of middle Slavonic vessels from the Baltic to the Balkans shared common designs, and the undecorated wares of earlier centuries were also similar in shape. They reached up the Danube and the Baltic coast; and on the Danube, where their approximate date can be determined by their association with the ornament of Romans and of other barbarians, they run on from the 5th century, but they are rarer in regions that the Slavs first occupied in and after the later 6th century. No evidence yet argues that they are significantly later in the north than in the south, and in the north their western limit is the town centre of Hamburg. The city is surrounded by earlier German burials, but none are reported from within its ancient walls. The accessible published illustrations of the Hamburg cemetery include Slavonic forms that on the Danube would hardly be later than the early or mid 6th century, together with vessels that recall late Roman provincial forms; though some German scholars admit them to be Slavonic products, others claim them as 'late Saxon', and most assert a later date.

The evidence that argues that Hamburg was founded by 6th-century Slavs naturally offends modern national sentiment. But though the frontier was later pushed back some 20 or 30 miles to the east of Hamburg similar evidence from other sites and from place names concurs. Slavonic place names have as yet received hardly any of the study that has been devoted to English, Scandinavian and Germanic names. The early spellings have rarely been studied, and only broad generalities can be extracted from a survey of their modern forms. Yet these forms show one outstanding contrast. The commonest terminations that are exclusively Slavonic end in *-itz* or *-in*, as in Chemnitz, or Berlin; but though the names in *-itz* extend to the furthest frontier of the Slavs, those in *-in* do not. They reach southward from the Baltic and northward from the Danube, but they are not found in a wide central territory between, that extends across the upper Elbe into Poland and Slovakia; and it is in this area, in the Elbe about Dresden, that Germanic burials last longer than elsewhere. Place names give no date; but the 6th-century Roman historian Procopius knew of Slavs by their final furthest Baltic frontier early in the 6th century.

So marked a frontier has a cause. Where place names are better studied, the immediate cause of such difference is regional dialect, but commonly a difference in date and stage of settlement underlies the frontier of dialect; so the varying forms of English names that end in *-ing*, *-worth* and the like differ in local and linguistic usage, but each usage was common at a particular time. The evidence can be no more than a pointer until Slavonic place names have been seriously studied. But the combined implication of the place names, the archaeology and the texts is that the Slavs pushed westward along the Danube and the Baltic at much the same time, during the 5th and earlier 6th centuries. In the north their advance is matched by the retreat of the English, whose Mecklenburg burial-grounds went out of use about the middle of the 5th century, a generation or more before those by the Elbe.

The pressure of the Slavs was subtler and more insidious than the assault of German armies. The centralised forces of the Germans were trained to war. Their excavated settlements show that successive peoples occupied the same cleared areas, separated by tracts of uncleared land; their history is clearest in the hillier south, especially in Bohemia, where hundreds of settlements were jammed together in a strip of fertile land in the north, no larger than an English county, where large rivers flow together below Prague, while in the upland that constitutes most of Bohemia scarcely more than half a dozen sites are known to have been cultivated before the coming of the Slavs. Throughout their history, the Germanic peoples had learnt to conquer districts already settled; and when they needed more land, they were readier to attack their neighbours than to clear wild woodland; for their historical experience equipped them to cut down people rather than trees. But the Slavs had as yet no centralised organisation, no armies, kings, or princes richly buried; they fought in armies only when they were themselves mastered and swept along by others, as by the alien Hunnic Avars in the Danubian lands. Otherwise, their pioneers advanced in large numbers of small groups, and held their lands because a different agricultural technology enabled them to clear scrub and woodland, and to till heavier soils that their predecessors had left wild. In the future, their technology was to revolutionise the economy and the warfare of Europe, for they and the Avars brought with them the stirrup, that enabled a mounted man to thrust with a heavy lance and to strike more strongly with his sword; and probably also the horse collar, that enabled medieval agriculture to plough the soil and transport loads four or five times more effectively than in the past. The Slavs did not conquer their predecessors; they surrounded and stifled thinly peopled regions, for they had no army to be destroyed in a single heroic engagement, leaving its lands defenceless; each settlement had to be attacked individually, and their settlements were very numerous, scattered in difficult terrain, well-placed to wear down and engulf any early German army that ventured among them.

In the mid fifth century, the homeland of the English was secure, and beyond it a choice of broad and open ways invited emigrants. But by the end of the century the expansion of the Franks, the Danes and the Slavs closed in upon the English. They were not expelled, but their possibilities of expansion on land were checked, and their territory was threatened. Icel led the remainder of the Angles to join the strongest of their colonies, who were in urgent need of reinforcement; and most of the Saxons followed their example. Together they formed the English nation in Britain; they left Europe because they could no longer maintain their ancient homes. The English came to Britain because they were squeezed out of Germany by the pressure of the Franks, the Danes and the Slavs.

After Badon

Britain was partitioned after the victory of Badon; and the main frontiers may well have been drawn before the last campaign. The English remained in a number of separate territories (see Map 8, p. 135). Their extent was reduced. In a wide stretch of country between Northamptonshire and the Thames, in the zone of the main fifth-century wars, where English settlement had been thin and scattered, few burials are known for three generations, except around Dunstable and Luton; and in Northamptonshire itself, the English were restricted. The normal brooches of the earlier 6th century are rare; the graves contained many of the little brooches termed 'small long' that are cheap imitations of Anglian cruciforms; but their dating has not yet been worked out, and it is uncertain whether any or many of them date early in the century. The meaning of the Northamptonshire burials cannot be learned until these brooches, and the urns, are more closely studied. At present it can only be remarked that the English who remained in the region did not have access to much of the ornament that their neighbours used. Elsewhere, harsh frontiers prevented the movement of fashions. Cruciform brooches were confined to the Anglian districts, saucer brooches to the Thames and the south, to the Dunstable area and to the Eslingas; and each district developed its own regional variations, that rarely passed beyond their own borders. Regional fashions in the naming of places also hardened, as

-ingham among the Angles, and others elsewhere. Gildas complained that the British did not visit the lands occupied by the barbarians; it is equally evident that the barbarians did not visit each other.

The cemeteries have little to say of the political government of those buried in them. Other texts do, and serve to explain something of the little that can be learned from the burials. English tradition is clear that only two kingdoms yet existed, that of the Oescingas in Kent, and of the Iclingas among the Angles. It is confirmed by the European contemporary notice of Procopius, who reported that in the 530s,

> three populous nations inhabit the island of Britain, each of them ruled by a king. These nations are named the *Angiloi*, the *Frissones*, and the *Brittones*, from whom the island is named.

Procopius was well-informed about the northern nations; he wrote of a time when Arthur, the last single king of the British, was recently dead. The heirs of Icel ruled the Angles and king Eormenric ruled the Jutes of Kent, who had not yet forgotten that their ancestors had come from Frisia. English tradition confirms Procopius, for it has preserved separate notices of the dates when other kingdoms came into being, all of them late in the 6th century; and it remembered that previously their peoples had been led by notables, not ruled by kings. The graves give some evidence of the notables. Burials of the 5th century show little social difference; the men were buried with spear and shield, the women with simple jewellery, few of them better adorned than others. But from the beginning of the 6th century, especially among the Middle Angles, datable swords become commoner in men's graves, and some women were buried with richer jewels and with emblems of authority, a spherical or faceted crystal slung between the thighs, a ceremonial iron blade by the arm. Differences of wealth and rank increased throughout the century, but the monumental barrows of kings and under-kings were not constructed before its last decades.

Most of the main territories contained a multitude of small peoples, each with their individual names, Wissa, Wixna and the like. None of these names are known to have been brought from Germany, and though some may have been, most are likely to have been adopted in Britain, as the men of each locality, often drawn from different continental origins, formed themselves into new political units. These were the communities that bred men of power and wealth, whose dignity the graves sometimes preserve. Some of the small English districts, about Abingdon or Luton, or the Sussex Ouse, may well have been grouped in a single community; but the larger Anglian regions each contained several peoples, many of whose names are known. Patient local study of variations in ornament and burial custom may in the future help to identify some of them, and determine their borders.

A few obvious inferences are yet possible. Since the lands of the Middle Angles in Leicestershire and Nottinghamshire were separated from the East

Angles of Norfolk and Cambridge, the same king could not effectively have ruled both; and since the Iclingas are reported in both territories, it may be that a cadet branch was established among the Middle Angles. Further north the settlements of Kesteven, south of the Lincolnshire Witham, formed a distinct unit; Lindsey, north of the river, accepted few of the later 5th-century inhuming immigrants, and may have remained a British territory less open to new settlement, except perhaps near to the Humber. Across the river the English of the East Riding had two main centres, about Market Weighton and Driffield, not yet joined into a single territory; in the Driffield area at least, British and English appear to have lived side by side, and the government may have been British. But the power of British York was still strong enough to be suzerain over both, and over the other scattered English communities south of the Tyne. Beyond the Tyne, the Bernicians still contained four separate small peoples in the later 6th century; these peoples may well have existed earlier, doubtless raiding their British neighbours when occasion served, but they were not yet able to assert effective independence.

Throughout Britain the English lived in very small communities each developing a class of notables. Only Kent and the East, and perhaps the Middle Angles, yet combined under a king; some of the small isolated communities may have accepted a local monarchical chief, for the Irish report of the pagan English at Abingdon at the end of the 5th century described their chief as a king. His people were no larger than an Irish *tuath*, whose ruler would not have been styled 'king' in later English usage. But English tradition gave them their own name, the *Gewissae*, and derived their dynasty from the Anglian element in their population, heirs of Wig, traditionally lord of Schleswig in Offa's time. Others may have been so ruled, for military insecurity and growing social differentiation encouraged a tendency towards individual authority, that is likely to have developed sooner in some regions than others. But whatever their internal structure, all the English were surrounded by stronger British neighbours; some of them were doubtless directly ruled by British kings, and all were confined within their borders.

In the earlier 6th century none of the English territories in Britain expanded significantly. But there was some new settlement. In the Thames estuary new immigrants arrived. Frankish fashions spread in Kent, numerous enough to suggest that Frank settlers as well as traders came, and the native English craftsmen developed Frankish ornament into the splendid jewellery of Kent, that became the greatest glory of all Teutonic art. Scandinavian influence is also noticeable in Kent, but its strongest impact was upon the opposite shore of the estuary. The Gippingas of Ipswich are the only English people whose well-furnished cemeteries contained neither the Anglian cruciform brooch nor the saucer brooch. Instead their women wore the earliest forms of the brooch described as 'great squareheaded'. It came into use in the earlier 6th century, and its wearers, who buried their dead unburnt, soon penetrated northward into the older East Anglian territories of Norfolk. But they did not join the old communities and share their cemeteries; some of their settlements were located immediately next to those of their predecessors, and may sometimes have superseded them, but others were placed between older communities. They were conquerors, for when the East Anglian kingdom achieved independence towards the end of the 6th century, its dynasty was not the Iclingas, but southerners, whose chief royal centre was at Rendlesham by Woodbridge, near Ipswich. Thenceforth the East Angles distinguished two distinct regions, of the North Folk and the South Folk, Norfolk and Suffolk; in defiance of natural geographical divisions, the South Folk annexed the lands by the Lark, between the homes of the original early 5th-century regions of Norfolk and of Cambridge, which had been peopled in Icel's time, in the later 5th century. The older North Folk were surrounded, contained and infiltrated. In Norfolk the conquerors brought with them their squareheaded brooches, but they also adapted and developed the native cruciform jewellery; and as the English expanded they carried their fashions westward into the lands of the Middle Angles and beyond.

One fragment, copied from a lost East-Anglian Chronicle, that was probably put together in or before the 8th century, remembers the newcomers.

> Pagans came from Germany and occupied East Anglia; and some of them invaded Mercia, and waged many campaigns against the British. But they were not yet organised under a single king. Many leaders occupied these regions by force, and fought many wars from there. But since the leaders were many, they have no name of their own.

Their first arrival is inserted into the narrative of medieval chroniclers at the year 527, but it is unlikely that the date meant anything more than early in the 6th century; and the advance of some of the raiders into the region that was later called Mercia is not likely to have been earlier than the mid or late 6th century. 'Germany' has no closer meaning than Germanic northern Europe, but the great squareheaded brooch gives a somewhat nearer indication. It is an English version of a popular Scandinavian brooch, that the Langobards and others spread widely in Europe; most of the Scandinavian and Langobard brooches are differently shaped from those of the English, but the nearest parallels to the English version, few in number, are found in the far north of Norway.

The Scandinavian invasion of East Anglia is dated to about the time of Arthur's death. It may have been a wholly independent movement, disregarding the British rulers; but the invasion was confined to lands already English, and did not touch British territory; and the interest of British rulers was served by the disruption of the most powerful English kingdom. It may be that they welcomed the invaders, or even invited them. Medraut perhaps opposed Arthur, and perhaps ruled in Suffolk; he might have introduced the *Gippingas* to fight at Camlann. But, however they came, they stayed in East Anglia, and did not subdue Colchester and Essex.

Other foreigners came to Deira in smaller numbers, at a date not yet determined.

A few English graves contained Alamannic grave goods and one place name locates a body of Alamanni, and suggests the manner of their coming. *Almanne Bire*, now corrupted to Almondbury, is the name of a prehistoric fort south-east of Huddersfield. It is very far from English territory, near to the natural frontiers that separated Reged from the eastern Pennine kingdoms, and its situation suggests that the kings of York stationed a Germanic force upon their borders, after Reged had asserted its independence, towards the end of the 5th century. That is also near to the time when the Alamanni were overwhelmed by Clovis the Frank, when some among them are likely to have sought new homes. They were not the only Germans to be deployed in British territory; for at half a dozen northern Roman forts, small cemeteries or burials with Deiran ornament of the late 5th or early 6th century have been observed.

It was not only in the north that English garrisons lined British frontiers. Map 18 shows their distribution. Some are of uncertain date. In Derbyshire south of the Trent, near to the probable border between the Cornovii and the Coritani, a few cemeteries have no known grave goods that seem earlier than the 6th century; they may mark new settlements, or it may be that they were earlier foundations, whose first burials chance has not yet detected. But the south-western borderlands of the Cornovii have plainer evidence; four large mixed cemeteries guarded the main crossings of the Avon on their side of the river, near Coventry and at Warwick, Stratford and Bidford. Their burials began very early in the 6th century, and their main ornament derived from the Middle Angles. Further south a larger number of smaller burial-grounds encircled the territory of Cirencester and Gloucester on the north, the west, and the south, approximately on the borders of the Roman Dubunni. The earliest of them, Fairford, may be as early as the Avonside cemeteries, but the ornament of most seems somewhat later, and was drawn from the Abingdon English; it passed on to Bidford, the nearest of the Avon garrisons, but only a little of it reached further north, though the Cotswold sites about Cirencester took little or nothing of the Anglian

---

Map 18

close shading areas shown on maps 3 and 6 (pp. 59 and 107) where early sixth century burials are numerous

wide shading areas shown on maps 3 and 6 where early sixth century burials are few and uncertain.

One dot beneath a symbol indicates period D 1 (510/540)
Two dots indicate period D 2 (530/560)
Symbols without dots indicate period C (490/530)

Other symbols as on Map 3

MAP 18 PAGAN ENGLISH SETTLEMENT 3
THE EARLIER 6th CENTURY

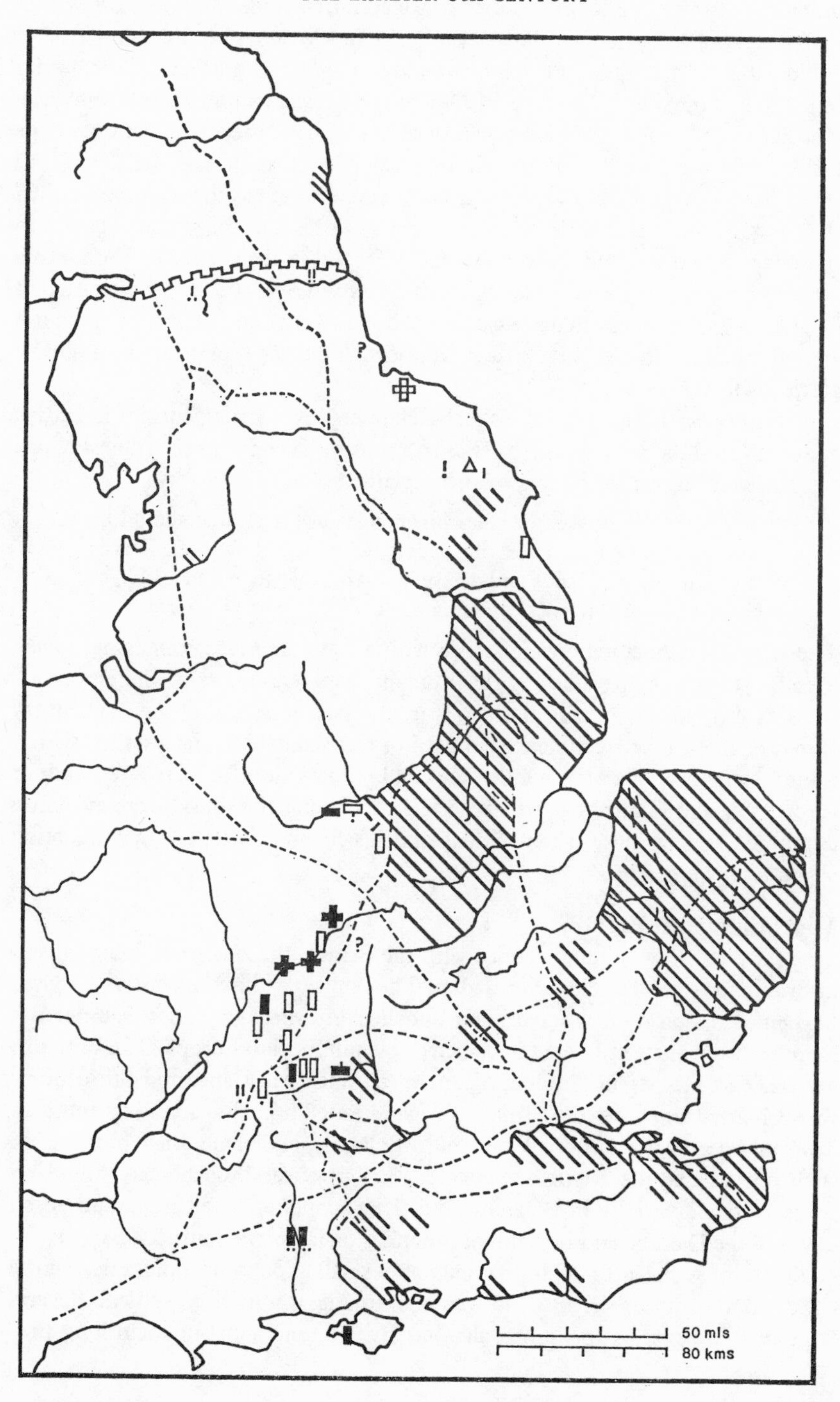

ornament of the Avon. Cornovian territory admitted brides and peddlars within its borders, but Cirencester allowed no traffic in the opposite direction.

No other such English detachments are known until a group of cemeteries immediately outside Salisbury, by Old Sarum, came simultaneously into use. The date is probably a little later than that of the Cirencester sites, but is perhaps earlier than the rebellion of Cynric in 550. The situation and the date of all three groups suggest that they moved to their new homes as the allies rather than the enemies of their British rulers, on similar terms and for similar reasons to those which had brought their ancestors to Britain in the service of Vortigern a century before. The British rulers needed dykes and rivers to deter the invasion of neighbours, who sought to drive cattle and other booty home; but they could not easily find native forces to hold their frontiers, and some found English infantry garrisons fit for their need.

Not every British king hired English defenders, for a strong current in British opinion feared the national enemy. Gildas reports and endorses the protest of one contemporary or earlier Briton, who complained that

> it is greatly to be desired that the enemies of the church should be regarded as the enemies of our people, without any kind of alliance; and that for the friends and defenders of our people we should have not only the federate allies, but also our own fathers and lords.

The writer is deliberately using words with a classical, archaic meaning; *amici*, friends, is used of the allies of the Roman people, and also of the emperor's advisers and officials; *patres*, fathers, is used of senators, and in the 4th century *foederati*, allies, is the technical term used of Germanic barbarians settled within Roman territory, like the Goths in Gaul. The rulers of Wroxeter and of Cirencester and Gloucester, perhaps of Lichfield and Salisbury, were evidently numbered among those whom Gildas and his fellows criticised for welcoming pagan English *foederati*.

Migration from Britain

Save for the few who found service with the British, the English did not expand in Britain for some 70 years after Badon. They stayed within the borders assigned to them and won no new territories; but their growing population had need of more land; for they emigrated in considerable numbers to Europe. The Frankish cemetery at Herpes in Aquitaine contained much early and mid 6th-century Kentish ornament; the small Kentish squareheaded brooch is found in numbers in Frankish graveyards from Flanders to Bohemia, and some other brooches in such burials may be Kentish. Scattered Saxon saucer brooches are found on several sites, especially in Belgium, and their adaptations and imitations reach down to the Danube and beyond, occasionally as far as the southern Balkans.

These are the traces of individuals and small groups of emigrants, whose children were absorbed into the nations among whom they settled. Several large well-organised expeditions also left Britain, and some of them long preserved their identity in Europe. Procopius describes and dates one English invasion of the Low Countries, and explains its root cause; in Britain

> there was such overpopulation that every year large numbers migrated with their wives and children to the Franks, who settled them in the emptier parts of their territory.

One major incident in this general movement was an English attack upon the Varni, whose ancestors had been their neighbours in Europe, located between Angel and Jutland, in what is now Denmark. In the 530s, all or part of the Varni were briefly settled on the northern bank of the Rhine mouth. Their widowed king married a sister of the Frank king Theudebert, who reigned from 533 to 548, and betrothed his son Radiger to the sister of the king of the *Angli* of Britain; but he died soon after, and advised his son to reject his English bride and marry his Frankish stepmother, since the Franks were more immediate neighbours. The outraged English virgin crossed the sea with a vast armament conveyed in 400 ships, commanded by another brother, defeated the Varni, and captured Radiger. The terrified prisoner expected torture and death, and was delighted to escape with no harsher sentence than a command to honour his broken promise and marry his captor.

This general movement, that Procopius observed in his own time, has left tangible traces in many English burials in northern Frankish lands, notably in the large cemetery of Anderlecht, near Brussels, and at Rhenen, by Arnhem on the Rhine; some among them may be the graves of those who fought the Varni, and settled among the Franks rather than return to their overpopulated homes. But the fleet that came to the Rhine brought warriors, and most of them went home, for no clear signs of large and permanent English settlement have yet been detected in the Low Countries.

Such signs are plentiful to the west, where the coasts of Gaul are nearer to Britain. There, over a hundred villages behind Boulogne, extending eastward as far as Lille, bear English names, like Ledinghem, slightly disguised in French spelling. More than three-quarters of them are of early types that are common among the East Angles of Norfolk, and are relatively rare elsewhere; their date appears to be indicated by the discovery of one or two Anglian cruciform brooches of the early 6th century in the same region. A migration so extensive and so concentrated is not easily explained as the casual spontaneous movement of landless individuals; it was plainly one part of the deliberate Frank policy that Procopius remarked in the decades before 550, of planting English colonists in lands that they could not themselves people; for the conquests of Clovis had recently annexed vast territories, far too large to be occupied and policed by men of Frankish birth alone. The dense settlement behind Boulogne suggests the enlistment of a particular English force at a particular moment; that force may have been the origin of the 'Saxons of Egwin', who formed one of the eleven divisions of the Frank army, and were prudently resettled on Montmartre,

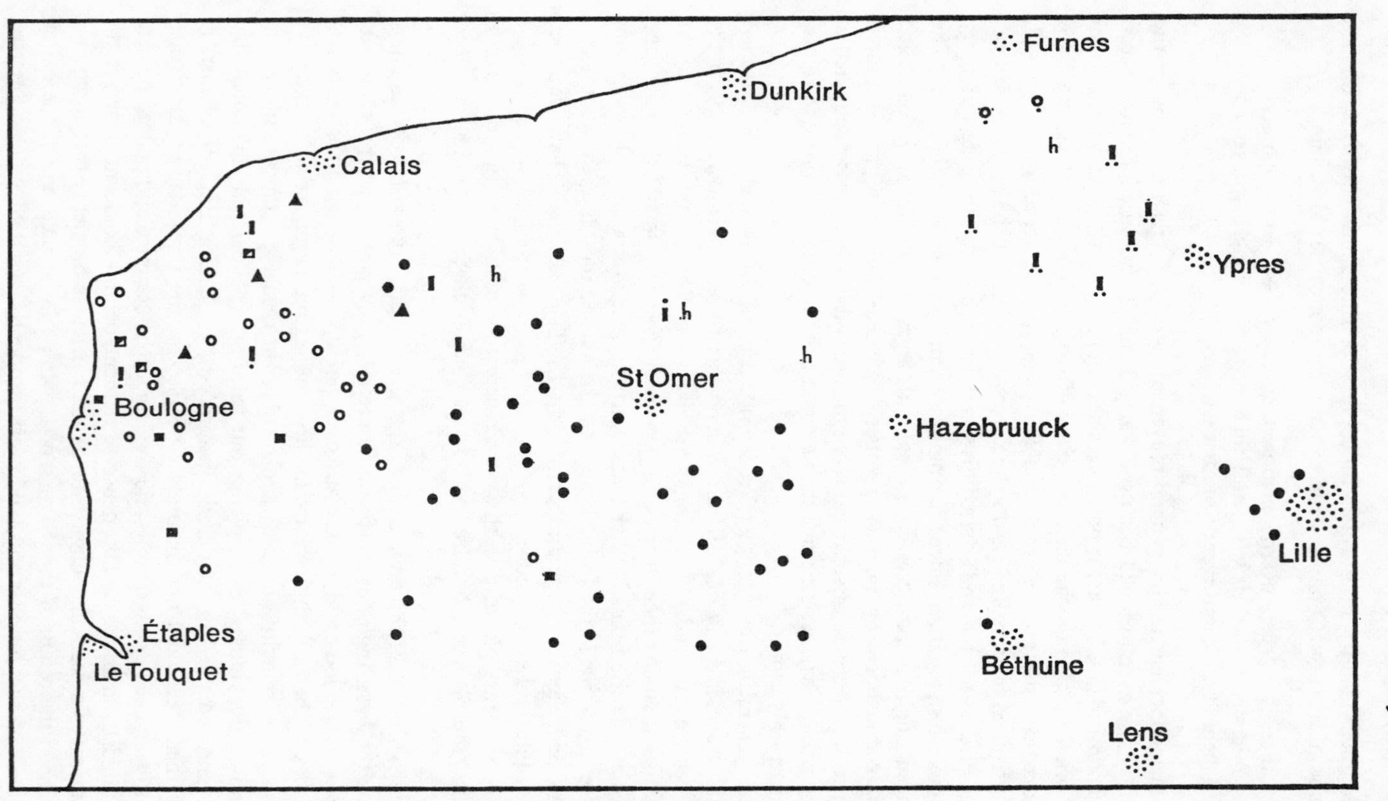

A ARTOIS AND FLANDERS (Legend p. 290)

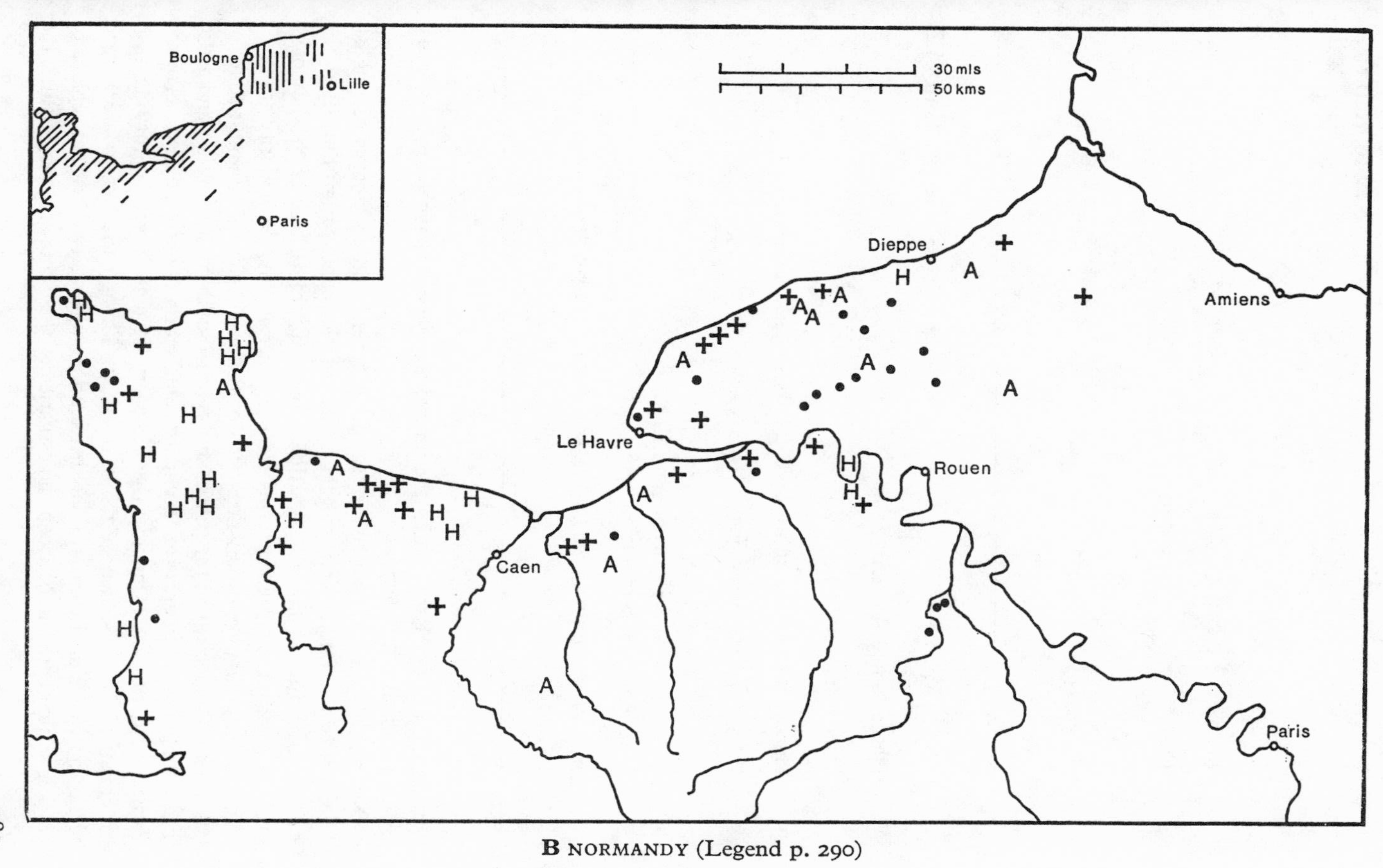

B NORMANDY (Legend p. 290)

Key to Map 19 A

Place names in

-ingues	ı	*-inghen*	○	*-thun*	▲
-ingue	!	*-inghem*	●	*-incthun*	■
-inge	.!.	*-ingem*	♀	*-enthun*	◩
-inghe	i				
-inckhove	h				

Key to Map 19 B

A Places named *Anglesqueville*

H Place names in *-hou* and variants

+ Place names incorporating an Old English personal name

• Other English place names

Inset

III Summary of symbols on map 19 A

/// Summary of symbols on map 19 B

No comparable study is available for several of the areas here shown blank.

---

outside the walls of Paris, under the immediate eye of the picked royal guards, by king Clothaire II in 627.

Not all colonies were so concentrated. Another hundred villages of English origin extend throughout the coastal regions of Normandy, from Picardy to the borders of Brittany. Their names differ markedly from those of the Boulogne area. The early East Anglian forms are altogether absent; the majority are those that are found all over the English parts of Britain, but are commonest south of the Thames, especially in the central and eastern south coast counties; and are in Britain more usual in areas of secondary colonisation than in the districts of the earliest settlers. In Normandy the discovery of a little 6th-century English ornament has also been uncertainly reported. Though the names are spread along the whole of the coast, their distribution suggests two distinct regions of thicker settlement, one between the estuaries of the Seine and the Somme, the other in and about the Cotentin peninsula, behind Cherbourg; and there Gregory of Tours knew of a substantial independent body of Saxons, established in the territory of Bayeux well before the end of the 6th century.

These considerable English colonies were installed by the western Franks in recently conquered Roman lands, that had previously adhered to the kingdom of Aegidius and Syagrius; and had accepted a large number of British refugees in the previous century, whose descendants inherited a profound hostility to Germanic invaders in general, and to the English in particular. There the colonists were in time absorbed, their earlier differences ultimately obliterated by the Scandinavian Northmen of the 9th and 10th centuries, who imposed upon the whole area its lasting name of Normandy. But other English expeditions were enlisted by the kings of the eastern Franks, and retained their identity. A later German chronicler transcribed an account of one of them, asserting that

> the Saxon people . . . leaving the *Angli* of Britain, urged on by the need and desire to find new homes, sailed to Hatheloe on the German coast, when king Theodoric of the Franks was at war with the Thuringian leader Hermenfred. . . . Theodoric sent envoys to these Saxons, whose leader was called Hadugat . . . and promised them homes for settlement in return for victory.

The date is probably 531. The place is Hadeln, the small district around Cuxhaven that had been the Saxon homeland, and includes Wester Wanna, Galgenberg and other early cemeteries.

Hadugat's men came back to the land of their ancestors. He sent some of them to help the Franks to victory, and they were settled in the Thuringian lands they subdued; they were perhaps the same Saxons who 'rebelled' against the Franks, with Thuringian support, a generation later, in 555. Others stayed by the Elbe, to become the nucleus of later Lower Saxon people, who halted the advance of the Slavs, recovered Hamburg, and held the frontier until their remote descendants overran and subdued the Slavs of the north European plain and made it a German land. They brought with them from Britain quantities of plain rough pottery, that is most closely matched among the Middle Angles, and continued to manufacture it for some generations; they also brought the characteristic Anglian place name *-botl*, a defended stronghold, that in Britain was most used by the Northumbrians and Mercians, and in Germany marks the concentrations of the Saxons, and is nowadays spelt *-büttl*. In Germany later chroniclers believed that the continental Saxons descended from the colonists who came from Britain in the 6th century. That tradition was unknown in Britain; in the 8th century Bede and others called their continental namesakes the 'Old Saxons' and assumed that the Saxons of Britain were the emigrants, a portion of a people who had remained continuously in their European homes. The archaeological evidence now available is not conclusive; but it suggests that both were largely right. In the ancient cemeteries by the estuary of the Elbe, burials all but ceased by the end of the 5th century, when the bulk of the population crossed to Britain; but a few later burials are known on some of the old sites, and it is probable that Hadeln was not as entirely deserted as Angel. Yet those who remained were few and weak. The strength and capacity of the continental Saxons was restored by large scale 6th-century immigration from Britain.

The identity of these various groups is not easily determined, for migration had already altered the meanings of national names before the middle of the 6th century. Procopius, writing about 550, already used *Angli*, English, as the general term for the Germanic settlers in Britain who were not Frisian, and the story of Hadugat observes the same usage, distinguishing the Saxons who made their homes in Europe from the *Angli* who stayed behind in Britain. Most European writers indiscriminately applied the word Saxon both to the Germanic inhabitants of Britain and to the people of the Lower Elbe; but in Thuringia the immigrants from the Elbe lands were called *Angli* and *Varni*, and there Anglian pottery and the widespread place names in *-leben*, confined to Thuringia and to Varnian and Danish territory, confirm their usage. Other historians report other peoples elsewhere who were known as Saxons; but the word does not contrast 'Saxon' with 'Angle'. Just before the Langobards invaded Italy in 568, they were joined by 20,000 of their 'old friends' the Saxons, with their wives and children. They could have come from Thuringia; or they might have been descendants of Hadugat's men or of other recent emigrants from Britain; perhaps of the Angles who had lived with the Langobards in fifth-century Bohemia; of those who had come to Italy with Odovacer; or of other unrecorded emigrants. Whoever they were, they quarrelled with their Langobard allies soon after the conquest of Italy and sought new homes in southern France, but without success; they were driven thence to their previous homes in Germany, to find that the Franks had installed Suevi in their place, and most of them perished in a vain effort to expel the intruders. Chance records name a few groups of Angles and Saxons, some of them from Britain; others are likely to have lived and moved without record.

These notices of English migration from Britain to Europe are confined to the earlier 6th century; and so is most of the archaeological evidence that matches them. The movement is most marked in the years between 520 and 560. The cause is plain. A very large population had come to Britain in the closing years of the fifth century, and had been confined within precise borders by the victory of Arthur. When their children grew to manhood they needed more land. Though the area of their reservations looks large upon a map, the extent of light alluvial soil was more restricted; and nothing suggests that the pagan English, before the coming of the monks, were any more accustomed to the clearance of wild woodland than other Germanic peoples. They could not find land at home, so they went abroad. Most of the few who were able to find new homes within Britain appear to have moved with the consent of the British authorities; it is evident that the English still considered the British states too strong to challenge or to defy. They accepted the consequences of their grandfathers' defeat at Badon, and continued to do so until after the great plague of the mid sixth century.

CHAPTER SIXTEEN
ENGLISH CONQUEST

Rebellion

The second Saxon revolt was no concerted national rising, like Hengest's rebellion in the 440s. It began as a trickle and became a flood. The memory of Badon had contained the English within their borders for three generations; though the military strength of Arthur's empire soon dissolved, fear of superior British power long outlived its reality. Its weakness was revealed when Cynric seized Salisbury in 550; though he made no further conquest, his little local victory demonstrated that British supremacy might be challenged with impunity.

The challenge was not taken up elsewhere until 568, and then at first it failed. Young Aethelbert of Kent broke out beyond his frontiers, evidently towards London, into the lands of the settled Saxons of the North Downs; the armies of Ceawlin and Cuthwulf came to the defence of the city, and 'drove him back into Kent'. The main military forces on both sides were English, and victory emboldened the victors. In 571 Cuthwulf destroyed the midland British at Bedford, and marched to Oxford; six years later his heir joined Ceawlin in the conquest of the lower Severn. In less than ten years British political authority in the south had been abolished. The crumbling dam crashed suddenly, and the English flooded over open lands.

Ceawlin commanded the English of Winchester and Salisbury. Various testimonies point to the homeland of Cuthwulf, called Cutha for short. The Eslingas of Haslingfield (Map 20, p. 295), south-west of Cambridge, had developed a new technique in the manufacture of saucer brooches; their jewellers punched the ornament on to a thin plate from the rear and soldered it to a base plate. In the later sixth century they evolved elaborate designs in this technique, most popular among them a Maltese Cross enclosing comic faces; these brooches are found beside the route of Cutha's army down the Icknield Way to the Thames and beyond, and so are some other related brooches; they also reach westward from the Eslingas towards the Middle Angles. Places named from Cutha also clustered along the Icknield Way, to Cutteslowe in north Oxford, probably his burial-mound, and mark the settlements that held the newly conquered military route. The genealogists give the same origin. A late gloss on the Saxon Chronicle explained Cuthwulf as the 'brother' of his ally Ceawlin, and the name of Ceawlin's predecessors, Cynric and Cerdic, are intruded into his pedigree. But the pedigree descends from Esla 'Gewising'; Gewissae was the earlier name of the middle Thames Saxons, whence the Eslingas had originated. Cuthwulf seems to have come from the Cambridge region, and to have died as the ruler of Oxford. His was the tiniest of all the earlier English territories, and Ceawlin's people were also small; yet it was they who seized the initiative and destroyed the British. They had much to gain and little to lose, for in their isolated territories their small forces lived more precariously than their greater neighbours, and also had less room for internal expansion. Ceawlin's people lived many scores of miles from the nearest English, and in the past a little local frontier had prevented the Eslingas from carrying their ornament to nearby Cambridge, and had exposed them to a double danger, from the British of the midlands and from strong unfriendly English neighbours.

Cuthwulf's victories liberated the rest of the southern English. The spread of late 6th century burial grounds, shown on map 21 (p. 297), describes the immediate consequence. A flood of immigrants colonised the lands between the districts in which the English had formerly been confined, and so joined the scattered English territories into a single block of territory. The most important further advance was the seizure of Ilchester. Half a dozen small sites surround the town, the furthest four miles to the north-west, at Pitney, by Somerton. They are known from chance finds, but from several of them chance has preserved grave goods fashionable well before the end of the century, earlier than any others known so far west of the old centres; and the unimportant little village of Somerton gave its name to a distinct people, the *Sumorsaete*, whose expanded territory is still known as Somerset. The seizure of Ilchester was clearly a deliber-

---

Map 20

⚔ 571 Approximate site and date of battles

C Places named after *Cutha*

\+ Saucer brooches with Maltese Cross design

I Saucer brooches with Six Face design

□ Great Squareheaded brooches
with border of free standing faces
(Leeds type B6, 95-100)

● *-tuns* taken by Cutha in 571

○ Modern towns

See Notes to the Maps

MAP 20 THE ENGLISH CONQUEST OF THE SOUTH

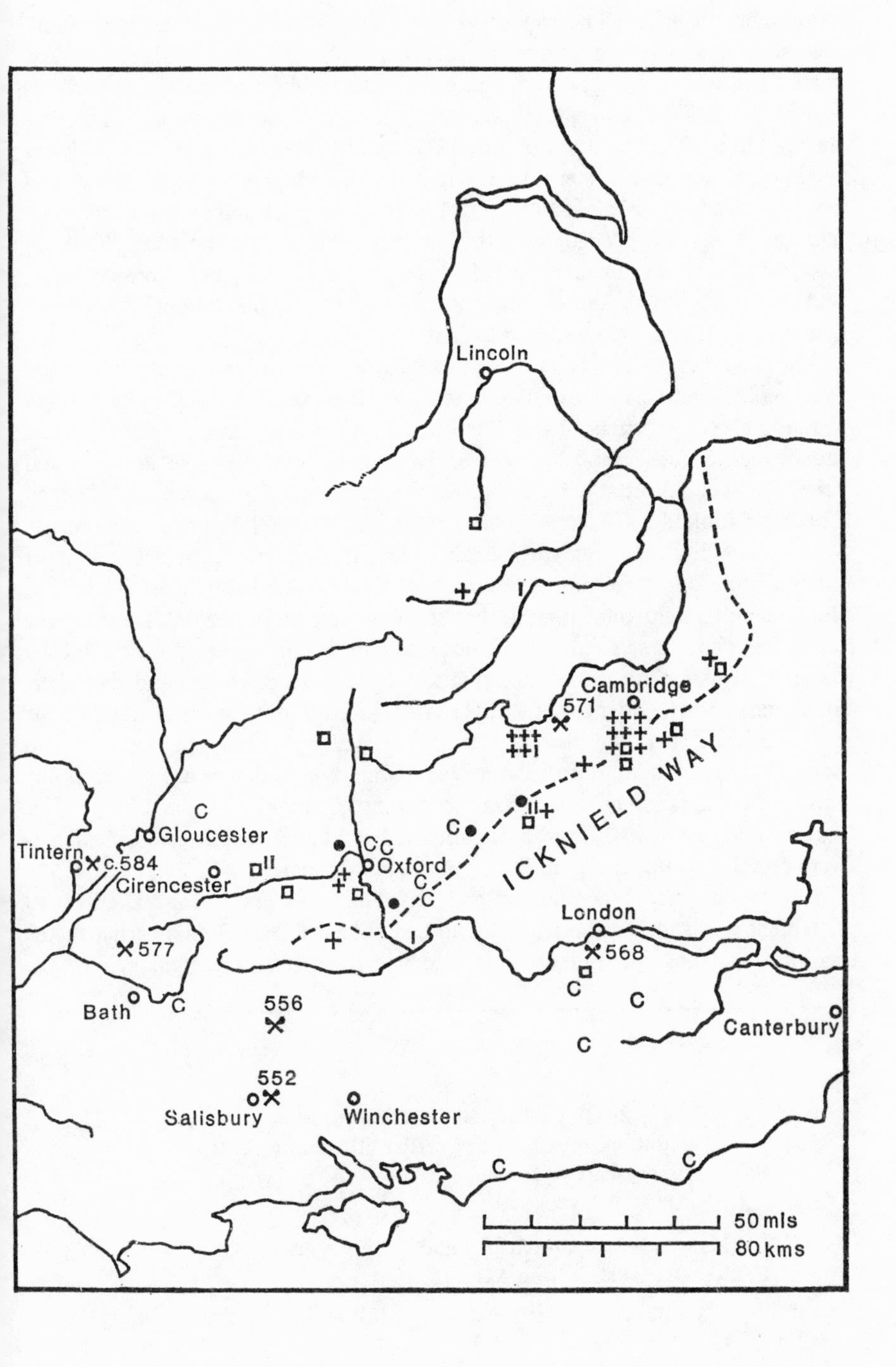

ate military decision. The town was the strategic focus of the region, where several Roman roads converged; there the Fosse Way from Exeter forked northwards towards Cirencester, Leicester and Lincoln, and westwards towards Salisbury and Winchester, Silchester and London; it was cut at right angles by the road from Dorchester and from Portland and Poole harbours to the mouth of the Parrett, that had formerly been one of the main highways from Ireland and South Wales to Europe. At Ilchester, the first English of Somerset constituted a garrison. They were needed, for in the marshes ten miles to the north Glastonbury is reported to have remained in British hands for several generations to come, and at the mouth of the Parrett the large British population who used the cemetery of Cannington endured as long.

The colonies that followed Cuthwulf's victory were not haphazard settlements, founded by carefree adventurers on their private initiative. Within a few years of 571, the several districts of the English are reported to have proclaimed their independence and established permanent monarchies. Records are few and brief, for Bede reported almost nothing of sixth-century history, and the Saxon Chronicle limited its selection of events to those that interested 9th-century West Saxon kings, together with a scanty botch of northern history. The story of the midlands is lost, for only a few fragments of the Anglian Chronicle survive. But these fragments remembered the foundation of future kingdoms, noting the 'first king who reigned' in each region; and their tradition was also accepted by the genealogists, who name the dynasties after the same rulers, and date their foundation. Independent monarchy is said to have been asserted among the East Angles in 571, the year of Cuthwulf's victory, and among the East and South Saxons by a king of the same generation, whose deaths are noted in 587 and 590; the creation of the Mercian monarchy is placed in 584, and its founder is also named as the first English ruler of Lindsey. The late sixth-century colonies were established under the authority of the new monarchies.

There is no record of midland and East Anglian wars, beyond the general statement that some of the pagans who had occupied East Anglia earlier in the century went on to 'invade Mercia' and to fight many campaigns against the

---

Map 21

o sites with 5th century and later 6th century burials, without clear evidence of earlier 6th century burial

◠ primary barrow burials

▲ excavated royal centre

Other symbols as on Maps 3 and 18 (pp. 59 and 285)

\\\ Areas shown on Map 18

MAP 21 PAGAN ENGLISH SETTLEMENT 4
THE LATER 6th CENTURY

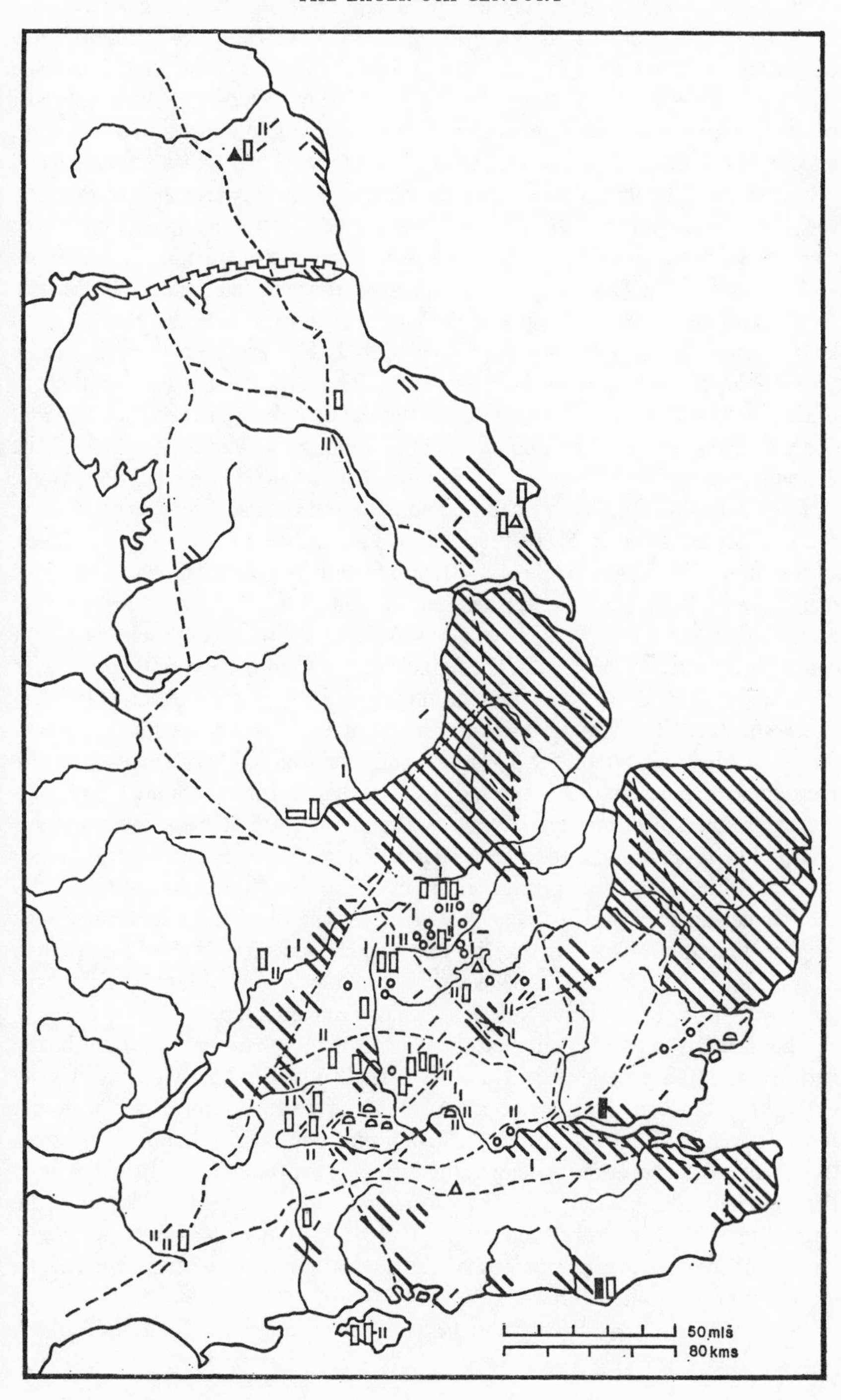

British. A few notices suggest a little of what happened. The East Anglian dynasty, named Uffingas from its first king, Uffa, were the dynasty of Suffolk. They displaced the Iclingas in Norfolk, perhaps in 571, perhaps earlier; and it may be that it was the pressure of their new kingdom that impelled the Eslingas, or part of them, to move westward against the British. Grave goods attest their advance, erasing the frontiers of the earlier sixth century. Their great squareheaded brooches are difficult to date; it may be that one or two had reached Sussex and the northern Angles in the middle of the century, but later versions swept in the wake of Cuthwulf's armies; they are especially numerous among the Eslingas and on the middle Thames, like the punched brooches, and among the Middle Angles and on the Avon. Those who took them did not give the East Anglian kings political sovereignty in these regions, but their spread argues that some East Angles had moved into these territories. There they settled; and at the end of the century their jewellers evolved a monstrous hybrid of the cruciform and squareheaded brooches, particularly popular among the Middle Angles and the Deirans.

The augmented English of the midlands united behind Creoda, a king who claimed descent from Icel. His kingdom was a federation of very small peoples, who assumed the general name of the 'frontier men', the Mercians, the men of the march, or border. The text termed the 'Tribal Hidage' knew of an 'original Mercia' that was half the size of 7th-century Mercia; the figures suggest that it comprised numerous peoples of the Middle Angles and the Avon, together with those of the Banbury area on the borders of northern Oxfordshire and Worcestershire. Their main territory approximately coincided with that of the former Roman *civitas* of the Coritani, and the frontier they held faced the Pennine British across the Trent and the Cornovii on the west. One list records the early rulers of Lindsey. It regards Creoda as its first king and notes his origin. The first name listed after Woden is 'Cretta Vinting'; and Vinta, 'son of Woden', is the name of no person, in English or in British, but of a place, Venta, the Roman name of Caistor-next-Norwich, the centre of the 5th-century East Anglian kingdom of Icel. It may be that Creoda was himself the East Anglian king whom Uffa of Ipswich expelled; or that he was heir of a cadet branch of the dynasty, whose origin in the Norwich area was remembered.

The creation of Mercia entailed the overthrow of whatever British authority had previously been asserted in the north midlands. But the Mercian dynasty emerged in the course of wars between different English dynasties, and is not reported to have fought against the British for many centuries. Campaigns across the Trent are not recorded so long as the further shore remained in British hands; the Mercians remained allies of the Cornovii on their western border until the middle of the 7th century, and of the Welsh kingdoms thereafter; all that is known of Creoda's own campaigns is that his death is linked with the wars of the Gewissae on his southern border.

The Saxon Chronicle briefly noted events that its editors did not understand.

They recorded the victories or deaths of kings, for these were the notices that they found in their sources; but they knew little of the kings' subjects. Their archaeological remains proclaim the important consequences of the wars. Map 21 outlines the expansion of the English in the years of Ceawlin's supremacy, and immediately thereafter. Most of the new sites are small poorly furnished cemeteries, or else the isolated graves of individuals, often wealthy, in sharp contrast with the large undifferentiated cemeteries of the fifth century. The majority of the new sites were in the midlands, around and between the borders of earlier English reservations. There the subjects of Ceawlin and Creoda lived secure, in small groups and family units, often settled immediately beside a Roman British farmstead, that was either still inhabited, or not yet reverted to the wild, or else beside a small town that was now under English political control.

Ceawlin's capture of the Cotswolds and Cirencester had made him great, and tradition honoured him as the first supreme commander of the southern English since Badon. He inherited small forces in Winchester and Salisbury; his rule was accepted by the Gewissae, and he is said to have annexed the South Saxons. But his power did not endure. The English were badly beaten by the British on the Wye, and in 584 Ceawlin returned home 'in anger'. In 591 a new king is said to have ruled in his place, evidently over the Gewissae, and in 592 Ceawlin was 'expelled' after a great battle at Woden's Barrow, near Alton Priors, east of Devizes, just south of the Wansdyke. Wars between the English had driven him back into his original territory. The Mercians were involved, for in the next year, 593, the Chronicle entry reads 'Ceawlin and Cwichelm and Crida died'. The name Cwichelm is rare, used otherwise only by a later Wessex king and perhaps a Kentish bishop; but it names one of the earliest Wessex royal burial-mounds, of the late 6th century, by East Hendred, near Wantage, evidently the district that Cwichelm ruled. The name of Crida, Creoda or Cretta is rarer still, otherwise known only through a few place names, near Cirencester and elsewhere.

The Chronicle entry does not say who fought whom, or whether the deaths were connected; one tradition says that the enemy at Woden's Barrow were British, and it may be that Creoda fought with Welsh allies; one West Saxon tradition included him among their kings, and it may be that he annexed part of their territory. But whatever the combinations, the strength of the Gewissae and the Mercians was reduced, and southern hegemony passed to Aethelbert of Kent. Little is known of how he acquired or held it; his sister married the king of the East Saxons, whose pedigree is attached to Saxon gods. But the pedigree abounds in Anglian names, that recall those of the dynasty of Deira; and some grave goods of his time are common to Deira and to the Thames estuary. It may be that Aethelbert allied with Aelle of Deira to establish the new East Saxon dynasty, for its next king, his nephew, accepted his suzerainty. Elsewhere, Kentish ornament spread widely in the south, and a few specifically Kentish burial-grounds in the south midlands suggest the posting of Kentish garrisons and perhaps of Kentish royal officials in subject territory. But the reality of Aethelbert's supremacy is known only from Bede's emphatic statement.

Consolidation:
Aethelferth and Aethelbert

A few years later Aethelferth of Bernicia won a like supremacy in the north, first destroying the British kingdoms and then annexing English Deira and York. At the beginning of the 7th century, the English were grouped into two large and powerful realms, both recent, but very different from each other. In the north, two small kingdoms had suddenly overwhelmed a large British territory, thinly peopled. The more numerous English of the south were divided into many kingdoms, a few of them large, many very small. Greater kings overawed the smaller, and the king of Kent asserted suzerainty over all of them; the accidents of their history had prepared them for a hierarchy of kingship, whose future was uncertain. The power of the sovereign dynasty might prove permanent, rooting in England a wide authority like that which king Diarmait had briefly held in Ireland; or it might dissolve into a loose and nominal superiority over numerous kingdoms that were in practice independent, as had already happened in Ireland, and was in the future to happen in Europe, under the revived Roman empire of the west.

Men knew that their present kingdoms were insecure, for power quickly won may as soon be lost; and the strength and structure of the several kingdoms greatly varied. In the north the Bernicians and the Deirans had little in common but their language. The ancestors of the Deirans had settled in a prosperous sophisticated countryside, where well-educated gentlemen were masters of obedient tenants, near to a great city; but the Bernicians had always lived among barbarians beyond the border. The Deirans controlled infinitely richer resources, but the Bernicians were a simple and hardier folk, greatly more experienced in warfare. The southerners were even more diversified. In the older kingdoms men lived on lands that their forbears had tilled for nearly two hundred years; between these kingdoms, pioneers established new homes quietly, in safe lands far removed from the surviving British states; but on the western borders colonists had to contend with a still obstinate Welsh resistance.

The political and social structure of the English was not uniform. After five or six generations the population of the old kingdoms was already divided into great men and small. But the pioneers and the colonists were of mixed origins. Some were coherent bodies detached from a single parent kingdom; others were small groups or individuals drawn from different kingdoms, not yet fused into political entities in their new homes. Their allegiance lay open to whichever ruler might offer greater security at any given moment, whether he were king of the West Saxons, of the Mercians, or of Kent, king of a small people or of a restricted region, or simply a capable leader of their own. In the early seventh century there were as yet no accepted institutions valid for all the English.

Their society and their political government was infinitely varied, its outline still to be formed.

In the time of Aethelbert and Aethelferth, the issue of a single battle might enable one of the two great kingdoms to subdue the other, and establish speedily a united England. Men weighed such possibilities, for when the men of Kent accepted Christianity from a Roman missionary the pope instructed him, in the summer of 601, to carry the faith to the north and to establish a bishop in York, with equal metropolitan authority. The pope's ruling plainly answered a query first raised by the Kentish church; and the proposal could not have been put forward without the approval of the king, for it concerned politics as deeply as religion. In 601 Deira was still independent. Aethelferth had destroyed the British of the Pennines, but had not yet turned south. But the writing was large upon the wall; his future invasion was already a danger to be dreaded. If the Deirans accepted a bishop in York, sent from Kent, they thereby riveted a political alliance with the king of Kent, admitting his stronger power in the north as well as the south. If Aethelbert took Deira under his protection and alliance, he automatically confronted Aethelferth of Bernicia; if he prevailed against him, his victory would make him sovereign of all the English in Britain.

The alliance did not mature. Aethelferth's victories overwhelmed Deira, bringing him to the Humber, and perhaps beyond, within three years of pope Gregory's letter. Later in the century, the pope's ruling became the legal foundation for the permanent division of the English church into two metropolitan provinces, but it had no immediate effect. After 604 Aethelbert led no crusade against the pagan north. When he died, in 616, the kings of the south refused allegiance to his son, and ended Kentish hegemony for ever; they also rejected Christianity. It was Aethelferth who marched south, against king Redwald of the East Angles, who for a short while asserted primacy over the southern kingdoms, and sheltered Aethelferth's exiled rival, Edwin of Deira. Victory might have made Aethelferth acknowledged sovereign of all the English. But he failed, and Edwin took his place in the north. The Bernicians accepted Edwin, and Aethelferth's sons went into exile.

Edwin and Oswy

Edwin overshadowed the south; when he married a Kentish princess he accepted her Christian religion and made friends and allies among those numerous southerners who adhered to the new faith or returned to it. He made war upon the Welsh, and the patriotic pride of Bede asserts his power at home. To later generations his strong rule seemed a golden age, for

> such was the peace of Britain at the time . . . that it is even today a proverb that if a woman with a new-born babe then wished to walk across the land from sea to sea, she would come to no harm. . . . King Edwin so considered his subjects' comfort that when he saw clear springs by the highway, he had posts set up with bronze cups

> attached for the refreshment of travellers, and no man dared . . . or wished . . . to touch them beyond his need.

He left a different reputation in the south. There the West Saxons were again united under strong kings. Ceolwulf campaigned against the South Saxons, and repeatedly fought the 'Angles and the Welsh'. His Anglian neighbours were Mercian, and nothing is remembered of the then Mercian king save that he had at one time befriended the exiled Edwin. Cynegils, who succeeded Ceolwulf in 611, crippled British Dumnonia, destroying its army near Axminster, and planting colonies in Dorset and north Somerset just before pagan burial rites passed from use. He reigned for more than 30 years, and was the only over-king of the West Saxons before the 9th century to bequeath his sovereignty intact to his son. He came nearer than any other early king to establishing a powerful West Saxon monarchy, and from Cirencester he looked north against the Angles.

Edwin broke the power of the West Saxons in 626. One of their under-kings attempted to assassinate him, and he replied with a full-scale invasion, killing five West Saxon regional kings and a 'great number of people'. The Mercian kingdom was reorganised; Creoda's grandson Penda began to rule in 626, and until 642 divided the kingdom with his brother Eowa. The new kings were enthroned when Edwin's armies overthrew the West Saxons, clearly with his approval; and they pushed back the West Saxon borders. In 628 Penda fought their kings at Cirencester and 'reached agreement'. Thenceforth the northern Cotswolds were Mercian, and the West Saxons were permanently cut off from the lower Severn crossings; their energies were thenceforth directed against Dumnonia, no longer against Wales.

Edwin's empire was as fragile as his predecessors'. He overran north Wales, but his invasion ended in defeat. Catwallaun of Gwynedd recovered his own kingdom, defeated Penda, and then enlisted him as his own subject ally. His Welsh and Mercian army defeated and killed Edwin in 633, and for a year British hegemony was restored. But the Northumbrians rallied. Oswald, the son of Aethelferth of Bernicia, returned from exile among the Scots and Picts, killed Catwallaun, and was accepted by both Northumbrian kingdoms. He immediately recovered Edwin's wide authority, constraining Cynegils of Wessex to accept Christian baptism and chastising the Welsh upon the Severn. But he too failed to hold his power. The 'English rose against Oswald' in 636, without success; but Penda soon after revived the grand alliance of the Welsh and the southern English, and killed him in 642. Penda plundered the north, and a contemporary Welsh record remarks his splendid distribution of the spoils by the Forth, the *Atbret Iudeu*. Penda's victory made him master of his allies as of his defeated enemies, and a few quick campaigns enforced the obedience of the West Saxons and the East Angles. Thenceforth, Mercian sovereignty lasted for 150 years. It was interrupted only for three years, when Oswald's brother Oswy killed

Penda in 655 and briefly reasserted the dominion that his brother and Edwin had held before; but in 658 the Mercians recovered their independence, under Penda's son Wulfhere; they quickly regained control of the south, conquered the West Saxons, re-established a separate kingdom of the South Saxons, to whom they gave control of Wight, and subdued Kent.

Northumbria was not conquered and did not at once accept defeat. Oswy looked north, making 'the greater part of the Picts and Scots tributary'. The Pictish king was killed, and an English under-king established over part of his kingdom; the king of the Clydeside British was also killed, and replaced with Oswy's brother-in-law. But Oswy's son Egferth tried to recover his father's southern authority, until he was compelled to accept the Trent as a permanent frontier in 679. Checked on the south, he turned his arms against foreigners, invading Ireland in 684, against the strong protest of his churchmen. But when he was killed by the Picts in 685, the lay and clerical leaders of Northumbria deliberately rejected their military past, and chose as their new king the elderly and pacific scholar Aldfrith, who had spent most of his life among Irishmen and monks. He ruled for 20 years and was patron of the monasteries where Bede grew to manhood, whence came the glories of Northumbrian art and learning; but on his death, the political fabric of eighth-century Northumbria dissolved amid the personal and dynastic discord of weak kings, brutal or feeble, whose authority commanded little respect at home and none abroad.

The Mercians

South of the Trent the kings who followed Penda built a powerful monarchy, which retained its supremacy into the 9th century. The dynasty, the Mercian peoples, and the lesser southern kingdoms clung to their unity. Wulfhere left a young son, not old enough to rule; his younger brother Aethelred therefore succeeded him, but no factions raised civil war in his nephew's name, or impelled him to make away with his nephew. When he abdicated and retired to a monastery, in 704, the nephew succeeded him, in preference to his own son; and when the nephew also retired to a monastery, Aethelred's son succeeded, for a brief and vicious reign. He was replaced by Aethelbald, descended from Penda's brother Eowa, and after forty years of sovereignty a distant cousin, Offa, also heir of Eowa, reigned as long and as secure, sovereign of an undivided realm now long-established. The five great kings of Mercia consolidated the English into a nation and a kingdom, whose identity proved strong enough to survive the fearful strains of Scandinavian invasions, that followed hard upon the death of Offa, in 796. When Egbert of Wessex destroyed the Mercian power he did not found a new united kingdom. He imposed a new dynasty upon a nation that had been formed long before.

Expansion

The Mercian dynasty enabled England to grow from origins immensely diverse.

The conquering English acquired vast territories and numerous foreign British subjects; and their own English past varied greatly. The second Saxon revolt was the work of three of the smallest peoples, the Bernicians, the Eslingas, and the Hampshire Jutes. The older and larger states profited from their success, but played no recorded part in its leadership. They had small cause. When the revolt began their inhabitants farmed the lands where they were born; they had lived at peace since their grandfathers' time, sending their adventurous youth and surplus population to Europe. They gave no sign that they felt able to attack their British neighbours, or wished to do so; and the princes of the British were still free to make war upon their relatives and rivals without fear of English attack. To outward appearance a Celtic Britain seemed able to absorb the English in course of time. Yet in a generation the tiny forces of three enterprising local captains were able to blow away the British power and to make the fairer parts of Britain permanently English.

The British collapsed because their states were rotted and hollow. The English prevailed because each initial success recruited larger and bolder armies, which had no need to guard against counter-attack. The circumstances of their victory bequeathed to their successors a remarkable and unforeseen consequence, the predominance of the north and the midlands, of Northumbria and Mercia. In all previous and subsequent history, Britain has been dominated by the fertile lowlands of the south and south-east, rich in easy soils, easily co-ordinated, strategically placed to rule the rest of the country. Now, war had wasted the fertile lowlands, and strengthened the hardier north.

The North and the East

At the beginning of the 7th century, each English kingdom inherited a different past, and fronted different present needs. In Northumbria, a very few English ruled a large British population. In the last generation of pagan burial their ornament spread through the East Riding from its original centres in Deira, and extended to the Bernicians and the lands between; but hardly any of it penetrated or crossed the Pennines. A few place names suggest the strongholds of English lords in the dales and in strategic west-coast regions, but the bulk of the English lived east of the road from York to Corbridge and Edinburgh, and were for centuries too few to colonise the west. The west offered no threat; and such

---

Map 22

Areas shown on map 18, p. 285

Areas shown on map 21, p. 297

Other symbols as for Maps 3 and 18 (pp. 59 and 285)

MAP 22 PAGAN ENGLISH SETTLEMENT 5
THE 7th CENTURY

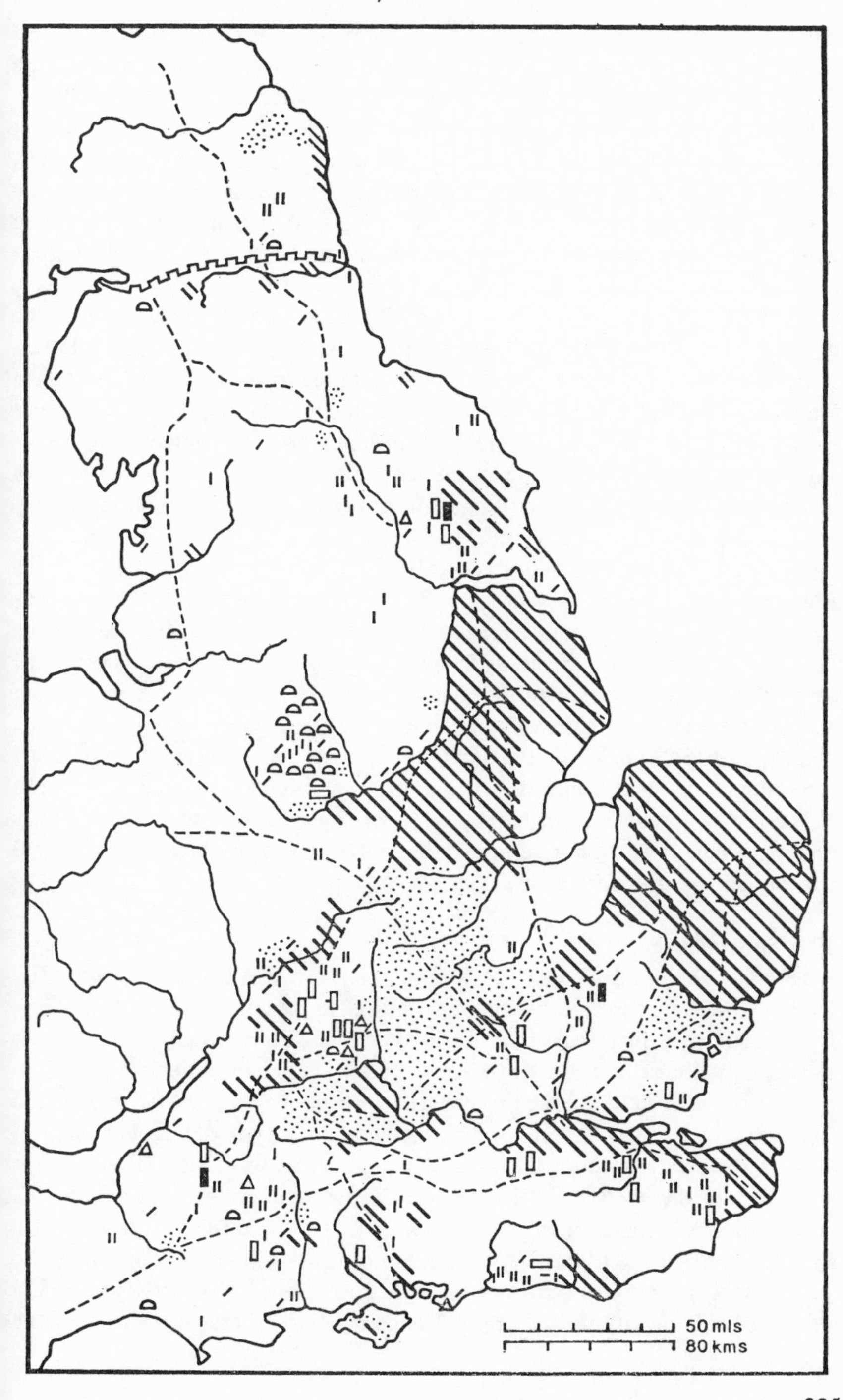

colonies as the English could afford went to lands that needed them. The wide ambition of their early kings asserted suzerainty over the southern English, and were content when it was acknowledged. Their military victory also carried them northward to the Forth and beyond into southern Pictland, in Strathmore. These were the lands of untamed foreigners, who would not yield to absent conquerors; and it is there that the English place names witness the migration of colonists. Northumbria expanded northward near to the east coast, and accepted the submission of the Pennines and the north-west. It had no need of external expansion, and ended southern wars when the midland and southern English decisively rejected northern suzerainty.

South of the Trent the older kingdoms of the east were set in their ways. Some of their excess population spilled into the lands that had formerly separated them from one another, and others doubtless contributed to the needs of the western kingdoms who had larger lands to colonise. But the old kingdoms had neither the incentive nor the means to enlarge their dominion. The scattered Lindissi of Lincolnshire were unhappily placed. Their lands had loomed large in the story of Arthur's wars, and after the English conquest, they were at first repeatedly wasted in the border wars of the Mercians and Northumbrians: not until the border was finally determined, in 679, did they win peace, as a province of the Mercian kingdom. Further south, the East Angles were isolated from the Mercians by their fenland frontier, and separated from the Thames basin by the Essex forests; and formidable dykes guarded their natural approaches to the south and west through Cambridge and the Icknield Way. They preserved their ancient division into a North Folk, descendants of the earliest Anglian settlers, and a South Folk, heirs of later immigrants, whose dynasty ruled both. They were numerous enough and well enough protected to offer a stronger resistance to Mercian supremacy; but they were not strong enough to reject it. They retained their dynasty, but admitted the greater power of Mercia, and stayed within their borders with little expansion.

The South East

Across the Thames the English of Kent had taken over a Roman society in full working order, by agreement with the then Roman government of Britain. Their first settlers were planted in their formative years within a Roman society, that was sharply differentiated between great landowners and servile tenant cultivators. They acquired their Roman lands half a century before the Franks mastered Roman Gaul, and the dazzling wealth of their jewellery is the outward sign of lords as aristocratic as those of Frankish Gaul. But they were cut off from the rest of Britain by the sea, the Weald, and the Medway, whose exceptional breadth prevented the integration of their colonies west of the river with the main Kentish homeland to its east. They made no further conquests. They failed to take London in the fifth-century wars, failed again in Aethelbert's youth, and failed to hold the city on his death. London passed to the direct rule of the weaker kings of the East Saxons. They, and the small peoples of the regions that later ages knew as Middlesex, the Middle Saxon land, and the Southern District, Surrey, were easily subjected to Mercian rule; when the Mercians went on to invade Kent in 676 and sack Rochester, the port of London passed permanently into the control of the Mercian kings, whose supremacy was challenged only on the rare occasions when West Saxon kings were strong enough to threaten Kent and the East Saxons.

The early settlers of Surrey and Sussex were confined to the easy Downs and coastland. From the early seventh century onward, they and the men of Kent spread into the Wealden country between, and tamed it by an arduous agricultural technology unknown to their ancestors. Their kinsmen north of the Thames also spread more thinly over the uninviting London clays. Throughout the south-east, expansion was slow, and empty lands sufficed to absorb the offshoots of the small early kingdoms. But in the west the frontier kingdoms of the West Saxons and the Mercians had other opportunities and other needs. In the early 7th century the men of Wessex were few, and the lands they mastered large. Their two small peoples had overrun huge parts of the most fertile soils in Britain, and in many of them no English had settled before the conquest. But their borderlands made stronger demands upon their manpower, for their ill-defined frontier faced the still unconquered power of British Dumnonia and was defended by no natural obstacles of hill or river.

The West

The West Saxons were obliged to fight continuously on two fronts, against the Mercians on the north and the Dumnonians on the west, and had also to contain the Welsh within their borders. The latest pagan burials, early in the 7th century, shown on Map 22, mark the first stage of their expansion. Most sites lie in secure lands, on the edges of earlier settlement; as yet there was little penetration beyond Cirencester, below the Chiltern escarpment into Gloucestershire. A few colonists lined the Bristol Avon, and the Dorset coast, but none are yet known to have penetrated into Devon.

The recorded western wars of Wessex are confined to the years when Wessex was least harassed by other English kingdoms. In 614, just before the death of Aethelbert of Kent, the kings

> Cynegils and Cwichelm fought at *Beandun*, and slew 2,065 of the Welsh.

The only known place so named is Bindon, by Axmouth, just on the Devon side of the Dorset border, just west of the furthest known pagan burial-ground on the south coast; and is near to the Roman road that runs from Ilchester to the mouth of the Axe. The precise figure of enemy casualties is exceptional among the Chronicle entries; it may be that the battle was celebrated in a poem that the Chronicle cited; the size of the figure proclaims that the victory was regarded as unusually important. The location suggests that the garrison of Ilchester, 25 miles away, may have marched south to intercept an invading Dumnonian army, that used the quickest road eastward from Exeter.

The date implies that the Dumnonians co-ordinated their effort with the kings of south Wales, for the traditions of Glevissig held that the peace on their borders also was broken in 614, 30 years after the campaign of 584, and another report remembers a victory in Gwent early in the 7th century. If it were so, the English won the campaign, for fighting in Gwent meant that they had advanced beyond Gloucester; and the Welsh claim no gains in English lands. Thereafter, the West Saxons were concerned with Northumbrian and Mercian enemies, and the Welsh remained the allies of the Mercians. No further western wars are reported for nearly 40 years, until king Cenwalh, son and successor of Cynegils, fought at Bradford-on-Avon, east of Bath, evidently against the Welsh or the Mercians or both. Mercian pressure was eased with the fall of Penda in 655, but was renewed after Wulfhere's accession in 658. The Welsh of Glastonbury are said, however, to have been reinforced by the arrival of the Cornovian Morfael, the last British lord of Lichfield, probably expelled by Oswy in 655, and in the next few years the last efforts of the British to recover the fertile lowlands are recorded. In 658

> Cenwalh fought at *Peonna* against the Welsh, and drove them in flight as far as the Parrett.

The place is probably Penselwood, deep in English Wessex, almost halfway from Ilchester to Salisbury. The pursuit to the Parrett implies that the river then became the boundary; the new frontier entailed the English occupation of Glastonbury and secured the region that the garrison of Ilchester had hitherto controlled. Easy contact between the Dumnonians and the South Welsh across the narrows of the Severn estuary was ended.

Cenwalh is then said to have recovered territory from the Mercians, and to have invaded southern Dumnonia thereafter. In 661, he fought at *Posentesburh*, probably Posbury by Crediton, beyond Exeter. Then, or soon after, Exeter was opened to the English. English place names attest heavy colonisation that spread inland from Exeter; and the city itself was long partitioned between the English and British. The date was not long after Cenwalh's campaign, for Boniface, the future apostle of Germany, was educated from childhood in an English monastery in Exeter, and is said to have been a native of Crediton. He was born in the 680s, and was presumably a son of one of the first colonists.

The English conquest of south Devon outflanked the northern Dumnonians, but they long resisted; in 682 Cenwalh's grandson 'drove the British as far as the sea', probably in a campaign that swept from the Parrett through north Somerset; but the region was not secured, for the fortress of Taunton, only eight miles west of the Parrett, was not constructed until the time of king Ine, perhaps when he 'fought Geraint, king of the British', in 710. Ine tried and failed to reduce

Dumnonia, for the Cambrian Annals claim the heavy defeat of an English invasion in Cornwall in 722, and in the same year the English acknowledged that Ine's queen dismantled his own fortress of Taunton, perhaps again withdrawing behind the Parrett. The West Saxons were also pressed from the north, for eleven years later the Mercians annexed Somerton. The ultimate conquest of Dumnonia was postponed. Egbert of Wessex invaded Cornwall in 815, but ten years later the Dumnonian kings fought back in Devon, and Egbert failed to take Launceston. A dozen years thereafter the Cornishmen found new allies in the Danes, and the fate of Cornwall was henceforth merged in the struggle against the pirate host. Independence ended in the later 9th century; the Cornish bishop at Bodmin acknowledged the authority of Canterbury in 870, and five years later the last known Cornish king, Dungarth, died by drowning, perhaps in battle. Final conquest was delayed for another half-century, but from about 950 the Cornish permanently acknowledged English kings, and accepted bishops with English names.

The conquest of Dumnonia was delayed because the West Saxon kings were continually harassed by the Mercians. In 661, the year when Cenwalh fought at *Posentesburh*, Wulfhere overran Wessex, and detached the South Saxons and the Isle of Wight, to form a separate kingdom. The South Welsh seized their opportunity, and the Cambrian Annals noted that in 665

> Easter was celebrated among the Saxons for the first time. The second battle of Badon. Morcant died.

The Easter entry confirms the date, the year after the Synod of Whitby, in 664. The entry probably means that Morcant of Glevissig was killed at Badon; but even if the statements are not linked, the British had crossed the Severn in arms. No victory is claimed, and it was their last recorded attempt to recover western Wessex. They failed, but Wessex was not free to counter-attack. Cenwalh had moved his capital from Dorchester-on-Thames to a safer centre at Winchester, but after his death the under-kings ruled on their own, and the central government of the West Saxons lapsed. It was restored by a king with a British name, Ceadwalla, who revived West Saxon supremacy in the south-east, recovered Wight, enlisted the South Saxons as subordinate allies and went on to conquer Kent. The West Saxon grip on Kent was soon loosened, but West Saxons remained united under the long rule of Ine, though at times he admitted Mercian supremacy, perhaps after an unsuccessful attempt to challenge it in 692. But Ine founded no dynasty and for 80 years his successors fought their own under-kings and the Mercians, until Egbert established a stable dynasty and broke the Mercian power, in the 9th century, in an age when the Norsemen were already savaging the old political structure of England.

The West Saxons expanded westward in two centuries of warfare, repeatedly planting colonies in newly conquered lands that still needed defence against the British. The expansion of the Mercians was peaceful. The neighbouring Welsh were their allies, with little sign of war until the middle of the eighth century. Then king Eliseg of Powys

> seized the inheritance of Powys, and recovered it from the power of the English for 9 years with sword and fire.

The years may lie between 743, when Cuthred of Wessex combined with his life-long enemy Aethelbald of Mercia to fight against the Welsh, and the events of 752, when Cuthred fought Aethelbald at *Beorgford*, perhaps Burford by Tenbury, near Ludlow, and of 753 when Cuthred 'fought the Welsh'; the causes and combinations of the conflicts are obscure, but these are the only wars involving the Mercians and the Welsh that the Saxon Chronicle records anywhere near the time of Eliseg. The threat persisted, until Offa marked the permanent frontier with a formidable dyke some decades later.

The Midlands

The Mercians had need of military colonies on their northern border, and some scores of earlier 7th-century warrior chiefs were buried in barrows in the Derbyshire and Staffordshire upland; several places in Cheshire are also named from English burial-mounds, though none have yet been excavated; and a few names that end in *-bold* derive from Mercian strongholds placed on the Northumbrian border. Similar names lie near the borders between Mercia and other English kingdoms, and Mercian names extend into the West Riding about Halifax; but there is no sign of defence against the Welsh until Eliseg's time. The latest pagan burials stop short of the allied British borders, and suggest that significant English settlement had not begun when the burials ended, early in the 7th century. But before the middle of the century an incidental story reports English settlers on the upper Severn, in lands not conquered by the Mercians, while the place names of Cheshire and the north-west suggest that the British states admitted the peaceful immigration of their Mercian allies well before the middle of the century. Further south the names of the constituent peoples of Mercia, the Hwicce, the Magonsaete and others, penetrated into the border regions and beyond without sign of wars and conquest; by the 670s the English were well established in Bath and Gloucester, Hereford and Leominster, where many of the names of people and of places suggest an untroubled mixture of English and Welsh.

Integration: the English

In the time of Bede, in the early 8th century, there was not yet a country called England. He lived in the island of Britain, in one of the regions that he called 'districts of the English'. He meant the districts where the English ruled. Their population was mixed, and included many British, whom the English commonly described as Welsh. Geography and recent history were none the less beginning to shape national and regional identities and loyalties. Permanent boundaries took shape in the age of conquest, and were thereafter adjusted, but not radically altered. The independent *Cymry* still called themselves *Britones* when they wrote in Latin, and remembered that they were a single nation who had lost their inheritance; but their segregation into the three separate highland zones ended cultural and political contact between them, and the Welsh who lived under English rule in time forgot their kinship with their unconquered fellow-countrymen.

Bede's countrymen called themselves English from the 7th century onward, *Angli* when they wrote in Latin. *Saxones* and *Saxonia* were literary affectations, as common in Northumbria as in Wessex, and were never used to distinguish Saxons from Angles; the East Saxons felt no closer kin to the West Saxons than to the East Angles, and no individual Englishman is ever termed a Saxon in his own language. Only in the 9th century, when supremacy passed to a West Saxon dynasty that lacked the description Anglian, was it necessary to invent the words *Angligena* and *Angelcyn*, to adapt the continental usage of *Angli Saxones*, English Saxons, in contrast to the Saxons of Germany, or to rename the West and South Saxons the West and South *Angli*. But these terms were short-lived Latin political devices, and no form of *Engle-Sexe* or the like ever took root in English language. The whole nation was English, though the territorial name *Engle Land* did not come into general use until the 11th century and was then first used to distinguish the English districts from the Danish.

These words are more than curiosities of language. They show what the early English felt about themselves. They sensed their national identity sooner and more keenly than the peoples of Europe because foreigners of different speech lived in the same island, beyond their borders and within their borders. But the English states were a compact group, geographically contiguous, while the Cymry were split between the three highland zones and Brittany, and many lived among the several English kingdoms. The bonds that united the Cymry looked to a fading past; those that united the English belonged to the present and the future.

The English were one people in the face of strangers, but their internal differences were many. Each Englishman belonged to his own small people, the Hwicce, the Wigesta or the like, and was also a subject of the kingdom that incorporated them into larger units, as the East Angles or the Mercians, the Northumbrians or the West Saxons. The ties that bound one man to another varied. The customs of the older kingdoms were already hardened, and were little changed by conquest. All were conservative, but each had its own conventions. The North Folk, the men of Kent, and some of the Middle Angles had settled in a world that was still Roman, and their first generations had learnt much from it; but many of the Middle and East Angles had come to England in large coherent communities, bringing with them ancestral custom, whereas Kent was a kingdom formed in Britain from diverse origins, and its situation readily exposed it to continuing European influence. The colonial lands differed from each other and from the old kingdoms; the Northumbrian English lived together in the east, in one part of their huge kingdom, but the Mercians and West Saxons were more evenly scattered throughout their territories. Their ways were not yet set; men whose adventurous ancestors had moved from Germany to Sussex, from Sussex to Hampshire, from Hampshire to Berkshire, and thence to Devon or Dorset, were readier for innovation than those whose ancestors had moved once, in a community, two centuries before, into Norfolk or Leicestershire.

The grave goods of the early western settlers indicate that men drawn from diverse English origins were often thrown together in their new homes; and the burial grounds show something of their formation. In the 5th century and much of the 6th most of the English lived in close packed villages and buried their dead in large communal cemeteries; many of these cemeteries remained in use until after the English conquest, and in some parts of the old kingdoms, especially in Kent and Cambridgeshire, the habit of burying the dead fully clothed, with brooches, belts and other articles of dress, continued after pagan burial had ceased. But in regions where there are no English burials before the later 6th century, large cemeteries are few; one or two bodies, or very small cemeteries are commonly found in isolation. The English no longer needed to concentrate for defence. They were the superior ruling element in the population, and their pioneers could afford to live in separate farmsteads without fear of effective native British assault. The new communities that grouped these pioneers were necessarily looser than those that united older villages; their population was also more open to the influence of their British neighbours; but the native population from whom they learnt were the heirs of the 6th-century warlord kingdoms, wholly different in outlook from the Roman British who had influenced the formative years of the old kingdoms.

The Subject Welsh

Most of the 7th-century English kingdoms included a large number of native British, whom the English sometimes knew by their native national name of *Cumbrogi*, or *Cymry*, but more commonly described in English as foreigners, *Wealh* or *Wylisc*. They are most prominent in Wessex, where the late 7th-century laws of king Ine contain many clauses that legislate for Welshmen. As in Wales, the Welshmen of Wessex might belong to a free or unfree kin, and the free landowners are divided into three classes, like the Welsh of Wales. Some were men of substance, for a Welshman who owned five hides rated with the middle grade of English nobility, and five hides was a great deal of land. The Welsh also held royal office, and the Welshman who rode on the kings' service ranked with the lower English nobles.

The laws do not show how many the Welsh were, or where they lived. Bede's language suggests that they were numerous, for he comments that Aldhelm's open letter to the king of Dumnonia in 705

> led many of the British subjects of the West Saxons to the celebration of the Catholic Easter.

They doubtless included the inhabitants of the newly conquered border regions; but place names in central Wessex like Andover, Candover, Micheldever indicate a substantial Welsh population, in a region that is a more probable home for noble Welshmen entrusted with royal missions than the borderlands of dubious loyalty. The limits and extent of these names cannot be determined until the survey of the place names of Hampshire is published, but the personal names of king Ceadwalla, his brother Mul and his grandfather Cadda, of the 8th-century *ealdorman* Conbran, abbot Catwal, and others, suggest that at least one among the small kingdoms of the West Saxons retained a strong Welsh element for a long time.

Kings and nobles so named must have been at least bilingual, their English as fluent as their Welsh; and perhaps they spoke little or no Welsh. But since their parents gave them such names, Welsh origins remained respectable, and imply intermarriage among the well-to-do. It is probable that most children were soon given names common among the dominant English; and Welsh names went out of fashion among the nobility after the middle of the 8th century, though they lasted longer, with the language, among the poorer cultivators. The inferior status of the Wessex Welsh persisted in Norman England, for when Henry I reissued the laws of Ine, he dropped the obsolete provisions for noble Welshmen, a class long extinct, but retained those that concerned Welsh bondmen; and since he revised the compensation due, to bring it into line with 12th-century values, he was not mechanically copying an ancient ruling, but was dealing with a law and a class of persons who were still a reality.

In Wessex, where English colonists were dispersed through extensive fertile lands that had recently been British, a class of wealthy Welshmen is more prominent than elsewhere. But for that reason it was more quickly assimilated among the ruling English. Yet equivalents existed in other kingdoms. The laws of Kent provided for an inferior class of cultivators, known by the Germanic term *laet*, who were divided into three classes, like the Welsh, and rated at the same inferiority as the Welsh of Wessex. Some Kentish notables also used Welsh names; Dunwald was an 8th-century royal officer who owned substantial property in Canterbury, and the extensive rural territory of *Dunwalinglond*. Dunwallaun, perhaps a relative, also witnessed charters, as did the priests Welhisc and Maban. Malvinus, Kentish ambassador to Mercia in 787, also bore a Welsh name.

The numbers and the status of these Welshmen cannot be clearly assessed until the early English charters are adequately published, the names of peoples and places indexed and studied. Comparable evidence is not available for the East and Middle Angles and East Saxons, whose laws and charters are not preserved; but in Sussex, whence a few charters survive, the names of king

Nunna and others may be Welsh. In western Mercia, however, where charters are numerous, British magnates are few, for most of the midlands lay beyond the region of rich Roman villas, and wealthy British landlords did not survive the long interval between the collapse of British authority in the lower Severn and the imposition of settled English rule.

In Northumbria, evidence is stronger. Chad, Caedmon and others had Welsh names. Earlier 7th-century pagan English burials are plentiful in the East Riding, but they barely extend into the North and West Riding. When the Pennine British kings disappeared, their subjects remained; and they were still Welsh enough in the 10th century to fall naturally and without struggle under the control of the Strathclyde British. Until then, their lords were English. When bishop Wilfred was granted lands in the regions of Ribble, Yeadon, Dent and Catlow, in the late 7th century, he received the estates of British monasteries whose monks had fled. The grant that he troubled to secure did not entitle him to unpeopled waste, but to cultivated farmland, whose British cultivators remained; and from the Mersey to the Tyne, British administration and land tenure lasted till the 12th century. Even east of the Pennines, near Harrogate, about 670, Wilfred had difficulty with an independent British village, whose obedience he could not command without a posse of armed men. York itself retained a class of *Wallerwenta* at least until the 10th century, and some of them were men of substance, for the laws provide for Welshmen who prosper, and own a hide of land.

Men of inferior Welsh status persisted as late and later in the south. The laws of 10th-century London sentenced a runaway bondman to be stoned 'like a Welsh thief', implying a different status from an English thief. In Cambridge, an 11th-century guild insured its members against the contingency that they might slay a Welshman, and so be liable for a compensation payment set at half the value of a free Englishman; there the nearby village of Comberton suggests the home of some of the Welsh whom the guildsmen might encounter. These laws imply that a class of persons with inferior Welsh status existed in some numbers in much of England from the English conquest until after the Norman conquest and later. Laws tend to illuminate the unusual, and do not show its size and extent; nor do they imply that men of Welsh status still spoke the Welsh language, for established interest may perpetuate the inferior status of a minority long after the circumstances that brought it into being have disappeared. Spoken Welsh was common in the 7th century. The river Beane in Hertfordshire was known to the later English by a Welsh name. British monks probably preached in Norfolk, and also in Hertfordshire, about the 590s; their activity implies a considerable population who understood their language. Near Peterborough, Guthlac was troubled about 705 by the still independent British of the Fenland, who were to retain their speech and untamed hostility into the 11th century. In Northumbria the poet Caedmon, Welsh by name, was an elderly layman of substance before he received the gift of song, and entered the monastery of

Whitby. But when he sang, he sang in English. He had been born and named not long after the English conquest, perhaps before, and English was an acquired language.

Men born British and reared in an English environment are likely to have become bilingual early. Some are also likely to have abandoned their ancestral language early, so that their grandchildren forgot that their grandfathers had been born Welsh. Among others, two languages are likely to have stayed longer in use; and in closed communities, Welsh may well have persisted for many generations. The old language is likely to have been dropped at different times in different regions, often influenced by purely local circumstances. But among most bilingual peoples, the minority language may linger for centuries, like Cornish, or Wendish in modern Saxony. It may recede gradually, or may disappear in a generation, like Irish, when some considerable upheaval suddenly extinguishes it. In Britain, both the Norse invasions and the Norman conquest were upheavals severe enough to kill what remained of peasant Welsh in many parts of Britain.

Something of the extent of the 7th-century Welsh in the English kingdoms may in time be learnt from the study of place names. Places whose Roman British names are preserved are few; apart from large towns, they are naturally most numerous in the West Riding, in the Welsh marches and in other border regions. Those that the English called villages of the Welsh or British are considerably more numerous. Some names carry dates, for forms like Comberton, Camberwell, Cumberlow were taken from British speech, before Welsh had transmuted *Cumber* into *Cymry*, hardly later than the 6th century, and are more plentiful in the areas of early settlement. Much more numerous are those described as *Wealh Tun*, Welshman's village, Walton and the like. Their study has been hindered by a curious modern myth, that

> the old English word *wealh* also meant 'a serf, a slave' in general,

which led to the speculation that such places

> might conceivably have been named from non-British serfs,

and thereafter grew to an assumption that many or most were so named.

The myth is quite untrue. *Wealh* never meant a 'slave or serf' in general. It carries that meaning only in West Saxon texts of the 10th century and later, written when in Wessex the only Welshmen left were servile. The usage did not extend to Mercians and Northumbrians, where free Welshmen remained unassimilated to a later date; it had not arisen in Wessex in the 7th and 8th centuries, when places were named in large numbers. The laws of Ine are explicit; when he provided for a *Wealh gafolgelda*, a Welsh taxpayer, valued at 120 shillings, he did not mean a servile person; when he referred to a servile Welshman or Englishman, he called him a *Wealh theow* or an *Englisc theow*, bondman. Some modern places called Walton and the like may take their names from a wall or a wood; but, when they derive from *Wealh*, they indicate the homes of Welshmen who lived among the early English, as do names that incorporate Cumber-, Britte-, and similar terms. Their study has been inhibited by a naïve and somewhat nationalistic reluctance to admit the existence of a considerable Welsh element among the ancestors of the modern English. The extent of these names cannot be assessed until they have been properly mapped and critically examined. Yet the evidence of the names of places and people, of laws and other texts, is ample. The population of the English kingdoms in the seventh century consisted of an uneven mixture of men of mixed Germanic origins and of descendants of the Roman British, called Welshmen, who are likely to have constituted the larger number in many regions. The history of the early English kingdoms is the story of the integration of this mixed population into a single nation.

CHAPTER SEVENTEEN

ENGLISH MONARCHY

Early Tradition

Englishmen, and the Welshmen within their borders, were integrated under the government of kings. The early history of the English monarchy is disguised by the sources which describe it. Bede emphasised the past power of his own Northumbria, and the editors of the Saxon Chronicle looked back from the standpoint of ninth-century Wessex. Both relate the main events of Mercian history, and silently ignore their meaning. No Mercian view survives. Later ages therefore easily absorb the viewpoint and accept the bias of the Northumbrians and the West Saxons. Bias there was. Bede listed the succession of English kings who 'held empire' over the southern English, and ended with the king who died a year or two before his own birth, Oswy of Northumbria. He did not remark that Oswy's supremacy lasted for no more than three years in a reign of nearly thirty years, although the evidence that he reports elsewhere told him so; and he ignored the southern supremacy of the three Mercian kings who reigned after Oswy's defeat, though he reports their victories in other chapters. Bede might legitimately close his list in his father's day; but when the Saxon Chronicle took his list, and added the 9th-century Egbert of Wessex immediately after Oswy, leaving out the great Offa as well as his Mercian predecessors, it deliberately falsified history; for the hegemony of Offa and the earlier Mercian kings was a great deal more substantial than that of Aethelbert of Kent and of others in the list.

The bias extends beyond a list and a viewpoint; it governs the selection of events and the context to which they are related. It is redressed by the evidence of charters, supplemented by the genealogies and other texts; but the Northumbrian and Wessex view of early England still predominates, for the charters have not yet been seriously studied, while the texts of Bede and the Chronicle have been repeatedly examined in detail. The evolution of the English monarchy is wholly misconceived if the empire of the Mercian kings is overlooked.

These misconceptions chiefly concern the matured monarchy; but they also cloud its first years. Its origins were many, for the early English learnt from different exemplars, from their own Germanic past, from the Roman and Frankish traditions of Europe, from the British of the 5th and 6th centuries, and from their Irish clerics. The institution of monarchy had developed among the

European Germans during the Roman centuries, but unevenly. The most glaring contrast was that between the Angles and the Saxons, whose traditions altogether differed, though they were near neighbours, closely connected. The Angles were believed to have obeyed a long-established monarchy in Europe since at least the late third century AD; and their monarchical convention differed from that of most other Germans, in that the undivided succession passed to the late king's nearest adult male relative, usually to his eldest son, unless he were a child or otherwise unfitted to rule. Their northern neighbours, the Jutes and the Varni, and some of the Scandinavian peoples, had similar traditions; but on their south

> in the old days, the Saxons had no king, but appointed rulers over each township. They regularly held a general meeting once a year . . . where the leaders met with twelve nobles and as many freedmen and bondmen from each township. There they confirmed the laws, judged important legal cases, and agreed upon the plans that would guide them in peace or war during the coming year.

The European Saxons did not establish a permanent monarchy until the 9th century, and the practices of the 'old days' continued to annoy 8th-century Franks, who were exasperated at the difficulty of pinning down a multitude of local rulers and assemblies to a binding agreement.

Kent

From their first arrival, the English of Britain inherited something of both traditions. Hengest the Dane was their first leader, and he established a monarchy among his own immediate followers in Kent. They were Jutes, accustomed to monarchy, and on his death they fetched Oesc, the heir of his lieutenant in Bernicia, to found a hereditary dynasty; the later royal house was known as the Oescingas, not as the 'Hengstingas'. Oesc had high ambitions, for he named his son after Eormenric, the founder of the great Gothic empire of the fourth century. The aspirations symbolised by a great name were not realised, for Oesc fell at Badon, and Arthur's victory compelled Eormenric to keep within his narrow borders for the whole of his long reign. Yet ambition remained, for just before his death Eormenric married his son Aethelbert to a daughter of the Frank king of Paris, and Aethelbert twice attempted to assert wide empire; but his power died with him, and later Kentish kings stayed within their frontier. Though they were the earliest English kingdom, settled in a Roman world whose economy and social structure heavily influenced them, their monarchy leant more heavily on German experience than most; the king's notables were known by a Frankish

MAP 23 THE 7th CENTURY ENGLISH KINGDOMS

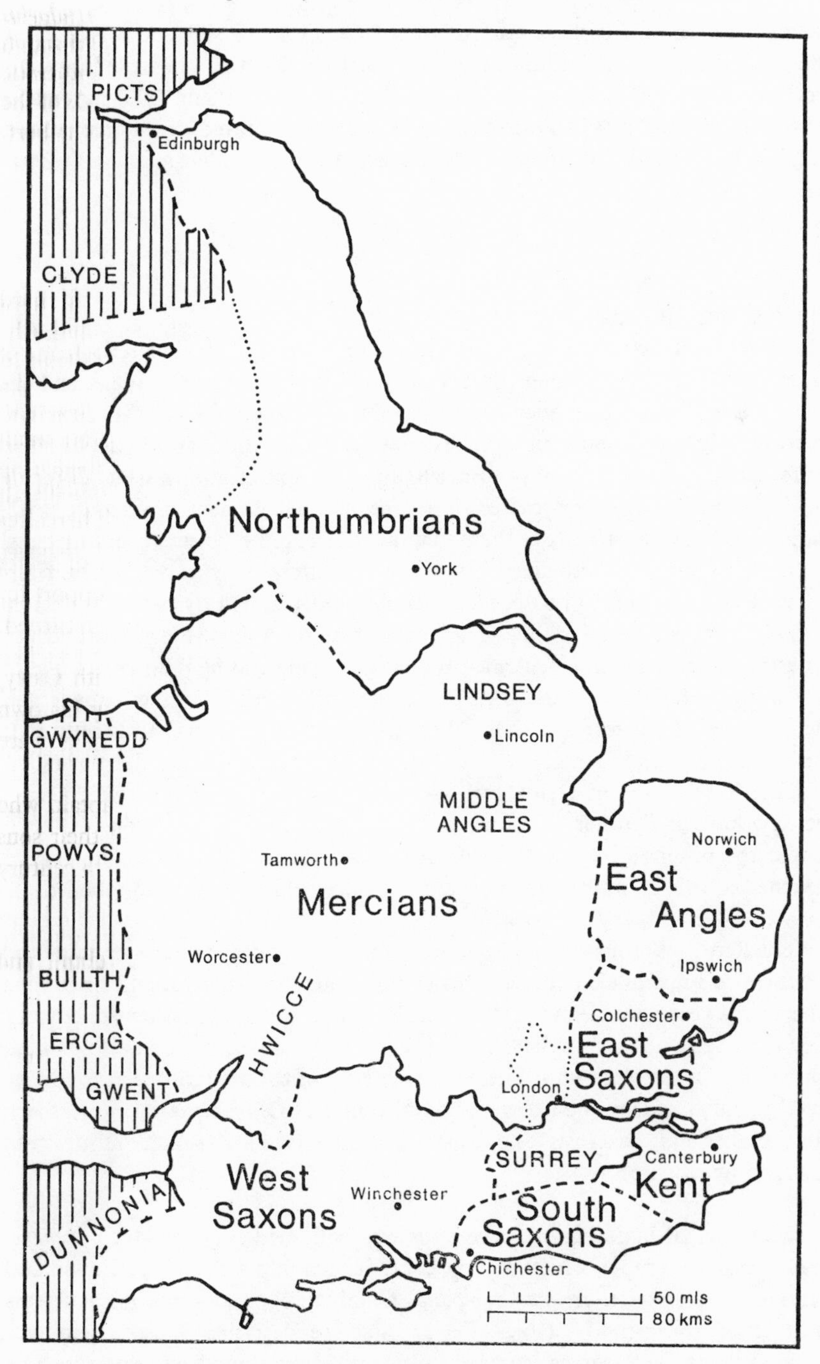

British and Pictish territory shaded.

name, *leode*, and his earliest ministers used the Frankish titles of *referendarius* and *graf*; there is less sign than elsewhere that the Kentish king ruled through local or central meetings of his subjects, or consulted them. The autocratic monarchy of Kent, cast in a European mould, proved unfitted to the needs of the English, and failed to hold their allegiance after the brief authority of Aethelbert.

The Northumbrians

The Northumbrian monarchy was differently constituted. It grew in hard fighting, its main root among the Bernicians. Revolt began with Ida, and 8th-century English tradition tidied the record of his successors into a neat scheme of dated orderly succession; but its dates contradict each other and Bede, and the contemporary observation of the British argues a form of government nearer to the Saxon model, with four leaders simultaneously in command of separate small territories. Near disaster drove them to unite under Aethelric, and the staggering successes of his son Aethelferth made the monarchy permanent. Aethelferth annexed Deira, expelling its newly constituted independent dynasty. Thereafter both kingdoms showed that they preferred unity under a single king, of whichever dynasty, rather than independence under local kings. When Edwin of Deira overthrew Aethelferth, the Bernicians accepted him, with no sign of support for their own exiled princes; and when Edwin fell and the Bernician Oswald returned, Deira accepted him as readily. When Penda of Mercia killed Oswald, he installed a Deiran under-king in Deira, but when the Deiran king clashed with Oswy, the new king of Bernicia, he could not find sufficient support among his own people to sustain his separate rule; and when sons of Bernician kings were detached to rule Deira, the Deirans did not rally behind those who rebelled.

Aethelferth's Bernicians were a nation united behind a military captain who led them to unparalleled success; his subordinate commanders, and their sons after them, were rewarded with territorial lordships, but in the earlier 7th century they developed no intermediate class of hereditary nobles, placed between king and subject, as in Kent and Wessex. Something of the way in which the kings ruled is illustrated by the excavated royal centre at Old Yeavering in northern Northumberland, that was established in Aethelferth's time and rebuilt and enlarged by his successors.

The principal buildings are a large oblong hall, evidently the king's, several smaller halls, a temple, which was probably turned into a church by Edwin and Paulinus, and an open-air meeting-place, plainly designed for periodical assemblies of the Bernician notables. Its architecture describes those assemblies. Planned like a slice from a Roman theatre, its several hundred seats rose row behind row, tapering downward to focus the attention of the audience upon a small dais, barely large enough to accommodate the king's throne, with a couple of attendants. This auditorium was not designed for the debate and discussion of contentious issues. It permitted the king to declare the policies resolved in council, and allowed the audience to shout approval, or to sit in silence. In such a structure, no district leader could rise from the rear or middle benches to question the policy propounded from the royal platform, nor be heard against the wind if he tried. The king's hall might permit the deliberation of a council, but the assembly place was designed for the king to communicate decisions to men who were expected to approve.

The kings had reason to expect approval. The men who met at Yeavering were the leaders of the most powerful kingdom in Britain. They had won their stature by their own effort, for men who were children when Urien and his allies shut the English up in Lindisfarne lived on into the reign of Oswy. They and their followers were proud of their achievement, and the kings who had led them from the edge of disaster to splendid strength deserved and earned their confidence. The architecture of Yeavering proclaims a popular monarchy, a trusted king respected by an equal people.

The purposes of the royal hall and open-air auditorium of Yeavering are explained by Bede's account of the debate in the Deiran royal centre of Goodmanham in 625, when the Northumbrians decided to accept Christianity. In Kent, the king had been converted, and sent priests endowed with ample estates and royal authority to recruit his subjects to the king's religion; there is no hint of consultation, and on his death his successors and their people rejected Christianity, and were won back with difficulty. But in Northumbria, Edwin first assembled his council of notables in the royal hall to hear the Christian priest; when a majority welcomed the new faith, he left them to urge it upon the people, by a dramatic demonstration of the impotence of the old religion.

The old Northumbria, and with it the buildings of Yeavering, survived into Oswy's time. The veterans preferred the austere piety of the Irish monks to the ostentation of the Roman church of Wilfred and of Kent. They were succeeded by a landed nobility in Deira and by unruly lords in Bernicia, whose licence Bede deplored. Their violence was checked in Oswy's time, but it brought military disaster under his son. The old austerity, fortified by the monastic church, regained control with the accession of Aldfrith, but on his death in 705 the disruptive ferocity of the new nobility ensured the quick decline of the monarchy, under a succession of child kings and weak kings. At the end of the century, their rivalries installed upon the throne a son-in-law of Offa of Mercia; though he was murdered when Offa died, his successors had no time even to attempt the restoration of the kingdom before the Norsemen swept upon their coasts.

Authority concentrated upon a trusted leader was based upon continuing Northumbrian victory; but it failed in adversity, when kings lost respect at home; and even the greatest kings came to the south as enemy tyrants, arousing a fierce resistance too resolute for them to quell. Aethelferth was destroyed when he ventured south of the Trent; Edwin conquered Wessex, and his victory inspired a grand alliance of the south that soon destroyed him; Oswald killed its British leaders, but the English Penda revived the southern alliance and overthrew him; Oswy in time broke the allied army, but the south threw him out within three years; his son tried and failed to regain control, and in 679 he was forced to accept the Trent as his permanent boundary. Northumbria began the long war with immense military superiority, sending a well-tempered and apparently invincible army of veterans against southerners who were in disarray after the dissolution of Kentish hegemony, and who had as yet no comparable military experience. But the south altogether rejected Northumbrian supremacy, doggedly renewing their resistance after each defeat. Devotion to a hero king was alien to their past and their present, and could not serve as a focus for the union and integration of the English nation.

The East Angles

Before they conquered the British, the southern English were grouped into a multitude of very small independent peoples and two considerable kingdoms. They briefly submitted to the empire of Kent, but they demolished it on its founder's death. Bede reports that Redwald of East Anglia then asserted a southern primacy similar to Aethelbert's. His was the only other kingdom with a large army capable of claiming the inheritance of sovereignty. Nothing is said of the nature of his monarchy, for East Anglia has left no written record. But the excavated royal tombs of the early 7th century bespeak its splendour. The great mound of Sutton Hoo, by the East Anglian royal centre near Ipswich, contained the funeral furniture of Redwald, or of one of his immediate successors. It is the most magnificent royal burial in Germanic Europe, the witness of a sovereignty no less exalted than the Northumbrian. It is not paralleled by any tomb of earlier or later generations yet known in Britain, but in its own day it did not stand alone. A burial at Broomfield, near Chelmsford, is similar in concept, though less splendid; and is probably the tomb of one of the early seventh-century East Saxon kings. A third burial, on the Buckinghamshire bank of the Thames opposite Maidenhead, approaches the wealth of Sutton Hoo. It is a tomb on a royal scale, and the place, Taplow, the burial-mound of Taeppa, preserves the name of the king there buried. Neither he nor his kingdom is otherwise known. The grave furniture resembles Sutton Hoo, and it may be that Taeppa was a regional king installed to hold the frontier against the West Saxons during Redwald's brief dominion, perhaps a son or a relative. The name and nature of the kingdom is suggested by its neighbour. Surrey, south of the Thames, is *Suder Ge* to Bede, the southern district; the usage implies that it was at one time paired with a 'Norrey' north of the Thames. Neither endured as independent kingdoms, and the origin of these districts is unknown; it may be that they were creations of

Redwald, for Taeppa's kingdom did not survive into the better documented generations of the mid and late 7th century; but the wealth of his tomb fits the ruler of a kingdom larger than the little territory in which he was buried.

Nothing is known of the later constitution of the East Anglian and East Saxon monarchies, save that their kings stayed within their borders, and won no authority over other English peoples. Political primacy passed to the frontier kingdoms, composed of small independent units, whose numbers greatly increased as colonists consolidated new lands to the west. They could not be bound together by a centralised absolute Germanic monarchy, on the model of Northumbria, East Anglia and Kent, or of the Goths, Franks and Burgundians in Europe. The form of government that they evolved was the starting point of one essential difference in the future history of the English and the peoples of Europe; in Europe Germanic monarchy was imposed upon a peasantry cowed into submission by late Roman institutions, but the circumstances of the early English forced them to adopt a looser authority, which was obliged to rest upon a stronger regional and local autonomy.

The frontier peoples of the 6th and early 7th centuries were heirs of the settlers whom the Anglian Chronicle described; they were grouped 'under many leaders', not yet 'organised under a single king'; their constitution resembled that of the continental Saxons, whose local leaders drew their authority from regular annual meetings of their people. The larger frontier monarchies were formed after the late 6th-century conquest, in the course of wars against the Welsh, against the Northumbrians, and between the Mercians and the West Saxons.

The West Saxons

The early history of the West Saxons is disguised by the ingenuity of the authors of the Saxon Chronicle. They needed to pretend that their own royal house was as ancient, as venerable, and as coherent as the dynasty of the Mercian Angles whom they had replaced. Their scholars did their best, but the evidence before them was stubborn and plentiful, and could not be compressed into the doctrine they proclaimed. Their own mutual contradictions, the numerous statements of Bede, and the evidence of the charters and many other texts disprove their thesis.

The central core of that thesis was that all West Saxon kings were sovereigns descended from Cerdic and formed a single dynasty. The genealogists tried to trace the descent of each king from Cerdic. They failed. They were unable even to contrive such ancestry for the more recent 8th-century kings, for living memory knew their immediate ancestors, and the genealogists had to be content with a generalised assertion that each king 'descended from Cerdic', without naming their fathers and grandfathers and with no attempt to link them with their 7th-century predecessors. Men still lived who knew that there were no such links. But the genealogies of the seventh century were more easily doctored; each sequence of two or three names was attached to either Cuthwulf or Cuthwine, who were turned into the brother and son of Ceawlin; and he became son of Cynric and grandson of Cerdic.

These authors did not fabricate. They adapted the conventions of British genealogists, who made no clear distinction between a pedigree and a king list. The British had attempted to show the succession of political power, and did so with rough and ready accuracy; but they agreed to assume that, as in their own day, son succeeded father, so that each Roman emperor was described as the son of his predecessor, and the last emperor in each table was treated as the father of the British ruler who inherited his authority. So the English transcribed the list of 6th-century West Saxon rulers, from Cerdic to Ceolric, as a succession from fathers to sons and brothers, confused by the intrusion of Creoda of Mercia into some texts. But their difficulties were greater in the 7th century, when texts and tradition remembered the fathers and grandfathers of some kings who were known not to have been kings themselves. Versions of the pedigrees therefore contradict each other; Cynegils, the contemporary of Edwin and Redwald, is given three fathers in different texts, and other kings have two fathers. Other reigning families, not connected with his, are traced to one or other Cutha by unlikely links.

The reality behind the fiction is discoverable, because some of the evidence that the genealogists manipulated is known independently of them. Bede knew that in Edwin's time Wessex comprised at least five distinct kingdoms, each ruled by an underking, who at times acknowledged varying degrees of sovereignty to a West Saxon overking. The still unstudied evidence of the charters names many of the people named in the pedigrees, and many more besides, as distinct regional kings; and the entries of the Chronicle itself name three contemporary kings in 661, two of whom died at the time of Wulfhere's invasion, doubtless in battle against him. Bede describes the failure of the early overkings. Cynegils was an effective sovereign, and was succeeded by his son Cenwalh. Between them they reigned for more than 60 years, from 611 to 672, but no other king is said to have been succeeded by his son, or any near relative, for more than 200 years thereafter, in the Chronicle or in any other text. Bede says that on Cenwalh's death the overkingship was discontinued, and the West Saxons were ruled by underkings for ten years. The overkingship was revived and maintained for 40 years by Ceadwalla and Ine; they came from different dynasties, and in the next hundred years half a dozen sovereigns are reported, whom no record links with one another or with previous dynasties, until an unconvincing list traces the descent of Egbert from Ine's brother. The Chronicle reports their frequent wars against underkings who refused to admit their authority, and reveals that some were forced to tolerate the independent defiance of local kings for decades.

The titles and the status of the regional kings varied with the power of the overking; sometimes in different contemporary texts, the same ruler is termed *rex*, *regulus* and *patricius*, king, underking and patrician, and sometimes some of the western regional kingdoms were altogether detached from Wessex, and were directly ruled by the Mercian kings. Exact study of the texts is likely to explain a good deal of the detail of the early history of Wessex; but the evidence that has already been collected is sufficient to show that no stable and lasting West Saxon monarchy was erected until the 9th century; then it was consolidated in the course of wars against the Scandinavians, out of the inheritance of the Mercian monarchy.

The Mercians

Early 7th-century Mercia also consisted of small independent peoples, some settled since the 5th century, others first established during the colonisation of the west. But its constituent peoples were much more numerous, and were quickly able to coalesce behind a powerful overking without internal wars. Their stability was grounded upon early success, and upon shrewd policies evolved by early kings that hardened into lasting principles of government. The Mercian kings won supremacy because they organised and headed southern resistance against the Northumbrians, and took the brunt of their attack. Thenceforth their northern border was secure, firmly marked by the lower and middle Trent. The Northumbrian danger had impelled them to make allies of the Welsh; and the long-standing alliance saved them from western wars, until the lowland was thoroughly settled by English speaking colonists, its border defined by the foothills of the mountains; a couple of sharp campaigns tamed the East Angles and permanently prevented further threats from their distinct and self-sufficient territory. The only open frontier of the Mercians faced the West Saxons on the south, and the Mercians retained superiority, periodically invading but never invaded, for they had one enemy only, while the West Saxons were distracted by wars against Dumnonia, by campaigns in Sussex and Kent, and by their own internal conflicts.

The first Mercian kings presided over the several peoples of the Middle Angles and the Avon. Some, perhaps all of these peoples retained their own local rulers, heirs of those who had led them before the English conquest, and before the central monarchy was established. The monarchy itself was at first small and weak, unable to withstand the Northumbrians; when Edwin subdued the West Saxons, his route took his armies through Mercia, with or without opposition. The Mercian kingdom was divided. Penda's rule began when Edwin was supreme, and included the western territories; his brother Eowa also reigned until 642, perhaps as king among the Middle Angles.

The Mercian Empire

The dynasty of Penda was acceptable because it claimed descent from the ancient kings who were held to have ruled all the Angles in Europe, the Iclingas, descendants of Icel, the king who transferred the monarchy to Britain. The claim may have been true, for one cadet branch of the Iclingas were already respected local rulers among the Middle Angles in the time of Penda's sons. But whether the claim was true or false is relatively unimportant; what matters is that it was believed and accepted. The local kings among the West Saxons and the British could brook no overlord, for each of them could claim ancestry as eminent as any potential sovereign; but the venerable antiquity asserted by the Anglian royal house gave it a stronger title to universal obedience than any rulers in Britain had been able to command since the last legitimate Roman emperors in Italy.

Penda's monarchy could claim ancestral right, but it could not rule by the simple direct authority that Offa of Angel or the Northumbrian kings had exercised over an equal people. The mechanics of government had yet to be worked out, to fit the conditions of the present. Penda learnt from his British allies, and from the experience of Ireland, the nearest established monarchical government. Like an Irish king, he exacted hostages and enforced tribute; he impressed British tradition by a distribution of gifts to his subordinate rulers, made in the manner of an Irish king or an 'open-handed' British king. He did not dethrone conquered kings and annex their kingdoms, as Aethelferth had annexed Deira, and as Oswy annexed most of Mercia in 655. He expelled Cenwalh from Wessex, but he left the regional kings alone; he restored the dynasty of Deira, but he left Oswy in Bernicia; and though he twice killed rebellious kings of the East Angles, he permitted their heirs to succeed them as his subordinate allies.

The clumsy Irish practice of levying tribute by forcing the tributaries to give hostages is not reported under Penda's successors; the relics of Roman administration showed more efficient ways of collecting taxes. Irish influence was strong at first, for the kings were Christian, and many of their decisions were guided by the advice of Irish priests, who drew upon the experience of their homeland; these decisions became formative precedents, that hardened into conventions of government. The Mercians adapted the principles of Irish monarchy, but did not imitate its detail. The high king ruled over many lesser kings, with an authority as strong as that which Diarmait had asserted in Ireland a century before. But the schematism of the Irish provincial kings, grouping smaller kingdoms behind a sovereignty intermediate between the high king's and the local king's, found no echo among the Mercians. Though Lindsey, the Middle Angles and the western territories were distinct geographical regions, each with its own individual history, the Mercians did not place regional kings over them, although the Northumbrian conquerors had in their time installed dependent rulers. The Mercian overking reigned over many separate kingdoms of different size. The far western lands between the upper Severn and the Wye were ruled by a dynasty that claimed descent from a son of Penda; on their east, the large kingdom of the Hwicce obeyed for centuries a dynasty of Northumbrian origin, that had perhaps been installed by Oswy.

Throughout their long history, there is no record of dynastic wars within these kingdoms, of wars between them, or of rebellions against Mercian supremacy. The titles of their kings vary; as among the West Saxons, the same ruler is sometimes described as king, sometimes as underking, sometimes as minister of the king of the Mercians; and in the rest of Mercia, lesser rulers, termed patrician or prince, ruled smaller peoples, equally without rebellion or internal discord. Within the Mercian dynasty itself, the succession was at times disputed. But the disputes were quickly settled; as in Ireland, men were chosen whose remote ancestors had once been king, and when they were chosen, they reigned for a generation or more without serious challenge. Loyalty to a stable dynasty built a monarchy stronger than the precarious sovereignty of Northumbrian, Kentish or continental kings. The Mercian monarchs retained their subjects' loyalty and increased their majesty because they continued the forms of government they inherited from the past, tolerating and encouraging the autonomy of dependent rulers, and leaving large areas of administrative, judicial and political decision in the hands of periodical local representative assemblies. They were content if their subjects accepted their supremacy, and kept peace with one another. Their sovereignty contrasts with the autocracy of Oswy, who, in 655, 'ruled almost all the English directly, or held empire over their rulers.'

Penda and his predecessors learnt from the British and Irish. His sons and their successors had other teachers. Their first priests and monks were Irish, but in the reign of Wulfhere the English church was reorganised by the flexible genius of Theodore of Tarsus, who brought to Britain the experience of the eastern Roman empire as well as of the church of Rome. The rapid spread of monasteries, bound together by common notions of what was right and wrong in the world of the living, profoundly influenced the practice of English government. Theodore found an apt pupil in Aldhelm, who had been taught by the Irish, but devoted his life to training English clerks and administrators as learned and as capable as the Irish. Aldhelm absorbed Theodore's experience, became the friend and counsellor both of the Mercians and of the West Saxons, and educated the next great Mercian king, Aethelbald, whose reign continued to 757, when Offa succeeded him. More than any other individual, Aldhelm gathered together the varied examples that could teach the English the practices of government, and sorted them into principles that their successors could observe. He and his royal pupils were the architects of the English monarchy.

The restrained might of the Mercian monarchs preserved their authority over all the English. They acquired sovereignty by conquest, but they retained it because their rule did not provoke the same lasting resentment that Northumbrian conquest had aroused. Penda twice invaded East Anglia, but no third invasion was needed. Wulfhere overran Wessex, and made Wight and Sussex a separate dependent kingdom. Aethelred annexed western Wessex, and in 676 invaded Kent. Thereafter the Mercians retained control of London, and from London controlled the south-west. Only the West Saxons renewed and maintained resistance; but the resistance of their fragmented kingdom failed to break Mercian supremacy. Mercian arms prevailed, and reinforced submission after each repeated victory.

The substance and the titles of Mercian supremacy are set down in the charters. Wherever charters survive, many of them are confirmed by the Mercian king. Some are preserved in their original manuscript, others are close copies of their originals, but many are much doctored by later copyists, who add particulars that enlarge or strengthen the claims that monasteries later founded upon the grants. The texts have not yet been assessed, for their interpretation has been obscured by an oversimple attempt to classify them as either wholly 'genuine' or wholly 'forged'; yet hardly any of them can be squeezed into these rigid categories. Most are in varying stages of corruption and manipulation; those that are closer to their originals commonly include a large number of witnesses, who were not contemporary with each other, but were near in time; for the original grants were commonly confirmed two or three times, not long after they were made, by subsequent kings, bishops and lords, and the earlier transcripts ran the successive witnesses together; but later copyists often left out large numbers of names that had lost their meaning, and sometimes put in their place the names of a few well-known potentates who lived at other times.

Normally the confirmatory signature of a Mercian king to a grant of land outside Mercia admits Mercian suzerainty, even if it is inserted by a copyist; for texts were not manipulated at random, but for the specific purpose of strengthening the title that the grant claimed. In and after the 9th century, when the Mercian power was broken, no monastic interest was served by adding Mercian authority in a kingdom that Mercia no longer mastered; even when the name of a Mercian king is wrongly intruded, the copyist who first inserted it did so when Mercian supremacy still prevailed, and thereby acknowledged that supremacy.

Many recipients did not require the sovereign's confirmation, or did not bother to obtain it. But many others did, and a close study of the wording of the texts is likely to explain changes in political power that often endured for only a few years; in some extreme cases, as when the West Saxons for a short time mastered Kent, a grant may be made by a Kentish underking or lord, witnessed by the overking of Kent, by the West Saxon king as overlord of Kent, and by the Mercian king as suzerain over the West Saxons. Such instances are rare; usually the king of each kingdom signs alone, and when another king signs, it is the Mercian monarch alone; and when the Mercian king grants Wessex lands without the West Saxon king, or grants exemption from the London customs dues without the king of Kent, he is commonly exercising direct authority.

The ideas that underlay Mercian sovereignty are expressed in the kings' titles. In most signatures, the king is content to be called simply 'king of the Mercians', for secure sovereignty did not need to be flaunted. No ruler is called 'king of England', for England did not yet exist, but 'king of Britain' is often used. 'King of all the southern English' is more frequent, with variants like 'king not only of the Mercians, but also of all the provinces commonly called southern

English'. Some drafting clerks used the grander style of the 'empire of the Mercians', and in 798, Coenwulf, the last of the Mercian kings to exercise effective supremacy, called himself *Imperator*, 'emperor', in a grant whose original manuscript survives.

The arresting title illuminates another of the main influences that gave the Mercians supremacy. Their monarchy had borrowed something from Germanic experience, something from Irish, and something from Europe. The concept of an island emperor was British. Nowhere in Europe is the title emperor used of any ruler but an emperor of Rome before the time of Napoleon; it is confined to the emperors in Constantinople, and to the successors of Charlemagne in the west. But from the time of Arthur, it remained in the political vocabulary of the British Isles, used only occasionally, but used by all peoples on occasions. One seventh-century Irish writer called an earlier high king of Ireland *imperator*, and another used the same title of Oswald of Northumbria, calling him 'emperor of Britain', not of the English; and in the 11th century, Brian Boru, the last great Irish king, himself asserted the same title. An Armorican British writer of the 9th century called the Frank king an emperor, and British poets celebrated the emperor Arthur.

The title was used rarely, for all men knew that emperors should be emperors of Rome. It was only in Britain that legitimate emperors had ruled who did not claim to rule the rest of the Roman empire. Men were chary of the high-sounding word, and archbishop Boniface sneered at its upstart use in the time of Aethelbald. But both the British and English perpetuated its substance in language more circumspect. The Welsh coined the title *Gwledic*, ruler of the country, and bestowed it upon Maelgwn, Urien and a few others, who came nearer than most to reviving the wide dominion of Arthur. The English early made the concept their own, and before Bede's time contrived a list of those who were sovereigns of the southern English. Bede put it into Latin, avoiding the personal title; he lists the men who were held to have 'held empire', *imperium*; the English language gave them the title *Bretwalda*, ruler of Britain; it came near to the imperial title, for a similar word, *Brytwalda*, 'wide ruler', was occasionally used of Roman emperors.

The list was artificially constructed. It began with Aelle of Sussex, who was no conqueror, but probably earned the title as commander of the force that was beaten at Badon. The next name is Ceawlin, whose conquest sealed the defeat of the southern British. Then came Aethelbert of Kent, who first reduced the southern English, and after him Redwald and the Northumbrian monarchs. Mercian historians may or may not have adapted and extended the same list in their own texts. Their texts have not survived, and it is possible that they ignored Bede's list, for if they had accepted it they would have been compelled to acknowledge past Kentish, East Anglian and Northumbrian overlords as legitimate sovereigns of all the southern English, in preference to their own royal house. But the West Saxon historians made much of Bede's list, exploiting it to justify the claims of their kings to inherit an authority over all Britain that was older than the empire of the Mercians.

The Northumbrian and West Saxon lists each make their own selection of English overkings. But the imperial sovereignty from which they made their partial selection was real and continuous; and its usages outlived its reality. *Imperator* became a favoured title of some later West Saxon kings. Official 10th-century documents style Edred 'king of the English' and 'emperor' of the Northumbrians, or of the 'pagans', or 'Caesar of all Britain'; and in the 11th century Aethelred's formal phrases define the meaning of the titles. He is king of the English, sometimes of 'Anglo-Saxony', and 'ruler of the Northumbrian monarchy'; he is also 'emperor of the British and of the other provinces'. Other documents bestow upon him and other kings Greek titles proper to the Roman emperor in Constantinople, 'emperor of the whole world of Britain' or of 'all Albion'. Sonorous titles are commonly proclaimed by the feeblest kings; just as the shrill and silly adjective *invictissimus*, 'most unconquered', was used by those later Roman emperors whose armies suffered heaviest defeat, so the pretentious assertions of later English kings increased, until the melancholy ruin of Aethelred made them wholly absurd. But his empty title, 'king of the English and Emperor of Britain', justly described the authority of his Mercian predecessors.

Aethelred's phrases none the less defined a solid reality of the recent past. His father Edgar had enforced acknowledgement of the supremacy he boasted, and Edgar had reasserted an ancient right. From the 7th century onwards the overkings of the English claimed to inherit empire over the whole of Britain. The inheritance came to them from the dispossessed British, for the British kings who earned the title *Gwledic*, like the early English *Bretwaldas*, had tried and failed to unite the whole island under a single imperial dynasty; the Mercian monarchy was more successful, and bequeathed the name of emperor to later kings. But whatever their title and whatever the substance of their power, the kings who claimed superior authority, from Maelgwn to Aethelred, all revived the ghost of an ancient reality, the short-lived empire of Britain, whose last and most famous emperor was Arthur.

Ghosts work powerfully when men believe in them. Arthur's empire left a consciousness that all Britain had once obeyed a single emperor, and could and should in the future unite under a single paramount sovereign. The high title was dropped, but the claim persisted throughout the middle ages. Its repeated assertions had long prepared Welshmen and Scots to accept it in practice, and to acquiesce in formal genealogical claims, when the accidents of royal marriage and royal mortality bequeathed the throne of England to the real or alleged descendants of Welsh and Scottish kings, the Tudors and Stuarts. But no tradition incorporated Ireland within the empire of Arthur; English rule in Ireland was based on force alone, and no latent beliefs encouraged English kings to marry their daughters to Irish princes, or served to persuade Irishmen that the kings of England were the legitimate heirs of Irish dynasties.

The concept of a single government of Britain lingered feebly until the middle of the 7th century. It gained strength and permanence during the long quiet rule of the Mercian kings; they were effective overkings of the English and paramount allies of the Welsh, from Penda's time on. Mercian supremacy endured unchallenged until the last years of their greatest king, Offa, who died in 796. Its long continuance placed him among the mightiest western rulers of his day, second only to his greater contemporary, Charlemagne. But Mercian power died of its own greatness. Offa's overpowering majesty induced him to cut away the props on which it rested. He abolished the underkings, executing the last king of the East Angles, ending the Kentish monarchy, reducing the rulers of Sussex to the status of *dux*, introducing his dependants upon the thrones of Wessex and Northumbria; and called himself 'king of the English', no longer, like his predecessor, of the southern English alone.

Offa observed the immensely powerful centralised monarchy of Charlemagne, and endeavoured to transform his English empire into a Germanic and Roman absolutism. His innovations drove his subjects to rebellion; Kent rallied round a local rebel who claimed no royal ancestry, and though the rebel was crushed, the peoples of the other kingdoms, formerly obedient to native kings who admitted Mercian supremacy, now viewed direct Mercian rule with abhorrence. In the next generation, they transferred their support to Egbert of Wessex, enabling him to unite his own people, and to challenge and end Mercian domination. Mercian power briefly revived, but Egbert's descendants inherited Offa's centralised monarchy; the old regional dynasties were gone, and the Scandinavian invaders had come, at the moment when the English most needed self-reliant regional leadership. The evil was immediately apparent to contemporaries; a few months after Offa's death, when the first few pirate ships had recently landed upon unguarded coasts, the greatest scholar and statesman of the day, Alcuin of York and Tours, warned of coming disaster and explained its cause.

> An immense threat hangs over this island and its people. It is a novelty without precedent that the pirate raids of a heathen people can regularly waste our shores. Yet the English people are divided, and king fights against king. Saddest of all, scarcely any heir of the ancient royal houses survives, and the origin of kings is as dubious as their courage. . . . Study Gildas, the wisest of the British, and examine the reasons why the ancestors of the British lost their kingdom and their fatherland; then look upon yourselves, and you will find amongst you almost identical causes.

The great age of the united English had died with Offa, and the nation was left leaderless in the face of peril. It had grown great because it had learned from the past of the British as well as from its own traditions. The long governance of Mercia had formed a nation tough enough to survive. Though the arrogance of Offa had destroyed the bonds that held it together, his successors salvaged their fragmented people. The cost was fearful. The noble prose of the Saxon Chronicle describes the wars of Wessex kings, who rescued half the country from gentile conquest. But they could not restore the stable government of the Mercian past; the resolute energy of the Scandinavians destroyed strong kings and exploited the vacillation of feeble monarchs, until in 1066 the English succumbed to a section of the Norsemen whose barbarism had been tamed by long residence in France. In the end the English recovered their national strength, in the course of prolonged passive and local resistance to the ignorant brutality of Norman rule. They did so because the inherited traditions of English monarchy enabled the kings to curb their magnates as no European sovereign could. To maintain their own power the alien kings were forced to submit to the ancient usages of the conquered English and to reject the language and the crude political notions that their ancestors had brought from Europe.

Charlemagne's Empire

The example of the Mercian monarchy stirred the imagination of Europe in its own day. It was a novel concept of kingship, that had learnt to comprehend immense diversity within one organic whole. It combined the tradition of Roman imperial authority with a loose hierarchical kingship adapted from the Irish, and with a secure law of succession inherited from the continental English; and thereby offered a security unknown to the emperors of Rome. It provided a model that Europe welcomed; for in the same generation in which Offa infected and corroded the English monarchy with the brittle centralisation of Europe, Charlemagne endeavoured to strengthen Europe by adapting the experience of the English.

During Offa's reign, Charles the Great won a wider dominion than any western European ruler since the fall of the Roman empire. To organise his dominions, he looked to the English, and in 782 acquired the services of Alcuin of York, under whose guidance the clerks of the Frankish lands were trained, with the help of some English and many Irish teachers. Alcuin became the close friend and counsellor of Charlemagne, and began to talk to him of empire, in the same years in which the Mercian kings are first known to have displayed the imperial title in Britain. His letters address him by the affectionate but challenging pen name of 'king David', and in 799 he hailed 'David' as ruler and defender of the 'Christian empire'. In the same year he formalised his political advice.

> Hitherto, three persons have been highest in the world. The Apostolic Sublimity (the Pope); the imperial dignity of the second Rome (Constantinople), though now the ruler of that empire has been wickedly deposed.... The third is the royal dignity wherein the dispensation of Our Lord Jesus Christ has made you the ruler of the Christian people.

Alcuin's 'hitherto' advised that the future should be different; and that the moment was now, when the surviving Roman empire in the east lacked an emperor.

Charles determined to go to Rome next year, and urged Alcuin to accompany him. Alcuin excused himself on grounds of health and age, and Charles asked for a deputy to 'undertake his responsibilities' in his stead. Alcuin sent the English monk Witto, called *Candidus* (White), but emphasised that the 'responsibilities' now fell on Charles alone, and he clearly defined them in biblical imagery.

> David adorned the temple . . . when his general Joab had conquered Syria. But David himself placed the crown upon his own head, though Joab had borne the labour of the fighting.

Alcuin, like Joab, had borne the labour of the political and diplomatic fighting that prepared the way; but Charles must crown himself without the aid of an English deputy. Charles hesitated, but was crowned Roman emperor in Rome on Christmas Day, 800. Many pressures and many circumstances determined his decision. But the strongest advice had come from the English Alcuin; it was the English who had developed the concept, alien to the Roman past, of an emperor who reigned over subordinate kings; it was an English sovereign who had first used the title emperor in an official document, two years before Charlemagne was crowned. The English usage was half-hearted, for the English did not rule Rome; Charlemagne had conquered Rome, and could exploit the English precedent to the full.

The substance of Charlemagne's imperial authority died with him, leaving an honorary title that persisted into the 19th century. But the substance of the Mercian empire lived on, without the title. Nations of half a dozen different languages grew accustomed to a single monarchy, supreme among the English, dominant throughout Britain, and accepted the guidance of a national monarchy more strongly rooted in the hearts of men than the kingdoms of Europe.

The English emerged as the permanent heirs to the ruins of Arthur's empire; the multiple origin of their population obliged their kings to admit infinite local and social difference, that hindered attempts to impose uniformity or to merge small units into unwieldy amalgamation. The flexibility of English administration was from the beginning able to avoid much of the arrogant ineptitude that centralised European governments inherited from Rome and the Germanic kings. Rulers were taught to respect the limits that each generation set upon the legitimate authority of king or lord; though the limits were repeatedly overriden, they were repeatedly reasserted. Kings who earned their subjects' respect found themselves more powerful than those who sought to command obedience by force alone. Their tempered leadership tolerated a greater local independence and a larger personal liberty than was possible in most of Europe.

English political society was formed in the age of Arthur and consolidated by the Mercian monarchy. From the beginning it was an unusual blend of local responsibility and strong central government. Though local potentates frequently overawed popular assemblies, each local and occupational community customarily decided its own affairs; central governments that guided and coordinated their mutual interests earned their respect, but those that overstepped their proper bounds were ignored or resisted. Excessive concentrations of property and power, in the hands of noblemen or the church, of foreigners or other interests, were repeatedly broken up when their size became a threat.

Direct rule by the central government provoked resentment, in the time of Oswy, of Offa, and of many later rulers. It was tolerated only in emergencies, and rarely for more than a few generations at a time, when severe disturbance crippled or destroyed existing forms, as in the age of conquest and conversion, after the destructive victories of the Northmen from the 9th century to the 11th, and in modern times; but after each emergency, established custom curbed the temporary extension of central authority, and devised new forms of local and occupational control. English society tamed the Scandinavian and the Norman, and outlived the tyrannical corruption of Angevin royal officers. Effective local power persisted for five centuries more, until its organs were corroded and destroyed by the violent impact of the industrial revolution.

Most of the familiar centralised institutions of modern society are at present little more than a hundred years old, and are already beginning to face criticism. They seem older than they are, for men cannot help reading the present into the past. Medieval writers equipped king Arthur and the Romans with the weapons, the clothing and the political morality of their own day; and in the last few generations many historians have dwelt at length upon the ancestry of modern institutions and ideas. Those aspects of parliament and other bodies that most nearly concern their present form have been emphasised, and the workings of earlier England have been explained in terms of modern notions of economics, government and morality; but until quite recently the important realities of local history have been ignored and even derided.

Nineteenth century forms of centralised government may or may not prove more durable than their predecessors. Critics who withstand ministries and national executives may be condemned or commended. But they cannot justly be represented as innovators, for they appeal, usually unconsciously, to the oldest traditions of English administration. Political prophecy is not the business of the historian, but he is obliged to stress the powerful influence of the past. Present tendencies in any society are easily misjudged if its origin and formative years are disregarded. The fundamental assumptions of English society were hardened under the Mercian kings, and were first fashioned in the age of Arthur. From the outset they have rested upon an equal balance of local or sectional autonomy and of national coordination. In the past these inbred assumptions have repeatedly curtailed the dominance of centralised authority, whenever it has exceeded the bounds deemed proper by public opinion, rarely more than a century or so after the central government has overstepped its traditional limits.

ANALYSIS

CHAPTER EIGHTEEN

THE FIFTH CENTURY CHURCH

Before 410

The Christian religion scarcely touched Latin Europe before the late second century, and until the end of the fourth century British Christians are rare in the records of the Church. Alban of Verulamium, executed in 209, is the earliest known Latin Christian of the European provinces, though others doubtless existed. His fellow Christians in Africa and Egypt noted with pleasure and surprise that Christ was worshipped in distant Britain, even beyond the Roman frontier. But these stories have no sequel. A century later four British sees, probably metropolitan, were represented at Constantine's first church council at Arles. No more is known for another forty years; then the catholics of Gaul praised the steadfast orthodoxy of the British in the Arian crisis, and remarked upon their light-hearted contempt for the government; the bishop of London was perhaps among the few who held out to the end and suffered exile.

Bishops and clergy existed. Nothing suggests that they were more numerous than in northern and central Gaul. There Christianity was hardly known before Constantine, was still weak half a century after his accession, and did not widely prevail until the end of the century. The archaeological evidence in Britain consists of a number of buildings that may or may not be churches, and of a variety of Christian symbols. Hardly any of it can be closely dated, and it is probable that, as in Gaul, more of it concerns the fifth century than the fourth; and that Christians were strongest in the major towns. London was one of the largest cities in the western provinces, big enough to have contained a Christian community even in the third century that could afford a church building; but it is unlikely that in other towns the Christians were better placed than in Gaul, where, in provincial capitals like Tours, they were too few to build or maintain a church before about 350.

In the fourth century almost nothing is known of British Christianity, save that it existed. Its detailed history begins with the visit of Victricius, bishop of Rouen, about 396. He is the best known of Martin's admirers, and Martin, then still alive, was a controversial symbol. Sulpicius Severus' biography, probably published about the same time, emphasised his plebeian dress and habits, and presented him as the miraculously gifted champion of the weak against oppression, of the subject against the government, detested by well-bred established bishops who bowed to the will of emperors. Victricius, himself perhaps of British birth, extended Martin's reforms. Martin had preached to peasants, but Victricius was the first missionary, converting the peoples of the barbarian frontier districts, in modern Belgium, so that

> where once barbarian raiders and native robbers made woodland and coast unsafe, now the angelic choirs of the saints sing.

Victricius made a theory of Martin's egalitarian practice, proclaiming that

> men do not differ by nature, but only in time and place, in their occupations and ideas; for difference is foreign to divine unity,

and warning the mighty that

> divinity spits upon degree, breaks beyond time and place; . . . greater is the glory of your authority if you protect those who toil, defend the oppressed against their enemies.

Pope Innocent was disturbed, and warned Victricius that Rome condemned innovators, whose presumption violated the purity of the church by seeking the favour of the people rather than by fearing the judgment of God. But Victricius was heart and soul with the reformers. His letter, describing his journey to Britain, was addressed to Ambrose, apologising that his visit to Milan had thereby been delayed. His excuse is that he had carried to Britain the 'precepts of the martyrs'; he defined them by praising

> hands heavy with the relics of the saints, whence the crowds of monks, refined by fasting, are thickened.

He called himself the 'interpreter of the views' of the martyrs, in Britain, and explained that he had gone to Britain because

> my worthy fellow bishops summoned me to make peace. . . . I filled the sensible with love of peace, taught the teachable, overbore the ignorant, attacked the opposition.

Victricius does not spell out the issues in dispute, but his letter makes them plain. Ambrose and Martin were old and near to death; he was their foremost adherent in northern Europe, advocate of the veneration of martyrs who had defied unjust authority in their lifetime and inspired living men to similar independence; he was the organiser of monks who condemned and renounced secular society, the pioneer of the extension of Christianity from townsmen and gentlemen to peasants and barbarians. Pope Innocent protested that bishops should not interfere outside their own diocese or rouse plebeian support, but Victricius was the spokesman of all bishops everywhere who found strength in 'the favour of the people', and was the impassioned champion of equality among all men, irrespective of rank and station. He was invited to Britain by British bishops, who knew his views; they could not have invited him unless the reformers were already strong in Britain. They were a party within the British church, for he faced a stormy synod and fierce opposition; but he judged that his views had prevailed. The issue which divided the bishops was the impact of Martin's reforms, offensive to many established bishops in Gaul, and also in Britain. The synod strengthened the reformers, and perhaps made them the majority.

Victricius' visit powerfully affected the future Christianity of the British Isles. Echoes of his radical thought abound in the scanty records of the British church, whereas in the fuller record of Gaul Martin is honoured, but rarely imitated. There, urbane bishops akin to Martin's critics still predominated, and tamed the monastic impetus. But in Britain, the causes that Victricius championed prospered immediately. Lay monks were still rare outside the senatorial aristocracy of Rome and their dependants; yet, though few Britons of the early fifth century are known by name, half a dozen of them were monks, and by 411 wandering monks were common. Within thirty years of Victricius' visit, the shrine of St. Alban had become the centre of an important national cult, too influential to have been left without the protection of a church building; and lesser local martyrs' shrines abounded in Britain. The name of Martin was venerated; Bede describes a Canterbury church

> built in antiquity in honour of St. Martin, while the Romans yet inhabited Britain.

Nearly half the major towns of Roman Britain have a similar church; but it is impossible to tell whether their re-used Roman stones were first made into a church in 400, or in 1100, or in between, for no text dates any but the Canterbury church. Any or none may be as old; but some such churches existed, and one or two seem to have maintained schools, like Martin's at Tours.

Victricius' missionary work on the barbarian borders of his diocese was an innovation, and no tradition gives him contemporary imitators, except in Britain. Patrick, in the mid 5th century, knew of lapsed Picts; some had been baptised, hardly later than about 400. Bede was told that the southern Picts had been converted by a bishop born in Britain and trained at Rome, named Nynia, who built a church 'in the name of Martin' at *Candida Casa*, 'the White House', Whithorn in Galloway, so named because its stone construction was then unfamiliar to the British of the far north. It is likely that Bede's Nynia, better known as Ninian, is identical with Patrick's unnamed missionary who preached about 400.

At that date Whithorn can scarcely have been a bishop's see; Victricius was a bishop of Rouen who built monasteries in Belgium, and Ninian was evidently bishop of a recognised urban see, probably Carlisle, who also built a monastery by the barbarian border of his diocese. The name of the church proclaims the influence of Martin, and argues a date not long after his death; its place bespoke the influence of Victricius. Irish tradition knew it by the name of Rosnat, and knew it as an important monastic school from the mid fifth century onward, while British tradition gives a precise date for its foundation, 398, just after Victricius' visit. Excavation has uncovered the remains of a very early stone church at Whithorn; if it be not the church of Ninian, then a similar church awaits discovery nearby.

Barbarian missions, monks and schools, shrines and the veneration of Martin, are all novelties advocated by Victricius, and they concentrate in the ten years or so after his visit. In these years British ideas first made an impact upon mediterranean Christian thought. The ideas are fresh, logically formulated, expressed in clearer and more polished Latin than was then usual among Italian and African theologians. They are deeply tinged with a radical egalitarianism that echoes Victricius, but extends beyond his elementary concepts. Though most of these British works were published abroad, they reveal something of the Britain where their authors were brought up, so that its intellectual climate is better documented for the early fifth century than for the Roman past, or for generations to come.

The Early Fifth Century

Before the fall of Rome changed men's thinking, the British monk Pelagius was esteemed in Rome as the most polished writer of his day, a Christian Cicero. But the shock of the city's capture overwhelmed the comfortable Ciceronian past and drove men to seek new remedies. Some urged the wholesale rejection of secular society, on the model of the monks of Egypt. John Cassian instituted at Marseille the first Latin monastery on the Egyptian pattern, but his success was limited; imitators were few, and Cassian complained that the Gauls did not respond to the principles of monasticism; they preferred to receive gifts of land, living upon their rents rather than upon their own labour. A few houses were founded in remote deserted districts, especially in the Jura, but most of them became quiet and ineffective retreats for men of property, sheltered from the wreck of their orderly world. They made little impact on the Christianity of Gaul, and by the middle of the century were easily subjected to close episcopal control. In the words of Montalembert, the modern historian of the western monks, the monasteries of the west had declined into 'torpor and sterility' before the end of the fifth century.

The example of Egypt did not yet appeal; others pioneered new types of monastery. On the island of Lérins, off the coast of the French Riviera, the fruitful initiative of Honoratus established a select monastic community of high-powered intellectuals, devoted to the reform of the practice of the church. Lérins was heavily imbued with the ideas of Ambrose. Its aim was reform from above, by securing the election of learned monks to bishoprics in Gaul. Many were elected. Among them was another Briton, the third abbot, Faustus, who became bishop of Riez in southern Gaul; whose prolific writings are the foundation of later Gallic theology. In tune with the teaching of Ambrose, and with much of Martin's thinking, the Lérins reformers encouraged another form of monasticism, the institution of a celibate diocesan clergy, and cathedral monasteries multiplied. Among their closest allies were Martin's pupil Amator, who founded the cathedral school of Auxerre before his death in 418, and also his illustrious successor Germanus. The best-known of Amator's pupils and priests was another Briton, Patrick, who may also have spent some time at Lérins.

Monastic reformers planned for the future, but the present was urgent. The most important Christian reaction to the fall of Rome was the speedy triumph of the views of Augustine, bishop of Hippo in North Africa. Augustine's central thesis was simple; all men inherited the sin of Adam, and could only be redeemed by the grace of God. Logical conclusions followed like links in a steel chain. A good life and good works were of no avail without grace; salvation depended more on God's predestined gift of grace than on the individual's free choice between good and evil; babies were damned at birth, unless they received grace through the sacrament of baptism. Pelagius was horrified when these views were first published, especially at Augustine's prayer, 'Grant what thou dost command, command what thou dost will'. Pelagius saw Augustine as the innovator, against whom he defended the humanist, classical, traditional values that Christianity inherited from its Roman past.

At first Augustine's views aroused only interest and comment. But the disaster of 410 ended the world that bred Pelagius' gentler philosophy. Churchmen listened more keenly to Augustine; though the deeper implications were not immediately spelt out, responsible ecclesiastics sensed that the gentle individualism of the past must cause the church to fragment into as many diverse hostile units as the secular state, whereas the logic of Augustine made man's salvation dependent on sacraments administered by a duly ordained priest, obedient to bishops, metropolitans and popes, in a disciplined hierarchy that might preserve the unity of the church, though political authority dissolved. Augustine's first attack was unsuccessful, but he made considerable use of the extreme tenets of a radical wing among the Pelagians, and secured an imperial edict, over the pope's head, outlawing and banning their beliefs, in 418. The government's statements made clear its reasons for aiding Augustine; the radicals had 'split Rome into factions', they had excited the minds of the common people, and had sapped 'the authority of the catholic law', and with it the Majesty of God, itself 'the source of our imperial rule'. Their leaders went into hiding in Rome, and 'corrupted the minds of the ignorant' by distributing 'secret pamphlets'. The pope died, and plebeian riots at the ensuing election taxed the strength of the police; the successful candidate proved a strong supporter of Augustine, and the laws against the Pelagians were rigidly enforced by church and state.

All the known leaders of the radicals in Rome came from the British Isles. The government denounced Pelagius' most prominent supporter, Coelestius, as their chief inspirer, perhaps rightly. He was probably Irish; and an educated

Irishman in early fifth-century Rome probably came from an Irish colony in civilised Britain, perhaps from Demetia. But the authors of the surviving tracts are British, foremost among them a young man who wrote in Sicily, called the Sicilian Briton, since his name is unknown. His half-dozen pamphlets have a single starting-point, the text 'If thou wouldst be perfect, go sell all that thou hast'. He condemns social inequality more fiercely than any Christian writer since the second century, turning Victricius' philosophical propositions into vivid rhetoric.

> One man owns many large mansions adorned with costly marbles, another has not so much as a small hut to keep out the cold and heat. One man has vast territories and unlimited possessions, another has but a little stretch of turf to sit upon and call his own. . . . Are these riches from God? . . . If God had willed universal inequality, he . . . would not have permitted . . . equal shares . . . in the elements. . . . Does the rich man enjoy the blessing of fresh air more than the poor man? Does he feel the sun's heat more keenly or less? When earth receives the gift of rain, do larger drops fall upon the rich man's field than upon the poor man's? . . . What God himself distributes . . . is shared equally; what we own in unjust inequality is everything whose distribution was entrusted to human control. . . . Is there one sacrament, one law for the rich, another for the poor? . . . inequality of wealth is not to be blamed upon the graciousness of God, but upon the iniquity of men.

The viewpoint is not new. But it had not been put so sharply for two hundred years, nor ever in such compelling language; for the direct plain vocabulary and strong balanced periods have more in common with the Latinity of Caesar than with the turgid prose of late Roman theologians.

Wealth was not merely unjust; it was the cause of misgovernment and oppression:

> Look you now, I pray you, at the pride and arrogance of those who . . . would take on the power of a master where Christ took the form of a slave. With that proud ambitious spirit which covets all earthly glory for itself, the rich commonly sit themselves upon that tribunal before which Christ stood and was heard. What is this, Christian? . . . You sit upon the tribunal. . . . Under your eyes the bodies of men like you in nature are beaten with whips of lead, broken with clubs, torn on the claws, burnt in the flames . . . It is the rich, dripping with excessive wealth, whom the will to cruelty leads into acts of such savage wickedness.

He was scornful of the excuses that the Christian rich found in the scriptures to justify the retention of their wealth, and scorn rises to fierce satirical humour when he faces the rich man's 'explanation' of Christ's assertion that 'it is easier for a camel to pass through the eye of a needle than for the rich man to enter into the kingdom of Heaven'.

> 'But,' you say, 'it does not mean a camel, which cannot possibly pass through a needle's eye, but a *camelus*, which is a kind of ship's hawser'. What intolerable subtlety when human greed . . . grasps at the names of ropes to keep its earthly wealth! . . . It is a rotten argument that will do the rich no good. As if it were easier to get a huge rope through the needle's eye than that well known animal the camel! If you want an excuse to live estranged from heaven's throne with an easy mind . . . ships are no good to you, with their huge great fittings. . . . You had better try the weaving trade, and search for some kind of thread called *camelus*. Such idiocy may amuse men . . . but it will carry little weight with God. But you quote . . . 'What is impossible for men is possible for God'. Of course it is 'possible' for Him to let the rich into heaven, 'possible' to let them bring all their estates and their mobile property and their wealth into heaven too, and the camels with them into the bargain. If it were just a matter of 'possibility' no one would be shut out of Heaven, for everything is possible to God.

The Sicilian Briton was not a lone idealist, but the spokesman of a movement. The rich were on the defensive against vocal plebeian critics.

> Listen to your rich man calling your poor man 'wretch', 'beggar', 'rabble', because he dares to open his mouth in 'our' presence, because in his rags he reproaches 'our' morality and conduct, . . . as if the rich alone had a right to speak, as if the understanding of truth were a function of wealth, not of thought.

He had evidently encountered poor men who voiced a protest, and rich men who condemned them. He cried aloud the age old resentment against social injustice, expanding ideas that the Fathers of the early church had cemented into the structure of orthodox Christian theology; but he added an entirely new theoretical analysis:

> Mankind is divided into three classes, the rich, the poor, and those who have enough.

The problems of human society are to be solved by transferring the superfluous property of the rich to the poor, so that everyone has enough. The argument culminates in a practical slogan.

> Abolish the rich and you will have no more poor . . . for it is the few rich who are the cause of the many poor.

Nineteenth-century theologians rightly compared these views with modern socialism, for the causal analysis and the proposals based on it are unique in antiquity, whose Christian tradition went no further than simple denunciation of wealth and property as evil and un-Christian. But the disintegrating Roman empire was not a society ready for socialism. The Sicilian Briton's ideas were turned against him. Augustine seized upon his major work, *On Riches*, and used it against Pelagius, who disclaimed responsibility; Augustine reluctantly accepted his denial and blamed Coelestius instead. The government denounced him as the author of sedition and ordered his arrest, for the Sicilian Briton's slogan, 'abolish the rich', in Latin *Tolle Divitem*, has a rhythm that a crowd might chant in anger; and an organised urban movement that rallied behind it, under the leadership of educated lawyers who went underground to escape arrest, was disturbing enough to any ancient government. Pelagius was no radical himself, but the government made no scrupulous distinction between the views of one Pelagian and another; Augustine might justifiably argue that it was the loose liberalism of Pelagius that permitted alarming subversion to riot outside the control of ecclesiastical discipline. Pelagianism became heresy.

The controversy flared up and was settled in the short space of eight years. But the outlooks that then clashed were the most fundamental in all Christian thinking; they disputed whether man might commune directly with his God, or must depend upon the intermediary of a priest. Modern theologians have properly remarked that Pelagius' philosophy has much in common with the later Protestantism of northern Europe; in its own time it was near to the need of the monk, who sought solitary communion with God in the desert. The similarity is not an accident. Though the Pelagians were universally condemned in name, their teaching was preserved. Not a word survives of any other of the major early heresies, save what their orthodox opponents cite against them, or fragments salvaged from papyri. But some seventy Pelagian works were copied and recopied through the centuries, most of them in northern European lands where monasteries inspired by monks from the British Isles were most numerous, and where protestant reform aroused its earliest and most enduring response a thousand years later.

In its own day, Pelagianism was eclipsed. Faustus and the church of Gaul formally accepted its condemnation, but strict Italian Augustinians reproached them as 'semi-Pelagian'. They had cause, for in northern Gaul a mid fifth-century layman might still treat Augustine as a distant heretic of small importance. Gaul was upon the margin of controversy, and soon accepted the ruling of Rome. But in Britain Pelagianism was no heresy. Most of the Pelagian writers were British, and their works were still read and cited as orthodox a century later in Britain. Britain escaped the controversy.

The one Pelagian author who is known to have written in Britain, Fastidius, takes it for granted in 411 that his readers share his assumption, and expresses incredulous amazement at rumours that abroad men urged the dogma of original sin. His social outlook is that of Pelagius rather than of the Sicilian Briton, but he too gives ample witness that plebeian protest was strong in Britain. In the course of his address to a young widow he welcomes a new government, of men of property, which had recently ousted a previous government, also of men of property. The previous government had oppressed the poor, and some of its members had been lynched by crowds, acting in support of the new rulers. He instructs the new government, with heavy emphasis, that it must use wealth rightly for the benefit of the poor, without oppression. Exhortations to charity addressed to individuals are a commonplace of late Roman sermons; used to exhort a government and a ruling class they are unusual. European churchmen uniformly preached obedience to ruling emperors, condemning all rebellion, while they urged emperors to heed their bishops; even the conflicts of Ambrose with Justina and Theodosius centred on a power struggle between bishop and emperor, unconcerned with the rights of rich and poor. Though the plebs frequently rioted in the great cities of the Mediterranean, they made little impact upon theological writing; and, except where Martin's influence was strong, the peasants of Latin Europe were as yet scarcely concerned with the church. Salvian of Marseille deplored their oppression, and Germanus of Auxerre sought a pardon for peasant rebels in Gaul after their defeat, but the active pressure of the poor upon the government made little impression on Christian writers, except upon the British.

Nothing is known of the British church for ten years after the condemnation of Pelagius, and its reaction thereto is not recorded. There is little trace of Augustine's thinking in the later writings of the British, and there is no reason to suppose that any considerable body of British opinion welcomed it during his lifetime, though there is ample evidence that Pelagian views persisted. The attitude of the British clergy, now outside the empire, can have mattered little to Rome so long as it did not impinge upon the affairs of Italy and Gaul.

Germanus

Something changed about 428. The chronicler Prosper, a strenuous Augustinian, records that the Pelagian heresy was 'revived' by Agricola, a bishop in Britain. The words must mean that he and his fellows openly and vigorously asserted the heresy, and began to affect Gaul. Doubtless some unrecorded incident, the condemnation of a British bishop in Gaul or the like, sparked off a dispute hitherto latent. It was clearly of importance, for both the Pope and the Gallic bishops bestirred themselves, sending Germanus of Auxerre to Britain in 429. Like Ambrose, he had been a secular officer, in command of troops, and had been forcibly chosen bishop by 'all the clergy, the whole nobility, and the people of town and country' when Amator, Martin's pupil, died in 418. As austere as Ambrose, he 'turned his wife to a sister, and gave his substance to the poor', and became an outstanding champion of reform, a vigorous ally of Lérins and of its foremost leader, Hilary, now bishop of Arles and metropolitan of Gaul. He was accompanied to Britain by Lupus, the young bishop of Troyes, who survived to describe his experiences to Germanus' biographer, Constantius.

Germanus found in Britain the same active hostility of the poor towards the rich that the Sicilian Briton and Fastidius knew, and turned it to his advantage. The bishops began by preaching 'not only in the churches, but also in the streets and in the countryside', until they won 'the whole region to their opinion', so that the Pelagians, who had hitherto ignored them, were compelled to challenge them to public debate. The debate was not held in a church council, as was normal, but in public. Ordinary people came for the day with their wives and children, and the Pelagians made a bad impression because their clothing was ostentatious, their 'crowd of flatterers' offensive. The people voted victory to Germanus by acclamation; the victory was sealed by a curative miracle, and the *suasio iniqua*, the subtle evil, was wiped from men's minds. The word *suasio*, appropriate to the legal plea of a professional orator, carries an overtone that the heretics were clever intellectuals, refuted by the plain man's common sense of Germanus.

Germanus tried to win the population for the cause of unity with Europe and Rome against separatist bishops. The only other ecclesiastical occasion that the biographer describes is a visit to the shrine of St. Alban. Germanus had the tomb opened and placed within it

> relics of all the apostles and of various martyrs . . . since . . . the saints . . . of different countries . . . were of equal merit in heaven.

It was an extraordinary action; saints' tombs were commonly opened to verify, transfer or remove relics, but not to intrude alien bones. The biographer admits a 'pious sacrilege', though the British bishops may well have questioned its piety. Germanus' intent is plain. The shrine was of great importance; otherwise Germanus would not have made his dramatic gesture, nor would his biographer have selected the isolated incident for full description. The shrine was evidently already the centre of a national cult, which clearly warranted a church building and a monastic community for the protection of the relics. Alban was already the national saint, and Germanus' strong assertion that the saints of all countries were equal claimed the tomb as the common property of Christendom, not merely the pride and symbol of a heretical national church. But the fame of Alban was not successfully merged with the generality of martyrs whose remains now shared his tomb. The shrine and church remained and remain the church of St. Alban, not of All Saints.

What Germanus did not do is as significant as what he did. He was sent to Britain to root out the Pelagian heresy, and his biographer selected the most convincing incidents he could to show that he succeeded. He worked miracles; he took part in a military campaign, and therefore clearly had the support of the secular government, who were in no position to quarrel with the imperial power in Gaul, or with the churchmen it favoured. But his only ecclesiastical success was to be cheered at a public meeting, and to make a demonstration at the chief national shrine. He held no synod; no heretics were condemned and no bishops were deposed, though there can be no doubt that Germanus would have had the Pelagians condemned if he could, and that his biographer would have reported any success that he had. Though he is said to have rallied at least a part of the laity, especially the rural population, against their bishops, he is not said to have won ecclesiastical support of any kind. What is set down in his biography is that which his assistant Lupus remembered. It is direct contemporary evidence that Germanus failed, that the church of Britain remained united, uncompromisingly Pelagian.

Palladius

Rome reacted swiftly. Germanus' visit had been prompted by the pope's deacon, Palladius, whose office made him one of the most important ecclesiastics in Europe, a potential successor to the papal throne. Palladius now took the remarkable decision to absent himself from Rome, and to visit Britain himself. The pope had no power to impose a bishop or a legate on an existing see, and Palladius was therefore given the novel post of 'bishop to the Irish Christians'. It is quite impossible that the propagation of the faith among the pagan Irish could have been the whole, or even the main reason. Missions to the heathen were new; a native Goth or Abyssinian might receive consecration if he travelled to Constantinople or Alexandria, but no Romans were sent to barbarians. Victricius had pioneered the conversion of pagans on the borders of his own diocese, and Ninian in Galloway had set a precedent, as yet not imitated. It is likely that Germanus had already decided to follow that precedent, for the biographers of Patrick believed that he was a priest of Germanus at Auxerre, and that the post of bishop to the Irish had been proposed and approved, Patrick named thereto, before Palladius decided to go himself.

It was an astounding decision. The proper person for a new and uncertain mission was an obscure priest from a provincial diocese, like Patrick; the choice of the pope's personal deacon was as eccentric as would have been the despatch of the most eminent cardinal of the mid nineteenth-century *curia* to Arizona or China. So unusual an appointment requires explanation, and Prosper gives the reason. Pope Celestine

> in consecrating a bishop to the Irish, while he was striving to keep the Roman island catholic, also made the barbarian island Christian.

The main object was to rout the Pelagians in Britain; the conversion of the Irish was secondary. The creation of a new see enabled Palladius to establish himself in Britain, among the heretics. The see had been created for straightforward missionary work alone; its success was an integral part of the British government's political policy towards the Irish, and Patrick was the kind of man required. Palladius was not. Yet, though the bishops and rulers of Britain might be confounded and dismayed at the pope's choice, they could not gainsay it;

the best they could do was to try to ensure that Palladius spent as much as possible of his time on his official business in Ireland, as little as possible in organising an anti-Pelagian faction in Britain.

Palladius was not successful. Prosper, who knew him well and wished him well, wrote two or three years after his appointment. He claims that Palladius fulfilled his nominal duty, for though the bland statement that he 'made Ireland Christian' is a patent exaggeration, it was acceptable to Italian readers, if he was known to have visited Ireland and to have made a few converts. But Prosper does not even claim that he converted the Pelagians, merely that he strove to do so. Prosper says no more of Palladius or of Ireland, though his wording implies that the mission was over, no longer in progress. Irish tradition makes it short, believing that Palladius failed, and died within the year, on his way home.

The see existed, and after Palladius' failure there was no longer reason to vary its original purpose or to hold back the original nominee. Irish tradition is unanimous that Patrick landed about 432. Patrick himself relates that his appointment was delayed by controversy and opposition, but ultimately received the support of British bishops. Opposition is understandable. In addition to the handicap of a broken education, which he felt unfitted him for the post, he was, though British born, the nominee of the foreigners who had tried and failed to discipline the British church. Trained abroad, he was no Pelagian, and no theologian; in his surviving works there is no Pelagianism, but also no trace of Augustinian opposition to the Pelagians; he was plainly dominated by a single-minded devotion to his mission. His attitudes must have been as clear to those who knew him as they are in his writings, and he could only have seemed a second Palladius to men who had not met him. Grounds of opposition were not strong enough to warrant further dispute with Rome and Gaul; he suited the lay government, and Rome and Gaul had no reason to complain when British bishops endorsed their choice.

Later Fifth-Century Britain

The church of Roman Britain lasted ten or twenty years more, and kept its character to the end. When Patrick was again at odds with British bishops, about the early 440s, he reproached them as urbane prelates, 'learned, skilled at public speaking and all else'. It is the same judgment that Germanus and Lupus had made of their Pelagian opponents a dozen years before. The British bishops were products of the same schools and the same society as Pelagius and Faustus, Fastidius and the Sicilian Briton. Before the sudden disaster of the Saxon revolt, their world had been spared the barbarian inroads that had convulsed Italy and Gaul; it had been able to preserve its institutions and its culture undamaged; it had had no need to undergo the bitter experience of the Augustinian controversy, and could afford to retain the older humanist theology. Only when the outbreak of the Saxon revolt caused its world to crash in ruin did it begin to yield; Germanus on a second visit in the mid or late 440s secured the deposition of two bishops. It was a small gain, too late to matter to the church of Gaul or of Britain.

Contemporary records of the church last a generation longer than those of the state, and serve to explain secular society, for the opulent cultured bishops whom Germanus and Patrick encountered were the contemporaries of Vortigern and his councillors, products of the same society, educated in the same schools, housed in similar buildings, bound by the same institutions. They were also influenced by the same ideas, heirs both to the attitudes that the Sicilian Briton urged and to those that he condemned, and to the gentility of Fastidius and Pelagius. Their material world was destroyed by the Saxon rising and the fifty years' war that followed; but the ideas outlived the buildings and the institutions, for Arthur's victory came just in time to save some of them. Children who had been born and baptised just before the revolt, who had seen their first Christian services in sophisticated Roman buildings, on the mosaic floors of the Roman mansion at Hinton St. Mary in Dorset, in the chapel at Lullingstone villa in Kent, or in the churches of Roman British towns, were aged sixty or seventy when Arthur was emperor and the monastic reformers of the sixth century were growing boys. The continuity of ideas is obscured, Roman Britain and the Welsh monks are made to seem unrelated worlds, by the break in historical tradition, as savage in the history of the church as in the history of laymen. Yet the older teachers of Gildas and his fellows were themselves children of an undamaged Roman Britain. To the young, ruined buildings and tales of the life lived in them were meaningless ancient history, ghosts of a dead past; but old ideas of the relation of man to man and man to God still mattered.

The memorials of the church after the Saxon revolt are scattered chiefly among the Lives of the Saints. Their outlook is usually repellent, their stories superficially absurd; but their indigestible mash of fiction, fantasy and folk-lore is rooted in the ruins of contemporary record, and needs careful excavation, like the vegetation that covers material archaeological ruins.

Patrick

The earliest of the British saints is Patrick, and he is the only one whose own writings survive. His history has been obscured by his later eminence, which has inspired the most elaborate falsifications in the ecclesiastical history of medieval Europe. In the course of 7th-century controversies, centred upon the proper date for the celebration of Easter, the adherents of conformity with Rome took Patrick as their patron. Their principal contrivance was to assert that all the churches of their day in Ireland that were not already under the control of major monasteries, and many that were, had been founded by Patrick. He was therefore made to consecrate some 450 bishops and a corresponding quantity of priests, establishing himself in Armagh as primate of Ireland. Though Patrick's own writings admit no other bishop but himself, and do not name Armagh or any other place, and though the authors of the fiction admitted that Irishmen in their own day did not believe them, the victory of their cause won acceptance for their story, and the tragic later history of Ireland hardened it into an article of national faith.

One by-product of the fiction has recently confused the straightforward account of the early texts. A 7th-century writer compared Patrick with Moses, who lived for 120 years; symmetry gave him 60 years before he came to Ireland, 60 thereafter. All writers agreed that Patrick landed about 432, and early tradition entered his death at 459 or 460. But his 120-year life-span added alternatives; since he died in 460, his birth was entered at 340; and since he taught for 60 years after 432, his death was also entered in the 490s. The Annalists repeated all these dates; and from the two death-dates an intelligent 8th-century writer advanced the thesis that there were two Patricks, and suggested that the earlier was perhaps identical with Palladius. The thesis had little sequel until it was revived in the middle of the 20th century, by writers who overlooked Moses and the early birth-date, and transferred the landing and the death of the second Patrick, author of the *Confessio*, to the later fifth century. Yet no writer earlier than the twentieth century admits any date other than about 432 for Patrick's landing, and his own writings treat of urbane bishops and a settled municipal life in Britain that ill accord with the disasters of the second half of the century.

These views have attracted little support outside Ireland, but they have inhibited serious study of the earlier and sober accounts of Patrick. Apart from his own writings, only two informative texts are immune from the extravagance of the Armagh tradition, a mid 7th-century Life by Muirchu, and one that forms the basis of a still unpublished anonymous Life. All the other early accounts of Patrick must be discounted, for their incentive, clearly expressed, was to invent stories that were not believed at the time when they were written. They are sources rich and fruitful for the study of the churches of 7th and 8th-century Ireland, and of the traditions of their founders. A few among them may have been Patrick's converts, for some lived in his time in the regions where Muirchu records his preaching, but the fabricated texts cannot be used to argue for or against such connection, or to provide any information whatsoever about Patrick himself.

Patrick's own writings record that he was the son of a British landowner, whose ancestors had been Christian since the early fourth century. Their names suggest that they had been Roman citizens for at least two hundred years. At the age of sixteen he was captured by Irish raiders; he served as a slave for six years, and escaped by sea. When he returned to Britain he dreamt that a man named Victoricus, Victoricius, or Victricius in various manuscripts, who was possibly Victricius of Rouen, charged him to preach in Ireland. Many years later, he was consecrated bishop, with the support of a boyhood friend who seems to have been a prominent ecclesiastic. He wrote after a number of years in Ireland, refusing to answer accusations brought against him by British bishops in a formal meeting, reminding the British that though he would dearly love to visit his homeland, he also had friends in Gaul. He had travelled widely in Ireland, he had occasionally been imprisoned, but was normally tolerated by local kings, and had made numerous converts, including both slaves and the children of kings, many of whom had taken monastic vows. He calls himself the 'bishop established in Ireland', and refers to priests who served under him, but not to any other bishops.

Muirchu and the anonymous Life send him to Gaul between his captivity and his consecration, under Amator and Germanus of Auxerre, and state that Germanus intended to send him to Ireland before Palladius' appointment; his mission was delayed until Palladius' death. He then coasted Ireland to the territory of the Ulaid, where he made his headquarters at Downpatrick, paying one visit to the former Ulaid capital of Emain, where he founded Armagh, and another to the High King's court at Tara. Patrick's own words suggest somewhat wider travels, and there may therefore be some substance in the northern Irish traditions of his journeys in the texts that do not make him 'primate' of Ireland or locate him in a single centre, at Armagh or elsewhere. Muirchu does not make him consecrate any bishops in Ireland, but associates him with two British bishops in the consecration of an Irish convert as bishop of Man.

The Annals record that Patrick was 'approved' by pope Leo the Great, who ruled from 440 to 467, and had earlier succeeded Palladius as papal deacon. Patrick's *Confessio* rejects the jurisdiction claimed by the bishops of Britain, and refers to friends in Gaul. Leo's policy throughout Europe was concerned to weaken the power of metropolitans and synods, and to establish the direct dependence of provincial bishops upon Rome. It is probable that Leo 'approved' Patrick's rejection of British metropolitan supremacy and welcomed Ireland as directly subordinate to Rome, independent of Britain; possible that Patrick's complaint was carried by Germanus on his last visit to Italy in the late 440s. It is not probable that the episcopate of Britain was in a position to assert authority over Ireland after the outbreak of the Saxon revolt.

Patrick was not the first missionary, even in the north of Ireland; for when he claimed that he had penetrated to

> the farther regions ... not previously reached by anyone who baptised or ordained priests,

he assumed that his readers knew that in the nearer lands someone had previously ordained and baptised. But he was the first regular bishop, appointed by Rome, and he made a considerable number of converts, including a number of highly placed younger men and women, at least in the north. He established an organised church, which his successors maintained. But the mass conversion of the Irish to Christianity in the next century was not the work of that church. Patrick, and the bishops who succeeded him, are almost unknown in the early traditions of the Irish monastic movement. The only modern scholar who has made a thorough study of documentation of early Irish Christianity, James Kenney, rightly remarked that for almost two centuries Patrick

> was not entirely forgotten, but . . . his memory had slipped into the background of old and far-off things.

His memory was revived and reasserted during the Easter controversy, when the framework of his episcopalian church was found to provide a means whereby the monasteries of Ireland might gain communion with Britain, Rome and Europe, without losing their independence.

Patrick wrote his *Confessio* while Roman Britain was still in being, just about the time of the Saxon revolt. When he died, towards 460, Roman Britain was destroyed, its political leaders were massacred, and a great part of their surviving relatives were emigrants in Gaul, while others were preparing to join Ambrosius' resistance movement. There is no further mention of British bishops in the low-land cities exposed to Saxon raids, though it is probable that Verulamium, London and a few other cities whose walls withstood the raiders still maintained bishops. In the west, less savaged by the wars, several bishops are named on both shores of the Severn.

The earliest of them, Docco, is the worst recorded of all the early British saints; he is named in a dozen unrelated English, Irish and Welsh texts, and in a couple of extremely corrupt Lives. Statements that do not appear to serve their authors' purpose are few and unconfirmed; but they match the circumstances of south-western Britain in the mid fifth century. Docco, also called Congar, is said to have belonged to one of the leading Cornovian families, young when they moved south to Dumnonia, probably about the 430s. He was apparently re-garded as a son or grandson of an emperor Constantine, evidently the British emperor of 407. Whether he was a relative or not, he acted like one; for Constantine's known son Constans had taken monastic vows, probably a year or two before Docco's birth. In Dumnonia, Docco's home was his estate at Congresbury, that preserves his name, in Somerset, south of Bristol. There he lived as a monk, as some of his European contemporaries lived ascetic lives on their own estates. He maintained a school, as did Martin; at least three other monasteries bore his name, St. Kew in northern Cornwall, and the two Llandough's in Glamorgan-shire. St. Kew is attested as a fifth-century foundation; the others are perhaps as early. Somewhere about the middle of the century he is said to have been conse-crated bishop, presumably in the chief town of a *civitas* where his monasteries made him known, either Exeter, or possibly Caerwent. His death is placed at 473, and he is said to have died an old man.

Later Fifth-Century Ireland

Docco was honoured in Ireland as the first author of the Irish Christian liturgy, and a number of notices suggest the reason. Patrick died about the same time as pope Leo, perhaps a year or two before, and his death left an organisational problem in Ireland that only Rome could solve. The law of the Church required that a bishop must be consecrated by two or more existing bishops; therefore, unless there were a number of bishoprics in a country, new bishops must either travel abroad for consecration, or hold office irregularly. In the generation after Patrick's death, the Irish record four or five new northern sees; either they were authorised by Leo in Patrick's lifetime, or by his successor after his death. The churchmen were either Irish, products of the church that Patrick founded, or British; and several of the prominent Irish leaders were trained in Britain, some by the abbots of Whithorn.

These northern sees derived from the concepts of Roman Europe, that assigned one bishop and one only to each political unit. In Europe the unit was the Roman *civitas*, but Ireland had no towns. The distribution of the late fifth-century bishops points to the commonsense principle evolved; a bishop is attested for each of the main kingdoms. There is no sign of a metropolitan. It is probable that the bishop of Armagh was from the beginning accorded some greater deference, but the earliest recorded claim to the title 'Archbishop' was advanced at Kildare in Leinster in the earlier seventh century, not at Armagh. The early canons of the Irish church attest a normal married diocesan clergy; Patrick had encouraged monastic vows, and speaks more often of the women than of the men who took them, but the church did not yet insist on celibate priests. Beside the bishoprics, two or three fifth-century monasteries are remembered in the north, together with a number of small cells of consecrated virgins.

Further south, traditions differ. Northern Leinster went its own way. Its earliest Christian record is dominated by the formidable energy of Brigit, whose large monastery and splendid church lay hard by the principal residence of the king. Her bishop, Conlaed, is depicted as a kind of domestic chaplain, necessarily employed to perform those ecclesiastical functions for which women were ineligible. The account is distorted by the prominence of Brigit in later legend; but the concept is early, set down a little over a century after her death, only just out of living memory. Brigit, who is said to have lived from 455 to 525, was a small child when Patrick died, but the inspiration that led her and Faencha and other young women of her day to take the veil was plainly his.

Brigit's house overtopped the rest; her miracles and activities are mainly concerned with cattle, butter, milk and other aspects of dairy farming, so that she appears as the patroness of women and of peace; she was also the champion of north Leinster. Other women practised women's virtues, and local patrons abounded, but Brigit became a national saint, second only to Patrick; she reached her eminence earlier than him, within a century of her death. It is evident that Irish society needed a female cult. In Ireland, as in European Christianity, congregations of religious women preceded the male monasteries; but they did not survive in Ireland, and separate houses for women play little part in later Irish monasticism. The choice among female saints was therefore restricted to those who lived in the late fifth century, and it must be presumed that among her contemporaries Brigit's personality excelled, attracting more numerous followers. It was perhaps a slight additional strength that she happened to bear the name of an ancient goddess, but the name Briga, in various forms, was almost as common in early Ireland as Mary in modern England, and the name by itself brought no closer identity with a mother-goddess.

Later tradition accommodated a female counterpart of Patrick. But the rest of the south remembered origins independent of Patrick. Ailbe of Emly, Ciaran of Saigir in Ossory, Declan of the Dessi, from the three main divisions of Munster, and Ibar of south Leinster went to Rome during the pontificate of Hilary, that lasted from 461 to 468. Another Irishman, Enda, and a Briton, Kebi, or Cybi, cousin or nephew of bishop Docco, visited Rome at the same time. The date was immediately after Patrick's death, which obliged Rome to consecrate one or more northern bishops to succeed him. The southern Irishmen had had difficulty in finding priests at home; Ailbe had British teachers, Ibar was a pupil of the Briton Mocteus of Louth, and Ciaran had had to go abroad to find Christian instructions; only Declan had found an Irish teacher, who had himself been trained abroad. A little later other Leinstermen, Eugenius and Tigernach, were sent to Whithorn for schooling.

Ibar and the three Munstermen were consecrated bishops in Rome and sent back to Ireland. Their biographers insist that they were consecrated before Patrick, and overcome the chronological difficulties by giving them life-spans of up to 300 years. Paragraphs in the medieval texts recount how they reached agreement with Patrick, with varying degrees of politeness, retaining southern independence without prejudice to Patrick's rights; these stories were plainly added in an age when the priority of Armagh was admitted in the south, but only grudgingly. The bishops founded sees, but Enda was a man of a different stamp, with other ideals. He was already a monk. In his youth he had been a dynastic chief. Leading his men home from battle, singing a victory song, he passed the cell of the virgin Faencha.

'That horrible yelling comes not from the grave of Christ,' she protested, and denounced Enda as a murderer.

'I keep my father's inheritance, and I have to fight my enemies,' he replied indignantly.

'Your father is in hell, his inheritance is crime and wickedness,' answered Faencha.

Enda was converted and joined the community. Soon after, raiding neighbours attacked his men; Faencha saw him put down the plank he was carrying as though tempted to help. She took no chances.

'You must get out of Ireland' she told him, 'or you will be seduced by the things of this world. . . . Go to Britain to the monastery of Rosnat.'

'How long must I stay there?' Enda asked.

'Till I hear good reports of you,' she retorted.

But from Britain he went to Rome, with Ailbe and 'Pubeus'. On his return he asked king Angus of Munster, who ruled from about 463 to 492, to grant him the desert island of Aran for a monastery. Angus was astounded, because the teaching of Patrick had enjoined that he should offer to clerics only 'good agricultural land near my royal residence'. But he agreed when Enda insisted. Few tales more clearly illustrate the basic differences between the bishops and the monks. Patrick's concept is the normal and proper attitude of the church of Rome and Gaul; bishops Ailbe and Declan followed it, and their churches were built by royal residences; most fifth-century bishops settled near royal centres, rarely more than a couple of hours' drive away, often within easy walking distance. Like most continental bishops, their duty was to guide kings. Enda's unusual attitude foreshadowed the future. The monk sought to escape from political society, not to reform it.

In the Life of Enda, the most eminent of the three companions was 'Pubeus'. Like several other island visitors to Rome, in the fancies of the biographers he was elected pope by the admiring Romans, but immediately resigned in favour of Hilary. As they left the city, Hilary gave the party sacerdotal vestments, and then recalled them; Pubeus protested, but Enda submitted, and Hilary foretold that thanks to his humility Enda would become chief of the three. Later, in Aran, a dispute arose as to which of them was *princeps*, chief, in the island; the polite redaction of the surviving text makes each defer to the other, Enda admitting that Pubeus was 'senior' and 'of higher authority', *auctoritate dignior*. The dispute was resolved by an embassy to Rome, consisting of a Finnian, of MacCriche, who was Ailbe's subordinate cleric in Clare, to whose territory Aran belonged, and of Erlatheus, bishop of Armagh, who died in 481. One story brings Ailbe with MacCriche to Aran. The pope, guided by a miracle, decided in Enda's favour.

The Life of Kebi is an exceedingly corrupt British text, but it is independent of the Irish tradition, and tells a similar tale. Kebi visited Hilary, who is confused with Hilary of Poitiers, dead a hundred years before; he returned to Wales in the time of king Etelic of Gelvissig, in the later 5th century. He crossed to Ireland with his aged 'cousin' Kengar, Docco, who died in 473. They settled on Aran, but after four years 'Crubthir Fintan' denied Kengar the cow that fed him and quarrelled with Kebi; though abbot 'Enna' for a time pacified him, Fintan succeeded in driving Kebi from Aran and Ireland, to make his permanent home in Llangybi, the Roman fort that bears his name on Holyhead, off Anglesey. The tale is packed with nonsense, but rests on a less banal original; the later editor had no idea who Hilary or Enda were, and took the Irish word *crubthir*, priest, for a proper name; he did not know that Fintan was a protégé of Mocteus of Louth in the late 5th century, or that these people were contemporaries of one another and of Etelic. These were statements that he found in his source. Yet the essence of the tale is similar to the Irish account; Kebi and Kengar were expelled from Aran after claiming disputed rights; as in the Irish story the superior authority of 'Pubeus' over Aran was disputed, and rejected after an appeal to Rome.

The name 'Pubeus' is unknown in Ireland, Britain or elsewhere, and is plainly a corrupt form; but it is a spelling natural to an Irish scholar who thought that Kebi was the Irish form of a British name, which should properly be rendered in Latin and in British by replacing an Irish K with a British P. It is not probable that Irish and British tradition remembered two separate people with similar names whose claims on Aran were both rejected by the same pope; it is more probable that the two traditions differently remembered the name of one person. The connection with Docco explains the context. He is the only late 5th-century British bishop known to monastic tradition, and he is honoured as the earliest episcopal patron of the monks, both by the Irish and by the British. He was the contemporary of pope Hilary, and the Roman church required that monasteries should be placed under episcopal supervision; it is likely enough that when Enda visited Rome, Hilary required that his intended monastery should be subject to an established bishop of south-western Britain rather than to untried Irishmen, consecrated to sees not yet formed; and it may well be that Hilary, faced with the problems of reorganising the Irish church on Patrick's death, sought and welcomed the advice of a British bishop who knew Ireland. Irish tradition distinguished the 'first order', Patrick's episcopalian church, from the 'second order', the monastic church, that multiplied in the sixth century. It named Docco as the earliest author of the liturgy of the second order. It may be that he was the author of the whole enterprise, and sponsored the visit of the five young Irish ecclesiastics to Hilary in Rome. But Welsh and Irish tradition agree that Aran, the first of the great Irish monasteries, soon threw off the tutelage of the British clergy.

These vigorous churchmen were Irish. Though they owed their organisation and perhaps their papal sanction to British help, their enthusiasm sprang directly from native tradition. They baptised the Irish as they found them, giving a Christian future to the weaknesses as well as to the strengths of their society. They were the heirs of Patrick's mission, but not of his outlook; his writings reveal his love for his Irish converts, but also his detestation of their society and his anxiety to replace it with the ideals of Christian Europe. But Conlaed and Ibar, Ailbe and Ciaran, became bishops of large Irish kingdoms, their priests spiritual heads of similar constituent kingdoms, and the clergy took on something of the colour of the society they served. The rugged Life of Ailbe's priest, MacCriche, portrays a wonder-worker whose supernatural authority was principally exerted to make good the military weakness of his people.

The Life is late and unhistorical, but the situation it outlines was real. It foreshadowed a danger that was long to haunt the Irish church, that the bishop or abbot might shrink to the status of the king's wizard, little more than the *magus* of pre-Christian Ireland, enlarged by the majesty of Roman Christendom. The danger was ultimately averted by the large monasteries; their ethic abhorred the violence of dynastic chiefs, and it was proclaimed when the dynasties were still relatively new, when their violence was keenly resented by humbler Irishmen. At first it was the women saints who led the struggle for peaceful living. Faencha told Enda that the virtues he respected were vices, and persuaded him. Darerca in the north, Ita in the next generation, and the many-sided cult of Brigit denounced violence and exalted maternity, dairy farming and all that belongs to the craft of women, against the bellicosity of men.

The bishops acted by practical example. Ciaran of Saigir intervened to prevent a war between the high king and the king of Munster, and the southern bishops found new outlets for the energy of men. The end of overseas raiding had accentuated internal warfare and the savagery of the chiefs. The bishops reversed the trend by reviving the ancient tradition of overseas voyages, called *Imramma* in lay saga, pilgrimage or *peregrinatio* in the language of the church. At first, not all voyages were peaceful. The followers of Senan and of the saints of the Shannon went with armies to Cornwall, and those who succeeded in establishing themselves brought with them the name of their own bishop, Ciaran, transliterated to Pyran or Perran in Britain. But the military expeditions had little success, and were not repeated. Ailbe preached peaceably to the Irish of Demetia, and baptised the infant David. But the main stream of the voyagers looked westward. Ibar and Ailbe are said to have been the first who dreamed of looking for an undiscovered Land of Promise in or beyond the Atlantic Ocean, and to have sent men to seek it. The first explorers are not reported to have reached further than Iceland, but the traditions of Brendan in the mid sixth century tell circumstantial tales of the sunny and fertile lands of north America. Whether these tales draw upon vigorous imagination or upon actual experience, the decision of Ailbe and Ibar to look for new lands beyond the Ocean added a new dimension to European thought.

Throughout the 5th century, in north and south, the church of Ireland was held to have been organised by British Christians and their native pupils, its organisation sanctioned and approved by Rome. That organisation approximated, as nearly as was possible in a land without towns, to the structure of the church of Rome and Britain. It was based on territorial sees, with a few monasteries under episcopal control, most of them, apart from Enda's Aran, concentrated in and about eastern Meath, Brega, the central regions of the national monarchy. But almost nothing is known of the late 5th-century church in Britain, save for its work in Ireland, and for the existence of a few monastic schools. Political disaster had cut away the foundations of the urban church. The Saxon wars had destroyed the lowland society of the educated early 5th-century bishops, and, though men were doubtless consecrated to urban sees, the decayed towns no longer ruled the countryside. The only part of the lowlands that had escaped continuing warfare was the Severn estuary, Dumnonia and South Wales; there Docco and other unnamed bishops survived; but elsewhere the bishops of the highland areas of Britain, who served a rough rural and military population, can never have attained to the strength and status of their lowland colleagues.

CHAPTER NINETEEN
SIXTH CENTURY MONKS

Britain

Good order prevailed in Britain so long as the victors of Badon lived. Gildas approved of the older bishops and clergy who, like the lay rulers, had 'each kept their own station'. Evil had come quickly, during the 520s and 530s. Tyrannical warlords who overawed laymen also appointed their own creatures to bishoprics, thereby spreading indolence and corruption among the lower clergy. Until the end of the fifth century, men like Docco and Illtud had been reared in the manners of a steady pre-war civilisation. But the men born two generations later, the adults of the 520s, had known nothing of past gentility; they had experienced only the violence of their own time, and they behaved as their education had taught them.

In the past, a few individuals turned away from society to find comfort in monasticism. Fastidius and the Sicilian Briton had known some monks early in the fifth century, direct followers of the teaching of Martin and of Victricius. By the middle of the century their example was followed in south-west Wales. Brioc, born of Irish colonist parents in Cardiganshire about 468, sought solitude in Cornwall, and later in Brittany; in his old age he attracted numerous disciples, when the monastic movement blossomed, but in younger years he was a lone hermit. Samson's father Ammon was born within a few years of Brioc, in nearby Demetia, then still Irish. His parents were sufficiently acquainted with the history and ideals of the monks to give him the name of the father of Egyptian monasticism; their fathers were younger contemporaries of Coelestius, who was perhaps also Demetian, and the distinctive names used by this family, Anna, Enoch, Samson, Umbrafel, denote an evangelical outlook that was alien to the polite British bishops of Patrick's time, and to the churchmen who served the warlords in Gildas' day. Monks were known, but they were few. Some monastic retreats had been founded by landed gentlemen, during and before the wars, but they are represented as comfortable places, recalling the milder austerities of Latin Europe, akin to those whose outlook John Cassian deplored. They obeyed the bishops, and made no known impact upon churchman or layman; they were as 'torpid' as the monasteries of Gaul.

Samson

Reform was the work of a single generation. Many of the earliest and best-remembered leaders were students at the school of Illtud, at Llanilltud Fawr, or Llantwit, in Glamorgan. Samson, Paul Aurelian, Gildas, Leonorus and others entered the school at the age of about five; and stayed there a dozen years or more. Their motive, method and achievement is most clearly seen in the Lives of Samson and Paul, both of which survive in early versions and rest upon contemporary originals. Samson is independently attested; he was present at a church council in Paris, about 557, and Gregory of Tours dates the events that brought him back to Brittany to the last weeks of 560. He died soon after, in old age. The oldest surviving Life was written some thirty or forty years later, about the year 600 or shortly before, and rests upon a contemporary original, composed 'in an elegant style' by Samson's cousin, Enoch, who had obtained stories of the saint's youth from his mother. Enoch's nephew gave verbal detail to the author, who also visited Britain to collect additional information.

He tells a vivid tale, whose incidents depict the reformers as their contemporaries saw them more clearly than any later description. Samson's father was a Demetian landowner, and also an *altrix*, companion of the king, probably Agricola; at the request of

> a learned master who lived in the far north and was much sought after by many provinces,

young Samson was sent to Illtud's school at the age of five; the northern master was perhaps Maucennus of Whithorn, who seems to have visited Demetia just before 500. When Samson said goodbye to his parents at the school gates, he

> did not cry as children usually do when they are taken from their father and their mother

but immediately began to learn his letters. By the age of fifteen his learning was precocious, his fasting immoderate; and he knew some practical medicine. At an early age he was ordained priest and deacon by bishop Dubricius, and aroused the jealousy of Illtud's nephews, who feared that he might succeed their uncle as head of the school and so deprive them of their 'earthly inheritance'. He sought and gained a transfer to another monastery of Illtud's, newly founded by Piro on Ynys Pyr, Caldey Island, where his austerity and theological scholarship astounded his fellows.

One winter's evening messengers rode to Caldey to tell him that his father was gravely ill and not expected to live. Samson

> was obdurate, and answered 'Tell your master I have forsaken Egypt and must not return thereto. God has power to heal the sick'. . . . Piro was shocked . . . and said, 'Why do you answer like that, saint? You ought not to do God's work carelessly. It is your business to care for the passing of souls'. . . . Saint Samson looked

> at him, and stood still awhile. Then he answered 'God's will be done; for the Lord and for the winning of souls I am ready to suffer in all things . . . I will go.'

The old man recovered when Samson reached home; he and his wife, his brother and younger sons all took monastic vows; but Samson rejected his sister, 'given over to worldly pleasures', adding grudgingly, 'but we must maintain her, since she is a human being'. Most of the family property was given to the poor, a little retained; the sister was no doubt not the only dependent. But on his three days' journey home, accompanied by a young deacon, Samson's zealous severity occasioned an unhappy incident.

> As they passed through a great forest, they heard a wild voice near them, shrieking horribly. The terrified deacon . . . let go the pack horse . . . and fled. . . . Samson . . . followed . . . and saw a hideous hairy witch, a decrepit old woman, with a three pronged spear in her hand. Samson, trusting in Christ, tied his horse to a tree . . . and chased her. The witch ran into the deacon and knocked him down. . . . Samson . . . cried out 'In the name of Christ Jesus I order you to stay where you are.' She stood still trembling, and dropped the spear, as Samson came up, asking 'Who and what are you?' 'I am a witch,' she answered . . . 'there is no one left of our family but I; my eight sisters and my mother are still living, but all nine are in another wood. I was married to a husband on this estate, but my man is dead, so I cannot leave the wood.' 'Can you cure the

---

Map 24

Main concentrations of dedications to

David and Teilo

Cadoc

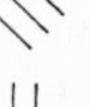

Illtud

Beuno

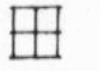

Tysylio

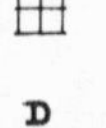

D Houses of Docco

Roman towns

• Main monastic centres

\+ Bishops' Sees

MAP 24 MONKS IN WALES

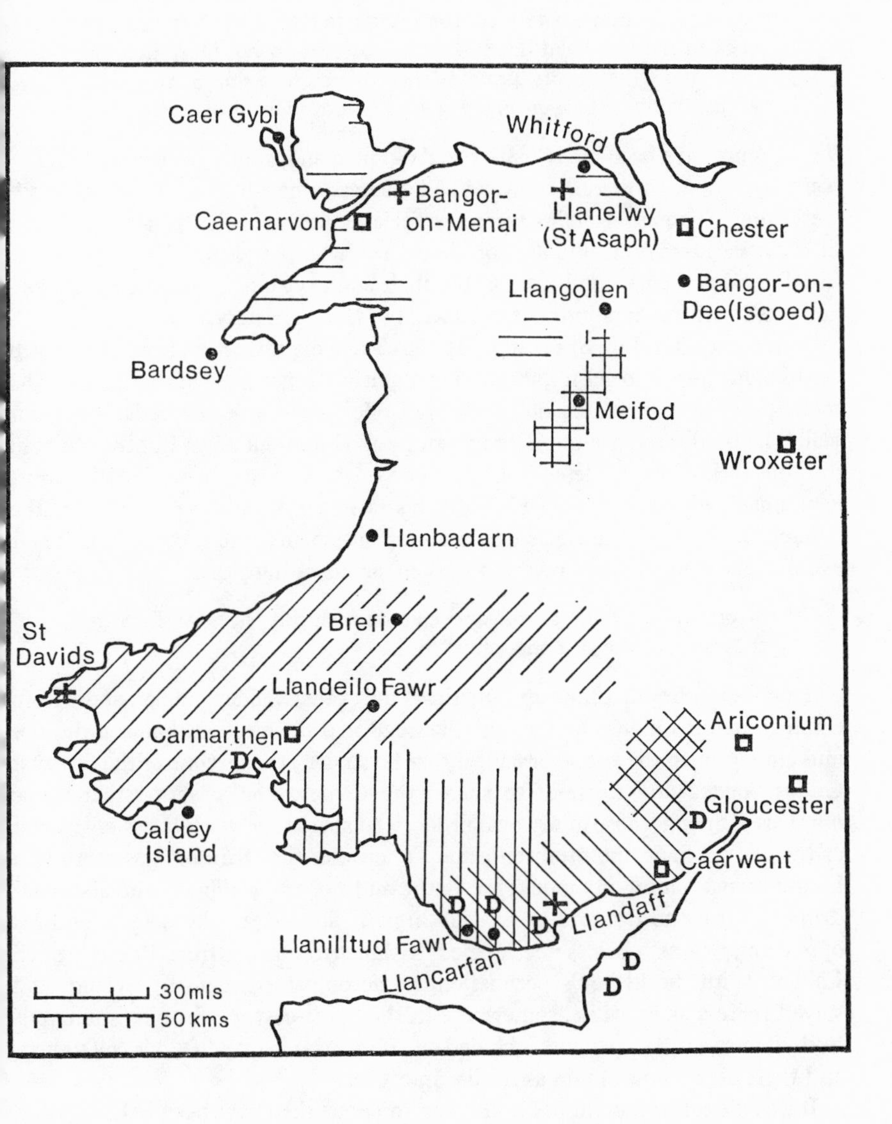

> man you have knocked down?' Samson asked. 'I cannot and will not . . . do good' she answered. 'I call upon the name of Almighty God,' Samson replied 'to prevent you doing any more harm to anyone . . .' Immediately . . . she fell down and died. Samson ran back to the half dead deacon, who recovered in not more than an hour and a half, very grateful that thanks to Saint Samson the wicked witch's three pronged spear had not pierced his skin.

There must have been many half-crazed old men and women, as terrified as they were terrifying, subsisting in woodland shelters when their normal livelihoods were gone. Though witches were fearful and loathsome creatures, Samson's fatal curse caused murmurs. Bishop Dubricius, who was visiting Ynys Pyr, 'as he usually did at Lent', conducted a thorough enquiry; but he acquitted Samson, and confirmed his appointment as steward of the monastery.

Some time later, Piro drank more at dinner one night than his head or stomach could hold; forced to get up, wandering alone in the darkness in the *claustra*, the monastic enclosure, he fell down the well. He let out a *magna ululatio*, a great yell. The brethren came to his rescue and pulled him out alive, but the old man died of shock. None the less, in the eyes of Samson's cousin, he was 'a saint and a gentleman', *vir sanctus et egregius*. But his fate reinforced the preaching of the stricter moralists, and the chastened monks chose Samson to succeed him. Their comfortable standards are revealed in their praise of him, that

> no one ever saw him drunk, or even talking thickly; he never forbade the cup, but the cup never hurt him.

The praise implies that the cup sometimes hurt other Caldey monks; and within eighteen months monks and abbot alike regretted the election. Samson did not find among them the passionate ideal that he sought, the fervour of the few that Gildas 'longed and thirsted' to share; the Caldey monks were rather to be numbered among 'those of my own order' who shared the worldliness of the rest of the clergy. Soon the brethren came to consider that Samson was more of a hermit than a community monk, for 'in the midst of ample dinners and abundant drink he strove to fast and thirst'. He himself 'longed for the desert', and his opportunity came when 'some learned Irishmen returning from Rome' visited Caldey. With the bishop's permission, he accompanied them to Ireland, and stayed there a short while, somewhere in the north-east, performing numerous healing miracles. His patients included an abbot, who bequeathed his cell to him, and thereafter followed him as his disciple.

It was the turning-point in his life. Samson must then have been in his thirties, the date somewhere in the 520s. The travellers from Rome cannot but have told tales of Benedict of Nursia, a Roman noble who had withdrawn from secular life soon after 500, at the age of about twenty, to live in a cave on the banks of the river Arno; after a quarter of a century, as his fame spread throughout Italy and attracted numerous disciples, he found the banks of the Arno too accessible to the envious and curious, and removed, about the year 530, to his permanent retreat on Monte Cassino. Samson had long seen his own vocation as 'quitting Egypt', as two centuries before the monks had left the cities to live in the Egyptian desert. Their example had long been admired in his family. On his return from Ireland he left Caldey. He sent his uncle to take charge of his Irish cell, and himself withdrew to an abandoned fort on the Severn, but soon left it for a nearby cave.

He was not allowed to remain long in solitude. A synod appointed him, against his will, first as 'abbot of the monastery which Germanus is said to have founded', and then as bishop of an unnamed diocese north of the Severn. Throughout his life Samson, like Patrick, was guided by dreams and visions, and on this occasion a vision warned him to accept the bishopric. But soon afterward another vision told him to emigrate; he settled the affairs of his diocese, said farewell to his mother and his family, and excommunicated his sister, who was 'living in an adulterous union'. He crossed to Cornwall, to the monastery of Docco, at St. Kew, where he suggested to the abbot Iuniavus that he should stay for a while. With polite embarrassment Iuniavus answered

> beloved father, it is better for the servant of God to continue his journey . . . your request to stay with us is not convenient, for you are *melior*, better than us; you might condemn us, and we might properly feel condemned by your superior merit; for I must make it clear to you that we have somewhat relaxed our original rules. . . . You had better go on to . . . Europe.

Samson was 'stupefied at this doctrine'. It was the same unresponsive hedonism that he had met at Caldey, perhaps also in his brief episcopate, the same indifference that distressed his contemporary, Gildas. Samson

> dismissed his ship, loaded his books and spiritual vessels on to his waggon, and harnessed to his carriage the two horses he had brought from Ireland, and . . . made his way to the southern sea that leads to Europe.

His stay in Cornwall was somewhat longer than the wording suggests, for in Tricurium, now called Trigg, the district of north Cornwall in which St. Kew lies, he dispersed a crowd of the subjects of count Gwedian, who were celebrating heathen rites about a standing stone, and with his pocket knife carved on it the sign of the cross; and the Life of Saint Petroc reports that when he landed nearby he found Samson in residence in a cell on the Padstow estuary. After some dispute Petroc evicted him. Samson moved again, to Castle Dore by Fowey, the insular capital of the Cornovian ruler Conomorus, where a chapel bore his name a few years later, and still does. But soon after he sailed abroad.

In Brittany he became bishop of the kingdom of Jonas of Dumnonie, with his see at Dol, in the north-east. When Conomorus mastered Brittany and killed Jonas, his son Iudual fled to Paris, but was imprisoned by king Childebert.

MAP 25 MONKS IN CORNWALL

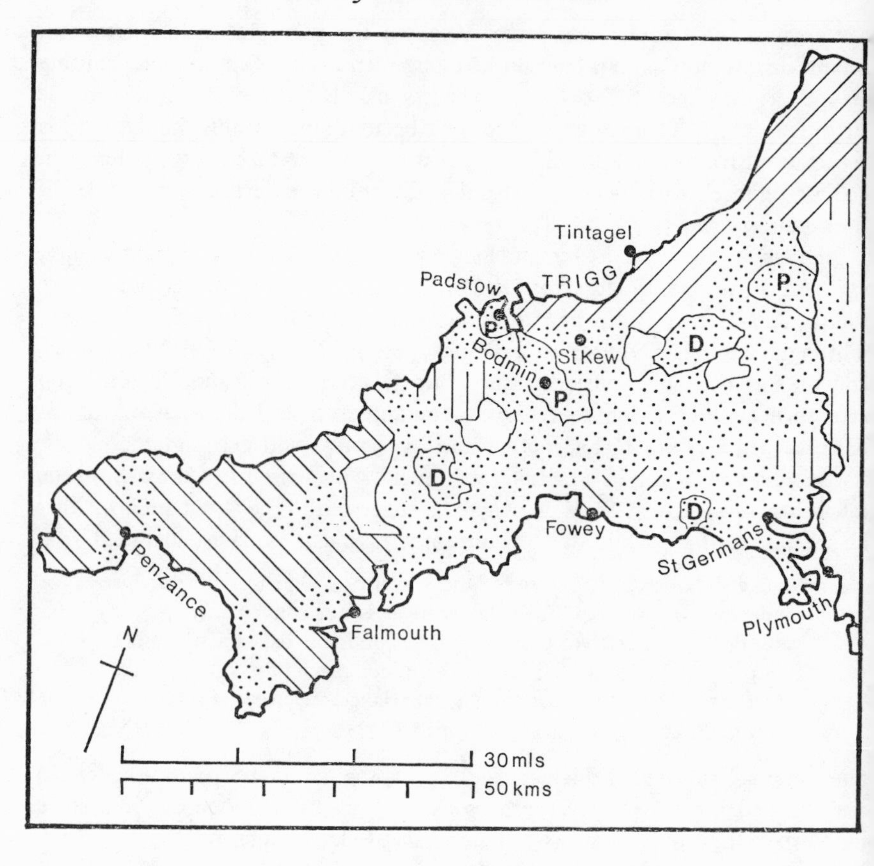

Parishes now or formerly named after

IRISH monks

The Saints of the Shannon

The Children of Brychan

Other Irish saints

BRITISH monks

D David and Nun

P Petroc

Old names not known

Samson, like many other saints of Brittany in Conomorus' time, also went to Paris. He is the only one among them who signed the acts of a church council held at Paris about 557, for thanks to his brief tenure of the Severn see he, unlike them, was a canonically consecrated bishop. He cured a court noble, whose support he enlisted, but found an enemy in the queen, whose machinations he miraculously defeated. In the end he prevailed, though the author of the Life was not aware that the occasion was the death of Childebert and the succession of Clothair. He came back with Iudual to Brittany in 560, and soon after died, 'his life and age completed'.

Paul Aurelian

Samson's biographer is mainly concerned with his life in Britain. Wrmonoc's Life of Paul Aurelian is chiefly concerned with Brittany, but contains some details of the saint's youth in Britain. The present text was set down in the ninth century, but uses a number of sixth-century spellings taken from a contemporary original Life. Paul's father was a landowner in Dumnonia who served as a military companion to a local king in Glevissig. The boy entered Illtud's school 'at a tender age' and left at sixteen because he felt the urge 'to penetrate the desert wilderness and live apart from civil society'. He settled with a few followers 'on a deserted site that belonged to his father's estates'. The fame of the hermit spread, and he was summoned to the court of 'king Mark, also called Quonomorius', who ruled 'different peoples who spoke four languages' from 'Villa Bannhedos', Castle Dore above Fowey, where Samson had been before him. Paul refused Mark's invitation to become the bishop of his kingdom, and crossed to Brittany, where he founded St. Pol-de-Leon and became 'bishop of the Osismi', the Roman name for the people and the bishop's see of the region. The date is plainly indicated. Mark Conomorus died in 560, Paul had then been long established in Brittany, but he crossed after Samson. His migration can hardly be much earlier than 540 or later than 550.

Samson and Paul were two among many hundreds of emigrant saints. Where dates are given, almost all are said to have crossed in the time of king Childebert, who reigned from 511 to 558. When dates are closer, they lie in the latter part of his reign. Leonorus died at the age of fifty-one, soon after 560; he was five when he entered Illtud's school, fifteen when he left. His migration cannot be earlier than 530, and was probably somewhat later. Winwaloe died in a year that was probably 583, and was already adult when his father reached Brittany. Teilo made a number of foundations in Wales before he crossed to Brittany in the hope of escaping the plague, about 550, and on the same occasion the aged Brioc hurried home to comfort his plague-stricken kinsmen in Cardigan, after he had been in Brittany for some years. Numerous other indications point to the same conclusion. The large-scale migrations to Brittany did not begin until after 530; Samson, Paul and probably Leonorus crossed the sea nearer to 540 than to 530. But there was an extensive migration well before the plague, and by about 545 many had crossed. Though new arrivals followed the pioneers later, the main weight of the emigration falls in the decade from 540 to 550.

The emigration to Brittany was one among several ways of achieving the ideals of new monks. Their aim was to get away from the 'society of man', to live alone with a few companions in caves or 'desert wildernesses'. Their Lives constantly cite by name the fathers of the Egyptian desert, especially Antony, and they deliberately imitated their practice and regulations. Very many found remote and deserted sites to hand in Wales and Dumnonia. Place names attest the scale of the movement and its locality. Sixth-century Latin usage calls the monastery *claustra*, enclosure, whence comes the English word 'cloister'. Its equivalent in Welsh was *llan*, whose literal meaning is enclosure. Well over six hundred Welsh towns and hamlets bear the name Llan, as do many hundreds in the Dumnonian lands and in Brittany. The numerous names that begin with *Tre-* or *Plou-* also derive from the terminology of the 6th century monks, and many of them were so named in the 6th and 7th centuries. The scale of the migration was large enough to entail a considerable transformation of society.

The saints did not set out to reform society. They gave it up as an evil to avoid. But, as in Egypt, the pioneers found that so many men flocked to the desert that they were driven to build a new society of a different kind, whether they liked it or no. Theirs was the first experience of a mass conversion to monasticism in the Latin west. Their experience differed from Egypt in one important respect. The eastern deserts were natural wildernesses that no effort of early man could make fertile; the deserts peopled by British saints were man-made, in lands depopulated by the decay of Rome; the effort of new cultivators easily reduced them to tillage and pasture.

The reasons that prompted men to move are not hard to see. Though the Roman civilisation of western Britain had not been physically destroyed, as in the lowlands, its strength had been sapped. It was a limb detached from a tree now dead. The unpredictable violence of the warlords weighed upon landowner, tenant and churchmen alike. At first, pioneer individuals who led a dedicated life in solitude were termed 'holy', *sancti*. The modern connotation of 'saint' did not arise until a later age, when the authority of Rome limited the use of the title in Europe to a restricted number of outstanding men long dead, and forbade its application to living persons; but in the fifth and sixth centuries, in Europe as in Britain, 'saint' was the normal and proper term for a living person of outstanding religious virtue. In late Roman Britain it applied not to monks in general, who were relatively few and unimpressive, but to men of notable piety who rejected the normal assumptions of lay society. The movement grew slowly, until a decisive moment, when public opinion approved the example of the *sancti* and began to see in them a possible protection against the ills that beset ordinary men. That moment was reached when the 'best councillors of the congregation' chose Samson for bishop, a man who had hitherto been regarded as an uncomfortable extremist even by his fellow monks; and when king Conomorus judged it wise to seek a monk, Paul Aurelian, as bishop of his kingdom. The date of both events is close to 540.

The turning-point coincided with the publication of Gildas' manifesto. It became the favourite text of the reformers, and accelerated their success. It denounced the *duces* who had usurped the authority of kings; and went on to arraign the churchmen who ought to have withstood them, but had connived at their crimes. Gildas protests that bishops and priests buy their places from the tyrants, and if they meet resistance in their diocese, they spend their substance on travelling overseas to seek consecration, to impose themselves on their country, proud and puffed up, on their return. They conduct services and preach in the churches, but instead of attacking the sins of the rulers and the people, they condone them and share in them. The evil extends even into the 'clergy of our order', priests who have taken a monastic vow. There are however a 'few, but very few' who have 'found the narrow way', whose life Gildas longs to share before he dies. These are the *sancti*, men like Samson and Paul Aurelian. The work was written late in the reign of Maelgwn, who died about 550. It cannot be much earlier than 540. But since the saints are still a 'very few', it cannot have been written after they inspired a mass movement in the early 540s. It was published just before the movement grew great, about the later 530s.

Gildas' book gave the new monasticism cohesion, and justified it in the face of existing society. The book succeeded because it came at the right moment, giving a voice to inarticulate men who were ready to reject that society. Such men were numerous. The Saints' Lives abound in tales of wicked persons who withstood the monks, but also record many who welcomed and protected them. Men of property gave them land; others led lay migrations in company with the monks, and some turned monk themselves. There were ascetics in small numbers elsewhere in Europe; but they became a mighty movement only in western Britain, because there men were able to heed them. In Italy, where the armies of Justinian were expelling the Goths, and in Gaul under the sons of Clovis, ascetics found no such response. There the ancient bond of landlord and peasant remained intact; the secular and ecclesiastical institutions of Rome were still strong. Benedict of Nursia thought and acted like Samson and Paul Aurelian. But he impressed Italy because he was exceptional. Few others imitated him and it was not possible to sprinkle the Italian countryside with hundreds of local copies of his monastery on Monte Cassino.

Almost nothing is known of the church that Gildas denounced. He says that until his generation ecclesiastics, like laymen, had 'kept their station'. The proper ordering of the church was still a diocesan episcopate, with monasteries subject to the bishops. The Saints' Lives record one such bishop, because he was well disposed to their aspirations. Dubricius visited Illtud, and Piro on Caldey Island, as a superior, investigating complaints and ordaining priests and deacons. The churches that bear his name are most frequent in the district called Ercig or Archenfeld, on the right bank of the Wye, opposite and below Hereford.

Archenfeld takes its name from the Roman town of Ariconium, Weston-under-Penyard, the other side of the Wye, nearer to Gloucester, but Dubricius' churches extend more widely, covering almost the whole of Gwent, the former *civitas* of the Silures; his see was probably its capital town, Caerwent, possibly Gloucester.

Episcopal sees had been designed to correspond with lay political states, Roman *civitates*. They functioned ill when the *civitates* ceased to be coherent states, and the remnant of their identity cannot long have survived the fall of Arthur's empire, shortly before 520. Gildas complains that kings appointed their own bishops, who sometimes sought consecration abroad if they could not get it at home. Though established bishops doubtless clung to their undivided sees, the kings might plead with justification that new political realities needed new diocesan boundaries; the principle of the church had always been one bishop for one state, and now that the Roman *civitates* had been replaced by new states, the bishops' sees should correspond to their frontiers.

Mounting pressure brought change. Samson was consecrated bishop north of the Severn. It may be that Dubricius had resisted the establishment of a new see designed for a royal nominee, but agreed to its creation if Samson was accepted as bishop. In Dumnonia, king Mark Conomorus sought Paul Aurelian as bishop of his own small kingdom, and bishop Wethenoc, whom Petroc encountered in the region of Bodmin and Padstow, had nothing of the status of a bishop of all Dumnonia, enthroned in Exeter. He too was clearly the bishop of a local king. By the 7th century, the new frontiers had become relatively stable; the greater abbots functioned as bishops of large kingdoms, Gwynedd and Powys, Cardigan, Demetia. But in the sixth century, the organisation of the episcopate was a matter of change, dispute and confusion. Once the monasteries were established, monks had little need of bishops; church order consigned to them certain necessary functions, chiefly the ordination of priests and the consecration of churches, but they were otherwise little esteemed, and are rarely mentioned unless they were monks themselves, or encountered them. Most early monks, like Samson and Paul Aurelian, rejected pressures to accept sees in Britain, and yielded only to the needs of colonists in Brittany. In south Wales, after Dubricius, only Teilo is regularly styled bishop; his chief monastery, at Llandeilo Fawr, commands the routes from Demetia to Glamorgan and Brecon; he was the patron of the reformers in Glevissig, and received grants from Agricola of Demetia. He was probably bishop of all Demetia, his nominal see Carmarthen, until in his old age the separate bishoprics of Glevissig and of St. David's were established. But Roman administrative divisions disappeared earlier, and a bishop of Gwent could no longer complain if his colleague poached within his diocese; each abbot had the effective power to choose the bishop whom he invited to ordain his priests, until established frontiers and hardening custom limited his choice.

The new monasteries became numerous in the 540s, and some of them were large. They were the first form of Christianity that the bulk of the countryside encountered at close quarters, for it is doubtful if the bishops and priests of the old sees had much effective contact with scattered local homesteads. The monasteries aroused eager support, and also fierce opposition. The numbers of single men who entered the new 'enclosures' as monks was in itself considerable; the Saints' Lives also emphasise that from the beginning monasteries, small and large, also maintained lay brothers, as Cassiodorus did in Italy, who brought their families to work the lands around them. Some monasteries, like Llantwit and Llancarfan, began upon the estates of large landowners who had turned monk. Others were built upon lands granted by a king or landowner, and the Lives have many tales of monks who were several times refused lands by wicked notables before a pious donor gave them ground. The original grant was often rapidly supplemented, and the Lives of the earliest founders, as well as later charter memoranda, frequently mention landlords' offers to make over estates, with their cultivators, to the monastery.

Grants of lands were doubtless often inspired by simple piety. But more practical consideration also operated. Once the monks had earned a wide respect among the population at large, they became powerful protectors. Kings and warlords might levy exactions upon lay landlord and peasant with little fear of opposition; but demands upon monastic lands and monastic tenants were sacrilege, not lightly to be risked when all men condemned it. Yet kings, and landlords who kept their estates intact, had good reason to resent the migration to the Llan. Each new recruit to the monastery, each estate placed under its control or protection, meant a loss of labour to the landlord, the loss of taxpayers and of army recruits to the king. Kings did not readily acquiesce, and the commonest miracles in the Lives of early saints are those that secure for the Llan a right of sanctuary and immunity from billeting, conscription and taxation. Commonly, in the fancies of the Lives, the evil king, Arthur, Maelgwn, or some local ruler, is blinded, swallowed up by the ground, or stricken with illness by the anger of the Lord; when he repents, the supernatural virtue of the saint cures him, and in gratitude he grants sanctuary or immunity. Miracles apart, the contest was a trial of strength between the old order and the new. The monks won early success because public opinion backed them, and their dependents enjoyed an enviable security against the exactions of royal government.

David

The monks sought solitude. Public support made them reformers, who transformed the character of the church and founded a new civil society within the kingdoms of the warlords. Their success divided them. There were many variant attitudes, but two sharply opposed outlooks crystallised, the practices of David of Demetia and those of Cadoc and Gildas. David is said to have been born in the 520s, and to have died in 589. He was baptised by Ailbe of Munster, who died in 528, and was taught by Paulinus, who was probably a pupil of Kebi and Docco, and was probably also the Paulinus who is styled 'defender of the faith, patriot, champion of justice', in Latin verses engraved upon his tombstone in a monastic churchyard near Pumpsaint, ten miles north of Llandeilo Fawr.

David was the pattern of the stricter monks, styled *meliores*, or 'better', the term that Iuniavus of St. Kew had apprehensively applied to Samson. Like Samson, his aim is said to have been to 'imitate the monks of Egypt'. His Rule rested on vigorous manual labour throughout the daylight hours, the evenings devoted to reading, writing and prayer. His mottoes were 'he that does not work, neither shall he eat', and 'comfortable ease is the mother of vice'. His monks therefore farmed without draught animals; their shoulders pulled the plough, 'each his own ox', their arms 'driving spades into the earth'. Their food was bread, cabbage and water, and David was therefore called *Aquaticus*, the water-drinker; there was 'no *meum* and *tuum*', no mine and thine, and even to speak of 'my book' was a punishable offence, since all was held in common. Unlike most other abbots, David resolutely refused to accept land or other endowments from laymen. 'Clothing was cheap, commonly of skins'; conversation was kept to the minimum, and discipline enforced absolute obedience. Aspirants to the strict rule were tested by being kept outside the gates for ten days, their patience tried by abuse from within, and thereafter by submission to a long probationary period before acceptance.

This extreme rigidity was a reaction against the comfortable ease of St. Kew and Caldey Island, and it also contrasted with the moderate conduct of Illtud. The *meliores* felt themselves to be superior, and provoked criticism as well as respect. In his later writings Gildas fiercely attacked them.

> Abstinence from bodily foods without charity is useless. The real *meliores* are those who fast without ostentation . . . not those who think themselves superior because they refuse to eat meat . . . or to ride on a horse or in a carriage; for death enters into them by the windows of pride. . . .

He accused them of social egalitarianism; it was a legacy of earlier British thought that he did not himself inherit; for

> they criticise brethren who do not follow their arrogant conceits. . . . They eat bread by measure, and boast of it beyond measure; they drink water, and with it the cup of hatred. Their meals are dry dishes and backbiting. . . . When they meditate their 'Great Principles' it is from contempt, not from love. They put the serf before his master, the mob before its king, lead before gold, iron before silver. . . . They set fasting above charity, vigils above justice, their own conceits above concord, their cell above the church, severity above humility; in a word, they prefer man to God. It is not the Gospels they obey, but their own will, not the apostle but their own pride. They forget that the position of the stars in heaven is not equal, and that the offices of the angels are unequal.

Gildas vigorously defended those whom the *meliores* attacked, the

> abbot . . . who owns animals and carriages, because he is physically weak or because it is the custom of the country.

Such an abbot was less sinful than

> those who drag ploughs about and drive spades into the earth with arrogance and prejudice.

What was virtue to David was vice to Gildas. Like Paul and Samson, Gildas had been brought up at Illtud's school. Illtud was a nobleman on his own estates who taught classical learning and the scriptures. He gently rebuked Samson's excessive asceticism, and gave no encouragement to Paul's urge for the desert, though he did not hinder it. Even the strict Samson is praised not as a water drinker, but as a moderate drinker of wine, whom 'no man ever saw slightly mellow'. Illtud is also said to have maintained a hundred labourers, and to have continued to receive the rent of his tenants. His school lies in a full Roman tradition, akin to that established in Italy in the next generation, about 540, by Cassiodorus, a learned noble who had been the minister of successive Gothic monarchs; his monks lived well upon the rents of their peasants, but they treated them benevolently, according to their founder's precept,

> teach your peasants good conduct; do not exploit them with new and heavy impositions, but call them often to your feasts.

Cadoc

Gildas was a conservative admirer of the old social order, of its privilege of rank and property. He deplored David's extremism, but he found himself on the defensive against the growing strength of the radicals, and was driven to reach commonsense compromise as more and more monks adopted the rule of David, or moved to houses where it was observed. He advised that

> abbots of the stricter rule should not admit monks from an abbot somewhat less strict; but similarly, less strict abbots should not restrain monks who are inclined to the stricter rule.

Sampson's outlook lay somewhat nearer to David's than to Gildas' and Illtud's. But the opposite pole to David was the monastery of Cadoc, Llancarfan, also called Nantcarfan, in Glamorganshire. The son of a local king, schooled by an Irish teacher at Caerwent, Cadoc sought ample estates with numerous rent-paying tenants, and kept his own labourers; unlike any other recorded British saint, he also maintained a hundred men-at-arms in the hill-fort above his monastery. He inherited his father's secular kingdom and ruled it without renouncing his abbacy, 'abbot and king over Gwynnliauc after his father', 'holding both the secular government and the abbacy of Nantcarfan', 'appointed by his father to rule after him'. The concepts of David and Cadoc clashed in the middle of the century. The Synod of Brefi is described in the Lives of both. In the David version, the saint accused his enemies of Pelagianism, perhaps with reason, and won a resounding victory. The Cadoc version admits defeat, excuses it by alleging that David deliberately and unfairly chose a time when Cadoc was absent abroad, and recounts Cadoc's fury on his return, that was cooled by his Irish pupil Finnian, but was ended only by the direct intervention of an angel. The opposing viewpoints were welcomed most widely by different social classes, among different nations in different regions; the adherents of David and of Teilo have left plentiful traces in the poorer uplands where Irish settlers were most numerous; but the tradition of Cadoc and Illtud is strongest in the wealthier Vale of Glamorgan.

The initial vigour of the British monks was confined to the decades about 550, and its strength lay in south Wales, Dumnonia and Brittany. Elsewhere reform was late and limited. In north Wales, Maelgwn resisted the monks; it was probably only after his death that Daniel came from Demetia to found the great Bangor on the Menai Straits. Most of north-west Wales traced its monastic inspiration to a dimly remembered mission from southern Brittany, headed by Cadfan, whose most important foundation was the monastery of Paternus at Llanbadarn by Aberystwyth. The few effective saints of Powys belong to the end of the century, and the monastery of Bangor-on-Dee was comparatively new when the Angles massacred its monks about 614. Throughout north and central Wales, places named Llan, followed by a saint's name, are rarer than in the south.

The Rest of Britain

Elsewhere in Britain traces of monks are fewer. Northern Britain knew a single outstanding leader, Kentigern. Exiled in youth, he is recorded as bishop of Senlis, near Paris, in 549 and again about 557. Some years later a change of government recalled him to the kingdom of the Clyde, where his principal monastery, Glasgow, became the nucleus of a great city. In southern and central England the traditions that might have remembered saints were lost when the British language gave place to English. A few notices survive. The story of Collen sends him east from Glastonbury and brings him to Southampton, though his best-known monastic foundation is Llangollen, on the Dee. The names of David and of Samson are remembered at a dozen places up the Fosse Way from Exeter to Newark, and thence to York; but they are absent on most of the central section of the road that was settled by the English in the fifth century. Irish monks are reported to have founded Abingdon and to have visited other pagan English peoples, perhaps in Norfolk. The Armorican British Winwaloe was remembered at the farther end of the Icknield Way, in Hertfordshire and in Norfolk; Cadoc is said to have preached on the further borders of the kingdoms of the Clyde, and to have established at least one monastery in a

MAP 26 MONKS IN THE NORTH

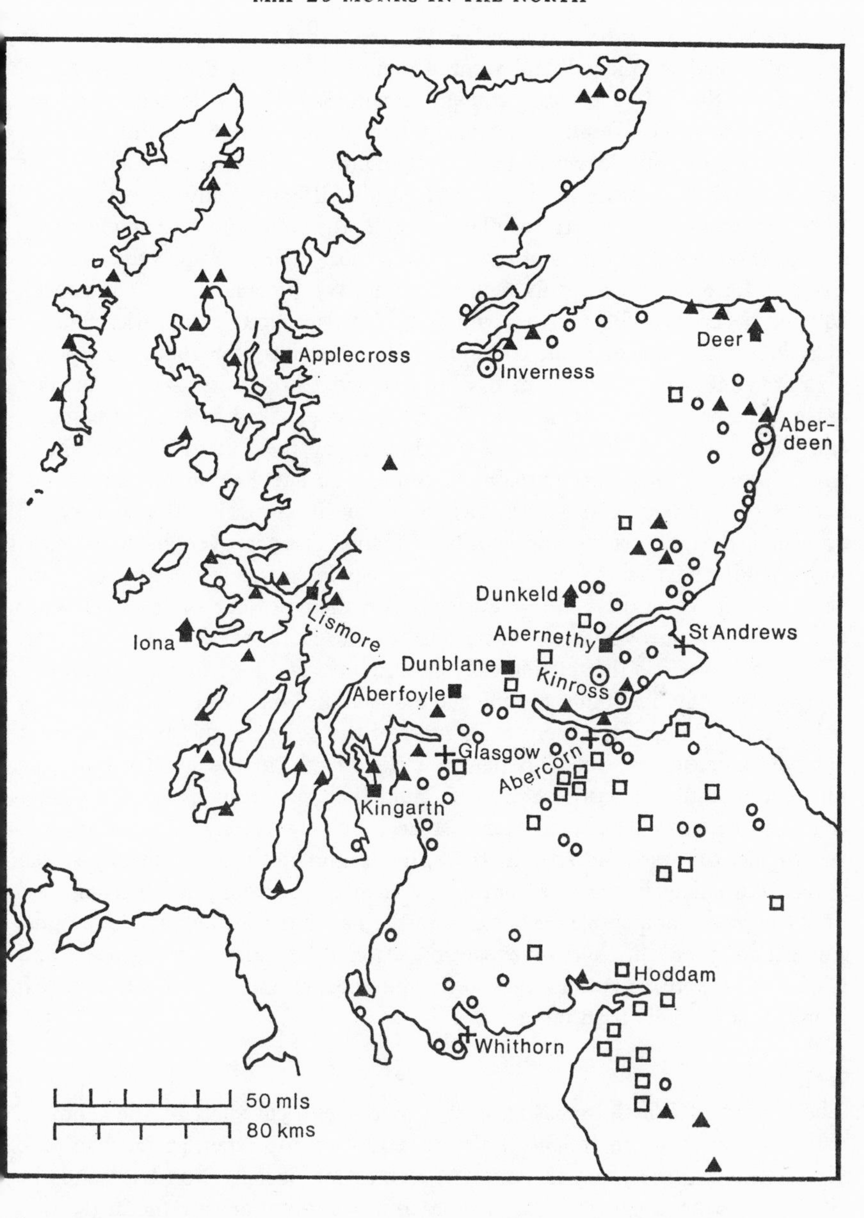

+ Bishops Sees

Dedications to ○ Ninian □ Kentigern ▲ Columba

■ Main centres of Irish monasticism ⊙ Other places

Pennine kingdom. In the north, bishop Wilfred 'listed the church lands . . . that the British had abandoned' and secured them for himself; British monasteries had existed there. In the south, enough remained of the old Roman monastery of St. Alban by Verulamium for king Offa to refound it in the eighth century.

The fragments of evidence do no more than prove the obvious, that a Christian church survived into the 6th century in most of Britain, ready to be reformed by the monastic pioneers. It was plainly feeble, the ghost of an urban church in a land where what remained of the towns had lost their grip upon the country. Even in Europe, where towns retained authority, the language of the church equated the country folk, *pagani*, with non-Christians, and for centuries churchmen had cause to condemn continuing heathen rites; for though no other organised religion remained, men who accepted Christianity did not thereby cease to be pagan. In Britain, Samson and others attacked heathen ceremonies and their successors were obliged to admit many pre-Christian observances, which were tolerated for centuries to come. The late Roman missionary adherents of Victricius and Martin had little time to evangelise the countryside or establish rural priests and churches before disaster overwhelmed them; and when the advancing frontiers of archaeology learn to recognise the religious beliefs of the early 6th-century warlords and their peasant subjects, they are also likely to uncover rites outrageous to the faith of devout Christians. Christianity was still the religion of kings and lords and townsmen, and nothing suggests that anything but the name had touched the bulk of the rural population before the coming of the monks. To most of the peasants, the monks brought not only monasteries, but Christianity itself. Thanks to the upheavals of the fifth century, the monastic reformers found their first response and strongest centre in the lands about the Severn estuary, the only region of Roman lowland wealth that the wars had spared; there, the example of the reformers inspired a mass movement in the 540s, but in less than a generation, before it had had time to arouse comparable enthusiasm in the north and in the fertile lowlands, English conquest cut short its expansion. After the conquest, monasteries and Christianity were carried to the north and the lowlands, not by the British monks, but by their Irish pupils.

Ireland

The fervour of British monasticism was soon spent, cut short by the agony of national defeat; but in Ireland the monasteries were to retain an inexhaustible vitality for centuries, and to impart it to most of Europe. The Irish and the British movements grew up together, each constantly renewing the inspiration of the other. The traditions of both countries acknowledge their mutual debt without rivalry. Christianity itself had come from Britain, in the time of Patrick. After him Mocteus, Mael and many others of the first Irish Christian leaders were British; the earliest Irish abbot, Enda, was schooled in Britain and guided in his novel experiment by British monks. But from the beginning the Irish

MAP 27 MONKS IN IRELAND

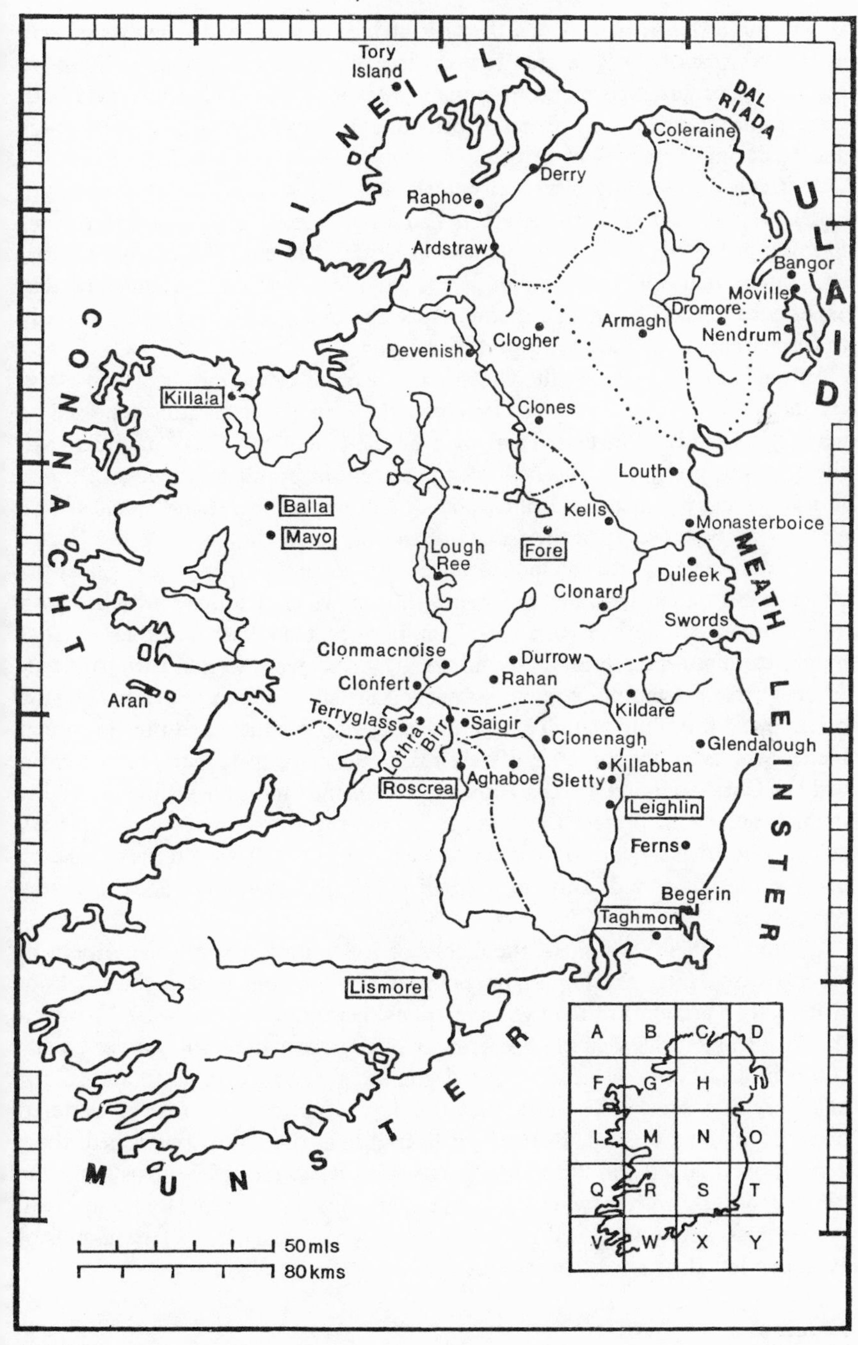

Chief Foundations of ● The 6th Century; ▭ The 7th Century, Inset Irish National Grid

also inspired the British; it was the visit of Irish monks, and a few years' stay in Ireland, that enabled Samson to break free of the easy European traditions of early British monasticism and to found a mass movement. He and David both came from the most Irish region of Britain, and David had both Irish teachers and Irish pupils, as well as British.

Monastic Christianity blazed as fiercely and as fast in Ireland as in Britain, and at the same time; for Irishmen had similar reasons to welcome the reforming preachers. The Irish colonists in Britain had experienced the material and intellectual sophistication of Rome, and had transmitted some of that experience to their kinsmen at home, especially in the south. Ireland was ready to learn from Rome, and to respect its religion.

In the later 5th century, the Christian religion of Rome meant bishops, who consorted with kings. To most Irishmen the bishops necessarily appeared as new style Druids, wizards strengthened by the power of a Deity mightier than the ancestral gods; but they had not the stature of prophets, capable of transforming society. Then, in Britain and in Europe, as in Ireland, monks were a minor excrescence upon the fringes of the Christian church.

In Britain in the 530s the monks voiced the protest of the subject against the violence of tyrants. Irishmen suffered a similar evil. For a hundred years Irish attacks upon Britain had been stilled; military captains had used their arms at home, to found kingdoms great and small, whose wars wasted their subjects. Abortive recent attempts to revive assaults on Britain had been beaten back by the brief power of Arthur's empire, and returning warriors increased the violence at home. Soon after, the successes of the British reformers made their faith the main form of Christianity on the coasts that faced Ireland, and gave visible proof that monasteries could protect the humble against the worst excesses of arbitrary rulers. The Irish welcomed their example, and for most Irishmen the monastery became the first and only form of Christianity that touched their lives directly.

Thanks to their early links, the monks of Ireland grew from small groups of eccentrics to a large and important community at the same time as the monks of Britain. The accounts of the two generations that intervened in Ireland between the death of Patrick and the foundation of the great monastic houses chiefly concern the labours of bishops, in a dozen territorial sees, in north and south; of a very few monasteries, mostly in the north; and of a number of scattered hermits, many of them British. Irish tradition rightly distinguished these generations, named the 'first order', whose leaders were 'all bishops', and the 'second order', with 'few bishops and many priests', when large and small monasteries were established in great numbers, and many tens of thousands of Irishmen left their homes to join them.

Finnian

The Irish records are much fuller than the British, and give the same close dates many times over. The 'second order' began in the last years of king Tuathal, who reigned from 532 to 544. The 'master of the saints', called the 'abbot of the second order', the 'best of the saints', was Finnian of Clonard. He died in the plague, about 550, after many years' work. He was baptised by Abban, nephew and companion of bishop Ibar, who had died in 499, and he was educated by Foirtchern, Patrick's royal convert, who was born about 440, the grandson of Loegaire of Ireland and of Vortigern of Britain. Finnian was an almost exact contemporary of Samson and of Gildas, born about the years 490 to 500, very near to the time of Badon. At the age of thirty Finnian went to 'study with the elders of Britain', and on his return brought two British monks with him. He was well received by king Muiredach of south Leinster, who reigned about the years 530 to 560, and set out on a missionary tour through Leinster and Connacht, preaching the ideas that he had learned in Britain, at first founding a few small monasteries, at one of which, Mugny, he is said to have stayed for 'seven years'.

After his travels, Finnian established his permanent home at Clonard and made it the nursery of Irish monasticism. The date cannot be far from 540, since a previous incident is dated to the reign of Tuathal, and is therefore later than 532; it was also some considerable time before his death about 550. The place was central, on the borders of Meath and Leinster, about twenty miles from the royal capital of Tara, and the same distance from Brigit's great house at Kildare, previously the largest monastic centre in Ireland. The area was peculiarly suitable, and deliberately chosen, for many of the principal houses founded by Finnian's pupils, Durrow, Birr, Clonmacnoise, Clonfert, Terryglass and others, lie close together, south-west of Clonard, concentrated in a small area barely thirty miles square, which straddles the frontiers between the four provincial kingdoms of Meath and Leinster, Connacht and Munster. Unlike their fifth-century predecessors, the monks chose a territory as withdrawn as possible from the seats of power of the main kings, and its many monasteries early made it a compact region, the heartland of the new society. In eastern and central Ireland men responded to its promise, but in the west, in Donegal, Connacht and western Munster, no major mainland houses are recorded till the seventh century, and then they are few.

Finnian's teaching was reinforced by the success of his monastic colleagues in Britain. 'The saints of Ireland came from every point to learn wisdom from him' at Clonard. The claims made by the authors of his Life are also accepted by the biographers of his pupils. Many of them came to him from other teachers, Columba of Iona from Gemman, Columba of Terryglass from Colman Cule, Ciaran of Clonmacnoise, the 'smith's son', from Enda's Aran. They, and many others who left a great name in Ireland, were for a few years contemporaries at Clonard. Women came too. Finnian had to assign a king's daughter for a short time to the care of the embarrassed Ciaran, 'until we can build a house for virgins'. The house was soon built, and placed under the care of Finnian's mother and sister. His pupil Dagaeus, and others later in the century vigorously encouraged double monasteries for both sexes.

Finnian's monks lived by their own labour, not on rents. He was

> full of knowledge, like a scribe most learned in teaching the law of God's commands. . . . With great tenderness he healed the minds and bodies of those who came to him. . . . From a pure heart he loved others. . . . He ate nothing but bread and vegetables, and drank nothing but water, save that on feast days he partook of a little wheaten bread, a small piece of fish, and a cup of beer or whey. . . . He never slept on a bed, but on the bare ground, with a stone for a pillow. . . . He was kind to others, austere and harsh to himself.

His diet and habit are akin to the rule of David, though the tenderness, emphasised again and again in the Irish tradition of his pupils, is not matched in the tradition of David in Britain. The Irish-language Life of Finnian tells a picturesque tale, that while in Britain he was called upon to adjudicate between David, Cathmael (Cadoc) and Gildas, contestants for the 'headship and abbacy of the island of Britain', and decided for David. The setting is unhistorical, for the controversy did not mature until after Finnian's death; but it enshrines a historical truth, for the discipline that Ireland learnt from Finnian was nearer to the rule of David than to the attitudes of Cadoc or of Gildas.

Finnian died in the plague, not much more than ten years after the foundation of Clonard. Several of his pupils had already left him. Ciaran, born about 517, and Columba of Iona, born about 521, were in their twenties, Columba of Terryglass probably somewhat older. Their lives were modest, but less austere than Finnian's. Ciaran went to an island in Lough Ree, and left it to found Clonmacnoise a year before his death, in 550. Tradition makes Ciaran's Clonmacnoise less strict than Clonard. He performed a miracle with wine brought by 'merchants from Gaul', but wine was a drink as alien to Finnian as to David, and so was the commercial agriculture that made such imports possible.

The plague wasted the Irish saints even more severely than the British. But the survivors outdid the energy of their predecessors, and the movement was spread by Finnian's pupils and by their pupils thereafter; the heirs of Columba of Iona were to win the greater part of the English to Christianity and monasticism. Fintan of Clonenagh was a pupil of Columba of Terryglass, and Comgall, who lived from 515 to 605, studied at both Clonenagh and at Ciaran's Clonmacnoise before he founded the great Irish school of Bangor in 559. There his outstanding pupil was Columban, who left Bangor for Gaul in 590, at the age of fifty, to found the monasteries of Luxeuil and Bobbio and to initiate the monasticism of the Franks and Lombards. Columban's numerous surviving letters are almost the only contemporary words that survive from early Irish monasticism, and are our only authentic guide to the outlook and aims of a sixth-century Irish monk, born within a year or so of the foundation of Clonard. That outlook is in essentials the same that the medieval Lives attribute to Finnian, Comgall and their fellows.

Columba

The greatest of the second generation monks was Columba. He was born an heir to the throne of Ireland, and in adult years his tremendous personality overshadowed his cousins, to whom the throne passed. Royal status as well as his personal stature set him apart from other men and other monks. Tradition contrasted him with the plebeian Ciaran, with whom he is said to have quarrelled in youth. The Columban version emphasises that the dispute turned on conflicting views, both widely held, and not on personalities alone, for Ciaran died at the age of 33 leaving a golden memory, but Columba's long life was stormy; he is made to comment

> Blessed is God who called Ciaran from this world in his youth. If he had lived to old age, he would have aroused many men's hostility.

Columba cannot have been much more than twenty when he came to Finnian, and in his early years he did not forget his birth. He placed his first principal monastery at Derry, in his own territory, hard by the court of his royal cousin. Plain monks might well trust a man of Ciaran's plebeian origins more readily. Yet though some might fear, many more men joined the monasteries of the royal monk than those of any lesser founder. By the time of his decisive quarrel with king Diarmait in 561, he commanded by far the largest body of monks in Ireland, as well as the largest secular army. He fought for the rights of an independent church against a king who opposed its claims. But the armies that won the battle of Cuil Dremhni were those of his dynastic relatives and their allies. Columba was personally present at the battle, praying for his own side against his monastic rival Finnian of Moville, who prayed for his enemies. Men believed in the power of prayer and attributed both the Ui Neill victory and the fearful slaughter to the greater efficacy of Columba's prayer. There was a real danger that the Christian saint might inherit the authority of the Druid, and also of the pagan king, that one man might become both head of the church and master of the secular kingdom.

Adomnan, writing a century after Columba's death, reports the sequel. Columba was excommunicated by a synod 'on certain pardonable and excusable charges', wrongly as the future showed.

> When St. Brendan of ... Birr ... kissed him, some of the elders protested ..., 'Why do you ... kiss the excommunicate?' Brendan answered, 'I have seen a column of bright fire going before the man of God whom you reject, and angels accompanying

> him'.... They did not then dare to proceed with the excommunication.... This happened at Telltown.

Adomnan elsewhere sets down what he considers 'excusable charges'; among his list of Columba's merits, he includes the claim that

> in the terrible clash of battle, the power of his prayer obtained from God that some rulers should be victorious and other kings be conquered.

Prayer so used seemed a virtue to Adomnan in Iona a century later; but it was a dangerous offence to Columba's contemporaries. The tradition of Derry is more prosaic, told with greater detail and less apology.

> When the news of the battle came to the ears of the saints of Ireland, Columba was assailed as the author and occasion of so great a loss of life. A general meeting decided that it was proper for him to perform a solemn penance, to be determined by Saint Lasrian.... Lasrian enjoined him to leave Ireland and his family, and to spend the rest of his life in exile abroad, where he might win more souls for Christ than he had caused to die in battle. Columba sadly undertook the penance prescribed, saying to Lasrian 'So be it'.

Lasrian of Devenish was the eldest of the Irish saints. His wisdom and the courage of Brendan solved an intolerable dilemma. Events had passed almost beyond the control of personalities, for the pardon or the punishment of Columba equally threatened to destroy the monks. Their movement had been born in protest against dynastic warfare and military violence, but now the greatest of the monks was seen to have caused slaughter on an outrageous scale; yet all men knew that he had fought chiefly to uphold the churchman's right of sanctuary. It was impossible to ignore his offence, but also impossible to abandon the cause he had defended. Excommunication threatened a still greater danger, underlined because the synod was convened at Telltown, in the territory of his enemy Diarmait. To have condemned Columba then and there invited the convocation of a counter-synod in Ui Neill lands, whose opposite anathema might threaten a religious war fought with sword and spear. If Columba's action were condoned, then the churchman's prayer became a military weapon necessary to the armament of all kings; if he were excommunicated at Diarmait's behest, the church submitted to the will of the High King on earth.

Exile without excommunication, voluntarily accepted, removed an appalling danger. Columba remained head of the community of Columban monasteries; his exile stilled the threat inherent in his royalty, and warned future churchmen against over-involvement in the political ambition of kings. The lesson was learnt, and the records of the next century are rich in stories of monks and abbots who deemed it proper to aid their kings with prayer in defence of their own subjects against enemy invaders, but condemned their own rulers when they attacked their neighbours. This was the attitude that Irish monks were to bring to Northumbria, and to teach to Bede, and that the Irish and the English were to impress upon the churchmen of Europe.

Gildas in Ireland

More than twenty years had passed since the initial outburst of monastic enthusiasm. The monks had met and overcome the enmity of great kings, even before Columba's wars. As in Britain, they had run foul of the lesser lords whose manpower they took away, and had been denounced as seducers, *seductores*. Now the monasteries were established beyond challenge; but rapid spontaneous growth had brought differences of outlook, practice and discipline, whose danger the crisis signalled. It was time to take stock and consolidate.

The Irish looked abroad for guidance. The tradition of Gildas, preserved in Brittany, held that he was summoned to Ireland by king Ainmere to 'restore ecclesiastical order'; he taught the Irish 'the rule of regular discipline', and put emphasis on the recruitment of new monks from among 'the poor as well as the nobility', and on freeing those 'enslaved by the tyrants'. Irish tradition also held that after Columba's exile

> the elders of Ireland sent trustworthy envoys with a letter to Saint Gildas. . . . When he read their letters, and also Columba's . . . he commented 'The man who wrote this is filled with the holy Spirit.' One of the envoys answered 'Yes, he is. But he has none the less been censured by a synod of Ireland, because he ordered his family to flight, when they were in danger of death.'

Irish tradition also attributed its liturgy to Gildas, together with David and Docco. Among the British, the Cambrian Annals enters Gildas' journey to Ireland under the year 565, two years after Columba's exile. The tradition survives independently in the three countries, and is confirmed by contemporary notices. Thirty years later, Columban cited to Gregory the Great a ruling given by 'Gilta' to 'Vinianus', Finnian. Columban reported Gildas' advice to an Irish monastic leader. He was a contemporary, and also a first-hand witness. Aged about 25 in 565, the year in which Gildas is said to have visited Ireland, he was a monk at Comgall's Bangor. Comgall was a close associate of Columba, deeply involved in the crisis, and visited him in Iona, also in the year 565. In making such a visit in that year he cannot but have conveyed Gildas' views to Columba, or Columba's to Gildas, or both. Bangor was already a pre-eminent monastery, that must have entertained Gildas during his visit. It is likely that Columban then met Gildas personally and heard his advice himself. Parts of the advice are extant, in a number of extracts from the letters of Gildas, preserved in Irish texts, that deal with various problems of monastic discipline, and also in the Penitential, or monastic Rule, that bears Gildas' name and is probably substantially his work.

The Rule of Gildas contrasts sharply with the Penitential ascribed to David. David's rules are limited to prescribing heavy punishment for grave sins, sexual offences, murder, perjury, drunkenness, usury and the like. They had little influence on later Irish regulations. But Gildas' Rule and the late sixth-century Penitential of Finnian, perhaps the Vinianus to whom he wrote, underlie the seventh-century Rules of Cummian, and of Columban, which form the main basis of later Irish monastic discipline. Unlike David, Gildas ignores murder, perjury, usury, and concentrates on a score of commonsense rulings concerned with the normal problems of day-to-day monastic life.

> A man who nurses anger long in his heart is in death . . . for anger breeds murder. . . . A monk who thinks another has wronged him must tell his abbot, not as an accusation, but as a genuine effort to heal the breach.

Penances are lighter, and vary with the circumstances of the individual and of the monastery, as well as of the offence; the punishment of three hours' standing night vigil is to be enforced only

> if there is plenty of beer and meat in the monastery, and the man is of strong physique; if the food is poor, let him recite twenty-eight or thirty psalms, or do extra work.

Common sense enjoins masses for good kings, not bad ones, and prompts the final tactful exhortation,

> if a monk sees one of the brethren breaking rules, he must tell his abbot. He should not be deemed an informer . . . provided that he first tries to persuade the wrongdoer to make a private confession to the abbot.

In his letters Gildas pleaded with the clergy to accept the authority of a superior without dispute, and with ecclesiastical superiors not to despise their clergy. The language and detail of the regulations imply that they were first devised for Britain; but they were preserved in Ireland, by Irishmen who adapted them from Gildas. Their controlled and disciplined austerity discountenances fierce asceticism, and matches the concept of the abbot's rule patterned by Finnian of Clonard, 'kind to others, harsh and austere to himself'.

Irish monasticism easily accepted a workable blend of the divergent interpretations of the monastic ideal. It lacked the tensions that had sharpened conflict in Britain. It had inherited no Roman legacy of wealthy landowners who lived a monastic life in their own mansions; it was equally free of the zealous radicalism that was provoked by the great inequalities of wealth in Britain, and was continued by the traditions of David. Gildas' tolerant conservatism discouraged extreme asceticism, but the society of Ireland did not permit the opulent ease that had distressed Samson and David. The quiet, simple and affectionate life derived from Finnian and Gildas was now guaranteed against secular interference; unembarrassed by the cares of administering monastic estates, the monks were able to develop an astonishing outburst of creative energy.

Art

Their energy was many-sided. Bold inventions in agriculture changed the economy of much of Ireland. Contemplation of the universe prompted searching enquiry into scientific phenomena, as uninhibited as any speculations since those of Hellenistic Greece. Irish ideas were to disturb the received dogma of the church, but they stimulated the education and the learning of Europe for several centuries. Probably towards the end of the sixth century, and probably a little earlier than in Britain, the monks pioneered a vernacular alphabet, and began to write down both the scriptures, and thereafter the stories and traditions of their homeland, in the spoken language of the people. Irish became the first medieval European language to be written. Ireland needed literacy, for it had less Latin than Britain; but Irish example soon taught the British and the English to write their own tongues.

Literacy brought important consequences; but the outstanding intellectual achievement of the sixth-century monks was their art. Dagaeus, who probably died about 586

> ingeniously and wonderfully constructed for the abbots and other saints of Ireland bells ... staffs, crosses, reliquaries ... cups ... and book covers ... sometimes plain, sometimes decorated with gold and silver and precious stones.

He spent some time at 'the little monastery called the school' at Devenish where he 'taught reading and writing and manual skills', and thereafter passed 'many years' at Bangor, where, among other works, he

> wrote an outstanding Gospel, and made for it a marvellous case.

The Book of Durrow was written not many decades later, and the splendid manuscript art, that Dagaeus is held to have initiated, matured through the succeeding centuries.

A few books and some ornaments survive to illustrate the splendour of early Irish monastic art. But their greatest pride was in the churches that these works adorned. Most of the great churches have been altogether rebuilt in later ages, and in the few early buildings that remain the rough exterior masonry, now unplastered, and the bare interior give little idea of their original magnificence. One vivid picture is preserved in words. Cogitosus, the biographer of Brigit, described the great church of Kildare as it was about 650.

> I must not omit the miracle which attended the repairs to the church in which rest the bodies of Bishop Conlaed and the virgin Saint Brigit. They are placed in elaborate monuments, to right and left of the decorated altar, and are splendidly bedecked with gold and

> silver, jewels and precious stones, and have gold and silver crowns hanging above them.
>
> As the numbers of the faithful of both sexes grew, the church was extended, both in area at ground level and in height projecting upwards, and was decorated with paintings. It has three oratories within, divided by painted walls, under a single roof that spans the larger building.
>
> In the eastern part, a cross wall extends from one wall to the opposite wall, decorated with pictures and covered with linen. In its ends are two doors. Through the southern door the Bishop enters with his regular choir and those deputed to celebrate the rites and sacrifices to the Lord; through the other door, in the northern part of the cross wall, the Abbess enters with her girls and faithful widows to enjoy the feast of the body and blood of Jesus Christ. Another wall extends from the eastern part as far as the cross wall, and divides the paved floor of the buildings into two equal parts.
>
> The church has many windows, and on the south side one ornamented gate, through which the priests and the faithful people of the male sex enter the church, and another gate on the north side, through which the congregation of virgins and faithful women enter. So in one great basilica a large people may pray with one heart to Almighty God, in different places according to their orders and ranks and sexes, with walls between them.
>
> When the workmen set on its hinges the old door of the north gate, through which Saint Brigit used to enter the church, it could not cover all the newly constructed gate . . . unless a quarter were added to the door's height. When the workmen were deliberating whether to make a new and larger door, or whether to make a picture and add it to the old door . . . the leading craftsman of all Ireland gave wise advice, to pray that night to the Lord, with Saint Brigit. . . . Next morning the old door . . . covered the whole gateway.

Kildare was one among many great churches; many others are likely to have been as lavishly adorned, in the sixth century as well as the seventh.

Travel

The creative energy of the Irish monks was not confined to their homeland. Irishmen had travelled abroad for centuries, usually in arms. Peaceful travel had long been natural to pious Christians of all nations. Deep reverence drew churchmen and kings to Rome and Jerusalem, and humbler pilgrims also travelled easily. The curious document from fifth-century Gaul entitled the 'Pilgrimage of Aetheria' is a chatty letter written home by a middle-aged nun who toured the holy places of the east. Her journey was somewhat more strenuous than a modern tourist's, but her simple curiosity, her interest in her fellow-guests at the houses where she boarded, and her relentless questioning of her guides differ little. Pilgrimages like hers, to Rome or to Jerusalem, were normal, and wealthy Christians constructed numerous *xenodochia*, or lodging-houses, to accommodate the stream of pilgrims. Such relatively light-hearted tours lasted through the sixth and seventh centuries, and many tales in many Irish Lives name pilgrims, while several report attempts by senior abbots to discourage them. They had good reason, and so had monks in other lands. In the eighth century Boniface urged archbishop Cuthbert of Canterbury to get his synod and his princes to

> forbid matrons and nuns to make frequent journeys to Rome. Many of them die, and few keep their virtue. In most towns of Lombardy and Gaul, most of the whores are English. It is a scandal and disgrace to your church.

Boniface perhaps exaggerated; the scandal doubtless arose because the tourists ran out of money on their way home; and the eighth century was perhaps more depraved than the sixth and seventh. But Rome was a magnet that attracted tourist pilgrims in some numbers from the fourth century to the eighth. Fewer could afford the greater expense and effort of a visit to Jerusalem. But Gregory of Tours has a pathetic tale of a British monk who set out for Jerusalem in 577, clad in sheepskins. He got no further than Tours, where the brethren wondered at his extraordinary asceticism. But after eight years his excesses deranged his mind; he seized a knife and made violent attacks upon several people, whom he evidently mistook for the devil. Gregory had to chain him for two years until he died.

Exploration

Travel was normal. The evangelical journeys and the migrations of dedicated monks had a deeper purpose than those of the tourists. The sixth-century British pioneered. About 550, a British hermit, John of Chinon, encouraged the Frankish queen Radegund to renounce her rank and establish her monastery at Poitiers; she left her royal ornaments with him, lest she be tempted to return to the world. When Columban settled in the Vosges forty years later, he was saved from starvation during his first winter by Carantocus, abbot of Saulcy, in the Haute Saône. His name is British, but the monks he had recruited included natives, since his steward was called Marculf. No Lives and no traditions remember these British monks abroad; a few chance mentions notice their existence. In northern Gaul they were evidently numerous, for many scores of churches and places, from Brittany to central Belgium, are or were named after their leaders, and a substantial number also settled in northern Spain, where they preserved their identity for centuries. But in most of Europe, the memory of the British monks was overwhelmed by the larger and later influx of the Irish and the English.

The energies of Irish travellers at first sought a more ambitious goal outside Europe. The southern bishops Ailbe and Ibar are said to have been the first to send men to seek the Land of Promise, whither the pious might emigrate, across the Atlantic Ocean. The voyages continued, and Adomnan records three unsuccessful explorations of Cormac Ua Liathain in the northern ocean. A considerable fanciful literature concerns the explorers; most of it, in Irish language texts, is a jejune repetition of banal wonders that plainly bored its authors; but several of the Latin texts, especially those that concern Brendan of Clonfert and his companion, the British Malo, contain vivid detail. The stories are evidently travellers' tales conflated under the name of an individual. In one version, Brendan made his first voyage in large coracles containing up to forty men apiece, but the virgin Ita warned him:

> You will not find the promised land in the skins of dead animals. Seek out a shipwright who knows how to build you a timber vessel.

Brendan found the necessary skills and wood in Connacht, and

> the shipwrights and workmen asked that their only wages should be that they should be allowed to sail with the man of God.

He was told stories of a previous voyage made by Ternoc, apparently from Iceland, and made the same voyage himself. In the first account, the saints

> sailed westward. . . . We encountered a fog, so thick in all directions that we could hardly see the prow from the stern. . . . After what seemed like an hour, a great light shone around us and we saw a spacious land, full of plants, flowers and fruits. . . . We disembarked . . . and explored the island, and after fifteen days' effort failed to find its further shore. . . . On the fifteenth day we encountered a river flowing from east to west. . . . Then appeared a man in great splendour, who told us . . . 'The Lord has revealed to you this land, which is to be given to his saints at the end of time. By this river you are in the middle of the island. You may not go further. Return whence you came.' . . . He accompanied us back to our ships on the coast . . . and we returned through the same fog to the Island of Delight, where our brethren waited for our coming.

This was the tale Brendan was told. He made the same voyage, taking forty days to reach the fog bank and spending forty days on the island, whose climate reminded him of autumn in Ireland. But when he reached the river, it was a youth who appeared to him, and told him,

> this is the land that you have sought so long. Yet you may not discover it now, for the Lord has desired to show you his secrets in the ocean. Go back to your native land, and take with you as many of the fruits of this island and its jewels as your ships can carry. . . . For after the lapse of many centuries, this land will be made known to your successors, at a time when there will be a great persecution of the Christians.

Brendan is later made to prophesy that 'Britain will cleave to a great heresy before the day of judgement'. These extraordinary prophecies naturally suggest to the critical reader that he is confronted with a nineteenth-century text composed after extensive Irish migration to the American continent. But the manuscripts are assigned to the thirteenth century, or, at latest, early fourteenth, long before the voyage of Columbus, and both derive from a common original, which itself draws on an earlier lost Latin Life. The substance of the story dates to the ninth century. These tantalising tales invite speculation as to whether the Irish reached North America in the 6th century. They might be true, for though much might be the product of a lively imagination, details like the fogbanks in the area of Newfoundland are less imaginary; Iceland had an Irish population when the Norwegians arrived, in the 9th century, and the study of blood-groups suggests that it was larger than Norse tradition admits; seamen who could reach Iceland might as easily sail on to Newfoundland and beyond. But the question has little more than romantic interest. The Irish tales specifically assert that there was no settlement in the Land of Promise, whose permanent discovery was postponed. The importance of the stories lies less in speculation about their possible truth than in the fact that they were told and believed. If they were believed in Ireland, they were certainly known in Iceland, to hand for the Irish of Iceland to tell to Leif Erikson, before he sailed for Vinland. The Irish stories were well known in the middle ages, and contributed to the hopes of undiscovered land that made men willing to sail westward with Columbus to seek it.

Brendan's travels were not confined to the ocean. His journeys in Ireland involved him in violent dispute with king Diarmait. He warned him:

> Your kingdom is brought to an end, and will be given over to holy churchmen.

Deeds evidently followed words, for

> fifty royal towns were emptied at his word, and remained unpeopled, for their inhabitants had offended the holy man.

A boy was drowned through Brendan's fault, and the saints of Ireland decreed a penance, to be fixed by the virgin Ita. She sent him abroad, as Lasrian had sent Columba, though not for life. He visited Britain and Brittany, recruited British disciples and miraculously read Gildas' Greek texts, as easily as though they had been written in Latin. These fragmentary notices evidently condense passages in the original that the editor judged unfit to repeat. They imply that Brendan was involved in wars like Columba's. Detail is not preserved, for Brendan's endeavours in Ireland are known only through the standard collections of polite medieval Lives, and similar Lives of Columba also leave out his stormy vicissitudes. Other older tales survive of Columba, because he was a great prince, and founder of many houses. Brendan was not.

Missions

Voyages continued, but the great age of exploration is limited to the first generation of the monks. Brendan retired from the sea and from wars, and settled at Clonfert about 560; and his young companion Malo settled in Brittany in or about the same year. The lure of the transatlantic lands had appealed to hermits who longed to abandon the world. But monks of the second generation set a different ideal. Lasrian enjoined Columba to 'win more souls for Christ', but there were no souls to be won in the empty ocean. A few missions to the heathen are recorded in the early years of the movement. In the last years of the 5th century, a monk of Leinster on his way to Rome founded and named the monastery of Abingdon in the centre of a pagan English kingdom. The story was transcribed in circumstantial detail by the medieval Irish, who normally take small account of Irishmen abroad; it was preserved because it was in Irish eyes a minor incident, the occasion of a few miracles in the Life of a saint whose important work was performed in Ireland. It is confirmed by the medieval English monks of Abingdon, who had even less incentive to regard a fifth-century Irish founder as an honourable distinction. Their tradition told them that the history of their house began with 300 monks established on the 'hill of Abendoun' by the Irish Aben, 'in the time of the British', after the Romans, but before the English mastered Britain; their account noted archaeological confirmation, by the frequent excavation of 'crosses and statues', but placed its emphasis on the first English foundation, in the 7th century, when the monks and the name were transferred from the hill to the riverside. The detail of their story is corroborated by modern archaeological discovery. The Irish were well aware that the British were Christians, but they knew that 5th-century Abingdon was the centre of a pagan kingdom. The medieval English also knew that in British times, before the English conquered, Abingdon had been an English 'royal seat, where the people used to meet to deal with the . . . business of the kingdom'. Yet no one knew that they were right until 1934, when a sewer trench exposed a major pagan English burial-ground, a mile to the south-west of the Abbey.

The two independent accounts, that both show accurate knowledge of fifth-century history, agree too closely for coincidence. There is nothing unusual about the story except its early date, half a century before the main monastic movement matured; for other pagan English kingdoms permitted British and Irish monks to preach within their territories. The East Angles received Winwaloe of Brittany; the South Saxons tolerated the ineffectual cell of the Irish Dicuil at Bosham; and Malmesbury was founded and named by Maeldubh, another Irishman, among the west Saxons, about the time of their conversion to Christianity. No Lives record how and why these missionaries came, but one Irish tale preserves some details of the visit of Columba of Terryglass to an unnamed pagan Saxon kingdom. On his way home from Tours in the 540s he stayed with a king whose children had just died; 'he turned to the ashes and prayed, and called two sons and two daughters . . . back from the ashes to life.'

The children asked to be allowed to return to the life of the just in heaven, so 'they were baptised and slept again in their grave'. The miracle is a conventional consolation story, where the saint's comfort to the parents, that the children are better off in heaven, is coloured by a temporary resurrection, so that the children may personally assure the parents that they agree, and may be baptised to guarantee heaven. The use of the word 'ashes', *cinis*, emphasised by repetition, is startling. If it were deliberately invented, the author would have made much of his hero's unique miracle, for many saints revived corpses, but no other restored a cremated body to life. But the Irish knew nothing of pagan Saxon cremation, and it is not easy to see how the words got into the text unless they derive from a contemporary, more rational story that involved cremation. Such tales are all that was remembered of missions to the sixth-century English; though there were doubtless other forgotten incidents, it is likely that the missionary effort was slight before the later sixth century, without great effect.

The lasting impact of Irish monasticism upon foreigners begins with the exile of Columba of Iona. From the beginning it was two-edged. Irish monks converted pagans to Christianity; they also converted more mundane Christians to the monastic ideal. Columba emerged from his crisis greater and stronger. Exile transformed him into the 'dove of peace'. At first, exile was hard and bitter, a greater loss than the renunciation of the throne; in the poems ascribed to him he is made to sing of

> the homeless land of my sojourn, of sadness and grief.
> Alas, the voyage that I was made to make . . .
> For the fault that I went myself
> To the battle of Cuil. . . .
>
> I have loved Erin's land,
> Its waterfalls, all but its government. . . .
>
> Death is better in reproachless Erin
> Than everlasting life in Britain.

But it was in Britain that his name won everlasting life. He settled in the island of Iona and was welcomed by the Irish colonists, who had recently been subdued by the pagan Picts. He did not rally the Irish for a holy war of Christians against the heathen; he went alone to convert the Picts, and in time they were converted. Their conversion transformed the north. No longer alien barbarians, marked off by a separate culture and a hostile faith from the British of Clyde and Forth, they became one among several states who shared a common culture. Columba kept the northern powers at peace for most of his lifetime and enabled them to set in motion the processes that were to form Scotland. But he was much more than the national patron of northern Britain. His successors at Iona undertook the conversion of the English, and in the next century the Irish and the English began to infect Europeans with their monastic experience. Columba was the mightiest of the monastic founders within Ireland, the first to carry their example overseas; he left behind him successors who transmitted that example to the furthest regions.

Monasticism was born and nurtured by the British of the Severn lands, but grew to maturity in Ireland. There, the monk's urge to seek deserts ever further removed from the seats of kings blended with the national tradition of the Irish, that had long encouraged their adventurous youth to win new homes overseas. They had colonised Britain until Vortigern checked them; thereafter they explored the Atlantic, and found it barren; then their energy carried the faith that swept their country to the nations of Europe. Ireland remained the homeland of monastic enthusiasm and learning for centuries; Europe welcomed what had been a limited and local form of Christian organisation, and developed it into a principal institution of the medieval church.

CHAPTER TWENTY

THE SEVENTH CENTURY CHURCH

The Conversion of the English

Columba's government moved contemporaries and later ages by its impressive austerity, discipline and simplicity. Its greater glory lay in the future and, if a great man's stature is fitly to be judged by the quality of his successors, then Bede's cautious judgement must stand:

> whatever may have been the character of the man himself, it is quite certain that his successors were outstanding in their abstinence, their love of God, and in the discipline of their organised life.

He died in 597. In the same year Augustine landed in Kent, sent by Gregory the Great to convert the pagan English. The history of English Christianity is told in sources utterly different from those that preserve the records of Irish and British monks. Bede, born in 672, grew up within living memory of most of the events he recounts. He is also one of the world's great historians, ranking with Thucydides, Tacitus and Shakespeare in his ability to select an incident that describes an age and forms a judgement.

There are ample other sources. Lives of English saints are fewer, but several of those that survive are contemporary, and have been preserved in their original form. Bede and the Saxon Chronicle provide dates that in the 7th century need little question; and the English church was soon in regular contact with Europe, whose documented history confirms the main story. But though the nature of the sources changes, there is no break in the nature of the story that they tell. Bede has much to say of Irish Christians, something of British, and his picture of their outlook and behaviour does not differ from that which lies beneath the native texts. Change there was, for Christianity brought the English into the European community, and the conversion of the English profoundly affected the native British and Irish. But the Christianity of the British Isles is a continuing whole, and the absorption of the English appears as a new starting-point only if its earlier history is disregarded.

Augustine and Edwin

Augustine was well received. The men of Kent were converted at the instance of their king, who had long been married to a Christian Frankish princess.

Bede in a sentence calls Augustine's life austere and simple, but he paints him as a proud authoritarian priest, conscious of the majesty of a constituted hierarchy. Appointed bishop by the pope, he expected instant obedience from the British abbots of the west, though they had lived long without organised contact with Rome. He knew nothing of their previous religious experience, and showed no wish to understand it. At first, a large party among the British were ready to submit. But the advice of a wise and humble hermit persuaded them to test the manner of Augustine's authority. At their second meeting they were to arrive after him. If he rose courteously to greet them, they would know him as a true servant of Christ, and hear him obediently. But if he sat enthroned like a master, they would despise him as he despised them. Augustine sat, and the British rejected him. Bede's story is doubtless over simple in its detail; the deep distrust plainly required more than a single polite gesture to allay it, and the shrewd hermit no doubt suggested his test because he anticipated Augustine's reaction. But the philosophies that the story portrays are accurate enough.

At first, Kentish Christianity is not known to have reached further than nearby London, and it was rejected when its royal patron died. But within a decade it revived, and was carried to the north. Edwin of Northumbria married a Kentish princess and received bishop Paulinus from Kent. Bede describes the dark, stern, hook-nosed prelate, remote and intense, simple and compelling. After hearing him, at the old pagan capital of Goodmanham by Sancton, in the East Riding, one of Edwin's councillors epitomised the strength of the Christian appeal to the barbarian.

> This present life on earth seems to me, my king . . . as though we were sitting at supper . . . in the winter time, warmed by a bright fire burning in the middle of the hall, while the storms of wintry rain and snow rage without; when a single sparrow flies swiftly in through one entry and out by the other. In its little time indoors, the winter weather touches it not, yet its brief moment of security lasts but a second, as it passes from the winter to the winter, escaping our sight. So seems the life of man in its little season; what follows, and what went before, we know not. Therefore, if this new teaching brings anything more sure, we should follow it.

These deep emotions were reinforced by the robust materialism of the high-priest Coifi, who proclaimed:

> I am convinced that our old religion has nothing good and no advantage about it. For no man has been more zealous in the worship of the gods than I; yet there are many who gain larger gifts and great dignities from you, my king, and prosper more in all they aim to do and to acquire. If these gods of ours were any good, they would rather have helped me, who have served them eagerly.

Coifi then mounted the king's charger and speared the idols he had served, though weapons and stallions were taboo to priests, and commanded the assembly to burn down the temple. So violent a profanation, undertaken with impunity, on the authority of the high-priest and with the complicity of the national assembly, jolted men's minds into an irrevocable breach with the old faith. Edwin was baptised on Easter Eve 627, in a hastily constructed timber church at York, soon to be replaced by a stone building, and the rest of the Northumbrians were baptised in crowds in the ensuing years.

A few years later Edwin was destroyed by the British king Catwallaun, aided by the Mercians. Catwallaun's aim was the expulsion of the enemy, 'exterminating the whole English race within the boundaries of Britain' without regard for age, sex, or religion. He proved a 'barbarian crueller than a pagan', and was shortly driven out by the sons of Aethelferth, who had adopted the Christianity of Iona while in exile among the Scots. In the disaster, Paulinus hastily took ship for Kent, with the queen and the church plate. Only James the Deacon stayed, to teach Gregorian plainsong in quieter times, to converts who remembered his courage in adversity.

Oswald and Aedan

Oswald and Oswy, the sons of Aethelferth, naturally applied to Iona for a bishop. Iona had preserved its austerity, sending exemplary humble monks to serve the political communities of the north, so that Bede called it the 'head' of all the Scot and Pict houses, 'presiding over the ruling of their peoples'. Its authority was the stronger because it depended upon no enforceable royal grant, but upon the affectionate respect and free consent of entire populations; and it was stable because custom enjoined, as in many other Irish and British monastic communities, that the abbacy descend among the heirs of the founder's family. In 634 the abbot of Iona was a grandson of Columba's cousin, and also third cousin to the reigning High King of Ireland.

The first bishop was defeated by the 'indomitable barbarism' of the English, but his successor, Aedan, less 'rigid with unlearned listeners', preferred 'nourishment by the milk of milder doctrine, leading gradually towards the higher and more perfect commands of God'. His apostolic simplicity contrasted both with the land-hungry monks of Wales and with the ceremonial dignity of Roman priests. Bede observed:

> what chiefly won men to his teaching was that he lived with his monks the life that he preached. He made no effort to acquire worldly advantage. . . . all that kings or rich men gave him he cheerfully gave away to the first poor man he met. He travelled everywhere . . . on foot, never on horseback unless he had to. . . . Timidity or obsequiousness never restrained him from criticising the sins of the rich, and he never gave money to great men.

Aedan's gentle dignity blended the best traditions of the British and Irish, the austerity of David, without the arrogance that had disgusted Gildas; the wisdom of Illtud, without the embarrassment of inherited estates; and the authority of Columba, without the violence of his earlier years.

Aedan's church was spread by the conquering armies of Northumbria, who made themselves masters of England. When the West Saxon king was persuaded to accept Christianity, his Northumbrian suzerain stood sponsor at his baptism; the kings of the East Saxons and the Mercians went north for baptism by the banks of the Tyne. In the south and the midlands, as well as in the north, monasteries modelled on Iona proliferated, often double houses, for women and for men, on the pattern of Whithorn, of Finnian of Clonard, and of Dagaeus of Bangor. Barking and Chertsey near London were among the greater foundations, and Irish teachers established themselves in ruined Roman forts or towns, at Burgh Castle by Yarmouth and elsewhere. Churches were constructed in the central squares of the Roman towns, ancestors of the medieval cathedrals, and at other centres of government. They were often impressive buildings; at Brixworth near Northampton, possibly a principal royal centre of the south Mercians, an

---

Map 28

+ EARLY BISHOPS' SEES

□ NORTH ITALIAN CHURCHES

MAIN MONASTIC FOUNDATIONS

■ of Irish origin

● of Anglo-Irish origin

○ of English origin

× of British or Roman origin

⊗ possibly of British origin

DEDICATIONS TO BRITISH SAINTS

C Cyngar (Docco)

D David

G Gulval

M Melor

S Samson

W Winwaloe

MAP 28 MONKS IN THE ENGLISH KINGDOMS

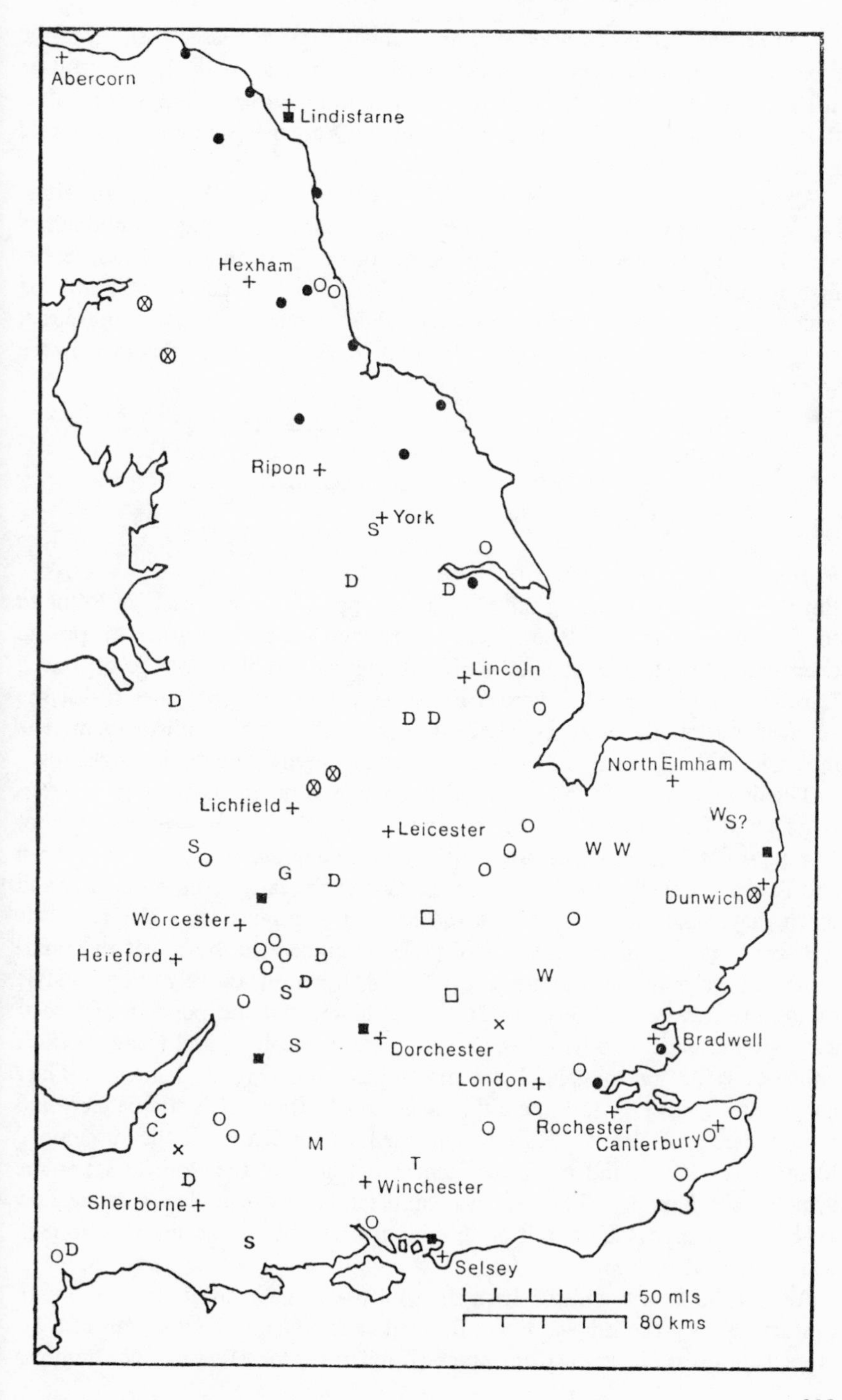

Italian architect imposed upon the midland countryside a large basilica, of the type most familiar at Ravenna, which has survived as a parish church, with its aisles and portico removed. It is almost unique in Europe north of the Alps, though a few other similar churches, notably at Wing in Buckinghamshire, were built in English lands at about the same time.

Many of the new abbots and bishops were Irish, and they brought some monks and clergy with them; but most of the members of the new communities were English, many of them of noble or royal birth. The simplicity of Iona was at first unchallenged. Aedan avoided Paulinus' metropolitan church of York; the ecclesiastical centre of Northumbria was established on the island of Lindisfarne, where the concepts of Iona more easily endured. Bede observed that even in the second generation the monks of Lindisfarne

> owned no money and no cattle. . . . They refused to accept land or estates for the building of monasteries, unless constrained thereto by the secular government. This custom continued in the churches of Northumbria for a long time after.

Rome and Easter

But there were many among the English who preferred the majesty of Rome to the humility of Ireland; they found their spokesman in Wilfred. A prelate determined to establish and uphold in Britain the visible power of organised European Christianity, he chose York as his centre and took pains to list the endowments of his churches, securing a royal charter to confirm them. His intransigent determination forced the issue to a speedy decision in England.

The dispute was new and many-sided; so long as the monasticism of western Britain and Ireland stayed within its remote Atlantic homelands, the church of Europe was not greatly interested in its unorthodox practices. But when Irish and British monks began to preach in Europe in the early seventh century, and when they came into contact with the mission of Augustine in England, differences began to matter. Successive popes reminded the Irish that their old-fashioned reckoning of the date of Easter and their provocatively different style of tonsure threatened the unity of Christendom; and the popes found their theology Pelagian. The Irish were uninterested in theology, and made no effort either to refute or to uphold the philosophy of a long-dead heretic. Their concern was with practical morality, the defence of the monk's simple piety and independent conscience. Wilfred demanded conformity with the disciplined hierarchy of Rome, and made the Roman tonsure and the Roman Easter the symbols of submission. The issue was simple in outline, complex in detail; how far must the monastic church of Britain and Ireland change in order to gain communion with Europe?

Among the British and the Irish the controversy lingered on into the eighth century. Among the English it was decided at the Synod of Whitby in 664. Its immediate occasion was a plain practical nuisance, for Oswy of Northumbria and his Kentish queen were obliged to observe Easter on different dates. Bishop Colman defended Irish usage on the authority of the third-century bishop Anatolius and of Columba. Wilfred disputed the mathematics attributed to Anatolius and impugned Columba as a false prophet, but he based his case upon the universal practice of Christians elsewhere, obedient to the successors of Peter, to whom Christ gave the keys of heaven; to which the king replied simply and shortly, 'I will not quarrel with such a doorkeeper'. Northumbria accepted the Roman Easter. Colman withdrew to Ireland with the minority among the English and the Irish. Like Aedan, he had been both abbot of Lindisfarne and bishop of the Northumbrians. The twin functions were now separated; an Englishman succeeded to the abbacy, the Irish Tuda to the bishopric.

Whitby was a commonsense compromise, excluding the extremists of both sides; for Wilfred also spent much of his life in exile. He strove not merely for outward conformity with Rome, but to create a church conceived in the Roman manner, headed by potent bishops who sat beside the kings, and to eliminate the anarchic, spontaneous independence of the Irish monasteries. He continued his fight, and failed. When Tuda died, the underking of Deira put Wilfred in his place, with his see in the royal city of York, and sent him to Europe for consecration. But while he was away Oswy took control of York and installed as bishop an English pupil of Aedan, Chad of Lastingham, whose name was British. Oswy sought to combine the best of both churches, to gain communion with Rome and Europe, but to retain the Irish piety and the independence of the new English church; for Chad was

> dedicated to humility, abstinence and study; he preached in town and country, in cottage, village and fort, not riding, but walking on foot like the apostles; for he was a pupil of Aedan, and endeavoured to instruct his hearers according to Aedan's principles and practice.

When Wilfred returned, Oswy refused to accept him; he retired to Ripon, whence he was summoned as bishop to the new frontier kingdom of Mercia.

Theodore and Wilfred

The conflict of opposing philosophies was resolved by Rome. The see of Canterbury was vacant, and the pope made an extraordinary appointment; his nominee, Theodore, was a Greek of Tarsus in Asia Minor, an elderly scholar, seventy years old when he arrived in 669. The aged academic seemed altogether unfitted for his task, too old to tackle it before he died. But he lived to the age of eighty-eight, and shaped the English church for all time. His tact successfully blended the pious energy of the Anglo-Irish monasteries with episcopal discipline, and did so by encouragement rather than by command. When Wilfred complained that Chad's consecration was uncanonical, Chad replied,

> I will gladly resign. I never thought myself worthy, but I agreed to do as I was ordered, for obedience sake;

for he much preferred the quiet of Lastingham. Theodore removed the complaint by consecrating him canonically, but advised him to ride henceforth, gently enforcing his advice by helping him into the saddle with his own hand; for the spiritual needs of a vast diocese were inadequately served by the slow progress of a walking bishop. Wilfred's grievance was appeased by an exchange of diocese; Wilfred went to York and Chad to Mercia, establishing his see at Lichfield, in 669, barely fifteen years after the English conquest of the region.

Wilfred was given the opportunity to prove himself; within eight years his overweening pride had brought about his downfall. He endeavoured to assert the Roman concept of a great bishop who stood behind his king and guided him to greater glory. His ambition deeply affronted both the secular and ecclesiastical morality of Irish and Northumbrian Christianity; but he at first found an eager ally in Egferth, the new king of Northumbria, who succeeded his father Oswy in 670. Wilfred's close companion and biographer, Eddius, attributes to the favour of Wilfred the military successes of the king, who 'filled two rivers' with the corpses of 'vicious Picts', reducing them to 'slavery', and slew the Mercians in 'countless numbers', thereby making Wilfred 'bishop of the British, the Irish, and the Picts as well as of the southern English'. Bede, who was a boy at the time, expressed the monastic attitude; he condemned Egbert's second Pictish expedition as 'rash', undertaken 'against the emphatic veto of his advisers, especially of . . . bishop Cuthbert'; and denounced his invasion of Ireland as a

> wretched devastation of an inoffensive people, who had always been distinguished by their friendship towards the English nation,

also undertaken against the protest of 'the most reverend Father Egbert'.

Wilfred made his worldly ambition as evident at home. Eddius called him 'head of the church', *caput ecclesiae*, and delighted in the splendour of his abbey at Hexham, adorned with

> magnificent ornaments of gold and silver, and altars decorated with purple and silk.

Irish monasteries took pleasure in beautiful and valuable ornament, for the greater glory of God, but Wilfred made them symbols of the bishop's glory. The king soon came to resent his

> worldly glory and wealth . . . his vast army of retainers, equipped with royal livery and weapons

and exiled him in 678. Like Cardinal Wolsey long after, he had served his king too well. Archbishop Theodore endorsed the king's action, split the great northern diocese, and opposed Wilfred's appeals to Rome.

The contest was decided. Though Wilfred's determined resistance won him a brief return, the structure of the Anglo-Irish church was secure. Wilfred proclaimed that his life's aim had been to 'root out from the church the foul weeds sown by the Irish'. He failed, for the Northumbrian laity as well as the churchmen preferred the Irish plant to Wilfred's. When Egferth's rash expedition cost him his life, they chose as their successor his half-brother Aldfrith, born of an Irish mother, reared in Ireland and Iona, in the full knowledge that he was an eminent scholar, patron of the monks, resolutely opposed to aggressive wars and to prelacy. His guidance consolidated the monastic church, built upon the Irish principles of the simplicity and independence of Iona. Northumbrian art and scholarship equalled its Irish original, outshining the cathedral monastery of Canterbury and the enfeebled survivors of Roman Britain, Whithorn and St. Albans. The English converts brought discipline, and during the years of Wilfred's struggle, Benedict Biscop and Ceolfred introduced the rule of Benedict of Nursia, patterned in their new foundation at Wearmouth and Jarrow, in 674. One of their early pupils was Bede, who entered the monastery in 680. He was not only a great historian, but a philosopher and a mathematician as well, perhaps the most influential European scholar of the early middle ages. The quiet strength of Bede's wisdom is the measure of the church that the Irish built in England.

The Irish founded the Northumbrian church, but the English organised it, under the guidance of archbishop Theodore; and the Northumbrian church was the principal influence in the conversion of the rest of England, outside Kent. Its early organisation, before the time of Theodore, was modelled on the practice of Iona. But the organisation of Iona already seemed strange to Bede; writing ninety years after Aedan had come to Lindisfarne, he remarked that

> it is the custom of the island to have a governor who is an abbot and a priest, to whose authority the whole province, even its bishops, must defer, a most unusual form of organisation. Therein they follow the example of their first teacher, Columba, who was not a bishop, but a priest and a monk.

Bishops and Abbots

The early ecclesiastical organisation of the British Isles surprised and surprises all who are accustomed to the Roman hierarchy of Europe. The British, the Irish and the English each came to Christianity from a different starting-point; each was dominated by the great number of their monasteries, that were still not matched in Europe, and each adapted itself to Rome and Europe in a different manner. In Wales the greater abbots of each kingdom served as bishops, at St. David's in Demetia, Llanbadarn in Cardigan, Bangor in western Gwynedd, and later St. Asaph in eastern Gwynedd; the successors of Tyssilio in Powys and of Teilo in Ystrad Tywi are at times styled 'bishop'; and in Glevissig the kings were served by three principal abbots, while the seats of bishops varied with the union and division of the political kingdom until a permanent see was settled at Llandaff, by Cardiff, probably in the 9th century.

Fifth-century Ireland was also provided with territorial bishops, with seats near the royal residences of major kingdoms; and at first they and their priests constituted a normal married clergy. But as monasteries multiplied in the sixth century, more and more monks became bishops, and some great abbots, like Maedoc and his successors at Ferns in Leinster, became bishops of their kingdoms, as in Wales. But such examples were few. Most of the dynasties sought bishops for their own kingdoms, and some obtained them, nearly always accepting monks. The bishop who was a monk remained under the discipline of his abbot. The office of bishop was less esteemed; the greater eminence of the abbot was so generally admitted that Irish usage sometimes describes the Pope as 'abbot of Rome', and Christ as 'abbot of Heaven'.

This was the ecclesiastical organisation that Columba brought to Iona, and Aedan to Northumbria. In the far north, one bishop sufficed for the Picts and one for the Scot colonists; and when the Scot king acquired the Pictish throne, a single bishop seemed natural and adequate for the combined kingdom until the coming of English and Norman influence; and as far as is known, a single bishop also governed the church of the Clyde. So at first in Northumbria, Aedan was both abbot of Lindisfarne and bishop of the Northumbrians, and sent his monks where they were needed, as priests or as bishops; so Cedd, brother of Chad, was sent as bishop to the East Saxons, and in the tradition of Aedan was also abbot of a monastery, sited far from the royal residence, in the ruined Roman fort of Othona, Bradwell-on-Sea. But political and ecclesiastical problems soon eroded Irish precedent; when Irish monks became the first bishops of the Middle Angles and the Mercians, they remained subject to an abbot who was also the Northumbrian bishop; but when their kings rejected Northumbrian political supremacy, they could no longer tolerate Northumbrian primacy over their church. Moreover, since the early initiative of Gregory in Kent had made the metropolitan of Canterbury primate of all the English, the authority of Rome required that bishops should be subject to him, not to a remote island abbot.

The political events of the 660s and 670s enabled Theodore to find a convenient solution, that reconciled ecclesiastical hierarchy with practical needs. The Mercian kings brought all the southern English under their political control, but failed to reduce the Northumbrians. In 664, while the kingdoms still disputed sovereignty, the Northumbrian abbacy and bishopric were divided, so that the southern monks who obeyed the abbot of Lindisfarne no longer owed allegiance to the national bishop of the Northumbrians at York. Permanent solution was reached a few years later. After a fearful battle in 679, Theodore's insistence persuaded the Northumbrian and Mercian kings to forgo claims to sovereignty over each other, and to accept the lower Trent as their lasting frontier. Ecclesiastical organisation matched the political agreement. The northerners and the southerners were each provided with an archbishop; the Northumbrians acquiesced in the nominal precedence of Canterbury; since the superior might of the Mercian armies was admitted in Kent, the Mercian kings remained content with the ecclesiastical primacy of Canterbury, save for a few years, when the vanity of Offa sought and obtained the rank of archbishop for his own Mercian bishop at Lichfield. From the time of Theodore, the secular and ecclesiastical government of the English was divided between the empire of the Mercians and the kingdom of the Northumbrians. The solution satisfied the church, for the old causes of divided loyalty dwindled; thirty or forty years after the conversion of the southern English, Irish clergy from Lindisfarne were no longer needed; kings might be served by a new generation of home bred English bishops, untrammelled by personal ties with a rival kingdom. The problems of the past had been by-products of the contrasting structure of the Irish and the Roman church; among the English they were solved by the compromise of Whitby and the tact of Theodore. The English church retained its independent monasteries, but it accepted territorial bishoprics subject to metropolitans, in conformity with Roman usage. In remote Wales conformity was of less moment, and the externals of Easter date and tonsure that symbolised conformity were not accepted until 768, on the initiative of Nennius' teacher, bishop Elvodug of Gwynedd.

The Irish Church

The problems of Ireland were more complex. There was no metropolitan see whose authority an Irish equivalent of Theodore might exercise, and deep differences divided north and south. The majority of the southerners early favoured conformity with Rome, but most of the north long resisted. The monasteries were grouped, not as in northern Britain, under the tutelage of a single great foundation, but in a dozen different substantial groups, with a large number of small independent houses as well. Organisational unity of some sort was urgent, and partisans on both sides felt the need of a metropolitan episcopate. The earliest candidate, put forward about 650, was the southern see of Kildare, in northern Leinster. But the claim of Kildare was wholly alien to the north, and is not mentioned save in the contemporary literature of the controversy. The ultimate basis of organisational unity was prepared by bishop Aed, of Sletty in south Leinster, who ostentatiously placed his own church under the patronage of Armagh. Armagh was not only the principal bishopric of the north. It was the senior bishopric of Ireland, named first in the early 7th-century papal lists. It had been founded by Patrick, and remained the most important of his monasteries. Its abbots had commonly been bishops, who were regarded as the successors of Patrick, and Patrick had been consecrated in Rome, first bishop of the Irish, and in his own day sole bishop. He was the only man who had ever been supreme bishop of all the Irish. The half-forgotten memory of Patrick was revived, and employed to unite the contending parties under his neutral name. The extraordinary fictions of Tirechan and his imitators pretended that in the middle of the fifth century Patrick had been recognised as metropolitan by nearly 500 bishops, and had founded innumerable churches all over Ireland; no one believed these absurd stories, but they were happily accepted by northern patriots, and prudently endorsed by the southern champions of unity with Rome.

The southern partisans of the Roman Easter offered allegiance to a northern metropolitan before the north conformed; and the honorary primacy of Armagh was proved to be inoffensive, not irksome to the independence of existing monasteries. At the end of the seventh century, the efforts of the principal northern champions of conformity, Adomnan and the English-born Egbert of Iona, induced their colleagues to accept simultaneously the Roman Easter and the primacy of Armagh; with it came the priority of Patrick over Brigit and the southern saints, and the enhancement of episcopal authority. The struggle was long and slow. Adomnan failed to convince his own monks, and Iona itself did not conform until 716, after his death. The conflict ended with an episcopate independent of the monks, directed by its metropolitan, concerned with the guidance of kings and the spiritual needs of laymen, while monasteries concentrated upon their art and learning, and upon the despatch of missionaries to foreign lands.

Monks in Europe

Columban was the first of the insular monks to make a weighty impact on Europe. For a quarter of a century he had served his abbot, Comgall, Columba's close friend. When he landed in Gaul in 590, he had behind him their experience, and the teachings of Finnian, David and Gildas; he quoted Gildas with respect, and may have known him personally. His stern simplicity shattered the conventions of Frankish Christianity. When he strode into the court of one Merovingian king and denounced his lechery and misgovernment to his face; when he adjured another to forswear his earthly crown for the greater glory of a tonsure; when

---

Map 29

- ▬ Churches and monasteries of British origin or inspiration
- ● Monasteries of Irish origin, inspiration or influence
- O Monasteries founded by Boniface, Willibrord and their English, Irish and German associates
- ? Churches and monasteries possibly of Irish or English origin, inspiration or influence

MAP 29 MONKS ABROAD

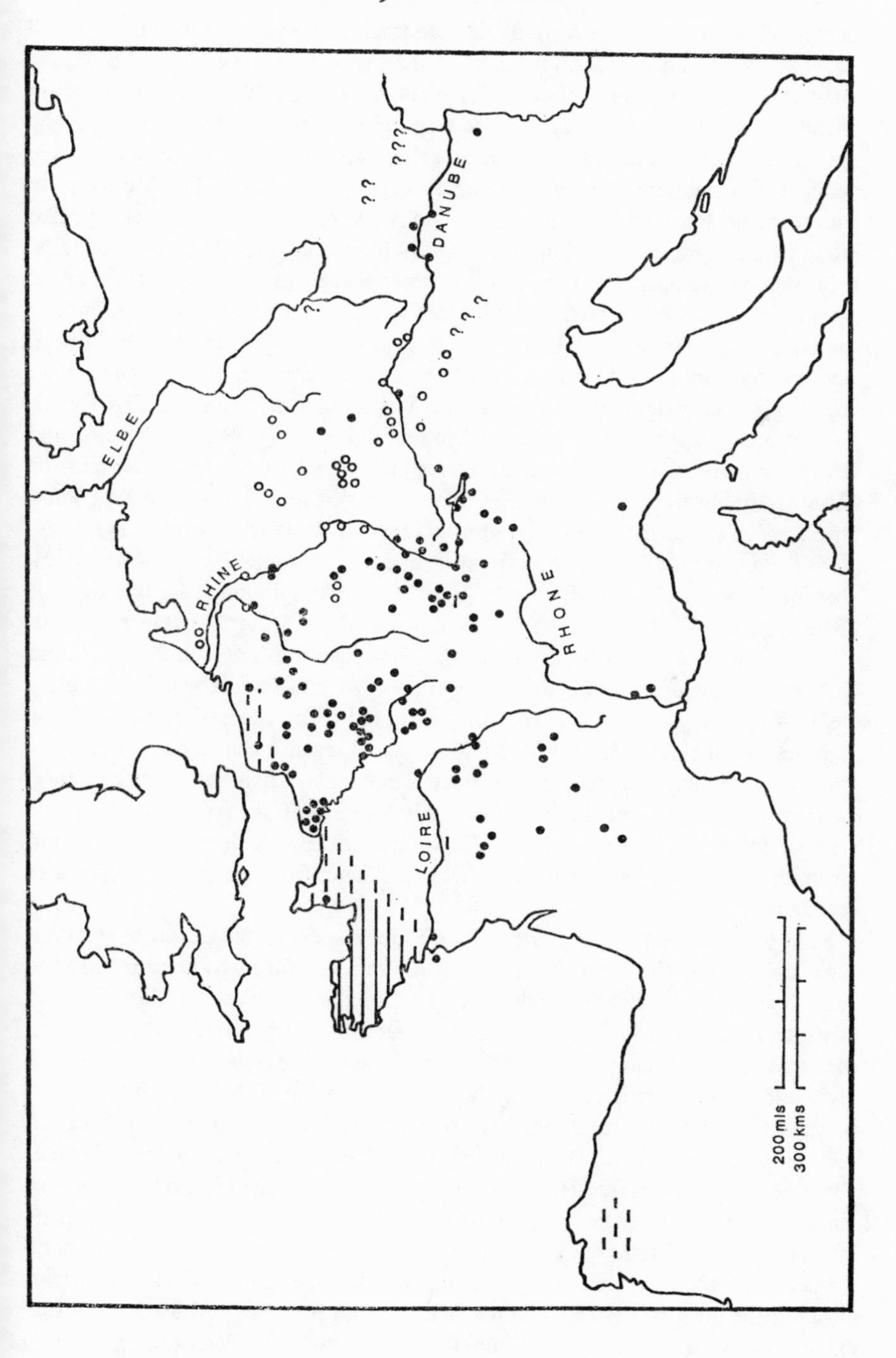

he publicly rebuked their formidable grandmother Brunhilde for crimes that all men knew but did not mention, then he sharply and openly expressed a disgust that their subjects had harboured in silent resignation. When he politely but firmly lectured pope Gregory the Great upon his mistakes in theology and in the government of the church, the pope and those accustomed to his authority were baffled by a sincerity that was neither subservient nor defiant. The Merovingian government deported him, but they could not suppress the monasteries he had founded, nor prevent him from founding Bobbio among the Lombards of Italy.

Columban enthused a number of Merovingian notables, as well as humbler men. He was soon followed by an increasing number of Irishmen from Ireland and Northumbria, and of English men and women. The English Willibrord evangelised Holland. The Irish Fursey spent ten years in East Anglia before moving to the neighbourhood of Paris. The Frankish queen founded Corbie under Fursey's guidance, while his brothers, his pupil Cellan of Peronne and their companions established some scores of houses between the Seine and the Meuse. Frankish noblemen entered these houses or founded their own; Didier, treasurer of Clothair II, and Eloi, mint master of Dagobert I, established monasteries and became bishops; their friend Iudicael, ruler of the British of Armorica, became a monk. The daughter of an East Anglian king founded Farmoutier-on-Brie, and the English wife of Clovis II refounded Chelles. St. Ouen and St. Vandrille were counts of the palace who were inspired by Columban to found houses, and his other disciples, among them St. Gall in Switzerland, St. Valery in Picardy, St. Omer of Therouanne, recruited many more Franks. Monastic fervour swept eastern Gaul in the middle of the seventh century as intensely as in contemporary England, or as in Ireland and Britain a century before. Merovingian society was in decay and ready for inspiration; the inspiration came almost entirely from the Irish and Anglo-Irish monks, with some contribution from the British, but with hardly a trace of influence from the earlier monasteries of Gaul or Italy.

The force of the movement west of the Rhine was expended during the seventh century. Beyond the Rhine it was constantly renewed for many centuries. In the eighth century the English and Irish began to evangelise the heathen German and their further neighbours. Boniface of Devon became archbishop of Mainz and apostle of Germany. Many of the bishops and abbots whom he directed were Irish; the most remarkable among them was Virgilius of Salzburg, who outraged orthodox opinion by teaching that other worlds besides our own exist in the universe. From Austria, later generations reached eastward. An Irish Colman became the patron saint of Hungary; others preached in Poland; and Brandenburg in Prussia perhaps owes its name to an Irish Brendan. The Scandinavian invasions of Ireland temporarily stemmed the flow of emigrants, but the monastic impetus revived thereafter. In 1076 Donald Rafferty, or Domnall mac Robartaig, head of the monasteries of Columba at Kells, sent his cousin Muiredach, better known as Marianus Scottus, to found the Irish house of St. Peter of Regensburg.

His vigorous successors established a chain of *Schottenkloster*, 'Irish Monasteries', at Vienna, Nuremberg and elsewhere, their furthest outpost at Kiev in the Ukraine. The Irish house at Kiev was destroyed by the Mongol invasions of the 13th century, but most of the monasteries in Germany remained Irish until the Reformation; a few, notably Erfurt and Regensburg, though in deep decay, continued as Scot houses into the 19th century, into an age when men had forgotten that Scot had once meant Irish and accepted emigrants from Scotland as the proper inmates of the *Schottenkloster*.

The quality of the Irish monks in Europe was as remarkable as their expansion in time and space, from north America to the Ukraine. Though evangelists continued to convert remote heathens, many of the Irish in western Europe transferred their emphasis from preaching to learning. From the seventh century to the eleventh the terms Irishman and scholar were virtually interchangeable; and until the Norse invasions, the English fully shared their scholarship. When Charlemagne needed schools to train the administrators of his revived western Roman empire, he induced Alcuin of York to become their first director; for Alcuin was the foremost scholar in Europe, York the finest library, Charlemagne the most munificent patron. At the central palace school Alcuin was assisted by the Irish geographer and astronomer Dicuil, and succeeded by the Irish grammarian Clemens; and in the next generation, the schools of Italy were directed by the Irish scholar Dungal of Pavia. These Carolingian foundations were the remote ancestors of the later schools of Paris and northern Italy, whence sprang the universities of medieval and modern Europe. Contemporaries, hostile and friendly, noted the comparative strengths and weaknesses of their teachers; the success of the schools stemmed from a blend of English discipline and administrative ability with Irish initiative and imagination.

The qualities that the Irish brought to Europe were those that their native monasteries had formed. To Europeans unacquainted with the origins of monasticism in Britain, the irruption of Irish monks seemed an act of God, as unpredictable as an earthquake, unexplained and in little need of explanation. Chroniclers noted that individuals were Irish, or pupils of the Irish, but did not wonder why they came, or why Europe responded to their coming. The story of the rise of monasticism in the British Isles is plainly told by the Saints' Lives, the Annals and related documents, once they have been stripped of the fancy dress in which medieval editors disguised them. The monastic explosion was not due to chance or wonder, but to the specific circumstances of early sixth-century western Britain and Ireland.

Seventh century Europe remarked that reforming monks came from Ireland and Britain. But nationality did not then arouse the powerful loyalties and resentments of modern nationalism. Large scale monasticism in the west originated among the British and the Irish, and its first and most notable founders in Europe were Irish and English. But they immediately drew to them many Franks, Germans and others, who shared and upheld their outlook, and in time their successors adopted the Rule of the Italian Benedict. Franks and Englishmen were received into monasteries in Ireland as readily as Irish and Englishmen settled in Germany. Men of Irish and English birth were long active in Europe in the movement that their countrymen had initiated, and were more numerous in some monasteries than others. But the common character of the movement rested upon its beliefs, not upon the birthplace of the men who made it. There were differences of emphasis; men often tended to settle among or near those with whom they had most in common, and the speech and background of their fellows were among the influences that brought men together. At some specific times and places men of one nation were more numerous than those of others; but no significant distinctions can isolate Irish or German, English or French monks from one another. All were deeply indebted to the British, Irish and English pioneers; the nationality of later generations marked only differences of detail.

Early monasticism, however disciplined, was by its nature subversive. In his communal life the monk owed strict obedience to his abbot; but the community was a necessary convenience, and in the monasteries of the 6th and 7th centuries each monk normally lived apart in his own cell, preserving the hermit's isolation within the community. The ideal of monk and hermit was direct access to God, in solitary communion that was often rewarded by heavenly visitation, in a dream or a vision, without the intermediary of the priest; but the hierarchy of the secular church, modelled upon the political society of men, interposed the priest between God and man, and thereby made the priest, however humble, in some degree an ecclesiastical politician. The monk was a student; though he must conform to the observances of his community, in his cell he was free to meditate on matters divine and human. The priest must accept the assumptions of the established authority he served; the monk might question them, and often did.

The early history of Christianity in the British Isles is a continuing whole; it is the first chapter in the history of European monasticism. In Europe the established church survived the barbarian invasions and tamed the first advocates of monastic meditation. The monasteries of Egypt had flourished in waterless deserts, and the efforts of late Roman ascetics to transplant them to the green lands of the west were unsuccessful; similar initiatives were no better received in the ensuing centuries. Cassiodorus, Benedict of Nursia, Radegund and other ascetics of Gaul and Italy who shared the aspirations of the British reformers were individually honoured, but inspired no large-scale movement on the model of Egypt, and did not prompt their contemporaries to enter and found monasteries in great numbers. But in Britain the destruction of the Roman economy and its institutions also brought down the established church; the failure of the church left men defenceless in face of dynastic violence and prepared them for Christian reform. The first and only European monastic movement that matched the scale and rapid growth of the original Egyptian monasteries was that which began in Wales in the 530s, and spread to Ireland, and thence by way of Iona to the English; and thereafter sent its missionaries to Europe.

The greater part of the early monasteries of Europe north of the Alps were founded by Irish, English or British monks, or by their native converts; to them most of the peoples beyond the Rhine and Danube frontiers of Rome, save for the eastern Slavs, owed their first conversion to Christianity. In the second and third generations the undisciplined enthusiasm of Irish founders no longer sufficed, and these houses sought an orderly rule; most of them ultimately observed the Rule of Benedict of Nursia, to form the nucleus of what was later termed the 'Benedictine Order'.

The monasteries of medieval Europe owe their being to Arthurian Britain. Most of the early houses were founded by men from the British Isles, or by those whom they inspired. The tenuous ancestry of British monasticism reaches back through Illtud and Docco to the teachings of the Sicilian Briton and Pelagius, of Victricius and Martin; but though it derived from the fourth-century Christian experience of Rome, it was spared the harsh necessities of Augustinianism. It won men's hearts because it adapted an older and kinder Roman Christianity to the needs of the shattered remnants of Roman Britain, and of the barbarians who had entered its ruins. Though the wars of Ambrosius and Arthur destroyed almost all that they fought to defend, their victory preserved one element of the Roman past, its radical, individualist and humanist Christian tradition. Though Arthur and his captains could not rebuild their old society in the land they had recovered, the ideas that they strove to defend did not wholly perish.

CHAPTER TWENTY-ONE
LETTERS

Language

In any society, education and literacy rest upon language. Most modern European peoples have achieved simplicity; they are monolingual, communicating in one language each, that is both written and spoken. Other modern societies, especially in Asia and Africa, are multilingual. They use more than one language, and are often handicapped because the language they know best is not written. But some societies are bilingual, equally at home in two languages. In the narrow zone of Switzerland where French and German overlap, neighbours in conversation may switch language unconsciously, and in some villages in Brittany French and Breton alternate as easily, though only French is written. The mark of a fully bilingual man, rare today, is that he does not notice which language he is speaking.

In early medieval Europe, most men were monolingual and illiterate; but the educated were multilingual, speaking their own language and Latin, writing in Latin alone, but keeping the languages apart. But in the Roman empire, language was more complex, bilingualism commoner. In the west, at the end of the empire, a few writers describe the relationship of Latin and Celtic. In the late 4th century, St. Jerome visited Trier on the Moselle, now in Western Germany, and also Ankara, now the capital of Turkey, but then the chief town of the Galatians, who were descendants of the Gauls who had invaded Asia Minor nearly 700 years before. He described what he observed.

> I have seen Ankara, capital of the Galatians.... The Galatians, apart from the Greek language that the whole east speaks, have their own native tongue, that is almost the same as that of Trier; and ... just as the Africans have somewhat altered the Phoenician language, so Latin itself is varied in different districts at different times.

Trier was typical of northern Gaul. Soon after 400 Sulpicius Severus issued a sequel to his Life of Martin, in the form of a Dialogue; a participant from Latin-speaking Aquitaine gibed at a student from Tours in the north.

> Go on. Talk in Gallic or Celtic if you like, so long as you talk about Martin.

Gallic was the speech of all classes, not only of the rustics, for seventy years later

Sidonius, a great nobleman of the Auvergne, congratulated his younger relative Ecdicius, because

> if our nobles have been inspired with a love of elegant language and poetry, if they have decided to abandon their hideous Celtic speech, it is thanks to your initiative.

Sidonius doubtless exaggerated Ecdicius' personal influence and the speed of change, but he wrote of his own time, for readers who knew what languages they and their fathers spoke. Gallic lingered among the nobility into the middle of the fifth century, and doubtless lasted longer among the peasantry; it outlived the Roman empire, and was effaced by the Latin dialect that grew into medieval French only when Christianity spread into the countryside. But, as Jerome remarked, it penetrated local Latin usage; a few Gallic words survive in French, like *alouette* or *pièce*, and Gallic constructions pervaded the Latin of Gaul. Sidonius strove to attain a classical purity, as far removed as possible from popular idiom, but he nevertheless used *quod* and *quia* as the modern French use *que*, and his *vir litterarum*, 'man of letters', perpetuated by the French *homme de lettres*, is as alien to classical usage. The idiom that he heard in contemporary speech occasionally penetrated his polished writing.

In Britain, Celtic and Latin were similarly related. British, akin to Gallic, was everywhere spoken, and Latin was widespread. The pens used for writing on wax tablets, called *styli*, are found in numbers in towns, and are not uncommon in the countryside; they are evidence not only of literacy, but of Latin, for British was unwritten. Several tablets survive, recording small-scale business transactions, and London artisans could write Latin jokes on wet clay in good grammar and a legible hand. In at least the larger towns, in London as in Trier, and among the nobility, men were fluent in both languages, and many were fully bilingual. As in Gaul, the languages interacted; British imported and passed on to modern Welsh a very large number of Latin words, used for the commonest objects of everyday life, that often displaced equally serviceable native words. Up to the middle of the fifth century, British, like Gallic, was on the road to absorbing so much Latin that it must soon yield to a spoken Latin language, but the destruction of Roman institutions halted and reversed the process, for in Britain spoken Latin died away, and the native speech endured.

The impact of the native idiom on Latin was less than in Gaul. Kenneth Jackson's study of the Latin loan words concludes that, to a European ear, British Latin

> seemed stilted and pedantic, . . . upper class and 'haw-haw'. . . . British Latin peculiarities . . . tend to agree with the pronunciations recommended by grammarians. . . . Schoolmasters . . . succeeded in . . . enforcing certain archaisms. . . . The standard of Latin language, thought and culture was capable of being a high one.

The precise observation is followed by a more dubious conclusion, that British

Latin was the language of 'the well-to-do landowners of the Lowland Zone', contrasted with their 'half barbarian' peasants, who learnt their Latin from their lord's bailiff. The inference underestimates the rural pens and the artisan's literacy. It does not explain why the 'archaisms' of the pedant and the bailiff 'succeeded' in Britain while they failed in Gaul, nor why they prevailed in Snowdonia and Cornwall, where lowland bailiffs were unknown.

The standards of British Latin are more simply explained. It was old-fashioned because it was recent. The sophisticated wealth of aristocratic Romanity spread later in Britain than in Gaul, during the fourth century, and British Latin had no time to evolve colloquialisms on the scale of Gaul. The Latin of the fifth-century British writers, Pelagius and Faustus, the Sicilian Briton and Fastidius, is not merely 'archaic'; it is a clearer and more graceful Latin than the turgid prose of Jerome, simpler than the resonant rhetoric of Augustine, more fluent than the language of their pedestrian contemporaries in Italy and Gaul. By contrast, Patrick, whose education was interrupted, was throughout his life ashamed of his rough Latin, that he had to acquire in Gaul. The only known comparable non-literary work preserved from Gaul in his time, the travelogue of Aetheria, emphasises the contrast. Her constructions are better disciplined, for she passed her life among Latin speakers, while Patrick lived long among the Irish, but the paucity of her vocabulary and her insensitivity to sound and syllable are akin to his, infinitely removed from the polish of educated British Latin.

The writers of the early fifth century cared for language, and bequeathed their standards to the British of the south-west, who retained the leisure and the schooling to prolong a cultivated literacy, that the war destroyed elsewhere. Docco, Illtud, Paulinus and others passed on their tradition to their own pupils, among them Gildas, whose original experiments in the use of language were followed by the heady, zestful Latin of many of the later Irish and English monks. But in their day, as in the rest of Europe, Latin was spoken only by scholars. It died from ordinary conversation and the future lay with the native speech. The Celtic languages are exceptionally conservative. The Celtic name for the Baltic in the 2nd century BC, '*Mori Marusa*, that is, Dead Sea', is recognisably similar to the modern Welsh for Dead Sea, *Mor Marw*; when the Romans first encountered the same place name, Sorbiodunum, at Salisbury in Wiltshire and also on the Danube, current pronunciation dictated exactly the same spelling, though the Celts who named both places had parted company some seven centuries before; after fourteen centuries of separation Breton remains readily intelligible to Welsh children and is easily acquired by adults; Welsh has changed much less than English since its earliest sixth-century poems were written.

But, because the languages are conservative, change is sudden and sharp when it comes. Spoken British was jolted by the catastrophe of Roman Britain, and the transformed language is commonly called Welsh, in contrast to earlier British or 'Brittonic'. The change, centred on the end of the sixth century, seems somewhat sharper than it was, for it is also a change from old-fashioned

Latin spellings, hardened by custom, to new spellings devised when the native language was first written. Latin Cun-o-belin(us) became Kynvelyn, Maglos became Mael, and a host of other changes matured at much the same time. But oral change there was, evidently maturing first in the north, for English ears heard southerners pronounce names in *-maegl* as late as about 580, when Taliesin in the north was already composing poems in Welsh; though they were doubtless not written down until some decades later, their rhyme and metre make them products of the transformed language.

These changes coincided. The population ceased to speak Latin after Roman civilisation was destroyed; British turned into Welsh in the same years in which the Irish, British and English languages were first written, in the decades on either side of 600. Vernacular literacy gave a new orientation to education and literature, lowering the barriers between the learned and the unlettered. The earlier Irish annalists wrote sentences half in Irish and half in Latin with no more embarrassment than any other fully bilingual people, and continued to do so into the 11th century. They wrote as they spoke; and some schools sought to preserve Latin from contamination by forbidding their pupils to talk Irish to one another, or to converse with the local Latinless population. The Welsh and the English kept their languages and Latin apart, but the same scholars wrote as easily in the vernacular as in Latin, in an age when no European scholar could write in German or French, Italian or Spanish, even if he wished to address the unlearned. Their multilingual training gave them a far wider public than Europeans could reach; it enabled them to learn more from and about their own society, and to preserve customs, beliefs and social and historical traditions that in Europe died out or were suppressed.

Education

The schools of late Roman Britain resembled those of the rest of the empire, and are described by the Sicilian Briton. When his relative urged him to bring his daughter home for schooling, he told him to think of her as of a boy, who is normally sent to school away from home; in another context he cited the analogy of a school, where the pupils strove to reach the top form, *gradus*, but did not thereby leave the lower forms empty. The boys' boarding school, divided into forms, was normal, though most of the students lived out in lodgings. Literacy was commonly enforced by the cane, despite the protests of the most distinguished academics, but with lessening effect. In the early empire, westerners of breeding had been reared to fluency in Greek as well as Latin. In the 4th century Greek was still taught in the greater cities, Carthage, Trier, and doubtless also London, but the wide scholarship of Jerome was a rarity; most boys left school with one language only, like Augustine, to whom Greek remained a foreign language after a long education in Africa and Rome, or like the great eastern orator Themistius, who knew no Latin. Britain was exceptional; Augustine complained that Pelagius prevailed in debate in Jerusalem by reason of his fluent Greek, whereas Augustine's representative, the historian Orosius, failed because he had to rely on a faulty interpreter.

In the last days of the empire British education was reinforced by adaptations of Martin's monastic school; Whithorn in the far north was founded early in the 5th century and later emerged as a major school; and Coelestius, who was probably Irish and perhaps from Demetia, was educated in a monastery, probably in Britain, before he practised as a lawyer in Rome, not long after 400. Illtud in the later 5th century inherited and developed the experience of Europe and of Britain. Like Paulinus of Nola, Cassiodorus and other Roman noblemen, he withdrew to live a personal monastic life on his own estates; but unlike them, he maintained a school, whose pupils boarded with him. As in Martin's school, the pupils were sons of laymen, whose parents expected most of them to return to the world after a long schooling. Illtud's teaching techniques were ancient, for five year old infants learnt their alphabet from twenty pieces, termed *eleae* and *tesserae*, as the great Roman educationalist Quintilian had prescribed four centuries earlier, insisting that primary schooling must begin with the handling of physical letters, cut from ivory, bone or wood.

Illtud's school is described in the Lives of Samson and Paul Aurelian, which both draw on first-hand accounts. They illustrate the gentle wisdom with which he guided his pupils. When visions of the Egyptian hermit Antony prompted the sixteen year old Paul, heir to a great estate, to seek a desert solitude, Illtud probed his motive, warning that

> our thinking may have three origins, either from God, or from the Devil, or from ourselves; from God . . . by the infusion of the Holy Spirit . . . as it now seems to you in your case; . . . from the Devil . . . by hidden traps, shrewd and subtle . . . ; or from ourselves, when our ordinary natural thought recalls to our conscious memory things we have experienced or heard in the past.

He made him take time to reflect, but did not restrain him when he freely decided. When Samson, a year younger, fasted to excess, to the damage of his health, Illtud restrained him; years later, when Samson was already a senior, he too felt the impulse to solitude and

> was seeking to escape from the cenobite community without causing offence to his master.

Illtud then took the initiative, made him speak his mind, and arranged a transfer to the newly founded house of Piro on Caldey Island. The practical lessons on how to deal with human frailty that Gildas later imparted to the Irish were those that he had learnt in youth from Illtud.

Illtud's was the best known of the early schools, but it was not the only one. Paulinus soon after, and probably Docco a little earlier, were regarded as great teachers, and Tatheus maintained a well-reputed school in Caerwent. Some texts call the schools *Gimnasia*, and Winwaloe's is described as *scolasticorum collegium*, a college of scholars. Detail is rare in the later Lives; Cadoc taught the infant Malo to write his letters on a wax tablet; the cane, not mentioned in the tradition of Illtud or of other Welsh schools, is recorded at Ninian's Whithorn and at Servanus' school in Fife. Very many Lives stress that the schools taught both sacred and profane letters, 'both disciplines', or 'liberal studies'. The exception is Demetia. The Life of Teilo goes out of its way to denounce the 'figments of the poets', and the 'history of antiquity'; though David's Life remembers that in youth he learnt *rudimenta* as well as the scriptures, and was instructed by Paulinus in a 'tripartite' discipline, teaching plays no part in the record of David's adult work. In Demetia the tradition of David and Teilo prevailed, and there is little later sign of profane letters.

The first Irish monks had to travel to Britain for Christian schooling, for their own secular schools were pagan and were tight technical institutes devoted to the training of professional scholars in a set tradition immemorially old. In the 5th century, Enda and Darerca, Tigernach, Eugenius and others were taught at Whithorn, and many more 'went abroad' or 'visited Britain' in their youth. A few early teachers in Ireland had Roman names, like Boecius and Natalis, and may have come from Gaul or Britain, but the first influential school in Ireland was that of the British-born Mocteus at Louth. Like Cassiodorus in Italy, but unlike Illtud, he exempted his pupils from agricultural work; but the exemption seemed odd, even improper, to the Irish, and most of the early monks were proud to grow their own food. The first great native Irish school was founded at Clonard in the 530s by Finnian, who had previously gone for some years to 'study with the elders of Britain'. He was universally regarded as the 'teacher of the Irish saints', as well loved as Illtud in Britain; and from the middle of the century new monastic schools multiplied, many of them founded by Finnian's pupils.

The Irish schools differed from the British in that they were coeducational from the start. Patrick had brought to Ireland the experience of Christian Rome; the church of Italy had discovered that women were at first readier to withdraw from the world than men, and had early learnt that prudence and economy more wisely housed widows and unprotected single women in supervised hostels than in scattered lodgings. In later 5th-century Ireland the houses of Brigit, Darerca, Faencha and other women were more prominent than monasteries for men; and several early monks, like Enda, had been obliged at first to live with a minority of men attached to a community of women. The claims of women to equal monastic right were well established when the first schools opened, and Finnian of Clonard and his pupil Ciaran of Clonmacnoise are reported to have attached houses for girls to their monastic schools; though there was opposition, coeducation prevailed, stoutly defended by Dagaeus, the father of the art and craftsmanship of the Irish schools, who taught in turn at a number of the major monasteries.

A few Lives report the inevitable occasional problems. In her youth,

Darlugdach with difficulty resisted the temptation to steal from the bed she shared with Brigit to meet her lover. She lived chastely to succeed Brigit, but other men and women yielded to temptation; their sins are recorded when they went abroad to repent and returned to become austere abbots in their later years. A grave scandal disrupted the school of Whithorn in about 550. Drusticc, daughter of the king of the Picts, bribed Finnian, the future founder of Moville, to induce a fellow student with the British name of Rioc to her bed; but he sent a young Irishman from Cork in his place. The girl is also said to have tried to seduce Finnian. Both were expelled; the authorities are said to have used violence against Finnian, and the students retaliated with violence against the abbot. The story is no more likely to tell the whole truth than accounts of other scandals in other times. It outlines a situation often repeated, when a disciplinary incident sparks off a major clash; but it carried deeper undertones, for the girl was more than a king's daughter. The succession to the Pictish throne passed through the woman; if she had married Finnian or Rioc, the son of an obscure Irishman or Briton would have acquired a title to the kingship, as yet not held by any foreign-born king.

Yet scandals were infrequent. The double monasteries and their schools survived and multiplied. In both Britain and Ireland, numerous children are reported to have begun a ten-year curriculum at the age of 5 or 7, and intending priests continued their schooling until they were ordained deacon at the age of 19 or 20. In the monastic school, in contrast with Patrick's secular education, spoken and written Latin began in infancy, so that children grew up fully bilingual. At first, parents of means were expected to make an initial down payment. Some poorer schools were also sometimes compelled to invite the families of the district to make voluntary contributions to their funds, and some students are reported to have received free meals from nearby laymen. But most of the major monasteries had land and manpower enough to feed their pupils, and their status grew when the Convention of Drumceat incorporated the old learning within the Christian framework. Their influence encouraged the monastic schools to add both classical Irish and classical Roman learning to divine studies, so that the hostility to profane letters, advocated with success in Britain by David and Teilo, found fewer adherents in Ireland.

Educational opportunity made the Irish rather than the British houses the main centres of Christian learning. In the 7th century, students from Britain and Gaul began to frequent the Irish schools. Early in the century, Agilbert, later bishop of the West Saxons and of Paris, left his native Gaul to spend a long time in Ireland 'in order to read Divinity', for Ireland offered an advanced education that he could not find at home. Bede was amazed at the open-handed ease of the Irish educational system in the middle of the century, remarking that

> there were many Englishmen in Ireland, both noble and plebeian, who left their homeland in the time of bishops Finan and Colman

> either to read Divinity or to live more continently. Some soon bound themselves to a monastic vow, but others preferred to travel around the cells of different teachers for the joy of reading. The Irish welcomed them all, gave them food and lodging without charge, lent them their books to read and taught them without fee.

Societies that find the means to offer higher education to all comers, native or foreign, without fee, with expenses paid, and without requiring proof of qualification, are not numerous in human history; and are more easily paralleled in Asia than in Europe. For the next several centuries Ireland prospered by the excellence of her schools. Men trained in Ireland were in demand throughout Europe; monied men as well as penniless students came to learn in Ireland. The freedom and the vigour of the schools was designed for learning, but it also brought material reward. Love of learning inspired a superb art, whose products, on paper and in metal, were exported in considerable quantity and earned a rich return by the receipt of corresponding gifts. At home, as in most societies, technological skills leapt ahead when a high standard of art and design was universally expected, and when its craftsmen were generally respected. Advances in mechanical engineering, in plant and animal biology, and above all in the cheap application of technological knowledge, rapidly increased agricultural and manufacturing production; the sudden widespread exploitation of waterpower, by devices long known and long unused, and the intensification of arable farming, were initiated by the same monasteries whose skills illuminated manuscripts and worked beautiful metal objects; both were the direct consequence of the educational system, whose expense was borne by rulers, who were compelled by public opinion to make land and resources available.

Irish inventiveness took its skills to Europe, especially to Italy and Germany, while its eagerness to learn enabled it to borrow and bring home something of the technological novelties that Slavs, Avars and others had brought to central Europe from further east. Inventiveness had its quirks, but common sense curbed the unfruitful and harmful; when at Ruadan's monastery of Lothra the commercial exploitation of a new and over-stimulating distilled drink threatened to overshadow the primary purposes of devotion and education, the pressure of other monasteries compelled Ruadan to limit the man-hours spent upon a specialised product of doubtful value to society.

Technological advance was an unforeseen fringe benefit. The business of the schools was to think and to teach, for the physical protection of a sacrosanct cloister was the only shield that could preserve the human intellect from the hideous violence of secular society. The same shield was welcomed abroad, by men who needed defence against the brutal administration that the uncouth rulers and lords of Europe had inherited from Rome. At first, the Irish came themselves. But other nations soon endeavoured to imitate and equal their learning. Among the English, double monasteries multiplied from the 660s onward; Benedict Biscop and others encouraged houses of purely English foundation and travelled to Italy to bring back books, that their *scriptoria* copied and circulated; Aldhelm tried without success to persuade English students that they could find at Canterbury in Theodore's time a Greek and Latin education as good as any to be had in Ireland. In Gaul, Columban brought the learning of Comgall's Irish Bangor to the Vosges at the end of the 6th century. The movement that he began swept Gaul in and after the 640s, as the original monastic reform had swept Britain and Ireland a hundred years earlier. Large numbers of monasteries founded by the Irish and English and by their native Frankish adherents also established libraries and copied books; if Agilbert had been thirty years younger, he would have had no need to go to Ireland to advance his education. Some Franks and many Englishmen still studied in Ireland, for the Irish libraries and learning were older than their own, and a journey to the land whence their monastic Christianity had come was in itself a pilgrimage. But the substance of Irish education had already spread abroad, and was in the next century carried to Germany.

The Irish brought not only books, but also men who loved to copy them, and did so with surpassing skill and beauty. They brought with them an understanding of what books were for, and a training in how to use them. The new education arrived when it was most needed, just after the old learning of Rome was dead beyond recovery. Half a century before the rash of new foundations, Gregory of Tours began the preface to his *History of the Franks* with a lament.

> Culture and education are dying out, perishing throughout the cities of Gaul. . . . There is no grammarian to be found, skilful enough in dialectic to depict the present age in prose or verse. You often hear people complaining 'Alas for our times; literacy is dying among us, and no man can be found among our peoples who is capable of setting down the deeds of the present on paper'.

The monks came just in time to replace the dying education of antiquity with a new learning, alert to seize upon what suited the needs of its own day.

Latin Literature

Latin learning persisted in the schools, at least in south-western Britain; but the work of one writer alone survives from 6th-century Britain, Gildas. The style of his letters is simple and vigorous, but his book, intended for publication, is an astounding and original development in Latin literature. Its construction is 'firm and monumentally wrought', put together 'on the grand scale, conscious and calculated'. The style and concept of language is altogether new. Gildas knew and studied the controlled elegance of the early 5th-century British writers, and the rhythmical rhetoric of his contemporaries in Europe. He rejected both. He learned more from poets than from prose writers, writing for the ear rather than the eye, striking at his readers' feelings. His paragraphs are an ordered series of impressions, painted in gaudy and unusual words, unusually arranged; their sentences run on in 'shapeless splendour' like the exhortation of a platform orator. Their impact is forced upon the reader by a wealth of colourful adjectives and images, the words placed together by sound and syllable, in defiance of the ordinary conventions of word order. When he contrasts Maelgwn's poets with Christian choirs he opens with powerful alliteration, *arrecto aurium auscultantur non Dei laudes*, 'the excited ears of the auditors are seized not by praises of God'; soft words compare the 'gently modulated tones of Christ's soldiers', *tironum voce sauviter modulante*, with the frenzy of the warband's bards, *spumanti flegmate proximos quosque roscidaturo*, 'bedewing all near him with foaming phlegm'.

Gildas' extraordinary style is unique. He was born beyond the Clyde, outside the frontiers of Rome, and sent to a good southern school because his father was an eminent military captain. His unsophisticated enthusiasm was fired by the possibilities of a long cultivated language, hitherto politely disciplined. His style appears as his alone, elaborated without precedent or parallel. Yet what he wrote was no literary exercise, but a political pronouncement of major importance, that was intended to move the hearts and minds of great numbers of readers, and achieved its aim. Gildas wrote as he did because he judged that a work so written would be welcomed and understood; and he judged rightly. His book was plainly designed to be read aloud to large audiences, as well as in private armchairs; it presupposes a considerable audience who could still understand some Latin, even if they could not read it. His work may have stood alone in his own day; but it may also be that he was the foremost among a school of new-style writers, that grew up among the pupils of Illtud's and similar schools, whose other writings have not been preserved.

What Gildas inherited from the British Latin authors of the past was above all a care for language. His idiom was original, without known antecedents. But it had a long sequel. Bizarre words, often newly concocted, put together for oral effect without regard to the precepts of grammarians, became a widespread literary form, termed 'Western Latin', that long flourished in Ireland and found occasional European imitators, like Virgilius Maro, though living Latin soon ceased in Britain. The Irish taught the new style to their English pupils, notably Boniface and Aldhelm, whose far-reaching influence established it firmly in the tradition of English Latin. But Western Latin was chiefly a literary exercise, and begot an extremist fringe, termed 'Hisperic', whose elaborate conceits defeat understanding.

Western and Hisperic fashions endured for a few centuries, but they contributed to one important permanent development. The experiments of Welsh and Irish poets exploited the regular and frequent use of rhyme, within lines and at their end, in Latin, in Irish and in Welsh. Rhyme was not new to Latin, but it was hitherto weakly developed. It well matched the alliteration of classical Irish verse and, from the 8th century onwards, monastic poets who called themselves the 'new writers' pioneered new metres, whose roots lay both in the late Latin hymn and in classical Irish. Their innovation was not confined to form; and was earlier matched in vernacular Welsh. Delicate and lovely lyrics described the beauties of the countryside, that monks had leisure to observe; their contemplation extended to humanity, to the sadness of withered age and the splendour of youthful vigour. The descriptive verse of Roman poets had commonly appealed to the intellect and the ear; Irish and Welsh observation appealed to the eye, using words as a painter uses colour. The new poetry of the Welsh is almost entirely confined to the vernacular, but the continuing bilingualism of the Irish scholars rooted it in Latin as well, and imparted its concept to the English. Their successors made their themes the familiar common stock of European verse; but in early Christian Ireland they were new and unique.

The ornament of Western Latin and Hisperic extravagance enlivened the Latin of the southern English, but the Northumbrians outgrew their Irish teachers, and under the guidance of Benedict Biscop and king Aldfrith they matured their own monastic learning. The finely chiselled austerity of Bede's Latin silently reproves the riotous imagery of Gildas and Aldhelm. It learnt from Europe, but its roots were English. It also permeated Europe, for Bede's wide scholarship placed him among 'the most widely read authors of the early middle ages', an influence as potent as the Irish on form and style. In prose as in verse, the literature that Irish and English monks brought to Europe was powerful, and helped to renew the vitality of languishing Latin culture.

Welsh Literature

Welsh vernacular literature was a new creation. Four hundred years of Roman civilisation had drowned all memory of the bards and the ancient learning of pre-Roman times. The past was altogether gone. When national sentiment required historical legends, early in the 6th century, Welsh scholars had to look to Roman historians, and from a late Roman mis-spelling of Cunobelinus, the last great pre-Roman king of the south-east, they contrived 'Belin, son of Manocan', who had ruled in London; for the real Cunobelinus was forgotten. In four centuries, the Welsh had lost all memory of the past when they had not been Roman, though for fifteen centuries they have remembered that they are not English.

The first mention of a bard in Britain is beyond the Roman frontier, at the court of Coroticus of the Clyde in the mid fifth century; and Gildas inveighed against Maelgwn's bards three generations later. None of their works survives, and a text preserved by Nennius dates the beginning of Welsh poetry to the mid 6th century, in the north, when Talhaern Tataguen sang in Outigern's time. He then names Aneirin and Taliesin, to whom some extant works are attributed, probably rightly, and Bluchbard and Cian, 'called Gueinth Guaut', whose name is Irish. Irish literature is drenched in the remote past, but the surviving works of the early Welsh know no history; all concern the present. The poets depended on royal patrons. Rhyme and alliteration abound in their diction, as in the Irish tradition that the 'new writers' later formulated. The oldest poems date to the end of the 6th century, but they were doubtless not written down until some decades later; for nothing suggests that the Latin schools of 5th- and 6th-century Britain encouraged or designed a vernacular alphabet. Deliberate intellectual effort was needed to adapt Latin letters to the sound of native speech, and it is probable that that effort was first made in Ireland, in the later 6th century, where Latin and writing itself were both novelties.

The Welsh may have owed the mechanics of writing to the Irish, but the content of their writing was their own. The odes that Taliesin and Aneirin addressed to their dead kings are finer literature than any that a trained Irish poet sang about the heroes of his own day; though they are the work of royal minstrels, they have nothing of the polished flattery of court poets in other societies. The poets mourned a world they loved, and that they knew was dying; Aneirin's *Gododdin* describes the grandeur of a final ruin; Taliesin found in Urien and his son a personal magnetism that won his affection; and Cynddylan also aroused in his unknown poet a like admiration and respect.

The epics of the northern British became the classics of the Welsh. For many centuries a succession of great poets wrote songs in praise of their own day. Lyric verse began early, with an isolated poem copied by chance into the manuscripts of Aneirin, sung to a child.

> Dinogad's coat is coloured bright
> I made it from marten skins. . . .
>
> When your Dad went a-hunting
> A spear on his shoulder, a club in his hand,
>
> He'd call his fast dogs
> 'Giff! Gaff! Catch, catch; fetch, fetch'. . . .
> Whatever came near your father's spear
> Boar or wild cat or fox
>
> Unless it had wings it could never get clear.

Later Welsh medieval verse is rich in love poems, and in nature poems that owe much in form to the Irish; but they remained vigorously secular, their delight in life keener than the quiet observation of the monks.

Since Welsh tradition had no history earlier than the fifth century, the poems of the sixth century became the starting point of historical verse and myth. The Merlin Cycle, the *Armes Prydein* and many other medieval poems plundered the older epics to weave mystic, nervous prophecies of an ultimate reconquest of the lost lands of England; and in so doing they preserved in allusion something of lost early epic. The concept of constructing a long past history told in detailed stories was in itself Irish. But its main vehicle was prose.

The Welsh story-teller had greater need of foreign borrowings than the Irish. The principal collection of tales is grouped in the text commonly called the

Mabinogion. It comprises a mythological cycle, the 'Four Branches of the Mabinogi', properly so-called, whose form and content is heavily indebted to Irish mythological tales, their setting transferred to West Wales; an Arthurian cycle, whose core probably derives from the same sources as the Norman romances; and a few historical tales. Some of them, like Lludd and Llevelys, are late attempts to picture conquering kings of pre-Roman Britain who ruled from London, but others are finer literature. One of them, the 'Dream of Maxen Wledig', is among the best told tales in the early prose of any land.

> Maxen was emperor of Rome, comelier, better and wiser than any emperor before. . . . Maxen slept, and he saw a dream. . . . Valleys he saw and . . . rocks of wonderful height. . . . Thence he beheld an island in the sea, facing this rugged land. . . . From the mountain he saw a river, and at the mouth of the river he saw a castle, the fairest that ever man saw. . . . He went into the castle, and in the castle he saw a fair hall. Its roof seemed to be all of gold, its walls of glittering precious gems. . . . Golden seats he saw in the hall, and silver tables. He saw two fair haired young men playing at chess . . . a silver board for the chess and golden pieces thereon. Beside a pillar in the hall he saw a hoary headed old man, in a chair of ivory, with the figures of two eagles of ruddy gold thereon. Bracelets of gold were upon his arms, and many rings upon his hands, and a golden torque about his neck; and his hair was bound with a golden diadem. He was powerful to look upon. A chessboard was before him, and a rod of gold, and a steel file in his hand, and he was fashioning chessmen.
>
> He saw a maiden sitting in a chair of ruddy gold. No more easy was it to gaze upon the sun at its brightest than to look upon her, by reason of her beauty. . . . She was the fairest sight that ever man beheld. . . . The maiden arose, and he put his arms about her neck. . . . But when he had his arms around her neck, and his cheek rested upon her cheek, then through the barking of the dogs . . . and the clashing of the shields . . . and the neighing of the horses . . . the emperor awoke from his dream.
>
> He was the saddest man that ever was seen. . . . The wise men of Rome said . . . 'Send messengers . . . to seek thy dream'. . . . So the messengers journeyed . . . and came to the island of Britain . . . to Snowdon . . . to Arvon. . . . They saw the youths . . . the hoary headed man . . . carving chessmen . . . and the maiden. . . . The emperor set forth with his army . . . and conquered Britain . . . and came to Arvon . . . into the castle and into the hall. And there he saw Kynan the son of Eudav and Adeon the son of Eudav playing chess; and Eudav the son of Caradawc sitting on a chair of ivory fashioning chessmen . . . and the maiden . . . upon a chair of ruddy gold . . . and that night she became his bride.
>
> The next day in the morning, she asked her maiden portion, to

> have the island of Britain for her father, with the three nearby islands . . . and the three chief castles . . . Arvon . . . Caerleon and Carmarthen. . . . Then Helen bethought her to make high roads from one castle to another; and for this reason they are called *Sarn Helen*, the roads of Helen of the Hosts.
>
> Seven years did the emperor stay in this island. . . . So the men of Rome made a new emperor. . . . So Maxen set forth towards Rome . . . and sat down before the city. . . . A year was the emperor before the city, no nearer to the taking of it than on the first day. . . . Then came the brothers of Helen from the island of Britain, with a small army, and better warriors were in that small army than twice as many Romans. . . . They came to the city, and set their ladders against the wall, and came into the city . . . and none could give it to the emperor but the men of the island of Britain. Then the gates of the city of Rome were opened, and the emperor sat upon his throne.
>
> Then the emperor said to Kynan and Adeon, 'I give you this army to conquer what regions you will'. . . . So they . . . conquered lands and castles and cities. . . . Then Kynan said to his brother 'Will you stay in this land, or go home to the land from whence you came?' He chose to go home to his own land, and many with him; but Kynan stayed with the others, and dwelt there . . . and the men of Armorica are called Britons. This is the dream called the Dream of Maxen Wledig, emperor of Rome, and here it ends.

The tale is a straightforward historical narrative, its main facts accurate, their context altogether unknown and misunderstood. Maximus was a fourth-century Roman emperor, who conquered the city of Rome with the help of an army from Britain; his wife, described in her lifetime by Sulpicius Severus as the pious woman who waited silently upon St. Martin while her husband discussed theology with him at dinner, may have been British. The story used a description of Roman Segontium by someone who had seen its buildings and its furniture before time wore them, and who knew something of his remoter ancestors' ornament and dress. It is possible that a part of Maximus' army settled in Armorica. The context is amiss, for the author supposed that Maximus ruled Rome before he came to Britain, and led the Roman army that conquered Britain.

The 'Dream of Maxen' and the legend of Belin embody the Welsh concept of early history. It was formed early in the 6th century, when Rome died with Arthur. It already pervaded the outlook of Gildas; though he knew of Roman armies and governors, law and gentility, he had no notion that Britain had once been an integral part of Roman civilisation; though he saw the scale of Roman buildings he did not associate them with Rome, but with the *cives*, the *Cumbrogi*, his fellow-countrymen. The past was forgotten, but the present needed a past. It was learned from Roman writers, but recorded in the manner of the Irish. The Cambrian Annals begin as a text of the Irish Annals, into which some British notices are inserted; its account is supplemented by genealogies modelled on the Irish, and by tales drawn from Irish mythology.

Later Welsh literature was built on history and mythology. They were consolidated in the 8th and 9th centuries. The documents collected by Nennius took British history back to the 5th century and prefixed it with an Irish account of the origins of the peoples of the British Isles. They included a satisfactory explanation of the coming of the British themselves. It was a convention of the age to supply national names with a fanciful etymology, and to personify them. Early in the 7th century Isidore of Seville had explained that the British were so-called because they were *bruti*, 'stupid'; some twenty or thirty years later the Irish annalist Cuanu accepted his unflattering view, admitting that the British were 'odious' (*exosus*), but personalised their founder as Brutus, great-grandson of Aeneas the Trojan, legendary founder of the Latins.

Brutus the Trojan was welcomed in Britain and long retained his fame. When the English mastered the island, he acquired three sons, Loegrius of England, from *Lloegr*, the Welsh word for England, Albanus of Albany, the heartland of the future Scotland, and Camber of Wales. The fancy was so universally accepted that later national leaders of Scotland did not dispute its substance, but protested only that it erred in detail, wrongly making Loegrius ancestor of the Plantagenets, and thereby entitling them to supremacy.

The nonsense filled a vacuum and pointed to a need. When once the Welsh had learned to record their history, they took care to see that their known national heroes were not again allowed to lapse from memory, and enshrined the rest of their history in a continuing literature, deeper in their consciousness than elsewhere in Britain. The rest of the peoples of Britain forgot or suppressed their history. The language and the memories of the British of the Clyde were preserved in Wales, forgotten at home; the faint traditions of the Picts are preserved only by the Irish, and the Scots project romantic medieval institutions back into a mythical past; among the English, the legend of Brutus the Trojan survived until the 16th century, and even today tradition distorts national history by beginning in the middle, with the Norman conquest. For nearly half of their known history the English are disguised as 'Anglo-Saxons', remote blondes with their legs in thongs, a quaint and irrelevant prelude whose study may safely be relinquished to a few specialists, while the Roman and pre-Roman past is normally abandoned to archaeologists and younger school-children.

Welsh literature has given the Welsh a saner and more balanced understanding of their origins than the romanticism of the Scots or the cultivated ignorance of the English. It has helped the Welsh to retain their identity, even when most of them have forgotten their language. History was its starting point, but from the 6th century onward it has continued to produce great verse and prose in each generation, so that even today the bulk and quality of Welsh literature is not less, in proportion to the numbers of those who read the language, than that of any other European nation. In spite of the language decline, it has also created a modern literature that is no less Welsh because it uses the medium of the English language.

It remains free and natural, unembarrassed by the artificial stage brogue that hampers the modern Irish; for though the serious Irish writer who would develop a national idiom must tread cautiously, lest he look like an English comedian aping the Irish, the Welsh writer is less exposed to such risk. The immediate impact of Welsh literature is handicapped because it has not yet come to terms with the comparatively recent fall in the numbers of those who read the language with ease and pleasure; but the riches of many centuries give it powerful reserves, and when it finds translators worthy of its content, it is likely to enlarge the dignity of national sentiment far beyond the bounds of the spoken language, and to enrich the literary inheritance of Europe.

English Literature

English vernacular writing began almost as early as the Welsh and Irish, but it matured more slowly. The earliest known text is the law code of Aethelbert of Kent, published in about 600. Its title, the oldest surviving words of the English language, is spare and terse. *This syndon tha Domas, the Aethelbirht Cyning asette on Augustinus daege*, 'there are the Laws that King Aethelbert fixed in Augustine's days'. The promulgation of laws in the spoken tongue caused wonder; more than a hundred years later Bede singled them out as the only benefit of Aethelbert's reign that he found worthy of remark. It was to be many centuries before any vernacular laws were written down in Europe; though later Kentish kings added new codes, and Ine codified the laws of Wessex about 690, Bede, in about 730, emphasised a desirable innovation, evidently not yet imitated in Northumbria.

No literature but law is known from Kent. Written verse is first recorded in the north. Caedmon bore a British name. He was an elderly layman who lived near Whitby, about 670. He often dined out, in company that was evidently predominantly English, where the lyre was passed round from guest to guest. He regularly left the dinner and went home before the lyre reached him, since he could not sing, perhaps because he could not yet trust his mastery of English. But one night it was his turn to undertake the job of policing stables, that evidently belonged to the monastery, and in the small hours divine inspiration prompted him to compose a hymn to the Creator. He subsequently entered the monastery, and in his old age men copied his verses into books, and perhaps on to stone.

Few other English poets are known before the 9th century. The excellence of Bede and the brilliance of Aldhelm kept Latin the language of literature; king Aethelbald of Mercia and other poets chose it as the natural language of verse. The Mercians and the West Saxons, like the Irish, wrote down traditional historical verses, notably *Beowulf* and the *Widsith*. But in the 9th century quantities of Latin literature were published in translation, and the learning of Wessex pulled together earlier monastic record into the Saxon Chronicle; its form and its earliest entries are Irish, but towards the end of the 8th century its terse notices are interrupted by the dramatic story of king Cynewulf's murder; thereafter an increasing number of long passages in resonant prose transform its character, and from the 10th century its entries include numerous poems of simple dignity. Thenceforth other authors strengthened the tradition of English writing, so that it survived the darkness of the northmen, and re-emerged when the English regained literacy in the 13th and 14th centuries.

Irish Literature

The Irish, unlike the Welsh and English, inherited an immensity of ancient tradition. Ireland was the first large territory outside the Roman empire to become Christian. It had no Latin; Christian scholars were therefore compelled to write the Irish language in Latin characters, that the scriptures might be communicated. They were also compelled to come to terms with the old learning while the old learning was compelled to make use of the new technique of alphabetic writing. The learned orders of 6th-century Ireland retained the ancient names of *drui*, *bard* and *faith*; Roman writers had used the same words six centuries and more before to describe the religious orders of the Gauls, *druides*, *bardi* and *vates*, which in their view were already older than the learning of the Greeks. The superior order of the Druids, who included learned 'philosophers' and *theologoi* who understood the words of the gods, was then divided into specialised colleges. Caesar was impressed by the number of their pupils, who travelled from afar to study for twenty years or more, memorising immense quantities of verse, for the Druids refused to permit their sacred lore to be committed to writing, though they permitted the use of Greek letters for 'public and private records'.

In Christian Ireland the name of *drui* was restricted to a class of minor scholars; bishops and abbots assumed the duties of the *theologoi*, but the colleges of learned men, termed *filid*, remained. The secular schools of the 7th century comprised three main faculties, classics (*leigind*), law (*fenechas*), and poetry and philosophy (*filidhecht*). Students were expected to study for at least 12 years and the graduate *filid* were divided into seven classes, the lowest qualified to recite 20 stories, the highest 350, which he was expected to 'synchronise and harmonise'. Many of these tales survive, in more recent versions, and the titles of hundreds more are recorded.

The pagan Irish had no alphabet, but they adapted Latin letters to a script termed *Ogam*, wherein each letter was represented by notches cut against or across the edge of a squared wooden stick; no sticks remain, but many stone memorials are so inscribed. Ogam remained the chief form of learned record until the middle of the 7th century; then Cennfaelad is said to have written down the learning of the schools 'on slates and tablets', evidently of wax, and to have fair-copied them into 'vellum books'. Columba had persuaded Christian Ireland to accept the ancient learning half a century or more before, but

Cennfaelad's innovation opened its preserves to monastic scholarship; the Annals preserve many of the ancient verses that he copied; and together with Aileran, and with his own cousin's son, Flann Fina, the future king Aldfrith of Northumbria, he is remembered among the principal doctors of 7th-century Irish learning.

The volume and antiquity of the old learning swept over Christian Irish literature. The early Irish historians were sceptical, protesting that the tales they rendered were 'not genuine history'. Nevertheless though the tales of early times are full of fancies, folk memory accurately reported some essential features of the remote past. The *filid* grouped the tales into four main cycles. The Mythological Cycle was followed by the Heroic Cycle, centred on the Ulaid heroes of about the first century AD; the Finn Cycle was concerned with Cormac's wars in the third century, and the Historic Cycle treated of more recent kings. The stories of the last three cycles abound in details of barbarian Ireland, which lasted into the 6th century, and have rightly been termed a 'Window on the Iron Age', for no other western people has preserved such vivid record of the remote past.

The weight of ancient story made the Irish more conscious of an ageless past than any other European people. It constrained the Christian Irish to continue to report the present and developed the forms of record that the Welsh and English later adapted. But it divided monk and layman. The Annalists ignored the story-tellers as often as they could, and the Latin-language Lives of the Saints were severely restricted to incidents factually related, concerning named peoples and places of the saints' own time and region. Though each story is the setting of an imaginative miracle, the Lives are cast in the mould of rational history. But the laity who knew no Latin were provided with the vernacular Irish versions, whose translators borrowed from the wonders of the story-teller without regard to time or place. Yet the quantity of stories kept them continuously alive; the Lives were recopied without interruption, suffering no periods of oblivion and revival like the tales of Welsh saints.

The Irish literary tradition was imprisoned by its own wealth and age. The discipline of the *filid* was prolonged until the Elizabethan conquest and the Cromwellian settlement; the last of the ancient scholars, Duald MacFirbis, after poverty had forced him to sell the last of his books, was murdered in a Sligo tavern in 1670, at the age of 80, by a drunken English gentleman. Learning that was older than the Greeks was ended by a sordid crime. But its discipline had long been oppressive; new literary forms were hard to evolve in a conservative tradition that issued degrees to those who mastered a set syllabus, and had no use for unqualified talent. The 'new writers' of the 8th century had forced their way into the approved canon of Irish literature, but their innovations evoked a keener response in the more receptive minds of the Welsh and of the nations of Europe than at home. The Irish poets were the first to move men deeply by tales of the tenderness of tragic love that overrides all else, but they were confined by fixed forms, traditional themes and a language unknown outside their island. They inspired the poets of the Welsh and English, and passed their stories of romantic love to the French, who permanently implanted them in the literary tradition of Europe. But they could not enrich the future of their homeland with a lasting native literature, renewing itself in successive generations with the vigour and flexibility of Welsh or English letters. The splendour of Irish learning and letters, like the inheritance of Irish art, was centred upon its Latin monasteries, not upon its secular schools or vernacular literature. That literature was not an article of export; its content and idiom were insular, and stories set in Ireland had little interest for foreigners. Its contribution to other lands was its aim and method, the recording of the past and the present and, above all, the gift to the Welsh and the English of the ability to write their own spoken language, in an age when all other literature was still composed in Latin alone.

Humour

One notable by-product of Welsh and Irish Literature was parody and satire. Though a few men wrote masterpieces and others wrote well, most produced dreary texts, pompous and jejune. Their banality provoked quiet mockery. One well worn pious theme, first elaborated in Adomnan's Life of Columba, praises the simple ignorance of children who tried to milk a bull. One author, transcribing such a tale, notes the 'columbine innocence' of Fechin of Fore who

> did not know the difference between a bull and a cow, and went up to a bull, and squeezed its genitals like a cow's udder.

The bull not only tolerated the assault, but gave milk. The author drily comments on

> a remarkable and unusual novelty. But that is what is possible in a country where honey is commonly produced from stones, and oil from the hardest rocks,

for such marvels were commoner in the Lives of the Saints of Ireland than of other lands.

Many authors vaunt the magic of the saint's curse, that kills the impious; and avoid the implication of a divine murderer by making the saint's prayer restore his victim to a penitent life. When the author of the verse Life of Senan met such a tale, he turned it to irreverent doggerel,

> The pious father's prayer
> Produced a sweetly flowing spring
> That the brethren largely used
> And thanked him for as often. . . .

There the holy Finan
The blessed man's disciple . . .
Came as was his wont
To sit beside the well,
Praising life's creator.

There came a peasant girl
And sat herself beside him.
She brought her little boy
To wash him clean. . . .

Most ill the monk regarded
The interruption of his prayer
By the washing of a child,
Polluting holy liquor.

So, moved to anger
For the wronging of the well,
He prayed to God
To sink the child beneath the waves.

Soon the waters' flux
That daily mounted there
At God's command took off the lad
And bore him out to sea.

When the mother saw him
Carried far from shore
Straightaway she sought the bishop
Wailing for her son. . . .

Stern the bishop summoned him
And bade him straightaway
Fetch back the wretched child
Or else be drowned himself.

No sooner said, the holy man
Ran off to brave the danger,
Sparing not his feet,
His holy staff in hand.

Carefully he measured
How deep the waters were
Wishing to wade no deeper
Than his holy middle.

For he was fearful
And had a firm intention
To go no deeper in
Than his staff would show was safe. . . .

Then, lo, a miracle.
The sea beneath his feet
Turned hard as rock
Although it was most deep. . . .

And there he found the lad
Not dead, but playing happily. . . .

The credit for the miracle
The master gave to the disciple,
The disciple to the master.

Yet in the eyes of each
Both of them were very humble,
And seeing what was done
They honoured one another.

Such elaborate parody is unusual; but light irony is not uncommon. Another convention gives many saints long conversations with angels. One author protested. Transcribing the tireless energy with which the virgin Attracta pestered the Deity to add a minor miracle to a mighty wonder, he made the angel of the Lord warn her solemnly

The Lord thy God is getting bored with thee.

Sometimes irony preached common sense; the strongest of conventions required saints of eminence to revive many from the dead, but such wonders normally belonged to the remote past. The author of an Irish Life of Adomnan dealt severely with an embarrassing consequence. When the body of the king of the Picts was brought to Iona for burial in 691 Adomnan and his clergy kept vigil by the bier. During the night a limb of the corpse moved, as rigor mortis set in. Movement naturally caused excitement, and raised expectation of a latter-day resurrection. But a 'certain pious man' warned Adomnan

> if you try to raise the dead, your precedent will become a reproach to your successors, who cannot do so.

Adomnan was made to reply

> There is something in what you say. It will be more proper to confine ourselves to blessing the body and soul of the king.

Irish irony was occasionally echoed by the Welsh. A favourite mythological theme is the hero who takes the shape of an animal. In the late Mabinogion tale called *Taliesin*, Ceridwen pursued Gwion Bach, who turned himself into a hare; so she became a greyhound, an otter when he became a fish, a hawk when he flew away as a bird; as he dived into a heap of corn to become a wheat grain, she became a hen and gobbled him up. The pursuit ended, and

> she bore him nine months, and when she was delivered of him, she

found him too beautiful to kill, so she put him in a leather bag and threw him into the sea. And it was the 29th day of April.

Welsh prose authors were of sufficient intellectual calibre to protest against the sterility of a worn-out convention as vigorously as Cervantes' *Don Quixote* protests against the rubbishy late romances of chivalry.

Parody courts disaster when it is so subtle that men do not perceive it; and Welsh parody aborted in catastrophe. The eccentric genius of Geoffrey of Monmouth in the 12th century protested against the arid academics of his day, notably Henry of Huntingdon and William of Malmesbury, and gleefully refuted them with a pretended Welsh book which, he warned his more sober readers, stemmed from Walter Map of Oxford, who was then well known as a satirist, a wit, and a literary practical joker. He should have been safe enough, for he used the standard texts known to the academic historians, and made fun of them. He repeated the Roman historian's account of the defeat of a third-century British rebel by the Caesar Constantius and his prefect Asclepiodotus; but when he decorated known history by appointing Asclepiodotus to the dukedom of Cornwall, and marrying Constantius to the daughter of Old King Cole, he and the historians knew that he was satirising. When he reproduced Bede's account of the wars of Catwallaun and Penda, he and they knew that he was guying history when he made Catwallaun outlive Penda, that the British might bury him in a bronze horse on the top of Ludgate; any educated man might read Bede for himself.

Geoffrey's wry fancy stirred his many sources into a soup of names. But his jest took himself and his readers captive. Whether he liked it or not, he was taken seriously. His mock solemnity aped the formalism of academic teaching, as bitingly as Selman and Yeats' *1066 and All That* in our day; he was as convincingly soaked in his material as Tolkien, author of *Lord of the Rings*. But Geoffrey confused satire with sincerity, putting into his book his own deeply held philosophy. Of Armorican origin, born in Wales, he was a patriotic servant of the English king, convinced that Britain was a family of nations among whom the English were senior; the fiction that made Loegrius of England the elder brother of Albanus and Camber of Scotland and Wales personified his conviction, and was a potent immediate political ideal, acceptable not only to the English but also to propertied Welshmen and Scots, who welcomed an excuse to decline futile national resistance that risked their lands and property.

Geoffrey's convincing fantasy was immediately accepted; it remained the received account of British history for many centuries, the foundation upon which Great Britain was built. It was not seriously challenged until the Renaissance, and was widely believed into the 18th century. Even today a thick dust of Geoffrey's imagination obscures understanding. Since countless names and incidents that Geoffrey annexed occur in other records, it is still quite common to cite Geoffrey as though he might be evidence for some tradition otherwise lost. Yet most of his sources are known; and his riotous plunder of the names they mention regularly and deliberately conflicts with what they say; even if he plundered an unknown source, his use of it was perverse. It ought not to be necessary to warn that no word or line of Geoffrey can legitimately be considered in the study of any historical problem; but the warning unfortunately remains necessary.

Parody can be powerful, even when it is known for what it is. But it is rare. The main body of Irish, Welsh and English literature in the 6th and 7th centuries is sober and straightforward. It was one of the formative influences in the literature of Europe. It stimulated the renewed vigour of Latin, and enriched it with a delight in language and a zest for experiment that classical tradition had long since stifled. But its most important influence was the precedent it set. Because the native languages of the British Isles were written, they became a model and an encouragement to the nations of Europe, who ultimately freed themselves from the exclusive use of Latin letters and took to writing original work in their own tongues. Modern European literature was born in the peculiar conditions of the British Isles in the sixth century, and was nursed by bilingual monks. The short life of Arthurian Britain brought into being a society that needed a modern literature, and knew how to create it.

CHAPTER TWENTY-TWO

THE ECONOMY

Roman Britain

Almost all men lived by the land, and fared better on good lands. But the fall of Rome left lands good and bad peopled by farmers of unlike skills and experience. The fertile lowlands were wasted; from the sandy coasts of Germany the first English brought techniques fitted only for alluvial lands by river banks, and for soils as easy. The wealth of the Severn estuary escaped the wars, but not the ruin of the Roman economy; the Pennine north, the Welsh hills and the Dumnonian moors were less affected, for they were poorer lands, that had never shared in the prosperity of the lowlands, and the north had always obeyed a hungry army. Beyond the Roman frontiers little changed, and in Armorica British immigrants resumed the cultivation of lands untilled for many years, but still recognisably cleared. The sources that described the agriculture of each region are as varied, and are imperfectly assessed; most of them are published but the texts are often indifferently edited, and rarely analysed. The ancient laws of the Welsh, the Irish and the English illuminate much of Britain, but the histories of churchmen, and the land grants of the Irish, Welsh and English are preserved only from a few regions. There is plenty of raw evidence, but until it has been sifted, the links between the several texts are hard to recognise; their undigested statements provoke a turbulence of ideas, whose ordering and assessment must await the labours of the future.

Roman Britain had integrated widely different economies. In the lowlands, towns large and small were set close together, 8 to 12 miles apart, joined to one another and to the surrounding rural population by main and minor roads. The owners of mansions, of substantial farms and of small cottages were all able to buy large quantities of pottery and other commercial products. But the highlands were poorer and more isolated; often a scrap of metal or a couple of pot sherds is the only evidence that a pre-Roman Iron Age farm lasted into and through the Roman period; and many others that lack such scraps may have lasted as long. Small regions differ greatly from each other, but the overall contrast between the two main divisions of Britain is sharp and clear. The peasants of the lowlands were exploited by their lords, but they were fully absorbed into Roman civilisation, customers in its markets; the small farmers in much of the highlands were little affected by Roman economy, but they were integrated into the Roman state by the agencies of government, language and law, that made them Roman citizens.

The last generations of Roman Britain brought important change to the lowlands. The ownership of land was concentrated into the hands of fewer great landowners, including the emperor, many of them absentees; many isolated farms of the early empire were deserted, and in several areas peasants congregated in poorly built villages and hamlets. On absentee estates the mansions rotted, but rents were collected, and unwanted living rooms were sometimes used as storehouses or workshops. Periodical fairs eroded the trade of some towns and many renders were paid in kind. Currency disappeared from much of the countryside, and concentrated in some great ports, like Richborough, in some towns, or parts of towns, and on fairgrounds, where peasants and their masters sold their produce to pay their dues, and spent what cash was left. Beyond these centres distribution proceeded by barter and exchange, and by the management of bailiffs.

The root cause of change was the crushing weight of taxation. Its consequence, the uneven circulation of late money, does not mean that more people lived in areas where money was more plentiful, or that people died or went away where money ceased to circulate. But it does mean that the fibres which bound countrymen to the urban economy were weakening. Farmers whose ancestors had been poor freeholders or tenants became *coloni*, semi-servile bondsmen, squeezed hard to pay their dues to the factor of an alien owner, less able to afford the manufacturers' products. Until the quantities and proportions of late objects on different kinds of sites have been studied more closely, it is not possible to discover how these changes progressed in different areas. But the direction of change was to detach the lowland peasant from Roman civilisation, to approximate him towards the status of the highland cultivator. It also prepared him for the future. His ancestors had been citizens of Roman *civitates*, poor, but none the less citizens. He became the servile dependent of a distant lord. That bond was easily snapped by political crisis. In Europe, the grandson of Ausonius of Bordeaux found it impossible to collect his rents from Macedonia in the Balkans, where Goths were settled as local landlords. After the political separation of Britain from Rome in 410 some Europeans who owned estates in Britain may have continued to receive their rents; but the disasters of the mid fifth century clearly smashed all alien obligations, as well as many of those due to the native magnates who were massacred or emigrated abroad.

In lowland Britain the old landlords were not replaced by new Germanic landowners, as in Macedonia or Gaul, for the English were not yet able to settle most of the territories they raided. In many areas the peasants of Roman Britain were freed from their old tribute. Those who remained on their land during the wars of the later fifth century faced the irregular demands of British war bands and the risk of plundering English forces; when the lowland areas were recovered by the forces of Ambrosius and Arthur, they were exposed to more regular impositions, at first their patriotic contributions to the war effort of their fellow-citizens, the *cives* or *Cumbrogi*, later the tributes of corn that fed the warlords' horses. The changes of the late empire had prepared them to become tributary subjects. The peace of Arthur directly subjected them to the demands of a new government. But in the interval no force had compelled them to grow more than they needed for their families; and a government that had to exact tribute direct from peasants, without the intermediary of landed nobility, cannot have enforced anything like as large a surplus of food production as the empire had enjoyed. The sixth-century economy was agricultural alone, admitting no role for towns; that is why in Gildas' day the towns were 'no longer inhabited as they used to be'.

Arable and Pasture

Arthur and his successors inherited two quite different kinds of agriculture, both established for many centuries. In simple language, the economy of lowland Roman Britain was arable, the economy of the highland west and north pastoral, geared upon cattle; and the economy of the barbarians beyond the frontier, in Ireland and the north, was also pastoral. The words are over-simple. The pastoral, cattle-raising peoples grew some corn, fodder for beasts, bread or porridge for themselves; arable farmers kept cows for milk and butter, and sometimes ate meat, if only on festive occasions. Britain was renowned for one specialised breed, exported to Ireland. But, variations apart, the extremes are the economy of Ireland, where cattle loomed large and corn was secondary, and that of the rich lowlands, where corn mattered more than cows.

An important indication in the balance of the economy lies in the proportions between different kinds of animals. Normally, settled farmers with acres to plough tend to have more sheep or pigs. The quantities of animal bones are not always thoroughly analysed; but the recent report of the excavation of a small chieftain's fortress at Dinas Powys near Cardiff examined bones from the kitchen refuse of the 5th and 6th centuries, and compared them with the figures available from Irish sites of the same period, as well as with three downland Wessex sites, one pre-Roman, one Roman, and one of the Arthurian period. The proportions in the three periods in Wessex are roughly similar to one another. But the regions contrast. In Dinas Powys, in the Vale of Glamorgan, an extension of lowland Britain, cattle bones make one-fifth of the total; in arable Wessex they are about one-third, but in Ireland they are well over three-quarters. In the Wessex chalklands sheep are as numerous as cattle, pigs fewer. In the wooded country of Dinas Powys, pigs constitute nearly two-thirds of the total, sheep barely one-eighth. In Ireland pigs and sheep are both few, and horses are numerous only in Wessex.

Ireland

The texts concur. Cattle obtrude into every Irish story. In the Irish reckoning of value, the unit of the *cumal*, 'slave girl', derived from the raiding days of the 4th century, was equated with three cows, and became the standard unit of price. In Wales, grants ascribed to the 7th and later centuries in the Llancarfan and Llandaff registers normally price swords, horses and other commodities as worth so many cows, usually three or four. Lists of renders emphasise that cattle remained less important than in Ireland. Payments due in the early 9th century to Llandeilo near Carmarthen, extant in the original, specify stated quantities of sheep and of bread and of butter, but not of live cows; those of Wessex, a century earlier, demand 300 loaves, much beer and butter, but only 2 cows or 10 wethers from each 100 hides; Llancarfan and Llandaff grants relating to the 6th, 7th and 8th centuries fix payments in beer and bread, meat and honey. They specify quantity only for the beer, and do not distinguish the kind of meat. But the tributes claimed in the Irish Book of Rights, set down much later, after arable agriculture had greatly extended in Ireland, still require no bread, corn or beer, and cattle still outnumber other animals.

Monastic economy transformed agriculture. Until the fifth century Irish cattle and Wessex corn marked the extreme variations; but the sixth century brought a large extension of agriculture, most marked in Ireland, where arable had hitherto been least in evidence. The chief agent of change was the monastery. Monasteries were many, and some were very large. All were stable communities in need of food; many refused to eat meat on principle, and all required a great deal of corn and many vegetables. They were established in south Wales, where the elements of an arable economy already existed; in Brittany where abandoned Roman estates were not yet wholly overgrown; in Ireland; and on a lesser scale in north Wales and northern Britain, where the cattle economy was not yet adapted to their needs.

The accounts of the first monks are shot through with conscious enthusiasm for pioneering agriculture. The austerity of David, Carthacus, Fintan Munnu and others required their monks to pull their own ploughs, but most houses used animals. All were eager for results. Ciaran of Clonmacnoise experimented with a horse-drawn plough, Aed with a three-ox plough. David's tradition boasted of his enormous yield, despite his lack of oxen, and Illtud's king is made to encourage him to 'till the land until it is rich in harvests', for 'it is land that ought to be cultivated', more fertile than 'the soil of Italy'. The Irish experimented with new fruits, and imported bee-keeping from Britain. In Brittany, Paul Aurelian, Fracan and others took over Roman estates, where their first concern was to beat the bounds and secure legal entitlement, their second to establish a secure water supply; for the saint whose staff tapped the ground to call forth a miraculous spring was archaeologist enough to know that a Roman site must have a well, that probing might discover. Elsewhere, on overgrown land, Maudetus burnt the scrub, and Leonorus felled trees, though he could not move the trunks until a miraculous storm swept them away.

In Britain and Ireland there was less empty land. In north Wales, Beuno secured the grant of particular estates already defined, but found that one of them already had a legal occupant, whom the king had dispossessed without his knowledge. In Ireland Berachus and others acquired land that had formerly belonged to druids, while king Angus of Munster, in the late 5th century, took it for granted that churchmen, if granted property at all, should receive 'good fertile lands near my royal residence'. But many saints deliberately sought solitude, removed from the territories where men ordinarily lived. Samson sought and found isolated lands in Cornwall and Brittany; Irishmen looked for them in or across the Atlantic, and some found them, in Ocean islands and in Iceland. In Ireland itself numerous accounts imply the establishment of monasteries on land not previously cultivated; for the crops of their early years were frequently disturbed by the horses, or sometimes the cattle, that had formerly pastured there.

Several texts minutely list the farmer's tools and furniture. The most striking innovation in Ireland and in Brittany is the water mill, named in many Lives, usually powered by the diversion of a river or the construction of a canal, occasionally worked by the tides; and in Italy the novel skills of Irish water engineers seemed miraculous to Gregory the Great. The baker (*pistor*) is frequently mentioned in all countries, but few stories are told of mills in Britain. Harvesting is as common an occasion for miracles as ploughing; harvested corn needed threshing and drying. Cainnech's monks complained that 'in wet weather we cannot thresh the corn without a building to protect it'. Cainnech's monastery did not then have

> craftsmen and workmen capable of building a shed for the drying and threshing of corn,

so he solved the immediate problem by blessing the 'open floor', which thereafter stayed dry without a roof while rain fell around it.

Skill was needed less for the shed itself (*canaba*), than for the kiln within. The Life of Ciaran of Clonmacnoise names the apparatus, *zabulum*, and describes it as

> a wheel made of interwoven brushwood, covered with ears of corn, placed over a fire, for drying and threshing in the manner of the westerners, that is of the British and Irish.

It differed from the stone and tile flues for drying corn that have been recognised on Roman farms in Britain, and could leave little archaeological trace beyond a burnt patch on the ground, with holes for supporting the posts. But corn kilns, whatever their construction, are in the Roman centuries peculiar to Britain, and have not yet been noticed in the European provinces; they are also frequently named in early medieval Welsh and Irish texts. Many Irish saints had such kilns, and one Irish monastic poem defines the process of corn production as 'ploughing, reaping, scorching'. In both Welsh and Irish law the corn kiln was regarded as essential to any well stocked farm; it is likely to have been brought by monks from Britain to Ireland.

At first, monks aroused hostility in many kings and lords, who lost manpower and revenue. Many kings sought to use the concentrated resources of the monasteries to maintain their men, by billeting or tribute; and very many tales of early monks record grants of exemption secured by the miraculous punishment of wicked kings who demanded secular service. Some rulers were thoroughly hostile to the expanding monks; a few were friendly from the first and gave them land, the more readily because many monastic founders preferred remote and underpopulated regions, of little profit to the kings. But some lords demanded and obtained compensation; Patrick had to pay a price for the individuals he converted and Finnian of Clonard paid an ounce of gold for a site in Leinster. Many Welsh and a few Irish grants detail the expensive gifts that brought permanent exemption from dues and claims from a variety of lay proprietors and rulers.

Enclosures

Monastic agriculture required the enclosure of open lands. Illtud and Paul Aurelian built sea dykes to reclaim coastal tracts; Tyssilio planted hedges in north Wales; Blaan built field walls in Bute; Lasrian of Devenish helped Aed to bring woodland under the plough. But the monks were not the only enclosers. Ireland was full of growing dynasties, and local warlords multiplied in Britain, while kings great and small sought horse pastures. Many Irish saints suffered from the encroachment of royal horses; in Wales Illtud was troubled by a royal *praepositus* who took over his meadows and impounded his cattle to make room for the king's horses.

Most of the stories told of monastic enclosure concern the clearance of waste land for arable farming, but most accounts of early secular enclosure concern the seizure of grazing land for horse pasture; but there are exceptions. Some monasteries were planted in well-populated lands, and sometimes aroused popular resentment. In Brittany Malo was accused of engrossing so much land that the next generation would have nothing to live on, and was expelled by the indignation of the 'godless' population. Beuno in Wales and Berachus in Ireland were among those who faced angry dispossessed owners. Arable farming among laymen was denounced when it enclosed former open grazing lands. Resentment is strongest in the traditions of Brigit of Kildare, who lived and died before male monasteries became numerous, about the late 530s. Her economy is principally concerned with dairy farming, rather than with the growing of crops, and an early Life, by Ultan, vividly expresses popular hostility to lay enclosures. A wealthy nobleman of Macha, Armagh, was

> cursed by everyone in the district, as a farmer who surrounds his lands with hedges, changing all the open straight roads.

On another occasion when Brigit drove in her carriage in Leinster she found a man fencing his land. He refused to let her drive through and told her to go round; her driver disregarded her advice to avoid a quarrel, and tried to force his way through. The landowner resisted and the carriage was overturned, but a speedy death brought to the enclosing farmer his just deserts. Nevertheless cornlands were spreading by the 550s, when the child Lugid fell foul of a secular miller.

Over the next hundred years enclosure greatly increased, and many men hungered. Famine sealed the change. The most detailed account is preserved in the Life of 'Gerald' of Mayo. About 665, shortly before the great plague, the pressure of a starving population constrained the high kings Diarmait and Blathmacc, sons of Aed Slane, to convene clerics and laymen in an assembly of all Ireland at Tara. The kings' edict proposed to allot to each *colonus*, or subject tenant, a minimum holding of 7 to 9 *iugera*, about 10 acres, of good land, with 8 of rough land and 9 of woodland, because

> the population was so great that the whole land did not suffice them for agriculture.

The nobility, encouraged by abbot Fechin of Fore, opposed the edict, and prayed to the Lord to send some sickness that might relieve them of

> a part of the burdensome multitude of inferior people, that the rest might live more easily . . . since overpopulation was the cause of the famine.

Gerald denounced the monstrous proposition, inhuman and immoral, on the ground that

> it is no harder for God to augment the food supply than to increase the population.

Fechin's prayer was granted, but Gerald's humanity was justified, for God's anger killed Fechin in the plague, together with the kings of Ireland and many other notables, but Gerald was spared. Plague solved the immediate crisis, and weakened resistance to enclosures, for the reduced population pressed less upon the land, and in the next generation arable agriculture took too firm a hold to be overset thereafter.

Tradition looked back upon the plague and the Tara convention as the turning point in Irish agriculture, dramatically condensing the processes of two centuries into the years of crisis alone. The Life of Flannan of Killaloe explained that until his time, in the early and mid 7th century

> the earth was unsown and no seed was sown.

Another tradition held that

> there was neither mound nor hedge nor stone walls round land in

> Ireland, . . . until the time of the sons of Aed Slane, but all was unbroken plain.

These are the tales that later Irishmen set down. The central dispute reported from the convention of Tara is not confined to seventh-century Ireland; it is the enduring argument between those who hold that hunger should be stopped by keeping down the numbers of the population, and those who would change the economy to increase the food supply.

The stories give no detail of who went hungry; but the core of the problem is written into the circumstances of expanding arable agriculture. Those who managed to enclose sufficient land prospered; those who starved were men whose livelihood had depended on grazing the lands now enclosed; and when possessions were few, famine struck easily. Throughout Ireland, the scale of property was small. A law tract, set down a generation or so later, after arable farming was well established, defines the minimum qualification that entitled a man to the rank of noble, *bo-aire*, 'lord of cattle'. But, by the time of the law tract, the cattle lord needed land as well. The lowest grade required 7 *celi*, 'vassals' or dependent labourers, 12 cows, 16 sheep, and land worth 14 *cumal* or 42 cows, with a corn kiln, mill and barn. The possession of a plough, with twice as much land and proportionately more animals, bestowed a more honourable rank; the highest grade, the *aire forgaill*, who commanded a hundred in war, needed no more land, but must have a minimum of 28 dependents, 30 cows and 30 sheep. Twice that mobile property, 40 dependents, with 60 cows and 60 sheep, was the qualification of the lowest grade of king, the king of a *tuath*, or people. The higher grades are distinguished from their inferiors by the ownership of more cattle, and the control of more dependents, but not by any larger acreage. It is therefore probable that the basis of the grading dates back to the centuries before the enclosures, and that the extension of arable farming added to a pre-existing system the need for 14 or 28 *cumals* of land, with the accessory equipment for harvested corn, the kiln, the mill and the barn.

These herds are not large, but they match the dimensions of the smaller excavated *raths*. Commonly a roughly circular enclosed area, about 100 feet in diameter, contained a barn, a few querns, occasionally a kiln, and a house, with a superficial area of between 100 and 200 square feet, enough for the parents and children of a single family; it might accommodate the cattle of the *bo-aire*, when weather or danger constrained him to congregate them within his defences. Ploughs, discovered on about 10% of the sites, are listed as the mark of the higher grades of *bo-aire*; while the very small enclosures, surrounding a single house without a barn, suggest the homes of the dependent *celi*.

When 12 cows made a nobleman, plebeians were poor. Their few cows and a little land were at the mercy of a cattle plague or a poor harvest, and they lacked any communal reserve. Another law tract defined 'the full property of the *tuath*, the legal equal right of men of all degrees'; the common property was limited to defined rights on wood and water, both of them regarded as private property on which the public retained a few minor claims, but only the upland, 'the unenclosed above the rest', remained common. Whatever the *tuath* had owned earlier was gone; enclosure was thorough and complete. Private pasture and private arable fields had replaced 'unbroken plains'.

Tradition outlines a double-sided process. At first, dynasts and local lords enclosed chiefly for cattle and horses, monasteries for arable farming; but later laymen also turned to arable, and by the middle of the 7th century enclosure provoked the insurgent demand for the distribution of the land, the familiar demand that runs through the history of peasant societies from the Hebrews, the Greeks and the Romans to the present day.

The aftermath of the plague consolidated change. Arable enclosure riveted the grip of little local lords in Ireland upon their dependent herdsmen and cultivators. It also opened new possibilities to agriculture abroad. It brought the economy of Ireland closer to the economy that Britain had inherited from the Roman past, and made new ideas easier to exchange and imitate. The difference was chiefly in outlook. In the former provinces of Rome the techniques of arable agriculture were old and conservative. But since arable farming was itself new to the Irish, they were as open to new techniques as to old ways. They made the water mill a commonplace instead of a rarity, pioneered horse-ploughing and other novelties. They were still innovators when they carried the faith and the economy of the monastery to Europe. They came at a time when important new technical possibilities had entered Europe from the east. The sixth-century Avars and the Slavs brought with them the Chinese devices of the metal stirrup and the horse collar. The stirrup in time transformed warfare, and the collar made the horse economic. In antiquity the horse that pulled against a trace exerted hardly more than four times the strength of a man, and cost four times as much as a man to feed; but the collar quadrupled the power of the horse, and more than justified his cost.

The innovations spread slowly and unevenly, for they could not be fully exploited until they were fitted to the heavy horse. The heavy horse was bred in antiquity, but is not known to have been common outside the small territory of Noricum, roughly modern Austria. Its first familiar breeding-ground elsewhere is in Flanders, in or shortly before the 11th century. It was bred because the collar and the stirrup needed it. Little is yet known of who disseminated the new devices, or when and where, between the 6th century and the 11th; but it is likely that the monasteries of Irish and Anglo-Irish origin in Europe were a principal agent in making men familiar with the new possibilities. They developed a concentrated agriculture, much of it in lands hitherto lightly tilled; and were readier than others to seize upon new methods. The monks were the first westerners who made peaceful contact with the Slavs, hitherto sundered from Christendom by the pagan Saxons and Thuringians; and were first able to appreciate the value of the horse collar. Their close contacts with one another enabled new knowledge to travel fast from Bohemia and the Danube to the low countries and France. Direct evidence is wanting, for early monastic records in Europe concentrate upon churchmen and rulers, and have little to say of agricultural practice. What is known is that the monks were better placed than others to observe and make known the new agricultural possibilities.

The Picts

Monasteries transformed the economy of Ireland, and opened new possibilities in Europe. Elsewhere their impact was less dramatic, though often important. Among the Picts evidence fails. Some had slaves; elaborate tombstones and the text of Adomnan betoken a nobility; some property was private, and was bequeathed by inheritance. Roman writers assert that the Picts were wholly unacquainted with tillage, but doubtless generalise from the rougher highlands, for the cultivation of the more fertile regions, ample in the middle ages, is likely to be as old as the Romans, or older. Irish monasteries spread in and after the 7th century, stimulating arable farming, and in time the Irish absorbed the Picts. But the evidence is not yet enough to show how, when and where the economy changed.

The British and the English

Among the northern British monasteries were few, and were soon overtaken by English conquest, before they had time to bring significant change to the older economy. In the shattered lowlands of Britain crops were grown and horses reared to feed the wartime armies and the warbands that succeeded Arthur. But there is as yet hardly any evidence for their economy before the English conquest.

The English themselves brought from Germany a mixed economy, whose balance of corn and cattle fitted well with the economy they found in Roman Britain. At first they were confined to lands easily tilled, but in time they learnt to plough heavier soils; their adaptation and diffusion will be known when care is taken to observe the local geological situation of the sites of successive periods. But their most striking difference from the British is in their homes. Most of the British, like the Irish, lived in isolated homesteads; small towns were numerous, and some peasants gathered into villages in some regions at the end of the empire, but the great majority still lived on isolated farmsteads, commonly rectangular. But the first English, in Britain as in Germany, normally lived in concentrated villages. In the less permeable soils of Britain they changed the architecture of their cottages. Their rural homes in Germany were also rectangular timber buildings, often long and thin, with cattle sheds built onto the living room. Though some such houses are found in Britain, the overwhelming majority lived in short rectangular dug-out houses; a foot or two of soil was removed and piled into a low wall around the edges of the excavation to keep out the water that would not drain away. Groups of such houses were built within the walls of

Canterbury, Dorchester-on-Thames and other Roman towns, and in the open country, often closely adjacent to Roman farms. The graveyards are similarly located, and, until the colonising period of the late 6th and early 7th centuries, the great majority are the burial-grounds of small communities; only a very few sites contain one or two burials in each successive generation, suggesting the burial-place of a single family homestead.

In the colonising period, from the late sixth century onward, many more single burials and many place names suggest a much higher proportion of homestead than of village settlement. But the homestead, like the village, practised a mixed economy, attested by the laws and by the words used for new settlements. It is probable that English farming technique had learnt something from its short fifth-century apprenticeship to the economy of Roman Britain. But there is no reason to suppose that there was significant change in the balance of the economy, the type of crops cultivated, the breeds of cattle raised. Nor had the English the same need of monastic agriculture. Monasteries were proportionately fewer; though many extended the arable acreage, secular colonisation opened up far more empty lands. The impact of monastic economy is more noticeable as a stimulus and example to the lay farmer than as a source of change in his methods.

Among the Welsh, monasteries are relatively few in the north, though some of them were very large. In the south, they were many. Most were quite small, but their number attests a considerable withdrawal of population from their old homes and a noteworthy extension of arable farming, much of it in areas where evidence for earlier cultivation is weak or wanting. The British Lives have more to say than the Irish about estates that paid rent to monasteries. Their stories more often illustrate the breaking of fresh lands to the plough, by existing methods, than a change in the economy, for in several regions, arable farming was already extensive. Throughout, Welsh miracles have more to do with corn and less with animals than the Irish. Few concern the water mill, for the techniques of an established arable economy were less responsive to innovation than in a land where arable farming was itself relatively novel; from the early 7th century onward, it became increasingly easy for dependent peasants to feed the Welsh monasteries. The impact of the monasteries extended the area of cultivation, and change has more to do with social organisation than with farming methods. Wealth increased, and its increase is confirmed by excavation, for the quantities of imports discovered on substantial sites argue that kings and monks were rich enough to pay for them. Their riches were not drawn from monasteries modelled upon the practice of David, whose inmates provided all their needs by their own labour, but from those who were supplied by the labour of *operarii*, dependent cultivators, in the tradition of Cadoc and Illtud, or by the dues furnished from estates instanced in the grants of Llandeilo, Llancarfan and Llandaff. Such dues were evidently already paid in the 6th century, for it is not probable that the tiny monastery of Tintagel, on an isolated rock off the coast, found the means to pay for the imports that excavation has there revealed solely from the acreage that the monks were able to till or pasture themselves. Their meditations are likely to have been sustained by food contributed by lay farmers on the lands above the cliffs, in sufficient quantity to afford a surplus for the purchase of foreign produce.

Craftsmen

Throughout the British Isles the economy was agricultural, and during the 6th and 7th centuries, the quantity of corn produced increased. Much of it went to monasteries and kings, and both were able to maintain specialised craftsmen. Simpler trades required few special skills; monasteries and their churches were normally of wood, save in Cornwall and parts of Wales, where abundant stone had always been cheap and easily available. The *artifex*, the craftsman, protected by his status in the older ordering of barbarian Irish society, was in short supply and high demand. Cainnech could not find a craftsman to make a kiln; Brendan had to go to Connacht to find a man who could build a timber boat; the father of Ciaran of Clonmacnoise was a carriage-wright, free to migrate from one lord to another, all of whom were eager to receive him; Findbarr was also the son of a smith, of considerable personal independence.

But from the beginning monasteries as well as kings kept their own craftsmen. Brendan of Clonfert maintained goldsmiths. Mo-Choemog's father was Ita's smith, 'skilled in wood and stone'. Expanding agriculture created a demand for the *artifex* who could build a mill, and several houses produced their own engineers. Irish carriages and carriage horses were prized, and Samson's biographer makes a boast of those that the saint brought back with him from Ireland. But the principal effort of the monastic artisan was directed to the production of things needed by the monastery that were elsewhere unobtainable, church furniture, books and bookbindings, bells, croziers and the like. Tradition celebrates Dagaeus as the founder of the Irish ecclesiastical art, in enthusiastic detail, but it also especially honours Columba of Iona as the inspirer or organiser of Irish calligraphy, of the dissemination of Gospel Books, and as the protector of traditional learning within the new Christian society. The outstanding achievements of Irish art, the Books of Durrow, Lindisfarne and Kells, are all products of Columban houses; the exquisite pillow stones of Lindisfarne, and the great stone crosses of northern England, also derive from the Columban inspiration, adapted by pupils.

Among the British, the technology of the Roman engineer and builder died with urban civilisation. The English brought with them skilled jewellers and potters, whose products were at first used in quantity in every village; in the 7th century, the craftsmen of Kent took hold of Frankish decorative tradition and transformed it into the short-lived splendour of Kentish ornament, that ranks among the noblest achievements of the jeweller's craft in any age in any country. But its splendour confined it to the rich, and as the craftsmen found wealthy patrons, so the tradition of fine ornament made for simple villagers faded away. It did not long outlive the pagan religion. Thenceforth pottery and ornament are rare in farm and village; where they survived, in towns and among the well-to-do, they soon lost their vitality. The arts and skills of Christian England are not those of the potter and the jeweller, but of the church, of its literature and its art. There the craftsman prospered, for in the lay society of Rome, and of the German barbarians, the craftsman was a humble servant, but the craftsmen of the church inherited something of the high honour accorded to the artisan in the tradition of Ireland.

Exchange and Trade

Some foreign trade persisted at all times, from the Roman empire to the late middle ages. But often there was little of it, and that little reached only to the surface of society. Wine came to Britain and to Ireland. In Muirchu's account King Loegaire drank wine at Tara in the 430s; whether he did or not, Muirchu in the 7th century thought it normal that he should. 'Merchants who came with Gallic wine' visited Clonmacnoise, but their visit was isolated and long-remembered; and Muirchu also regarded the 'wonderful foreign bronze vessel' that Daire gave to Patrick as a rarity. But though wine and foreign bronzes were rare, traffic of some sort was less unusual. Columba learnt of a disastrous eruption in Italy from the crew of a Gallic vessel that put in to a Kintyre harbour. Columban was deported a few years later from Nantes on a 'ship engaged in the Irish trade'. Early in the 5th century Patrick had embarked 200 miles from Sliabh Mis in Antrim, scarcely nearer than Wexford or Cork. As well as direct voyages to Europe there was plenty of traffic through Wales and Cornwall; the commonest landfalls in Britain were Porth Mawr, Whitesands Bay, in Pembrokeshire, and Padstow, and the main port of embarkation for Europe was Fowey. Little is said of the manner of travel, save for those who crossed on miraculous leaves or stones, but most voyaged like Finnian of Llancarfan 'with merchants, but with a different purpose, he seeking to purchase the kingdom of heaven, they to gain worldly lucre', in a journey that brought him to St. David's by Porth Mawr.

What was traded is less clear than the fact of trade. The pottery imports are of two main kinds. Mediterranean vessels, including a fair proportion of wine jars, are common in Cornwall, Somerset and south Wales, and are also found on some southern Irish sites; Gaulish vessels are found on the same sites, and also in Meath, Ulster and south-west Scotland. The Irish distributions may prove misleading when other sites elsewhere are excavated in greater numbers, but the present pattern is clear. The mediterranean trade is evidenced from the other end by a single passage in the Life of an Egyptian saint of the early 7th century, John the Almsgiver; a vessel sailed to Alexandria from Britain with a cargo of tin, doubtless from Cornwall. The products of Irish monastic craftsmen circulated among foreign monasteries and were rewarded with corresponding ecclesiastical gifts, but they had less value in secular society; in the one recorded transaction, about 800, a layman sold the Book of Teilo, or Chad, to the monastery for no more than a 'best horse'. Irish brooches are occasionally found in Britain, but a lead pattern, prepared for the casting of an Irish brooch-maker's mould, found at Dinas Powys, near Cardiff, suggests that the craftsman exported himself rather than his product. Similarly, the splendid scroll escutcheons attached to hanging bowls that are often found in rich late pagan English graves are of Irish workmanship; but it is likely that their makers worked in Britain.

The mediterranean trade brought wine, perhaps in larger quantities than later Irishmen knew, and carried back metals; it was essentially trade with the Severn estuary, a very little of which spilled over into Munster. The Gaulish trade is another matter. It brought domestic pottery, jugs, plates and bowls, and doubtless other perishable goods whose nature is guesswork. It may have taken away cloaks, dogs, horses and the like. Its currency was precious metal. The merchants who sailed to Pembrokeshire sought 'lucre', and 'lucre' was known and feared in monasteries; abbess Ita so abhorred it that she washed her hands if she touched silver; but she evidently sometimes had to touch it, and Finnian of Clonard had to pay for land in gold. Some of the metal currency is identifiable; some silver ingots found in Britain, Ireland and Germany are dated to the early 5th century by their maker's name, and unstamped rings or bars of gold and silver that carry no date doubtless circulated then and later. Men traded; but the volume of trade was small enough to manage without coinage.

Internal trade is less in evidence. The monks of Ireland prevented Ruadan's attempts to market a new drink, and the economy of monks and laymen was self-sufficing in Ireland and Wales, its import chiefly restricted to foreign luxuries. Among the English, specialist jewellers and potters worked within local limits before the conquest, while the movement of their products after the conquest is more likely to be the consequence of the movement of their owners than of their makers. Roads fell out of use. Burials cut into the metalling of the Watling Street, at Cestersover in Warwickshire and elsewhere, are proof enough that roads were out of use and grass-grown. A road was a *herepaeth*, an 'army path', and early settlements are commonly discreetly set back from roads, for the passage of an army threatened the farmer's livestock and his daughters. The roads did not revive for centuries; the Roman towns along the Icknield Way at its junctions with the northward roads from London, at Dunstable, Baldock and Royston, reverted to woodland until all three were refounded in the 12th century, when new towns were planted on their sites, as traffic along the road resumed, and charters were granted for fairs. In the 6th and 7th centuries churchmen, kings, armies, and a few well-to-do notables travelled, but there is little sign of the exchange of goods.

What trade there was was suspect. At the end of the 7th century, the laws of the West Saxons forbade trade without witnesses, and fined the merchant who could not prove that his goods were not stolen, while Kentish law insisted that purchases in London must be registered with the king's officer and required that 'traders and other strangers who cross the border' must have a sponsor responsible for their good conduct. Later laws confined trade to towns. The merchant was by definition a suspected thief, a foreigner of ill repute, rare and unwelcome. Trade there was. But it was largely in foreign hands, limited in kind and in scope, and to a few places, to London above all. It was an incidental phenomenon on the margins of the economy, irrelevant to the lives of nine-tenths of the population.

Throughout the British Isles, tribute mattered more than trade. Native traders are rare in the records of the Irish, the Welsh, or the English, for the exchange of commodities was more the business of kings and lords than of merchants. In Ireland, the 'Book of Rights' sets down an elaborate, and perhaps ideal list of tributes exacted by the greater Irish kings, and of gifts they dispensed. The kings received large quantities of animals, and some clothing. They distributed weapons, armour, horses, horns, ornaments, and occasionally a few animals and a little clothing. Though the figures are late and perhaps unreal, the principle is amply attested in the Lives, the Annals and the stories. The payment of tribute was secured by the retention of hostages, and was enforced by war when it was withheld. British kings followed the Irish example; Maelgwn and others levied cattle to maintain their military companions; the poems praise northern kings, like Owain, who 'hoarded' wealth exacted from his subjects or looted from his enemies 'like a miser', and 'gave it freely' to his retainers. Penda of Mercia held Oswy's son as a hostage, exacted tribute from subject Northumbria and distributed it to his British and English allies. The British king who collected and distributed more tribute and booty than others commonly earned the epithet *Hael*, 'open-handed' or 'generous'. The process by which animals taken in tribute were turned into weapons and ornaments involved either using the food rent to maintain craftsmen, or exchanging cattle for the smith's products.

Only the English minted money. It priced fines. It served kings and abbots for the payment of rents, and for the purchase of great men's needs; it circulated within towns. Close examination of what coins have been found where may help to show how far and when it began to link lesser men. Present evidence suggests that trade between towns, and outside towns and fairs, was slight before the 9th and 10th centuries, not considerable until the 12th. Most men lived upon the produce of their lands, and paid a tax or tribute to lords and kings. The principal commodities that circulated internally, salt, iron, fish and others were paid as annual tribute to the lords, who most commonly paid two-thirds of their price to the king if and when they sold them. The earliest articles of export were slaves, usually prisoners of war, though the stronger kings forbade and often curtailed the export of men. By the 8th century, cloth, wool and cheese were shipped to Gaul, though they were principally sold by lords who had received them in tribute, chiefly in exchange for silks, wine, precious stones and metals and other luxuries. A little commercial production prospered in a few towns, mainly through craftsmen whose raw materials came through the lords' tribute. Before the Scandinavian disturbances, the principal source of raw material was tribute rather than purchase and the craftsman and distributor were bound to the lord from whom they received the raw material. Trade, the buying and selling of commodities, was still a relatively insignificant element in the exchange of goods.

CHAPTER TWENTY-THREE

WELSH, IRISH AND NORTHERN SOCIETY

The Family

Throughout the British Isles, the unit of society was the single family of parents and their children, living in a family house. All other associations of people, social or political, were no more than groups of such families, differently organised for different purposes. Welsh law made intimate provision for a secure family, with personal equality for both parents, and care for the upbringing and rights of children. It dealt with the ordinary contingencies of private life in pragmatic detail, with respect for the feelings and dignity of the individual. The law defined the signs of a well inhabited land as 'little children; dogs; and cocks'. Obligations were incurred by actual relationships, not only by their legal registration. A man who slept three nights or more with a girl must give her three oxen if he deserted her; cohabitation ranked as marriage after 7 years. A child 'begotten in brake and bush' must be wholly maintained by the father. The boy came of age at 14, the girl at 12; she then 'possesses her own property, and need not remain at her father's table, unless she so wishes.'

On marriage the girl received an *agweddi*, dowry, from her father, and also a *cowyll*, marriage gift, from her husband. Occasions of dispute were foreseen. The girl's kin might choose to certify her a virgin bride if they wished; if they did so falsely, the husband might shame her by slitting her shift in the presence of the bridal guests, provided that before consummation, he jumped out of bed 'immediately on his discovery; but if he stays in bed through the night, he is deemed to have accepted her as a virgin'. The father must provide for the children's upbringing until they came of age; thereafter he might not chastise them. In Irish law, where 'fosterage', the education of the children away from home, is more prominent than in Wales, both parents had equal responsibility for the children's education.

If a couple divorced within seven years, the woman took only her dowry and marriage gift, whether she were the innocent or guilty party. If she went off with another man, he must compensate the husband. After seven years, the whole property of the homestead was equally divided on divorce. The meaning of equality was not left to the embittered couple to dispute, but laid down in exact detail. The wife took one-third of the children, the husband two-thirds, including the oldest and the youngest. If the wife was pregnant, the husband must pay for the child till he came of age. A detailed schedule apportioned every object likely to be found on a farmstead, the general principle being that the tools of agriculture and stock raising went to the man, dairy farming and the household gear to the woman.

The grounds for divorce were 'leprosy', meaning all incurable illness, bad breath, and impotence. Adultery was not included. Adultery was punished by the payment of *wyneb-werth*, *faciei pretium* in Latin, payment for loss of face by the guilty husband to his wife, or the guilty wife to her husband; and the adulterer must also pay a fine to the husband. Wife beating by the husband, or shrewish scolding by the wife, were normally punishable by a fine, payable to the injured party; but were permitted in the case of adultery, though if the husband beat up an adulterous wife he forfeited his 'face payment'. The wife was also exempt from normal penalties for assault if she attacked her husband's mistress. But if the husband committed adultery three times, the wife who did not leave him received no more 'face money'.

Kissing or cuddling another man's wife was punishable by a fine to the husband, except on festival occasions. Illegitimate children were accepted into the *cenedl*, kindred, if acknowledged by the father, or if paternity was proven; children of untraceable fathers belonged to their mother's kin. The laws provided full defence against accusations; 'leprosy' must be proved incurable by a doctor's certificate; a charge of impotence might be rebutted by a public demonstration in a form prescribed in uninhibited detail; charges against women were examined by elder women, denied by a formidable oath, or tested before witnesses, the trials and tests being conducted by the *penncenedl*, chief of kindred.

Irish law had similar grounds for divorce, with numerous additions of detail. Impotence and infertility were distinguished; the taking of a monastic vow and long absence were added; some texts add chattering to strangers about prowess in bed. In both Wales and Ireland the church contested the marriage laws, but with little success. The text termed *Hibernensis*, which commonly offered a judge a choice of rulings, cited Deuteronomy (24,1), 'if she find no favour in his eyes ... let him write her a bill of divorcement', but it also added from the Gospel (Matthew 5,31–32) 'a man shall not put away his wife, save for the cause of adultery'. It then cited from Isidore

> What if she be barren, deformed, a hag; fetid, violent, cross; an evil liver, luxurious and gluttonous, cursing or swearing? Do you keep her or reject her? Whether you like it or not, you must keep her as you took her.

In Britain one text observed that its provisions on the inheritance of illegitimate children were counter to 'Church Law', which prescribed that the patrimony should go only to the 'father's eldest son by his married wife'; but it replied that 'the law of Howel ... decides that the father's sin, or his illegal act, is not to be brought against the son's patrimony'.

These were the practical regulations of a small community where everyone knew his neighbours. Family quarrels were brought to open court as soon as they erupted into violence in word or deed, and the pressure of public opinion, under the guidance of the *penncenedl*, was brought to bear to sober the pair. But when a marriage had irrevocably broken down, the troublesome division of the home was automatically regulated, and the law ensured that the children were protected.

Welsh law treated the family as an association of responsible individuals, not as an institution. The law protected the privacy, the dignity and the freedom of man and wife, and of sons and daughters who had reached puberty. Each was legally independent, of equal rights and status. Their personal relationships were their own affair; the law intervened only to protect children and to prevent violence. Safeguards for bastards, and for adolescents against their parents, contrast with the provisions of most legal codes. The law and custom of most of Europe and Asia interferes in family relationships and encourages outsiders to impose taboos upon them. Roman law forbade adultery and enhanced the father's authority, though without savage penalties. Brutal repression of women remains a chief means of perpetuating peasant poverty in many Asian societies, while the persecution and slaughter of unchaste girls and soured old women was sanctioned in the name of honour and virtue among many Germanic peoples, and constituted one of the principal barbarian contributions to the doctrines of the medieval Christian church.

Kindred

In Welsh and Irish law, the kindred had two main functions. It regulated the inheritance of men who died without sons, and it ensured the payment of damages to the victims of violence. Its terminology varied. In Wales, the *cenedl* protected freeborn subjects; but the Irish *cinel* is most prominent as a ruler's kindred, and variations of the word *fine* described family groupings.

Welsh and Irish legislation on violence was mainly concerned with compensation to the victim and his dependents. It contrasts with the moral outlook of the laws of Rome and of most modern states, whose chief concern is punishment, theoretically justified on the grounds that fear of the law will deter the criminal, and that if vengeance is not exacted by society it will be exacted privately by the victim's friends and relatives. The law of terror commonly kills, maims or imprisons the wrongdoer, and places emphasis on his motives, inflicting lesser penalties on those who acted in momentary anger or by accident. Welsh and Irish codes were more concerned with the consequences of the offence than with the offender's motive and with preventing violence rather than with punishment. They imposed damages rather than fines; the scale began with small payments for an insult or a blow of the fist, and rose through the loss of limbs and physical ability to the loss of life. Since the offender might lack the means to pay the damages himself, his relatives must make good the deficit, the nearer relatives contributing the larger share. Each individual in the community was therefore given a powerful incentive to restrain a relative who was temperamentally prone to violence, and to do so early, before violence passed beyond rowdiness.

Inheritance

Welsh and Irish law compelled men to bequeath their most essential property to their family and kin. In Wales, the youngest son took the family house, with a few acres of land, on the assumption that his elder brothers were more likely to have married and moved into their own houses. He also took the cauldron, the axe and the coulter, with the harp. The youngest son divided the rest of the land into equal portions, and the brothers chose in turn, the eldest first. There is no mention of cattle in the division between brothers, or between husband and wife on divorce; for cattle were personal property and were also currency. The laws carefully distinguished the *tir gwelyauc*, family land, divided by inheritance, from *tir cyvriv*, usually Englished as 'register land', the property of the *tref*, or township, that might be granted to the dead man's son, but could not be inherited.

Most men had sons, and when they did the inheritance laws worked simply. Complications arose when there were no sons. Claims of kinsmen were harder to accommodate, both in law and in practice. In Ireland and Wales inheritance passed only from father to son, never directly from brother to brother or from uncle to nephew. A childless man's land passed back into the inheritance of his father or grandfather, even when they were dead, and through them to their heirs. Irish law retained a series of terms for *fine*, family, with differing rights. In the prime of life a man's *Geil Fine* comprised his father, his sons, his brothers and their sons, a three-generation family containing all his father's male descendants. His *Derb Fine* added his grandfather's other descendants, his uncles and his cousins and their sons, a four-generation family. The *Iar Fine* comprised five generations, descending from his great-grandfather, the *Ind Fine* six generations from his great-great-grandfather.

In practice, most important rights fell to his *Derb Fine* of four generations, both in inheritance and in the mutual respect and self-help which society expected of a family. The wider groups of remoter cousins retained marginal rights in certain contingencies, and owed small shares of the compensations due from the kin. The *Derb Fine* was the normal word used in the law books for a man's immediate relatives; at least from the 10th century onward, succession to political sovereignty was, in theory at least, confined to the king's *Derb Fine*, whose members were *Rigdomna*, royal heirs. A man might claim a throne that his great-grandfather or nearer relative had held, but could not claim succession from his great-great-grandfather. The custom is likely to have established itself piecemeal over a long period, earlier among some dynasties than others, before it was formally and generally recognised; but it is in practice reported among the Ui Neill from the fifth century onward.

Welsh law also confined effective inheritance to the four-generation family, the equivalent of the Irish *Derb Fine*. By the later middle ages it had acquired a general name, *gwely*, 'bed', but the laws spell out what they mean in detail without using a generic term. The land of the childless is divided three times, between brothers, between cousins, and between second cousins, who constitute the members of a four-generation family. Thereafter, 'there is no division'.

These laws concerned a time when the kindred was no longer the political unit; the Welsh *tref* and the Irish *tuath* and *baile* included many different unrelated kindreds, and men related to the fourth or ninth degree might farm lands in different communities. The laws regulated inheritance of land, houses and gear rather than of cattle, and therefore mattered more where arable agriculture was more extensive. They persisted in an age when the bulk of the free population was dispersed in separate family homesteads, and the kindred of four generations or more no longer lived together, farming lands that lay in one block. But it is likely that they had their origin in an earlier age, when the kindred lived together, with all its land in walking distance of its home. Societies so organised still exist in Asia, in parts of the Balkans, and elsewhere; they may have existed in parts of Ireland and in Britain into the Roman period. Such extended families are the likely builders of the 'native villages' of Roman Britain, that consisted of a few houses clustered together, as at Chysauster in Cornwall or Ewe Close in Westmorland; or of the large round houses, 30 foot or more in diameter, known in the earlier generations of the Iron Age of southern Britain. But from at least the sixth century onward, though the kindred retained important rights and responsibilities, it was no longer the main basis of political society.

Community: the Irish.

Class Difference

Families and kindreds, with their inheritance laws, each lived within a particular political society. Society contained a number of recognised divisions, of different origins, which the lawyers endeavoured to arrange into an orderly structure, and distinguished by technical terms.

The oldest division of Irish society was between the *nemed*, 'sacred persons', and the *celi*, 'plebeians', who became vassals dependent upon chiefs. The concept is pre-Christian, for the term *nemed*, meaning 'holy' in all the Celtic languages, was intimately associated with pagan religion and subsisted in Christian times only when it could not be avoided.

By the time of the oldest lawbooks both classes were divided into *soer* and *doer*, 'free' and 'unfree'. The freemen of the sacred class, *soernemed*, included kings and chiefs; the learned professions, the *filid*; churchmen, the *feni*, military officers, who were equated with the *airig*, nobility, graded by their wealth in cattle, and later in land; and the rise of the kings added a number of royal officials. The 'sacred unfree', *doernemed*, were primarily the craftsmen, builders and metal-workers, doctors and lawyers, and included the humbled *drui*. The dependent plebeians were divided into freemen, *soercheli*, who owed military service and annual tribute and must contribute to a king's ransom, and the unfree *doercheli*, who paid rent, provided maintenance for royal officers and owed menial services. The *celi* were all owners of cattle and of land, but the *doercheli* might not leave his land, nor be evicted, so long as he retained his cattle.

Below these landowners stood the landless, classified in the law books according to their supposed origin. The *fuidir* was a free stranger from another *tuath*, or political state; he was the equivalent of the Greek *metic*, the Latin *advena*. The *senleithi*, 'old refugees', were descendants of prisoners and hired fighting men; the *bothach*, cottager, was a native without property. Below them all were the slaves, male and female, *mug* and *cumal*, rarely encountered outside the law books, save as the personal servants of chiefs and kings.

The terminology echoes successive layers of forgotten conquest and migration, for even the word *doer* has the root meaning of 'stranger', 'foreigner'. The classification of the status of persons was cut across by the classification of peoples. The word *tuath* denotes people in the most general sense, as varied as the Greek *ethnos*, more varied than the Latin *civitas*. The Israelites were the *Tuath De*, the *civitas Dei*, people of God. Time hardened the meaning, until *tuath* normally denoted a tiny state, often subject to a greater neighbour. The Ireland of the 1st century AD, as described by Ptolemy, comprised fifteen political states; Irish names record other still older peoples, usually called by their distinctive names, Lugne, Galenga and the like, or known by the appellation *Fir*, 'men of', the *Fir Domnann* and others. In a pastoral society enclosed within an island, groups of such older peoples wandered widely to different districts, sometimes losing their identity, sometimes imposing their name. When a people lived long in a defined territory the word *tuath* denoted both the people and the territory.

By the time of the early Christian writers Ptolemy's fifteen states had divided into something over a hundred, whose schematic hierarchy grouped them into five provinces, though several large kingdoms, like Ossory or Airgialla, were at best nominally and intermittently subject to provincial kings. Almost all were subject to dynastic chiefs, who awarded lordship and lands to their nearer relatives. A law of the 7th or 8th century prescribes distinctive dress for different classes, yellow or black or white for subjects, grey, brown and red for nobles; purple and blue for kings. Later texts limit the number of colours that each class might wear, rising from one for slaves to two for subjects and six for the learned *filid*, seven for the king.

The spread of dynastic kingship divided the Irish states into three categories, the *Soer Tuatha*, free states; the subject states, *Aithech Tuatha*; and the intermediate *For Tuatha*, autonomous but tributary. Most, though not all, of the free states were known by the name of their dynasty, while *tuath* was commoner among the subject states. The principal origin of the difference lay in conquest; the *tuath* whose kings had subjected weaker neighbours was free, the subject neighbours unfree.

The Irish: Village and Hundred

Kings and chiefs needed armies and a stable mechanism to raise them. As among most Indo-European peoples, the unit of military organisation was the hundred. Later texts schematise its developed form. The higher grades of *aire*, 'nobles of property', were qualified to command a hundred, a *cet*, in war; the standard concept of a large military formation was the *tricha cet*, 'thirty hundreds'. But the *tuatha* were of varying size. Each comprised a number of *baile*, the origin of the common Irish place name element 'Bally-'. In its civil function the word meant 'enclosed farmstead', or 'town', almost the precise equivalent of the English *-tun*. In its military aspect it is alternatively described as the *baile biataigh*, 'supply *baile*', its duty to supply a hundred men, a *cet*. Though schematised, the terminology is deeply embedded in Irish stories and in the notices of the Annals. It lasted as long as Irish independence. The muster of the last native army, destroyed at Kinsale in 1601, enjoined the 'constable of each hundred' to levy 84 men, but to receive and distribute the pay of a full hundred.

The actual organisation that underlies the scheme is preserved in a late 7th-century text of the Irish colonists in British Dal Riada, the *Miniugid Senchusa Fir n-Alban*, the 'Explanation of the History of the Men of Britain'. It divides the Dal Riada Scots under their three dynastic *Cinel*, and subdivides each *Cinel* into groups, some with territorial names, some with the names of small chiefs. Each group comprises a number of houses, *tech*, reckoned in multiples of 5 and 10, 20 and 30 being the commonest numbers; and it gives the total land and sea muster for each *Cinel*. The average demand is for about 3 men from every two houses for the land muster, 2 men from every three houses for the sea muster. These are the houses of individual families. The larger groupings of 60 or 100 houses correspond to the future *baile*, the smaller groupings of 20 to 30 houses to a half or third of a *baile*. The harsh geography of Argyle, dividing its people among islands and headlands of unequal size, prevented any simple schematic equalisation of areas; the term 'Bally-' did not extend to the place names of the Argyle Irish, and was probably not developed when the *Senchus* was written. But the easier geography of mainland Ireland made such simplification easier.

The power of the people was greatly less among the Irish than among the Welsh or the English. The assembly of the local *tuath* did not control its lands; local political authority was vested in its king, who was himself the tributary of a greater king, and formed the lowest grade in a hierarchy of despots; jurisdiction was the business of professional lawmen, rather than of local courts. The popular assemblies that tradition remembers are those of large regions or of the whole country, called together at fairs and conventions. Such meetings were necessarily restricted to delegates and representatives, and met under the presidency of kings, their debates dominated by the nobility, their decisions regulated by professional custodians of the law. It was only on rare occasions, like the great famine of the 660s, that desperation gave the plebeians courage to voice their independent initiative.

In Ireland the institution of the monastery was widely and rapidly welcomed by the subjects of the dynasts. The monks themselves were divided between those who welcomed a strong high king, and those who saw him as the arch tyrant, and proclaimed the power of the church as the alternative to all secular authority. They prevailed, and broke the power of the monarchy. But they were not able to unseat the regional and local kings and lords; the monasteries remained islands of independence, a refuge and a shield against the excess of tyranny, but they were not the authors or patrons of an alternative social order. At the convention of Drumceat, the church blessed the ancient learned class and in time fused with it; and it thereby opened the doors of learning more widely to men of humble birth.

The extreme subjection of the Irish peasant gave the monasteries their first inmates, and maintained for centuries a continuing supply of fresh recruits and a steady flow of learned emigrants abroad. It also conditioned the nature of Irish lordship. The Irish lord cared little for the ownership of land or the enjoyment of its revenue, in the manner that Rome had taught to Britain. Like the patrician of Rome, his power and his prosperity rested on the number and the status of his dependent clients; he was a lord of men rather than a lord of land. These ancient notions of submission to authority enfeebled Ireland for centuries. The lord who exacted submission from his own clients readily acknowledged himself the client of a greater lord; so that when the Norman and the English conqueror asserted his superiority by force, he was more easily accepted as a still greater lord, entitled to the obedience of his clients. Ireland submitted, for peasants who had never ruled themselves knew not how to organise effective resistance when their lords failed them. Medieval Ireland found no plebeian national leader; and until after 1916, English rule rarely faced a challenge more serious than local or regional risings, conspiracy or parliamentary protest; half a century of independence has not yet wholly eliminated the old habits that were formed in remote antiquity and hardened in early Christian Ireland, of grudging submission occasionally goaded into sporadic violence.

The North

The nations of the north slowly combined into the kingdom of Scotland. The dynasty of the Dal Riada Irish acquired the Pictish throne in the 9th century, and subsequently annexed the English of the Forth and the British of the Clyde; in time its authority prevailed beyond the Great Glen, and in the 15th century it subdued the western and northern Isles. Its records deal with rulers, nobles and churchmen, and have little to say of the early society of their subjects. As yet, the archaeological evidence is too little and too loosely dated to make good the silence of the written record.

The Irish dynasty brought with it the society of its homeland. The church was Irish, and disseminated Irish notions; their impact was strongest among notables, and in the lands where lords and wars were most frequent, but little of the pace and detail of change can be traced. Almost nothing is known of the society of the Picts, save that the inheritance of land and property as well as of political sovereignty passed through the woman; and that there were lords and great men who could afford to purchase slaves and to erect elaborate stone monuments.

In the sparsely populated lands beyond the Great Glen the brochs and duns are the memorials of unremembered peoples, whose military might had faded before the fall of Rome. The earliest coherent accounts of their way of life were set down by the 18th and 19th century travellers to the islands. There, very small independent communities of 4, 6 or 12 families then met annually to decide what lands to crop and to divide them by lot; the land was unfenced and the cattle were herded by day, pounded by night. The numbers that might graze the land were limited; excess cattle must be kept on the croft, or grazed by renting the rights or the land of a neighbour. Though earlier evidence fails, there is no reason to suppose significant change in their society over very many centuries. They were unharassed by king or landlord, without need of armies or commanders, chiefs or rulers, long isolated by geographical and political frontiers. Their institutions, or lack of them, fit the peaceful economy of some prehistoric peoples, whose excavated homes show no signs of kings, wealth or violence; but they do not fit the military vigour of the Argyle Scots or of the peoples of the Pictish lowland.

The Clan

Little is known of the early peoples of the future Scotland, but much is fancied. The understanding of what little evidence there is has long been bedevilled by the romantic myth of a 'clan society'. Its pretended antiquity is altogether bogus. 'Clan' is a modern word with a modern meaning, albeit foggy and changeable. In the circumspect language of the 19th century it meant

> a tribe . . . regarded as having a common ancestor;

but in the looser popular idiom of the 20th century Oxford dictionary it became

> Scotch highlanders with common ancestor; tribe.

The definition is confusing, for though 'tribe' is identified with 'clan', 'tribe' is itself defined as a 'group of barbarous clans'.

The dictionaries are accurate, for their business is to report current usage, not to correct its muddles. The meaning of 'clan' is shrouded, for it is simultaneously a subdivision of a 'tribe', and the 'tribe' itself. The word is misty, because the term 'tribe', to which it is related, is even vaguer. It is nowadays commonly used to lump together peoples little influenced by European technology, and often distorts enquiry into their separate customs.

The uncertainties are chiefly caused by confusing the modern meanings of these words with their origin and evolution. The *tribus* was an administrative division of the Roman people. The Latin Bible used the Latin word to describe the twelve stocks of the ancient Israelites; and the English Bible transliterated *tribus* into 'tribe'. The Old Testament Israelites practised a simple economy, rare in renaissance Europe, and European explorers therefore applied the familiar biblical term to newly discovered peoples whose way of life was simple. In consequence, it has acquired racial and patronising overtones, stigmatising the peoples to whom it is applied as 'backward', or even 'barbarous'.

The modern notion of a 'clan', a population supposedly descended from a common ancestor, was brought into frequent English usage by the romantic writers of the 18th century, and popularised by the novels of Sir Walter Scott. Generations of imperial administrators thereafter used biblical tribes and Scott's clans as shorthand labels for the societies of distant continents; the carefree use of such labels inspired belief in an abstract 'tribal society' and 'clan system', whose imaginary institutions were assumed to have been shared by the ancestors of the modern Scots, and many other peoples. Various attempts to define these words failed, for it is not possible to classify real institutions in the language of romantic fiction; and many anthropologists now avoid the words. They linger however among historians. The Macedonians of Alexander the Great are commonly termed 'clansmen' because they also inhabited a hilly homeland and felt its impact; the word 'tribe' is still often applied both to the migrating nations of the Germans and also to the sophisticated Roman *civitates* which they attacked, though no ancient writers described either by any word that corresponds to English 'tribe' or 'clan'; and these words abound in most short accounts of early Ireland and Scotland.

Many peoples trace their origin to a legendary common ancestor. The Hebrews and the Christians descend all mankind from one individual. But many other nations do not, and among them are the Irish and the Scots, whose myths record few traditions of a common national ancestor, except in some medieval tales that imitate Christian idiom. The word 'clan' seems ancient only because it derives from an Irish word that had a precise but different meaning. *Clanna*, like its Welsh equivalent, *plant*, means 'children', and by extension 'descendants'. It was one of many words used to distinguish the descendants of a ruler from the rest of his subjects, and in this sense meant 'royal family' or 'dynasty'. It was a late comer among these numerous equivalent terms, and is rarely used of a dynasty whose founder was held to have lived earlier than the 9th century; but in later medieval Scotland it became the commonest of such words. It outlived the Irish language, for successive foreign conquerors used it to induce their subjects to accept their rule.

The corporate *clanna*, or dynasty, is first reported in Scotland in the 12th century, in Buchan, in the fertile lowland territory of the northern Picts. The founder of the *clanna* Morgan was held to have lived some three centuries earlier. His name was British in origin, but had long been adopted through marriage into the royal family of the Argyle Scots; his dynasty were *mormaers*, Irish rulers imposed upon the native population, and the latest of them assumed the prouder title of Kings of Moray.

The power of the dynasty of Morgan died with its last great king, Macbeth. He was overthrown by English invaders, who installed the heirs of the exiled southern dynasty of Albany. They brought with them English and Norman barons, to rule men of Irish speech. The coming of the English overlaid the old antagonisms between Pict and Irish, and the new lords found an Irish pedigree useful. Their genealogists traced the Campbells to the Bronze Age Kings of Ireland by way of King Arthur; the Earls of Lennox were represented as descendants of the Kings of Munster by the assertion that a 12th century Norman was the son of 6th century Irishman, and Albany was peopled with his supposed descendants by the alteration of a single letter in an ancient text. These early *clanna* were limited to lowlanders, or to lowland rulers imposed upon the fringes of the highlands; and they still sharply distinguished members of the ruling dynasty from their subjects. In 14th-century Fife, membership of the ruling *Clanna* MacDuff was still rigidly restricted to nine generations in descent from an acknowledged ruler. The restriction shut out plebeians, and denied them the right to wear the multi-coloured clothing proper to nobility.

By the end of the 14th century, the prestige of the Irish past had dwindled in the lowlands, and lowland *clanna* passed from record. But at the same time, lowland authority began to be asserted powerfully in the Irish-speaking highlands. Hitherto, resentments were little enflamed, and a 14th-century lowland gentleman could still describe the 'Highlanders and peoples of the Islands' with distant tolerance as

> savage and rude, independent, ease-loving, of a docile and warm disposition, comely in person but unsightly in dress, hostile to the Anglic people and language . . . They are however easily made to submit if properly governed.

The 'Anglic people' were the lowlanders of Scotland, whose speech was English. 'Proper government' entailed obedience to a co-operative local lord and his dynasty, still termed in Irish his *clanna*. The first highland *clanna* are recorded in 1396, and the earliest known chief of a highland *clanna* bore the English name of Johnson. Little lords multiplied, many of them of local birth and Irish speech. The sovereign authority of the 'Anglic' lowland government was strengthened if the highland chiefs fought each other in savage feuds, and if each dynasty engulfed its population. The end result was described by a shrewd 18th-century observer.

> The lands are set by the landlord during pleasure, or on a short tack, to people . . . of a superior station . . . These are generally the sons, brothers, cousins or nearest relations of the landlord or chief. This land . . . they, their children and grandchildren possess at an easy rent, until a nearer descendant be . . . preferred. As the propinquity removes, they . . . degenerate to be of the common people. As this hath been an ancient custom, most of the farmers and cottars are of the same name and clan as the proprietor.

Over a period of four centuries the 'common people' of each valley assumed the 'name and clan' of their rulers. In a small enclosed population it was not easy to disprove a man's claim to noble rank and clothing by descent through nine generations, from a ruler dead for three hundred years; nor was there incentive to challenge such claims, for 'as propinquity removed' it was more decent to dispossess a distant cousin in favour of a near relative than a stranger who owed no family allegiance. When the dynastic *clanna* was extended to admit the whole population, its founder was necessarily accepted as their common ancestor. The modern clan was born.

The clan owes its origin to a peculiar combination of Scottish geography and Irish customary law. Peoples and regions elsewhere take their name from an individual who ruled long ago, but no one pretends that the whole population of Lorraine or Tirconnel are descendants of Lothaire or Connel; and few Lorrainers remember ancestors older than their grandfathers. But Irish and Welsh custom had always devolved rights and obligations upon a nine generation family; and the population of many highland valleys was small enough to be credibly accommodated within a nine generation family, isolated enough to make marriage outside the community a rarity.

In a more tranquil age the highland clan might have remained a short lived local institution, confined to the mountains and to the age that created it. But the convulsions of the 16th and 17th centuries enlisted neighbouring valleys on opposing sides in greater wars, and loosed them upon each other and upon lowland supporters of the opposite party. Repeated raids taught the lowlanders to fear and abhor highland savagery; but fears faded when William III fortified the Great Glen, and the Act of Union inclined many lowlanders to sympathy with highland dislike of English rule. Fashionable ladies whose mothers shuddered at the sight of highland dress began to wear highland ornament. In 1745, the romantic failure of the Young Pretender, clad in a 'Royal Stewart tartan' that would have startled his royal ancestors, made heroes of the highlanders, so soon as they were safely defeated. The English government banned the tartan from the highland hills, but when the ban was lifted the tartan spread to lowland streets. The magnificently blended colours evolved by the weavers of the valleys delighted elegant urban taste, and Scott's novels endowed the clansmen of the past with a generous nobility.

The pageantry of pipe and tartan has become the symbol of modern Scotland, rooted in the highlands, but no longer confined within them. Nineteenth century lowland gentlemen discovered that they too were clansmen, and devised their own tartans and their own ancestors. The modern clan is a recent institution. An institution is none the worse for being modern; but when a modern institution asserts a sham antiquity, it degrades those whom it pretends to ennoble. The ceremonies of the Scottish clan are far removed from the trivial modern romances of the rest of Britain, King Arthur's Tintagel among the English, or the latter day Druids of the Welsh; for the innate good taste of the highlanders has invested the clan and its observances with a dignity that makes them a worthy symbol of a modern nation.

The clan is embedded in modern society. But neither clan nor tribe have any legitimate place in an account of early Ireland or Scotland. They need explanation, because they still frequently corrupt such accounts, even though scholars intimate with the evidence have stigmatised their irrelevance for more than half a century. Eoin MacNeill is judged by the most learned of his successors to have 'done more than any other to place the history of pre-Norman Ireland on the basis of sound historical criticism'; and, as leader of the Irish Volunteers, he is also numbered among the creators of modern Ireland. In 1921 he summarised the evidence in words too little heeded:

> the only technical meaning that *clann* has in Irish is that of 'children'. All this solemn classification of family, sept, clan or . . . tribe is so much rubbish, . . . rubbish . . . imposed by the careless, the presuming and the ignorant.

The judgement is as valid for Scotland as for Ireland. The evidence for Scotland was assembled and surveyed by W.F. Skene more than a hundred years ago, and interpreted in the light of mid Victorian assumptions. No study of early Scotland on a comparable scale has since appeared; until it does, fancy prevails, and the nation is robbed of its history. Reality is a surer foundation for national sentiment than make-believe; and reality discredits sweetened romance, but honours the men and women who created a single and confident nation out of numerous discordant peoples with unlike customs, beliefs and institutions.

Community: the Welsh

Class Difference

Welsh and Irish society were not alike, for in Britain four centuries of Roman government had absorbed the notables and modified their relations to the poor. The society of early Wales is most fully described in their laws. Welsh law is difficult to interpret, since the only texts preserved are late and have therefore been unduly disregarded. They have not yet received sufficient historical study, and their enactments are sometimes uncritically dismissed as late invention. But a few commonsense rule-of-thumb principles pinpoint the main stages in their evolution. They contain little medieval English law, for the Edwardian conquest tended to impose English law, to abrogate Welsh law rather than alter it. Values expressed in English pence cannot be earlier than the 10th century, when English money began to circulate freely, and may be later; but they commonly translate values previously expressed in cattle. Some sections transcribed from West-Saxon law are unlikely to be earlier. But the dating of older sections rests primarily on comparison with legal practice outside Wales. Institutions that are also found in Cumberland, in Brittany, or among the Welsh of Wessex are likely to have existed before the 6th century, when English conquest sundered these regions from one another; what is paralleled in Irish law, and not found elsewhere, is likely to date back to an earlier age, before the Roman conquest separated Britain from Ireland.

The social divisions of early Wales are akin to those of the late Roman empire, that distinguished the *ingenuus*, the free-born native citizen, from the bond *colonus*, and the slave, *servus*. But changing late Roman economy altered the meaning of words used for bondman and slave; Latin *servus* in law denoted the marketable human property, whom the modern English language calls slave, in contrast to the serf, who is bound to the soil, but cannot be sold apart from his land. But in practice the *servus* so often remained on his land that the word gave birth to the English term 'serf'. The process was so far advanced in Wales that Welsh Latin writers commonly preferred the clarity of the alternative Latin word *mancipium*, a 'purchased or captured slave'. There were plenty of men of servile legal status, but marketable slaves were rare.

Welsh laws distinguished three categories of native Cymro, the free, the bond, and the slave, as in Roman law. Free men included the *boneddig*, free-born, whether he owned land or no; the *priodaur*, who owned land; and the noble *uchelwr*, upper man, who owned much land. Below them were the *taeog*, a cultivator bound to the soil, termed *rusticus* or *servus* in Latin, and the *caeth*, slave, commonly called *mancipium* in Latin. The language of the Saints' Lives uses similar terms; *liberi* were free men in general and included *possessores* and *domini*, owners of the land and masters of men, and *nobiles*, nobles; below them were bond rent-paying *rustici* and *servi* and slave *mancipia*. These provisions echo the central distinction of later Roman law, between *honestiores* and *humiliores*, 'worthier' and 'humbler' citizens.

These Roman categories date back in Wales to the 6th century. Somewhere about 560, Gildas warned that David's radicalism 'preferred serfs above their masters, the commons above their kings' (*servos dominis, vulgus regibus*). The parents of Samson were *nobiles* and landowners; when they took monastic vows, they 'gave alms to the poor, relaxed their claims upon their debtors, lightened the tribute of their serfs' (*tributa servis suis levigantes*); the near-contemporary author got his information, at one remove, from Samson's mother. Hervé in Brittany encountered the chief of a *plebs* who was chasing runaway rustics; both Roman and Welsh law are clear that the rustic who escaped might find plenty of other lords who were ready to receive strangers on their lands. On Ramsey Island by St. Davids, the hermit Justinian was killed by his *servi*. In 7th-century Wessex the Welshman's kin might be free or unfree. The distinction was plainly inherited from the independent British of the 6th century.

Large landowners are frequently named. Illtud's monastery was his 'earthly inheritance'; it contained the ruins of a mansion. Paul Aurelian's father was a nobleman and landowner, and his sister had trouble with 'wicked co-heirs' near Exeter. Both these texts rest on 6th-century originals. Tatheus was entertained by a rich man near Chepstow, who still heated his bath on Saturdays in the manner of his Roman forbears. Lesser freemen are also common; many saints were entertained by small farmers who lived in a *tuguriolum*, a cottage; by men of modest means who owned a few cows; or by the swineherds of wealthier men. Land was measured in the laws by the *erw*, acre, but in the Llandaff texts its value was assessed in units of so many cows, or by its arable yield, reckoned by the *uncia* and the *modius*.

The earlier texts of Brittany emphasise the gulf between the free classes and the rustics. Malo lost and regained his cloak; when he learned that a cottager had used it as a blanket he refused to wear it, 'thinking a garment that had lain upon rustics unworthy of him'. Winwaloe fed the poor and his 'usual custom' was to offer them 'the hope of eternal reward and the solace of prayer'; but 'the high master did not deign to call them brothers', though he accepted 'lesser brethren' as labourers in his monastery, as did Illtud, and Cassiodorus in Italy. These are the poor whom Roman usage called *rustici* in their social status, *coloni* in their economic condition. Medieval Welsh law used different words for men of the same status and condition.

The Welsh: Village and Hundred

The 6th-century emigrants to Brittany were organised into *plebes*, composed of a number of *tribus*, each of which contained a number of *domus*, houses. The names were borrowed from Jerome's account of the monks of Egypt, but they were used of secular as well as monastic organisation. The three words were translated as *Plou*, *tref* and *ker*; all are common in place names, and are often followed by a personal name. In Wales, *plwyf* meant a parish, but is rare in place names; *tref* is as common in local names, while *caer* was normally reserved for substantial fortifications, except in parts of Dumnonia, and the usual word for a house is *ty*, or its variants. In north Wales a number of *tref* were commonly termed a *maenol*, in the south a *mainaur*; though the schematism that assigned 64 houses to each *tref* and 4 *tref* to each *maenol* is late, the word *mainaur* was already established by the 8th century.

The native inhabitants of the *tref* were free, bond or slave. But the laws have much to say of the *aillt*, glossed as *estron*, stranger. He was normally a Cymro, from another part of Wales, a refugee or a landless freeman who sought to better himself elsewhere. The strangers also included the *alltud*, defined as 'from overseas, from another country, speaking a different language', among them shipwrecked sailors. The law prescribed that the stranger, like the rusti *taeog*, must have a lord. The reasons repeated in the texts echoed laws older than themselves. Strangers must be prevented from plotting; the foreigner must not acquire Cymric land; nugatory marriages and illegitimate children must be avoided. The last reason had troubled 5th-century Rome. In 451 Valentinian III tackled the troubles of *coloni originarii*, native rustics, or tied tenants, disturbed by *advenae*, strangers, 'often poor . . . who accepted food and clothing, thereby escaping the squalor of indigence', by 'pretending to undertake labour and duties', but who,

> thinking nothing of the misery they caused, chose women belonging to the estate, and, when they had had enough of them, went off, unmindful of their former state, ignoring their cohabitation and their lovely sons, with no law to stop them.

Valentinian enacted that the stranger must register on a particular estate, and might not thereafter desert his home or his wife. The Welsh law re-enacted Valentinian's.

The stranger is prominent in the law books, for the unusual is commonly more difficult for lawyers to describe, and needs more words. But the stranger played a large part in the economy, especially in unfree *tref*; for the *tref* was of two kinds, *rhydd*, free, and *taeog*, unfree. The land of the free *tref* was divided by the free man's law, but in the unfree *tref* it was assigned by the *arglwyd*, the lord, though it commonly went to the dead man's heirs, since the laws prescribe fees paid for the son's succession to his father's land. The land of the unfree *tref* was *tir cyvriv*, 'register land'; the modern Welsh *cyfrif* means 'counting' or 'reckoning', its derivative *cyfrifeb* a 'return', a 'census' or 'statistics', what is entered in a written record; *tir cyvriv* is land registered in a document or book. The laws measure land by area, by the *erw*, 'acre'; but the Llandaff documents measure by capacity, by the *modius*, or bushel, and *uncia*, a 'twelfth', perhaps of the *iugum* of Roman Britain.

Taxation of free and unfree land differed. Booked land paid *cyllid*, rent or tax, in Latin *vectigal*, to lord or king, but was exempt from the food tribute, *gwestva*. The king exacted *gwestva* from free *uchelwr*, nobles; Roman law had called it *pastus*, and it was held to have been originally levied when the king was on progress, dispensing justice. Taxes were differently collected. The twice yearly *cylch*, or 'circuit', of royal officers called *cais*, collected the unfree tax, but not the nobleman's food tribute. The Saints' Lives record the visits of these officers to each *pagus*, the equivalent of *tref* in the sixth century, and describe them by their late Roman name of *exactores*. Sometimes they demanded payment in the valuable ancient breed of white cattle with red ears; but in the laws these special cattle are demanded only as compensation for insult or injury to the king, his *saraad*.

The extent of unfree land is not known. Medieval schematism reckoned it at about one-third of all Welsh land; though the figures are unreal, the proportions are closer to reality, but they do not show how and when the amount of servile land grew. The free and unfree *tref* were envisaged as physically different. The houses on the free man's heritable land, partitioned among his sons, are treated as scattered separate farmsteads, but the unfree *tref* is regarded as a compact village. The laws on fire prevention enact that its bath must be built at a specified distance from the nearest house, that its smithy must be roofed with tiles or sods, not thatch; and require that accusations of arson must be cleared by the oath of 50 men, half of them *Gwyr Nod*, in Latin *viri noti*, respectable persons, or 'men of note', an oath that is normal for the bond *taeog*, not for the free man. These physical distinctions are recognisable on excavated sites. The compact hill-top village of Tre'r Ceiri in Caernarvonshire corresponds to the inflammable *taeog tref* of the laws; the chieftain's residence of Dinas Powys by Cardiff was a fit home for a lord, *arglwyd*; and the known numerous farmsteads of varying sizes suit the landowners and nobles, *priodorion* and *uchelwr*, of varying degrees.

The laws were written down for the benefit of kings and have most to say of the servile *tref*, which lay directly in his power; there he settled his strangers, who did not acquire free Cymro status until after nine generations of marriage with native women and therefore tended to increase in numbers. Their rents were earmarked for the king's dogs, horses and progress, and over them he placed his lord, who received part of their revenues. Less is said of the free *tref*, save that it was a unit of taxation, with fixed bounds. There is no sign that it had its own assembly or council, or any administrative or judicial function; but its notables met the king at regular times and places in the assembly of the *cantref*, the unit of a hundred *tref*, which constituted a principal court for civil and criminal offences; and might also censure a king and compel him to right an individual deemed to have been unjustly wronged.

The laws assign the political administration of the free Cymro not to the residential *tref*, but to the *cenedl*, the kindred of related families. It was a nine-generation group, whose functions included the defence of the free *bonheddig* against the encroachments of the king and the *taeog*. Its head, the *penncenedl*, in Latin *caput gentis*, was elected. Under his guidance it undertook a wide range of civil and criminal jurisdiction. In particular, though *saraad*, compensation for injury, was borne by the four-generation *gwely*, the more expensive *galanas*, compensation for manslaughter, was spread among the *cenedl*, with exact practical provisions to meet the difficulty of finding out who belonged to the eighth and ninth degrees of kinship. Some texts give the *penncenedl* a war leader and other assistants, but all agree that he must be a noble *uchelwr*, and emphatically repeat that no lord or royal official might be chosen.

The *cenedl* is rarely named outside the laws, and there is therefore no guide to its effective reality. But its name and form are closely paralleled by the earliest form of Scottish *clanna*, whose earlier names had included *cinel*. The functions differed, for the *clanna* organised a dynasty, while the *cenedl* organised freemen independently of kings. The similarities imply an ancient institution that the Welsh and Irish put to different uses; among the Welsh, the name may be later than the institution, for the earliest original texts, dated to about 800 or earlier, knew a kinship group called *luidt*, not recorded later; it may have been the ancestor of the *cenedl*.

Land Tenure

Welsh law mixed Roman and native precedent. Roman law classified men by status and domicile, native law by kinship. The dynasties that succeeded Arthur added the new claims of kings, and the spread of monasteries brought new problems, at first hard to resolve, that centred upon the tenure and inheritance of land. The claims of king and church conflicted with the rights of kin. The new problems are illustrated in the Life of Wenefred. Early in the 7th century, Teuyth of Tegeingl, Flintshire, was the *possessor* of three *villae*. He had no sons and decided to grant a *villa*, *tref*, to St. Beuno. He asked king Cadfan to 'fulfil for him his intentions about his patrimony'. Cadfan, whom his tombstone honours as the 'most learned of kings', replied

> The decision is neither mine nor yours; for we ought not to harm your interest or my need by separating land from the community of the province. But I will make you a free grant of whichever *villa* you choose, if you will be content to leave me the others.

The text is late and much corrupted; but what it reports is a problem of the 7th century, when monks were relatively new in north Wales, and the mechanics of how to grant them lands still needed careful thought. By the time the Life was written the problem had been solved for centuries.

The words and clauses are expressed in awkward Latin, but the problem and solution are clearly defined. Seen solely from the standpoint of Roman law and its modern heirs, in terms of the simple polarised abstractions 'private property' and 'communal property', the transaction bristles with apparent contradictions. Teuyth was a *possessor* who could not alienate; the decision was not his or the king's, but he and the king decided. They alienated part of Teuyth's 'possessions' from the 'community', but what Teuyth retained was the king's.

Seen in the language of early Welsh law these statements are more easily intelligible. Teuyth was lord of a *maenol*, comprising three unfree *tref*. The land was *tir cyvriv*, the documented property of the *tref*, not legally inherited, paying *cyllid*, tax, to Teuyth and to the king. Its transfer from the community to the individual involved other interests besides the loss of revenue to king and lord, for the nearer relations of Teuyth's *gwely* were his heirs, and his larger *cenedl* also had claims upon his inheritance. These interests were appeased or overridden by the cession of one *tref*; the others remained the king's, for the principal renders were his. The grant to the monk entailed further complication. Later law enacted that when the king authorised the construction of a church in a servile *tref*, its inhabitants were freed; they ceased to pay servile tax, their land ceased to be registered communal property, and passed by family inheritance. The later law generalised claims that monks had advanced from the beginning in respect of individual estates, and may have been secured by Beuno.

King Cadfan's learning found the problems difficult in the early 7th century, chiefly because of the claims of kin. The residual claims of distant heirs mattered most in times of expanding population, when good land was short. Exact detail is recorded in 14th-century surveys. Then, in one district, the heirs of four landowners numbered more than 200 persons after 150 years, and their holdings were drastically partitioned. One of the four ancestors had held five whole *tref* and fragments of others, together equivalent to a sixth. Some heirs had divided their inheritance, but others jointly farmed undivided lands. The undivided holding had become the property of the ancestor's *gwely*, his four-generation family; its separate divided portions were termed *gavell*, and fines had confiscated tiny portions, as exact as five eighths or seven sixty-fourths of a gavell, that became the king's property. He might either assign them to his unfree cultivators, or allot them to free *bonheddig*, provided that they paid servile tax. Though each man knew his own acres, the revenue officers faced a mathematical nightmare.

The result was not only the subdivision of large estates into small holdings. The wealth and status of families changed. The proprietor of six *tref* had been a great landlord. The descendant who held fragments of a few *gavell* was a poor peasant. The principles of the law operated, but their operation was far more complex than the simple legal contrast between a *tref* that was entirely free, and another that was unfree. Two parts of the holding of one *gwely* were held on servile *taeog* tenure, paying servile tax, but the rest was held in free tenure; and one *gwely* might hold several *tref*, differently partitioned among its members, so that beside the free and unfree *tref* there were others that were part free, part unfree.

The survey is late, but it illuminates an older system. It shows what happened when the birth rate was high. Holdings then fragmented. But in times of falling population they consolidated. Over centuries of fluctuating population inheritance by kin divorced land-holding from territorial political organisation. But the chief gainer was the king; his lands were enlarged by fines, and he also acquired the 'extinct *erw*', the acres of a free man who left no heir in his four-generation *gwely*; and death without heirs was commoner when population contracted. Crown lands grew, and when population rose the freeman's demand for more acres sharpened, strengthening his need of his *cenedl*, and inciting him to bring a suit of *dadenhudd*, 'recovery of patrimony'.

The claim of patrimony threatened church lands, for the church did not die and did not partition its estates. The legal problem was real, for a free man was entitled to inheritance by ancient custom, that no king or lord had power to override in native law. The church therefore asserted the tenures of late Roman law, *ius perpetuum*, everlasting right, or *ius ecclesiasticum*, church right, against *ius hereditarium*, the claims of kin. But when two legal systems conflicted, force was the arbiter between opposing rights. Commonly, an individual's grant of land, ratified by the king, sufficed to deter the claims of his heirs to recover the land in law; but not infrequently a great-grandson might disregard a grant made a century before, sometimes with no greater violence than withholding rents claimed by the church; and many charters are re-grants of old donations ignored by later landowners.

But prudence dictated that all possible steps should be taken to satisfy the claims of heirs, and to make a suit for recovery of patrimony legally invalid. The most sensible way was to compensate the heirs in advance. The medieval charter memoranda of the Books of Llancarfan and Llandaff altered much of the wording of the grants they transcribed to suit the needs of their own day, but they often retained elaborate details of the gifts made to redeem the rights of all the interests involved; their transcripts illustrate the efforts of early 7th-century Welsh lawyers to fight their way through to safe legal forms.

The Llancarfan texts give most detail. Guorcinnim bought an estate from the king 'into his own inheritance', for a sword worth 25 cows. The king freed servile land and made it the 'perpetual inheritance' of Guorcinnim; but it was still subject to the law of kin, so Guorcinnim gave another gift to Mesioc, 'whom it concerned by hereditary right', and then assigned the estate to the monastery of Cadoc 'in perpetual possession'. But Cadoc's heirs also had claims upon his monastic lands, for his immediate successors were lay abbots chosen from his kin; so Guorcinnim also gave gifts to the son and grandson of the lay abbot. In addition he compensated the son and grandson of the king, and also Guengarth, styled *procurator*, who had previously levied services and dues upon the estate. The whole transaction was termed an *emptio*, 'purchase'.

A little later Guengarth himself was given an estate by the king. He gave its rents to the church, and gave 'his guilded sword Hipiclaur, worth 70 cows' to the abbot, who then gave it to the king, in exchange for confirmation, for the remission of all secular dues and for an assurance that the estate should never be subjected to any lord but Guengarth and his heirs. On another occasion the king himself gave a sword and a cloak to the abbot, who used them to buy an estate; he then held it in *ius perpetuum* from two laymen, evidently joint-heirs, who themselves gave two cows to the lord, to free it from royal dues, and 'held a charter on the hand of the abbot', who beat the bounds in token of 'private possession', *propriae possessionis*. Another landowner gave an estate that was his 'by hereditary right' to the abbot, in 'perpetual right'; he also 'bought' it from another man, 'to whom it had devolved', evidently a kinsman and heir. Another estate belonged jointly to two brothers and a sister, together with two parts of a second property, and was granted by the king, who himself 'held a charter on the hand of the abbot'; the abbot then gave the king a horse, which he passed on to a royal officer.

The texts that report these details are late, but their matter is not. Most of the later grants, in the Llandaff book, are content to record that a man gave an estate, transferring it from 'hereditary right' to 'perpetual right', for the procedures were then standardised and recognised. They hardened early, for late 8th-century grants preserved in the original in the Book of Teilo, or Chad, found no such detailed explanation necessary.

Similar problems beset the grant of land to Irish monasteries. The earliest records date from the late 7th century, and the scribe who copied them into the Book of Armagh a little over a hundred years later found them difficult to understand. In the fullest of them, two persons, the virgin Cummen and Brethan, bought Oughteragh in Leitrim from property bequeathed to Cummen and two other virgins. The estate was the half of her own inheritance. The value of the personal mobile property due to her was paid in animals and old plate, which she presumably passed on to her co-heirs. She then wove a cloak and gave it to the chief of the ruling dynasty; he gave her a horse, which she gave to 'Colman of the Britons', who sold it for a *cumal* of silver; and the *cumal* went to the price of the estate. Not everything is clear in the difficult language; but the substance is that the donor bought out the rights of her kin and of the king. Colman was probably the former bishop of the Northumbrians, the date about 665 or soon after.

Kin were not always bought out in Ireland. In another text in the same collection Feth made a formal oath to the monks and nobility that there should be no kin over the monastery of Drumlease in Leitrim save his own, and that the abbot should be chosen from his kin so long as there was a qualified candidate. These practices remained normal. For more than a hundred years the successors of Columba at Iona were chosen from his kin, and many other abbots were kinsmen of the founder of their house. Very many houses also remained in secular law the property of the founder's kin, whose head was an *erenarch*, 'lay proprietor'; the normal word for the religious abbots of the greater houses was *comarb*, 'joint heir', jointly with the lay heir.

The institution of the lay abbot is not reported in Wales after the early 7th century, and the kinsmen of abbots are less in evidence throughout. But in Ireland the *erenarch* took firm root. Early in the 9th century the notice of Foirtchernn's foundation of Trim, in the middle of the 5th century, is followed by a list of eight religious abbots who succeeded him, and also of eight generations of 'secular heirs', *erenarchs*, who descended from his brother. But, as in Wales, procedures were standardised, and in the 9th century it was sufficient to record that the kin, *genus*, of Binean's mother 'gave him the inheritance' on which he built a church.

Irish and Welsh society shared a remote common past. But the Welsh had also experienced four hundred years of Roman rule, which differentiated them from the Irish, even though their monasteries transmitted some of that experience to Ireland. Their lawyers had to improvise, but their solutions endured at home and became one of the influences that bore upon the formative years of the English. The men who faced and solved the problems that Arthur's successors passed to the British and Irish contributed to the common culture of medieval Britain.

CHAPTER TWENTY-FOUR
ENGLISH SOCIETY

Local Difference

Early English society is more difficult to comprehend than Welsh or Irish. It was more varied and changed more quickly. Much more is known about it, but large sections of the evidence are still unsifted. Its simplest outlines are clearer. At the beginning of the seventh century the English conquerors had no common custom and no fixed social order. The conventions of the Welsh and the Irish had hardened over many centuries, but English society was new, unformed, and full of local variation; and the speed and extent of recent conquest brought violent upheaval. From the seventh century onward lawyers struggled to impose uniformity, but found that words were more easily standardised than the things they represented. Uniformity of custom could not be achieved by the pen of the administrator, for diversity was deep seated. The chief difference was that which separated the old kingdoms from those that had acquired vast lands in need of colonisation, the Northumbrians, the West Saxons and the Mercians. But within this general distinction, the needs and outlook of each kingdom, and of regions within kingdoms, differed greatly.

The English brought their national monarchy to Britain in the late fifth century. But partition long prevented it from uniting the English in Britain. Each monarchy had its own tradition. Kent alone was ruled by a long established monarchy. Monarchy was old among the East Angles, but the dynasty was new. The East and South Saxon kings were too weak to assert lasting independence against their greater neighbours, and Lindsey was long buffeted between the Northumbrians and Mercians. In Northumbria repeated military success endowed the kings with enormous personal prestige, but the affection inspired by the sincerity of Irish monks gave churchmen power to curb the kings. The numerous small peoples of the midlands were still loosely adjusted to the growing power of the Mercian monarchs, and the five West Saxon kingdoms admitted the suzerainty of an overking only when they must.

Within each kingdom the proportions of great men and small varied, and variation caused different relations between them; in addition, the proportions and relations between the English and the native British, or Welsh, were as diversified. All these differences were accentuated in the newly subdued lands, that invited settlement by young men of energy, particularly in the west, beyond the furthest frontiers of their forefathers. There men risked destruction by native rebellion, or by invasion from the still unconquered Welsh kingdoms, but those who secured their lands became lords of native subjects, more than the possessors of lands that they must cultivate by their own labour.

The Sources

The main witness to the evolution of English society in the 5th and 6th centuries is the mass of material interred in pagan graves; thereafter, evidence comes chiefly from place names, supplemented by laws, charters and other texts. The different kinds of evidence are dissimilar. The 7th-century law codes of Kent and Wessex survive as they were written, and report the lawyer's view of their society. Charters are preserved from several regions of the south and midlands, but their rich reserves of information have as yet scarcely begun to be explored. The texts are available only in imperfect modern editions, inadequately indexed, whose shortcomings hamper their study; a few texts survive unaltered, and a very few are wholly the invention of later ages, but most have been altered in the copying to suit later interest. The alterations are sometimes trivial, sometimes extensive, but it has not yet been possible to distinguish systematically between the original content and later additions, and the charters are therefore still often herded into the oversimple categories of 'forged' or 'genuine', though few of them are properly described by either term. The study of place names suffers from a different handicap; the greater part of their evidence cannot be assessed until the survey is complete, but nearly a third of the counties are not yet published. These several sources also overlap in time. The earliest Kentish law-code was drawn up at the beginning of the 7th century, the earliest West Saxon code at the end of the century. With few exceptions the charters do not begin until the 670s, but much of the place name evidence concerns earlier generations, and some of it reaches back into the 6th century, when pagan cemetery burial was still normal.

Graves

The pagan burials illustrate the beginnings of social difference. Most of the 5th-century cemeteries were the graveyards of communities, and most of the graves were of equal wealth; the women were buried with a pair of simple brooches, the men with spear and shield. Swords, and emblems of female wealth and authority increased during the 6th century, and were matched by greater numbers of poorly furnished burials. Contrast is more marked after the conquest. A majority of the latest burials were the tombs of individuals or of families, often wealthy. Prominent barrows were erected over the remains of the local kings of the West Saxons; early in the 7th century the Mercian barrows in the uplands beyond the Trent sometimes contained costly armour, and in the south the dazzling royal tombs of Taplow, Broomfield and Sutton Hoo witness the sudden emergence of splendid kingship. Many lesser men were also buried richly, for the institution of monarchy required the support of a nobility, graded by differing degrees of wealth and power.

Place names

The evidence of place names confirms and continues the evolution traced by the graves. Many kinds of names carry their date with them. No place, save sometimes a region or a large town, could acquire an English name before its first English settlers arrived, and their arrival is dated by the graves, by the Saxon Chronicle, Bede, and other texts who report either the first arrival of the English in particular districts, or the existence of particular names at specific dates. It is rarely possible to know when a name form altogether passed from use, for isolated instances lingered long; but it is frequently observed that some forms are common in older areas, rare in regions settled later, while others are rare in old areas, common in lands first settled after the conquest. It is hardly ever possible to date the name of a particular place, for when a name form was established in a district, it often remained long in use; but the texts and graves frequently indicate when and where particular types of name came into widespread use.

Communities

Only a fraction of the evidence can yet be studied, but understanding has been greatly helped by the publication of volumes analysing the meaning and distribution of the main elements used in forming names, and by recent thorough study of the element *-ing*. Interpretation of its various forms demands nice attention to Old English spelling and grammar and usage, but the basic meaning

---

Map 30

	single sites	frequent
Names in *-ingas*	ı	|||
Names in *-ingaham*	○	≡
Names in *-inga-*	■	///

Sites outside the areas of frequency are marked individually

-.-.-. Boundary of counties examined

—— Approximate limit of 6th century pagan burials within the area *(cf. Map 21, p.297)*

MAP 30 ENGLISH COLONISATION: PLACE NAMES I

The South and the Midlands, names in *-inga(s)*

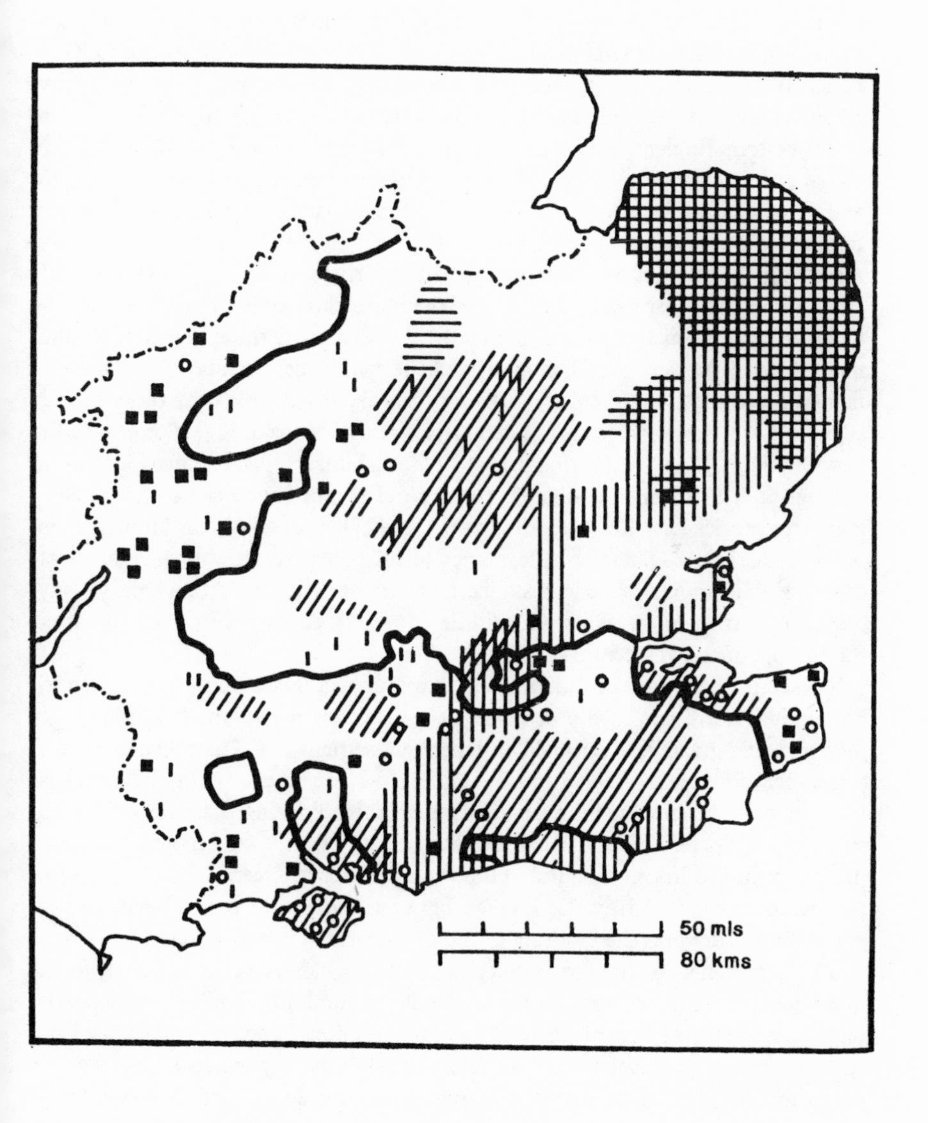

is clear. It is a word ending, not unlike the modern *-ine* or *-ite*, but more widely employed, meaning a place or people who belong in some sense to the word that precedes it; the *Haestingas*, who named Hastings, were Haesta's people, and Tyningham means the home of the people who lived by the river Tyne.

Maps 30 and 36 show where these names were mainly used in England. Names in *-ingaham* abound in East Anglia, and extend to the Middle Angles and to Kent in smaller numbers. Elsewhere they are common only among sixth-century English emigrants to Gaul, in Artois and western Flanders (Map 19A, p. 288); in south-eastern England a few exist upon the immediate margins of the pagan burial areas, but they are very rare in districts that were first colonised in the 7th and later centuries. Names in *-ingas* are somewhat more widespread in the districts of the 5th and 6th-century English, but they are also rare in 7th-century areas. But they do not mark the names of the earliest English. Though they are common in the older areas, very few of them are close enough to known cemeteries to have been the names of the villages that used those cemeteries; and many among the few burial grounds that lie within half a mile of villages so named are cemeteries of mid or late 6th-century origin. Most of these names surround cemeteries or groups of cemeteries at a distance of several miles, or lie between them. Map 31, showing part of Bedfordshire, is typical of many localities. Though it is in theory possible that many old names have been lost, and that many cemeteries have not been discovered, the evidence of what is known is too plain to disregard. These are the names of offshoots from the first villages, of colonists who moved a little distance from home. Names of this type plainly began to be used in or before the middle of the 6th century, but were rare after the middle of the 7th century.

These are the names of independent communities. Names in *-inga-* followed by another word, commonly *denn*, swine pasture, or *hyrst*, wooded upland, or *fold*, enclosed grazing, describe later dependent settlements. Their distribution is altogether different. They are rare in the older areas, except in the districts between reserves in which the English were confined during the years of British supremacy. There the English came in the late 6th century; and these dependent names continued in common use in the western lands between Avon and Severn, that were first peopled by the English between the end of pagan burial in the early 7th century and the granting of the first charters, fifty years later.

The commonest of the community names, *-tun*, cannot yet be studied, for it is frequent in the counties not yet published, and its significance depends chiefly on the words that precede it. Its basic meaning, 'fence', is perpetuated by the modern German word *Zaun*. In Old English it usually means a fenced area, sometimes agricultural, as in *gaerstun*, grass enclosure, and is used for a house in a couple of exceptional passages. But its ordinary meaning in the 7th century and later, when places were receiving their names, was 'village', a collection of houses, compact or scattered, forming a single political unit. In place names it has no other meaning. It is regularly translated in Latin by the word *villa*, that was

MAP 31 ENGLISH COLONISATION: PLACE NAMES 2

Central Bedfordshire, names in *-inga(s)*

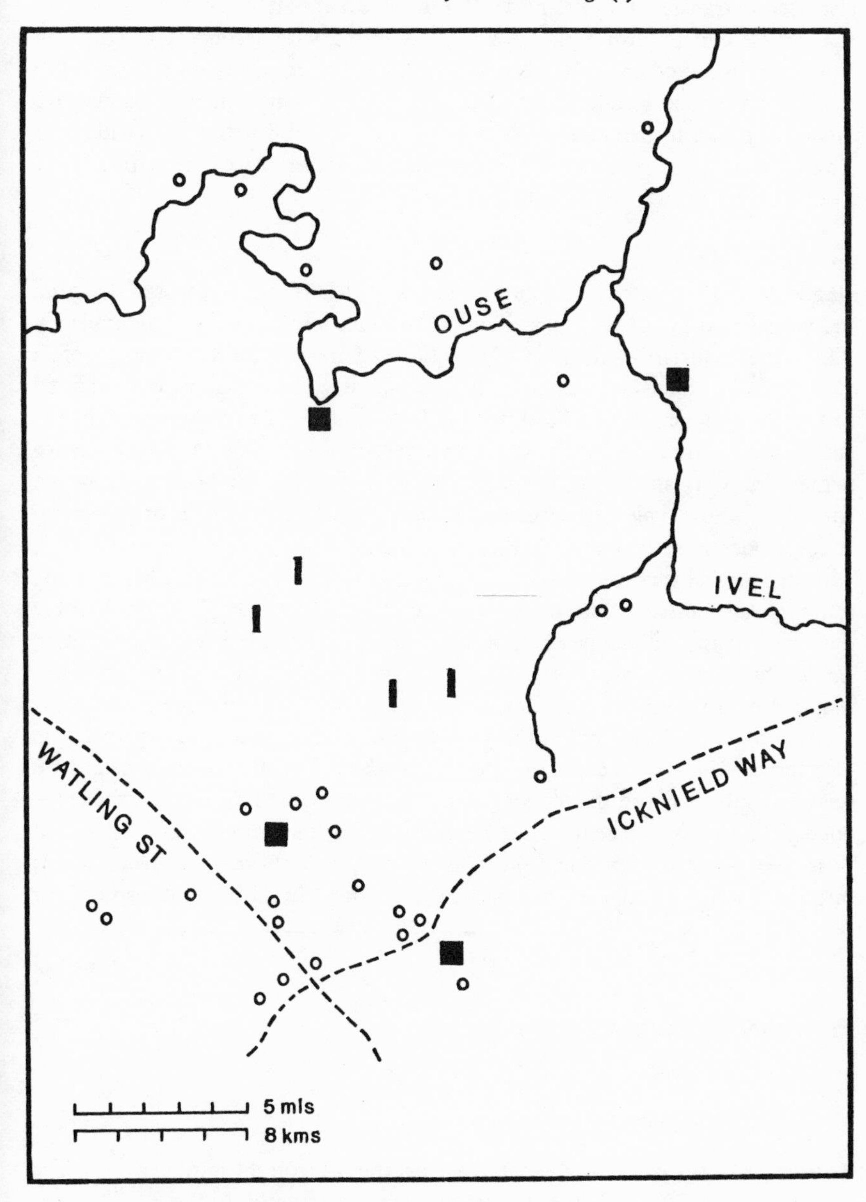

■ Main early pagan cemeteries

○ Other pagan English burial grounds

I Place names in *-ingas*

also used to translate the Welsh *tref*. But in place names it 'was not so common in the earliest Old English period', and is 'associated with secondary colonisation from established centres.' It was not until the 12th century that men needed to distinguish the size of unfortified places by different words; then the diminutive *villagium* began to denote smaller places, and to establish the word village in English usage; the old words were restricted to larger places, becoming 'ville' in French and 'town' in English.

Individual Colonists

Besides the words for communities and collections of houses, words denoting individual holdings of varying size and importance were used for naming places. The Northumbrian *-botl*, as in Harbottle, had the specialised meaning of 'a superior hall, a mansion, a castle'. The word is early, for in Europe it is confined to the Elbe regions where Saxons from Britain are said to have settled in the earlier 6th century, and there it is now spelled *-büttl;* but in English place names (Maps 35 and 36) its use is restricted to the Northumbrians, and to the Mercians, whose dialect gave the form *-bold* or *-bald*, as in Bolton or Newbald. A commoner word is *-worth*, defined as an 'individual and personal possession'; with its regional variants *-worthy* and *-wardine*, it distinguished the home of the ordinary substantial freeman, the *ceorl*, from the *-cote*, the 'cottage, humble dwelling' of the poorer peasant. Besides these descriptive names, the ending *-ingtun*, usually preceded by a personal name, most often describes a village founded by a prominent individual, accompanied by his dependents.

Map 32 displays the numbers of places named *-worth*, *-cote* and *-ingtun* in the counties that have been surveyed, and of *-worth* in all counties. These names are relatively infrequent in the old kingdoms. They are most numerous in the lands opened to English settlement in the 7th century, in the Weald of Kent and Sussex, in western Mercia and the West Riding, and, above all, in Devonshire; but they were no longer in common use when English names spread in

---

Map 32

Place names in *-worth* etc.

-cote

-ingtun

The length of the columns, measured against the scale on the left, indicates the numbers of each type of name in each county. In the counties shaded comparable information is accessible only for *-worth*.

MAP 32 ENGLISH COLONISATION: PLACE NAMES 3

Settlement by or through individuals: *-worth, -cote, -ingtun*

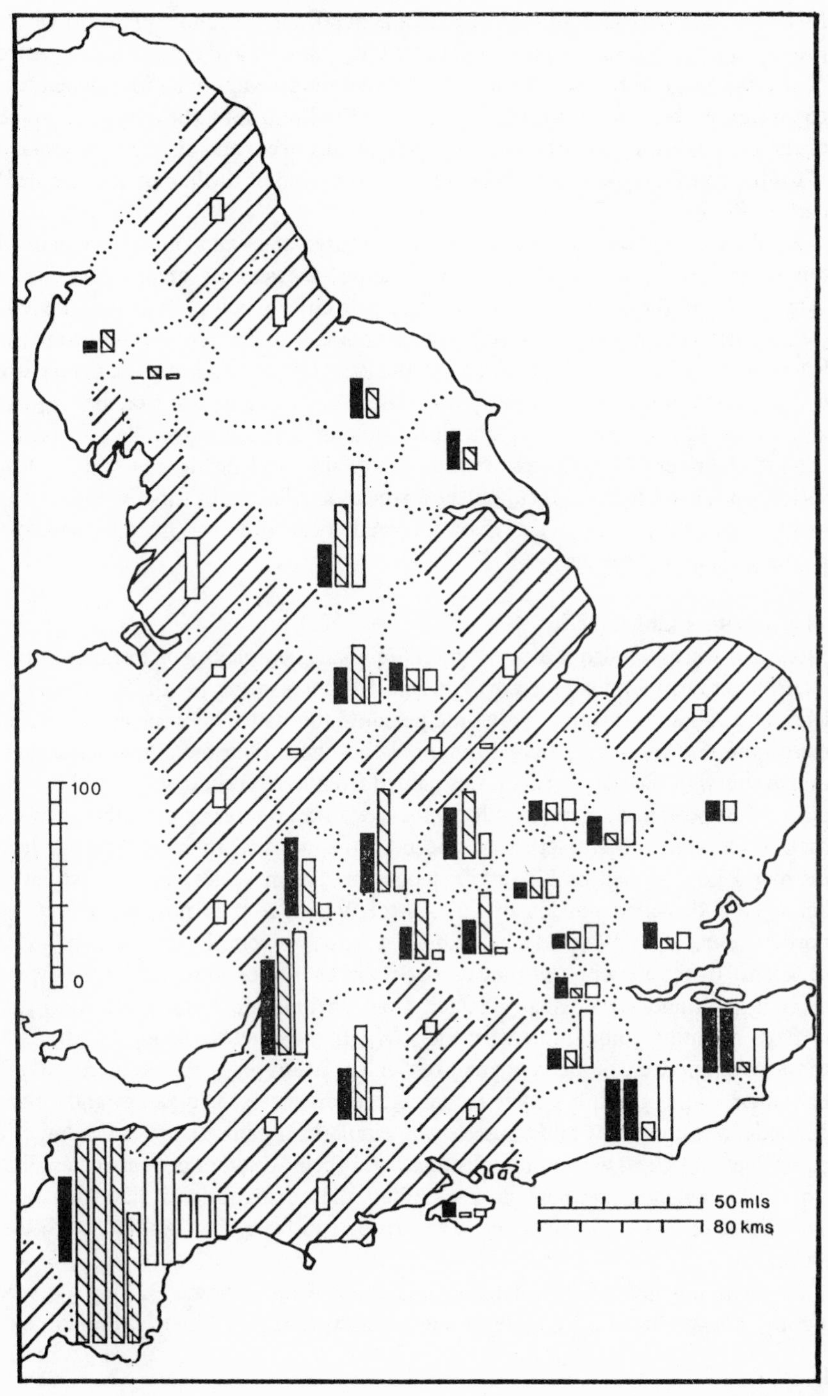

Cumberland and Westmorland, and are also relatively rare in north-western Mercia, in Staffordshire and Cheshire. In general, they are most plentiful where the *-ingas* and *-ingaham* names are fewest. They confirm and extend the evidence of the pagan graves, that in the old kingdoms most men lived in independent communities, but that in the lands opened to the English by the conquest, much of the colonisation was conducted by individuals, great and small. There many of the humbler *-cote* names are likely to have been used of the homes of dependent native Welshmen.

Small scale maps of the whole country or large areas can only show general tendencies. It is possible to examine some districts in greater detail. In Warwickshire, the river Avon still marked a frontier when pagan burial ended; the English did not master and settle the former Cornovian territories beyond the river until well after the beginning of the 7th century. There the *-cotes* are equally distributed on both sides of the river, but three quarters of the *-ingtuns* and all the *-worths*, together with nine-tenths of the clearings called *-leah*, lie beyond the river. The 6th-century English plainly did not live in the kind of society that used these names, but in a world of villages; but many of the 7th-century colonists beyond the river followed local lords, or lived in separate homesteads and clearings.

The Regions Colonised

Preliminary studies also indicate something of the complexity of Kentish settlement. There, the English took over an intact Roman society, with its great landlords and its native custom of dividing peasant inheritance between all sons. The towns and villages were grouped in nine 'lathes' with their own jurisdiction, not unlike the *cantref* of Wales; each was named from a royal centre, that had been a place of importance since the 5th century, with a large early cemetery, and in each of the seven coastal lathes had been a Roman town. In each the king had his own lands, farmed by his servile dependents, as in Wales; and to each lathe belonged a detached portion of the central Weald, usually not adjacent to its borders. But, as in Wales, land holdings were more complicated than political divisions. In the Downs and the coastlands, large estates were many; they were termed *land*, and were usually named from an individual, sometimes British, or from a family, comparable with the *gwely*, like *Welkechildeland*, the estate of the *childe*, children or descendants, of Welke. Many or most of these estates had their swine pastures, their woodland, their enclosed grazing and other dependencies in the Weald. Sussex was similarly organised into nine 'rapes', equivalent to lathes, with numerous *lands* and their Wealden dependencies; but when Sussex names are more closely studied, their distribution is likely to differ from those of Kent, for more roads and rivers run from the Weald through the Downs.

Kentish and South Saxon colonisation of the Weald, shown on Map 33, was plainly not pioneered by independent communities and hardy individuals, penetrating into the forest at random, but was planned and organised by kings and lords. The freeman's *worth* seldom reaches beyond the fringes of the Weald, and the humble *-cote* is rare, though somewhat commoner in the more loosely organised territories of Surrey, but *-inga*, *-ingtun* and the estate names spread throughout the Weald, to face each other across the modern county boundaries. Other regions show a different kind of colonisation. In Hertfordshire and Middlesex (Map 34), *-ingtun* and estate names are rare; *-worth* and *-cote* reach into the London clays from the pagan settlement districts by the Thames and the Icknield Way, but they do not meet; the first settlers in the difficult soils between them used other forms of name, many of them perhaps at a later date.

Northern regional difference is marked; *-worths* are many in the southernmost Pennines, and also in Durham and on Tyneside, but there are hardly any in between, from the East Riding to Cumberland; there the *-ingtuns* reach into the eastern Pennines, and the *-botl* strongholds guard the passes and the coasts. The blend of different kinds of settlements established lasting local customs, whose consequences may be detected only in the local history of each area. They will be better understood when a far wider range of place names can be studied and compared.

These are preliminary indications, that serious local study will clarify and correct. They suggest three main stages in the expansion of the English, the first delineated by the pagan cemeteries of the 5th and 6th centuries, the second in the nearer regions opened to settlement in the later 6th and early 7th centuries, and the third indicating the extensive colonisation of the 7th century. The community names are commonest within the 6th-century frontiers and just beyond their borders; but in the 7th century most colonisation was undertaken by lords who led their followers. The exceptions are the dangerous borders where enemies might be expected in arms. There, large concentrations of lesser freemen defended their own lands. Their *worths* are most numerous in Devon, where they are four times as many as in a dozen eastern counties put together; in Gloucestershire; and on the frontiers between the Mercians and the Northumbrians. Though new villages continued to be founded and named for centuries, it is probable that the great majority of the districts rich in colonising names had already been settled before the end of the 8th century, and that the derivative names became more usual thereafter.

The three stages of English expansion are the century and a half of war and partition, when the pagan English survived beside and among stronger Christian British neighbours; the age of conquest and conversion; and the age of colonisation. Cemeteries are the main evidence for the first stage of war and partition; place names are the chief witness of where the conquerors and early colonists settled.

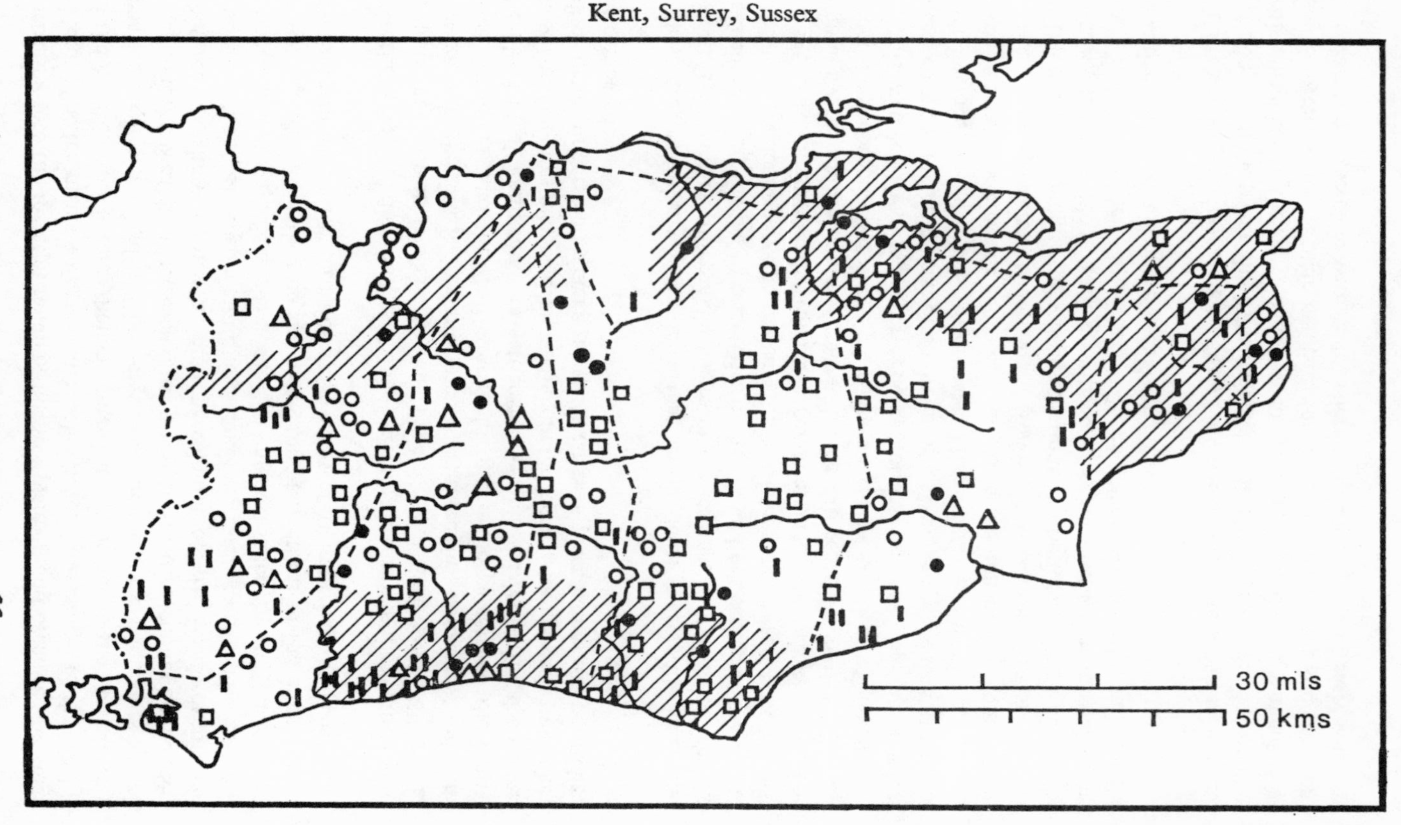
Kent, Surrey, Sussex
30 mls
50 kms

MAP 34 ENGLISH COLONISATION: PLACE NAMES 5

Essex, Hertfordshire, Middlesex

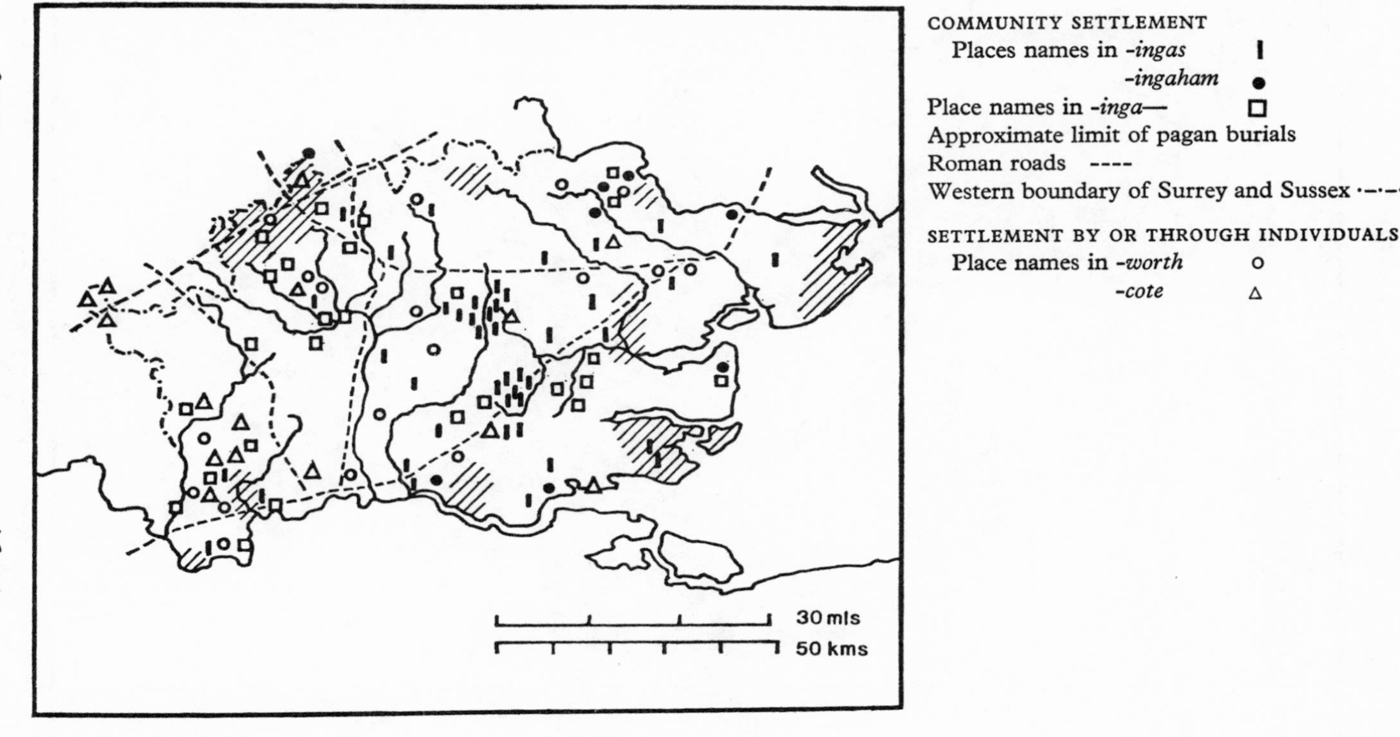

MAP 35 ENGLISH COLONISATION: PLACE NAMES 6

The North and West

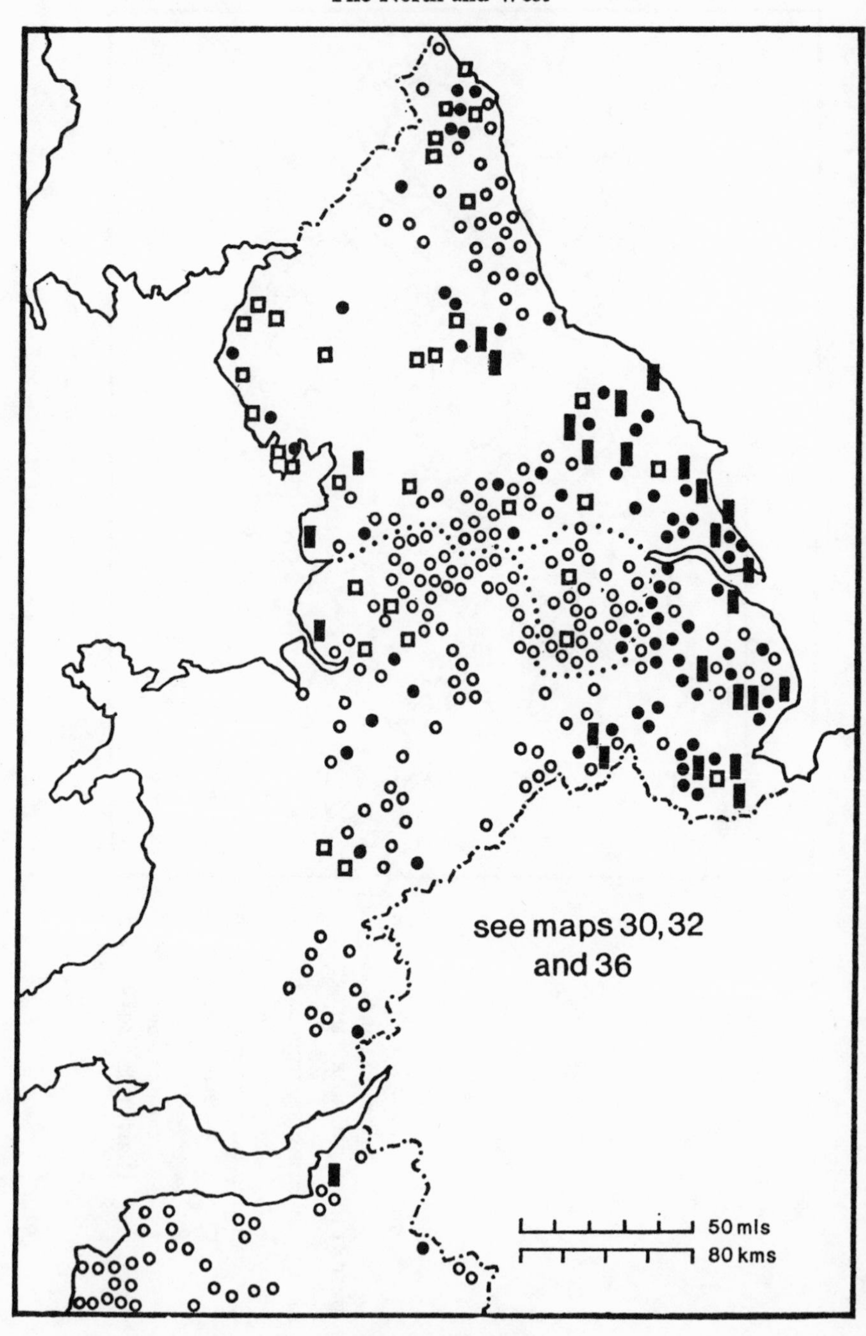

Symbols, see p. 479

MAP 36 ENGLISH COLONISATION: PLACE NAMES 7
-botl and variants in the South

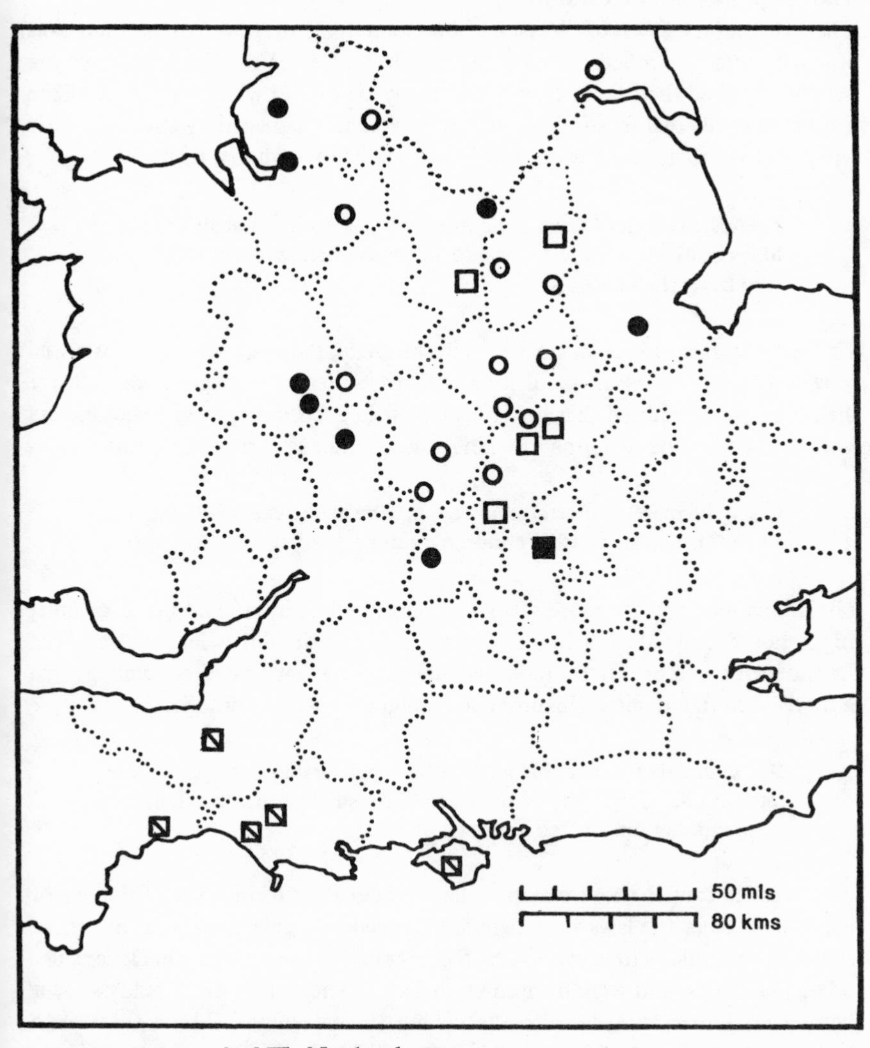

NORTHUMBRIAN: *-botl* ■; Newbottle □
MERCIAN: *-bold, -bald* ●; Newbold, Newbald ○
WEST SAXON: *-buddle* and variants ⧅
The dotted lines represent modern county boundaries

Map 35

COMMUNITY SETTLEMENT: Place names in *-ingas* ▮; in *-ingaham* •
SETTLEMENT BY OR THROUGH INDIVIDUALS: Place names in *-worth*, etc. o; in *-botl* and variants □
Approximate frontiers of Mercia and Elmet · · · · Limit of area surveyed –·–·–·

The Organisation of Colonies

The 7th-century laws of Wessex show something of how colonisation was organised and controlled. It was not a haphazard affair of adventurous young men who moved their families and belongings when and where they liked. Care was taken to see that existing communities were not damaged by sudden erratic withdrawal of their manpower. The laws provide that when a man

> intends to depart (*faran wille*), he who has 20 hides shall show 12 hides cultivated; he who has 10 hides shall show 6 cultivated, he who has 3 shall show 1½.

The man with 20 hides was a powerful magnate, the man with 3 a substantial *ceorl*. The laws envisaged the likelihood that freemen of all degrees might leave their lands, and required that the lands be left in good heart, tilled by cultivators who would continue to supply the king's needs. The laws also enact that

> if a nobleman (*gesithcundmon*) depart, he may take with him his reeve, his smith, and his children's tutor.

The limitation matters more than the permitted retinue. The noble colonist might not depopulate his homeland by taking with him a large part of its dependent cultivators. If he took dependents, he must find them among men authorised to follow him. Unauthorised emigration was forbidden.

> If a man departs from his lord without permission and steals away into another shire, and is discovered, he shall return to where he was, and pay his lord 60 shillings.

Law codes cannot show whether the offences they forbid were frequent or rare, nor whether the laws were regularly obeyed or regularly broken. But these laws were enacted at a time when West Saxon colonists were arriving in Devonshire in large numbers, and were devised to check tendencies that had already shown themselves. Other laws concern the colonists' new homes. Those that relate to the *worth* of the *ceorl* were enacted for all Wessex; but the circumstances they envisage are likely to have been commonest among the *worths* that were multiplying on the western frontiers when the laws were enacted. They provide that

> a *ceorl*'s *worth* shall be fenced in summer and in winter. If not, and a neighbour's beast strays through the gap he has left, he shall have no claim on the beast; he shall chase it out and accept the damage.
>
> If *ceorls* have a grass enclosure, or other apportioned land to fence, and some have fenced their part and some have not, and (cattle

> get in) and eat their common arable or grass, those responsible for the gap shall offer compensation for the damage done to the others, who have enclosed their part. They shall demand from the (owners of the) cattle whatever reparation is proper.
>
> But if a beast breaks through the *hegas* and wanders within, since its owner cannot or will not control it, he who finds it on his arable shall take it and kill it. The owner shall have its hide and flesh, and accept the loss of the rest.

The *worth* is a self-contained individual farm; its fences, hedges or banks must be permanent. But, in addition to their separate *worths*, the *ceorls* may also have enclosed grass, a *gaerstun*, or other 'apportioned', *gedal*, land, in common. They must hedge or fence it, to keep cattle out; if the cattle get in, everyone's crop is damaged.

The *gaerstun* contains grass that cattle are not supposed to eat. The grass is therefore intended for hay, winter fodder. The enclosure may also be used for other crops, though the law primarily envisages hay fields. Within the enclosure there is no division. The 'arable or grass' is common. When an animal gets in it can eat the lot; if the enclosure were subdivided into individual portions, each separately fenced, then animals could only get at the unfenced portions, and those who had put up their barriers would suffer no damage and require no law to secure their compensation.

The part, *dael*, which each man must fence can therefore only be his portion of the bank or hedge which surrounds the whole enclosure. In calling the land '*gedal land*', divided or apportioned land, the law does not mean that it is to be subdivided; it means that it has already been doled out by allotment. Provision is made for a rough beast that forces its way through a hedge or fence that is judged strong enough to keep out normal animals. The procedure is normal sensible farming practice, among colonists in new lands. Each has his own farm, but they pool their resources for their winter fodder and may grow in common other crops as well as grass. The law prescribed that the *ceorl's* own fence must be permanent; and plainly supposed that the fence of the land they farmed in common should be as well protected. The 'fences' to be built were not temporary affairs; they might be hedges, or might be the steep banks of Devon fields. The law chiefly concerned land that was being enclosed by the English for the first time.

These are laws that compelled the free *ceorl* to respect each other's interests and common good. They presuppose communities where the English lived together. But when the great nobleman with his reeve conducted parties of lesser men who had obtained permission to leave, such regulations were more easily enforced by him, and many such parties did not live alone by themselves in their new homes. Very many of the 5th- and 6th-century settlers were located in or beside Roman towns and villages, mansions and farms, originally billeted upon their owners; and many of the earliest colonising settlements, marked by the small cemeteries and single graves common in the latest age of pagan burial, had also been established immediately beside British farmsteads. Often, the reason why the Roman British farmhouse was abandoned, and reverted to ploughland or pasture instead of continuing in use, was that an English farm or village had already been established nearby, its people working the same or adjacent acres, until the heirs of the native farmstead intermarried with the English, or moved into their village; their fusion is occasionally noticed by British burials in an English graveyard, sometimes marked by native hob-nailed boots, where the soil preserves their traces, on the feet of buried bodies.

There are many local variants. In parts of the West Riding, of central Wessex and elsewhere, places called Walton or the like and places with British names cluster together, with a few early English names among them. But in other areas a few English mastered many Welsh. One Sussex charter suggests a probable instance. At Heberden, now abandoned in Madehurst, north of Arundel, king Nunna in 725 granted to the bishop twenty tax-paying *tributarii* at 'Huga's hills and the *denn*', the pasture land, commonly for pigs. The district had not been English for much longer than a century; Huga had been dead for some time, since his heirs had disappeared and the land was now royal; he may well have been the original settler. The bounds are given, from Lavington Dyke to the Stane Street, stretching north to the Billingas of Billingshurst; they adjoin cleared land still unoccupied, termed 'No Man's Land'. They border on, and perhaps include, the arable land of the huge Roman mansion of Bignor. Huga doubtless brought his reeve, and perhaps some English dependents, but it is likely that many of the *tributarii* were the descendants of the peasants who had tilled the estates of the Roman magnate. They, and doubtless many of the inhabitants of a *cote*, a *botl* or an *-ingtun*, were conquered natives to be treated as the English Saxons treated the 'natives' whom they had conquered in Thuringia in the 530s. The Saxons there received the conquered territory, but

> because they were too few to occupy it all, they assigned part to dependent cultivators, subject to tribute, but held the rest themselves.

It may be that the Welsh of Bignor were obliged to guard and pasture English pigs, and that they were in time assimilated, for Huga's hills and the *denn* later merged into a single village, named Heberden. But whatever the speech of Heberden, conquered Welshmen and Englishmen with little land both became *tributarii* in English law.

Only a fraction of the evidence can yet be assessed. As far as it goes, it points to some regional characteristics. Institutions and ideas inherited from Roman landlords affected the English most deeply in Kent. Compact communities were most numerous in the old kingdoms inhabited by the English throughout the 6th century; separate farmsteads, great lords and subject Welshmen were most numerous in the lands colonised in and after the late 6th century. But the mixture varied. Men who lived in compact villages most easily preserved the tradition that all men's voices must be heard on matters of common interest; but colonists who came from such villages carried long established village attitudes with them to their new homes, and adapted them to a new environment when they were numerous. Lordship and patronage are most obvious in the colonial lands; but kings bred aristocracy, and imposed lords upon villages in the old kingdoms as well. The quality of lordship varied. The loyalties that men accorded to a great captain who had led them to a distant home and there protected them were not the same as those accorded to a lord imposed by a king over villagers who tilled ancestral lands. The attitudes of cottagers, Welsh and English, and of two hundred shilling *ceorls* were not identical. The nature of lordship therefore depended on the degree of obedience and the kind of rights and privileges that each local custom recognised as proper.

Time smoothed many differences, but it also hardened others. The disasters of the 9th and 10th centuries broke up old conventions, and subjected English society to the unchecked violence of brutal landlords and power happy magnates, whose mutual hatreds exposed England to conquest by the Normans. The ample evidence of late Saxon poems and of recorded individual instances depicts the misery of exploited peasants in the West Saxon period, but it has little direct relevance to the conditions of the age of colonisation and of the Mercian empire. The documents of this earlier age suggest an unusual blend of aristocratic privilege and of social equality, both of them prominent and widespread from the 6th century onward. Beyond this easy generalisation, their interaction can only be discerned by local and regional studies.

The Family

As among other peoples, the family was the basis of English social and political organisation. Their terminology differed slightly. The Dal Riada Scots organised their fighting force by houses, and assumed that each house had land; Welsh law grouped men by houses, and expected each house to have a minimum of 5 acres of land. But English usage listed family landholdings, and assumed that a house went with each holding, for the earliest English free men's homes were grouped in compact villages, that were more sensibly estimated by the extent of their land than by the number of their buildings. Seventh and perhaps sixth century documents, used by Bede, grouped and counted populations by such holdings, termed *hides*, and commonly equate one tax-payer with one hide. Like the Welsh and Irish, the English were a nation of two-generation families. Their excavated homes, grouped in villages or singly sited, are too small to accommodate more than parents and their children; such was the family of the great noble, who might take his children's nurse when he emigrated, and so also was the family of the *ceorl*.

The numbers and the economy of the Welsh and English family were much alike. But the English shared with almost all Germanic peoples a common attitude to marriage, divorce and children that differed radically from Welsh and Irish concepts. Custom harshly punished unchaste women, but condoned unchastity in men. It excluded and stigmatised the bastard, unless his father vigorously asserted paternity. The laws have little to say of marriage, divorce or adultery, for these are the concern of the customary popular courts and of the church; most of what the royal laws say concerns compensations to the cuckold and to the master of seduced servile girls. But Alfred's laws expressly authorised a man to kill the lover of his wife or sister without punishment, where Welsh law offered the alternative of a blow in anger or a 'face payment'. National attitudes harden and endure, and Alfred's outlook is not far removed from the lenient sympathy that some modern judges showed to the violence of returning wartime soldiers, outraged by the infidelity of lonely wives. The essential difference is that Welsh law rigidly asserted the equal rights of men, women, and adult children, while early English law upheld the superior authority of the husband, the father and the brother.

Kindred

As among the Welsh and Irish, the kindred legislation of the English mainly concerned the inheritance of the minority of men who left no sons, and compensation to the victims of violence. But the English legislators faced quite different practical problems. Most Welshmen lived and died near to the homes of their fathers and grandfathers, their cousins and second cousins; the rights and duties of the kin worked easily in communities that stayed together, where a man's second or third cousin might readily be identified. The bonds of kinship also retained their hold among most of the Germanic peoples of Europe, for the greater part of them moved to their new homes as coherent nations, or as large sections of such nations, so that in practice a great part of a man's kin moved with him. But repeated migration weakened the kindreds of the English. In the fifth century men of quite different continental origins shared the same cemetery, with most of their kinsmen left at home, or settled elsewhere in Britain. But the mass migration of the Angles at the end of the century was clearly able to maintain its ancient kin, and in the old kingdoms kinship had time to grow again by the end of the sixth century. But after the conquest, the colonists of Northumbria, Wessex and Mercia broke their kin connections a second time. Some doubtless moved with their relatives, but many were younger sons and landless men, given permission to move, who at first were not related to their neighbours in their new homes.

The main age of colonisation was the seventh century, but movement did not thereafter cease. Many laws seek to prohibit the unauthorised movement of men, but their wording and their frequency proclaim that considerable movement was permitted, and that much illicit migration continued. The disasters of the Scandinavian invasions, in and after the 9th century, clearly increased its volume.

There were at all times many Englishmen whose relatives could not be traced within the shire, or even the kingdom, in which they lived. English law therefore has no defined terms that correspond to Welsh and Irish *fine, cinel, cenedl, gwely;* it cannot particularise beyond the portmanteau term *maegas*, relatives in general.

The weakness of English kinship entailed important consequences. The laws of violence prescribed compensation for injury, as in other codes. Welsh law assumed that the offender's kin would in fact pay the sums due, and devised elaborate procedures to discover who was or was not distantly related to the offender. West Saxon law treated its Welshmen in the same way; the kinsmen must pay, if the criminal had a free kindred (*gif he maegburg haebbe freo*); only if he had not was he handed over to his enemies. But no such provision was made for the English offender. The law assumed that he would pay himself; his relatives are mentioned only rarely, and then were obliged to pay only a proportion of the sums due, if they could be found; if the offender did not pay he was exposed to *faehdhe*, 'enmity', and might legitimately be killed by his victim's relatives, who did not thereby make themselves liable to legal counter-violence from his relatives. A man's relations might ransom him; but they need not do so.

Enmity might satisfy revenge, but it earned no compensation. Other compulsions were necessary. The codes of Kent and Wessex devolved considerable responsibility on the lord. In Kent, he was called the *dryhten*, the personal superior, in Wessex the *hlaford*, the 'loaf-keeper'. Every poor man had his immediate lord, but even the *gesithcund* nobleman, master of numerous dependents, free and unfree, had over him his *hlaford*, who received dues and undertook to answer for him. The lords did not undertake to pay from their own pockets the fines and compensation due from their dependents; yet many men were too poor to pay a *wergild*, a man's worth; and means had to be found to meet the needs of the victim's kin. Wessex law therefore devised the *gyld*. The 'guild' was essentially an association of men who between them undertook to provide the *wergild* of a member; the earliest of references, in Ine's laws, assumed that the most natural association was between relatives; but membership could not be confined to relatives, and not all relatives were compelled to associate. In default of relatives, the most natural association was among residents and, later, among persons of the same trade in towns, whose groupings were the ancestors of the medieval trade guilds.

Inheritance

The inheritance laws of the continental Germanic codes were not repeated in the legislation of Kent and Wessex; among the English they primarily concerned local customary law rather than the king's law. Local custom varied, and was also modified by experience learnt in Britain. The Germanic codes were mostly set down in writing between the 7th and the 9th centuries, and they too vary. Sons inherited equally among the Salic and Ripuarian Franks, the Scandinavians and the Lombards; the Lombards and some of the Franks assumed that brothers might live together, jointly sharing their father's inheritance without division, provided that one at least must stay at home when others go to war. The exceptions were the English of Thuringia, who speak of a single son as heir, and the Frisians, who envisaged a single heir. In default of children inheritance passed to the mother's kin as well as the father's among the Franks and the Frisians, the Saxons and the Norse; the vague Lombardic *parentes* perhaps also denoted the kin of both parents. Exceptionally, the Thuringian English confined inheritance to the father's kin. The childless inheritance was shared among a four-generation family by the Frisians, among five generations by the Franks and the Thuringian English, seven by the Lombards.

A long history plainly underlies these considerable variations. It left no clear-cut distinction between a prevailing Germanic custom and a prevailing Celtic custom. The Irish, the Welsh and the continental English agreed with one another, and differ from the rest, in their emphasis on paternal kinship. The English and the Frisians differed from the Welsh and from the rest of the Germans in avoiding divided inheritance. But the most striking difference was that between the continental Saxons and the continental Angles. The Saxon law explicitly enacted that 'in default of sons, the whole inheritance passes to the daughters', but the corresponding Anglian law asserted 'to the daughter the movables; but the land to the nearest male paternal relative'. In Britain, West Saxon law allotted to the mother's kin a share in the payment and receipt of *wergild;* but in time the Anglian custom of the inheritance of political power and of landed property by the nearest paternal male relative prevailed throughout most of England.

Community:
Class Difference

Welsh customary law spells out its social classification. English customary law, *folc riht*, was never written down. Unlike Welsh law, original 7th-century texts survive from Kent and Wessex and fragments of later laws from other kingdoms are also known. These texts treat of the various classes of society, but do not describe or relate them to one another. Their terminology suggests a structure that was in origin not greatly different from the Welsh. The general term of *frigman*, 'free man', excluded the servile *theow* and the slave, *esne*. The Welsh of Wessex and the *laet* of Kent were graded into three classes like the Welsh of Wales, but the value of each class was rated lower than that of the corresponding English grade. As among the Welsh, the English distinguish two superior categories of free men, the land-owning *ceorl*, who in Kent at least was master of dependent 'loaf-eaters'; and the noble, called *eorl* in Kent, *gesith* among the West Saxons.

Wergild

These words denoted birth and status, and they gave rise to adjectives and categories, the nobility, *eorlcund* and *gesithcund*, 'noble kind'; and *cierlisc*, commoner. The laws imposed fines and obligations and admitted compensations, that were expressed in terms of currency or of land. The English, unlike the Welsh, minted money. The standard unit was the shilling; originally it was perhaps a valuation of cows, like the Irish *cumal*, but in long-established Kent, where the word may have been used of Roman coins before the English minted their own, its 7th-century value was twice as much as in Wessex; the *wergild* or *leod* of a Kentish *eorl* required 300 shillings, of a West Saxon *gesith* 600 shillings; but in both kingdoms the noble was worth three *ceorl*.

The Hide

The worth of men was measured in money after money was minted. The differences it measured were older, and rested on the extent of a man's land. Land was measured by its actual capacity, calculated by its extent, its fertility, and of the man power that tilled it; and was first measured by kings in need of men and money. The early English kings, like the Welsh and Irish, numbered and taxed their subjects by families. As the Dal Riada Scots listed the numbers of houses in each region, so Bede normally described the extent of kingdoms, districts and estates as the 'land of so many families'.

The Old English version of Bede translated the Latin *familia* by English *hide*. The language of the charters was similar. Where the Latin text granted twenty *tributarii*, tax-payers, the English version granted hides, save in Kent, whose lawyers preferred to grant 'ploughs', *aratra*. The notion of the hide, measuring the capacity of land, is alien to modern thinking, that prefers the less accurate measurement of crude acres, without regard to their quality or population. Later lawyers tried to equate the hide with a fixed number of acres, often favouring the figure of 120, but with indifferent success. The English hide calculated practical value, like the Welsh *uncia* and the late Roman *iugum*, and may well have originated in whatever form of *iugum* was standard in the taxation of late Roman Britain.

The hide, the land of a household and a taxpayer, became the standard English unit of land measurement. Like most standards, it became notional. But circumstances severely limited the extent to which it could depart from its original meaning. Governments counted hides and families for two purposes, raising men for the army and raising dues from the cultivators. The military assessment was the most severely limited; no estate could send more men to the army than its actual population. Taxation might bear heavily, demanding more than the cultivators could reasonably afford, particularly when population fell and revenue officers demanded the old dues; but in a subsistence economy, when men produced only for themselves with little surplus for the market, the excess that overtaxation could actually extract was not great. It was easier to undertax land than overtax it; great landlords might be assessed at fewer hides than they actually possessed. Yet, though there are plenty of individual vagaries, no convincing evidence yet observed suggests that there was any wide overall discrepancy between the actual and assessed capacity of the land, or any difference at all in the earlier 7th century. Difference was social rather than fiscal. Long before Bede's time, and before the 7th century laws were drafted, some men possessed many hides, while many poor men had no land at all, or much less than a full hide. 'Possession' bestowed the right to receive the cultivators' dues; and the possession of much land gave rank and standing that could be classified in shillings.

Military nobility: in Wessex

The noblemen and landowners were graded in the laws by shillings and hides. The development of the monarchy created higher ranks of nobility. Among the Welsh of Wessex the king's messenger and five-hide man were distinguished above the rest. English landowners were rated at three, ten and twenty hides, their worth or *wergild* fixed at 200, 600 and 1,200 shillings; and they were therefore classified as *twyhynde*, *syxhynde* and *twelfhynde*. These three classes were also named the *ceorl*, the noblemen 'without land', and the *gesithcundes monnes landhaebbendes*, noblemen with land. The title of 'landed nobleman' does not imply that other 'landless' nobles were paupers, literally without any land at all. The title describes holders of a special kind of land. Its status is explained by the law of compensation for *burgbryc*, 'breach, or violation, of a stronghold'. The landed nobleman was the lowest of the categories who owned a *burg*, ranking after the king and the bishop, the *ealdorman* and the thane. He differed from the 'landless noble' because he owned a *burg*; and other *burgs* belonged only to important officers of the king and the church. His land clearly went with his *burg*, and recompensed an obligation to the king. Another law defines the nature of the obligation. If a 'landed nobleman' neglected military service, he forfeited his land; other *gesithcund* nobles were fined, but forfeited no land. All nobles possessed inherited land; the greater noble whom the laws called 'landed' received additional land, granted for specific military service, which the king reclaimed if he failed to discharge his obligation. In the source of his land, though not the nature of his service, he was the equivalent of the Welsh *arglwyd*, the lord installed by the king on his 'documented land'.

Such royal land, revocable when service ended, and not inherited, was plainly only possible when kings disposed of ample lordless lands, when the English kingdoms were young and still expanding. It had doubtless been the original source of noblemen's estates in the old kingdoms in the pagan period; but the pressures of an aristocracy commonly constrain monarchs to renew a grant in favour of an old retainer's son, that in a few generations becomes in practice hereditary. The Roman and European *comes*, or count, and the English *gesith* had originally been royal companions, rewarded with land because they served the king in arms; but the succession of their sons and grandsons turned their titles to hereditary rank, too deeply rooted in national custom for kings to cancel, without the excuse of open treason.

In Northumbria

Such revocable military tenures are not again recorded among the southern English. But Bede describes similar lords of royal land in Northumbria. There nobleman and peasant were sharply differentiated. By 679 rustic Deirans served in the army's supply train, but their speech was far removed from their lords', doubtless distinguished by the influence of British idiom and pronunciation; so that a noble prisoner who tried to disguise himself as a rustic was immediately detected by his Mercian captors as soon as he opened his mouth. Deira was a land of peasant villages, some long settled, some new, but in the early 7th century there cannot have been many young Bernicians who could not make themselves masters of men if they had the will and the personality, for they were few in a very large British territory, recently conquered. The kings needed lords to place over their subjects. Bede records how they found them. Benedict Biscop was 'born of a noble English family', in the time of Edwin. His father plainly owned lands that he stood to inherit, but in his early twenties he became a *minister*, or thane, of Oswy, about 650, and the king gave him 'landed possessions adequate to his rank'. Biscop gave them up when he entered religious life at the age of 25, rejecting 'earthly service with its perishable donative'. Bede deliberately selected an old-fashioned word, rare in the Latin of his day, that meant the gifts that Roman emperors gave to their troops, donatives.

Allocations of land with military obligations continued into the early 8th century, and the grants were made by written charter. By Bede's time they had become a scandal. In a letter to Egbert, that he dated on the 5th of November 734, he complained of fraudulent grants authorised by

> a senseless pen . . . the lying pen of corrupt clerks.

Bede is chiefly concerned with the corruption of monasteries, but he saw the proper purpose of charters as twofold, monastic and secular. Lands were properly granted either

> that a regular life may be observed towards God

or that they be owned by

> the soldiers or military companions of the secular powers, who defend our nation against the barbarians.

His complaint is that since king Aldfrith's death, thirty years before, almost every reeve and thane and noble has bought such charters so that now

> there is absolutely nowhere where the son of nobles or of retired soldiers may acquire possessions.

Therefore the young men who ought to be fighting for their country could not do so; they stayed unmarried, and either emigrated abroad or led dissipated lives, seducing nuns. The fraudulent grants owed their authority entirely to 'royal edicts' and to the 'improper decisions of kings'. Egbert was therefore urged to induce the reigning 'religious king' to

> scrutinise the bad Acts and Documents of former kings, and pick out those which are useful to God, or to the laity.

The system had worked well throughout the 7th century and was still justified in the 8th, if its corruption could be cured. Some noblemen were granted lordships with military commitments, and relinquished them when they entered the church or otherwise ceased to discharge their commitment; some commoners spent their active lives as professional royal soldiers until they were too old to fight. Bede describes them as *emeriti*, the technical Roman army term for discharged veterans, and, like Roman *emeriti*, they were entitled to a grant of land on discharge. The corruption was especially rampant among grants nominally intended for monasteries, since a commitment to live a religious life in private could be disregarded with less flagrant publicity than a commitment to serve in the army; but it impinged upon military charters, because it left them no land to grant. Time had eroded the system, for grants of land in successive generations could function smoothly only when ample lordless land remained.

In the rest of England

The Northumbrian armies were static, guarding their borders and restraining their Welsh subjects, and assembled only occasionally for massive foreign expeditions, which altogether ended with Egferth's death in 685. But West Saxon kings were involved in continuous smaller wars, internally and on several distant frontiers. The welfare of king or kingdom was not served by requiring every land holder in Devonshire to serve in every campaign in Sussex or Kent; national security needed most of them at home to guarantee local defence. The 'landed nobles' provided a specialised force, more easily mobilised under the king's personal command; many of them were doubtless young men, nobly born, like Benedict in Northumbria, the senior among them called 'thanes'. The king's retainers also included humbler free men; before the conquest the English had long been accustomed to the warbands of the British, and early West Saxon stories praise in their own kings' military companions the same ruthless devotion of the professional soldier that the Welsh poets had honoured in the time of Urien and Cynddylan. The compact kingdom of Kent had less need of such mobile forces, and there the available land and lordships had been granted long before the early 7th century. Then Frankish terms were still in use; the king summoned his *leode*, and the great lord was a *grafio*. But later, when English words replaced them, there is no obvious sign of an equivalent of the 'landed noble'. The few fragments of the laws of the Mercians, whose armies also fought principally in occasional powerful expeditions, also observe only one class of nobles, the *twelfhynde*, rated at six times the *coerl*'s worth. East Anglian and East

Saxon needs are likely to have resembled those of Kent and Mercia, but no text survives to show their social categories.

The social order of the several English kingdoms differed greatly. In the old kingdoms difference had evolved over centuries; in the colonial lands some men lived under the tight and immediate control of their lords, others more freely; some were masters of the local native population, others were their neighbours, equal in all but legal worth. But the English nobility differed in one important particular from the Welsh. In Wales, most men had held their land by inheritance from ancestors time out of mind; but the greater part of the English had won their lands by recent conquest. All lands acquired since the English conquest were held by grant of the king, or by his confirmation of tenure; and so were all lands in the dominions of the Kentish and Anglian monarchies, that had been acquired since the dynasties were established in the 5th century. Old grants of heritable land could not normally be revoked, but new royal grants continued to make men great, and more closely related the landowner and the royal officer; they linked a man's hereditary status with his material wealth, for in time they expressly enabled a man who had acquired the land that befitted a higher rank to attain that rank.

Villages

Before the conquest most of the earliest English lived in compact village communities. Their insecurity reinforced the traditions of their homeland. But after the conquest many pioneers enclosed substantial individual farmsteads, and others obeyed those who conducted their migration. But compact or scattered, free or subject, each political community formed a *-tun*, or village, a basic unit of society already normal by the 7th century. Wider concerns grouped the *-tuns* into larger areas, whose common council was composed of representatives of each constituent *-tun*.

The Hundred

Monarchy and lordship were grafted on to older institutions. The beginnings of English administration, law and justice were rooted in the old kingdoms, whence colonists came, and where kings continued to reside. The royal law codes were founded upon these older laws and took them for granted; the aim of royal law was to assert royal and ecclesiastical rights, and to standardise local practice. They therefore refer only occasionally to the principal institution of everyday English administration, the *folc gemot*, called in Latin *populare concilium*, 'public assembly'. In Alfred's laws the assembly heard legal cases, in which one man brought an accusation against another, and was responsible for licensing traders and registering the number of persons each might take with him. It was a judicial and administrative body, meeting in the presence of the king's reeve and under the protection of the *ealdorman*, whose supervision is likely to have smoothed out local differences. It was already ancient by 800, when Coenwulf of Mercia liberated Harrow from

> all payments, works and services due to the Treasury, and from the judgements of the Public Assembly . . . save that it must give account for three Public Services, namely the building of bridges and of strongholds and the supply of 5 men when a campaign is necessary.

It was a district assembly, already long established and taken for granted in the late 7th century. Ine's laws rule that

> if a man wishes to deny on oath a charge of homicide, there shall be in the Hundred a king's oath of 30 hides, whether he be noble or commoner.

In later times, the English Hundreds were grouped into large shires, and many changed their boundaries and their names. But traces of their antiquity remain. Earlier usage, formed long before the creation of the large modern counties, described the hundred itself as a 'shire', literally a division, of a kingdom. A number of Hundreds are named from pagan barrows or burial-grounds, and some long continued to meet there; such sites cannot have been first chosen after Christianity had made bishops the advisers of kings and peoples; they remained in use when they had already been meeting-places in the 6th century or the early 7th. Such meeting places were familiar to the continental English; one, at Thorsberg in Angel, marked by a monument in the midst of a large cemetery, was an important regional centre, possibly the national centre.

The Hundred was the first fundamental form of English government. It is one of the earliest and most widespread institutions of the European peoples, known to the early Romans, the early Germans, the Welsh and the Irish. Its purpose was commonly to provide a hundred fighting men, in simple societies where it was originally normal for one man from each family to serve in the army. It remained the natural form of English organisation, so that when the lawless violence of the 10th century constrained the Londoners, *eorlisc* and *ceorlisc* together, to organise the fellowship or 'gildship' of the city, they did so by grouping the citizens into Hundreds, *hyndena*, each of 100 men under a *hyndenman*, subdivided into groups of ten. In any developed society the Hundred becomes a notional term, but its starting-point is the equation that a hundred fighting men in principle correspond to a hundred families, and to the hundred patches of land that support each family.

The Hundreds were grouped early into larger units. The text that is unhappily labelled 'The Tribal Hidage' is a late corrupt copy of ancient administrative lists of the Mercian kingdom and its subject states. It includes within the kingdom the Isle of Wight, entered separately from Wessex and Sussex, which Wulfhere annexed in 661 and straightway gave to Sussex; the kingdom also includes

Elmet, which is not known to have been in Mercian hands after the frontier was fixed on the Trent in 679; it was not acquainted with the name of Surrey, which came into use in the 670s. The list was evidently drawn up in 661, or immediately after; other later dates have sometimes been asserted, but not evidenced. It records an older list, drawn up 'when Mercia was first so named', in the late 6th century. The Mercian Hundreds are grouped into twenty small regions, each containing 12 Hundreds, or fractions thereof, 9, 6 or 3, and six larger districts of 70 Hundreds, two of them subdivided. Each territory is named, from its people, or from its terrain. Outside Mercia, only the totals of the kingdoms are given. The East and South Saxons are rated at 70 Hundreds, Kent at 150, the East Angles at 300, the West Saxons at 1000. The figures are deliberately reduced to manageable round numbers, for the total of the original Mercia is slightly adjusted to give an even 300 Hundreds; and the partial total is mistakenly added in to the grand total at the end, which adds up to 212,000 hides. It includes the Welsh within the English kingdoms, for the Cornovian *Wrocensaetna* of Wroxeter and Lichfield are entered, five or six years after the English annexed them, at 70 hundreds, long before they received substantial English settlement; and the former British kingdom of Elmet is also listed by its British name.

The text describes the planned organisation of a newly formed English kingdom, and its reorganisation when Wulfhere permamently reasserted the Mercian empire over the southern English. It has not yet been studied by a philologist familiar with the names of early English places, districts and peoples, and much of the detail remains obscure; but the total numbers of hides in each kingdom is roughly proportionate to the population listed for the same territory in the 11th-century Domesday Book, and the absolute figures do not differ widely, for the equivalent Domesday counties list about 250,000 persons.

The Mercian kingdom was from its first beginnings a federation of small peoples, who were organised in groupings of Hundreds; from them and through them it drew its revenues and its armies. Other kingdoms were similarly organised, though in Kent and Sussex the lathes and rapes inherited a stronger influence from the administrative practice of Roman Britain and of Europe. Later Hundreds were often larger, but they and their assemblies remained the principal administrative and judicial institution of early England, with the unseen workings of the village meeting behind them. The day to day importance of the Hundred was the greater because its proceedings were oral, not recorded in writing, so that little can be learnt of how it functioned, save by inference from casual notices in later documents, and from a multitude of chance references to its ancient meeting places in pagan times or in the earliest Christian centuries.

The later Hundreds normally met monthly, their chief business to ensure that every man had the protection of *folc riht*, public law, and that cases were heard with expedition by men who knew the litigants and the circumstances of their cases. It is not probable that the business and the form of the meetings reported in the 10th century differed greatly from those of the 7th century; but it is evident that in practice their internal political working differed greatly from one Hundred to another, from the 7th century onward. In all political assemblies men who are wealthy or powerfully connected carry greater weight than their fellows; among the English, the pagan graves and the place names of colonising settlements indicate that from the 6th century onward some communities were dominated by a single individual, while others contained a limited number of well-to-do families and some consisted of numerous *ceorls* with little social difference between them.

There is little sign of important change during the long Mercian peace; for the well documented transfer of revenues by charter grant, bequest or sale did not directly impinge upon the composition of the Hundred. But the continuing wars of the West Saxon and Scandinavian kings ruptured traditional ways, impoverished many men and brought wealth and power to a few. The pressures of local lords and the power of lawless violence increased within most Hundreds. But the Hundred itself retained and perhaps increased its importance; in the districts where they settled thickly the Danes named it the *wapentake*, the basis of their weapons and of their armed forces. In the 10th and 11th centuries the Hundreds were grouped into the larger units, called shires or counties, intermediate between them and the national government, whose boundaries have endured to the present day, with trifling local adjustments, and have defied repeated tidy minded efforts to abolish or rearrange their time honoured identities. But the Hundred remained the basic unit of English administration throughout the middle ages.

The Hundred proved a tough and resilient institution. Its substance long outlived its form, the principle that local affairs were the business of men of note in each locality. The Norman kings relied upon its sworn jury to verify and assert the facts of land tenure and ancient custom, and thereby to curb the licence of over-mighty magnates. It withstood the brisk efficiency of their Angevin and Plantagenet successors, who sought to impose upon the diversity of the English countryside the bureaucratic uniformity of their European dominions. Their success was limited. When local institutions had been weakened by the violence of great lords, the kings were suffered to withdraw the cognisance and profits of a wide range of legal cases from the traditional speedy justice of local courts, and to import the Roman institution of the professional judge, ignorant of local circumstances and person, assisted by a small number of picked assessors; for men acquiesced in the high cost and inordinate delays of professional lawmen when local justice was overwhelmed by the sword. But the apparatus of centralised administration did not endure. The sheriff and his bailiff proved as corrupt and incompetent as royal officers in other lands. English society rejected them, and reverted to its long established tradition of entrusting local administration to men of local substance. From the close of the middle ages the vestry and the bench of justices regulated the internal affairs of the county and its subdivisions; the officers of the central government did not regain detailed control of local affairs until the later 19th century. From the 7th century to the 19th, local lords and gentry increasingly overrode humbler men; but English society held to its tradition that each small community should properly decide its own affairs, under the presidency of a strong national government; and looked unkindly upon over-large concentrations of political or economic power.

Land Tenure: Charters

The community and its assembly were exceptionally strong in early England because the grip of ancient kin custom was weaker than in other lands. Accidental combinations of custom jostled each other in each kingdom, hundred, district and village; and soon hardened into local ancestral precedents whose just operation could be understood, interpreted and decided only by local inhabitants. Lawyers and royal officers sought uniformity, but found it easier to standardise their words than the institutions and tenures the words described. Their endeavours are illustrated by the early English charters. The texts are poorly published, and have therefore been incompletely studied. The names, the titles and the status of persons, the boundaries, population and history of estates, the circumstances of the grants and the uses to which they were put have not yet been systematically investigated; and Bede's emphatic statements about their use and abuse in his day have often been undervalued. The content of the charters has therefore received less attention than their form. Historians familiar with later medieval law have enquired whether they are 'conveyances' of 'ownership', or merely of rights and powers, though the lawyers of the 7th and 8th centuries had little interest in these distinctions. Words and phrases borrowed from the jargon of 'Roman' or 'Germanic' law have been noted, though it has often been assumed that the customs of different German nations closely resembled each other and English law, or that the usages of Roman law were uniform in the kingdoms of 7th-century Europe. The borrowings prove the obvious, that early English administrators plundered every possible convention to find words to fit their peculiar institutions; but their contradictory usages have sometimes prompted the over easy inference that the same words mean the same things in different texts.

Written charters are preserved from the 7th century onward. They usually authorised their recipients to build a monastery on the land allotted, and to receive the payments that the cultivators had formerly owed to the king, with the exception of the three public services. As in the Welsh grants, the king often gave land to a layman, who then gave it to the church. The surviving copies often conflate the two grants, but sometimes preserve only one of the pair, giving the superficial impression of a purely secular grant. Grants of land to laymen who undertook specific military commitments were older than the written charters of the church. None survive in writing from the early centuries, and they are directly evidenced only among the West Saxons and Northumbrians, who had ample new lands to settle in the 7th century. Such grants are not preserved, for they commonly allotted land for life, or for so long as the specified service was actually performed; though repeated renewal to the sons and grandsons often made them in practice hereditary, their wording bestowed no legal hereditary claim and gave later ages no motive to prescrve or copy them. Moreover laymen lacked the clerical staff to file and keep them; and before Christianity brought literacy they were necessarily unwritten, oral statements made before witnesses. Yet though they were unwritten and of little legal value to the future, they provided the first archaic model for the charters of the church. Kings had long granted land in return for a military obligation; Christian kings also granted land in return for the religious obligation of building or maintaining a monastery.

Grants to the church needed documents, and prudence preserved them. The lands and cultivators granted had belonged either to the king or to private persons; and both had heirs who might impugn their ancestors' grant. Moreover, individual churchmen, abbeys and cathedrals disputed the possession of the lands and revenues of dead hermits. At first, different kings and churchmen in search of safeguards borrowed from many different precedents. The earliest Kentish clerks learned from the northern Franks, and Augustine's monks brought Roman forms; Northumbrians and Mercians learnt from Ireland; Wilfred and his companions were instructed in Lyon, in central Gaul; Benedict Biscop carried the practice of Italy and Gaul to Northumbria; archbishop Theodore was trained in the conventions of the eastern Roman empire as well as of Italy; the western Mercians were open to the influence of their Welsh allies. In the later seventh century the energy of Aldhelm began the synthesis of these many precedents. He was the English pupil of an Irish teacher, he lived in a land full of Welshmen and was widely read in European literature; he served both Theodore of Canterbury, who successfully united the English church, and the Mercian kings who forged the cohesion of the southern English nation. The precedents were many, customs varied. At first, numerous local obstacles confronted the single aim of guaranteeing secure tenure to the church.

Monastic Tenure

The earliest records express the eager enthusiasm of recent converts. King Osric of the Hwicce, of Worcestershire and Gloucestershire, began his reign about 670, at a time when Theodore was pressing for the establishment of bishops' sees in each kingdom. The Synod of Hertford endorsed his proposals in 672. Four years later, in founding the monastery of Bath, Osric explained that

> when, after baptism, the evangelical and apostolic dogmata were explained, and all the ridiculous . . . idols destroyed, . . . we decided to found an episcopal see, in accordance with the decrees of the Synod.

But when the abbeys of Gloucester and Pershore were founded three years later, in 679, Aethelred of Mercia was forewarned of difficulties to come, and observed that

> disputes often arise between and among many clergy . . . and faithful laymen about landed possessions. . . . Therefore I, king Aethelred . . . will give a portion of land, that is 300 *tributarii* at Gloucester, and 300 *cassati* at Pershore, to my two ministers in the province of the Hwicce, Osric and his brother Oswald, in the *vicarium*, so that Osric may receive the *oba* (estate) of Gloucester, and Oswald may have Pershore. Afterwards, I . . . was asked by . . . Osric for permission . . . to found a monastic *locus* (site) and life in that city; . . . and he bought the city with a golden *sule* (measure), in which were 30,000 (pence?), with its land, with full power over everything, into his perpetual inheritance, to possess and to have, and after him to give to whatever hand he wishes in his own kin.

The text, though not the narrative thereto appended, is substantially original. Its eccentric Latin and cumbrous argument wrestle with problems that lawyers of the next century had smoothed into order. It uses two old German words not elsewhere preserved in English, *oba* and *sule*. It also uses the common British word *locus*, site, for monastery, and the British administrative term *vicarium*, for the more usual continental *vicariatus*, the territory or jurisdiction of a *vicarius comes* or *vice comes*, the subordinate ruler. The word is elsewhere recorded only in Brittany, where it is normal, typically instanced in the charters of Landevennec, as when

> Budic *comes* . . . gave . . . from his own inheritance . . . Caer Bullauc in the *vicarium* of Demett.

The word was doubtless also current in 7th-century Wales, though no 7th-century texts survive to witness it.

The grant served practical policy as well as the piety of converts. Gloucester was the key to the control and separation of Wales and Dumnonia, and in the 670s not many of its 300 *tributarii* are likely to have been English in speech or sympathy. The foundation of a substantial monastery was a surer way to win the city than the installation of a garrison. The need was there, but in the 670s men had not yet learnt how monasteries could legally be endowed with land. The wording was devised for the purpose. Some of it is taken from Roman and continental German usage. But Aethelred also learnt from his Welsh neighbours; the Hwicce and the Mercians themselves were too recently baptised to have had direct experience of the disputes of clergy and laymen over the inheritance of estates, but the monasteries of south Wales had encountered such difficulties for more than a century. The substance of the grant imitates the procedures outlined in the Llancarfan texts, that are dated to half a century earlier; the king sold the land to his *minister*, 'under-king', equivalent to the *praefectus* of the

Welsh texts, in exchange for valuable gifts. It then passed into the minister's personal inheritance, and his kin acquired rights upon it. But a different precedent is brought in to avoid the multiple claims of distant heirs that disturbed Welsh monasteries. The grant reproduced the succession practice of the Irish monarchy, whereby one among several qualified heirs within the kin might acquire the undivided inheritance. Chosen by Osric himself, he succeeded to the position of the Irish *erenach*, 'lay proprietor', as Foirtchernn's Trim descended to the heirs of his brother.

The innovation was important. English inheritance was as firmly entailed upon kin as Welsh. The difference was that the Welsh had one common custom, but the English had many different customs; some observed Anglian descent, undivided inheritance by the nearest paternal relative, some accepted the Saxon practice of a daughter's inheritance, and other variants abounded. The monarchy of the Hwicce themselves was shared among sons, but the Mercian kingship passed by Anglian custom to a single heir. Diversity gave the lawyers greater headaches than in Wales, and prevented the adoption of a single solution; but it also prevented collective resistance to change, and in time helped kings and churchmen to subdue the claims of kin altogether.

Aldhelm and Church Right

Time was needed. A few years after the Gloucester grant Aldhelm gave its principles an important twist. The South Saxon king and his West Saxon overlord granted Pagham to bishop Wilfred, with the confirmation of the superior king, Aethelred of Mercia. Aldhelm, writing 'at the instance of archbishop Theodore', added a clause, not contained in the body of the text, 'as the command of the king and the elders decreed'. It runs

> on their authority it is established that the mastery of this ... property is vested in the blessed Wilfred for life, and that on his death he should bequeath it in eternal possession to whomsoever he will by the law of inheritance.

Again, the bulk of the text has been much adapted by later copyists, but the addition is unequivocably Aldhelm's, in his own idiom, and is followed by a gay verse of his composition. Inheritance still passed by kinship law, as at Gloucester, but the founder who shall choose the heir is the churchman himself, not a lay proprietor; 'inheritance law' is used with deliberate vagueness, and is balanced by the equally vague Roman term of 'eternal possession'. As Aldhelm well knew, the terms conflicted; 'inheritance law', *ius hereditarium*, was the customary term of the Welsh grants for secular inheritance by kin, used in contrast to 'church right', *ius ecclesiasticum*, which was equated with the Roman concept of *ius perpetuum*, 'everlasting right', because the church did not die and had no heirs. The way was prepared to make 'church right' the usual form, and to override 'hereditary right'.

Bookland

The king might grant royal documented land belonging to the kingdom, or else his personal land, inherited from his own kin, on which his heirs had claims; he frequently states explicitly which he grants. Land inherited by the king by *folc riht* from his relations is often named; but when Nunna granted *tributarii* at Heberden in 725, the Latin charter is endorsed in English.

> This is the land book by which king Nunna booked, to bishop Edbert, at Huga's Hills, 20 hides.

His 'booked' or documented land was royal land, not his personal inheritance. But future kings might revoke such grants, and heirs could challenge grants that violated the claims of kin. Nunna, like many other kings, threatened a curse, or anathema, against 'any of my successors' who cancelled the grant. But not every king's successor was frightened by a curse. One of Aethelred's monastic grants was speedily revoked, in about 700. An under-king of the Hwicce claimed the land as the heir of Aethelred's queen, asserting that it was hers, not his, to give away; and won his claim. Such suits for the recovery of inheritance were a commonplace of Welsh law, termed *dadenhudd*, in Latin *actio possessoria*; similar suits, called *hereditaria proclamatio*, 'assertion of kin', long threatened English church estates. As late as the 11th century, a few years before the Norman conquest, the bishop of Worcester complained that

> Toki . . . left me land, by right of hereditary succession . . . in his will, because of our friendship. But his only son Aki, a powerful *minister* of the king, wished to set aside his father's will, and claimed the land by right of kinship succession, with the king's backing. . . . But, on receipt of 8 marks of purest gold, he restored it to me, free of suit for assertion of kin by himself and all his kin.

Grants continued to be made, bestowing church right; they ran the risk not only of challenge by kin, but of the abuses that angered Bede. The abuse was heightened by Aldhelm's formula of granting the recipient the right to bequeath the land to whichever of his kin he chose; and Bede complained that in his day Northumbrian charters caused

> an ever graver scandal, when straightforward laymen . . . buy themselves estates on the pretext of building monasteries . . . and in addition get them assigned in hereditary right by royal edicts, and then secure confirmation of these letters of privilege . . . by the signature of bishops, abbots and secular authorities.

Some southern English charters instance similar grants. About the 680s, Aethelred and the Hwicce king gave land at Withington to a woman and her daughter 'to build a monastery in church right'. The mother willed it to her daughter and grand-daughter, but in the grand-daughter's infancy it was entrusted to her mother, who refused to hand it over when the child grew up, alleging that the charter was lost. A church council restored the land to the grand-daughter, who became a regular abbess, 50 years after the original grant. Her mother and grandmother did not observe the 'regular discipline' that Bede required in a celibate monastery, and resembled the Northumbrian magnates who 'bought themselves a monastery and lived there with their wives'.

But what seemed an abuse to Bede became in time the principal form of English land tenure, the means by which it escaped from stultifying restrictions of kin. Bede's indignation at 'luxury and gluttony', where the name of monastery should mean 'chastity and continence', suggests orgies in a bawdy house, but his factual detail describes the purchase of estates by mature married couples; his objection is that secular estates are called monasteries and eat up the land. They were so called because there was no other way in which men who prospered could buy land. By church right, they acquired royal land, documented or booked by the king, burdened with no claims of other men's kin, and added it to their own inheritance. They were at first also bound to bequeath the land to those whom folk right prescribed as their heirs; but the devices of Theodore and Aldhelm enabled men who held by church right to choose which kinsman should inherit, in disregard of whatever inheritance custom bound their family.

Soon the restriction of choice to an heir within kin was removed. The recipient was permitted to sell the land, or bequeath it to whom he would. The source of such rights was the king's royal booked land, and 'bookland' came to mean land that could be sold or bequeathed without regard to kinship; so a 9th-century king explained that with the consent of his bishops and magnates, he booked estates to himself, 'in order that I may leave them after my death to whoever I wish in perpetuity'. The king's right to book his own estates enabled him to grant his inherited land. Ine of Wessex gave lands

> which I possess by paternal inheritance, and hold in perpetual lordship,

and at the end of the 8th century Beortric of Wessex assigned

> land that is mine by right, that my predecessors and my relatives bequeathed to me to possess by hereditary right . . . to . . . Hemele . . . to possess eternally, to have, to hold or to exchange, and to leave after him to whomsoever he will.

The quantities of available land were increased by exchange and transfer; a 9th-century Kentish king exchanged land that, like Beortric's, was his 'by right', for a subject's land. What he granted became 'bookland', what he received became his 'folk land', replacing what he relinquished.

Estates that became bookland were an extension of church right, and carried with them its important privileges, including exemption from normal taxation. The earliest Mercian grants had made no specific mention of taxation, but Aldhelm's weighty influence soon obliged kings to spell out a precise renunciation of their claims upon the cultivators' dues, in a clear formula that hardened into an inescapable standard clause. The urgent needs of government quickly obliged the church to accept one important qualification of Aldhelm's exemption clause, the discharge of the three public services of the maintenance of the army, fortifications and bridges; but otherwise immunity from normal dues was permanently extended to church right and booked land. Bookland was tax free; but its greater importance was that, in contrast with folk land and loan land, it was held in full private possession, free of claims by the kin of its former owner or of its new owner, unless expressly so bound. A law of Alfred defines the entail.

> If a man has inherited Bookland from his relatives, he may not leave it out of his kindred, if there are witnesses or documents to show that he was forbidden to do so by those who first acquired it, or those who gave it to him.

But if there were no such witnesses or deeds, he was free to leave it out of kin. As in Wales, booked land was free from normal taxes, and free from the claims of heirs.

Folkland

Yet folk right was still powerful; much land was not booked and not free from kin. The distinction was rigorously maintained. A 9th-century *ealdorman* left most of his bookland to his wife and daughter and asked the king to let his son, apparently illegitimate, inherit his folk land; unless the king admitted the son as legitimate heir, the folk land necessarily passed to his nearest legitimate paternal male relative. Folk land lasted long; its disputes were settled, not in the king's courts, but in the *folc gemot*, the public assembly, guided, but not ruled, by the king's reeve. Its function was emphasised in the 10th century. When king Edward the Elder enjoined his reeves to pronounce 'right judgment' in dealing with 'written law', but to 'interpret' public law, he expressly provided that disputes about folk land, but not about book land, should be heard in the reeve's presence, in the public court. The old claims of kin outlived the Norman conquest, and 12th-century London still found it necessary to rule that

> if a citizen of London wishes to sell land because of poverty, neither his sons nor his relatives can prevent him.

Some Londoners still maintained that a man's kin had rights upon his land, that prevented him from selling it. The 12th-century ruling extinguished the lingering claim of folk land. Bookland prevailed among men of substance. It emerged from church right. It enabled the powerful to sell, exchange or bequeath their property at will. It also avoided the growth of military tenures, that had been normal in Wessex, Northumbria, and perhaps also Mercia in the 7th century; and when the Norman conquerors sought to impose them, the maturity of the

English freehold prevented them from striking deep, and in time reduced them to an additional form of taxation, thereby shielding England from many of the worst excesses of European military lordship.

The Cultivators

Tenure by bookland was the privilege of greater men. What it granted was not acreage, but the right to receive the rents and dues of those who worked the acres, and to sell or bequeath those rights. No humble cultivator received such charters. The language of the grants distinguishes cultivators by three main terms. *Tributarius* is the Roman lawyers' word for a tax-paying provincial, and translates the English word *gafolgelda*, tax-payer, equivalent to the *boneddig*, the simple free man of Welsh law. The *cassatus* was also a Roman legal term, meaning a dependent established in his *casa* or cottage by his lord; it translates the English *cottar*, the occupier of a *cote*, and is equivalent to the Welsh *taeog*. The third class were the *manentes*, who 'stay' where they are, the dependent population of a *mansio*, a single undivided property; they doubtless included the population of villages named *-ingtun* or *-botl*, and of other places subject to a lord. The *manentes* are also likely to have included the bulk of the Welsh who lived in the 7th-century English kingdoms, with a status not unlike that of the *aillt*, the stranger, in Wales, or of the Latin *coloni originarii*, ancestral cultivators, who had once been free, in contrast to the *cassati* installed by their lord.

The terms are at first used with precision, though a grant that adds together *tributarii*, *cassati* and *manentes* often also used *tributarii* as the general word to describe the grand total; for from the point of view of the lord and the king all the cultivators were liable for tribute, tax or rent. The earliest texts grant persons, *tributarii*, except in Kent, whose documents from the beginning grant *aratra*, ploughs. But from the later 7th century more and more charters grant 'land estimated at (or of) so many *tributarii*', and later texts sometimes confuse the three categories. Their changing usage, and its local variations, cannot be determined until closer study is possible.

The tenures of these small-scale cultivators continued to be governed by kin inheritance, that eroded only slowly under the influence of the lord's bookland; at the end of the 11th century the Domesday Book entries in some counties baldly record many poorer peasants in phrases like '15 men have half a hide' between them. A few charters use similar words. They describe inheritance shared among kin. It lasted longest among the poorest; for though there is relatively little sign of lands divided into fragments, as among the Welsh, there is ample evidence of men who jointly farmed a joint inheritance. Undivided inheritance became usual. The king's concern for a stable nobility, and the influence of his reeve over the development of public law, helped Anglian primogeniture to oust other complex rules of kinship, with all their local variations. The free testamentary inheritance of bookland powerfully aided primogeniture, for most men who have a free choice prefer to leave their land to a son, but to have freedom to provide for daughters and younger sons, and to entail an inheritance if they doubt their heirs. Long custom bred a general opinion that expected men to leave the bulk of their estates to their eldest son, and enforced strict primogeniture upon the succession to rank and title. In contrast with France and many other European lands, the English nobility were able to conserve estates, and lesser men who prospered might grow to the status of gentry.

The Survival of the English

English society was loosely knit. Its numerous intermediate gradations avoided polarisation between the extremes of over-mighty nobles and servile cultivators, crushed, and powerless to voice their resentment. In the most general terms, it owed its cohesion to the simple fact that Britain is an island. Until the coming of the Scandinavians and the Normans, the English were free to choose the foreign customs that influenced their development, and to determine the manner in which those influences should operate. Their early training accustomed them to easy change, and constant contact with foreigners, readily accepted within their island, enabled change to continue by gradual adaptation, without sudden upheaval.

The comfortable England of Bede and Offa was shattered by the invasions of the 9th, 10th and 11th centuries. Damage was most severe at the top of society. The autocracy of Offa had seemed in his lifetime an unassailable sovereignty. But the sharp mind of Alcuin discerned its weakness; in destroying the ancient dynasties of the regional kings, the imperial power had destroyed its own support. Even before the full shock of the invasions, Offa's monarchy was in ruins, and the disappearance of the lesser kings left the English leaderless. Despite their handicap, they rallied behind the new Wessex monarchy. But in the long run, they failed. Not even the victories of Alfred and Athelstan were able to replace the vanished strength of royal government; the power of the monarchy had crumbled before the Norman host landed, and its disintegration made their conquest possible.

The conquerors eliminated the ancient nobility of England. But they could not eliminate the population, and could not suppress or replace the institutions of local decision. Customary tenures survived. The foreigners who were rewarded with the lands of the conquered also inherited their status and tenure; and in spite of the efforts of lawyers and churchmen to impose military fiefs, old tenures persisted. Though land lay in the king's gift in law, his actual power to grant and to revoke rarely reached beyond the mightier lords, whose mutual violence floated upon the top of society. The status of the peasant sunk to the level of the exploited serf, but the old tenures inherited from early England maintained an independent class of small and modest landholders. The yeoman and the franklin, the gentry and the squire were numerous enough and sufficiently secure to retain control of their own localities, and were thereby enabled to grant or withhold the revenues of the central government.

The power of the English Commons owes little but its form to the king's council, the *witan* of 'wise men' and magnates. Its roots lie in land tenure rather than in institutions. It has been less respected in periods when it has submitted to the control of magnates, powerful interests, or professional politicians; but public support has made it all-powerful when it has demonstrably represented the dominant interest and views of the localities that make up the nation. The national assemblies and estates of other nations withered in the middle ages. The English parliament survived because it became the organ of lesser local lords and of their urban equivalents, whose interests repeatedly aligned them with the peasant against the demands of king and baron. It was able to speak for lesser lords because they had asserted effective control of the localities, the shires, the hundreds and the parishes, and had restrained the power of the king's officials and of the nobleman's factor. Their existence and their collective strength ultimately derived from the tenures and the institutions of early England, that proved able to survive Scandinavian and European conquest.

Local tenures and local institutions trained English society to respect governments that coordinate, and to discipline governments that rule by command. From pagan and Mercian times onward, custom has expected that men of suitable standing should be heard before decision is reached; society has frequently disagreed about which men should be heard when, but when it has reached agreement, governments that ignored agreed opinion have been denied obedience and revenue. These attitudes have maintained the flexibility of English society, and secured an easier movement of men and ideas, a speedier and smoother social change than was possible in most of Europe. They were first formed by the piecemeal migrations of the early English, and by their need to absorb the alien natives in the lands they had conquered. The English mastered the fairer part of Britain, and emerged as the most powerful of the successor states within the territory of Arthur's empire. Though they were stronger, they could neither exterminate their neighbours nor drown their identity.

Early experience obliged the English simultaneously to create an unusually powerful central government, and to maintain an unusual degree of regional and local variety and independence. Later experience induced men of all classes and regions to respect the central government so long as it behaved sensibly and retained authority; and also compelled successive rulers to observe the restraints that custom set upon that authority. The English were unable to conquer and annex Wales and Scotland; they were forced to be content with the status of elder brother, their primacy admitted only when they themselves acknowledged its limits. Kings who asserted a loose suzerainty over the 'empire of Britain' also learnt to rule the several regions of the English as loosely, to refrain from annexation, from savage butchery or unbearable extortions after military victory. Time and effort shaped a tradition of firm leadership and light rule. The tradition was often flouted, and as often reasserted, when attempts at autocracy failed. But from its troubled origins and repeated buffetings, the conventions of

English government inherited a resilience that is not easily repressed. English society early learnt and practised the simple truism that the whole is no more than the sum of its parts, and is as strong as the links that bind them together.

CHAPTER TWENTY-FIVE

ARTHUR AND THE FUTURE

The age of Arthur ended Roman Britain, and created the nations of modern Britain. His short empire crowned the efforts of the fifth-century British to retain their island; its dismemberment compelled the peoples of the sixth century to define their identity. His victory briefly demonstrated that Britain was and could be a single political state; his failure obliged the separate nations to tolerate each other's existence, to fight for supremacy over their neighbours, but no longer for their extermination, and to accept the autonomy of regions and districts within each nation. In name he was the last Roman emperor; but he ruled as the first medieval king.

Many permanent institutions, customs and conventions that still influence modern political behaviour begin their history in the Arthurian age. Though the institutions have been transformed, and ideas been hardened and broadened, it is in this age that they were first formed. They were the response of the peoples of Britain to the awful catastrophe of fallen Rome, the sharpest and most sudden break in the history of Europe. Old conventions were everywhere blown into forgetfulness, and men devised new bonds to hold together the shattered fragments of their society. But the transformation of Europe was confined within narrower bounds than in Britain. When once the imperial government disintegrated and admitted independent barbarian nations in arms, without destruction of the Roman economy, the fusion of Roman and German was inescapable; the outcome of political and social initiative could only decide which Germans should rule where, and determine the nature and degree of fusion in each region.

But in Britain, no inevitable necessity compelled events to turn out as they did. When the old order was smashed, and not yet replaced, the issue of each crisis affected all succeeding time. Options were wide open, as they never had been before, and never were to be again. If individual leaders had taken different decisions, Britain might have become Pictland, or Vandalland; if the government of Vortigern had decided to deploy its English federates against the Irish, instead of against the Picts, then the English would have been settled in Snowdonia and Cornwall, not in eastern Britain. If the British had not rallied to the partisan forces of Ambrosius, Britain might have passed under the control of a miscellaneous Germanic soldiery, as mixed as Odovacer's in Italy, and have dissolved like Italy into tiny hostile states, disunited for fifteen centuries. But if the Roman aristocracy of Britain had joined Ambrosius instead of emigrating, they might have won the war before their society was destroyed, and permanently upheld in Britain a western state as Roman as the empire of the east, ruled from a London as imperial as Constantinople.

It is futile to explore the possibilities of what did not happen. But they need to be displayed, for the rigid complacency of historical determinism easily assumes that what actually happened was bound to have happened sooner or later, and easily credits events to the wisdom of individual leaders who perceived the necessities of their age, or to the folly of those who did not. Yet historical events are not determined by the will and understanding of great men alone. They are brought about by the sum of the manifold individual decisions taken by all the men and women concerned, great and small, separately and collectively, to fight or to flee, to obey or to disobey, to bestir themselves or to rest quiet. The quality that distinguishes a leader above his fellows is his ability to arouse sentiments that inspire effective decision, to realise men's hopes.

In settled ages men's aspirations and beliefs are limited by the ideas that they have inherited. Original thinkers may modify and extend their inheritance, but they cannot transform a society whose assumptions are taken for granted by the majority of their fellow-men. When the customary conventions of Roman Britain were suddenly and violently destroyed, all the old controls were overthrown. No later age was free to choose between so wide a range of possibilities. Even the invading Northmen were compelled to accept decisions already taken; from the 9th century to the 13th, five centuries of attempts to impose their languages and institutions yielded to the solid persistence of England, Wales and Scotland, and left native speech and custom modified, but intact. The decisions taken by the men and women of the fifth and sixth centuries moulded the whole future history of the British Isles, and fixed limits that succeeding ages were not able to overstep; if they had taken other decisions, the history of their descendants and the possibilities open to them would have been utterly different.

The debt that modern men owe to the energy of their remote ancestors is easily hidden behind foggy language. The term 'Dark Ages' is not the innocent invention of conscientious academics, stumped for the want of a clearer term. It has always been used to impose a viewpoint and to suppress evidence. It once comprehended all the 'Gothic' centuries of European history between the Romans and the Age of Enlightenment, and condemned them as inferior. The invention of the term 'Middle Ages' rescued several centuries from obscurity and contempt; but 'Dark Age' remained the designation of European society between the Romans and the Crusaders until the words Merovingian and Carolingian replaced it. It was thenceforth confined to Britain.

The term always confused, for it conveyed a two-fold meaning; it implied that the age was dark because men were ignorant, illiterate and brutish, authors of a dismal regression from the elegant splendour of Rome; and was also dark because it was little known. Most aristocratic societies have looked back with nostalgia upon the stable empire of Rome, when the lower orders were content to keep their station more obediently than in later times, and have looked gloomily upon the sequel; their viewpoint was challenged by a different outlook, that defined the 'Dark Age' as a time of 'less light for more people', as the period that initiated the struggles for human liberation that underlie modern ideas of equality and social justice. But 'darkness' remained a reproach, conveying a political judgement, as surely as the later variant, 'sub-Roman', that equally maligns the Romans and their successors.

These verbal controversies belong to the past. Nowadays the term is chiefly restricted to the notion that we cannot see clearly what happened. Yet darkness lies in the eye of the beholder; though much is not yet understood, and much can never be known, yet most darkness is the fault of modern vision. There is no lack of evidence, but there is still a lack of systematic study; and the use of a misleading term itself has dimmed understanding, for it hides the connections between events and people. The convention that normally and properly guides historical enquiry allots neutral distinctive names to defined periods, so that these connections may be recognised; the term Victorian links Swinburne with Gladstone and railway trains, Marx and Verdi, as the term Elizabethan relates Shakespeare and madrigals to American colonists and the Spanish Armada. But the want of sensible terms prevents even specialists from observing the connections between different events in Britain in the centuries after the fall of Rome, and hides their significance.

Yet the decisive events that separate coherent periods in early British history are well known, as self-evident as those that justify terms like Roman or Renaissance; periods, like persons, are not easily understood or described until they are identified. The term 'Roman Britain' conveys a clear meaning, even to those who know little about it. It ended in the middle of the fifth century; though the imperial government ceased to rule Britain in 410, yet the Roman civilisation of Britain and its political institutions lasted a generation longer, into the 450s, until about the time of Arthur's birth.

The end of Roman Britain was immediately followed by the age of Arthur. It includes his own lifetime, and the rule of his successors until the English conquest, half a century after his death. It constitutes a self-contained period, whose important achievement bore heavily on the future, and is thoroughly misunderstood if it is viewed as a vague 'transition' between Rome and the Middle Ages. Thereafter, the periods of English dominance are clearly marked. The Age of Conquest and Conversion reached from the 570s into the 640s, and included the short-lived military supremacy of the Northumbrians. Thenceforth, until modern times, defined periods are clearly marked by the names of the principal ruling dynasties. The Mercian period began with the victories of Penda in the 640s; interrupted only for three years, from 655 to 658, it continued for a century and a half, until Mercian supremacy was challenged and replaced by the sovereignty of the West Saxon dynasty, early in the 9th century. These periods might conveniently be subdivided; yet they are clear and significant stages in the evolution of Britain and England, separated by events that contemporaries recognised as decisive turning-points; and the dynastic names of the Mercian and West Saxon periods are as valid as those of the Norman, Angevin and Plantagenet periods that followed them.

The age of Arthur is the beginning of modern British history. For that reason, it cannot escape controversy. Men are always moved by their beliefs about the past, and the historians who mould those beliefs naturally emphasise aspects and periods that are in their view important. Views vary, for many historians share the outlook of established authority, and some reject it. Recent prejudice has preferred to avoid the origins of British history, and to pretend that modern society is rooted in the despotism of the Normans; as that pretence becomes increasingly untenable, medieval history is less studied, and attention concentrates upon the authoritarian rule of the Tudors and their successors. These attitudes are recent and temporary. Earlier generations lacked the formidable equipment of modern scholarship, but they judged honestly. The instinct of the middle ages began its tradition with Arthur of Britain, the champion of a legendary golden age, the pattern of a just society that should be, but was not; and the legend retained its dignity until it was degraded by the banality of Tennyson. The time of the early English kings remained the starting-point of national history, until ignorant contempt divorced the 'Anglo-Saxons' from their English descendants; and as late as the 17th century it still worked powerfully upon the minds of English revolutionaries, who rightly saw themselves as rebels against a 'Norman yoke', revitalised by Tudor authority, and strove consciously to revive what they held to be their native tradition.

Earlier instinct did not err. The origins of the modern nations of Britain may be swept aside or hidden, derided as remote, irrelevant and unimportant, but their essential story cannot easily be misrepresented. The brief rule, victory and failure of Arthur shaped sixth-century Britain and equipped the English for mastery over decaying native society. It also gave courage to native protest, whose monastic enthusiasm seized upon the Irish and the English, binding together peoples whom kings had sundered, and carrying their joint reforming zeal to Europe, at the moment when Europe needed and welcomed reformers. The endeavours of the early monks bequeathed as much to the future of Europe as the conflict of popes and kings, lords and landowners.

The history of Europe is nowadays the proper study of all mankind, for all nations now accept the technology and the political philosophies of Europe. National histories are a blend of their own past and of European experience. But the study of Europe is still hampered by exclusive national emphasis, that confines most English students to the history of England and of the nearer parts of Europe that directly concerned England, or of its overseas colonies; and is as cramped in most other countries. It has been freed from its earlier limitation to the record of kings and notables by the stresses of 20th-century disturbance, that have focused attention upon the subjects of the kings. It is now passing out of a rigid academic tradition that carved it into artificially separated compartments, labelled 'political', 'constitutional', 'economic', 'social', and the like. It is no longer sufficient for the 'economic historian' to confine himself to a flat description of the environment in which inert masses were imprisoned; for men now demand to know the ideas that have moved mankind to change their environment, and to enquire into the reasons for their success and failure.

The history of Europe, as of Britain, is misrepresented if it begins in the middle, and emphasises only parts of its origin. Its debt to Rome is plain to see. The social institutions and the urban Christian church of the empire withstood the invaders and absorbed them. But the ferment of ideas that the reformers from Ireland and Britain injected into the settled ways of seventh century Europe are less easily perceived, so long as their origin in their homeland remains in darkness. The future of the Germanic and of the western Slavonic nations owed as much to the monks as to bishops, emperors and kings. The faith of the monks was born and bred in Arthurian Britain, in an age that rewarded initiative.

Therein lies the importance of the little short-lived realm that Arthur salvaged from the ruin of Rome. The tales that immortalised his name are more than a curiosity of Celtic legend. Their imagery illuminates an essential truth. In his own day Arthur failed, and left behind him hope unfulfilled. But the measure of any man lies not in his own lifetime, but in what he enables his successors to achieve. The history of the British Isles is funnelled through the critical years of Arthur's power and of its destruction, for thence came the modern nations. The age of Arthur is the foundation of British history; and it lies in the mainstream of European experience.

TABLE OF DATES

Capital letters denote Emperors, Popes and major rulers. (W. . West; E . . East).
Italics denote battles. Italic capitals denote Irish Kings.
The span of years shown indicates either the reign or the effective adult life of t
individual concerned; birth dates are not given.

THE EMPIRE	THE CHURCH	BRITISH ISLES
350		
CONSTANS (W) 337–350	Hilary of Poitiers	*MUIREDACH* 325–355
CONSTANTIUS (E) 337–361	353–368	
MAGNENTIUS (W) 350–353		Paul the Notary 353
JULIAN (W) Caesar 355–361	Synod of Rimini 359	*EOCHAID* 356–365
360		
JULIAN 361–363	DAMASUS 366–384	Barbarian raids 360, 364, 367
JOVIAN 363–364	Ambrose of Milan	
VALENTINIAN I (W) 364–375	371–397	*CRIMTHANN* 365–378
VALENS (E) 364–378	Martin of Tours	Border dynasties founded c. 3
	372–c. 397	
370		
GRATIAN ((W) 375–383		*NIALL* 379–405
Adrianople 378		
VALENTINIAN II (W) 375–393		
THEODOSIUS I (E) 379–395		
380		
MAGNUS MAXIMUS (W) 383–388	Augustine of Hippo	First Migration to
	386–430	Brittany ?388
390		
Offa of Angel c. 390/420?	Victruvius in Britain	
ARCADIUS (E) 395–408	c. 396	Saxon raid c. 397
HONORIUS (W) 395–421	St. Albans, Whithorn ?	
	founded	
400		
THEODOSIUS II (E) 408–450	Pelagius c. 400–418	*NATH – I* 405–428
CONSTANTINE III (W) 407–411		
410		
Goths take Rome 410	Sicilian Briton 411	Britain independent
	Fastidius 411	COEL HEN dux ? c. 410/420
Visigoth federates in Gaul	Amator, Auxerre -418	AMBROSIUS the Elder
418	Germanus of Auxerre	? c. 412/425
	418–448	Drust (Picts) 414–458
420		
Eomer of Angel c. 420/460?	Jerome died 420	VORTIGERN c. 425–c. 459
VALENTINIAN III (W) 423–455	CELESTINE 422–432	*LOEGAIRE* 428–463
Vandals take Africa c. 429	Germanus, Britain 429	HENGEST and Horsa land c. 4

BROAD	THE CHURCH	BRITISH ISLES
30		
ëtius supreme in the west c. 433–454	Patrick in Ireland 432–c. 459 SIXTUS III 432–440	Cunedda, and Cornovii, migrations c. 430? *Wallop* c. 437
40		
ëtius consul III 446 HILDERIC I (Franks) c. 440?–481	LEO I 440–461 Patrick's *Declaration* c. 440/443 Germanus in Britain	First Saxon revolt c. 441/2 *Aylesford, Crayford* c. 445/449
50		
ARCIAN (E) 450–457 VITUS (W) 455–456 egidius in Gaul 455–464 EO I (E) 457–474	Patrick's *Letter* c. 450 Northern Irish sees c. 459	*Richborough* c. 450 Coroticus, Clyde, c. 450 Massacre c. 458. Aelle, South Saxons Second Migration to Brittany c. 459
60		
el of Angel c. 460/480? yagrius in Gaul 464–486 NTHEMIUS (W) 467–472	HILARY 461–468 Faustus at Riez 462–c. 495 Ibar, Enda, Kebi in Rome c. 465	AMBROSIUS AURELANIUS c. 460–c. 475 *AILLEL MOLT* 464–482 *ANGUS* of Munster c. 465–492
70		
ENO (E) 474–491 dovacer ends western emperors 476	Sidonius of the Auvergne 470–479 Docco died c. 473	ARTHUR c. 475–c. 515
80		
LOVIS (Franks) 481–511 *oissons* 486	Illtud's school c. 480–c. 510 Brigit c. 480–524	*Portsmouth* c. 480 Cerdic c. 480–c. 495 Migration of Angel kings c. 480 *LUGAID* 482–505
90		
NASTASIUS 491–518 HEODORIC in Italy 493–526	Abban and Ibar, Abingdon, c. 498	Irish attacks on Britain 495/510 *Badon* c. 495. Partition.
00		
oitiers 507 aul becomes France nd of main Elbe cemeteries	Benedict of Nursia c. 500–c. 542	Demetia recovered c. 500/510 Dal Riada Scots c. 500 Dyfnwal, Clyde, c. 500 *MAC ERCA* 505–532
10		
ONS OF CLOVIS 511–561* USTIN I 518–527	Dubricius c. 510–c. 540	*Camlann*, Arthur killed, c. 515
20		
eowulf c. 520/550 USTINIAN 527–565	Samson c. 525–c. 563	Vortipor c. 515–c. 540 MAELGWN c. 520–551
30		
frica reconquered 533, Italy 533–544 HEUDEBERT (East Franks) 533–548	Finnian of Clonard c. 530–551 Gildas' book c. 538	Saxon migrations from Britain to Europe c. 530/550 *TUATHAL* 532–548
40		
ubonic plague 543–547 HEUDEBALD (East Franks) 548–555	Kentigern exiled c. 540 Columba, Derry 544 Cadoc c. 545–c. 580 Brendan's voyages 545/560	Eliffer of York c. 540/560 Morcant, Clyde, c. 540/560 Gabran, Dal Riada, 541–560 *DIARMAIT* 548–564 Plague 547–551

TABLE OF DATES

ABROAD	THE CHURCH ABROAD	THE CHURCH IN THE BRITISH ISLES
550		
	Radegund at Poitiers 550–587 PELAGIUS I 555–560	David c. 550–589 Comgall founded Irish Bangor 558
560		
CLOTHAIR killed Chramn and CONOMOR 560 BRUNHILD 566–613 JUSTIN II 565–578 Lombards in Italy 568		Daniel at Bangor, Menai c. 560–584 Columba at Iona 563–597 Gildas in Ireland 565
570		
TIBERIUS 578–582	Gregory of Tours 573–594 PELAGIUS II 578–590	Gildas died 570 Kentigern, Glasgow, c. 575–c. 603
580		
MAURICE 582–602		Aedan of Ferns c. 585–627
590		
	GREGORY the Great 590–604 Columban in Gaul and Italy 595–615	Augustine Archbishop of Canterbury 597–604
600		
PHOCAS 602–610		
610		
HERACLIUS 610–641		
620		
PEPIN I Mayor 624–639	HONORIUS I 625–640	Edwin baptised 625
630		
DAGOBERT I 630–638 Arabs took Damascus 634, Jerusalem 637		Aedan of Lindisfarne 635–651
640		
Arabs in Egypt 640, Persia 642, Africa 647 GRIMOALD, Mayor, 642–656	Eligius bishop 640–659	Hilda of Whitby c. 640–680

RITAIN	IRELAND	THE ENGLISH
50 HUN of Gwynedd 551–580? RIDEI, Picts, 554–584		CYNRIC took Salisbury 552 AETHELBERT of Kent 555–616
60 EREDUR, York, c. 560–580 IDERCH, Clyde, c. 560–c. 600 ONALL, Dal Riada, 560–574	*AINMERE* 565–569 *BAETAN* c. 569–588	IDA, Bamburgh, c. 560–c. 570 *Wibbandun* 568; Ceawlin and Cutha beat Aethelbert
70 RIEN of Reged c. 570–c. 590 *rthuret* 573 EDAN, Dal Riada, 574–609		*Bedcanford* 571 *Dyrham* 577
80 OURIC, Glevissig, c. 580–c. 615 *aer Greu* 580. PEREDUR killed *intern* c. 584	*AED* m. Ainmere 588–601	ADDA, etc., Bernicia, c. 570–588 AELLE occupied York? AETHELRIC 588–593
590 *indisfarne* c. 590 WAIN of Reged c. 590–c. 595 *atraeth* 598?		CEAWLIN killed 593 AETHELBERT supreme c. 593–616 AETHELFERTH 593–617
	NORTHERN ENGLISH	**SOUTHERN ENGLISH**
600 *Degsastan* 603	AETHELFERTH in York 604	
610 *Chester* c. 613	EDWIN 617–633	CYNEGILS, West Saxons, 611–643
620		PENDA 626–655
630 Catwallaun killed Edwin 633	OSWALD 634–642	
640 Penda and Welsh killed Oswald 642	OSWY 642–670	CENWALH, West Saxons, 643–672

ABROAD	THE CHURCH ABROAD	THE CHURCH IN NORTHERN BRITAIN AND IRELAND
650		
EBROIN, Mayor, 656–681	Fursey died 649	
660		
Arabs took Syracuse 664		Synod of Whitby 664
670		
Arabs besiege Constantinople 673–675	Killian of Wurzburg c. 670–689	Wearmouth founded 674 Caedmon died c. 678
680		
PEPIN II, Mayor, 681–714		Bede at Jarrow c. 681–735 Adomnan, Iona, 686–704
690		
	Willibrord, Frisia, 695–739	
700		
Arabs in Spain 710 CHARLES MARTEL 714–741 *Poitiers* 732 PEPIN III 741–768	Boniface of Mainz killed 755 Alcuin of York and Tours 766–804	
800		
CHARLEMAGNE, 768–814		

*SONS OF CLOVIS

THEODORIC I,	East Franks, 511–533
CHLODOMER,	Orleans, 511–524
CHILDEBERT,	Paris, 511–558
CLOTHAIR I,	Soissons, 511–561
	Orleans, 524–561
	East Franks, 555–561
	Paris, 558–561

TABLE OF DATES

	THE CHURCH IN SOUTHERN BRITAIN	THE NORTH	MERCIA AND THE SOUTH
650		Oswy killed Penda 655 OSWY supreme 655–658	WULFHERE 658–675
660	Theodore Archbishop of Canterbury 669–690	Plague 664	Second *Badon*; Morcant killed 665
670	Barking, Chertsey founded 675 Aldhelm c. 670–709	EGFERTH 670–685 *Trent* 679	West Saxon underkings 672–c. 682 AETHELRED 675–704
680		ALDFRITH 685–705 Ferchar, Dal Riada, 680–696	CEADWALLA 685–688 INE 688–726
690			WIHTRED, Kent, 691–725
700		Pict and Scot wars Northumbrian civil wars	Coenred 704–709 Ceolred 709–716 AETHELBALD 716–757 OFFA 757–796 First Scandinavian raid 789
800		KENNETH MacAlpine 830–860 united Picts and Scots	EGBERT, West Saxon, 802–839 RHODRI MAWR, Wales, 844–877 ALFRED 871–?900

SUMMARY OF EVENTS

350–400. The Imperial Government, under pressure on the Rhine and Danube, kept the garrison of Britain under strength. Britain prospered, in spite of occasional raids. Christianity prevailed by the end of the century.

400–450. The Rhine frontier broke, 406/407. The emperor Constantine III, a Briton, cleared the barbarians from Britain and Gaul, but was suppressed by the legitimate emperor, Honorius. The Goths took Rome, 410. Honorius told the British to govern and defend themselves, legitimising local emperors. The British repelled foreign enemies, but divided in civil war. Vortigern (c. 425–c. 458) employed Saxons, or English, to defeat the Picts, barbarians beyond the Forth; he neutralised mainland Ireland and reduced Irish colonists in western Britain. The British nobility, led by Ambrosius the elder, rebelled against Vortigern and the Saxons; Vortigern enlisted more Saxons, who rebelled against both parties, c. 441, and destroyed Roman British civilisation. After heavy fighting, the political leaders of the British were assassinated, and much of the surviving nobility emigrated to Gaul, c. 459.

450–500. A national resistance movement of the citizens (*Cymry*) was initiated by Ambrosius Aurelianus the younger, c. 460, and triumphed under Arthur at Badon, c. 495. The English remained in partitioned areas, chiefly in the east. The political forms of the Roman Empire were revived, but its economy had been destroyed.

500–550. The central government disintegrated with the death of Arthur (c. 515). Numerous generals became warlords of regions, Malegwn of North Wales the most powerful among them, and provoked the resentment of civilians of all classes. A monastic reform movement on a mass scale freed the church from dependence upon the warlords; it spread to Ireland, and also prompted a massive migration to Brittany. Bubonic plague ravaged the mediterranean and also Britain and Ireland, 547–551.

550–600. The second Saxon, or English, revolt permanently mastered most of what is now England, destroying the remnants of the warlords. By 605, Aethelferth of Northumbria and Aethelbert of Kent were between them supreme over all the English. Kent was converted to Roman Christianity, 597. Columba of Iona established Irish monastic Christianity among the Picts, and among the Scot or Irish colonists of Argyle, 563–597.

600–650. The empire and Christianity of Kent collapsed, 616. Northumbrian supremacy, 617–642, was overthrown by Penda of the Mercians, with Welsh allies. The monastic impetus faded in Wales but renewed its vigour among the Irish.

650–800. The Mercian kings held empire over the southern English; the Northumbrian monarchy lost authority after 700. The Northumbrians and Mercians accepted monastic Christianity from the Irish, and the English and the Irish carried it to Europe north of the Alps. Its practices conflicted with those of Rome. Archbishop Theodore, from Tarsus (669–690), presided over the fusion of native monastic and Roman episcopal Christianity among the English; the Irish and the Welsh conformed later. Scandinavian raids began in 789, and sovereignty over the English passed from the Mercian to the West Saxon kings early in the 9th century.

ABBREVIATIONS
used in the Notes

Italic figures and letters give National Grid Map references:
Two letters and four figures, as *TL 01 23*, refer to Great Britain.
One letter and two figures, as *N 58*, refer to Ireland.
One letter and one figure, as *H 2*, refer to Brittany.
The National Grid for Great Britain is explained on Ordnance Survey maps, in the Automobile Association Handbook, and elsewhere.
The Irish National Grid is shown on Maps 9 and 27, pp. 153 and 373 above.
The Grid devised for Brittany is shown on Map 14, p. 255 above, and explained in the notes thereto.

A single bold capital letter, as **A**, refers to the appropriate section of *Arthurian Sources*, cf. p. xv above, whose contents are

A Annals
B Badon
C Charters
D Dedications
E Ecclesiastics
F Foreign persons and places
G Genealogies
- **G** A Armorican
- **G** B British
- **G** E English
- **G** F Foreign
- **G** I Irish

followed by the initial letter(s) of the territory concerned

H Honorius' Letter
I Inscriptions
J Jurisprudence, Law
K King Lists
L Localities, Geography
M Miscellaneous
N Names of Places
O Ogam Script
P Persons, laymen
Q Quotations from texts
R Roman institutions
S Saxon Archaeology
T Texts discussed

Roman numerals I, II and III refer to the sections of *Works cited in the Notes* below; I Sources, II Modern Works, III Periodicals.

AA	I MGH	AHS	I	Arch. Ael.	III
AASS	II Leeds	AI	I Annals	Arch. Camb.	III
AB	I *Vitae*; III	AIM	I Irish	Arch. Jl.	III
AC	I Annals	ALE	I	ARS	I
ACDS	II MacKinlay	Alfred	I; I LEEK	ASE	II Åberg, Stenton
ACL	II Stokes	ALI	I		
ACm	I Annals	ALW	I	ASH	I *Vitae*
ACR	II Fox	Ant.	III	ASP	II Myres
Aethelbert	I LEEK	Ant. Jl.	III	ASS	I *Vitae*
Aethelstan	I LEEK	AP	I Welsh	AT	I Annals
AG	I *Vitae*	Arch.	III	AU	I Annals

ABBREVIATIONS

BA	I Welsh
BB	II
BBA	I
BBC	I Welsh
BBCS	III
BCS	I Charters
BD	I Genealogies
Beds.	Bedfordshire
Berks.	Berkshire
BG	I Procopius
BGG	I Genealogies
BHL	II
BICS	III
BM	British Museum
BNE	I *Vitae*
Brev. Ab.	I *Vitae*
BT	I Welsh
BV	I Procopius
ByS	I Genealogies
c.	circa, about
CA	I Welsh
CArch	III
CASP	III
CEIS	II Hughes
cf.	compare
CGH	I Genealogies
ch.	chapter
Chron.	Chronicle
CHE	I Church
CIIC	I Corpus
CIL	I Corpus
CLH	I Welsh
CPL	II Bieler
CPNS	II Watson
CPS	I Chronicles
CR	III
CS	I Annals
CS	II Skene
CSEL	I Corpus
CSHB	I Corpus
CSW	II Davies
CT	I Welsh
CTh	I Codex
DAB	II
DAS	I
DB	I
DBB	II Maitland

DC	I ALW
DCB	II
DEPN	II
DSB	II Leeds
ECHR	III
ECMS	I
ECMW	I
ECPMS	II Cruden
ECW	I Charters
ECWM	I Charters
ed.	editor, edition
Edward	I LEEK
EETS	I
e.g.	for example
EHD	I
EHDS	I
EHR	III
EHS	I
EIHM	II O'Rahilly
Ep(p).	Letter(s)
EPNE	II
EPNS	II
ESSH	I
EVC	II Seebohm
EWGT	I Genealogies
f.	filius, son of
FAB	I Welsh
ff.	following
fig.	figure
FHG	I
FM	I Annals
FW	I
GC	I ALW
GCS	I
Gesetze	I Liebermann, Schmid
GM	II Vinogradoff
GP	I MGH
H	I Genealogies
HA	I Bede
HE	I Bede, Rufinus
HF	I Gregory

HH	I
Hlothere	I LEEK
HMC	Historical Monuments Commission
HMSO	Her Majesty's Stationery Office
HS	I
HW	II Lloyd
HWL	II Parry
HY	I
IANB	II Rivet
i.e.	that is
ILS	I
Ine	I LEEK
Iolo	I Welsh
ITS	I Irish
IWP	II Williams
J	I Genealogies
JBAA	III
JCS	III
JEPN	III
JRIC	III
JRS	III
JRSAI	III
JTS	III
KCD	I Charters
LB	I
LBS	II Baring-Gould
LEEK	I
LB	I
LG	I
LH	I
LHEB	II Jackson
Lismore	I *Vitae*
LL	I
LRE	II Jones
m	map, mac, son of
M	I

ABBREVIATIONS

MA	III
MGH	I
MHB	I
MHH	I *Vitae*
Mon. Ang.	II Dugdale
MS(S)	Manuscript(s)
Myv. Arch.	I Welsh
NC	III
n.f.	Neue Folge
NH	I Pliny
NLA	I *Vitae*
Not. Dig.	I
n.s.	new series
Occ.	West (cf. Not. Dig.)
OEN	II Chadwick
OET	I
OIT	II Jackson
Or.	East (cf. Not. Dig.)
p.; pp.	page(s)
passim	scattered (references)
PE	I *Vitae* Brev. Ab.
PFE	II Joliffe
PG	I
PH	I *Vitae* Brev. Ab.
Pinkerton	I *Vitae*
PL	I
pl.	plate
PLAC	I MGH
PLECG	II Chadwick
PLRE	II
PNK	II EPNS
P and P	III
PP	II Wainwright
PPS	III
PRIA	III
PSA	III
PSAS	III
PWP	I Welsh
RBH	I Welsh
RC	III
RCHM	II
RHS	Royal Historical Society
RIA	Royal Irish Academy
RIB	I
RIS	I Muratori
Rolls	I Chronicles
RS	Record Society
SAEC	I
SAL	Society of Antiquaries of London
Sal.	I *Vitae*
SANHS	III
SASI	II Chadwick
SC	I
SCD	II Arnold-Foster
SCSW	II Bowen
SD	I
SE	II Kemble
SEBC	II
SEBH	II
SEIL	II Thurneysen
SG	I Irish
SILH	II Carney
SRA	I
SRG	I MGH
SRL	I MGH
SRM	I MGH
SS	I MGH
STS	I
Sup.	Supplement
SyAC	III
Tac. Ann.	I
TCASL	II Seebohm
TCD	Trinity College Dublin
THS Cymm	III
TRHS	III
TRIA	III
Triad	I TYP
TSW	II Seebohm
TT	I *Vitae*
TYP	I
VC	I ALW
VCH	II
vita	Life of
vol(s).	volume(s)
VSBG	I Genealogies; *Vitae*
VSH	I *Vitae*
VT	I *Vitae*
WBT	I Welsh
WEW	II Hoskins
WHR	III
Wihtred	I LEEK
YC	III
ZCP	III

WORKS CITED IN THE NOTES

Space and time prevent the publication of a full bibliography. The works here cited provide a brief guide to the main printed sources; the modern works named are chiefly those which list, assess and discuss the sources, and which contain the fullest bibliographies. Many useful discussions are therefore excluded, but most of them are mentioned in the text or bibliographies of the works here cited.

I Sources and Collections of Sources

Some of the printed texts are hard to find and difficult to edit. It has therefore been necessary to consult the most accessible and useful editions; in a few instances it has been impracticable or inadvisable to cite the most recent publication.

Abingdon Chronicle	Rolls 2, 1858	
Adam of Bremen	*Gesta Hammaburgensis Ecclesiae Pontificum* MGH SS 7,267, ed. 2, 1876; PL 146, 451	
Aethelweard	*Chronicon* CHE 3; MHB 499; ARS	
Aetheriae *Peregrinatio*	CSEL 39, 35 ff.; cf. II Löfstedt	
Alcuin	MGH Epp. Karoli Aevi; HY 1,349	
Aldhelm	MGA AA 15; PL 89	
Alfred	*Alfred des Grossen Bearbeitung der Soliloquien des Augustinus* ed. W. Endtler, Bibliothek der Angelsächische Prosa 11, Hamburg 1922	
Ambrose of Milan	CSEL 73; PL 16	
Ammianus Marcellinus	ed. Teubner, Loeb etc.; ed. J. C. Rolfe, London 1939	
The Ancient Laws and Institutes of England	ed. B. Thorpe, London 1840	ALE
The Ancient Laws of Ireland	ed. W.M.Henessy and others, 6 vols. Dublin 1856–1901; cf. p. 445 above	ALI
The Ancient Laws and Institutes of Wales	ed. Aneirin Owen, 2 vols. London 1841. Vol. 1 contains the so called Demetian, Gwentian and Venedotian Codes; cf. p. 445 above	ALW DC GC, VC
Anglian Chronicle	see p. 283 above	
Anglicanae Historiae Scriptores	R.Twysden, 2. vols., London 1652	AHS
Anglicarum Rerum Scriptores post Bedam	H.Savile, London 1596; Frankfurt 1601	ARS
Anglo-Saxon Chronicle, see Saxon Chronicle		
Annales Fuldenses	MGH SS 1,343	
Annales Laurissenses (or *Regni Francorum*, or *Einhardi*)	MGH SS 1,126; SRG 1895, reprint 1950	
ANNALS Irish (see **A**)		

I SOURCES

Annals of Inisfallen	(1092) ed. S.MacAirt, Dublin 1951	AI
Annals of Tigernach	(1088) ed. W.Stokes RC 16, 1895, 375–419: 17, 1896, 6–33; 119–263; 337–420: 18, 1897, 9–59; 150–198; 267–303; 374–391	AT
Annals of Clonmacnoise	translated C.Mageoghagan (1627) from an original of c. 1408, now lost; ed. D.Murphy, Dublin 1896	AC
Annals of Ulster	(before 1498) ed. W.M.Henessy, Dublin 1897–1901	AU
Annals of the Four Masters	(1632–1636) ed. J.Donovan, 7 vols., Dublin 1851	FM
Chronicon Scotorum	(1660–1666) ed. W.M.Henessy, Rolls 46, 1866	CS
Annals of Roscrea	ed. D.Gleeson and S.MacAirt PRIA 56 C 1957–1959	
Annals from the Book of Leinster	VT 512–529	
ANNALS Welsh (see **A**)		
Annales Cambriae	Rolls 20, 1860; YC 9, 1880, 152; MHB 830; *Nennius* ed. Morris, forthcoming; cf. Welsh Literature, Bruts	ACm
ANNALS English (see **T**)	see *Anglian Chronicle*; Saxon Chronicle; Florence of Worcester; Flores; Henry of Huntingdon; etc.	
Anonymus Valesianus	ed. H.Valesius, Paris 1636; Muratori (ed. 1786) 25; (ed. 1913) 24,4; MGH AA 9 (Chron. Min. 1) 7 ff. and 306 ff.; ed. Rolfe, *Ammianus* 1939; ed. J.Moreau (Teubner) 1961; etc.	
Archiv, see II Stokes		
Asser	*Life of King Alfred* ed. W.H. Stevenson, Oxford 1904; MHB 467; SRA 2	
Augustine of Hippo	PL 34 ff.; cf. *The Anti-Pelagian Treatises of St. Augustine* ed. F.W.Bright, Oxford 1880; *de Gestis Pelagii* CSEL 42	
Ausonius	MGH AA 5; also Loeb	
Barnabas	*Epistula Catholica* ed. A.Hilgenfeld, Leipzig 1866	
Bede	*Opera Omnia* ed. J.A.Giles, 13 vols. London 1843–1845; PL 90 ff.	
	Opera Historica ed. J.Stevenson, EHS London 1838–1841	
	Historia Ecclesiastica Gentis Anglorum, *Historia Abbatum*, *Epistula ad Egbertum* ed. C.Plummer, Oxford 1896, reprint 1966;	HE HA

	Old English Version of HE in EETS 95–96, 110–111 London 1890–1898
	Chronica MGH AA 13 (Chronica Minora 3) 247 ff.
Benedict of Nursia	*Regula* CSEL 75
Beowulf	ed. R.W.Chambers and A.J.Wyatt, London 1914; also C.L.Wrenn, Oxford 1953; cf. II Chambers; see Finn's Burg Fragment, below
Hector Boece	*History of Scotland* STS series 3, 1946–; Rolls 6
Boniface	*Epistulae* ed. M.Tangl *Die Briefe des heiligen Bonifatius* MGH Epp. Selectae 1, Berlin 1910, reprint 1955
Book of Armagh	ed. T.Gwynn (diplomatic text) Dublin 1913; facsimile of Patrician documents, ed. E.Gwynn, Dublin 1937
of Ballymote	in the RIA; Kenney 24; facsimile, Dublin 1887
of Chad	see *Book of Teilo*
of Deer	ed. J.Stuart, Spalding Club, Edinburgh 1869; Kenney 656; K. Jackson *The Gaelic Notes in the Book of Deer*, Cambridge 1972
of the Dun Cow	*Lebor na hUidre* ed. R.I.Best and O. Bergin, Dublin 1929; facsimile, Dublin 1870; Kenney 15; in the RIA
Yellow Book of Lecan	in TCD; Kenney 24; 89; facsimiles, Dublin 1896, 1933;
Great Book of Lecan	in the RIA; Kenney 25
Book of Leinster	in TCD; ed. R.I.Best and others, Dublin 1954– ; facsimile 1880; Kenney 15
of Lismore	Kenney 308; facsimile, Dublin 1950; cf. Stokes *Lismore Lives* (*Vitae*, below)
of Llancarfan	*vita Cadoc* ch. 55–68
of Llandaff	see *Liber Landavensis*
of Rights	*Lebor na Cert*; ITS 46, 1962, ed. M. Dillon
Black Book of St. Augustine	ed. G.J.Turner and H.E.Salter, 2 vols., London and Oxford 1915–24
Book of Sligo	lost; cited in BM Egerton MS 1782, SG 72; 76; cf. viii
of Teilo	unpublished; in Lichfield Cathedral since the 9th century, therefore also called the Book of Chad; the

	Courtauld Institute has photographs. Memoranda are reproduced in LL	
Books, Welsh	see Welsh Literature, below, BA, BBC, BT, RBH etc.	
Book	see also Lebor, Liber	
Bower	see Scotichronicon	
Bruts	see Welsh Literature, below	
Caedmon	cf. Plummer *Bede* 2, 251; OET 125 ff. (cf. p. 421 above); etc.	
Caesar	*de Bello Gallico* ed. Teubner, Loeb etc.	
Cain Adomnan	(Law of Adomnan) ed. K.Meyer, Oxford 1905; cf. SEIL 269 ff.; Kenney 245	
Cartulaire de Landevennec	ed. Le Men and Ernault, 1882; ed. de la Borderie, Rennes 1888	
Cartulaire de Quimper	*Bulletin de la Commission diocesaine de Quimper* 1901	
Cartulaire de Quimperlé	ed. L.Le Maitre and P.de Berthou, Paris 1896	
Cartulaire de Redon	ed. A de Courson, Paris 1863	
Cartularium Sithiense	(Abbaye de S.Bertin) Guérard *Cartulaires de France*, 1840–1857, vol. 3; cf. Seebohm EVC 256, with map	
Cassiodorus	PL 69, 70	
Catalogus Ordinum Sanctorum in Hibernia	Sal. 161 (see *Vitae* below); AB 73, 1955, 206	
CHARTERS		
Cartularium Saxonicum	W.de G.Birch, 3 vols. London 1885–1893; Index of Persons 1899	BCS
Codex Diplomaticum Aevi Saxonici	J.H.Kemble, 6 vols. London EHS 1839–1848	KCD
Anglo-Saxon Charters	A.J.Robertson, Cambridge 1939	
The Latin Charters of the Anglo-Saxon Period	F.M.Stenton, Oxford 1955	
The Crawford Collection of Early Charters and Documents	ed. A.S.Napier and W.H.Stevenson, Oxford 1895	
The Early Charters of Wessex	H.P.R.Finberg, Leicester 1964	ECW
The Early Charters of Devon and Cornwall	H.P.R.Finberg, Leicester 1954, supplement in Hoskins WEW, cf II below	
The Early Charters of Essex	C.Hart, Leicester 1957	
The Early Charters of the West Midlands	H.P.R.Finberg, Leicester 1961	ECMW
The Crawford Collection of Early Charters	ed. A.S.Napier and W.H.Stevenson, Oxford 1895	

see also II Sawyer, below. cf. Cartulaire, Cartularium, Diplomatarium; Wills; Writs; Books of Llancarfan, Llandaff, Teilo.

Chronicles and Memorials of Great Britain and Ireland during the Middle Ages	under the direction of the Master of the Rolls, London 1858–	Rolls
Chronicle of 452	MGH AA 9 (Chronica Minora 1) 652 ff.	
Chronicles of the Picts and Scots	ed. W.F.Skene, Edinburgh 1867	CPS
CHRONICLES see also Annals above		
Church Historians of England	J.Stevenson, 6 vols. London 1852–1856	CHE
Claudian	*Carmina* MGH AA 10; CSEL 11	
Codex Theodosianus	ed. T.Mommsen, Berlin 1905, reprint 1954	CTh
Columban	*Opera* ed. G.S.M.Walker (Scriptores Latini Hiberniae 2) Dublin 1957; PL 80; cf. Kenney 186. *Epistulae* MGH Epp. 3	
Consuetudo West Sexe	Liebermann *Gesetze* 1,588	
Corippus	MHG AA 3	
Cormac mac Cuilenan	*Glossary* (Sanas Chormaic) ed. W. Stokes translated J.O'Donovan, Calcutta 1868; AIM 4, 1912	
Corpus Inscriptionum Insularum Celticarum	ed. R.A.S.MacAlister, 2 vols. Dublin 1945–1949	CIIC
Corpus Inscriptionum Latinarum	ed. T.Mommsen and others, Berlin 1863–	CIL
Corpus Scriptorum Ecclesiasticorum Latinorum	Vienna 1866–	CSEL
Corpus Scriptorum Historiae Byzantinae	Bonn etc. 1828–	CSHB
Cyfreithiau Hywel Dda	ed. S.J.Williams and J.E.Powell Cardiff 1942, ed. 2, 1966; ed. M. Richards, Cardiff 1957	
Cynewulf	C.W.Kennedy *The Poems of Cynewulf* London 1940, reprint New York 1949; cf. II Bateson	
DEDICATIONS to Saints	see II: *Wales* LBS, SCSW; *Ireland* O'Hanlon; *England* Arnold-Foster, Doble; *Scotland* Forbes, MacKinlay, cf. I *Vitae* Reeves *Adomnan*	
F.C.Diack	*The Inscriptions of Pictland* Aberdeen 1944	
Dialogue of Egbert	HS 3,403	
Dicuil	*de Mensura Orbis* ed. G.Parthey, Berlin 1870, cf. Kenney 546	
Dio Cassius	*Roman History* ed. Boissevain, Berlin 1895, Loeb etc.	
Diodorus Siculus	ed. Teubner, Loeb etc.	
Diplomatarium Anglicum aevi Saxonici	ed. B.Thorpe, London 1865	DAS
de Divina Lege	Jerome *Ep.* 7, PL 30, 104	

I SOURCES

Source	Edition	Abbreviation
Domesday Book	ed. Farley, London 1783; ed. with translation, Morris, Chichester 1973– ; facsimiles, Ordnance Survey, Southampton 1861–1864; many county translations in VCH; and others elsewhere	DB
Duan Albanach	Skene CPS 57	
The Early Christian Monuments of Scotland	ed. J.Romilly Allen and J.Anderson, Edinburgh 1903	ECMS
The Early Christian Monuments of Wales	ed. V.E.Nash-Williams, Cardiff 1950	ECMW
Early English Text Society	London 1870–	EETS
Early Sources of Scottish History	ed. A.O.Anderson 2 vols. Edinburgh 1922	ESSH
Einhard, see *Annales Laurissenses*		
English Historical Documents I	ed. D.Whitelock, London 1955	EHD
Select English Historical Documents	ed. F.E.Harmer Cambridge 1914	EHDS
English Historical Society	Publications, London 1833–1856	EHS
ENGLISH LITERATURE	cf. Alfred, Beowulf, Caedmon, Cynewulf, Finn's Burg Fragment, Saxon Chronicle, Widsith, etc.; cf. II Bateson, Baugh, Greenfield, Wrenn	
Eugippius	see *Vitae* Severinus	
Eunapius	*Fragments* FHG 4	
Eusebius	*Chronicon* ed. A.Schoene, 2 vols., Berlin 1866, 1875; PG 19, 99 ff. ed. R.Helm GCS 24 and 34 = 47, 1913, 1926, 1956, (Jerome's Latin translation only) ed. J.Karst GCS 20, 1911 (Armenian translation only, translated into German) ed. C.Siegfried and H.Gelzer, Leipzig 1884 (Syriac epitome only, with Latin translation)	
Fastidius	*de Vita Christiana* PL 40, 1031; translated R.S.T.Haslehurst, cf. Sicilian Briton, below	
Faustus of Riez	CSEL 21; PL 53; 58	
Felire, see Martyrology		
Finn's Burg Fragment	ed. J.R.Clark Hall and C.L.Wrenn, London 1950	
Florence of Worcester	*Chronicon* ed. B.Thorpe EHS London 1848–1849; MHB 522	FW
Flores Historiarum	Rolls 95, 1890	
John of Fordun	*Chronica* ed. W.F.Skene, Edinburgh 1871–1872; SRA 2; cf. *Scotichronicon*	
Fragmenta Historicorum Graecorum	ed. C.Müller, 5 vols., 1841–1883	FHG
Fredegarius	*Chronica* MGH SRM 2	

GENEALOGIES (see **G**)

Armorican (Brittany) Texts are few; the main sources are notices in the Lives of the Saints, especially Iudoc and Winnoc, and the lists of *Comites Cornubiae* in the Cartularies; see **G** A

English The principal texts are in Bede HE; SC: Nennius; OET pp. 170 ff.; FW; HH; and other chroniclers; cf. **G** E

Irish M.A.O'Brien *Corpus Genealogiarum Hiberniae* vol. I Dublin 1962; *The O'Clery Book of Genealogies* Analecta Hibernica 18, Dublin 1915; Keating, vol. 4 (ITS vol. 15), and other texts, including the MacFirbis Genealogies, cf. Kenney 45; O'Curry 121; cf. also T.O'Raithbheartaigh *Genealogical Tracts* Dublin 1932; cf. **G** I — CGH

Welsh The principal modern collections are Wade-Evans, cf. *Vitae* below [VSBG], and P.C.Bartrum *Early Welsh Genealogical Tracts* Cardiff 1960 [EWGT]. The principal texts are

- *Bonedd Gwyr y Gogled* EWGT 72; Skene FAB 2,454; TYP 238 — BGG
- *Bonedd y Saint* EWGT 51; VSBG 320 — BYS
- *Brychan Documents* EWGT 14–21; VSBG 313–320 — BD
- *Harleian MS 3859* EWGT 9; YC 9, 1888, 169 — H
- *Jesus College, Oxford, MS 20* EWGT 41; YC 8, 1887, 83 — J

Pedigrees are also given in a number of Saints' Lives, in Nennius and other sources. The texts printed in EWGT 35–40; 68–71; 75 ff. are mostly derived from the main texts, but are corrupted by antiquarians, often under the influence of Geoffrey of Monmouth, though a few preserve some incidental echoes of lost medieval origins; see **G** B.

Scottish The pedigrees of the several regions form part of the appropriate Irish, Welsh and English dynastic records; and are supplemented by the texts and incidental notices collected in CPS.

Gennadius — *de Viris Inlustribus* PL 58; ed. E.C. Richardson, Leipzig 1896

Geoffrey of Monmouth — *Historia Regum Britanniae* ed. A. Griscom, New York 1929, and many other editions

Gildas — MGH AA 13 (Chronica Minora 3) 25 ff.; ed. and translated M. Winterbottom, Chichester, forthcoming; ed. and translated H. Williams, London 1899

Giraldus Cambrensis — Rolls 21, 7 vols. 1861–1891

Gregory of Tours — *Historia Francorum* and other works MGH SRM I — HF

Gregory the Great — *Dialogi* PL 77, 149 ff.; *Epistulae* MGH Epp. 1–2

Die Griechischen Christlichen Schriftsteller der ersten drei Jahrhunderte — Berlin and Leipzig 1897– — GCS

ed. A.W.Haddan and W.Stubbs — *Councils and Ecclesiastical Documents relating to Great Britain and* — HS

	Ireland 3 vols. Oxford 1869–1871, reprint 1969	
Henry of Huntingdon	*Historia Anglorum* Rolls 74, 1879; MHB 689; ARS	HH
Hermas	*Pastor* GCS 48; PG 2; ed. A. Hilgenfeld, Leipzig 1866	
Collectio Canonum Hibernensis	in H.Wasserschleben *Die Irische Kanonensammlung* Giessen 1874; ed. 2, Leipzig 1895; cf. Kenney 247	
Hieronymus, see Jerome		
Hilary of Poitiers	*de Synodis* PL 40, 157	
Hisperica Famina	PL 90. 1185; ed. F.J.H.Jenkinson, Cambridge 1908	
Historians of the Church of York	ed. J.Raine, Rolls 71, 1879–1894	HY
Pope Innocent I	*Epp.* PL 20, 463	
Inscriptiones Latinae Selectae	ed. H.Dessau, Berlin 1902–1915	ILS
INSCRIPTIONS	see CIIC, CIL, Diack, ECMS, ECMW, ILS, RIB; II *Feil-Sgribhinn* 184	
Irenaeus	*adversus Haereseos* PG 7; ed. W.W. Harvey, London 1857; ed. A. Harnack, Leipzig 1907–1910; ed. A.Rousseau and others, Paris 1952	
IRISH LITERATURE translations include		
ed. Bergin, Best and others	*Anecdotes from Irish Manuscripts* Halle 1907	AIM
J. Carney	*Medieval Irish Lyrics* Dublin 1967	
T.P.Cross and C.H.Glover	*Ancient Irish Tales* New York 1936	
T.Fraser and others	*Irish Texts* London 1931–1934	
K.H.Jackson	*A Celtic Miscellany* London 1951	
P.W.Joyce	*Old Celtic Romances* Dublin 1879, reprint 1961	
A.G.van Hamel	*Immrama* (Voyages) Dublin 1934	
K.Meyer	*The Voyage of Bran* 2 vols. London 1913	
	Selections from Ancient Irish Poetry ed. 2 London 1913	
	The Death Tales of the Ulster Heroes Dublin 1906	
S.H.O'Grady	*Silva Gadaelica* (vol. 1 Texts, vol. 2 Translations) London 1892, reprint Dublin 1935	SG
The Cattle Raid of Cooley	*Tain Bo Cualgne* ed. and translated E.Windisch, Leipzig 1905; T. Dunn, London 1914; C.O'Rahilly Dublin 1967; and others	
Irish Texts Society	Publications, with English translation on facing pages, Dublin 1899–	ITS

Isidore of Seville	PL 81–83; *Chronicon* MGH AA 11; *Etymologiae* also ed. W.M.Lindsay Oxford 1911	
Jerome (Hieronymus)	PL 22–30. *Epistulae* CSEL 54–56. *Eusebii Chronicon* also GCS 47 (= 24 and 34); cf. Eusebius, above; *de Viribus Inlustris* also Teubner 1879	
John Cassian	PL 49, 50; *Collationes* CSEL 13; *Institutiones* CSEL 17	
Jordanes	*Getica*; *Romana* MGH AA 5; PL 69, 1251	
G.Keating	*History of Ireland* 1634, MSS; 4 vols. ITS 4, 8, 9,15 Dublin 1902–1914	
LAWS (see J)	see ALE, ALI, ALW, CTh, Consuetudo West Sexe, Cyfreithiau, Dialogue of Egbert, Collectio Hibernensis, LEEK, Leges, Lex, Liebermann, Schmid	
The Laws of the Earliest English Kings	ed. F.L.Attenborough, Cambridge 1922, reprint New York 1963; cited under the names of the Kings who issued the codes	LEEK
Lebor Bretnach	ed. J.H.Todd *The Irish Version of Nennius* Dublin 1849; *Nennius Interpretatus*, translated into Latin, MGH AA 13, 143 ff.; ed. A.G.van Hamel, Dublin 1932	LB
Lebor na Cert	see Book of Rights	
Lebor Gabala Erenn	ed. R.A.S.MacAlister, 5 vols. ITS 34, 35, 39, 41, 44 Dublin 1938–1956	LG
Lebor	see Book	
Leges Saxonum	ed. MGH Leges 5; MGH Fontes 5 (with *Lex Anglorum*)	
J.Leland	*Itinerary* (c. 1540) ed. L.Toulmin Smith, 3 vols. 1908	
	Commentarii de Scriptoribus Britanniae ed. A.Hall, Oxford 1709	
Lex Anglorum et Werinorum, hoc est Thuringorum	see *Leges Saxonum*	
The Irish Liber Hymnorum	ed. J.H.Bernard and R.Atkinson, 2 vols. London, Henry Bradshaw Society 13, 14, 1898; ed. J.H. Todd *The Book of Hymns of the Ancient Church of Ireland* 2 vols. Dublin 1855–1869	LH
Liber Landavensis	J.G.Evans *The Book of Llan Dav* Oxford 1893	LL
Liber Pontificalis	ed. L.Duchesne, 2 vols. Paris	

	1886–1891; ed. T.Mommsen (to 530) MGH GP 1898	
ed. F.Liebermann	*Die Gesetze der Angelsachsen* 3 vols. Halle 1903–1916	
LIVES of the Saints	see *Vitae*	
Loeb Classical Library	with English translation on facing pages, London and New York	
Sir T.Malory	*Le Morte d'Arthur* (completed 1469) Caxton, London 1485; many later editions, especially J.Rhys, reprinted in Everyman's Library 1906	
J.D.Mansi	*Sacrorum Conciliorum nova et amplissima Collectio* 1759; facsimile, Paris and Leipzig 1901	
Marcellinus Comes	*Chronicon* MGH AA 11, 60 ff.	
MARTYROLOGIES of		M
Donegal	ed. J.H.Todd and W.Reeves, Dublin 1864	
Gorman	ed. W.Stokes, London 1895	
Oengus the Culdee	ed. W.Stokes, London 1905 (often called the *Felire of Oengus*)	
Tallaght	ed. R.I.Best and H.J.Lawlor, London 1931	
Monumenta Historica Britannica	ed. H.Petrie and J.Sharpe, London 1848	MHB
Monumenta Germaniae Historica	ed. G.H.Pertz, T.Mommsen and others, Hannover, Berlin, 1826– AA: Auctores Antiquissimi GP: Gesta Pontificum PLAC: Poetae Latini Aevi Carolingi SS: Scriptores SRG: SS Rerum Germanicarum SRL: SS Rerum Langobardorum SRM: SS Rerum Merovingicrum	MGH
L.A.Muratori	*Rerum Italicarum Scriptores* Milan 1786; ed. R.Cessi, Citta di Castello 1913	RIS
Nennius	*Historia Britonum* ed. T.Mommsen MGH AA 13 (Chronica Minora 3) 143 ff.; ed. E.Faral *La Légende Arthurienne* (Bibliothèque de l'Ecole des Hautes Etudes 237) 3 vols. Paris 1929, vol. 3; ed. and translated J.Morris, Chichester, forthcoming; see also LB	
Notitia Dignitatum	ed. O.Seeck, Berlin 1876, reprint Frankfurt-am-Main 1962	Not.Dig.
The Oldest English Texts	ed. H.Sweet EETS 83 London 1885	OET

Author / Work	Edition	Abbreviation
Olympiodorus	*Fragments* FHG 4	
Ordericus Vitalis	*Historia Ecclesiastica* ed. A. le Prevost, Paris 1838–1855; PL 188; translated E. Forester, London 1853–1856	
Origen	PG 11–17; *Homilies on Luke and Ezekiel* (and others) Latin translation by Jerome, PL 25, 691; 26, 229; GCS 9; ed. H. Crouzel and R. Girod, Paris (Sources chrétiennes 87) 1962	
Orosius	ed. Teubner, 1889; CSEL 5; PL 31	
Pachomius	*Regula*, translated into Latin by Jerome PL 23, 275; cf. *Pachomiana Latina* ed. A. Boon, Louvain 1932	
Patrick	*Confessio*; *Epistula ad Coroticum* VT 357–380; ed. J.D. White PRIA 25 C 7 1905; ed. L. Bieler, Dublin 1952; ed. and translated A.B.C. Hood, Chichester, forthcoming	
Patrologia Graeca	ed. J. Migne, Paris 1857–	PG
Patrologia Latina	ed. J. Migne, Paris 1844–	PL
Paul the Deacon	*Historia Langobardorum* MGH SRL 45; translated W.D. Foulke, Philadelphia 1907	
Paulinus of Pella	*Eucharisticus* CSEL 16, 291; Ausonius, ed. Loeb, vol. 2	
Pelagius	*Commentary on the Pauline Epistles* PL Sup. 1, 1110 ff.	
Pliny	*Natural History* ed. Teubner, 1875–1906	NH
Priscus	*Fragments* FHG 4	
Procopius	*de Bello Gothico*; *de Bello Vandalico* ed. Teubner, CSHB, Loeb etc.	BG BV
Prosper of Aquitaine	*Contra Collatorem* PL 51, 213 *Chronica* MGH AA 9 (Chronica Minora 1)	
Prudentius	*Peri Stephanon* PL 60, 275	
Regesta Regum Scottorum	ed. G.W.S Barrow, Edinburgh 1960	
The Roman Inscriptions of Britain	ed. R.G. Collingwood and R.P. Wright, Oxford 1965	RIB
Rufinus	*Historia Ecclesiastica* PL 21	HE
SAINTS' LIVES	see *Vitae*	
Salvian	*de Gubernatione Dei* CSEL 8; MGH AA 1	
Sanas Chormaic	see Cormac *Glossary*	
The Saxon Chronicle	Rolls, 23, 1861, ed. B. Thorpe; MHB 291; ed. J. Earle, Oxford 1865;	SC

	revised C. Plummer, 2 vols. 1892–1899; D. Whitelock and others, text London 1952, translation 1961; translated G. N. Garmonsway, Everyman's Library 1953	
ed. R. Schmid	*Die Gesetze der Angelsachsen* Leipzig 1822, ed. 2, 1858	
Scotichronicon	(Walter Bower's revision (1437) of Fordun) ed. W. Goodall, Edinburgh 1759; T. Hearne, Oxford 1722	
Scottish Annals from English Chroniclers	ed. A. O. Anderson, London 1908	SAEC
SCOTTISH HISTORY	see Boece, CPS, ESSH, Fordun, Regesta Regum, Scotichronicon, SAEC, STS, Wyntoun	
Scottish Texts Society	Publications, Edinburgh 1883–	STS
Scriptores Rerum Anglicarum	ed. T. Gale and W. Fulman, 3 vols. Oxford 1689–1691	SRA
Senchus Fir nAlban	Skene CPS 308; *Celtica* 7, 1966, 154 ff.; cf. 8, 1967, 90 ff.; 9, 1968, 217 ff., etc.	
Sicilian Briton	ed. C. P. Caspari *Briefe, Abhandlungen und Predigten* Christiana 1890; PL Sup. 1 (*Ep.* 1, col. 1687; other works 1375 ff.; cf. JTS 16, 1965, 26 ff.); translated A. S. T. Haslehurst *The Works of Fastidius* Westminster, Society of SS Peter and Paul, 1927	
Sidonius Apollinaris	*Carmina*; *Epistulae* MGH AA 8; ed. Teubner, etc.	
Simeon of Durham	*Opera Omnia* 2 vols. Rolls 75, 1882–1885; MHB 645; CHE 5; AHS	SD
Solinus	*Collectanea* ed. Mommsen, Berlin 1864; ed. 2 1895; cf. II Walter	
Suetonius	*The Twelve Caesars* ed. Teubner, Loeb etc.	
Sulpicius Severus	*Chronica*; *Dialogi*; *vita Martini* CSEL 1	
Symmachus	*Epistulae*; *Orationes*; *Relationes* MGH AA 6	
Tacitus	*Agricola*; *Annals* ed. Teubner, Loeb etc.	Tac. Ann.
Tertullian	*adversus Iudaeos* CSEL 20; PL 2; ed. A. L. Williams, Cambridge 1935; ed. F. Oehler, Leipzig 1854	
Teubner	*Bibliotheca Scriptorum Graecorum et Romanorum*, Leipzig	

The Tribal Hidage	BCS 297; Rolls 2 ii, 1861, 626; cf. pp. 492–3 above	
Translatio Sancti Alexandri	MGH SS 2, 673	
Trioedd Ynys Prydein	ed. R.Bromwich, Cardiff 1961; cf. WHR Special Number 1963, 82	TYP
Victor of Aquitaine	MGH AA 9 (Chronica Minora 1) 686 ff.	
Victricius	*de Laude Sanctorum* PL 20, 443	
de Virginitate	Jerome Ep. 13 (PL 30, 162 = 18, 77 = 20, 227 = 103, 671)	

VITAE SANCTORUM (Saints' Lives)
see **E** for full references
see also II Dedications

COLLECTIONS OF LIVES

i General

Acta Sanctorum	Brussels 1643 –	ASS
Analecta Bollandiana	Brussels 1882 –	AB
Breviarium Aberdonense	Aberdeen 1509–1510; facsimile London 1854; *Pars Estivalis,* and *Pars Hyemalis*	Brev. Ab PE, PH

See also BHL; CSEL; GCS; MGH; PG; PL

ii Ireland and Scotland

(a) Latin Lives

Acta Sanctorum Hiberniae I	ed. J.Colgan, Louvain 1645, reprint Dublin 1948	ASH
Trias Thaumaturga	(Patrick, Brigit, Columba) ed. J. Colgan, Louvain 1647	TT
Vitae Sanctorum Hiberniae e codice Salmanticensi	ed. C.de Smedt and J.de Backer, Brussels, 1887; ed. W.W.Heist, (*Subsidia Hagiographica* 28), Brussels, 1965. (References are here given to the columns)	Sal.
Vitae Sanctorum Hiberniae	ed. C.Plummer, Oxford 1910	VSH
Lives of the Scottish Saints	ed. J.Pinkerton, London 1789, revised W.M.Metcalfe, 2 vols., Paisley 1889	Pinkerton
The Tripartite Life of Saint Patrick	ed. W.Stokes, Rolls 89, 2 vols., 1887 (*Vita Tripartita*); collection of principal Patrician texts	VT

(b) Irish Language Lives

Lives of the Saints from the Book of Lismore	ed. W.Stokes, Oxford 1890	Lismore Lives
Bethada Naem nErenn (Lives of Irish Saints; in Irish)	ed. C.Plummer, Oxford 1922	BNE
Miscellanea Hagiographica Hibernica	ed. C.Plummer (*Subsidia Hagiographica* 15) Brussels 1925	MHH

See also LH; Martyrologies; O'Hanlon

iii Wales

Vitae Sanctorum Britanniae et Genealogiae	ed. A.W.Wade-Evans, Cardiff 1944	VSBG

See also Doble, LBS

iv Brittany

Les Vies des Saints de Bretagne	ed. A. Le Grand, Morlaix 1636; revised edition, Rennes 1901	AG

See also Cartulaires; Doble; LBS

v England

Nova Legenda Anglie	collected by John of Tynemouth, c. 1340, and John Capgrave, c. 1440, ed. Wynkyn de Worde, 1516; ed. C.Horstman, 2 vols., Oxford 1901	NLA

See also individual Lives below, BHL and **E**

vi Gaul

Vitae Sanctorum	MGH SRM 3–7, 1896–1920
Vitae Patrum and *de Gloria Confessorum*	Gregory of Tours MGH SRM 1, 661
Vitae Sanctorum	in Venantius Fortunatus MGH AA 4

See also Individual Lives below, BHL and **E**

INDIVIDUAL LIVES

Normally only the principal versions are given; page references are not normally given to collections arranged in alphabetical order. The symbol † indicates that the Life is translated in one of the Collections cited below: for full references see **E.**

ABBAN	VSH
AILBE	VSH
ADOMNAN	CPS 408; cf. MHH 179, 2; AIM 2, 10; CR 5, 1908, 97
ALBINUS of Angers	by Venantius MGH 4, 2, 27; PL 88, 479
AMBROSE of Milan	by Paulinus PL 14, 27†
BEUNO	VSBG†; *Arch. Camb.* 1930, 315
BONIFACE	by Willibald PL 89, 603; MGH SS 2, 333; MGH SRG Schol., 1905, 1†
BRENDAN	VSH; cf. C.Selmer *Navigatio Sancti Brendani* Notre Dame, Indiana, 1959†
BRIGIT	TT
CADOC	by Lifris VSBG†; by Caradoc of Llancarfan AB 60, 1942, 45
CADROE	ASS Mart 1, 474; ASH 494; cf. CPS 106, MGH SS 4, 483
CAINNECH	VSH
CARANTOC	VSBG†
CIARAN of Clonmacnoise	VSH
CIARAN of Saigir	VSH; BNE; Sal. 805
COLUMBA of Iona	by Adomnan, ed. W.Reeves, Dublin 1857; also

	A.O. and M.O.Anderson, London 1961; J.T Fowler, Oxford 1894
	by M.O'Donnell TT 389; ZCP 3–5 and 9–11, 1901–1905, 1913–1916; ed. A.O'Kelleher and G.Schoepperle, Urbana, Illinois, 1918
COLUMBA of Terryglass	Sal. 445; cf. AB 72, 1954, 343
COLUMBAN	by Jonas MGH SRM 4, 1
CUTHBERT	by Bede, ed. B.Colgrave *Two Lives of St. Cuthbert* Cambridge 1940†
DAGAEUS	Sal. 891
DAVID	VSBG† ed. J.W.James, Cardiff 1967
DECLAN	VSH; ITS 16
DOCCO	NLA 1, 248; cf. AB 42, 1942, 100; JTS 20, 1918/19, 97, cf. 23, 1921/22, 15
DUBRICIUS	LL 78
ENDA	ASH 704; VSH
FINGAR	AG 812; ASS March 3, 454; ASH 387, cf. PL 159, 325
FINNIAN of Clonard	Sal. 189; ASH 393
FINNIAN of Llancarfan	vita Finnian Clonard, ch. 4–11
FINNIAN of Moville	ASH 634; NLA 1, 444; cf. LH 1, 22; 2, 11
FLANNAN	Sal. 643; AB 46, 1928, 122
FURSEY	Sal. ASH 75; cf. NLA 1, 461, Sal. 77 (Fursey's Vision)
GERALD of Mayo	VSH
GERMANUS of Auxerre	by Constantius MGH SRM 7, 259 (ch. 12–18, 25–27 transcribed by Bede HE 1, 17–21)†
	by Heiric MGH PLAC 3, 421
GILDAS	by Caradoc of Llancarfan, and by a monk of Rhuys MGH AA 13, 91; Williams *Gildas* 322 ff.(†)
GUTHLAC	by Felix, ed. B.Colgrave, Cambridge 1956; ASS April 2, 38; ed. W.de G.Birch, Wisbech 1881
GWENAEL	ASS Nov. 1, 674; AG 670
GWYNLLYW	VSBG†
IBAR	AB 77, 1959, 439; cf. Abban
ILLTUD	VSBG†
ITA	VSH
IUDICAEL	AG 819; cf. Meven
IUDOC	AG 806; Ordericus 3, 13
JOHN THE ALMSGIVER	AB 45, 1927, 19; PG 93, 1614; PL 73, 337; translation E.Dawes and N.Baynes, London, 1948
KEBI	VSBG†
KENTIGERN	by Jocelyn of Furness, Pinkerton 2, 1
LASRIAN (Mo-Laisse) of Devenish	VSH
LEBUINUS	by Hucbald, MGH SS 2, 361; PL 132, 627 ff., 875 ff.†
LEONORUS	ASS July 1, 121 (107)
MARTIN of Tours	by Sulpicius Severus CSEL 1†
MELOR	AB 5, 1886, 166; NLA 2, 183
MEVEN	AB 3, 1884, 142
MOCTEUS	Sal. 903
NINIAN	by Ailred, Pinkerton 1, 9; NLA 2, 218; AHS
OUDOCEUS	LL 130
PATERNUS	VSBG†

I SOURCES

PATRICK	by Muirchu, VT 269; AB 1, 1882, 545; PRIA 52 C 1948/50, 179; *Patrick*, ed. Hood, Chichester, forthcoming
	by Tirechan, VT 302; AB 2, 1883, 35
	Bethu Phatráic, VT 2; ed. K.Mulchrone, Dublin 1939 –
	by Probus, TT 51
	other Lives, TT 1 ff.
	see Kenney 319 ff.; Bieler CPL 16 ff.
PAUL AURELIAN	RC 5, 1881–1883, 417; AB 1, 1882, 209; cf. ASS March 2, 111 (probably by Vitalis of Fleury).
PETROC	AB 74, 1956, 145; NLA 2, 317
RUADAN	VSH
SAMSON	I: ASS July 6, 573; ed. R. Fawtier *La Vie de S. Samson*, Paris (Bibliothèque de l'Ecole des Hautes Etudes 197) 1912; translation T.Taylor, London 1925
	II: AB 6, 1887, 79, cf. 12, 1893, 56
	III, by Baldric: cited in II above
	IV: AG 409
	V: LL 6
	VI: NLA 2, 350
SENAN	Sal.
SEVERINUS	by Eugippius MGH AA 1, 1; SRG 1898; CSEL 9, 2; PL 62, 1167: translation G.W. Robinson, Harvard 1914
TATHEUS	VSBG†
TEILO	LL 97
WENEFRED	VSBG†
WILFRED	by Eddius Stephanus MGH SRM 6; HY 1; ed. B.Colgrave, Cambridge 1927†
WINNOC	(with Audomar) MGH SRM 5, 753; MGH SS 15, 775; cf. PL 147, 1179 ff.
WINWALOE	AB 7, 1888, 172

NAMED AUTHORS OF SAINTS' LIVES

Adomnan	COLUMBA of Iona	Muirchu	PATRICK
Ailred	NINIAN	O'Donell	COLUMBA
Animosus	BRIGIT	Paulinus	AMBROSE
Bede	CUTHBERT	Probus	PATRICK
Caradoc of Llancarfan	CADOC, GILDAS	Ricemarchus	DAVID
Cogitosus	BRIGIT	Stephanus, see Eddius	
Constantius	GERMANUS	Sulpicius Severus	MARTIN
Eddius	WILFRED	Tirechan	PATRICK
Eugippius	SEVERINUS	Ultan	BRIGIT
Felix	GUTHLAC	Vitalis	PAUL AURELIAN
Heiric	GERMANUS	Willebald	BONIFACEN
Jocelyn of Furness	KENTIGERN	Wrdestan	WINWALOE
Jonas	COLUMBAN	Wrmonoc	PAUL AURELIAN
Lifris	CADOC		

WORKS CITED IN THE NOTES

COLLECTIONS IN TRANSLATION include VSBG; BNE: Lismore; C.W.Jones *Saints' Lives and Chronicles in Early England* Cornell 1947; J.F.Webb. *Lives of the Saints* (Brendan, Cuthbert, Wilfred) Penguin, 1965; F.R, Hoare *The Western Fathers* (Martin, Ambrose, Augustine of Hippo, Honoratus, Germanus) London 1954; C.H.Talbot *Anglo-Saxon Missionaries in Germany* (Willibrord, Boniface, Sturm, Leoba, Lebuin) London 1954.

WELSH LITERATURE

ANCIENT POEMS

Author	Work	Abbreviation
J.G.Evans	*The Book of Aneirin* Pwllheli 1908	BA
	The Black Book of Carmarthen Pwllheli 1906	BBC
	The Text of the Book of Taliesin Llanbedrog 1910	BT
	Poetry from the Red Book of Hergest Llanbedrog 1911	RBH
K.H.Jackson	*Early Welsh Gnomic Poems* Cardiff 1935	
A.O.H.Jarman	*Ymddiddan Myrddin a Thaliesin* Cardiff 1951	
W.F.Skene	*Four Ancient Books of Wales* 2 vols. Edinburgh 1868	FAB
Ifor Williams	*Canu Aneirin* Cardiff 1961	CA
	Canu Llywarch Hen Cardiff 1935	CLH
	Canu Taliesin Cardiff 1960	CT
	Armes Prydein Cardiff 1955	AP
	Chwedl Taliesin Cardiff 1957	

BRUTS

Author	Work	Abbreviation
J.G.Evans	*Bruts from the Red Book of Hergest* Oxford 1890	
	cf. *Brut y Tywysogion* Myv. Arch. 685; MHB 841; Rolls 17, 1860	

MABINOGION

Author	Work	Abbreviation
J.G.Evans	*The White Book Mabinogion* Pwllheli 1907	
	Pedeir Keinc y Mabinogi Wrexham 1897	
J.G.Evans and J.Rhys	*The Text of the Mabinogion from the Red Book of Hergest* Oxford 1887	
Ifor Williams	*Pedeir Keinc y Mabinogi* (The Four Branches of the Mabinogion, from the White Book of Rhydderch) Cardiff 1930; cf. THS Cymm 1970, 263	

I SOURCES

TRANSLATIONS include		
Lady Charlotte Guest	*The Mabinogion* text and translation, London 1849, translation reprinted 1877 and Everyman's Library	
Gwyn Jones and Thomas Jones	*The Mabinogion* London 1949	
K.H.Jackson	*The Gododdin* Edinburgh 1969 (translation of CA)	
ANTHOLOGIES include		
E.Williams (Iolo Morgannwg) and others	*The Myvyrian Archaiology of Wales* London 1801; reprint Denbigh 1870 (based on medieval MSS)	Myv. Arch.
T.Williams (Taliesin ab Iolo)	*Iolo Manuscripts* Liverpool 1848, reprint 1888 (almost entirely antiquarian)	Iolo MSS
H.I. and C.I.Bell	*Poems from the Welsh* Caernarvon 1913	
	Welsh Poems of the Twentieth Century in English Verse Wrexham 1925	
A.Conran	*The Penguin Book of Welsh Verse* London 1967	
A.P.Graves	*Welsh Poetry Old and New in English Verse* London 1912	
E.A.Jones	*Welsh Lyrics of the Nineteenth Century* Newport 1907	
ed. T.Parry	*The Oxford Book of Welsh Verse* Oxford 1962	
Gwynn Williams	*The Burning Tree* London 1956	WBT
	Presenting Welsh Poetry London 1959	PWP
Widsith	ed. K.Malone, London 1956, etc.	
William of Malmesbury	PL 179; *de Gestis Regum* Rolls 90, 1887–1889; *de Gestis Pontificum* Rolls 52, 1870	
Anglo-Saxon Wills	ed. D.Whitelock, Cambridge 1950	
Anglo-Saxon Writs	ed. F.E.Harmer, Manchester 1952	
Andrew of Wyntoun	*Original Chronicle of Scotland* ed. F.J.Amours, 6 vols. STS 63, 50, 53, 54, 56, 57, Edinburgh 1903–1914	
Zonaras	*Epitome Historiarum* ed. Teubner; PL 134	
Zosimus	*Historia Nova* ed. L.Mendelsohn, Leipzig, 1887; CSHB ed. B.G. Niebuhr, Bonn 1837 etc.	

II Modern Works

(A few of the works listed below became available after the text matter of this book had been set, but before the notes were printed.)

* Lists of further books and articles are contained in several of the works cited, especially in those marked with a star (*).

* Nils Åberg *The Anglo-Saxons in England* Uppsala 1926 — ASE
L. Alcock *Dinas Powys* Cardiff 1963
L. Alcock *Arthur's Britain* London 1971
A. O. Anderson, see I ESSH
Angles and Britons (O'Donnell Lectures) Cardiff 1963
F. Arnold Foster *Studies in Church Dedications* 3 vols. London 1899 — SCD

A. Bach *Deutsche Namenkunde: II die deutschen Ortsnamen* 2 vols. Heidelberg 1953–1954
* G. Baldwin Brown *The Arts in Early England*, especially vol. 3, London 1915 — BB
S. Baring-Gould *A Book of Brittany* London 1901
S. Baring-Gould and T. Fisher *The Lives of the British Saints* 4 vols., London, 1907–1913 — LBS
* F. W. Bateson *The Cambridge Bibliography of English Literature* Vol. I Cambridge 1940
* A. C. Baugh *A History of the English Language* London 1935, ed. 2 1951
* A. C. Baugh *A Literary History of England* New York and London 1940, reprint 1950
* H. I. Bell *The Development of Welsh Poetry* Oxford 1936
Bibliotheca Hagiographica Latina Brussels 1898–1901, reprint 1949; supplement Brussels 1911 (*Subsidia Hagiographica* 12) — BHL
L. Bieler *Codices Patriciani Latini* Dublin 1942 — CPL
E. G. Bowen *The Settlements of the Celtic Saints in Wales* Cardiff 1954 — SCSW
J. Brøndstedt *Danmarks Oldtid: II Jernaldern* Copenhagen 1940
J. B. Bury *The Life of Saint Patrick* London 1905

W. Camden *Britannia* London 1586; ed. Gibson 1772; ed. R. Gough 1789; also ed. Holland 1610
* J. Carney *The Problem of St. Patrick* Dublin 1961
J. Carney *Studies in Irish Literature and History* Dublin 1955 — SILH
C. P. Caspari *Briefe*: see I Sicilian Briton
Celt and Saxon ed. N. K. Chadwick 1963
H. M. Chadwick *Early Scotland* Cambridge 1949
H. M. Chadwick *Origin of the English Nation* Cambridge 1924 — OEN
H. M. Chadwick, *Studies in Anglo-Saxon Institutions* Cambridge 1905 — SASI
* H. M. and N. K. Chadwick *The Growth of Literature* Cambridge 1932–1940
N. K. Chadwick *The Druids* Cardiff 1966
N. K. Chadwick *Poetry and Letters in Early Christian Gaul* London 1955 — PLECG
N. K. Chadwick, ed. see *Celt and Saxon*; *Studies*
* R. W. Chambers *Beowulf* Cambridge 1932
Christianity in Britain 300–700 ed. M. W. Barley and R. P. C. Hanson, Leicester 1968
The Civitas Capitals of Roman Britain ed. J. S. Wacher, Leicester 1966
* R. R. Clarke *East Anglia* London 1960

II MODERN WORKS

R.Collingwood and J.N.L.Myres *Roman Britain and the English Settlements* Oxford 1937

Fustel de Coulanges *La Monarquie Franque* Paris 1888

S.E.Cruden *The Early Christian and Pictish Monuments of Scotland* (HMSO) Edinburgh 1957, ed. 2 1964 — ECPMS

A.O.Curle *The Treasure of Traprain* Glasgow 1923

Dark Age Britain (Studies presented to E.T.Leeds) ed. D.B.Harden, London 1956 — DAB

Dark Age Dates John Morris, see Jarrett and Dobson pp. 145. ff

P.David *Etudes historiques sur la Galice et le Portugal* Lisbon 1947

E.Davies, ed. *Celtic Studies in Wales* Cardiff 1963 — CSW

P.Delamain *La cimetière barbare d'Herpes* Angoulême 1892

Dictionary of English Place Names ed. E.Ekwall, Oxford 1936; ed. 4, 1960 — DEPN

Dictionary of Christian Biography ed. W.Smith and H.Wace, 4 vols. London 1877–1887 — DCB

* M.Dillon and N.K.Chadwick *The Celtic Realms* London 1967

G.H.Doble *Dedications to Celtic Saints in Normandy* in *Old Cornwall* Summer 1940, 1 ff.

G.H.Doble *The Saints of Cornwall*, 48 booklets, 1923–1944, republished in volumes, Truro 1960–

C.Du Cange *Glossarium Mediae et Infimae Latinitatis* Paris, Niort etc. 1772, 1844, 1886, etc.

L.Duchesne *Fastes Episcopaux de l'ancienne Gaule* 3 vols. Paris 1907–1915

W.Dugdale *Monasticon Anglicanum* 3 vols. London 1655–1673; ed. 2., 6 vols., London 1817–1830

F.Duine *Saint Samson* Rennes 1909

F.Duine *Notes sur les saints bretons* Rennes 1902

H.J.Eggers *Der römische Import im freien Germanien* (Atlas der Urgeschichte 1) Hamburg 1951

T.P.Ellis *Welsh Tribal Law and Custom in the Middle Ages* 2 vols. Oxford 1926

English Place Name Elements A.H.Smith EPNS 25–26 Cambridge 1956 — EPNE

English Place Name Society Survey by counties, Cambridge 1924– — EPNS

The counties published are Beds., Bucks., Cambs., Cheshire, Cumberland, Derby, Devon, Essex, Gloucester, Hertfordshire, Hunts., Middlesex, Northants., Notts., Oxon., Surrey, Sussex, Warwick, Westmorland, Wiltshire, Worcestershire, Yorkshire.

Other studies of counties not yet published in the Survey include *Berkshire* W.W.Skeat, Oxford 1911; *Dorset* A Fägersten, Uppsala 1933; *Durham* see Northumberland; *Herefordshire* A.J.Bannister, Cambridge 1916; *Isle of Wight* H.Kökeritz, Uppsala 1940; *Kent* J.K.Wallenberg, Uppsala 1931, 1934; *Lancashire* E.Ekwall, Manchester 1922; *Northumberland and Durham* A.Mawer, Cambridge 1920; *Shropshire* E.W.Bowcock, Shrewsbury 1923; *Staffordshire* H.Duignan, London 1902; *Suffolk* W.W.Skeat, Cambridge 1913. — PNK

Most of these studies are less comprehensive than the Survey volumes.

The counties for which no considerable published survey is available are Cornwall, Hampshire, Leicestershire (cf. Philological Society Transactions 1917–1920, 57–78), Lincolnshire, Norfolk, Rutland and Somerset.

For Place Names in France, see Gröhler; in Germany, see Bach; Scandinavian names have been extensively studied, but virtually no work has been done on Slavonic place names, save for a few isolated regions of Germany.

Excavations at Richborough 5, SAL Report 23, Oxford 1968

E.Faral *La Légende Arthurienne* (Bibliothèque de l'Ecole des Hautes Etudes 257) Paris 1929
Feil-Sgribhinn Eoin mhic Néill (MacNeill Essays) Dublin 1940
H.P.R.Finberg *The Agrarian History of England* Vol. 1, 1972
H.P.R.Finberg *Lucerna* London 1964; see also 1 Charters
A.P.Forbes *Kalendars of the Scottish Saints* Edinburgh 1872
Sir Cyril Fox *The Personality of Britain* Cardiff 1932; ed. 4, 1943
Sir Cyril Fox *The Archaelogy of the Cambridge Region* Cambridge 1923, revised 1948 — ACR
* S.S.Frere *Britannia* London 1967

* A.Genrich *Formenkreise und Stammesgruppen in Schleswig-Holstein* Neümunster 1954
R.L.Green *King Arthur* Puffin Story Books 1955
S.B.Greenfield *A Critical History of Old English Literature* New York 1965, London 1966 (reprint 1968)
H.Gröhler *Ursprung und Bedeutung der französischen Ortsnamen* Heidelberg 1913–1937

* Isabel Henderson *The Picts* London 1967
T.Hodgkin *Italy and her Invaders* 8 vols. Oxford 1880–1899
E.Hogan *Onomasticon Goedelicum* Dublin 1910
W.G.Hoskins *The Westward Expansion of Wessex* Leicester 1960 — WEW
V.Hruby *Staré Mesto* (Momumenta Archaeologica 14) Prague 1965
* K.Hughes *The Church in Early Irish Society* London 1966 — CEIS
M.R.Hull *Roman Colchester* SAL Report 20, Colchester 1957

K.H.Jackson *Language and History in Early Britain* Edinburgh 1953 — LHEB
K.H.Jackson *The Oldest Irish Tradition; a Window on the Iron Age* (Rede Lecture) Cambridge 1964 — OIT
K.H.Jackson *The International Popular Tale* (Gregynog Lecture) Cardiff 1961
H.Jankuhn *Geschichte Schleswig-Holsteins* 3 vols. Hamburg 1957
M.G.Jarrett and B.Dobson (ed.) *Britain and Rome* (Essays Presented to Eric Birley) Kendal 1966
H.Jedin and others *Atlas zur Kirchengeschichte* Freiburg-im-Breisgau 1970
E.John *Land Tenure in Early England* Leicester 1960
J.E.A.Jolliffe *Pre-Feudal England* Oxford 1933, reprint 1962 — PFE
* A.H.M.Jones *The Later Roman Empire* Blackwell, Oxford 1964 — LRE
P.W.Joyce *A Social History of Ancient Ireland* 3 vols. Dublin 1913

J.M.Kemble *The Saxons in England* London 1848, revised edition ed. W.de G. Birch 1876 — SE
T.Kendrick *The Druids* London 1928
J.F.Kenney *The Sources for the Early History of Ireland* 1, Ecclesiastical (all published), New York 1929, reprint Dublin 1969
W.P.Ker *The Dark Ages* London 1904, reprint New York 1958
D.Knowles *Great Historical Enterprises* London 1963
* M.L.W.Laistner *Thought and Letters in Western Europe* London 1931
E.T.Leeds *The Archaeology of the Anglo Saxon Settlements* Oxford 1913 — AASS
E.T.Leeds *A Corpus of Anglo-Saxon Great Squareheaded Brooches* Oxford 1949

II MODERN WORKS

E.T.Leeds *The Distribution of Anglo-Saxon Saucer Brooches* in *Arch.* 63 1911/12, 159 ff. DSB
Lefebvre des Noëttes *L'Attelage et le Cheval* Paris 1931
* J.E.Lloyd *History of Wales* 2 vols. London 1912 HW
* H.R.Loyn *Anglo-Saxon England and the Norman Conquest* London 1962
* E.Löfstedt *Philologische Kommentar zur Peregrinatio Aetheriae* Darmstadt 1962

* J.M.MacKinlay *Ancient Church Dedications in Scotland* 2 vols. Edinburgh 1910–1914 ACDS
Eoin MacNeill *Celtic Ireland* Dublin 1921
Eoin MacNeill *Phases of Irish History* Dublin 1920
MacNeill Essays see *Feil-Sgribhinn*
* *Magna Moravia* University of Brno, Faculty of Philosophy Publications 102, Prague 1965
F.W.Maitland *Domesday Book and Beyond* Cambridge 1897, reprint (Fontana) London 1960 DBB
* M.Manitius *Gesichte der lateinischen Literatur des Mittelalters* Munich 1911–1931
H.I.Marrou *A History of Education in Antiquity* London 1956
H.I.Marrou *St. Augustin et la fin de la culture antique*, ed. 2 Paris 1958
C.L.Matthews *Ancient Dunstable* Dunstable 1963
* A.Meaney *Gazateer of Early Anglo-Saxon Burial Sites* London 1964
* R.Merrifield *The Roman City of London* London 1965
K.Meyer *Learning in Ireland in the Fifth Century* Dublin 1913
C.de Montalembert *Les Moines d'Occident* 7 vols. Paris 1860; English edition, *The Monks of the West* London 1861
* L.Musset *Les Invasions, les Vagues germaniques* (Nouvelle Cleo 12) Paris 1965
J.N.L.Myres *Romano-Saxon Potters* DAB 66 ff.
* J.N.L.Myres *Anglo-Saxon Pottery* Oxford 1969 ASP

Eugene O'Curry *Lectures on the Manuscript Materials of Ancient Irish History* Dublin 1861
J.O'Hanlon *Lives of the Irish Saints* 8 vols. Dublin 1875–
T.F.O'Rahilly *The Two Patricks* Dublin 1957
T.F.O'Rahilly *Early Irish History and Mythology* Dublin 1946 EIHM
Ordnance Survey *Map of Dark Age Britain* Southampton, ed. 1, 1936; ed. 2, Chessington 1966
Ordnance Survey *Map of Roman Britain* ed. 3 Chessington 1956
* A.Ll.Owen *The Famous Druids* Oxford 1962

* T.Parry (translated H.I.Bell) *A History of Welsh Literature* Oxford 1962 HWL
S.Pender *Essays and Studies presented to Tadg Ua Donnchadha* Cork 1947
G.de Plinval *Pélage* Lausanne 1943
* A.Plettke *Ursprung und Ausbreitung der Angeln und Sachen* Hildesheim 1921
* F.Pollock and F.W.Maitland *History of English Law* Cambridge 1895; ed. 2 revised 1968
H.Preidel *Slawische Altertumskunde des Ostlaender Mitteleuropas in den 9ten und 10ten Jahrhunderten* Munich 1961
* *The Prosopography of the Later Roman Empire* ed. A.H.M.Jones, J.R.Martindale, J.Morris, Cambridge, Vol. 1, 1971, Vols. 2 and 3 forthcoming PLRE

Recueil de Travaux offerts a M.Clovis Brunel Paris 1955

* A.L.F.Rivet (ed.) *The Iron Age in Northern Britain* Edinburgh 1966 — IANB
J.H.Round *Studies in Peerage and Family History* London 1901
Royal Commission on Historical Monuments, County Series — RCHM

* B.Salin *Die altgermanische Tierornamentik* Stockholm and Berlin 1904
* E.Salin *La Civilisation Mérovingienne* 4 vols. Paris 1949–1959
* P.H.Sawyer *Anglo-Saxon Charters* London 1968 (RHS Handbook 8)
L.Schmidt *Allgemeine Geschichte der germanischen Völker* Munich and Berlin 1909
G.Schoepperle *Tristan and Isolt* Frankfurt and London 1913
F.Seebohm *The English Village Community* London 1883 — EVC
F.Seebohm *The Tribal System in Wales* London 1904 — TSW
F.Seebohm *Tribal Custom in Anglo-Saxon Law* London 1911 — TCASL
R.C.Shaw *Post-Roman Carlisle* Preston 1964
W.D.Simpson *The Celtic Church in Scotland* Aberdeen 1935
W.F.Skene *Celtic Scotland* 3 vols. Edinburgh 1876–1880 — CS
W.F.Skene, cf. 1 CPS above
T.C.Smout *A History of the Scottish People 1560–1830* London 1969
* F.M.Stenton *Anglo-Saxon England* Oxford 1943 — ASE
C.E.Stevens *Sidonius Apollinaris* Oxford 1933
W.Stokes and K.Mayer ed. *Archiv für Celtische Lexicographie* Halle 1900–1907 — ACI
Studies in the Early British Church ed. N.K.Chadwick, Cambridge 1958 — SEBC
Studies in Early British History ed. N.K.Chadwick, Cambridge 1959 — SEBH
* B.Svoboda *Cechy v Dobé Stehování Národů* (Bohemia in the Migration Period) (Monumenta Archaeologica 13) Prague 1965

E.A.Thompson *The Early Germans*, Oxford, 1965
R.Thurneysen and others *Studies in Early Irish Law* Dublin 1936 — SEIL
F.Tischler *Der Stand der Sachsenforschung* (35 Bericht der Römisch-Germanischen Kommission) 1956, 21 ff.
J.H.Todd *St. Patrick, Apostle of Ireland* Dublin 1864
Torna Festschrift see Pender

Victoria County History of the Counties of England, County Volumes — VCH
P.Vinogradoff *The Growth of the Manor* London 1911 — GM

* F.T.Wainwright (ed.) *The Problem of the Picts* Edinburgh 1955 — PP
H.Walter *Die Collectanea . . des . . Solinus* (Hermes Einzelschrift 22) Wiesbaden 1969
W.J.Watson *The History of the Celtic Place-Names of Scotland* Edinburgh 1926 — CPNS
J.Werner *Münzdatierte Austrasische Grabfünde* Berlin 1935
G.K.Whitehead *The Ancient White Cattle of Britain* London 1953
G.K.Whitehead *Ancient White Cattle* London 1963
H.Willers *die roemischen Bronzeeimer von Hemmoor* Hamburg 1900
* Gwynn Williams *An Introduction to Welsh Poetry* London 1953 — IWP
M.Winterbottom *Gildas* Chichester, forthcoming
C.L.Wrenn *A Study of Old English Literature* London 1967

III Periodicals

Alt Thüringen 1953/4	
Analecta Bollandiana 1882 –	AB
Annales de Normandie 1951 –	
Antiquaries Journal 1921 –	Ant. Jl.
Antiquity 1927 –	Ant.
Archaeologia 1773 –	Arch.
Archaeologia Aeliana 1822 –	Arch. Ael.
Archaeologia Cambrensis 1846 –	Arch. Camb.
Archaeological Journal 1845 –	Arch. Jl.
Bedfordshire Archaeological Journal 1962 –	Beds. Arch. Jl.
Beiträge zur Namenforschüng n.f. 1966 –	
Berkshire Archaeological Journal 1895 –	Berks. Arch. Jl.
Britannia 1970 –	
Bulletin of the Institute of Classical Studies 1954 –	BICS
Bulletin of the Board of Celtic Studies 1921 –	BBCS
Cambridge Antiquarian Society Proceedings 1840 –	CASP
Celtica 1903 –	
Celtic Review 1904 –	CR
Current Archaeology 1967 –	CArch
Economic History Review 1922 –	ECHR
English Historical Review 1886 –	EHR
Eriu 1904 –	
Hertfordshire Archaeology 1968 –	
Journal of the British Archaeological Association 1846 –	JBAA
Journal of Celtic Studies 1949–	JCS
Journal of the English Place Names Society 1969 –	JEPN
Journal of Roman Studies 1911 –	JRS
Journal of the Royal Institution of Cornwall n.s. 1951–	JRIC
Journal of the Royal Society of Antiquaries of Ireland 1870 –	JRSAI
Journal of Theological Studies 1900 –	JTS
Lochlann 1961 –	
Medieval Archaeology 1957 –	MA
Norfolk Archaeology 1847 –	
Northern History 1966 –	
Notes and Queries 1849 –	
Numismatic Chronicle 1881 –	NC
Past and Present 1952 –	P and P
Proceedings of the Prehistoric Society 1934 –	PPS
Proceedings of the Royal Irish Academy 1837 –	PRIA
Proceedings of the Society of Antiquaries of London 1849 –	PSA
Proceedings of the Society of Antiquaries of Scotland 1852 –	PSAS
Revue Celtique 1870/72 –	RC
Rheinisches Museum 1827 –	
Somersetshire Archaeological and Natural History Society Proceedings 1851 –	SANHS
Speculum 1926–	
Studia Hibernica 1961 –	
Surrey Archaeological Collections 1854 –	SyAC
Traditio 1943–	
Transactions of the Honourable Society of Cymmrodorion 1[illegible]92/3–	THSCymm

Transactions of the Royal Historical Society	1868 –	TRHS
Transactions of the Royal Irish Academy	1787 –	TRIA
Welsh History Review	1960 –	WHR
Y Cymmrodor	1877–1935	YC
Zeitschrift für Celtische Philologie	1897 –	ZCP

BIBLIOGRAPHICAL NOTE

It is not yet possible to attempt a comprehensive bibliography of the period. Considerable lists of books, relevant to their own subject, are printed in many of the Collections of Sources given in I above, in the source surveys and in the works starred in II above, and also in

A.O.Anderson *Adomnan's Columba* see *I Vitae* above
P.H.Blair *An Introduction to Anglo-Saxon England* Cambridge 1956
R.Bromwich TYP see I above
W.Bonser *An Anglo-Saxon and Celtic Bibliography* Berkeley California 1957
J. Brøndstedt *The Vikings* Penguin 1960
Jan Filip *Celtic Civilisation and Its Heritage* Prague 1960
R.H.Hodgkin *A History of the Anglo-Saxons* Oxford 1935
T.G.E.Powell *The Celts* London 1958
A. and B.Rees *Celtic Heritage* London 1961
C.Selmer *Navigatio Brendani;* see I *Vitae* above
D.M.Wilson *The Anglo-Saxons* Harmondsworth 1971
and in numerous other publications.

NOTES

The notes aim to indicate the main sources relevant to each subject discussed. Space prevents discussion of many of the possible alternative interpretations that could be based upon them.

Proper names are themselves references, since they are discussed and indexed in *Arthurian Sources;* whose relevant sections, listed on p. 519 above, are here cited for many of the more important persons, places and subjects.

Introduction

xv.2 BIELER: *Irish Ecclesiastical Record* 1967, 2.

xv.3 GILDAS, NENNIUS, PATRICK: text and translation, ed. M.Winterbottom; J.Morris; A.B.C.Hood, Phillimore, forthcoming.

xv.3 ARTHURIAN SOURCES: Phillimore 1973 –.

xvii.2 CHADWICK: *Growth of Literature* I, xix.

1 Britain in 350 (pp. 1–9)

1.1 ARMED CONFLICT: see **R.**

2.1 CLAUDIAN: *de Laudibus Stilichonis* 3, 150–153.

2.3 CIVITAS, VICI, PAGI: see **R.**

3.3 INVASIONS, DEVASTATION, FRONTIERS: see **R.**

4.1 AUSONIUS: his estate, *de Herediolo* 29 ff.; his uncle, *Professores Burdigalenses* 17, cf. *Parentalia* 5; his father, *Parentalia* 3, *Epicedion*, etc.

4.3 PHILO: Ausonius *Ep.* 22.

5.1 IUGUM: the evidence is summarised by Jones LRE 62 ff.; the assessment varied from province to province, and was sometimes by area. In Syria, a *iugum* was reckoned at 40 *iugera* (about 25 acres) of average land, 20 of good land, 60 of poor land. The calculation of the British *iugum* is not known.

5.2 DIOCESE: see **R.**

5.2 MILITARY COMMANDERS: see **R.**

5.2 GARRISONS: see **R.**

5.3 GEOGRAPHY: see **R**, and Fox *Personality of Britain.*

6.2 PEASANTRY: see especially Jones LRE 774 ff.

8.1 BACAUDA: see especially E.A.Thompson in *P and P* 2, 1952, 11 ff.

9.3 AUSONIUS: *Mosella* 389 ff.

2 Ending of the Western Empire (pp. 10–28)

10.1 MAGNENTIUS: see PLRE I.

10.1 ALAMANNI: Ammian 16, 12, 4; cf. Zosimus 2, 53.

10.1 MURSA: casualties rated at 54,000, Zonaras 13, 8.

2 THE ENDING OF THE WESTERN EMPIRE (pp. 10–23)

10.2 CONSTANTIUS AT MURSA: Sulpicius Severus *Chron.* 2, 38, 5–7.

11.1 CONSTANTIUS' INQUISITION: Ammian 14, 5, 2–9.

12.1 TOIL AND SWEAT: Barnabas 10.

12.1 BARREN ELM: Hermas 3, 2.

12.1 IRENAEUS: *adversus Haereseos* 4, 46.

12.3 CHRISTIAN COMMUNITIES: see Duchesne *Fastes Episcopaux* 1, 31–32; Lyon, Paris, Sens, Rouen, Reims, Metz, Bordeaux, Bourges and Toulouse, with Arles and Vienne in Provence, Trier and Cologne in the Rhineland, are the known pre-Constantinian bishoprics; cf. Greg. Tur. HF 10, 31, and p. 335 below.

13.2 ARIAN CONTROVERSY: the clearest concise account, here cited, is that of Sulpicius Severus *Chron.* 2, 38 ff.

14.1 AUGURIUS: see **E**.

15.2 RAIDS: in 360 and 364, Ammian 20, 1 and 26, 4, 5; in 367, Ammian 27, 8 and 28, 3, 7–8.

15.3 COUNTRY HOUSES: notably Park Street near St. Albans, and Norton Disney on the borders of Lincolnshire and Nottinghamshire, see **R**.

15.3 LONDON: see **L**.

16.2 NIALL: see **G** INA and p. 157 below.

16.3 AREANI: variant *Arcani*.

16.3 YORKSHIRE SIGNAL TOWERS: see p. 51.2 below.

16.3 ANTICIPATORS: *Not. Dig.* Occ. 40, 31 *Praefectus numeri Supervenientium*

17.2 *Petueriensium, Derventione*.

17.2 CRIMTHANN: see **G** IML, and p. 157 below.

17.2 BRITAIN, CHANNEL: see **L** Alba, Icht.

17.2 IRISH COLONIES: see **L**.

17.2 VALENTIA: see **L**.

17.3 PATROL UNITS: *Exploratores* at Risingham and Rochester, *Raeti Gaesati* at Risingham and Cappuck, RIB 1235, 1243–4, 1262, 1270, 1217, 2117. Neither the forts nor troops of north-eastern Northumberland have yet been identified; see **R**.

17.4 NORTHERN LISTS: see **G** introduction, and BA, BN.

18.1 THEODOSIUS . . . AFRICA: Ammian 29, 5, 35.

18.1 AUGUSTINE: *Ep.* 199, 46: cf. Jones LRE 652 and note.

18.2 FRAOMAR: Ammian 29, 4, 7, *potestate tribuni Alamannorum praefecit numero*. He was doubtless *tribunus gentis Alamannorum*, analogous to the *tribunus gentis Marcomannorum* in Pannonia Prima, *Not. Dig.*, Occ. 34, 24. The *vir tribunitiae potestatis* whom Germanus met in 429 (Constantius ch. 15) was perhaps a similar *Tribunus gentis*.

18.3 DEMETIA: see **G** BD.

18.3 PATRICK: *Ep.*, 2.

19.2 SYMMACHUS: *Oratio* 4, 6.

20.2 GRATIAN: Rufinus HE 11, 13; Ausonius *Gratiarum Actio* 14. Ammian 31, 10, 18 compares him with Commodus.

20.2 MAXIMUS: see **P**, and PLRE 1 Maximus 39.

20.2 BRITTANY: see p. 250 below.

21.5 UNITS: Claudian *de bello Getico* 414 ff.

21.5 LEGION: the *Notitia Dignitatum* omits the 20th, but names the other legions of Britain.

23.2 JEROME: *Commentary on Ezekiel*, Prologue, and preface to book 3.

23.2 YOUNG BRITON: Sicilian Briton (see **E** and pp. 340 ff. below) *Ep.* 1, 1 (PL Sup. 1, 1687 ff.).

23.5 AMMIAN: 27, 3, 14.

24.3 EFFICIENT HEAD: e.g., Ambrose *Ep.* 11, 4 *totius orbis Romani caput Romana ecclesia.*

25.2 EUSEBIUS: Ambrose *Ep.* 63, 66.

25.3 MATTERS OF FINANCE: Ambrose *Ep.* 40, 27.

25.3 OLD TESTAMENT: Ambrose *Ep.* 20, 23.

25.3 MILAN: Ambrose *Ep.* 20, cf. 21 (*contra Auxentium*); Augustine *Confessio* 9, 7; Paulinus *vita Ambrosii* 13.

26.1 THESSALONICA: see especially Ambrose *Ep.* 51, 6 ff.

26.2 MARTIN: Sulpicius Severus; ELECTION *vita Martini* 9, cf. *Dialogi* 1, 26, 3; SCHOOL *vita* 10; AMATOR *Dialogi* 3, 1, 4; VICTRICIUS *Dial.* 3, 2, 4; CLERGY ALONE *Dial.* 1, 26, 3; VALENTINIAN *Dial.* 2, 5, 5; LAY JUDGE *Chron.* 2, 50, 5; BANQUET *vita* 20, 2; 20, 5–7.

27.3 SAME MOUTH: Gregory the Great *Ep.* 11, 34.

28 1 MARCELLINUS: *Chronicle* AD 454, on the assassination of Aëtius.

3 **Independent Britain: The Evidence** (pp.29–43)

29.1 HONORIUS' LETTER: Zosimus 6, 10; cf. **H**.

29.2 PROVINCIAL COUNCIL: see **H** and **R**.

30.5 COINS: see **R**.

31.5 ARCHAEOLOGY OF THE BRITISH: see **M**.

32.2 PAGAN ENGLISH: see also **S**.

32.2 PLETTKE: *Ursprung* 65 dates the migrations to Britain to some time before 441/442, citing L. Schmidt *Allgemeine Geschichte* 159 ff., who rightly based his conclusions on the Chronicle of 452 (p. 38 below). Plettke uses this date as a main criterion for the dating of German pottery and brooches; cf. e.g. pp. 44–45 where the latest forms of vessels of Type A 6 are prolonged 'perhaps into the early 5th century' because they are occasionally found in England, and type A 7 is centred on the early 5th century both because it derives from A 6 and because 'diese Form besonders haüfig in England gefunden ist und die Hauptüberwanderung der Angelsachsen doch wohl mit Sicherheit in die erste Hälfte des 5. Jahrhunderts zu setzen ist.' In general, Plettke's dating, and the reasoning behind it, remain the basis of modern German archaeological dates; so Tischler *Sachsenforschung* 41 'Unsere Chronologie . . . weicht letzten Endes nur wenig von der Anschauung Plettkes ab.' German estimates of Anglian and Saxon burial dates about the Elbe still ultimately derive from the Chronicler of 452; the notion that there exist independent 'German dates', which can be used to guide dates in Britain, is an illusion.

33.1 BROOCHES: see **S**

33.1 CRUCIFORM BROOCHES: cf. p. 269 below. The most useful study is still that of Åberg ASE 28 ff. The principal corrections are that Åberg's starting date is a generation too late; his groups III and IV are contemporary; and the border lines between groups need adjustment by closer attention to the foot of the brooch. The term 'cruciform' is restricted to the series of brooches that begin with Åberg's group I; it excludes the prototype brooches found at Dorchester, Beetgum and elsewhere, and also 'small long' brooches, sometimes miscalled cruciform.

33.1 SAUCER BROOCHES: see especially Åberg ASE 16 ff.; Leeds DSB; SyAC 56, 1959, 80 ff.; cf. p. 269 below, and **S**.

33.2 AFTER 400: until recently unnecessary uncertainty has bedevilled modern

English, but not German discussions of the date when the first pagan cemeteries came into use. Bede's date of '450' (p. 39 below) was long repeated without examination; an equally untenable date of about 360 has been advanced by Myres ASP 71 ff. The argument stresses some vessels that 'on the Continent are dated in the fourth or at latest the early years of the fifth century', i.e. about 400, not 360. Such relatively small numbers do not date cemeteries. Most migrating or conquering peoples bring with them a small proportion of objects that are at least a generation old; the Roman conquest of AD 43 brought with it a number of Arretine and other pots that were then 20 or 30 years old, but these vessels do not alter the date of the Roman invasion; and early English graves in Britain also contained a few brooches, as well as pots, that were fashionable in Germany about 400. A proportion of objects about 30 or 40 years old forms a necessary part of the furniture of cemeteries first used about 430. The extreme date of 360 appears to rest chiefly on a single vessel, typologically intermediate between one dated in continental English territory to the 3rd century and another of the early 5th century, and is for that reason placed halfway between, 'no later than the second half of the fourth century'. A vessel with so frail a date is not enough to alter the date of a national migration by two generations.

Equally important is the evidence of what is not found in Britain. Brooches that in Germany are normally dated to the later fourth century, notably the prototypes of the cruciform brooch, of the Beetgum or Dorchester-on-Thames pattern, and the latest Germanic 'crossbow' forms, have not yet been discovered in pagan Saxon cemeteries in England; and those that date to 'about 400', notably the 'equal arm, series 2' and the 'tutulus', are very rare; two of the former and one of the latter are known. The essence of the matter however is that the ultimate criterion that persuades German scholars to date a pot or brooch to the fourth century or to the early fifth is whether or not its parallel has been found in England. In general, the continental dates fit the rest of the evidence because they rest on the assumption that the pagan cemeteries of England began in the early fifth century; that assumption is securely grounded because it is based on the contemporary statement of the Chronicler of 452, reported by Schmidt, and adopted from him by Plettke. The dating based upon it has stood the test of time.

33.3 CHIP CARVED: or *Kerbschnitt*, cf. p. 51 below.

33.3 SCANDINAVIA ... DATING: the chief independent means of dating are gold bracteates (medallions) and coin hoards, from the late 5th century; but as yet they give few dates to other objects.

34.1 HALF A DOZEN PERIODS: based chiefly on cruciform brooches, the periods are A, 430/470: B, 460/500: C, 490/530: D, 510/590, subdivided into D 1, 510/540; D 2, 530/560; D 3, 550/590; E 570/610; F, 7th century. Maps 3, 6, 18, 21 and 22 (pp. 59, 107, 285, 297, 305) show the sites and areas where burials began in these periods. A number of sites on the margins of periods might alternatively be shown on the succeeding or preceding maps.

34.1 COINS: e.g. J.Werner *Münzdatierte Austrasische Grabfünde.*

34.1 WEAPONS: e.g. the axe termed 'francisca' is found in dated Frankish graves from the early 5th century, and might in theory be as early in Kent. Though it has not yet been reported in dated English graves before the later 6th century, it has sometimes been treated as though it were by itself evidence of a 5th century date in Britain. In general, dates assigned to weapons as yet inspire little confidence.

34.1 PURE TYPOLOGY: e.g. Harden's important study of glass vessels paid 'little or no attention to the evidence of associated objects. The omission is deliberate' (DAB 139). The neglect of evidence is in some particulars troublesome; the largest class of vessels (Cone beakers III a i and Claw beakers II a) are assigned by typology to the 5th and early 6th centuries, but have not yet been found in dated graves earlier than the mid or late 6th century, cf. MA 2, 1958, 37; SyAC 59, 1959, 115.

34.1 ANIMAL ORNAMENT: the fundamental work is Salin *Tierornamentik*. Animals clearly represented, mostly in the late 4th and earlier 5th centuries, present fewer problems; abstract motifs, part animal and part otherwise, tread upon uncertainties.

34.2 RECENT STUDIES: notably Meaney *Gazeteer*, that for the first time pulls together all known sites, though the information, dates and grid reference locations require close examination; Myres ASP is an important preliminary to a full corpus of the pottery, though the starting date of c. 360 is not tenable (p. 33.2 above). Hawkes and Dunning *Soldiers and Settlers* MA 5, 1961, 1 ff. have made a new and important class of object available for study, though it is still over easy for the unwary to treat late Roman metal as 'Germanic'.

35.2 BRITISH AUTHORS: especially Pelagius, Fastidius, the Sicilian Briton and his colleagues, with Patrick and Faustus of Riez, see **E**, and JTS 16, 1965, 26 ff. and pp. 338 ff. below.

35.5 GILDAS: see **T** and **E**.

36.2 ROMANS: Gildas 18, 1.

36.3 WHIPS: Gildas 7, 1.

37.1 ARMED FORCES: Gildas 14, 1.

37.2 NO EARLIER AGE: Gildas 21, 2 cf. p. 70 below.

37.2 COUNCILLORS: Gildas 23, 1.

37.2 AMBROSIUS: Gildas 25, 2 ff. cf. pp. 48 and 95 below.

37.3 NENNIUS: see **T**. The Kentish Chronicle, ch. 31, 36–38 and 43–46; the Chronographer, ch. 66.

38.2 CHRONICLE OF 452: see **T**.

38.2 ANOTHER . . . ALLUSION: in asserting his suzerainty over the Germanic peoples of Europe, in 448, Attila the Hun claimed to rule the 'Ocean Islands', evidently Britain, (Priscus, FHG 4, 90, Fragment 8); his claim implies that he then regarded the island as under German control, cf. C.E. Stevens EHR 56, 1941, 263.

38.3 BRITISH VICTORIES: Zosimus 6, 5, cited p. 70 below; cf. **H**.

38.4 MIGRATION: Sidonius *Ep*. 3, 9; Jordanes *Getica* 45; Greg. Tur. HF 2, 18; Mansi 7, 941; see **E** Mansuetus, and p. 90.5 below.

39.1 WHEN THEY DIED: Gildas 26, 3.

39.1 BADON: see **B** and p. 112 below.

39.2 AETIUS: Gildas 20, cf. **F**.

39.3 BEDE: see **E**.

40.1 BEDE . . . AETIUS . . . DATE: see **T**. Bede also corrected the error in the manuscripts of the Chronicle. He inserted the year date, '23rd year of Theodosius' into the middle of the entry, though it is placed at about Theodosius' 10th year. The correction was emphasised by the insertion of a correct date, the '8th year of Theodosius' at the end of the preceding entry. Elsewhere in Bede's Chronicle year dates are very rare, and are placed after the opening words of the entry, and at the right place in the sequence of events. The evidence is discussed in *Dark Age Dates* 152 ff., where however the date '443/4' on p. 154 is a misprint for 453/4; see also **T**.

40.2 SAXON CHRONICLE: see **T**.

41.2 BRITISH: some confusion arises from the use of 'Breton'. In English, its meaning is restricted to the British who have retained their national name in France, in Brittany. It is a valid modern geographical term, for the British of Brittany have long been sundered from Britain, save in their language. But when the word is applied to their 5th and 6th century ancestors, it implies a separation that had not yet occurred. The British who settled in Roman Armorica and gave it the modern name of Brittany were as fully British as their relatives at home; and were numerous elsewhere in northern France, not yet confined to Brittany.

41.2 COMBROGI, CYMRY: see p. 98, and **L.**

41.3 ANGLES, SAXONS: see **L**; cf. p. 311.

41.3 WEST SAXONS: Jutish and Saxon ornament is prominent in the early graves of the West and South Saxons, but not of the East Saxons. The earliest name of the West Saxons was however *Gewissae*, or Confederates, and the term Middle Saxons is not known before the late 7th century. The name did not arise from a belief that the southern English were descended from the Saxons of Germany rather than the 'Angles'; its use created that belief; cf. p. 294 below.

42.1 CONTINENTAL ORIGIN: cf. p. 269.

42.2 ANGLO-SAXON: see **L**; in 1865 Earle published *Two Saxon Chronicles Parallel*, not 'Anglo-Saxon', and Kemble published *The Saxons in England* in 1848. The titles were retained in revised editions in 1896 and 1876. The hybrid term was used earlier, but plain 'Saxon' lingered long.

42.3 SCOT: the origin of the Latin word is not known. It was not used in the Irish language.

42.3 PICT, CRUITHNI: see **L** and pp. 186 ff. below.

43.2 PERIODS: outlined in *Dark Age Dates* 1966; summarised Frere *Britannia* 1967, 381 ff.; cf. 'phases' Myres ASP 1969, 63 ff.

4 Independent Britain: Vortigern (pp. 44–70)

44.1 THE BRITISH: Zosimus 6, 5, probably citing Olympiodorus and other contemporaries, cf. **H.**

44.2 HORDES: Gildas 19, 1–4.

44.2 NATH – I: Yellow Book of Lecan 192 b 25, cited Watson CPNS 192, cf. Book of Leinster 190[a] 27 (4,836); cf. O'Curry 591. All that remains is the title of a lost tale.

45.1 IRISH SETTLEMENT: see **L** Dal Riada, Maps 7, p. 128; 25, p. 362; and p. 158 below.

45.2 HOMILY: *de vita Christiana*, PL 4, 1031 ff., ascribed to Fastidius in one MS; Augustine quotes a copy that had reached Sicily by 412, cf. JTS 16, 1965, 32 ff.; see **T** Fastidius.

45.2 FASTIDIUS: Gennadius *de Viris Inlustribus* 56; see **E.**

45.2 FASTIDIUS: *de Vita Christiana* 11 and 14.

48.2 PROCOPIUS: BV 1, 2.

48.2 KINGS ANOINTED: Gildas 21, 4.

48.2 AMBROSIUS: see p. 95 below.

48.3 SICILIAN BRITON: *Ep.* 2 *opto te semper Deo vivere et perpetui consulatus honore gaudere.* For the imagery, cf. Prudentius *Peri Stephanon* 2, 559–560 *quem Roma caelestis sibi Legit perennem consulem*, on St. Lawrence. The Saint earned office in heaven by martyrdom; the unchristian British magistrate's only qualification was earthly office, that reformed conduct might perpetuate in heaven. The metaphor is pointless unless he were a consul.

48.3 CONSUL: the elder Ambrosius is also called *unus de consulibus Romanicae gentis* in the fable of the dragons on Snowdon, Nennius 42. The fable is older than medieval usage of the word, and the title therefore may derive from early tradition.

49.3 NOTITIA DIGNITATUM: see **T.**

49.4 COMMANDS: *Comes Britanniarum* listed in *Not. Dig.* Occ. 7, 154–156, 200–205; *Comes Litoris Saxonici* Occ. 28; *Dux Britanniarum* Occ. 40.

49.4 SAXON SHORE FORCES: The *Anderetiani,* listed in the *Notitia* in the field army of Gaul, on the Rhine, and at Paris (Occ. 7, 100; 41, 17; 42, 22), probably came from Anderida, Pevensey; the units of the three southern forts of Portchester, Pevensey and Richborough, *Exploratores, Abulci,* and *Secundani* also appear in the field army of Gaul (Occ. 7, 109; 110; 84; cf. 5, 241). The duplicate names, as elsewhere in the *Notitia,* suggest that detachments, and occasionally whole units, were posted from the coastal forts to Gaul by Constantine and earlier emperors, from Pevensey on two separate occasions.

50.2 VALENTIA: see **L**, and p. 17 above.

50.4 OUT OF DATE: S.S.Frere, *Britannia* 230 ff., 354 ff., discards earlier views that the Wall list was more than a hundred years out of date, but deems it 'inconceivable' that 'old regiments survived' after the raid of 367. The frontier was then reorganised and reconstructed. But reconstruction does not imply that any units other than those named by Ammian were annihilated, disbanded or replaced. Valentinian had no new troops to spare, and on other frontiers retained the remnants of similar old units of the lesser schedule who had survived worse disasters.

51.1 REBUILDING: e.g. the Commandant's House at Housesteads, *Arch. Ael.*[4] 39, 1961, 279 ff.; cf. 38, 1960, 61 ff.

51.1 BURIALS: e.g. Saxon, see **S**, Cumberland, Birdoswald; Durham, Hurbuck (Lanchester); Lancashire, Ribchester and Manchester; Northumberland, Benwell and Corbridge; Westmorland, Brough-by-Stainmore and perhaps Low Borrow Bridge. British, Chesterholm, Brigomaglus, RIB 1722 = CIIC 498, late 5th century (Jackson LHEB 192 note 2) or later, probably also Old Carlisle, Tancorix, RIB 908.

51.2 YORKSHIRE TOWERS: p. 16 above; see especially *Arch. Jl.* 89, 1932, 203 ff.

51.2 FARMING SITE: see **S** Yorkshire, Scarborough, Crossgates.

51.3 WALES: see **R.**

51.3 IRISH: see p. 158 below.

51.3 KERBSCHNITT: see **S.**

52.1 TWO UNITS: Fraomar, under Valentinian, probably *tribunus gentis Alamannorum,* cf. p. 18.2 above; *numerus Hnaudifridi,* 3rd or 4th century, at Housesteads, RIB 1576, cf. 1593–4; the commander of the mid third century *numerus Maurorum* at Burgh-by-Sands RIB 2042, cf. *Not. Dig.* Occ. 40, 47, was Roman; and so doubtless was the commander of the early third century *cuneus Frisiorum* at Housesteads RIB 1594, cf. 1593.

52.2 GENTILES: *Not. Dig.* Occ. 42, 33 ff.

52.2 COMMERCIAL POTTERIES: 'Romano-Saxon' ware, cf. J.N.L.Myres in DAB 16 ff. Though some of the vessels there discussed are now held to be earlier, the majority are not.

52.2 PAGAN ENGLISH GRAVES: a very few contain an occasional sherd of 'Romano-Saxon' ware, for surface Roman sherds of all kinds are not uncommon; unbroken Roman, and perhaps Romano-Saxon, vessels are found, but very rarely.

52.2 SERVICE WITH ROME: for example, Silvanus the Frank, impeached before Constantius, dared not seek refuge with the barbarian Franks, since they would certainly either kill him or sell him, Ammian 15, 5.

53.1 AEGIDIUS, SYAGRIUS: see especially Greg. Tur. HF 2, 11, 18, 27; cf. **F**.

53.1 DALMATIA: see **F** Marcellinus.

53.2 ROMAN EMPIRE: Eugippius *vita Severini* 20.

53.2 BATAVIANS: *Not. Dig*. Occ. 35, 24; the MS reads *novae* for *nonae*.

53.2 MAMERTINUS: Eugippius *vita Severini* 4.

53.2 BARBARIAN GARRISON: Eugippius *vita Severini* 2.

53.2 REFUGEES: Eugippius *vita Severini* 30.

53.3 EGYPT: papyri, cited Jones LRE 662–3, with note 128.

54.2 COEL HEN: see **G** BN and BEB.

54.4 THE ISLAND: Gildas 21, 2–3.

55.2 VORTIGERN: see **P** and **G** BV.

55.2 AMBROSIUS: see **P**.

56.2 THE FEATHERED FLIGHT: Gildas 22, 1–2.

56.2 TRANSMARINI: Gildas 14; coracles, *curucae*, modern Welsh *cwrwg*, Gildas 19, 1; booty carried *trans maria*, in the plural, by Picts, as well as Scots and Saxons, Gildas 17, 3.

57.2 NORFOLK: an inscribed Pictish knife-handle found on the surface at a Roman farming site at Weeting in Norfolk, near the Devil's Dyke (*Ant. Jl.* 32, 1952, 71; *Norfolk Archaeology* 31, 1955, 184; cf. R.R.Clarke *East Anglia* pl. 44) might have been lost by a Saxon or Roman who took it from a Pict; or by a raiding Pict. There is no evidence to show how early the Picts adapted Ogam script (see **O**) to wood and bone; see p. 191 below.

57.3 TIME DREW NIGH: Gildas 22–23; 'keels', *cyulae*.

57.3 THREE KEELS: *ciulae* Nennius 31.

60.3 EXCAVATED EVIDENCE: See **S**. There is no evidence for the settlement of federates in Gaul before 418, or in Britain before the 420s (cf. p. 33.2 above). *Gentiles* are attested by texts in Gaul and Italy, perhaps by pottery in Britain, but not by cemeteries. Cemeteries in Gaul that contained both German and Roman grave goods were probably used by newly raised barbarian units of the Roman army, perhaps *Auxilia Palatina*.

61.2 HENGEST: Nennius 38.

61.2 ORKNEYS: a Saxon urn in Edinburgh Museum, see **S**, said to have been 'found in Buchan', may be mislabelled; or may be a relic of this expedition, a freak counterpart to the Pictish knife in Norfolk, p. 57.2 above.

61.2 FRENESSICAN SEA: probably the Forth, see **L**.

61.3 CEMETERIES: see **S**.

62.1 DUMFRIES: Watson CPNS 422 demonstrated that the name means 'Fort of the Frisians' linguistically, but proposed a fanciful alternative, solely because he did not think that Frisians settled in Scotland; Glensaxon (CPNS 356) and similar names might concern English settlement at this, or any other date.

62.4 GERMANUS . . . ARMIES: Constantius *vita Germani* 17, cf. Bede HE 1, 20.

63.1 LLANGOLLEN: see p. 64 below. The traditional site, marked by an obelisk, north of Maes Garmon, at Rhual (*SJ 223 647*), near Mold in Flintshire, is probably no more than an antiquarian guess from the place name.

63.2 NENNIUS: 32–35, placed at the beginning of Vortigern's reign; the second visit, Nennius 47, is placed at the end of the reign.

63.2 CATEL: see **G** BP.

63.2 POWYS: see **G** BP.

63.2 ELISEG: ECMW 182, see **G** BP.

63.2 BRITTU: see **G** BP; it is possible that the names derive from a single individual, Catellius Brutus.

63.3 PAGENSES: Jackson LHEB 443, cf. 91.

63.3 CORNOVII: see **G** BC.

64.1 WELSH POEM: *Angar Kyvyndawt* BT 21, 14 (FAB 529–530; 134) '*py dydwc garthan Gereint ar Arman*', 'why Geraint committed (?) the camp to Germanus'; the work is a late hotch-potch of allusions to earlier, lost poems.

64.2 PICT SAXON . . . ALLIES: late Welsh legend called the Powys foreigners *Gwyddyl Ffichti*, 'Irish Picts'; the earliest reference is in the 13th century Jesus Genealogy 23 (see **G** BGG 480); the phrase may originate from a misunderstood 'Scotti (et) Picti' in a version of the Germanus tradition.

64.3 MOEL FENLI: *SJ 163 601*, see **L.**

64.3 MOEL-Y-GERAINT: *SJ 202 419*, otherwise called Barber's Hill, see **L.**

64.3 GERMANUS CHURCHES: see **E.**

64.4 UNWARY CRITIC: e.g. PLECG 259 ff., cf. **E** 'German mac Guill'.

64.5 PALLADIUS, PATRICK: see **E** and p. 345 below.

65.1 SAXON RAID: see **A** 434; the texts do not support the translation 'raid from Ireland'.

65.2 MARRIAGE: see **E** Foirtchern and **G** BV, of p. 166 below.

65.2 IRISHMEN . . . CHRISTIANITY: e.g. **E** Coelestius, Corcodemus, Michomerus.

66.2 NENNIUS: 62, reproducing the 7th century spelling, Cunedag, cf. LHEB 458; *atavus* means ancestor in general, not only great-grandfather.

66.2 GENEALOGIES: see **G** BGG.

66.2 KIDWELLY: Nennius 14.

66.2 FIGURE . . . CORRUPTED: see **G** BGG 430.

67.1 VOTADINI: Gododdin, see **L.**

67.1 TRAPRAIN LAW: in East Lothian, *NT 58 74*, see **L.**

67.1 YEAVERING BELL: *NT 928 924*, see **L.**

67.2 INSCRIPTIONS: see p. 124 below.

68.1 SPLENDID IN BATTLE: BT 69, 11–12; 24; 70, 5–6; 11–12; cf. FAB 257,200. Durham and Carlisle, *Kaer Weir a Chaer Liwelyd*; Caer Weir, Durham, did not exist before the Norse invasions, and is an anachronism, comparable with a modern statement that a Roman fort is 'in Yorkshire'.

68.2 OCTHA: see p. 61 above.

68.2 GERMANIANUS: see **G** BNM. The dynasty of Decianus (see **G** BA and p. 17 above), probably Lothian, may also have originated at this time, but is more likely to have been established somewhat earlier.

68.3 CORNWALL: Cornovia, etc. The name does not come into use in any form until after the English conquest of Devon; see **L** and **G** BC. It means the land of the Cornovian Welsh.

69.3 COHORS: *Not. Dig.* Occ. 40, 34.

69.3 FORTS IN WALES: see **R.**

69.3 IUVENTUS: see **R.**

70.1 THE BRITISH: Zosimus 6, 5, cf. p. 38 above.

70.1 AFFLUENT: Gildas 21, 1, cf. p. 37 above.

5 The Overthrow of Britain (pp. 71–86)

71.1 THE PICTS: Nennius 31.

71.1 AMBROSIUS: see **P**, and p. 95 below.

71.2 AUGUSTINE, PELAGIUS: see pp. 339 ff. below.

5 THE OVERTHROW OF BRITAIN (pp. 72–84)

72.4 THE KING: Nennius 36.

73.1 RANSOMS: Alaric demanded 4000 lb. of gold in 407, rather more in 409; some senators are said to have received 4000 lb. of gold in rent annually; cf. texts cited in Jones LRE 185–6, 554.

73.4 CHRONOGRAPHER: Nennius 66.

73.4 VITALINUS: see **G** BV.

73.4 WALLOP: unduly ignored by Ekwall. Possibly *guoloppum* Jackson *Ant.* 13, 1939, 106; see **L.**

74.2 HENGEST: Nennius 37. Chartres MS 19 keels; other MSS 16, 17 or 18.

74.2 HENGEST'S DAUGHTER: Nennius 37.

74.4 HENGEST: Nennius 37.

75.1 CANTERBURY: see **L.**

75.2 OCTHA: see p. 61 above.

75.2 EBISSA: the name is perhaps Celtic, and, if so, implies a joint command by a Roman officer and a German Captain.

75.3 COMPLAINED: Gildas 23, 5.

75.4 BARBARIANS: Gildas 23–24.

75.4 GREATER TOWNS: *coloniae.*

76.1 CAISTOR-BY-NORWICH: JRS 21, 1931, 232 and plate xxi. The excavator's interpretation has been challenged, but without good reason.

76.1 COLCHESTER: Hull *Roman Colchester* 41. The north-east gate was twice stormed; the most likely occasions are the first and second Saxon revolts, about the 440s and the 570s.

76.1 LINCOLN: the burnt stones are preserved in place for public view.

76.4 CERAMIC INDUSTRY: see **M.**

77.2 SOEMIL: see **G** END.

77.3 SAXON CEMETERIES: see **S.**

78.1 AETIUS: Gildas 20, 1.

78.1 WATER TABLE: see **M.**

78.1 FIRE OF VENGEANCE: Gildas 24, 1.

78.1 WENT HOME: 25, 2.

78.1 THE EAST: Gildas 24, 1; cf. 23,3; cf. p. 57 above.

78.2 UNEXPECTED RAID: Eugippius *vita Severini* 4.

78.2 THE CITIZENS: Eugippius *vita Severini* 30.

79.2 VERULAMIUM OVEN: *Ant. Jl.* 40. 1960, 19–21; *Ant.* 38, 1964, 110–111; *Civitas Capitals* 97.

80.2 ELAFIUS: Constantius *vita Germani* 26–27. The name is Roman and needs no emendation, see **P**, and PLRE Aelafius.

80.3 SOUTHAMPTON: cf. the Gallic tradition that on one of his visits Germanus sailed from near Cherbourg, de Plinval *St. Germain* 46.

80.4 VORTIGERN'S SON: Nennius 43.

81.1 SECOND ACCOUNT: Nennius 44 assigns four battles to Vortimer, but names only three. If the figure 4 is not a scribal error, it may derive from a tradition that included the battle of the mid 450s (SC 473, cf. p. 86 below).

81.1 ARCH: *Excavations at Richborough* 5, 1968, 40 ff.; cf. RIB 46 ff.

81.2 HORSA: see **G** EK.

82.1 STRATEGY: cf. Map 3, p. 59.

82.5 VORTIMER'S PROPHECY: Nennius 44.

83.2 BARBARIANS RETURNED: Nennius 45.

83.2 BARBARIANS SENT ENVOYS: Nennius 45.

84.2 HENGEST . . . TOLD HIS MEN: Nennius 46. Most MSS read *Eu Saxones, eniminit saxas*, with minor variants; two read *nimed Eure* (or *hlore*) *saxes.*

84.3 VORTIGERN HATED: Nennius 48.
85.1 WRETCHED SURVIVORS: Gildas 25, 1.
86.1 FOUGHT AGAINST THE WELSH: SC 473.

6 The War (pp. 87–115)

88.1 WESTERN EMPIRE: cf. p. 28 above.
90.3 NORTH OF THE LOIRE: Sidonius *Ep.* 1, 7, 5 *supra Ligerim*; cf. p. 91 below; to Sidonius in the Auvergne 'beyond the Loire' meant to the north (and east) of the river.
90.3 BRETTEVILLE: *Annales de Normandie* 10, 1960, 312, based on M.H.Chanteux in *Recueil . . . Clovis Brunel*, 248 ff. A large number of churches and places named in honour of 6th century British monks, extending eastward into Belgium, also suggest a substantial British element in the population; see Map 4 and notes thereto, and **D**. The place name Breteuil, near Evreux, 40 miles south of Rouen, and near Beauvais, 60 miles south of Amiens, probably has the same origin.
90.4 RIOTHAMUS: Sidonius *Ep.* 3, 9; see **G** AC.
90.5 NEW LANDS: Mansuetus (see **E**) is termed 'Bishop of the British' in 461, Mansi 7, 941, cf. p. 38 above. His name is also inserted, at much the same date, in the episcopal lists (cf. p. 12.3 above) of Toul, on the borders of Burgundian territory, and of Meaux and Senlis, in Syagrius' dominions; both Senlis and Toul list subsequent bishops with British names, cf. **E** Amon and Conotigernus. The reason may be that substantial numbers of Mansuetus' British congregation settled in these towns. The place names and dedications of these regions have not yet been examined in the manner of those of Normandy.
90.5 BACAUDAE: cf. p. 8.
91.1 FREQUENT CHANGES: Jordanes *Getica* 45.
91.1 PREFECT: Sidonius *Ep.* 1, 7, 5.
91.2 LOWER LOIRE: Greg. Tur. HF 2, 18; see **T**.
91.2 ODOVACER: see **P** and p. 93 below.
92.3 FRISIANS: *vita Meloris* 1, cf. **E**.
92.3 JOHN REITH: see **G** AC.
92.3 GRADLON: see **G** AC, Wrdestan *vita Winwaloe* (cf. **E**) 2, 15.
93.1 GOTHIC ADMIRAL: Sidonius *Ep.* 8, 6, 13–15.
93.2 SOUTH COAST HARBOURS: Sidonius' words *de continenti in patriam vela laxantes* imply that their home was not on the European mainland; and was therefore in Britain.
93.2 ALAMANNI: see **G** AC Daniel, Budic, and p. 130 below.
94.1 AELLE: SC 477 (= c. 456); see **P**.
94.2 ARUN: cf. Map 6, p. 107.
94.3 ESSEX: see **S**; the sites by Tilbury appear to belong to the first settlement of the 420s, and are exceptional, remote from inland Essex.
95.1 SEALS: PSA 22, 1863, 235 cf. 87; cf. *Arch. Jl.* 16, 38; the objects, probably seals, contain about 75% tin and 25% lead.
95.2 SURVIVORS: Gildas 25–26.
95.2 LAST DEFEAT: Gildas 2 *postrema patriae victoria*; cf. 26, 1 *novissimaeque ferme de furciferis non minimae stragis.*
95.2 NENNIUS: 43, conclusion of the first account, after Vortimer's victories, cf. 56.
95.3 AMBROSIUS: see **P**.

95.3 ARTHUR: see **P.**

95.3 COMMANDER: *tunc Arthur pugnabat . . . cum regibus Brittonum, sed ipse dux erat bellorum* Nennius 56.

96.2 WELSH POEMS: see **T.**

96.2 GERMAN CAVALRY: see E.A.Thompson *The Early Germans*, especially pp. 127–130, with texts there cited; cf. *P and P* 14, 1958, 2 ff.

96.2 ENGLISH . . . HORSES: Procopius BG 8, 20, 28.

96.3 ARMORICAN CAVALRY: see **G** AC 520 Budic, 550 Conomorus, and p. 258 below.

96.3 ONE POEM: *Marwnad Gereint*, cited p. 104 below.

96.3 ECDICIUS: Sidonius *Ep.* 3, 3, 3–8. Sidonius was Ecidicius' brother-in-law, and was therefore well-informed. The story is reproduced by Greg. Tur. HF 2, 24, where the words *et octo* have falled from the text. See PLRE 2; for the date, cf. C.E.Stevens *Sidonius Apollinaris* 202.

98.2 COMBROGI: not *Combroges* Jackson WHR Special Number 1963, 85; cf. p. 41 above.

98.2 COMBERTON: see **N.**

99.2 CADBURY CASTLE: see **L**, and p. 137 below.

100.2 AMBROSIUS . . . NAME: see **P** and **N**. Discordant explanations advanced by various editors of older EPNS volumes include several types of plants and birds and the alleged personal name of an 'archaic Vandal'.

102.1 EXCAVATION . . . GROUPS: see **S**, and Map 5.

102.1 DUNSTABLE: *Beds. Arch. Jl.* 1, 1962, 40, C.L.Matthews *Ancient Dunstable* 71.

103.2 PEVENSEY: SC 491 (=c. 470).

103.3 WEST SAXON ENTRIES: see **G** EW; **T**, SC; cf. p. 323 below.

104.3 PORT: SC 501 (=c. 480).

104.4 GERAINT: BBC 71–72 (folios xxxvi a–b), RBH 1042 ff., cf. FAB 1, 266 ff.; 2, 37 and 274; translated WBT 43.

106.3 OESC: see **G** EK and **B.**

106.3 THE SAXONS: Nennius 56.

106.3 THE KINGS: cf. p. 272 below.

106.3 ANGEL EMPTY: Bede HE 1, 15; Nennius 38.

109.1 SURREY: see **S.**

109.3 DYKES: cf. Fox ACR ed. 1948 Appendix iv, p. 123.

110.1 HASLINGFIELD: EPNS Cambridgeshire 77, where the inferred name **Haesela* is a variant of Esla. Other Eslingas settled at Essendon near Hertford (EPNS 233) and at Eslington near Alnwick, in Bernicia, (DEPN 169), both probably in or after the late 6th century. See **S**, and **N.**

111.5 NENNIUS . . . POEM: Nennius 56, see **T**. The sites are 1, the river Glen; 2–5, the river Douglas in Lindsey; 6, the river Bassas; 7, Celidon Forest; 8, Fort Guinnion; 9, the City of the Legion; 10, the river Tribruit; 11, Agned Hill, or Bregion; 12, Badon Hill.

112.5 BADON: see **B.**

114.3 RICH GOTH: Theodoric the Great, cited in *Anonymus Valesianus* 61 (12).

7 **The Peace of Arthur** (pp. 116–141)

116.1 ARTHUR: see **P.**

116.2 POET: Aneirin *Gododdin* 1241–2.

116.2 HEIRS OF . . . ARTHUR: cf. p. 242 below.

116.2 NAME OF ARTHUR: the name of Arthur was given to their sons by Aedan of Dal Riada and his son Conang; Peter of Demetia; Pabo of the Pennines

(**G** IDR; BD; BN); by Coscrach of Leinster (CGH 78 R 125 a 41); and by Bicoir the Briton, probably of the Clyde, Annals 626. All these children were born and named in the mid or late 6th century; no other child is known to have been named Arthur for 500 years, until after the diffusion of the Norman romances.

The name of Arthur, father of Ascelin, whose land at Caen William the Conqueror appropriated about 1070 (Ordericus Vitalis 7, 13), suggests that tales were told of Arthur in Normandy at least a hundred years before the composition of the oldest known Norman romances of the Arthurian Cycle. There are also three or four Arthurs in DB.

The letters ARTR, inscribed on ECMW 287, probably about 700 AD, Jackson LHEB 668 note 1, are however not likely to represent the name Arthur.

117.2 RULERS: Gildas 26, 2.

117.3 ARTHUR LEGEND: see **P**.

118.1 PEREDUR: see **G** BN 560.

118.1 TRISTAN: see **G** AC 550 Conomorus, Drustanus; cf. *P and P* 11, 1957, 15–16.

118.2 PRINCE CONSORT: Tennyson *Idylls of the King*, dedication.

119.2 GREAT JEOPARDY: Malory *Morte d'Arthur* 1, 5.

119.2 IN THIS REALM: Malory *Morte d'Arthur* 20, 17.

119.2 SIR BORS: Tennyson *Holy Grail* 702 ff.

119.2 ARTHUR'S KINGDOM: R.L.Green *King Arthur* p. 11.

120.2 CERTAIN TYRANT: *vita Paterni* 21.

120.2 BUT LO: *vita Cadoc*, prologue. The hill 'Bochriu Carn' is Fochriw *SO 10 05*, cf. Map 7, p. 128 and notes thereto.

120.3 GREAT GENERAL: *vita Cadoc* 22. The place is named 'Tref Redinauc', now Tredunnock, *ST 37 94*, cf. Map 7, p. 128 and notes thereto.

121.2 CATO AND ARTHUR: *vita prima Carantoci* 4.

121.2 CUILL: *vita Gildas* (Caradoc) 5, Hueil; cf. *vita Gildas* (Rhuys) 2, Cuillus; cf. **G** BAB.

121.2 ILLTUD: *vita Iltuti* 2.

122.3 GILDAS . . . SIXTH CENTURY SPELLING: *Beatus Gildas Arecluta . . . oriundus, patre Cauuo* (misread as *Cauno* MGH) vita Gildas (Rhuys) 1; the names are 'clearly . . . sixth century . . . from contemporary manuscripts' LHEB 42, cf. 306, 307.

123.3 DUMNONIAN POEM: see p. 104 above.

123.3 NENNIUS POEM: Nennius 56, see **T** and p. 111.

123.4 DYFNWAL: see **G** BA and BNM.

124.2 MARIANUS: see **G** BGM.

124.2 INSCRIPTIONS: see **P** Cauuus. The relevant stones are

1 ECMW 282 Llanfor *SH 94 36*, near the Roman fort of Caer Gai. CIIC 417.
Cavo[s] Seniargii [filius] (hic iacit)
Possible variant readings *Cavoseni Argii* or *Cavos Eniargii*
Date: 5th to early 6th ECMW; early to mid 6th LHEB 521. The stone is extant.

2 ECMW 283 Caer Gai *SH 87 31*. CIIC 418.
Hic iacet Salvianus Burgo Cavi, filius Cupetian[i]
Possible variant readings: *hec* for *hic*; *Burso* for *Burgo*.
Date: 5th to early 6th ECMW; not noticed LHEB. The stone is lost; the reading derives from a 17th-century copy.

3 ECMW 284 Llan-y-mawddwy *SH 90 19*, seven miles south of Caer Gai. CIIC 419.
Filiae Salvia[n]- hic iacit Ve . . . maie uxsor Tigirnici et filie eius Onerat- [uxsor ia]cit Rigohene [mater? . . .]ocet- [et? . . .]ac-

Possible variant readings: *Verimate, Vetti[a] Maie*; [*hic iac*]*it Rigohene.*
Date: 6th century ECMW; not noticed LHEB. The stone is lost; 18th century reading reproduced ECMW.

4 ECMW 285 Tomen-y-mur *SH 70 38*, the next Roman fort on the road from Caer Gai to Caernarvon. CIIC p. 397.
D M Barrect- Carantei
Date: 5th ECMW, apparently solely on the basis of the formula DM; not noticed LHEB. The stone is lost; the reading is 19th century.

5 CIIC 514 Liddel Water, Roxburgh, between Newcastleton *NY 48 87* and Hawick *NY 56 96*. PSAS 70, 1935–6, 33.
Hic iacit Caranti fili Cupitiani
Date: late 5th to early 6th LHEB 290. The stone is extant.

6 CIIC 510 Kirkliston *NT 12 74*, 8 miles west of Edinburgh.
In [h]oc tumulo iacit Vett[i]a f[ilia] Victr[ici?]
Possible variant reading: *Vict*[*o*]*r*[*is*].
Date: early 6th LHEB 407. The stone is extant; it was found in a long cist cemetery.

Notes

1 and 2. *Burgo Cavi*, placed between the name of Salvianus and of his father, is not a personal name; it should indicate the place to which he belonged. *Burgus* is the normal late western Latin for a small fort, in this case 'the fort of Cavos'. Since Cavos is buried nearby, he is likely to have been the person who named the fort.

2 and 5; 4 and 5. The personal names Carant(e)us and Cupetianus are both otherwise unrecorded in these centuries in Britain; it is therefore improbable that two pairs of different people bore the names in the same context.

3 and 6. Vettius is a Roman family, not otherwise known in Britain in these centuries; the restoration is uncertain, but if it was inscribed on both stones, it suggests the likelihood that the persons were related.

The Persons

If the three pairs of people who have the same name were identical, as seems probable, the relations between them are

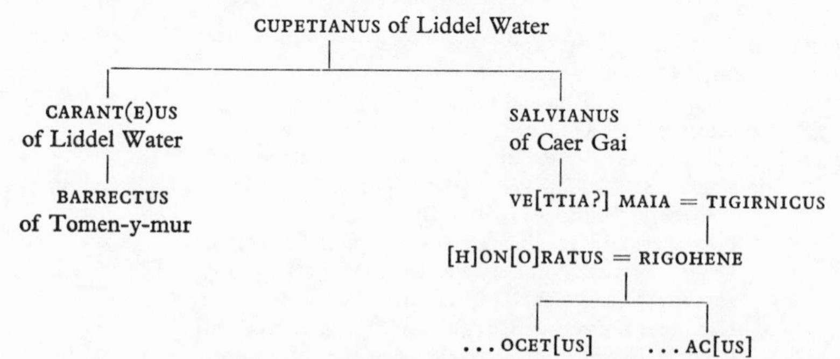

All dates suggested for British inscriptions of the 5th and following centuries rest upon somewhat fragile assumptions; but those advanced for these stones are consistent with the relationships that the stones report, except for the date given to the lost Barrectus stone, on the basis of a formula not otherwise known. The deaths of both sons of Cupetianus are placed '5th to early 6th'; Salvianus' descendants are allotted to the 6th century. Cupetianus' lifetime should therefore be mid to late 5th century. The stones suggest that Salvianus moved from his father's homeland, on the borders of the Selgovae and the Votadini, to central Wales, about the end of the fifth century; and that his nephew accompanied or followed him, while his daughter may have used the same family name as a native of the Edinburgh region.

Salvianus was an approximate, perhaps a younger contemporary of Cavos, who named the fort where he lived and died in Merioneth. A text in 6th-century spelling names a Cauuus, father of Gildas; his home was north of the Clyde, but his son was in Wales, in infancy, by about the year 500 (see p. 205.3). A late, but quite independent genealogical tradition lists half a dozen relatives of Gildas, two of them in or near Roman forts within ten miles of Caer Gai, the rest elsewhere in mid Wales, at Caersws, Clyro and near Abergavenny (**G** BAB).

Each separate strand of evidence bristles with uncertainties. They combine to suggest a migration from the lands of the Votadini and their neighbours to Merioneth and mid Wales at about the time when Cunedda's nephew Marianus is said to have moved from Votadinian territory to name Merioneth; and at a time when the lands by and south of Forth and Clyde are said to have obeyed Dyfnwal, apparently a firm ally of Arthur. The context suggests that the movement was Arthur's answer to renewed Irish attacks, matching the Demetian campaign in the south (p. 126).

124.3 FERGUS: see **G** IDR and p. 180 below.

125.1 CUNORIX, EBICATOS: see **P** and p. 137 below; for the dates, see **O** and **P**.

125.1 SILCHESTER: Ebicatos may have had a neighbour or successor, noteworthy in his own day. Berkshire is the shire of Barruc or Berroc, and until the 12th century the woodland in the south-east of the county, north of Hungerford and including the early English area about East Shefford, bore the same name; Asser (ch. 1) in the 9th century supposed that the county was named from the woodland. 'Barruc' is a pre-English regional name, and is commonly derived from British *barr* (top), with locative suffix *-aco-*. But, since elsewhere in Britain 'Barrock' names normally refer to single hilltops, and since British regional names that are not of Roman origin often derive from 5th- or 6th-century rulers, an alternative possibility is that Barruc was the personal name of a local lord, either of Silchester or of a small territory on its north-eastern border. If so, the name is probably Irish, cf. **L**.

125.1 CYNRIC: see **G** EW and p. 225 below.

125.2 CATWALLAUN: see **G** BGG and p. 168 below.

125.2 ILLAN: see **G** ILD and p. 168 below.

125.3 KIDWELLY: see Nennius 14, cf. p. 158 below.

125.3 DEMETIA: the dynasty were of the Ui Liathain, not of the Dessi, see **G** BD and p. 158 below.

126.2 BRYCHAN: See **G** BB and texts in VSBG and EWGT.

126.4 THEODORIC: see **P**. The significance of the name is easily overlooked because the Welsh form, Tewdrig, superficially resembles Tewdwr, which transliterates Theodore and is Englished as Tudor. There is no direct relationship between Germanic Theude-ric and Greek Theo-dorus. Tewdrig's Germanic ancestry is confirmed by the name of his father, Theudebald, transcribed in the Brychan documents as 'Teithfallt', or in similar spellings.

127.1 NAMED PLACES: see note to Map 7, p. 128. The distances are Brecon (Llan Maes) to Lan Semin 24 miles; thence to Methrum 28 miles; thence to Caer Farchell 31 miles (to Porth Mawr 35 miles).

127.1 LLAN MARCHELL: the name should normally denote the monastery of a monk named Marcellus, but might mean a monastery established at a place already named after Marcellus. In North Wales a Marcellus or Marcella named Llanmarchell, the old name of Denbigh; Ystrad Marchell near Welshpool; and Capel Marchell in Llanrwst, LBS 3, 438, but there is no trace of a monastic Marcellus in south Wales.

129.1 BOIA: see **P** and **E** David.

130.2 TRIGG: see **G** BB.

130.2 BROCAGNUS: CIIC 478 cf. **G** BB.

130.2 FINGAR: see **E** Fingar, Guiner and **P** Theodoric.

130.2 CORNISH PARISHES: see Map 25, p. 362.

130.3 BUDIC . . . MAXENTIUS: see **G** AC and p. 93.

132.3 RECTORES: Gildas 1, 14; for *speculator* in the meaning of bishop, not here relevant, see AB 76, 1958, 379.

133.2 MASUNA: Dessau ILS 859.

133.2 ARMORICA: Greg. Tur. HF 4, 4, cf. p. 251.3 below.

133.3 AMERAUDUR: e.g. BBC 72, 9 cited p. 104 above.

133.3 VORTIPOR: see **G** BD.

133.4 IUDICES: see p. 201 below.

133.4 MAGISTRATUS: ECMW 103.

135.2 RECTORES: Gildas 1, 14; cf. p. 132 above.

136.1 DIVORTIO: Gildas 10, 2.

136.1 KEMPSTON: see **S** and Map 18, p. 285. These sites will be better understood when 'small long' brooches have been more closely studied.

137.1 CITIES: Gildas 26, 2 *sed ne nunc quidem, ut antea, civitates patriae inhabitantur; sed desertae dirutaeque hactenus squalent*; cf. **T**.

137.1 JEROME: *Ep.* 1, 3; the city of Vercellae in northern Italy was in 370 *raro habitatore semiruta*; but its decay did not prevent a consular governor from holding his court in the city.

137.1 WROXETER: *Ant. Jl.* 48, 1968, 296, cf. **P** Cunorix, cf. p. 125 above.

137.1 SILCHESTER: CIIC 496 cf. **P** Ebicatos, cf. p. 125 above. Local tradition also named a former supposed ruler whose name may possibly have been British. Camden's *Britannia* 1, 222 (Gough) reported that local people gave the name 'Onion's pennies' to Silchester Roman coins, 'fancying this Onion a great giant who formerly lived in this city'. I am grateful to Mr K.R.Davies, who drew my attention to this statement and to the possibility that 'Onion' might derive from the Welsh name En(n)iaun.

137.2 VERULAMIUM, MAGIOVINIUM: unpublished, see **L**.

137.2 LATE CEMETERIES: see **M**.

137.2 COLCHESTER, YORK, LONDON see **L**.

137.3 CADBURY CASTLE: *ST 62 26* in South Cadbury parish, to be distinguished from nearby North Cadbury, and also from Cadbury, near Congresbury, *ST 43 64*, south-west of Bristol. The site has been dubbed 'Camelot' by antiquarians from the 16th century to the 20th; though not Camelot, it was an important fortress of the Arthurian period, cf. *Ant. Jl.* 47, 1967, 70; 48, 1968, 6; 49, 1969, 30; 50, 1970, 14; 51, 1971, 1; *Ant.* 41, 1967, 50; 42, 1968, 47; 43, 1969, 52; 44, 1970, 46.

139.2 WALES . . . TRIBUTE: see p. 220.3.

139.2 NO NEW EMPEROR: later traditions name two sons of Arthur, but do not regard either of them as rulers of any territory, cf. **P** Arthur.

140.3 CAMLANN: ACm 537 cf. **A**.

140.3 MEDRAUT: see **G** BLS, and **P**. The only other record of the name Medraut is BYS 51, Dyfnauc Sant m. Medraut; Dyfnauc (Domnoc) is a common name, but the only 6th or 7th century Domnoc known in Britain named Dunwich in Suffolk, Bede HE 2, 15.

141.2 WILLIAM OF MALMESBURY: *de Gestis Regum* 1, 8.

8 **Pagan Ireland** (pp. 142–163)

142.1 PATRICK: *Confessio* 46.

142.1 TOLD SEPARATELY: in the following narrative it has proved necessary to repeat the accounts of many events, and sometimes the comments made upon them, since they are viewed from a different standpoint in the context of the history of the Irish or the British, the English or the Northerners.

143.4 GENEALOGIES: see **G** Introduction, and **G** 1.

144.2 ANNALS: see **A** Introduction. The main European source seems to have been a Latin translation, no longer extant, of Eusebius' Chronicle, with continuations, fuller than the translation by Jerome which has been preserved (see BICS 19, 1972). This text was also a main source of Bede's Chronicle, since he and the Annals quote from it independently, and occasionally reproduce passages that are otherwise preserved only in the Armenian translation of Eusebius. Irish notices are said to have been collected from the 6th century onward. Most of the apparent inconsistencies are due to comments incorporated from corrupt genealogies or to mistakes, usually identifiable, in the European sources. Except for the Inisfallen Annals, most printed texts are faulty, and fail to distinguish the body of the MSS they reproduce from glosses added thereto.

145.3 MAELGWN . . . IDA: Nennius 62, cf. 61; 63.

146.1 SAINTS' LIVES: see **E** Introduction and p. 164 below.

146.1 EVIDENCE OF . . . DEDICATIONS: outlined by Bowen SCSW 6 ff., cf. **D**.

146.1 ARGUMENTS: cf. e.g. Simpson *Celtic Church* and Owen Chadwick SEBH 173 ff.

146.1 CHURCH OF MARTIN: Gregory of Tours, sensitive to the conventions of his own day, is careful to describe the church as 'the church which Briccius built over Martin'.

146.1 NINIAN: see p. 337 below. Bede's statements are explicit; it is most improbable that Ninian, devoted to Martin's then rare advocacy of monastic discipline and preaching to peasants and barbarians, could have avoided visiting Tours on his return from Rome in the 390s, and spending some time with Martin.

146.2 LOCAL . . . TRADITION: a clear instance is St. Asaph, formerly Llanelwy, the monastery on the river Elwy. The conventions of the medieval founders of the see did not permit a cathedral to be dedicated to a river; it was therefore given the name of a saint who was already widely honoured locally, but who was not, like others, the national saint of a Welsh kingdom.

146.2 NATIONAL TRADITION: Irish Norse brought Columba to Iceland, and Patrick and Brigit to Cumberland, and sometimes elsewhere in England; for the few dedications in England to Welsh and Armorican saints, see p. 370 below and map 28, p. 393 below. It is noteworthy that dedications to the numerous major or local saints of Normandy, Brittany and Flanders are not found in lands settled by lords from these territories after the Norman conquest.

147.1 KING LISTS: see **K** 1; martyrologies also supplement Saints' Lives, see **E** Introduction.

147.3 PREHISTORY: the main sources are *Lebor Gabala Erenn* (The Book of the Invasions of Ireland), the substance of whose tradition was known to Nennius, and to Cormac mac Cuilenan (**G** IMC 490 note) in the 9th century; Keating's

History of Ireland 1635; and the Annals. LG incorporates some 136 poems older than itself, varying in length up to about 150 lines. The synchronists supply dates, which the Annals repeat.

147.3 ANTIQUARIES: cited Keating 1, 5, 4 (ITS 1, 149). The 'Just Canon' is the Old Testament.

147.3 I LIKE NOT: CS p. 9.

147.3 NOT GENUINE HISTORY: Keating 1, 5, 4 (ITS 1, 147), cf. AT (Tigernach) 307 BC (RC 16, 1895, 394) *omnia monimenta Scottorum usque Cimbaed incerta erant.* Cimbaed, whose reign is dated 307–279 BC in the Annals, was the legendary founder of the Ulaid dynasty of Emain; recent excavation has shown that the great ceremonial mound of Navan (Emain, near Armagh), was constructed at a radio carbon date of 245 BC, + or − 50 years, cf. C. Arch. 22, 1970, 304 ff., where the date given needs slight adjustment. Tigernach accepts the historical reality of the Ulaid heroes, but rejects their mythological predecessors; recent discovery tends to confirm rather than to challenge his judgment.

148.2 BRONZE AGE . . . ROUTES: e.g. JRSAI 75, 1945, 94, fig. 6, cauldrons with conical rivets, a dozen by the Tyrrhene Sea, 4 about the headwaters of the Rhine and Danube, 10 in Denmark and Sweden, 7 in Ireland and 1 in Wales.

149.2 PTOLEMY: his account of Ireland is conveniently set forth in the Ordnance Survey's Map of Roman Britain, p. 20; cf. O'Rahilly EIHM, 1 ff., see **M.**

149.3 CRUITHNE: held to have been powerful in the distant past, cf. e.g. AI, AT (**A** 172 AD) 'Seven kings of the Cruithne ruled Ireland before Conn'; Tuathal's predecessor Elim was regarded both as king of Ireland and as king 'of the Domnann' LG 9, 95 (para. 593a) (ITS 5, 311), etc.

149.3 CRUITHNE . . . IDENTITY . . . LANGUAGE: change of language need not imply change of national identity; a modern Jones or Williams does not cease to be Welsh because he speaks English and bears a name of English origin.

150.1 JACKSON: OIT 44–45 note.

151.3 TUATHAL: extensively treated in AC 50–54, Keating 1, 39 (ITS 2, 243), LG 9, 95 (para. 593 ff.) (ITS 5, 309).

151.5 AGRICOLA: Tacitus *Agricola* 24, in 81 or 82 AD.

155.2 CAERNARVON: RIB 430; the repair of a ruined aqueduct implies rebuilding after disuse.

155.2 BENNE BRIT: see **A** 217 and note thereto; cf. also CGH 403 LL 328f 11, 14; Keating 1, 41 (ITS 2, 272), etc. The name is a corruption rather than an invention; invented foreigners were normally given Irish names, as 'Fergus the king of Spain's son', AC 59 etc.

155.3 CORMAC: see **A** 217–257, with note to 257; cf. also especially AC 60 ff., Keating 1, 43 ff. (ITS 2, 298 ff.) etc.

155.3 OBSOLUTELY: AC 60.

155.3 ALBA: see **L.**

156.1 REACHTAIRE: Keating 1, 43 (ITS 2, 306).

156.1 FINN: see especially **A** 257 note.

156.1 WISE, LEARNED: AC 60.

156.3 INSCRIPTIONS 244–264; of Philip (244–249) RIB 327 (Caerleon), 882–883 (Papcastle), 915 (Old Penrith); of Gallus (251–253) 2057–8 (Bowness-on-Solway); of Valerian (253–258, in Britain) 316, 334 (Caerleon), 913 (near Carlisle), 2042 (Burgh-by-Sands); of Postumus (258–268) 605 (Lancaster, dated 262/266).

156.4 COIN HOARDS: see **R.**

157.1 PLUNDER . . . SEVERN: see **R.**

157.2 AMARGEIN: e.g. Keating 1, 43 (ITS 2, 304); cf. Plummer VSH clxiii 6.

8 PAGAN IRELAND (pp. 157–162)

157.3 EMAIN: the ceremonial mount at Navan, p. 151 above, remained important for several centuries after 300 BC. The hill top of Armagh, 2 miles away, was fortified at a radio carbon date of AD 310, + or − 80 years, cf. CArch. 22, 1970, 308, where '5th century' is mistaken. Cf. 147.3 above.

157.5 CRIMTHANN: The Southern Irish texts do not refer to the Picts of north Britain; cf. **G** IML.

158.1 DIN TRADUI: **T** Cormac, and **L**.

158.1 CAIRPRE: see **G** IMW.

158.1 DERGIND: CGH 196 R 148a 31; see **L**. Inscriptions, CIIC 488, 489, 492, 493, 494.

158.1 AENGUS: see **G** IML.

158.2 UI LIATHAIN: see **G** BD and IML (especially CGH 228 R 151b 37 Lec.).

158.2 NENNIUS 14: *filii autem Liethan obtinuerunt in regione Demetorum et in aliis regionibus, id est Guir Cetgueli, donec explusi sunt a Cuneda et a filiis eius ab omnibus Brittannicis regionibus.*

158.2 CORMAC: see **T**.

158.2 EOGAN ALBANACH: see **G** IML.

158.2 MUNSTER: see **P** Builc.

158.2 LEINSTER: the peninsula of Lleyn, by Caernarvon, may take its name from the Laigin of Leinster; cf. also the later campaigns of Illan of Leinster (see **E** Brigit and p. 168 below), possibly fought in support of compatriots who had settled earlier in Britain.

159.2 NIALL: see **G** IN. King of Alba, king of the western world, CGH 122 R 136 b 27, b 23; king of the western world, invaded the kingdom of Letha (Letavia, Llydaw, see **L**), meaning Europe in general, or specifically Gaul, as here, and especially Brittany, LG 9, 114 (para. 612; ITS 5, 348).

160.1 CORCC: see **G** IMC, cf. **A** 439 Senchus Mor, FM etc.; Keating 1, 3 (ITS 1, 122–124), etc. Eoganacht genealogists legitimised his sovereignty by marrying him to Crimthann's sister Mongfind, whose other connections place her generations earlier, and make her the wife of Eochaid.

160.1 ULAID, LEINSTER: see **A** and **G**.

160.2 NIALL'S SONS: see **G** INA; *Eriu* 13, 1942, 92; Hogan *Onomasticon* Cenel, Tir, Ui etc.

160.3 NAMES: the fundamental discussion remains MacNeill's *Early Irish Population Groups* (PRIA 29 C, 1911/12, 59 ff.) cf. *Eriu* 3, 1907, 42 ff.

160.3 PATRICK: *Confessio* 41, cf. 52; *Ep. ad Coroticum* 12.

161.2 MUIRCHU 9: *imperator barbarorum regnans in Temoria, quae erat caput Scotorum, Loiguire nomine, filius Neill, origo stirpis regiae huius pene insolae.*

161.2 ADOMNAN: 1, 36, adding *deo auctore ordinatus.*

161.2 BRIAN BORU: Book of Armagh 16 v° *ego scripsi id est Calvus Perennis, in conspectu Briain imperatoris Scotorum.* Brian plainly authorised and accepted a title written under his eyes. The scribes name translates Mael Suthain, **G**.

161.3 ADOMNAN: Comgall, Cormac 3, 17; Columbanus 3, 12.

161.4 GLOSSES: e.g. *Cenel Conaill Cernaig*, Great Book of Lecan 190, Book of Leinster 312, cited Hogan 218; *Clann Cathair Mair* CGH 78 R 125 a 50, in contrast with the normal usage of e.g. CGH 358 LL 318 b 60 *Ic Cathair Mor condrecat Hui Falgi 7 Hui Enechglais . . . 7 Hui Crimthaind 7 clanda Cathair archena*, cf. e.g. CGH 44 R 121 a 19 ff., where Cathair is made ancestor of families named from persons elsewhere dated to the early 5th century; *Cenel Rochada* CGH 139 R 140 b 46. Such associations are not made in the main pedigrees or their headings.

162.1 BEC: AC 550.

162.1 ALL SUBJECTS: Ultan 66 (TT 534). The Life is early.

9 Christian Ireland (164–176)

164.1 SAINTS' LIVES: see **E** introduction.

164.1 COULANGES: *La Monarquie Franque* 9–12, cited Stokes *Lismore Lives* xci-xcii; cf. also JTS 17, 1966, 347 ff.; *Christianity in Britain* 65 ff.

164.2 SUPPRESSED . . . DOCTRINE: e.g. Jocelyn of Furness complained, *vita Kentigerni* prologue, that his sources were full of 'solecisms' and also *relatu perverso et a fide averso*; he took pride in his attempt, in rewriting them, *barbarice exarata Romano sale condire*, and tried to restore *sana doctrina*. Serious study cannot rest content with poking fun at Jocelyn's pretentious style and boundless ignorance of the times he described; the need is to get rid of the 'Roman salt' and 'sound doctrine', and to seek out the 'barbarisms' and 'perversity' that Jocelyn was unable to suppress.

164.2 GARRULITY: *Britannica garrulitate*, Vitalis of Fleury *vita Pauli Aureliani* ASS prologue, cf. RC 5, 1881/3, 415.

164.2 UNCOUTH . . . NAMES: *absona . . . barbara Britonum nomina*, Vitalis of Fleury, cf. note above, cf. AB 1, 1882, 209. The nature and extent of the omissions and alterations may be observed, since a version of the original which Vitalis abbreviated is extant.

165.1 HISTORICAL CRITICISM: the starting point of criticism is the comparison between those Lives that survive both in their original form, or in an early version that reproduces much of its names and content, and in 12th century or later recensions. The Lives of Samson, p. 357 below, and of Paul Aurelian, cf. note 164.2 above, are among the most important of those so preserved. Such comparison demonstrates how medieval editors actually altered their originals and disperses subjective speculation about what was or was not 'forged' or invented. No such comparison has yet been systematically undertaken.

166.1 ENDA: see **E** and p. 352 below.

166.2 CIARAN SAIGIR: *vita* (VSH) 18.

166.2 CIVIL VIOLENCE: Prisoners freed, e.g. *vitae* Ciaran Clonmacnoise 19; Colman Elo 24; Adomnan 1, 11. Cruelties, e.g. the tossing of a murderer's child, which survived to Viking times as *gall-cherd*, Macnissi (Sal.) 9; Cainnech 34, etc. Execution, e.g. Fintan 17, cf. Ruadan p. 170 below. Opposition to war e.g. Tigernach (VSH) 10, where the glory of the saint's deception was that 'the enemy army was put to flight without hurting anyone and without being harmed itself'. Comgall startled contemporary notions of justice by sentencing a slave girl, convicted of trying to poison her mistress, to be freed both of her slave status and of her prison, to spend the rest of her life in perpetual pennance. Other saints, however, became patrons of their people, whose military victory their prayers ensured.

166.2 VORTIGERN'S DAUGHTER: see **E** Foirtchern, and p. 65 above. The surviving notices report that Foirtchern, whose name is an Irish transliteration of the British Vortigern, was the son of Fedlimid, son of Loegaire, and of the daughter of an unnamed British king. Since she gave her son the alien name of Vortigern, it is probable that in the original version of the tale he was her unnamed royal father; for the surviving fragments are unaware that there was a British king so named. Foirtchern became a notable ecclesiastic, particularly active in South Leinster, and his name subsequently passed into common use for a short period, especially in the south, since he was the principal teacher of Finnian of Clonard, the father of Irish monasticism. The name is not recorded in Ireland before his time, and soon after disappeared.

9 CHRISTIAN IRELAND (pp. 166–174)

166.3 PATRICK ... POPE ... BISHOP: see pp. 64 and 348.

167.4 OCHA: cf. MacNeill *Phases* 190 ff., 231 ff. Though the Annals and Genealogies do not support the view that *derbfine* succession already obtained generally in the 5th century, the battle secured Ui Neill kingship.

168.2 DAL RIADA: see p. 180 below, also **L**, and **G** IDR.

168.3 ILLAN: see **G** ILD. *Novemque certamina in Britannia prospere egit* Ultan *vita* Brigit 90 (TT 538); variant *octosque* Animosus 2, 12 (TT 551).

168.3 CATWALLAUN: see **G** BGG.

168.3 SERIGI: (Triad 62, etc.) see **P**.

168.4 DEMETIA, CORNWALL: see **G** BB, BD; **P** Theodoric, and p. 125 ff. above.

168.5 MAC ERCA ... LIVED AT PEACE: the numerous featureless battles entered in **A** 530, 531, appear to derive from a saga, whose date should be 6th or 7th century, since the source is given as Cennfaelad (**E**); and are entered for convenience in the Annals at Mac Erca's death. The only other wars noted by the Annals are dated before his accession.

169.2 REIGN OF TUATHAL: *Secundus vero ordo ... ab extremis Tuthayl Maylgairb temporibus* Catalogus 2, confirmed by very many individual accounts.

169.3 DIARMAIT ... BRIGIT: Ultan 64 (TT 534).

169.3 CIARAN: *vita Columbae* (O'Donnell), 44 (TT 396; ZCP 74).

169.4 DERRY: the traditions are summarised in Reeves' *Adomnan* 160. The Annals' date agrees with the tradition that Derry was founded immediately after the death of Mobhi Clarainech (**E**).

170.2 RUADAN: *vita* 15–18; AC 85–88.

170.2 PEACEFUL KING: *vita* Ruadan 17, *Rex enim defensor patrie pacificus erat, adiutor ecclesiarum et pauperum, verax in sermone, equus in iudicio, et firmus in fide.*

170.2 ULAID POET: Beccan, *M. Oengus*, prefaces, pp. 6 and 14.

170.2 HIS OWN SON: Book of Leinster 358, Book of Lismore 94 b, cited Stokes *Lismore Lives* xxvii; *M. Donegal* April 5.

170.3 BRITISH KING: perhaps Peter or Arthur of Demetia, see **G** BD; the powerful Rhun of Gwynned is less likely to have feared Irish threats.

171.1 COUNTRY SECURE: *vita* Ruadan 17, *Ego firmavi regiones, et pactum firmum feci in omni loco, ut pax firma ecclesiis et plebibus esset ubique. Ego bonum defendo secundum legem Christi; vos autem malum operamini, defendentes reum mortis. De parva enim multa surgent.*

171.1 PRICE: the author of the Life understood an ordinary compensation, and resumes his own jejune narrative, and inferior Latinity, with a story of miraculous horses who acquitted the payment.

172.1 COLUMBAN HOUSES: Reeves *Adomnan* 276 ff. lists 37 Irish and over 50 Scottish houses. The list is not exhaustive, but is likely to include some later offshoots which claimed personal foundation; see Map 26, p. 371.

172.2 FINNIAN'S BOOK: the story is told many times, and is here cited from *vita Columbae* (O'Donnell) 2, 1 (TT 408 (misnumbered 402)–409), ZCP 168; see also **E** Columba, Finnian of Moville.

172.4 CURNAN: Annals 560; *vita Columbae* (O'Donnell) 2, 2 (TT 409), ZCP 168; the lost Book of Sligo, cited Egerton MS 1782, *Silva Gadaelica* 79, translation 84, cf. Stokes *Lismore Lives* xxviii; and other versions.

173.1 CUIL DREMHNI: *vita Columbae* (O'Donnell) 2, 3 (TT 409), ZCP 170 ff., cf. **A** 561, etc. The essential facts are reported by Adomnan, see **E** Columba, and p. 377 below.

173.2 BRENDAN OF CLONFERT: see p. 384 below.

174.2 COLUMBA ... CROWN: cf. p. 169 above and *Betha Coluim Chille* (Stokes

Lismore Lives 749), 'By inheritance his was the natural right to the kingship of Ireland, and it would have been offered him if he had not put it from him for the sake of God.'

174.2 THRONE OFFERED: vita *Columbae* (O'Donnell) 1, 44 (TT 396) *sceptrum antequam offeretur abrenunciavit*; 'it was offered many a time but he refused it' ZCP 74.

174.3 SYNOD . . . EXCOMMUNICATED: Adomnan *vita Columbae* 3, 3 etc.

174.3 LASRIAN: *vita* 31 (VSH) *Sanctus vero Columba visitavit sanctum Lasrianum, confessorem suum, post bellum de Cul Dremni, petens ab eo salubre consilium, quomodo post necem multorum ibi occisorum benevolenciam Dei . . . mereretur accipere. Beatus igitur Lasrianus . . . imperavit illi ut tot animas a penis liberaret quot animarum causa perdicionis extiterat; et cum hoc ei precepit ut perpetuo moraretur extra Hiberniam exilio.* Exile did not of course preclude frequent visits to Ireland; it forbade permanent residence.

174.4 GILDAS: see p. 379 below.

175.1 CAIN ADOMNAN: ed. Meyer; cf. Kenney 245; SEIL 269 ff.

175.4 MONASTIC UPSURGE: see pp. 357 below.

176.2 KING . . . BORN IRISH: Aldfrith, cf. p. 196 below, and **G** ENB.

10 The Dal Riada Scots (177–185)

177.1 SCOTLAND: see Maps 2, 10–12, 26 (pp. 47, 179, 187, 189, 371), and **L** Atecotti, Caledonii, Circinn, Fortrenn, Miathi, Picts, Scots, etc. The principal collection of the sources is still the work of W.F. Skene, more than a hundred years ago, especially in CPS and CS; selections thereof are translated, with some supplementation, by Anderson ESSH. Much of Skene's interpretation is coloured by the assumptions of his day; but since no comparable comprehensive history of early Scotland has since appeared, any discussion of the formation of the Scottish nation must admit a considerable debt, directly or indirectly, to the body of evidence which Skene assembled and used.

177.2 ATECOTTI: the official 4th century spelling of the *Notitia Dignitatum* means 'the very ancient peoples', see **L**.

180.2 IRISH LEGEND: Watson CPNS 213 ff. summarises a number of the main stories.

180.2 BEDE: HE 1, 1, *Brittania . . . Scottorum nationem in Pictorum parte recepit, qui duce Reuda de Hibernia progressi . . . a quo . . . hodie Dal Reudini vocantur, nam lingua eorum 'daal' partem significat.*

180.2 FERGUS . . . DAL RIADA: see **G** IDR and p. 168 above.

180.3 TWO TEXTS: *Senchus Fir nAlban*, History of the Men of Alba (Skene CPS 308) see **Q**; **T**. *Cethri prim cenoil*, The Four Chief Dynasties, (Skene CPS 316) see **G** IDRF 590 Gartnaid; cf. p. 451 below.

180.3 COWALL, GOWRIE: see **L** Dal Riada.

180.4 PICT RECORDS: see **K** P and p. 191 below.

181.1 IONA: granted by Conall, **A** 574; by Bridei and the Picts, Bede HE 3, 4.

181.2 IONA . . . BURIAL PLACE: *Bethu Adomnan*, cited CPS 408 cf. MHH 179, 2 (AIM 2, 10 ff.; *Celtic Review* 5, 1908, 97 ff.)

181.2 NINIAN, KENTIGERN, COLUMBA: see Map 26, p. 371.

181.4 SEPARATE PORTIONS: *ri Aodhan na n-iol-rann* (Duan Albanach, CPS 60); the verses single out the particular distinction of each king, and therefore imply their author's view that Aedan was the first to unite the portions, to master the Cinel Loarn and Cinel Angus.

182.1 CONSECRATE AEDAN: Adomnan 3, 5.

182.3 DRUM CEAT: see **L**.

182.4 PEACE . . . BRITISH: Aedan may have attacked the Clyde after Columba's death, see **G** IDRF 560 Aedan.

183.3 DOMNALL: see **G** IDRF and **A**.

183.3 FIFE: Skene CPS 315–316, variant note 7.

183.3 CUMMENE: Adomnan 3, 5.

183.4 GLEN MURESON: cf. Skene CS 1, 249.

184.2 CUMMENE: Adomnan 3, 5.

11 The Picts (pp. 186–199)

186.1 PICTS: see **L**, cf. especially Chadwick *Early Scotland* 1 ff. and Isabel Henderson *The Picts*.

186.3 KING LISTS: see **K** P.

186.3 INSCRIPTION: RIB 191 *Lossio Veda . . . nepos Vepogeni, Caledo*, cf. Vepoguenech, placed about the first half of the third century in the king lists, see **K** P.

188.2 PLACE NAMES: Map 11; Watson CPNS surveys Celtic, but not English or Norse names. 'Scotland north of the Forth' (206 ff.) is treated as a single unit, but the survey is almost entirely confined to districts east of the Great Glen. Four isolated Pictish place names opposite Skye suggest a garrison whose names endured; a few stones in Caithness, the islands and southern Scotland are probably memorials of lords and colonists in the years of Pictish supremacy.

188.3 DUNS AND BROCHS: see **M**, and Map 12. Many contained Roman objects of the early Empire but, unlike other native sites in Scotland, none has any of the late Empire; cf. *Britannia* 1, 1970, 202, cf. 210, 212; see **M**. See especially IANB 111 ff.; *Ant*. 39, 1965, 266; PPS 31, 1965, 93; *C.Arch*. 2, 1967, 27; 12, 1969, 5.

188.3 ORKNEYS: not part of Pictland, but situated 'beyond the Picts' (*ultra Pictos*), Nennius 8; their king was a subject foreign tributary of the Pict king Bridei, p. 193 below.

190.4 OTHER INDICATIONS: e.g. various confused Irish traditions, backed by Tacitus (*Agricola* II) 'the red hair and huge limbs of the Caledonians proclaim their German origin; the dark complexions and the frequency of curly hair among the Silures (of Monmouthshire) . . . justify the belief that their ancestors crossed from Spain and settled there'. Excavation has confirmed the tradition of migration from Spain to South Wales, some two thousand years before Tacitus' time, and thereby adds weight to his comment on the more recently arrived Caledonians. Tacitus uses 'Caledonia' as a general term for all north Britain; the dated evidence of the brochs and their situation suggests that in his time their builders were the dominant power in most of northern Britain. At the time of their arrival in Britain it is probable that the larger part of the Germanic peoples still dwelt in Scandinavia. See **L**.

190.4 SOME OTHER CONQUERORS: e.g. the Normans, in England, France and Italy, and the Bulgarians, among the Slavs of the eastern Balkans, etc.

190.5 ATECOTTI: see **L**, and p. 177 above.

190.5 ABORIGINES: they are unlikely to have been concentrated in a single area. Communities who cling to a dying language are often isolated from each other by considerable distances, as, for example, the pockets of Slavonic speaking peoples who survived into modern times in widely separated regions of Germany.

191.1 OGAM: see p. 422 below.

191.1 STONES INSCRIBED IN OGAM: ed. MacAlister *MacNeill Essays* 184 ff., cf.

Diack *Inscriptions*, see **O**. Of 17 such Ogam stones, 7 are in the Orkneys and Shetlands, where brochs are numerous, but only 3 in Caithness and Sutherland, and none at all in Skye and the Hebridean area, where brochs are equally numerous. There are 3 in the Northern Pictish lands and 4 in the southern; none in the regions where duns are frequent. In addition, there are three similar inscriptions on knife handles, in Orkney, in the Hebrides, and in Norfolk (p. 57 above); but portable knives are not evidence of settlement. One stone from the Isle of Man may or may not belong to the same series.

Three of the inscriptions were added to Christian crosses, five to Pictish memorial stones, and can therefore hardly be earlier than the 7th or 8th centuries, if so early. But these stones cannot date the others, for date depends upon the origin of the script. The chief consideration is that its authors were familiar with Irish Ogam characters; but no Irish Ogams are known in the countries whence these inscriptions came, and only two are known anywhere in Scotland, both in Dal Riada, in Argyle. The most likely of the several possible origins of the script is therefore Irish Ogams inscribed on wood, by the earlier Irish population of north-western Scotland. The inscriptions appear on stone only in those regions where stone memorials were familiar.

If the symbols represent Irish letters, if the modern transcripts are secure, and if they represent a language at all, it is possible to detect Irish and Norse words for son and daughter, and some Pictish and Latin personal names; but it is also possible that all are an illiterate ornamental borrowing by persons who had seen Irish Ogams, but could not read or understand them. If the symbols do represent a language, the language is unknown, and attempts to 'translate' it have not succeeded.

191.3 BEDE: HE 3, 4.

191.3 NINIAN: see **E**, and p. 337 below; cf. Map 26, p. 371.

192.2 INHERITANCE: see **L**, Picts; land and property inherited through the woman, CPS 328; 126; 319; sovereignty through the woman, CPS 40; 45; 329. The Picts perpetuated customs that had been more widespread in pre-Roman Britain, and which also survived in other parts of northern Britain. Sovereignty through or of the woman is reported of the Iceni and Brigantes in Britain in the 1st century AD. In the 7th century the queen of Eigg exercised wide authority among the *Iardomnan*, M.Oeng. April 17; in the 6th century or earlier the Hebrides maintained a king who was denied marriage, children and personal property, Solinus (Irish version), ed. Mommsen p. 219, cf. Walter *Solinus*, especially p. 38, and Chadwick ES 92. Matrilinear inheritance still survives in parts of Asia, especially south-western India.

192.2 BRIDEI: see **P**.

192.2 PICTISH GRANDMOTHER: see **G** BGG.

192.3 RHUN: see **J** and **G** BGG.

193.1 BRIDEI'S ROYAL FORTRESS: Adomnan 2, 35.

193.1 BEDE: HE 3, 4 *venit . . . Columba . . . praedicaturus verbum Dei provinciis septentrionalium Pictorum . . . gentemque illam verbo et exemplo ad fidem Christi convertit.*

193.1 ADOMNAN: 3, 3 *populorum ducem ad vitam*, cf. 3, 1 *animarum dux ad caelestem*; but Picts are one among several peoples in Adomnan's narrative, and are not the most prominent.

193.1 MAGI: Adomnan 2, 33–34, cf. **P** Broichan.

193.1 WINDS: Adomnan 2, 34.

193.1 LOCH NESS MONSTER: Adomnan 2, 27 *aquatilis bestia, bilua*, that bit and killed swimmers in the river Ness, below the Loch.

193.2 LORDS: e.g. at Urquhart, Adomnan 3, 14. Emchath was local, since his son Virolec was baptised *cum tota domu*.

193.3 ORKNEY KING: Adomnan 2, 42.

194.1 MEMORIAL STONES: Map 11, p. 187; see **L** Picts; cf. J.Romilly Allen and J.Anderson ECMS; Isabel Henderson *The Picts* 104 ff.; *Arch. Jl.* 120, 1963, 31, cf.118, 1961, 14; PSAS 91, 1957/8, 44; Wainwright PP 97; Cruden ECPMS.

194.1 STONES . . . DATE: a few of the earliest, e.g. Dunnichen, imitate 6th century Saxon saucer brooches too closely for coincidence.

195.1 PENTLAND . . . PEHTLAND: so Skene CS 1,238, without citation of evidence; cf. *Pettaland* (Pictland) for the Pentland Firth, between Caithness and Orkney, Watson CPNS 30.

195.2 AETHELFERTH'S SONS: his heir Osric was killed in an Irish battle shortly before Edwin's death **A** 631.

195.2 EANFRITH: Bede HE 3, 1.

195.3 ENGLISH KING: Talorcan filius Enfreth, see **K** P, cf. **G** ENB. It is likely that foreign-born Pictish kings who used Pictish names assumed them on their accession. Talorcan's English name is not recorded.

195.3 BEDE: HE 2, 5.

195.3 ENGLISH UNDER-KING: Beornhaeth (Eddius 19), apparently already in office on the outbreak of the revolt at the beginning of Egferth's reign.

196.1 BESTIAL NATIONS: Eddius 19.

196.1 WASTE . . . THE PICTS: Bede HE 4, 26.

196.1 ALDFRITH: see **G** ENB 650, and p. 176.

196.3 SCOTLAND: The most useful brief survey of Scottish history from the 7th to the 11th century remains that of Skene CS 1,240 ff., though much detail has since been corrected.

197.2 MORGAN: see **G** IDRL.

197.3 ALBAN: at the Battle of the Standard in 1138, the Scots from beyond the Forth *exclamant Albani! Albani!* HH 8, 9; cf. GESTA STEPHANI *Scotia quae et Albania dicitur*; Richard of Hexham *in fronte belli erant Picti*, Rolls 82, 3, 35 and 163.

197.4 EDINBURGH 960: CPS 365.

197.4 LOTHIANS 1018: Simeon of Durham *de Obsessione Dunelmi* 6.

198.1 DUNCAN KILLED: **A** AT (Tigernach) 379[2] (AD 1040) *Donncadh m Crinan, aird ri Alban, immatura etate a suis occisus est* ('Duncan mac Crinan, High King of Albany, was killed in youth by his own people'). Tigernach wrote within fifty years of the event.

198.1 MACBETH: see **G** IDRL.

198.3 WALTER OF OSWESTRY: cf. e.g. G.W.S.Barrow *Regesta Regum Scottorum* 1; for the genealogy see e.g. *Complete Peerage* 5, 391–2, Round *Peerage and Family History* 115 ff.; 129. Walter's grandfather was Flaald, brother of abbott Rhiwallon and son of Alan, steward of Dol; hence the later spread of the name Alan in England and Scotland.

12 **British Supremacy** (pp. 200–224)

200.1 SOURCES: see pp. 143 and 164 above.

200.2 ARCHAEOLOGICAL EVIDENCE: is still much less in the midlands and the south than in the west and north; and little of it can yet be dated with confidence. 'Grass tempered' pottery, recently recognised, and provisionally dated to the Arthurian centuries, cannot yet be clearly interpreted; Celtic metalwork, listed by E. Fowler in *Arch. Jl.* 120, 1963, 135 ff., with an extensive bibliography, is reported from a number of southern and midland sites; but the import of British or Irish ornaments and craftsmen does not always imply a British or Irish population. Hanging bowl escutcheons with unequivocally Irish ornament, mostly of the 7th century, are known almost entirely from English graves, since they survive only in burials; in living use they are likely to have been at least as common among the Irish and British, and among the English they argue only the purchase of objects manufactured by Irishmen, who are as likely to have worked in Britain as in Ireland. Major British sites of the 5th and 6th centuries, outside the north and west, are few, and are at present most numerous in the Home Counties, cf. London, Colchester, Verulamium etc.

What is now known is surveyed in Alcock *Arthur's Britain* 142 ff. As yet the material is disjointed and of uncertain date, and there is not much of it. But since it has only recently begun to be recognised, it is likely that twenty years hence much more will be known, its dates more surely estimated, and that recognisable sites and objects will be more evenly distributed throughout Britain. They may well provide the most useful means of resolving many present uncertainties.

201.1 GILDAS' KINGS: 27 ff.

202.2 EMESA: *Novella Theodosii* 15, 2 (CTh. Vol. 2, p. 36).

203.3 PERHAPS OF GLOUCESTER: see **P** (Aurelius) Caninus.

203.3 VIOLATED HIS DAUGHTER: the offence was no more startling than many other dynastic marriages, e.g. Radiger's with his step-mother (p. 287 below) or the suggestion of marriage between Henry VII and his widowed daughter-in-law; but papal dispensation was less familiar in Gildas' time than a thousand years later.

206.4 ILL-STARRED GENERALS: *infausti duces* Gildas 50,1.

207.5 CAERWENT: see especially **E** Tatheus and **G** BMG.

208.1 GLEVISSIG, GLIVIS: see **G** BM and **L**.

208.1 PENYCHEN: see **E** Cadoc.

208.1 DEMETIA . . . BORDER: *Venta provincia proxima eiusdem Demetiae* vita 1 Samsonis 1; *ultra Sabrinae fluminis fretum Demetarum sacerdotes* Aldhelm *Ep.* 4 (MGH p. 484), written from Malmesbury.

208.1 DUBRICIUS, TEILO: see **E**. David is freely called 'bishop' and 'archbishop' in the Lives; but no episcopal acts, comparable with those ascribed to Dubricius and Teilo, are related of him.

208.3 POMPEIUS, TURPILIUS: ECMW 198; 43. Cf. p. 251 below.

208.3 ILLTUD: see **E**.

208.3 CHEPSTOW: *vita Tathei* 4, see **E** Tatheus; the place is probably Portskewett.

208.3 CARRIAGE AND PAIR: Gildas *Ep.* 4 *habent pecora et vehicula vel pro consuetudine patriae vel sua infirmitate*, cf. *Ep.* 2. *vehiculis equisque vehuntur*.

210.1 DECANGI: Tac. *Ann.* 12, 32; Decanti ACm 822, cf. 812, cf. Degannwy by Llandudno, traditionally a royal centre of Maelgwn; Decangli, inscribed on lead pigs CIL VII 204–206; JRS 12, 1922, 283 15; cf. Tegeingl (Flintshire). It is possible but not probable that these spellings relate to two distinct adjacent peoples; cf. **L**.

210.2 WANSDYKE: see **L**. The frontier work included stretches evidently wooded in the 5th and 6th centuries, where it was not necessary to dig a dyke.

210.2 CATO: see **G** BC.

210.3 GREAT KINGS: e.g. Amlaut, Kassanauth, see **G**, index.

211.1 CARADOC VREICHVRAS: see **G** BLS.

12 BRITISH SUPREMACY (pp. 211–219)

211.1 SILCHESTER: see p. 137 above.

211.1 SILCHESTER DYKES: *Ant.* 18, 1944, 113, cf. 17, 1943, 188; cf. *Berks. Arch. Jl.* 54, 1954, 50.

211.2 ENGLISH TEXTS: SC.

211.3 CALCHVYNYDD: See **G** BLC, and **L**.

211.3 CATRAUT: see **G** BLC.

211.3 VERULAMIUM: cf. p. 137 above.

211.4 LONDON, COLCHESTER: see p. 137 above. The latest relics of British London are an *amphora* (wine or oil jar) imported from the eastern mediterranean, probably in or about the 6th century *Britannia* 1, 1970, 292 (where note 127 corrects the text), and several others excavated earlier, but first recognised after this discovery. The exact dating of these vessels is still uncertain.

211.4 ARTHUR'S CAMPAIGN: Nennius 56, see p. 111 above.

211.4 LINDSEY: one of its early 7th century rulers is said to have borne the British name of Caedbad, of **G** EL.

211.4 POETS: see **T** and p. 241 below.

212.1 WROXETER: see p. 241 below.

213.1 GENEALOGIES: especially **G** BA, BN.

213.3 DEIRANS: **G** END 430 Soemil, see p. 77 above.

213.5 YORK CEMETERIES: see **S**.

214.2 GERMANIANUS . . . KINGDOM: see **G** BNM.

214.3 YEAVERING: see p. 320 below.

214.4 REGED: see **L**.

214.4 DENT: *regio Dunotinga* is one of four districts of north-western Yorkshire overrun by the English in or before the 670s, Eddius 17. The passage is overlooked in EPNS WRY 6, 252, where the early spellings Denet(h) are rightly related to a British *Dinned* or the like, and Ekwall's derivation from a non-existent British equivalent of the Old Irish *dind*, hill, is properly dismissed. EPNS does not observe that Dent was, and still is, the name of a considerable region, and that the village is still locally known as Dent Town, in contrast with the surrounding district of Dent. The physical appearance of the village is still strikingly unlike that of any other in the Yorkshire Dales, and it has been aptly described as a 'Cornish village stranded in the Dales.' *Regio Dunotinga* plainly takes its name from a person named Dunawt, Latin Donatus, as does the district of Dunoding in Merioneth, named from another Dunawt, son of Cunedda. See **L**.

214.4 SAMUEL: see **G** BN and **E** Cadoc.

215.2 GUALLAUC: his memory caused later parents in the area to name their children Wallace.

215.3 KENTIGERN: see **E**. Cambria, Jocelyn 11; Morken, Cathen, Jocelyn 22; see **G** BA, BN.

215.3 MANAU: see **L**.

215.3 DYFNWAL: see **G** BA; **J**.

216.3 WELSH ACCOUNT: see **J** and **Q**.

216.3 ELIDYR: see **G** BNR.

216.3 RHUN: see **G** BGG, and p. 192 above.

216.3 BRIDEI: see p. 193 above.

216.4 LLYWARCH . . . PASSIVE: Triad 8, cf. **G** BNR.

217.2 CYNDDELW: references assembled in TYP 502.

218.2 ARDERYDD: see **G** BN 560 Gwendoleu.

219.1 CELIDON: Nennius 56, cf. **T**; see **L**.

219.2 URIEN: see **G** BNR; see p. 232 below.

219.2 ROYAL RESIDENCE: Llwyfenydd, near the Roman fort of Kirkby Thore, by Penrith; see **L**.

219.3 CERETIC: Muirchu 28 cited p. 416.4 below.

219.3 MAELGWN: Gildas 34 *auscultantur . . . laudes . . . propriae . . . praeconum ore ritu Bacchantium concrepante*, cf. p. 416.4.

220.1 DINAS POWYS: Coed Clwydgwyn cf. **G** BB 530 Clytwin and p. 431 below.

220.3 MAELGWYN . . . TRIBUTE: e.g. Maelgwn imposed a tribute of a hundred cows and a hundred calves on each pagus; his *exactores* collected them in Glevissig, with a force of three hundred men, *vita Cadoc* 69.

220.4 LAWS . . . OF WALES: see **J** and p. 445.

220.4 ROMAN: see Jones LRE, especially 672 ff.; cf. 258–259 and 449 ff., and the texts there cited.

220.4 EROGATOR MILITARIS ANNONAE: cf. e.g. the texts cited in Du Cange, *Erogator*.

221.2 CAIS etc.: see p. 460 below. The evidence is briefly surveyed by W.Rees in *Angles and Britons* 148; cf. G.W.S.Barrow *Northern History* 4, 1969, 1 ff. It will be better understood when the texts, including the Yorkshire documentation, have been more fully studied. Random observation suggests that survivals of British administration were not confined to the north. *Gwestva*, tribute of food to the king, was reported in Flintshire in the 11th century, as *hestha* (DB 269 b (Cheshire FM 7); in the East Riding, as *hestcorne* oats, and as *hestra(st)la* or *hest(e)rasda*, horse fodder (Mon. Ang. 2,367; 1,170; HY 1,298); and, in the 13th century, as *ghestum*, loaves, in Northamptonshire (Northants. RS 5,793) and in Somerset (Archaelogical Institute, Salisbury volume, 1851, 208; Somerset RS 5,83, cf. 89.90.93; cf. HMC Report 12, 1, 288, 329; SANHS 20, Supplement 67). I owe the references to *ghestum* to the kindness of Mr R.E.Latham. The obligation survived elsewhere without the name, cf. e.g. BCS 612 (Taunton, AD 904) 'one night's supplies (*pastus*) for the king and his kenneler and eight dogs, and nine nights' supplies for his falconers, and whatever the king may desire to convey thereof with waggons and horses to Curig (?) or Wilton'.

221.5 GILDAS: 1, 2 ff., quoting *Ecclesiastes* 3, 7.

222.1 MONKS: cf. chapters 18–20 below.

222.2 PLAGUE: see **M**.

222.3 TRADE: see p. 441 below.

223.1 EGYPTIAN SAINT: cf. p. 441 below.

223.2 PARTITION: see p. 134 above.

223.2 IRISHMEN: see **E** Abban, Columba of Terryglass and p. 386.

223.2 BRITISH . . . AMONG . . . ENGLISH: see **E** Gwenael, Winwaloe, and p. 314.

223.2 GIDEON: Gildas 70, 3; cf. 72, 3.

223.3 AFRICA: Corippus *Iohannidos* 3, 388–389 (p. 36 cf. xvi), *Gentes non laesit amaras Martis amica lues.*

13 **British Collapse** (pp. 225–248)

225.1 SAXON REVOLT: cf. p. 293 below.

225.1 CYNRIC: see **G** EW.

225.2 CEMETERIES: see **S**.

226.2 CIVIL WARS: the most likely cause of conflict between Winchester and Salisbury is a division of the *civitas* of the Belgae between the heirs of a former ruler, possibly Caradauc Vreichvras, cf. pp. 211 above, and 293 and 324 below.

226.2 CEAWLIN, CUTHA: see **G** EW, cf. p. 293 below.

13 BRITISH COLLAPSE (pp. 227–236)

227.1 GLOUCESTER . . . POPULATION: BCS 60, cf. Finberg ECWM 158 ff.; p. 497 below.

227.2 FETHANLEA: see **L**; the name might be a misreading of *Feranlea*, any of the several places now called Fernley or the like, which include the old name of Hereford HW 282.

227.3 MAEDOC: *vita* (VSH) 17 see **E**.

227.3 FINNIAN: *vita* (Sal.) 8 see **E**.

228.1 BOULDERS: the story might suggest to the unwary that it was borrowed from Bede's account of Germanus' Alleluia victory (p. 62 above). But Irish tradition knew Germanus only as Patrick's teacher; the point of the story is not borrowed, and battles in Wales are commonly fought among hills; it is not therefore prudent to assume the influence of Bede.

228.2 CADOC . . . PRAYED THE LORD: *vita Cadoc* 25, cf. **E**.

228.2 MOURIC: see **G** BM.

228.2 LLANCARFAN, LLANDAFF: see **T** Gospel Books.

228.2 THEODORIC: see **G** AC, BM and pp. 126 ff. above.

228.3 KING THEODORIC: LL 141–142.

229.1 BROCKWEIR: see **L**.

229.1 SIGBERT: Bede HE 3, 18.

229.2 AXMINSTER: *Beandun*, Bindon SC 614, see **L** and p. 307.

229.2 IDON: LL 123 see **G** BMG.

229.3 DUMNONIA: cf. p. 302.

230.1 BADON . . . MORCANT: see p. 309 below.

230.2 UNTIL 775: see **G** BM. The reigns of a father and son for 110 years, from 665 to 775, are unusually long; but not unduly longer than those of Louis XIII and XIV of France, 105 years, or of Attalus I and II of Pergamon, 104 years. Queen Victoria's last surviving child died 107 years after her mother's accession to the throne.

231.2 RECORD OF THE ENGLISH: see **T** SC; cf. p. 317 below.

231.2 WELSH POEMS: see **T**.

231.5 IDA: see **G** ENB.

231.5 NENNIUS: 62, see **G** ENB.

232.2 TALHEARN: Nennius 62.

232.3 URIEN OF ECHWYD: CT 3, 1–4; 7–11; 27–30, translated IWP 28.

232.3 ECHWYD: possibly Solway, see **L**.

233.4 TERRITORIES . . . SPLIT: see **G** ENB, cf. note 234 below.

233.4 CAER GREU: ACm 580, see **G** BN Peredur, ENB Adda.

233.4 GWGAUN: see **G** BN.

234.1 AELLE: see **G** END.

234.2 ULPH: CT 7, 11–12; 29.

234.2 FFLAMDDWYN: see **G** ENB sons of Ida, Aethelric; **G** BNR Owain, Urien.

234.2 FOUR ARMIES: CT 6, 10; the Bernician forces were still organised in four armies at Catraeth, *Gorchan Tudfwlch* CA 1296 ff.

234.2 ARGOED LLWYFEIN: CT 6, translated WBT 29, PWP 18; see **L**.

234.3 URIEN'S ELEGY: CLH 3 (FAB 359, 259).

234.3 PILLAR OF BRITAIN: *Post Prydein* CLH 3, 16, cf. T 5, bracketed with Pabo, father of Dunaut, and Cynvelyn Drysgl of Edinburgh, cf. **G** BN.

234.3 HUSSA: Nennius 63. The text is early, using the 7th century spelling Urbgen for Urien.

234.3 METCAUD: Lindisfarne, **A** 635 (Metgoit); cf. **L**.

235.1 FIACHNA: Fiachna Lurgan, see **G** IUA 570/580 note.

235.3 WHEN OWAIN: CT 10, 11 ff., translated Parry HWL 3, cf. IWP 27.

236.2 THE HEAD I CARRY: CLH 3, 8; 30–31; cf. 46; 51; 53; 56; 59.

237.2 CATRAETH: see **L** and **A** 598.

237.2 DEIRAN TREACHERY: CA 198–201 'The treacherous Deirans asked "Is there a Briton truer than Cynan?"' **L**; Jackson *Ant.* 13, 1939, 27; *Gododdin* **A** 18.

237.3 MEN WENT TO CATRAETH: CA 33 (372–375); 31 (361–2); 58 (670–674); 60 (689–694); Jackson *Gododdin* A 33; 31; 56; 59.

238.1 MAEL UMA: see **G** INE 570/580, IDRF Aedan note.

238.1 BEDE: HE I, 34.

238.2 DEIRA: see **G** END Aelle; the statement of SC that Aelle died in 588 is formally denied by Bede and other earlier texts.

238.2 CHESTER: Bede HE 2, 2 cf. **A** 614.

239.1 CONTEMPLATED CONQUEST OF NORTHUMBRIA: see p. 301 below.

239.2 CLYDE: see **G** BA.

240.2 GWYNEDD: see **G** BGG Cadman, Catwallaun, etc.

240.2 VESTIGES OF POEMS: BBCS 7, 1933, 24, cf. TYP 294.

240.2 MEVANIAN ISLANDS: Bede HE 2, 5, cf. 2.9; see **L**.

240.3 PENDA: see **G** EM and pp. 302 ff. below; one tradition held that he was first attacked and subdued by Catwallaun, another that Catwallaun married his sister or niece.

240.3 EDWIN KILLED: the campaign apparently involved two battles, near Welshpool and Doncaster, see **L** Meicen, Hatfield.

240.4 MERIONETH: Idris, see **A** and **G** BGM.

241.2 OSWALD IN WESSEX: SC 635.

241.2 CYNDDYLAN: see **G** BCW.

241.2 MAES COGWY: see **L**.

241.2 GAIUS CAMPUS, WINWAED: see **L**.

241.3 CYNDRWYN: Triad 60, his son Gwiawn at 'Bangor Orchard'.

241.3 CYNDDYLAN: CLH II, 3 and 4.

241.3 WROXETER: CArch. 4, 1969, 84; 23, 1970, 336; 25, 1971, 45; where however the word Germanic is misleading.

242.2 MAES COGWY: CLH II, III.

242.2 OAKEN COFFIN: CLH 13, 1; 25 ff.

242.3 MY HEART IS AFLAME: CLH 13, 42 ff.

243.1 LUITCOET: see **L**.

243.1 MORFAEL: see **G** BCL and p. 308 below.

243.2 OSWY . . . RAIDED: ACm 656.

243.2 TRIBAL HIDAGE: see **T** and p. 492.

243.2 WULFHERE'S FORD: DB f. 259 d, Shropshire IV, last entry, cf. HW 195.

244.1 CYNDDYLAN: CLH II, 6 (Tren); 15–16; 18; 27; 29; 31; 66; 69; 71–72; 85; 87.

245.2 WREKIN: CLH II, 81, 'Once I looked from Dinlle Wrecon, Down upon the land of Freuer'. Freuer is represented as the sister of Cynddylan.

246.1 BROKEN SHIELD: CLH II, 55–56.

14 **Brittany** (pp. 249–260)

249.1 ARMORICAN BRITISH: see **L** Llydaw and **G** A.

249.1 SAINTS' LIVES: see **E** introduction, and p. 164.

249.2 MANUSCRIPTS: many of the published texts were discovered by a deliberate search conducted by French scholars in the Bibliothèque Nationale, the libraries of Fleury, St. Germain-des-Prés, and other houses, chiefly between 1880 and 1914; further search in such libraries offers the most likely chance of finding unpublished texts that concern Britain and Brittany.

249.2 PERTINACIOUS ENQUIRY: *Cartulary of Quimperlé*, preface, pp. vi–ix.

249.2 LE GRAND ... TEXTS: including Breviaries and *Propria*, service books, in manuscript, or printed in the 16th and 17th centuries for the use of particular houses, which were also extensively consulted by Baring-Gould LBS; full publication is likely to add to knowledge; see **T**.

249.2 LE GRAND: see **E** introduction.

249.2 CHARTERS: see **C**.

250.1 GREGORY OF TOURS: see **E**.

250.1 PILGRIM: see p. 383 below.

250.2 MANY REGIONS: Nennius 27.

251.2 SECOND MIGRATION: cf. pp. 38 and 90 above.

251.3 BRITISH COUNTS: Greg. Tur. HF 4, 4 *nam semper Brittani sub Francorum potestatem post obitum regis Chlodovechi (511) fuerent, et comites non reges appellati sunt.* The language of the Lives is normally precise, using *rex* for 5th century rulers, *comes* for 6th-century rulers.

251.3 THIRD MIGRATION: for its date and nature see especially p. 364 below.

251.4 CONOMORUS, RIWAL: see **G** A; the most important of the 6th-century emigrant leaders was probably Arthmael (see **E**), but little is known of him.

251.4 CARADAUC: see **G** BLS.

251.4 RIWAL ... FROM OVERSEAS: *vita Winnoci*, cf. LBS 1, 297 note 3; cf. also *vitae Leonori, Tudwal*; see **G** ADW.

251.4 FRACAN: *vita Winwaloe* 1, 2.

252.2 HORSE RACE: *vita Winwaloe* 1, 18; cf. **E**.

252.4 PAUL TRAVELLED: *vita Pauli Aureliani* 15, cf. **E**.

253.2 ROSCOFF ... POTTERY: discovered by the late Professor J.B.S.Haldane.

253.3 BACAUDAE: see pp. 8 and 90 above.

253.4 VICTOR: *vita Pauli Aureliani* 15, cf. 19 *rex Philibertus istam mihi regionem sub suae potestatis conditione ad regendam tradidit.*

256.1 CYNAN: see **G** AG, AV.

256.1 DANIEL, BUDIC, THEODORIC etc.: see **G** AC and p. 130.

256.2 MACLIAVUS: Greg. Tur. HF 5, 16, cf. **G** AV.

256.3 MACLIAVUS, CONOMORUS: Greg. Tur. HF 4, 4; cf. **G** AC.

256.3 CONOMORUS: *iudex externus* in Armorican tradition, *vita I Samsonis* 1, 53; *vita Leonori*, a foreign ruler, in contrast with the immigrants who had forsaken their homes in Britain; to those in Britain, Armorica was also *externae gentis regio* (vita Pauli Aureliani 9). His kingdom is approximately located by the Life of Paul Aurelian, whose father took service in Glevissig, but whose ancestral estates lay on the Channel coasts and within the dominion of Conomorus. Conomorus' royal centre is explicitly located at Castle Dore by the Norman poets, see references in *P and P* 11, 1957, 15–16. No evidence locates him in South Wales, as THS Cymm. 1953, 47 ff., cf. TYP 446.

257.1 BANHEDOS ... MARCUS: *vita Pauli Aureliani* 8; variant reading *Bannhedos*.

257.1 DRUSTANUS: CIIC 487, corrected JRIC n.s.1, 1951, 117, *His iacit Drustanus Cunomori filius*; the name *Drustanus*, no longer legible, is restored, chiefly from earlier readings. It recalls Pictish Drust, but is rare, cf. Columba's pupil Drostanus, abbot of Deer, *Book of Deer* p. 91, who is however said to have been son of an Irish Coscrach, *Brev. Ab.* PH 19 d. The Tristan of the legends is transformed into a nephew of Mark and given alternative fathers, Rivalen in Brittany, Tallwch in Wales; both names are late additions, not related to the realities from which the legend originated.

257.3 CHRAMN: Greg. Tur. HF 4, 20 cf. 21, death of Clothair; cf. *vita Samsonis* (AG) 14–15; the AG Life of Samson concentrates upon events in Brittany; the early *vita prima* and its derivatives deal chiefly with events in Britain.

258.2 BURIED AT CASTLE DORE: *vita Pauli Aureliani* 8.

258.4 THEODORIC: Greg. Tur. HF 5, 16, cf. **G** AC, BM and p. 228.

258.4 WAROC: see **G** AV.

259.2 IUTHAEL, HAELOC etc.: see **G** ADe.

259.2 MALO: see **E**; the principal life is a 9th-century text, using 7th-century sources.

259.3 IUDICAEL, IUDOC, WINNOC: see **G** ADe, and **E**.

259.3 MEVEN: see **E**.

259.4 FITZALANS, STUARTS: see p. 198 above.

15 **English Immigrants** (pp. 261–292)

261.1 HOMELAND: see **S**.

261.2 GERMANIC LEGEND: especially the poem *Widsith*, notably lines 18 ff. and 57, and *Beowulf*.

261.2 OCEAN PEOPLES: see **F**.

261.4 MIGRATION: the fundamental survey of the texts is Thomas Hodgkin *Italy and her Invaders*. Lucien Musset *Les Invasions; les Vagues Germaniques* summarises more recent thinking. The viewpoint is Roman. From the barbarian standpoint the fullest study is L. Schmidt *Allgemeine Geschichte der Germanischen Völker*. There is no comprehensive survey of the archaeological evidence.

262.2 CHAMAVI: Eunapius, fragment 12.

264.3 SCANDINAVIA: *vagina nationum* Jordanes *Getica* 4.

264.3 OTHERS: e.g. the Burgundians, whose name is preserved in Bornholm and elsewhere.

264.3 GERMANIC NATIONS: the nearest equivalent to a comprehensive map of barbarian Europe is the *Grosse Gesamtkarte* in Eggers *Römische Import*; though it excludes sites that have no import, few areas had none, and the blanks on the map are usually devoid of native as well as of imported finds.

264.4 LANGOBARDI: Cassius Dio 71, 3, 1a; see **F**.

265.2 EORMENRIC: see PLRE 1, Ermanaricus.

265.2 JUTLAND . . . DEPOPULATED: see **F** and **S**.

265.3 OFFA: see **G** EM.

266.3 HENGEST: see **G** EK. Hengst and Hors mean 'Stallion' and 'Mare', evidently the nicknames, and perhaps the ensigns of the two leaders. One genealogy suggests that Hengest's name may have been Aethelbert. Bede HE 1, 15 says that the name of Hors was to be seen on a monument in East Kent. What was seen was doubtless the remnant of a Roman inscription erected by a [CO]HORS; if so, the place was probably Reculver, the only place in Kent or in southern Britain where a cohort was stationed in the period when such inscriptions were commonly erected.

266.3 BEOWULF: see **T**; Hengest, lines 1068 ff.

266.3 FINN'S BURG: see **T**.

267.5 GRAVE GOODS: see **S** and p. 32 above.

268.2 ROUTES: they were a particularly unhappy handicap to the sensitive and perceptive studies of E.T. Leeds; in other hands the concept often verged upon the absurd.

269.3 CRUCIFORM AND SAUCER BROOCHES: cf. p. 32 above.

270.2 THE NATION: Bede HE 1, 15.

270.2 HE KNEW: Bede HE 5, 9.

272.1 ENGLISH: Nennius 56, cf. p. 106 above.

272.1 PROCOPIUS: BG 4, 20.

272.2 ICLINGAS: see **G** EM.

272.3 NAME OF ICEL: in Sussex a few Icel names, together with Cutha names and great squareheaded brooches, suggest some East Anglian settlement in the later 6th century, cf. Map 20, p. 295. Personal names in Cutha are numerous at all periods, but, on the evidence so far published by EPNS, are relatively infrequent in place names outside the districts overrun by the Eslingas; the most noticeable other Cutha region is in northern Mercia.

273.2 ESLINGAS: see p. 110 above.

273.4 ENGLISH IN EUROPE: Map 16; see **S** and the particular peoples and regions in **F**.

274.1 EVERY OARSMAN: Sidonius *Ep.* 8, 6, 13 *Saxones . . . archpiratas . . . ita ut simul omnes imparent parent, docent discunt latrocinari.*

274.2 CORSOLDUS: see p. 92 above.

274.2 ODOVACER: see **P** and p. 91 above.

276.1 PRESSURES: exactly defined and keenly remembered in the native tradition of the continental Saxons, e.g. *Translatio S. Alexandri* 1, reporting that their ancestors had been continually obliged to defend their living space (*spacia*) against four named enemies who pressed upon them, *a meridie Francos . . ., a septentrione vero Nordmannos . . ., ab ortu Obroditos . . ., ab occasu Frisos.* The *Obroditi* were Slavs, the *Nordmanni* Danes.

278.1 DANISH INVASION: Greg. Tur. HF. 3, 3, cf. the Latin sources printed in Chambers *Beowulf* 3–4, cf. pp. 381 ff. Frisian territory, though not settled by Franks, seems to have been a subject *pagus* of the Frank kingdom before 520, see **L**.

278.2 DANES: see **F**.

278.3 SLAVS: see **F**. The main difficulty in the interpretation of the evidence is that the same grave goods are often given quite different dates by modern German and modern central European scholars. Identical pots are sometimes assigned to the 7th or 8th centuries if they are excavated in Baltic lands and published in Germany, to the 5th and 6th centuries if they are excavated by the Danube and there published. Until a thorough comparative study is available, it is only possible to observe that the Danubian dates are based on the evidence of associated Roman objects, while the north German graves have no such evidence. The Danubian material justifies the conclusion of, e.g. Preidel (*Slawische Altertumskunde* 2, 14 ff.) that Slav graves begin in the 4th century, and that the 'Prague Type', and related pottery vessels, were 'dominant' during the 5th and 6th centuries, rare thereafter. They are markedly absent from 7th century southern Slav sites. Such vessels are quite common in north Germany; though it is theoretically possible that their manufacture might have begun later and continued longer in the north, such a hypothesis cannot be maintained until decisive evidence is clearly demonstrated. The dating at present given by different scholars in different countries, and the reasoning upon which it is based, is discussed in **F**.

278.4 HAMBURG CEMETERY: Tischler *Sachsenforschung*, plate 29, p. 85, cf. H. Jankuhn *Geschichte Schleswig-Holsteins* 3, 1957, 100, citing local publications. The view that the large vessel there illustrated seems to be a normal Slavonic Prague Type, and that the smaller vessels are imitations of late Roman provincial wares, is endorsed by Czech scholars conversant with these vessels, who have been kind enough to look at the illustration. Present conditions preclude a more precise pursuit of the opinions expressed.

279.1 PROCOPIUS: especially BG 2, 15, 1 ff.; 3, 55; see **F** Slavs.

279.3 AGRICULTURAL TECHNOLOGY: it is sometimes schematically pretended that a 'slash and burn economy' is necessarily more 'primitive' than the cultivation of lands already cleared. But the opening up of virginal lands commonly requires greater application and a technology as 'advanced' as inherited cultivation, or more so; 'slashing and burning' is the most suitable technique for the clearance of lightly wooded lands. It may only be dismissed as 'primitive' when it is not followed by continuing cultivation. The nature of Slavonic agriculture in Bohemia and the Baltic lands will be better understood when adequate comprehensive and comparative study has been directed to excavated Slavonic objects; to old Slavonic words for tools; and to Slavonic place names. Circumstances have tended to inhibit such study.

280.1 STIRRUP . . . HORSE COLLAR: cf. p. 437 below.

280.3 MAP 8: Partition, p. 134 above.

281.2 PROCOPIUS: BG 4, 20.

281.2 BURIALS: see **S.**

281.3 SMALL PEOPLES: most are mapped on the Ordnance Survey's *Map of Dark Age Britain.*

282.1 BERNICIANS . . . FOUR PEOPLES: cf. pp. 233–234 above.

282.3 NEW IMMIGRANTS: see **S.**

283.2 ANGLIAN CHRONICLE: cf. Liebermann MGH SS 28, 11. Differently excerpted by Henry of Huntingdon and *Flores Historiarum*, both under the year 527. In the reconstructed text below, the words common to both are printed in capitals; those excerpted by Henry only are in italics, and those excerpted by the *Flores* only are in Roman type.

> VENERUNT *multi et saepe* pagani DE GERMANIA ET OCCUPAVERUNT EST ANGLIAM (id est regionem illam quae Orientalium Anglorum regio dicitur) *et* quorum quidam MERCIAM invadentes bella cum Brittonibus plurima peregerunt SED *necdum sub uno rege redacta erant. Plures autem proceres certatim regiones occupabant, unde innumerabilia bella fiebant,* quoniam PROCERES *vero* eorum *quia* ERANT MULTI NOMINE CARENT.

I am grateful to my former pupil, Dr. Wendy Davies, for drawing my attention to the significance of the *Flores* entry, cf. **T.**

283.3 MEDRAUT: see p. 140 above.

284.1 ALAMANNIC GRAVE GOODS: see **S.**

284.1 ALMONDBURY: EPNS WRY 2, 256.

286.3 GILDAS: 92, 3.

286.4 HERPES: it is possible that some of the Kentish objects catalogued in the British Museum as from Herpes did not come from there; but probable that most did; cf. Delamain *Herpes.*

287.1 PROCOPIUS: BG 4, 20; see **T** and **F.**

287.3 BOULOGNE: Map 19A, and notes thereto; cf. *Cartularium Sithiense*, c. AD 850; see **N** Place Names.

287.3 BROOCHES: said to have been in Boulogne Museum before 1940; none are known to have survived the war.

287.3 EGWIN: Fredegarius 4, 55, cf. 4, 78, see **P** Aigynd.

288.2 NORMANDY . . . VILLAGE NAMES: Map 19B and notes thereto; see especially *Annales de Normandie* 10, 1960, 307 ff.; 13, 1963, 43 ff.; cf. **N** Place Names.

291.1 SAXONS . . . OF BAYEUX: Greg. Tur. HF 5,26; 10, 9.

291.2 SAXON PEOPLE: *Translatio Sancti Alexandri* 1; cf. Adam of Bremen 1, 4 *Saxones primo circa Rhenum sedes habebant* [*et vocati sunt Angli*] *quorum pars inde veniens in Brittaniam Romanos depulit; altera pars Thuringiam oppugnans tenuit illam regionem.*

291.2 DATE 531: Greg. Tur. HF 3, 7.

291.2 HADELN: *Annales Regni Francorum* AD 797. '*Haduloha . . . ubi Oceanus Saxoniam alluit*' beyond the Weser, but not beyond the Elbe, therefore the region now called Hadeln, cf. **F**.

291.3 SAXONS REBELLED: Greg. Tur. HF 4, 10 cf. 4, 14.

291.3 ROUGH POTTERY: Tischler *Sachsenforschung* 79.

291.3 BUTTL NAMES: see Map 17, p. 277.

292.2 THURINGIA . . . ANGLIAN POTTERY: Map 16, p. 275, and notes thereto. The Anglian grave goods of the Czech and East German museums have not yet been sufficiently studied to determine their date; it may prove possible to distinguish two movements, from the lower Elbe in the 5th century, and from Britain in the 6th century. Most of the stray English grave goods in Hungary, Albania and elsewhere in the Balkans (see **S**) seem to be 6th century, matched in cemeteries in Britain, but not on the Elbe.

292.2 -LEBEN NAMES: see Map 17, p. 277. The names clearly remained in use for some time, into the earlier stages of German conquest of Slav territory.

292.2 SAXONS AND LANGOBARDS: Greg. Tur. HF 4, 42; 5, 15, cf. Paul the Deacon HL 2, 6; 3, 5–7. Since the Suevi were installed before the death of Clothair in 561, these Saxons left their homes earlier.

16 English Conquest (pp. 293–316)

293.1 CYNRIC, CEAWLIN, CUTHA: see **G** EW; cf. p. 225 above.

293.3 CUTHWULF: the story that he was Ceawlin's 'brother' is confined to guesses in late genealogies and insertions into the later texts of SC.

293.3 PLACE NAMES: see **G** EW 560 Cutha, and Map 20, p. 295.

293.3 CUTTESLOWE: now commonly spelt Cutslow, cf. *Ant.* 9, 1935, 96 and EPNS Oxfordshire 267.

293.3 ESLINGAS: see p. 110 above.

294.1 GEWISSAE: see **L**. The word probably means 'confederates', either a federation of different English peoples, whose burial rite attests a mixed origin, or else translating *foederati*, the status accorded to them by the British. Their ornament demonstrates that they included many immigrants from the Saxon country on the left bank of the Elbe estuary, whose descendants in time predominated (cf. p. 324 below), and, in contradistinction to the Mercian Angles, consented to be known by the collective national name of Saxons, which their British neighbours applied to them, as to other English immigrants.

296.1 ILCHESTER: see **S** and Map 21.

296.1 GLASTONBURY: William of Malmesbury *de Gestis Regum* 1, 27–28, in 601; Morfael, in or about 655, see p. 243.

296.1 CANNINGTON: *ST 25 40*, MA 8, 1964, 237; *Christianity in Britain* 195.

296.2 INDEPENDENT MONARCHY: see **G** E and **T** Anglian Chronicle, cf. p. 283 above.

296.3 EAST ANGLIAN WARS: see p. 283 above.

298.1 UFFINGAS: see **G** EA.

298.1 SQUAREHEADED BROOCHES: see **S**.

298.2 CREODA: see **G** EM.

298.2 TRIBAL HIDAGE: see **T** and p. 492 below.

299.2 WYE . . . 584: see p. 227 above.

299.3 KENTISH . . . MIDLANDS: e.g. Leighton Buzzard, Chamberlain's Barns Pit II, which endured, and Totternhoe (Dunstable), Marina Drive, which did not long survive, *Arch. Jl.* 120, 1963, 161; *Bed. Arch. Jl.* 1, 1962, 25; together with many of the sites listed *Arch. Jl.* 120, 190, beside others which contain Kentish material but are less specifically Kentish.

300.3 PIONEERS: see Map 22, p. 305. The latest pagan burials, most of them of the early 7th century, extend into a few concentrated regions, between Bernicia and Deira; in the Peak District; in the border lands between the West Saxons and the Mercians, about the Cherwell and the Cotswolds; on the south-western borders of the West Saxons; and on the edges of the Weald. Pagan English burials have not been reported from the British lands of the north-west midlands, allied with the Mercians, though some Cheshire place names ending in *-low* (burial mound), preceded by an English personal name, suggest some colonisation in the 7th century, perhaps beginning at the end of the 6th century, cf. p. 310.2 below.

301.2 BISHOP IN YORK: Bede HE I, 29 cites a letter of Gregory the Great, dated 22 June 601, elevating Augustine to metropolitan status, and adding,

> we wish you to appoint and send a bishop to York, provided that if the city and its neighbourhood receive the Word of God, he also may consecrate 12 bishops, and exercise metropolitan authority.

301.3 HUMBER AND . . . BEYOND: Bede HE I, 25 says that in 597 the *imperium* of Aethelbert extended 'as far as the Humber, the great river that divides the southern and northern English'; on Aethelbert's death in 616 he describes the frontier as 'the river Humber and its adjacent borders' HE 2, 5. In both passages the language is careful; the reason for the variation may be that in the meantime Aethelbert lost all or part of Lincolnshire, to Aethelferth.

301.4 GOLDEN AGE: Bede HE 2, 16.

302.3 EDWIN AND THE WEST SAXONS: Bede HE 2, 9; SC 626.

302.4 EDWIN AND WALES: see p. 240 above.

302.4 PENDA: see p. 240 above.

302.4 OSWALD . . . SEVERN: see **A** 635 and p. 240 above.

302.4 ENGLISH REBELLION: **A** 636 *congregacio Saxonum contra Osualt.*

302.4 ATBRET IUDEU: Nennius 64–65, see **L** Giudi (probably Stirling). The word *atbret* is British, 'older than . . . Primitive Welsh, and therefore not later than the seventh century', Jackson *Celt and Saxon* 38; cf. also **L** Winwaed.

303.2 PICTS AND SCOTS: Bede HE 2, 5.

303.2 PICTISH KING: Talorcan son of Enfrith **A** 656, see p.195 above; **K** P; **G** ENB; son of Oswy's elder brother, he had by Anglian law a better claim to the Northumbrian throne than Oswy himself.

303.2 ENGLISH UNDER-KING: see p. 195 above.

303.2 CLYDESIDE KINGS: see **G** BA.

303.2 EGFERTH: made Mercia tributary, before the death of Wulfhere (675), Eddius 20; constrained by archbishop Theodore to make peace after a disastrous battle on Trent in 679, where his young brother Aelfwin was killed, possibly at Elford *SK 18 10* near Lichfield, perhaps *Aelfwin's Ford*; Bede HE 4, 21; **A** 679; cf. Eddius 24.

303.2 EGFERTH . . . IRELAND: Bede HE 4, 26; **A** 684, in Breg (eastern Meath north of Dublin).

303.2 EGFERTH . . . PICTS: Bede HE 4, 26, **A** 685, SC 685. He was killed at Lin Garan, Nennius 57; at Dun Nechtain, **A**; Nechtansmere, Simeon of Durham HDE 9; Dunnichen *NO 51 48* near Forfar, north of Dundee, cf. **L**.

303.3 AETHELRED . . . NO CIVIL WAR: he faced and survived one major rebellion, **A** 692, 'battle against the son of Penda', which is probably not a doublet of the 679 entry; his enemy is more likely to have been Ine of Wessex than a relative or a Welsh invader.

303.3 EGBERT: he asserted Wessex independence in 803, and subdued Mercia twenty years later. 'The great battle between Egbert, king of the West Saxons and Ceolwulf, king of the Mercians, at *Cherrenhul* between Oxford and Abingdon, which Egbert won', Leland *Itinerary* (Toulmin Smith 2, 151), cf. *Ant.* 9, 1935, 99, probably preserves in Latin the full text of SC 823 (821) 'Ceolwulf was deprived of the kingdom.' The Saxon Chronicle dates the completion of the conquest of Mercia to 829, but Mercian independence was briefly re-asserted in the following year.

307.3 LATEST PAGAN BURIALS: there was no sharp and sudden end to the old funeral rites. Clothed burial lasted in some areas throughout the 7th century, and beyond. Some of the dead, especially wealthy women and young girls, were buried in their best clothes, with their finery. But in most of large midland and southern cemeteries the pagan convention that deliberately buried objects intended for use in the after life declined after the conquest and was almost entirely discontinued early in the 7th century. Strong evidence indicates the date at which weapons, emblems of office, pottery vessels and the traditional jewellery of ordinary women ceased to be normal in graves. The great royal barrows of the south, and some of the warrior graves of the Peak District, are securely dated to about the 630s by continental coins and ornament; the decorative styles of objects found in these tombs are slightly later than the latest normally observed on humbler brooches and ornaments in the large cemeteries, but not much later. Most pagan cemetery burial ended a generation or more before the coming of Christianity. Pagan burial was not ended by conversion, but by the causes that made easy conversion possible; the grip of the old beliefs upon men's minds was already weakening before the Mercian and West Saxon kings were baptised.

307.4 BEANDUN: see **L**. Bindon, Devon, unlike Bindon, Dorset, and Bindon, Somerset, probably derives from *bean dun*, 'bean hill', EPNS Devon 636; cf. Hoskins WEW 8.

308.2 GLEVISSIG: see p. 228 above.

308.2 MORFAEL: see **G** BCL (H 25) and p. 243 above.

308.2 PENSELWOOD: see **L**. The suggestion that the battle was fought near Exeter and that the British withdrew northward towards Bridgwater (Hoskins WEW 15) is possible, but not probable.

308.3 POSBURY CAMP: *SX 80 97*, 'Possebury' in the 13th century, EPNS Devon 406.

309.1 CORNISH BISHOP: HS 1, 674, cf. **E** Petroc.

309.1 BODMIN: HS 1, 676 ff., cf. **T** Gospel Books.

309.1 DUNGARTH: ACm 875.

309.2 MORCANT: cf. p. 230 above; *moritur*, died, is commonly used of death in battle, e.g. ACm 558 (for 560) *Gabran . . . moritur*; 580 *Gurci et Peretur moritur*.

309.2 INE . . . MERCIAN SUPREMACY: In 701 Aldhelm secured the confirmation of the Pope's privileges for Malmesbury by both Aethelred and Ine; they

> came to an agreement, and so concluded, that whether it were peace or war between Saxons and Mercians . . . the monastery should be ever in peace.

Aethelred signed first, as *Myrcena kyncg*, followed by Ine, *Wessexena cyng* BCS 106, end. In the 680s Wiltshire estates had been granted by Mercians alone (e.g. BCS 58, cf. 54); Ceadwalla and Ine had revived Wessex, but not thrown off Mercian supremacy. Coenred, who granted land near Shaftesbury in 704, could have been either king of the Mercians, or Ine's father, BCS 107.

310.1 ELISEG: ECMW 182 cf. **G** BP; *necxit hereditatem Povo[i]s [et recepit ?] per VIIII [annos ?] e potestate Anglorum in gladio suo parta in igne*. The grammar is too eccentric for exact translation, but the meaning seems clear.

310.2 DERBYSHIRE: see Map 22, p. 305.

310.2 NORTHUMBRIAN BORDER: the early place names of Cheshire and south Lancashire are chiefly Mercian rather than Northumbrian. Peaceful settlement of some Mercian English in allied Welsh lands may have begun quite early, for early in the 7th century a Welsh churchman was said to have been disturbed by Englishmen shouting 'Ker gia, ker gia!' at their hunting dogs on the upper Severn, far beyond lands yet conquered, *vita Beuno* 8. But extensive settlement is unlikely before Wulfhere's accession, cf. p. 300.3 above.

310.3 BEDE . . . ENGLAND: cf. e.g. for the territory *regio Anglorum* HE 3, 8; *Anglorum provinciae* 3, 3; cf. *Brettonum provinciae* 2, 2; for their dominion, *Anglorum regnum* 3, 24; 4, 26, etc.; for the population, *Anglorum populi* 1, 25; *natio Anglorum* 2, 2; 4, 26; *gens Anglorum* 2, 2; 3, 3; and *gentes Anglorum* 2, 3. These are samples of normal usage. 'Anglia' does not occur. 'Engelonde' in BCS 738, dated AD 939, may or may not belong to the original text.

311.1 CYMRY: cf. p. 41 above.

311.2 SAXONIA: cf. p. 41 above.

311.2 ANGLI SAXONES: first used in the later 8th century, in Europe, by Paul the Deacon *Historia Langobardorum* 4, 22, about 790, cf. Willibald, *Anglorum Saxonumque vocabulo*, vita Bonifatii 4 (11), about 760. *Angul Saxones* is common in 9th-century charters, usually in Latin, but found no wider popularity; Latin variants were used by Florence of Worcester and a few other medieval writers, citing from West Saxon usage.

311.2 WEST ANGLI: and *Suth Angli*, used consistently by the chronicler Aethelweard, himself a prince of the West Saxon dynasty, as substitutes for West and South Saxons; but the substitution would not work for East and Middle Saxons, since East and Middle Angles already existed; it found few imitators.

312.4 ALDHELM: Bede HE 5, 18 cf. Aldhelm *Ep*.4 (also excerpted HS 1,202).

313.1 CONBRAN: Combran BCS 169 (745), Cumbran SC 755, possibly a nickname, 'the Welshman', more probably the name Conbran, cf. LL index, LL 122 etc.

313.1 CATWAL: BCS 186.

313.2 HENRY I: *Consuetudo West Sexe* (70) 5, Liebermann *Gesetze* 1,588; cf. **J**.

313.3 LAET: the German word *litus*, or variants, including the *laeti* imported into Roman territory, denoted dependent cultivators, usually foreign, often conquered natives. The *laeti* of Kent were probably British; so Stenton ASE 300, cf. 311, and most who have studied the evidence in context.

313.3 DUNWALD, DUNWALLAUN: BCS 160, 175, 192 (about 747–772), cf. 332 (811) and 254 (788).

313.3 WELHISC: BCS 45, 72 (679, 688).

313.3 MABAN: Bede HE 5, 20, cf. Jackson LHEB 295[1].

313.3 MALUINUS: BCS 250.

314.1 NUNNA: very rare among the English, but a normal late Roman and British name, cf. Nonn(ita), mother of David, cf. **E**; Nunechia, wife of the early 5th-century British *magister militum* Gerontius **G** BC 380; Nunechius, the name of two bishops of Nantes, Duchesne *Fastes* 2, 365; 367; and of a *comes* of Limoges, Greg. Tur. HF 6, 22; Ninian, cf. **E** and p. 337, called Nynia by Bede, Nyniga by Alcuin.

314.2 CHAD: etc., from British Catu–, Jackson LHEB 554.

314.2 CAEDMON: Bede HE 4, 24, Welsh Cadfan, Jackson LHEB 244, etc.; cf. p. 421 below. Bede does not say that he was a 'cowherd', 'humble', or a 'lad'. He was 'elderly', *provectioris aetatis*, before he composed verses or entered a monastery. He had previously attended English-speaking dinner parties, where the *cithara*, 'guitar', or 'harp', was passed round in turn, but always left before his turn came, returning 'to his own house'. But on the particular night when his gift came to him, it fell to him to guard the stables (*stabula iumentorum*), for which he received payment from the steward, apparently of the monastery, next morning. The word *iumenta* means draught animals, oxen, horses or mules, who pull carriages or carts; not 'cows'. They were a valuable property, and the duty of night guard clearly went by rota; adequate guard against thieves plainly required a number of people under a responsible person. The implication of Bede's words is that landowners undertook the duty in turn, supplying a guard from their dependents; Bede does not indicate whether the obligation fell upon all landowners, English and Welsh, or upon Welshmen only. It was an imposition likely to fall on men of Welsh status; Caedmon's name was Welsh, but his language was English, at least in his later years; there were doubtless many Welshmen born who normally spoke English, but were held to the legal status of their birth.

314.2 PENNINES . . . STRATHCLYDE: *vita Cadroe* 17, Colgan ASH 497 and Skene CPS 116. In the early 950s Dyfnwal of the Clyde (see **G** BA) escorted Cadroe to meet the envoy of Eric Blood-Axe, king of York, *usque Loidam civitatem, quae est confinium Normannorum atque Cumbrorum*, 'as far as the city of Leeds, which is the border between the North Men and the Cymry'. The place could not be the Lothians, also called *Loidis*, Skene CS 1,241 note, which was not a *civitas* and was far from Eric's borders. The place name and other evidence for the British reconquest of the Pennines in the earlier 10th century is discussed by Kenneth Jackson, *Angles and Britons* 72 ff. Dyfnwal's short-lived reconquest, however, extended far to the south and west of the border there indicated; his suzerainty over remote and inaccessible Yorkshire dales implies the survival of a considerable Welsh-speaking population until the Norse settlement of the later 10th and earlier 11th centuries. That settlement was thorough enough to enable modern Norwegians to understand conversation in broad Yorkshire concerned with agricultural and topographical terms; what remained of Welsh speech and custom in Yorkshire was evidently extinguished after the devastation of the north by William I in 1069, except possibly in Dent.

314.2 WILFRED: lands, Eddius 17.

314.2 BRITISH ADMINISTRATION: see p. 221 above.

314.2 BRITISH LAND TENURE: R.C. Shaw *Post-Roman Carlisle* 55 ff.

314.2 WILFRED . . . VILLAGE: Eddius 18. Wilfred was in pursuit of a boy whom he claimed for his monastery, whose parents had fled to a British village to save the child. Wilfred was at *On Tiddanufri*, probably Tideover *SE 32 49*, in Kirkby Overblow, south of Harrogate; the British village was perhaps nearby Walton Head EPNS WRY 5, 43.

314.2 WALLERWENTE: the 'North People's Law' *North leodalage*, Liebermann *Gesetze* 1,460, cf. EHD 1,433; see **J**.

314.3 LONDON: VI Athelstan (*Iudicia Civitatis Lundoniae*) 6, 3, cf. IV Athelstan 6, 3.

314.3 CAMBRIDGE GUILD: Thorpe ALE 1,258, DAS 610, see **J**; translated Kemble SE 1,514, and, less accurately, EHD 1,557, with the strange suggestion that *Wylisc* means 'servile'. It does not. For the meaning of *wealh*, see p. 315 below.

314.3 BEANE: SC 913 *Beneficcan*, interpreted as *Bene fychan*, 'Little Beane' in Welsh, probably rightly, cf. Jackson LHEB 567. Many English rivers have Welsh names; but the retention of the Welsh adjective *fychan* argues that Welsh was commonly spoken when the English first settled by its banks, about the beginning of the 7th century, and perhaps for some time thereafter.

314.3 NORFOLK: Winnold House *TF 68 03* at Wereham, cf. Tanner 355 and *Norfolk Archaeology* 5, 1859, 297 ff., preserves the name of Winwaloe (see **E**) and incorporates much of the medieval monastic buildings. It was the site of a major fair on Winwaloe's day, March 3, until the late 18th century, superseded by Downham Market (*TF 61 03*) fair on the same day.

The cult of Winwaloe in Norfolk was not confined to Wereham. He is said to have had a church in Norwich (LBS 4, 361) and a widespread Norfolk weather rhyme on the windy first days of March runs

First come David, then come Chad,
Then come Winnell roaring mad.

The rhyme is cited LBS 4, 360; Arnold-Foster SCD 2,284. A radio broadcast request in the late 1950s elicited half a dozen versions, with slight variants, still known in different parts of Norfolk. David and Chad are extensively venerated in Britain on March 1 and 2; the observation of Winwaloe's day on March 3 is recorded only in Norfolk, and in Wales, Cornwall and Devon.

314.3 HERTFORDSHIRE: Wynnel's Grove *TL 41 35* in Cockenach, astride the boundary between Nuthampstead and Barley parishes, was *capella Sancti Winwaloei* in the 13th century, *Registrum de Walden* (BM Harleian MS 3697) folio 189, printed Dugdale *Mon. Ang.* 1, 462–3; traces of what may be the chapel are visible in the wood, but have not yet been excavated. A stretch of the Icknield Way near Royston was called *Wynewalestrete* c. 1470, EPNS 175.

Both Wereham and Cockenach were granted to St. Winwaloe's Abbey at Montreuil-sur-mer in Picardy about the end of the 12th century. At first sight these grants might seem to be the reason why Winwaloe became patron of the places granted. But the late acquisition of a small dependent priory is insufficient to explain the wide and persistent honouring of Winwaloe's name in Norfolk; and in Hertfordshire the grants refer to the chapel, with its monks, as already in existence at the time when the grant was made, while the grantor's son undertook to maintain it in good repair. Moreover, a late name for a little chapel cannot by itself explain the local name for a major Roman and prehistoric highway five miles distant.

No medieval reason explains or links the grants of the two sites, remote from each other, to a foreign abbey without other English connections. The likely cause is that at the time of the grants both houses already bore the name of Winwaloe, but were doubtless in deep decay. The Life of Gwenael, Winwaloe's successor at Landevennec in Brittany, states that in or about the 590s he visited Britain and founded one or more houses; several are known in Wales and the west (see **E**), and they may have included Wereham and Cockenach, named, as often, in honour of the founder's teacher and master.

314.3 GUTHLAC: Felix *vita Guthlaci* 34. A band of Britons fired the monastery in a dawn attack, and wounded the saint who was wakened from a 'light sleep'. The incident was not an 'unquiet dream', nor were the British 'devils in disguise', as Colgrave, *Felix* 185 (for the translation, see *Ant.* 8, 1934, 193); Guthlac lived among British neighbours, for, at Crowland, he was a 'pattern to many a Briton', Cynewulf III c. 140 Kennedy p. 268.

314.3 11th CENTURY: BCS 991 and Ramsey Chronicle, cited H.C.Darby, *Ant.* 8, 1934, 194.

314.3 CAEDMON: see p. 314.2 above.

315.3 CAMBERWELL: the well from which the place is named has been excavated and found to be Roman British.

315.3 WEALH . . . SERF: EPNS 1 i 18 (1924).

315.3 SPECULATION: EPNE 2, 242–3 (1956).

315.4 WEST SAXON TEXTS: the texts are cited and discussed by H.P.R.Finberg *The*

Agrarian History of England, vol. 1,2 ch.1; to whom I am indebted for permission to read the manuscript before publication.

315.4 INE: 23, 3.

315.4 WALL, WOOD: EPNE 2, 241; 244. These names are however far fewer than *wealh-tun*.

17 English Monarchy (pp. 317–334)

317.1 BEDE . . . EMPIRE: HE 2, 5, cf. p. 329; Aethelbert of Kent *imperavit* all the English *provinciae* south of the Humber; and was the third to hold such *imperium*. Bede adds details only of the Northumbrians, evidently commenting on a list already recognised. Its existence emphasises that the concept that the English should have one over-king who held 'empire' over all Britain was already established in the 7th century.

317.1 SAXON CHRONICLE: 827 (829), repeats the list, on Egbert's conquest of Mercia, adding Egbert, and gives these rulers the title *Bretwalda*, 'ruler of Britain', adapting the Welsh *Gwledic* (p. 206 above).

318.1 ANGLES: **G** EM and p. 265 above.

318.1 SAXONS . . . NO KING: Hucbald *vita Lebuini* 4.

318.1 FRANKS . . . EXASPERATED: e.g. *Annales Laurissenses* AD 798 *perfidissimos primores Saxonum*.

318.2 OESC: see **G** EK.

320.1 LEODE: Laws of Aethelbert 2.

320.1 REFERENDARIUS, GRAFIO: BCS 4; 5. The witness-lists are older than the body of the text; 'Hocca grafio' in 4 has been misunderstood by the copyist of 5, and turned into two persons, 'Hocca comes' and 'Grafio comes'.

320.2 FOUR LEADERS: cf. p. 233 above.

320.3 YEAVERING: publication forthcoming; the excavator, Brian Hope-Taylor, has kindly allowed me to give this short description; cf. p. 214 above.

321.3 GOODMANHAM: see p. 390 below.

322.2 SUTTON HOO, BROOMFIELD, TAPLOW: see **S**.

323.1 TAEPPA'S KINGDOM: the location of his tomb argues that his territory included south Buckinghamshire. Its splendour implies a wider kingdom. The then English settlements, whose ornament resembles that of the Taplow region, extended eastward along the Thames bank. Taeppa's 'Norrey' may therefore have been coterminous with Surrey, including the future Middlesex. In the poorly recorded conflicts that followed Aethelbert's death, Edwin of Northumbria overran Mercia and Wessex, and his ally Redwald was dominant in the south east, probably through most of the 620s; it is possible that Taeppa then took London from the East Saxon allies of the enfeebled Kentish kingdom. It is also possible that the king buried at Broomfield was an East Anglian, temporarily installed as ruler of the East Saxons under Redwald's suzerainty; alternatively, it might be that Taeppa was himself an East Saxon, but since all known East Saxon kings, except Offa, bore names beginning with S for almost 200 years, the alternative is less likely.

The evidence does not suffice to determine the origin of Taeppa or the precise limits of his kingdom; but the magnificence of his tomb demonstrates that he was a great king who ruled north of the Thames in a generation when the history of the region is not known, between the collapse of the Kentish empire and the consolidation of Mercian control. Whatever the vicissitudes of the London region (cf. p. 493.1 below) in these years, East Saxon control was probably reasserted by the middle of the 7th century; the weak record and uncertain dates of the East Saxon kings are discussed by Plummer, Bede, 2, 176; cf. **G** EE.

323.3 FRONTIER PEOPLES: the term chiefly applies to the western districts of the Mercians and the West Saxons, and to the Bernicians in the north.

323.3 ANGLIAN CHRONICLE: p. 283 above, and **T**.

323.4 SAXON CHRONICLE: see pp. 103 and 317 above; cf. **T** and **G** EW.

324.2 WEST SAXON RULERS: the older national name was *Gewissae* (p. 294 above), probably meaning 'confederates' (see **L**). It may have originated when Ceawlin and Cutha organised the separate southern English settlements into a single nation in the 570s and 580s, but was more probably the earlier name of the Berkshire English of the middle Thames about Abingdon, who began as an amalgam of immigrants from different parts of the continental homeland, who used differing burial rites, and ornament, and were also *foederati* of the British. They were known to the British as Saxons, as were all other English, and are first known to have used the collective term Saxons of themselves in the preamble to Ine's laws in the 690s, though the same laws describe the individual members of the population as English (p. 41 above). Thereafter 'West Saxon' was the common and usual national name, though for centuries the old name Gewissae occurs as an occasionally literary variant in Bede, Asser and elsewhere.

324.3 WESSEX: the territorial name Westsexe is rarer than the ethnic term West Saxons. The adjective 'West' was required when other kingdoms also accepted the name Saxon. The English of the former *civitates* of the Trinovantes and Regnenses are also first recorded as East and South Saxons in the 690s (BCS 81, 87, 78 ff.), those of the London region as Middle Saxons in 704 (BCS 111). All four names were well established by Bede's time. The extant late copies of the 'Tribal Hidage' (p. 492 below) use the terms Wessex, Essex and Sussex; since they are unacquainted with the term Middlesex, their usage may date back to the original of the document, probably drafted about 661. The name Saxon may have been first and most readily accepted by the Gewissae, since ornament that derives from continental Saxons of the lower Elbe is plentiful among the first immigrants, and continental Saxon political notions won acceptance in later generations (cf. note 324.4, Power of the Overking, below); but ancestry cannot explain the name of the East Saxons, whose archaeology and traditions have little to do with the continental Saxon area. A more compelling reason to accept a national name used by the British was doubtless dislike of the masterful assertion of sovereignty by the Northumbrian and Mercian Angles over all the English, that pressed acutely upon the West Saxons from the 620s, upon the East and South Saxons from the 640s and 660s.

324.3 WESSEX ... FIVE ... KINGDOMS: SC 626; Bede HE 2, 9; cf. p. 302 above. See **G** EW and **L** Wessex. The charters and some SC entries locate the kingdoms and name many of their rulers. The evidence has not yet been sifted, and has sometimes been swept aside by the easy pretence that the names are 'spurious'; it indicates however that the regions were in substance the future counties of Berkshire, Hampshire, Wiltshire, Somerset and Dorset. These kingdoms emerged from the former Roman *civitates*, Berkshire from the Atrebates, Hampshire and Wiltshire from the division of the Belgae (cf. p. 226.2 above), Dorset from the Durotriges, Somerset from the portion of north-eastern Dumnonia subdued by the English in the late 6th century (see p. 294 above), extended westward by later conquest. The subjugation of the rest of eastern Dumnonia in the mid and late 7th century added the new region of English Devon, which may thereafter have formed an additional kingdom. Some boundaries shifted; notably, some southern Atrebatic territory was incorporated in Hampshire.

324.3 THREE . . . KINGS: in 661, while Cenwalh was High King, SC notes the deaths, presumably in the course of Wulfhere's invasion of Wessex, of king Coenberth, father of Ceadwalla, and of Cuthred, son of Cynegils' contemporary king Cwichelm (SC 614–636). The wording of many of the charters, and of the pedigrees inserted into SC, suggest that each kingdom had its own hereditary dynasty; Cuthred may or may not have been ancestor of Cuthred, king in Berkshire and northern Hampshire in Ine's time, c. 700, (BCS 101, 102, 155 etc.) and of Cuthred, High King of Wessex 741–756.

324.3 OVERKINGSHIP DISCONTINUED: Bede HE 4, 12 'the under kings took over the government of the nation and held it divided between them for about ten years'. SC exploited a different tradition, that recognised a High Kingship continued, in name at least, by Cenwalh's widow for a year, by Aescwine from 674 to 676, and by Cenwalh's (grand)son Centwine from 676; Florence of Worcester (Appendix, *Genealogia regum West-Saxonum*, at 672, ed. Thorpe 1,272), on the authority of a *Dicta Regis Alfredi*, adds Aescwine's father Cenfus, from a tradition that evidently intended the dates 672–674. The variant traditions are not in conflict; it is likely that these rulers claimed the high kingship at or about these dates; Bede's words show that the claims did not then succeed.

324.3 OVERKINGSHIP REVIVED: by Centwine, who is said to have claimed it from 676. He was acknowledged as 'King of the West Saxons' by his Northumbrian contemporary Eddius (ch. 40) in 680/681, at the end of Bede's ten year period.

324.3 DIFFERENT DYNASTIES: the future form of the West Saxon monarchy was the result of a deliberate political decision taken at a particular time. The 60 years unbroken rule of a father and his son from 611 to 672 had threatened to establish the High Kingship permanently in one dynasty. In 672 the West Saxon magnates refused to perpetuate its supremacy. Though Centwine briefly regained his ancestors' title, he failed to re-establish his dynasty. Ceadwalla, the young son of a former regional king, soon 'began to contend for the kingship' (SC 685), and succeeded. Three years later he abdicated; the political pressures and personal motives which induced him to do so are not fully recorded. He was succeeded by Ine, the son of a regional king who was still alive. Nothing is recorded of the ancestry of his successors, save that none of them is said to have been the son of his predecessor before 839; and that one of them retained Hampshire, presumably his own kingdom, when deprived of the High Kingship (SC 757). The principle of an elective monarchy, whose conventions limited the choice of the supreme ruler to the kings of regional dynasties, closely resembles the practice of the Irish, who for centuries chose their High King from among the heads of the several Ui Neill dynasties in turn.

324.4 POWER OF THE OVERKING: the decision to abolish a permanent dynasty in 672 automatically restricted the High King's power. It marked the dominance of those who clung to the continental Saxon tradition of effective government by local rulers, and rejected the continental Anglian tradition, powerfully asserted in Britain by the Mercians, of a strong central monarchy. It coincided in time with the consolidation of Mercian supremacy over the southern English, and with the replacement of the old national name of Gewissae (see p. 324.3, Wessex, above) by the collective ethnic term Saxon, and was reached when the influence of monks trained in Ireland, familiar with Irish hierarchical kingship, was at its strongest throughout Britain.

324.4 DIFFERENT TEXTS: closer study is likely to suggest when the differences are no more than varying formulae, and when they imply differing political conceptions. Occasionally an underking is termed *minister*, e.g. BCS 60, whereby Aethelred of Mercia granted Gloucester, c. 680, to Osric and Oswald *duobus ministris meis nobilis generis in provincia Huicciorum*, though they are elsewhere regularly termed *reges*.

324.4 REX: still used of regional West Saxon kings of the later 8th century, cf., e.g., SC 757.

325.1 KINGDOMS . . . DETACHED FROM WESSEX: e.g. Wiltshire grants in 680–681 made to and by Cenfrith, *comes Mertiorum*, who is also called *patricius*, and *propinquus*, near relative, of Aethelred of Mercia, BCS 54, 58, 59.

325.2 MERCIANS: see **G** EM.

326.3 COLLECTING TAXES: cf. p. 460 below.

327.1 OSWY: William of Malmesbury *de Gestis Regum* 1, 50; he 'ruled (*praefuit*) the Mercians and the peoples of the other southern provinces', Bede HE 3, 24.

327.2 ALDHELM: e.g. BCS 108 *Ego Ine . . . rex cum consilio et decreto praesulis nostri Aldhelm.*

328.2 CHARTERS: see **C**.

329.1 EMPIRE: Bede regularly distinguishes the *imperium* of each over-king from his own *regnum*, e.g. HE 1, 25; 2, 5, cf. Plummer *Bede* 2, 43; 86. The Mercian charters and the 'Tribal Hidage' similarly distinguish between the *imperium* and the *regnum* of the Mercian kings; cf. Stenton ASE 234, and EHR 33, 1918, 433.

329.1 EMPEROR: BCS 289 *rector et imperator Merciorum regni.*

329.2 IRISH . . . IMPERATOR: Muirchu 9, cf. Loegaire, p. 161 above.

329.2 OSWALD: Adomnan *Columba* 1, 1 *totius Brittaniae imperator a Deo ordinatus*; earlier in the chapter *regnator Saxonum*, cf. p. 161 above.

329.2 BRIAN BORU: Book of Armagh, folio 16 verso, cf. p. 167 above.

329.2 ARMORICAN BRITISH: *vita Pauli Aureliani* 15, cf. p. 253 above.

329.3 BONIFACE: *Ep.* 78 *imperator vel rex* referring to Aethelbald, cf. *Ep.* 75. Aethelbald calls himself *gentis Merciorum regens imperium* in an original charter, BCS 162, ruling the empire held by the Mercian nation.

329.3 GWLEDIC: cf. p. 206 above.

329.3 BRETWALDA: cf. p. 317 above, and Athelstan's usage of *Brytaenwalda*, BCS 706, to translate *rector Britanniae* of BCS 705, dated AD 934.

330.2 10th CENTURY: occasionally used by Athelstan, e.g. *basileus Anglorum simul et imperator regum et nationum infra fines Britanniae commorantium*, BCS 700, dated AD 934, exactly defining notions of the respective meanings of king and emperor; cf. also BCS 746.

330.2 EDRED: king and emperor, e.g. BCS 874, 882, 884; Caesar BCS 909.

330.2 AETHELRED: e.g. KCD 1308 *rex Anglo-Saxoniae, atque Nordhymbrensis gubernator monarchiae; paganorumque propugnator, ac Bretonum ceterarumque provinciarum imperator.*

330.2 GREEK TITLES: e.g. *basileus orbis Britannie* KCD 1283; *basileus Albionis* KCD 1279 cf. note 330.2, 10th century, above.

331.2 ALCUIN: see **E**.

331.2 ALCUIN . . . IMMENSE THREAT: *Ep.* 129, also printed HS 3, 509–511, cf. *Ep.* 17.

332.3 THREE PERSONS: Alcuin *Ep.* 174.

333.2 DAVID . . . JOAB: Alcuin *Ep.* 178.

333.2 PRESSURES . . . ADVICE: cf. Ganshof *Speculum* 24, 1949, 524. 'It was . . . owing to Alcuin that he (Charles) went to Rome . . . it was under the same influence that he accepted there the imperial dignity.' The story that Charles was taken by surprise when the Pope crowned him is unconvincing government propaganda, that could have deceived no one who knew what Alcuin had been advising, or had read his letters.

333.2 CHARLEMAGNE ... ROME: at the moment of his coronation Charles was not crowned 'western' emperor. He was crowned Roman emperor while the imperial throne in Constantinople was vacant. But the elevation of a new emperor in Constantinople made him and his successors western emperors.

333.2 ENGLISH PRECEDENT: English practice grew from past English, Welsh and Irish experience. Irish political practice was the main root of government by a High King over subordinate kings who acknowledged his precedence, but denied his authority. The circumstances of Europe prevented the emergence of a sovereign high-kingship on the English model and condemned the emperors to a high-kingship as weak as the Irish. For the next several centuries the main political relationships of European rulers, that are at present commonly classified as 'feudal', were of necessity obliged to reproduce many of the features of Irish government, which had underlain their formation at several removes. The study of 9th, 10th and 11th century Europe is impoverished if Irish experience, secular as ecclesiastical, is disregarded.

18 **Fifth-Century Church** (pp. 335–355)

335.1 CHRISTIAN RELIGION: cf. pp. 12 and 23 above.

335.1 ALBAN: and other personal names, see **E.** Alban, *Hertfordshire Archaeology* 1, 1968, 1.

335.1 AFRICA AND EGYPT: Tertullian *adversus Iudaeos* 7, written before 209; Origen *Homily 4 on Ezekiel, Homily 6 on Luke.*

335.1 ARLES: Mansi 2, 466 (HS 1, 7); cf. *Ant.* 35, 1961, 316.

335.1 ORTHODOXY: e.g. Hilary of Poitiers *de Synodis* Prolog. and 1, PL 10, 457, 459 (HS 1, 9); cf. passages cited HS 1, 7–13, from Athanasius and others.

335.1 CONTEMPT: e.g. the British bishops who rejected government subsidies at Rimini, p. 13 above.

335.1 BISHOP OF LONDON: see **E** Augurius, and p. 14 above.

335.2 CLERGY: e.g. the priest (Calpurnius) Odysseus, great-grandfather of Patrick (see **E**) about the beginning of the fourth century.

335.2 ARCHAEOLOGICAL EVIDENCE: summarised in JBAA 16, 1953, 1 ff.; 18, 1955, 1, ff. *Christianity in Britain* 37 ff., cf. 51 ff., 87 ff.

335.2 LONDON: see **L.**

336.1 VICTRICIUS' LETTER: *de Laude Sanctorum* PL 20, 443; a long extract is reprinted in HS 2, xxi.

336.1 MARTIN: cf. p. 26 above.

336.1 POPE INNOCENT: *Ep.* 2 (PL 20, 471).

337.2 HALF A DOZEN ... MONKS: Pelagius, Coelestius, the Sicilian Briton and his fellow authors, Faustus, Constans Caesar (see **E**); Antiochus and Martyrius (Sicilian Briton *Ep.* 1) were monks in Britain, but might have been native or foreign by birth.

337.2 WANDERING MONKS: Fastidius, *de vita Christiana* 15 (PL 40, 1046), enjoins his widowed correspondent to delight in washing the feet of travelling saints.

337.2 SHRINE OF ALBAN: cf. p. 344 below.

337.2 MARTYRS SHRINES: Gildas 10; *sanctorum martyrum ... corporum sepulturae et passionum loca ... quam plurima.* He names St. Albans and Caerleon; St. Martha's, near Guildford, *TQ 02 48*, is probably another, cf. Arnold-Foster

SCD 2, 559, cf. 509; and EPNS Surrey 244. The place name Merthyr, usually joined with the name of a sixth-century saint, is common in south Wales, in and by the territories where Roman literate civilisation was deep rooted. Some of these shrines may have held imported relics maintained by monks.

337.2 BEDE: HE 1, 26.

337.2 SCHOOLS: see p. 409 and **E** Coelestius.

337.3 PATRICK: *Ep.*, 2 and 15, cf. **E**.

337.3 NYNIA: Bede HE 3, 4, cf. **E** and p. 191 above.

337.3 CHURCH . . . NAME: see **D** and p. 146 below.

337.4 ROSNAT: see **L**.

338.1 EXCAVATION: see **L** Whithorn.

338.3 PELAGIUS: see **E**, cf. JTS 16, 1965, 26 ff.; his *Commentary* on the Pauline Epistles, PL Sup. 1, 1110 ff.

338.3 JOHN CASSIAN: see **F**.

338.3 JURA: cf. Greg. Tur. *Vitae Patrum* 1, and BHL Lupicinus, Romanus, 5073–4, 7309.

338.3 MONTALEMBERT: *Les Moines d'Occident* 1, 288 (English edition, 1,514).

338.4 HONORATUS: see DCB.

338.4 FAUSTUS: see **E**. The suggestion that he was 'Breton' rather than British is anachronistic. Faustus came to Lérins 40 years before the second migration to northern Gaul, a century before the third migration turned Armorica into 'Lesser Britain'.

339.1 AMATOR: see DCB, and p. 349 below.

339.2 AUGUSTINE: and other European ecclesiastics, see DCB, cf. **F**.

339.2 AUGUSTINE: the texts of the Pelagian controversy are assembled in PL 45, 1679 ff.; 48, 319 ff.; 56, 490 ff.; cf. Mansi 4, 444 ff.; and are discussed in JTS 16, 1965, 51 ff.

340.1 ONE MAN: Sicilian Briton *de Divitiis* 8, 1–3.

340.2 LOOK YOU NOW: *de Divitiis* 6–7.

341.1 CAMEL: *de Divitiis* 18, 1–3.

341.2 LISTEN: *de Divitiis* 17, 3, concluding words.

341.2 MANKIND IS DIVIDED: *de Divitiis* 5 *tria enim ista sunt in quae humanum gens dividitur; divitiae, paupertas, sufficientia.*

341.2 ABOLISH THE RICH: *de Divitiis* 12 *tolle divitem et pauperum non invenies . . . Pauci enim divites pauperum sunt causa multorum.*

341.2 THEOLOGIANS: cf. C.P.Caspari *Briefe*, page v.

341.2 UNIQUE: the nearest parallels to the Sicilian Briton's concepts are expressed by his contemporary John Chrysostom of Antioch, Patriarch of Constantinople 398–404; but Chrysostom's argument is less analytical, simple and direct, his practical conclusion less sharp and positive.

342.2 PROTESTANTISM: cf. e.g., G. de Plinval *Pélage* 405 *combien d'éléments inconsciemment pélagiens ont reparu dans le protestantisme anglo-saxon ou scandinave.*

342.2 WORKS COPIED: listed in Migne PL Supplement 1. Many MSS are known by the name of the monastery from whose library they come; the origin of those known only by the catalogue number of a major central library has not yet been systematically explored.

342.3 PELAGIAN WRITERS: Pelagius, the Sicilian Briton, Fastidius, and the author of *de Virginitate* were British, Coelestius probably Irish; Julianus of Aeclanum was Italian, the author of *de Divina Lege* of unknown origin. The writings of several other continental Pelagians have not been preserved; the writings of Faustus, also British, imply a Pelagian background in youth.

342.3 CITED IN BRITAIN: Gildas 38 cites *de Virginitate* 6 as the work of *quidam nostrum*, 'one of us', of our fellow countrymen, cf. JTS 16, 1965, 36. The tract is one of half a dozen similar works similarly preserved, and it is therefore probable that the whole collection was known to Gildas, and approved by him; though the sentiment is repeated by the Sicilian Briton and others, the exact wording is used only in *de Virginitate*.

343.3 GERMANUS IN BRITAIN: Constantius *vita Germani* 12 ff., excerpted word for word by Bede HE I, 17 ff., cf. p. 62 above. Prosper says that he was sent by Pope Celestine, Constantius that he was sent by a Gallic synod at the request of anti-Pelagians in Britain. Both are plainly right; a Gallic synod could not intervene without the Pope's approval, nor could the Pope wisely intervene without Gallic support.

345.2 PALLADIUS: see **E**.

345.2 PATRICK: see **E** and p. 64 above.

345.3 POPE CELESTINE: Prosper *contra Collatorum* 21 (PL 51, 271).

346.4 PRELATES LEARNED: Patrick *Confessio* 13.

348.2 TWO PATRICKS: see **E**., and especially T.O'Rahilly *The Two Patricks*; J. Carney *The Problem of Patrick* and SILH 324 ff.; D.Binchy *Studia Hibernica* 2, 1962, 7–173; JTS 17, 1966, 358 ff.; for older views cf. e.g. Todd *Patrick* and Bury *Patrick*.

348.3 INFORMATIVE TEXTS: the *Hymn of Secundinus* LH I, 7 was probably composed in the 5th century, Kenney 260, CPL 16; but, though its author may have known Patrick, it gives little information about him.

348.3 MUIRCHU: see **T**.

348.3 ANONYMOUS LIFE: Colgan's *vita Secunda* TT 11 ff., cf. **E** Patrick; the texts and traditions that underlie this Life require study.

348.3 OTHER EARLY ACCOUNTS: Tirechan, 'Muirchu Book II', Probus, the Book of the Angel, etc. collected in Stokes VT and Colgan TT; several texts have been published independently; cf. Kenney 165 ff.; 319 ff.

348.4 VICTORICUS: see **E**, cf. also JTS 17, 1966, 359.

349.2 AMATOR: see **E**; Muirchu, and derivative texts, have Patrick ordained by Germanus and consecrated by Amator(ex), a neighbouring bishop; Muirchu's source did not make it plain to him that Amator was Germanus' predecessor, and died in 418; he understood *ordinatio* by two separate bishops to mean two contemporary bishops; since the bishops were successive, the original probably meant that he was ordained deacon by Amator, priest by Germanus.

349.4 FARTHER REGIONS: *Confessio* 51.

350.1 PATRICK . . . FORGOTTEN: Kenney p. 324.

350.3 DOCCO: see **E**.

350.3 ST. KEW: founded long before Samson's visit, c. 530, cf. **E** Samson.

351.1 BISHOP CONSECRATED: the normal reluctance of popes and patriarchs to permit a multiplicity of bishops and a potentially independent metropolitan is emphasised by the exceptional nature of the privileges granted to Augustine among the English and to Boniface in Germany. Results were sometimes bizarre; until the 20th century, only one bishop was permitted in Abyssinia, and each new bishop was obliged to travel to Egypt for consecration. The mid seventh century plague produced a comparable temporary difficulty in the English church; without sufficient bishops to consecrate new bishops, the episcopate could not have continued in Ireland in the fifth century after Patrick's death.

351.1 NORTHERN SEES: see **A** index. Few of the sees became permanent.

351.1 CHURCHMEN . . . BRITISH: e.g. Mel (Mael), Mocteus, etc., see **E** index.

351.2 ARMAGH . . . DEFERENCE: e.g. the bishop of Armagh is named first in the address of Pope John's letter to the Irish bishops in 640, Bede HE 2, 19.

351.2 ARCHBISHOP: Cogitosus, prologue (TT 518), writing not later than c. 650 (cf. **E**) calls Conlaed of Kildare (died 517, see **E**) *archiepiscopus Hiberniansium episcoporum* and describes Kildare as *caput pene omnium Hiberniensium eclesiarum . . . cuius parrochia per totam Hiberniensem terram diffusam a mari usque ad mare extensa est* 'head of almost all the Irish churches . . . whose diocese extends throughout Ireland from sea to sea'. The claims are no less extravagant than those put forward for Armagh half a century later; but are less remarked because they were not accepted, and not repeated. Some later Leinster clerics (e.g. Maedoc, see **E**) are entitled 'archbishop of Leinster', but not of Ireland.

351.2 DIOCESAN CLERGY: the sources are surveyed by Kathleen Hughes, CEIS especially pp. 79 ff.

351.3 BRIGIT: see **E**.

351.3 CONLAED . . . CHAPLAIN: Cogitosus, prologue (TT 518) is explicit; Brigit was 'prudently concerned' that the Kildare houses should be governed 'properly in all respects', and because

> without a bishop who could consecrate churches and appoint clergy . . . this was not possible, she summoned an illustrious hermit . . . to govern the church with her, with the status of bishop, so that her churches should not lack clergy.

Nothing is said of how she got him consecrated, or by whom.

352.2 AILBE, CIARAN, DECLAN, IBAR, ENDA, KEBI: see **E**.

352.2 EUGENIUS, TIGERNACH: see **E**.

352.3 FAENCHA: she is likely to have been one of the numerous Irish girls to whom Patrick gave the veil, see **E**.

352.4 ROSNAT: Whithorn, see **L** and p. 337 above.

353.1 ANGUS: see **A** 492.

353.2 POPE: the patriotic tale of the two-day British or Irish pope occurs in several Lives.

353.2 FINNIAN, MACCRICHE, ERLATHEUS: see **E**.

353.3 ETELIC: see **G** BM; made uncle of Cadoc and of Paul Aurelian, both born in about 500.

353.3 FINTAN: see **E**.

355.2 VOYAGES: cf. p. 384 below.

355.2 CORNWALL: cf. p. 130 above.

19 Sixth-Century Monks (pp. 356–388)

356.2 BRIOC: and other names, see **E**.

357.1 LIFE OF SAMSON: see **T**. The Life was written before the episcopate of Thuriau, bishop of Dol about 610.

363.2 LIFE OF PAUL AURELIAN: early spellings, e.g. Tigernomaglus (ch. 11); Quonomorius (ch. 8); villa Banhedos (ch. 8).

363.2 WILDERNESS: *ut heremi deserta penetraret, ibique a consortio mundalis vitae sequestratus . . . vitam duceret* (ch. 6).

363.3 CHILDEBERT: often called 'Philibert' in the Lives.

364.2 PLOU- . . . TRE-: Paul Aurelian (*vita* 12) found a still recognisable Roman estate (*fundus*) in the *Plebs Telmedovia*, now Plou-Dalmazeau (Map 14, p. 263, *D 2*, number 22) which became 'one of his hundred *tribus*' wherein his followers built their *habitacula* (houses); Fracan (*vita Winwaloe* 1, 2) found another estate, near St. Brieuc (Map 14 *N 2*) 'of the right size for a *plebs*', which 'is now named after its finder', to-day Plou-Fragan. Both Lives are 9th-century texts that used 6th-century written sources.

The organisational form of a *plebs* comprising a number of *tribus* containing houses has one precedent. Jerome's account of Pachomius' organisation of the Egyptian monks (PL 23, 69 ff.; 50, 275 ff.; preface 2, and *passim*) explains that 'three or four houses were federated into one *tribus*' with 'thirty or forty houses to one monastery', a *populus* or *plebs Dei*, a people of God; Bangor-on-Dee was also divided into seven *portiones*, equivalent to Jerome's *tribus*, 'none with less than 300 men', who necessarily lived in separate houses (Bede HE 2, 2).

The monastic terminology was riveted upon secular usage. *Plou-* and variants are the normal names of early district centres in Brittany and sometimes in Cornwall; *plwyf* is used for parish in Welsh, but does not occur in place names. *Tre-* is the commonest form of village name in all British lands where monasteries were numerous, Brittany, Cornwall, Wales and the Clyde kingdom (Watson CPNS 358 ff., with some possible extension as a suffix in Pictland), but not in Reged, between the Solway and the Mersey, (EPNE 185; EPNS Cumberland 116), where monasteries were limited to a small region (Map 26, p. 371). *Tref* (*trev* in Brittany) is the normal Welsh for village, equivalent to English *-tun*. *Ty*, house, and, in Brittany, *ker*, fortified enclosure, are also common in the names of farmsteads. Once established, the name forms remained in use, to give Treharris, Treherbert etc. in the 19th century; but very many of the personal names attached to *Tre-* are those of persons known to have lived in the 6th or 7th centuries.

The linguistic origin of *tribus* and *tref* is not known. It may derive from an Indo-European original, that might also underlie Germanic *terp*, *dorf*, *throp*, *thorp*, etc, but no such root is known; it does not occur among the very numerous Celtic place names of the Roman world, and is unlikely to be connected with Gallic *Atrebates*, since, apart from linguistic difficulties, 'those who live at home (or in houses)' is an unlikely name for nation. Irish *treabh*, village, also exceedingly rare in place names (Watson CPNS 357) is likely to derive from *tref*. The short vowel of *tribus* would by oral transmission be expected to give Welsh *trif*, or perhaps *trwyf*; but the term was no longer in normal spoken use in the late Empire; it was adopted by men who read what Jerome wrote; similarly the English read Jerome's *tribus* and pronounced it 'tribe', with a long vowel. The linguistic origin of *plebs*, *plou-*, *plwyf*, and of words for 'house', is clearer.

366.3 DEMETIA . . . GLEVISSIG: Teilo is said to have instituted bishops in both kingdoms, in or about the 570s, LL 115; 131. The appointments corresponded with the creation of the separate Glevissig monarchy, cf. pp. 228 and 208.

367.3 DAVID: see **E**. He was born *anno XXX post discessum Patricii* ⟨*de Menevia*⟩ ACm, at 458. The words *de Menevia*, 'from St. David's', are evidently a gloss added to the original by a copyist who mistook *discessus*, death, for 'departure', and allied it with a tradition that Patrick had sailed for Ireland in 432 from Porth Mawr, by St. David's. The round figure of 30 years after the death of Patrick, entered in most annals at various years in the 490s, gives a date in the 520s, consistent with baptism by Ailbe. He died in 589, **A** (AI, cf. AT, AC, CS). The corrupt entry or entries of ACm 601 *David Episcopus. Moni Iudaeorum* (perhaps for *Mons Giudiorum*, intending *Urbs Giudi*, Stirling), whatever their meaning or origin, do not evidence a belief in a variant death date at odds with the main Annals tradition. *David Episcopus* might derive from an Irish

Annal, not otherwise preserved, concerning Mobhi of Inch (see **E**), who is sometimes called David in Irish texts.

368.1 PAULINUS: ECMW 139, cf. **E**.

368.2 RULE OF DAVID: Ricemarchus *vita David* 21–30. The words transcribed by Ricemarchus, *suffosoria vangasque invicto brachio terre defigunt* (22), are also cited by Gildas *Ep.* 4 *suffosoria figentes terrae*, and therefore derive from a sixth-century original. Ricemarchus cannot have copied Gildas, for even if he had known his Letters, he could not have identified the unnamed monk whom Gildas abused with his own hero.

368.3 ABSTINENCE . . . : Gildas *Ep.* 2.

368.3 THEY CRITICISE BRETHREN . . . : Gildas *Ep.* 3.

369.1 ABBOT: Gildas *Ep.* 4.

369.2 CASSIODORUS: see **F**.

369.3 ABBOTS: Gildas *Ep.* 5.

370.1 BREFI: see **L**.

370.1 DIFFERENT REGIONS: see especially Bowen SCSW, particularly the maps on pp. 38 and 52.

370.3 PLACES UP THE FOSSE WAY: see **E** David, Samson.

370.3 FOSSE WAY: beyond it, Elphin of Warrington, and of North Frodingham in the East Riding, was Welsh by name.

370.3 IRISH MONKS: see **E** Abban, Columba of Terryglass, cf. pp. 386 ff. below.

370.3 WINWALOE: cf. p. 314.3 above.

372.1 WILFRED: Eddius 17.

374.3 SCATTERED HERMITS . . . BRITISH: e.g. Daniel of Hare Island (*vita Ciaran Clonmacnoise* 25).

374.3 FIRST ORDER: *Catalogus* see **T**.

374.3 MONASTERIES: most were far removed from the seats of kings; the few that lie near to royal centres include Columba's Derry and Kells, and the Leinster houses of Kildare, Glendabough and Ferns.

375.1 TUATHAL: cf. p. 169.2 above.

375.3 SAINTS OF IRELAND CAME: Irish-language Life, Stokes *Lismore Lives* 2640.

376.1 FULL OF KNOWLEDGE: *vita Finniani* 34.

376.1 DAVID, CATHMAEL: Irish-language Life, Stokes *Lismore Lives* 2527 ff.

376.2 WINE: *vita Ciaran* 31.

376.2 AGRICULTURE: cf. pp. 432 below.

377.2 BLESSED IS GOD: *vita Ciaran* 33 cf. p. 169 above.

377.3 CUIL DREMHNI: cf. p. 173 above.

377.4 ADOMNAN: *Columba* 3, 3; 1, 1.

378.1 WHEN THE NEWS CAME . . . : *vita Columbae* (O'Donnell) 2, 5 (TT 410), cf. ZCP 9, 1913, 268, paragraph 180.

379.3 TRADITION OF GILDAS: *vita Gildas* (Rhuys) 11–12 *Ainmericus rex . . . misit ad beatum Gildam rogans ut . . . veniens ecclesiasticum ordinem in suo regno restauraret* etc.; cf. *vita Gildas* (Caradoc) 5 *Gildas . . . remanens in Hibernia studiam regens et praedicans in civitate Ardmaca.*

379.3 ELDERS OF IRELAND: Colgan TT 463 (50), also printed Reeves *Adomnan* 193, note a.

379.3 COLUMBAN . . . GILTA: MGH *Epp.* 3, 158.

379.3 GILDAS' RULE: *Penitential* 17–18; 22; 27.

381.2 AGRICULTURE . . . ECONOMY: cf. p. 432 below.

381.2 SCIENTIFIC ENQUIRY: e.g. Virgilius, Dicuil, etc. cf. p. 402 below.

381.3 LITERACY: some of Taliesin's poems in Welsh were probably composed as early, but were probably not written down until the 7th century.

381.3 DAGAEUS: *vita* (Sal) 3, cf. 4–6.

381.4 KILDARE CHURCH: Cogitosus *vita Brigit* 35 (TT 523–4).

382.5 CHURCHMEN AND KINGS: e.g. Benedict Biscop; Ine and Ceadwalla, Coenred and Offa, Bede HA 2 ff.; HE 5, 7; 5, 19.

382.5 AETHERIA: CSEL 39, 35 ff., cf. **T**.

383.1 XENODOCHIA: e.g. the 4th-century British frequented the *Xenodochium in Portu Romano* Jerome *Ep.* 77, last paragraph.

383.1 BONIFACE: *Ep.* 78.

383.1 BRITISH MONK: Greg. Tur. HF 5, 21; 8, 34, cf. **E** Winnoc, and p. 250 above.

383.2 RADEGUND: see **E** John of Chinon, Radegundis.

383.2 CARANTOCUS: *vita Columbani* 7, cf. **E**.

383.2 NORTHERN GAUL: see **D** and Map 4, p. 89, cf. p. 90 above. Casual observation has remarked about a hundred place names and church dedications extending from western Normandy as far east as St. Pol (de Leon), the proper name of the Dunkirk beaches, and Samson near Namur; systematic enquiry, so far confined to Canon Doble's study of the records of the diocese of Rouen, is likely to discover more. Many of these names are due to the Armorican British, some to migration direct from Britain. On the Belgian littoral, Winnoc's name is still prominent, though it is nowadays most obvious in the names of boarding-houses, restaurants and branded goods. The monks probably often preached where their countrymen had settled previously.

383.2 SPAIN: see **E** index. Excerpts from the texts are reprinted in HS 2, 99 ff. and discussed by E.A.Thompson in *Christianity in Britain* 201 ff., citing P.David *Galice et Portugal*.

384.1 VOYAGES: *Immrama* cf. Kenney 406 ff. CEIS 233 ff. Some of the Irish-language tales are translated in P.W.Joyce, *Old Celtic Romances*, the *Navigatio Brendani*, in J.F.Webb, *Lives of the Saints*, cf. Selmer *Navigatio Sancti Brendani*.

384.1 BRENDAN AND MALO: see **E**. The two voyages, *vita I Brendani* 13; 64–66.

384.1 ITA: *vita I Brendani* 71.

384.1 SAILED WESTWARD . . . : *vita I Brendani* 13.

384.2 THIS IS THE LAND . . . : *vita I Brendani* 65.

385.1 BRITAIN . . . HERESY: *vita I Brendani* 87.

385.1 MANUSCRIPTS: date, cf. Plummer VSH 1, xxi ff., commenting 'the compiler . . . has earned our gratitude by preserving for us materials which exist nowhere else'; cf. xxxvii and Kenney 410 (ninth-century date).

385.1 ICELAND: see **L**.

385.2 YOUR KINGDOM . . . : *vita I Brendani* 95.

385.2 FIFTY ROYAL TOWNS . . . : *vita I Brendani* 80, where *oppida regum* probably means the raths of *tuath* kings.

386.1 ABINGDON: *civitatem que dicitur Abbaindun vel Dun Abbain* vita Abbani 14; cf. 13 *civitatem gentilem et deditam ydolis*. The early spellings *Aebbandun*, *Abbandun*, *Abbendun*, originally referred to another site, perhaps Boar's Hill, whence the name was removed to the later abbey and town DEPN 1; cf. MA 12, 1968, 26 ff.; see **L**. Medieval English tradition held that a Roman temple had formerly occupied the site; some 500 Roman coins are reported from Abingdon. The number is exceptionally large for a rural site away from a road; such concentrations are commoner in Roman temple enclosures than on farms.

386.2 COLUMBA OF TERRYGLASS: *vita* (Sal.) 10 cf. **E**. The direct route from Tours to Ireland passed through no English area at this date. Columba's detour suggests a visit to Abingdon, or possibly to Caistor-by-Norwich or Leicester, the nearest likely centres of royal cremation.

387.2 HOMELESS LAND: Reeves *Adomnan* 274; 266.

20 Seventh-Century Church (pp. 389–405)

389.1 BEDE: HE 3, 4.

389.3 AUGUSTINE: Bede HE 1, 26.

390.1 BRITISH ... MEETING ... AUGUSTINE: Bede HE 2, 2, at *Augustinaes Ac*, 'on the borders of the Hwicce and the West Saxons', perhaps Aust, *ST 57 88*, now the English end of the Severn Bridge.

390.2 THIS PRESENT LIFE ... : Bede HE 2, 13.

391.4 AEDAN: Bede HE 3, 5, cf. **E**.

392.2 WEST SAXON ... BAPTISM: Bede HE 3, 7; cf. 3, 22 (East Saxons), 3, 21 (Mercians, Peada).

392.2 BARKING AND CHERTSEY: Bede HE 4, 6.

392.2 BURGH CASTLE, BOSHAM: cf. **E** Fursey, Dicuil, Cedd etc.

392.2 BRIXWORTH: see **L**; cf. also Lyminge in Kent.

394.2 LINDISFARNE: Bede HE 3, 26.

394.3 WILFRED ... ENDOWMENTS: Eddius 17.

394.4 EASTER CONTROVERSY: see p. 399 below.

394.5 WHITBY: Bede HE 3, 25, dated 664 HE 3, 26, after Easter, but early in the year, since Chad left for the south after the synod, but had not heard of the death of Deusdedit of Canterbury (14 July 664) until he reached Kent (HE 3, 28).

395.2 CHAD: Bede HE 3, 28.

395.3 CHAD AND THEODORE: Bede HE 4, 3.

396.2 PICTS, MERCIANS, IRISH: Eddius 19–20, Bede HE 4, 26.

396.3 HEXHAM: Eddius 22.

396.3 WORLDLY GLORY: Eddius 24.

397.1 FOUL WEEDS ... IRISH: Eddius 47.

397.1 RULE OF BENEDICT: the Rule is named, and chapter 64 cited by Bede *Historia Abbatum* 11, cf. 16. The Rule was probably set down before 550, and made extensive use of an earlier Rule, probably of about 500 or soon after, perhaps drawn up at Lérins or Marseille; the arguments are discussed by David Knowles, *Great Historical Enterprises*, 1963, 137 ff.

397.2 IONA CUSTOM: Bede HE 3, 4.

397.3 LLANDAFF: see **T** Gospel Books, *Liber Landavensis*.

399.2 CONFORMITY WITH ROME: summarised by Kenney 210 ff., Plummer *Bede* 2, 348 ff., etc.; see **E** Aed of Sletty etc.

399.2 KILDARE: cf. p. 351 above.

399.2 MEMORY OF PATRICK: cf. p. 350 above.

400.2 MONASTICISM IN EUROPE: the sources are summarised by Kenney 486 ff., cf. **E** index.

402.3 VIRGILIUS: see **E**.

403.2 ALCUIN: see **E** and pp. 331 ff. above.

403.4 NATIONALITY ... MONASTICISM: much misunderstanding arises from the indiscriminate and undefined modern terminology of 'Irish' or 'English' missionary movements in Europe, particularly in accounts of the 8th century. Boniface and Virgilius of Salzburg disagreed deeply on matters of moment; but their disagreements had little to do with the accident that one was of English birth, the other Irish. Modern emphasis on their birth often leads to considerable confusion, cf. e.g. note to Map 29; and sometimes tempts historians to exaggerate the importance of their fellow-countrymen and to belittle the impact of the foreigner upon their own history. The initial driving forces behind the monastic movement in Europe, north of the Alps and the Massif Central, were a blend of Irish zeal and English discipline. But after the first pioneering generations these influences, together with those of the environment of each monastery, worked with differing strength on different individuals, English, Irish, French or German, whatever their personal national origin.

21 Letters (pp. 406–428)

406.2 ROMAN EMPIRE: the evidence is surveyed in Jones LRE 991 ff.

406.2 ANKARA: Jerome *Commentary* on the Epistle to the Galatians 2(3) (PL 26, 357).

406.2 SEVERUS: Dialogues 1, 27.

406.2 SIDONIUS: *Ep.* 3, 3, 2, *sermonis Celtici squarma.*

407.2 LONDON ARTISANS: Merrifield *Roman London* plate 101.

407.2 LATIN WORDS: Jackson LHEB 78–80 lists a selection.

407.3 BRITISH LATIN: Jackson LHEB 108 ff.

408.2 AETHERIA: the Rhone, ch. 18, 2. The date is probably early fifth-century, but might be later, as Meister in *Rheinisches Museum* 64, 1909, 337 ff. The Latinity is analysed and discussed by E.Lofstedt, *Peregrinatio Aetheriae.*

408.3 LATIN . . . DIED: the late 6th century Armorican British Latin of the first Life of Samson is as pedestrian as the language of Aetheria, but is still a living idiom; but in the 8th century Nennius is 'laboriously thinking first in Welsh and then translating', LHEB 121, cf. THS Cymm., 1946–7, 55–56.

408.3 MORI MARUSA: Pliny NH 4, 27, citing Philemon.

409.1 MAEGL: SC 577, which has 'the look of contemporary record' LHEB 677.

409.2 IRISH . . . SCHOOLS . . . PRESERVE LATIN: and Greek, see especially K.Meyer, *Learning in Ireland,* where, however, the statement of a 12th-century MS that 'all the learned of the whole empire fled abroad and increased the learning of Ireland' is unfounded (cf. **M** Gallic Migration); cf. LHEB 122 ff.

409.3 EDUCATION: the evidence for Roman education is collected and discussed by H.L.Marrou, *Education in Antiquity,* cf. *St. Augustin,* and is summarised by Jones, LRE 987 ff.

409.3 SICILIAN BRITON: away from school *Ep.* 1, 5; classes *de Divitiis* 12, 5; cf. **E**.

409.3 FLUENT GREEK: *eius responsionem Graeco eloquio prolatam* Augustine *de Gestis Pelagii* 4, cf. 2; and cf. 19 (Orosius).

410.2 WHITHORN: cf. **L** and **E** Maucennus.

410.2 COELESTIUS: cf. **E**; p. 339 above; JTS 16, 1965, 41.

410.2 ILLTUD: cf. **E**. His school is described in the Lives of Samson, written about 600, and of Paul Aurelian (9th century), both of which used written texts of the 6th century.

410.2 SONS OF LAYMEN: e.g. Maelgwn, Gildas, Faelan, Colman of Leinster, (*vita Coemgen* 31), and others.

410.3 OUR THINKING: *vita Pauli Aureliani* 6.

411.1 GIMNASIA: e.g. *vita Kebi* 1.

411.1 COLLEGIUM: *vita Winwaloe* 1, 11.

411.1 CANE: *vita Niniani* 10; *Kentigerni* (Jocelyn) 5; cf. e.g. Ausonius *Protrepticon* 33; Augustine *Confessio* 1, 28; Sidonius *Ep.* 2, 10.

411.1 TEILO: LL 101, cf. 98, *stultorum philosophorum.* These attitudes are noticeably rare in the accounts of other saints.

411.2 TEACHERS . . . GAUL AND BRITAIN: for the modern myth of a migration of Gallic scholars see **M** Gallic Migration, and p. 409 above.

411.2 MOCTEUS: see **E**.

412.1 DRUSTICC: see **E** Finnian of Moville.

412.2 CURRICULUM: in Britain, Samson was at school from the age of 5 to 18 or 20; Leonorus from 5 to 15; Kebi from 7; Brioc from 10 or 12 to 24; Malo and Paul Aurelian from 'an early age', Paul to 16. The curriculum seems to have regarded Leonorus' 10 years as normal; Winninus stayed for 'the two *lustra*', the ten year period, and Maudetus 'finished his curriculum in 7 years' and therefore 'did not complete his *decennium*'; cf. **E**. In Ireland, Brendan of Clonfert entered school at 5, Findchua Bri Gobban (*Lismore Lives* 2834) at 7; in England Bede's education lasted from the age of 7 until his ordination as deacon 12 years later, Willibrord's from 'weaning' till the age of 20.

412.2 PAYMENT: e.g. *vita Samson* (1) 7, cf. (2) 1, 5, *donaria secundum morem*; one cow, *vita Ciaran Clonmacnoise* 15.

412.2 FUNDS: e.g. *vita Columba Terryglass* 5; in the early days of Finnian of Clonard's school his pupils took it in turns to provide the common meal, by labour, by purchase, or *per postulationem ab aliis*, by asking from others, lay neighbours.

412.2 STUDENT MEALS: e.g. *Hisperica Famina* 303 ff., cf. 222 ff.

412.3 AGILBERT: Bede HE 3, 7.

412.3 IRISH EDUCATIONAL SYSTEM: Bede HE 3, 27.

413.2 TECHNOLOGICAL SKILLS: see p. 433 ff. below.

413.3 RUADAN: vita 14, cf. *vita Finnian* of Clonard 24–26, cf. **E**.

414.1 ALDHELM: *Ep*. 5., cf. 3.

414.2 GREGORY: HF, *Praefatio Prima*.

414.3 LITERATURE: comment is here restricted to matter relevant to the history and impact of the Arthurian period. Space does not permit a balanced survey.

414.3 GILDAS: see M. Winterbottom, *Gildas*, introduction.

415.1 MAELGWN'S BARDS: Gildas 34, 6, cf. p. 219 above.

415.3 VIRGILIUS MARO: see **F**.

415.3 BONIFACE: *Ep*. 9, written in youth to Nithard, is phrased in extravagant Hisperic. Boniface (Winfrith) was educated at Exeter and at Nursling, near Southampton, but in adult years in Europe wrote normal European Latin; cf. **E**.

415.3 ALDHELM: see **E**, and p. 498 below.

415.3 WESTERN LATIN: the main texts are summarised by Kenney, 250 ff.; cf. **E** Aldhelm, Boniface; **F**, Virgilius Maro. The word Hisperic is best confined to texts with fantasy vocabulary, as the *Hisperica Famina*, the word Western used for the wider literature, including Aldhelm.

415.3 HISPERIC: named from the *Hisperica Famina*, ed. F. J. H. Jenkinson, Cambridge, 1908, including related texts; cf. M. Winterbottom *Celtica* 8, 196, 126 ff., and Ker *Dark Ages* 31 note 4, etc.

416.3 CUNOBELINUS, BELIN: cf. **G** BE. The words of Suetonius, *Caligula* 44, *Adminio Cynobellini Britannorum regis filio* are transcribed by Orosius (7, 5, 5) as (*ad*) *Minocynobelinum Britannorum regis filium*; in Arthurian Britain the name was evidently read, with the corruption of a single letter, as *Minocyni Belinum*. The earliest person known to have been named Beli(n) was born about, or just before, the middle of the sixth century, see **G** BG. The name was readily accepted because it occurred occasionally in Irish and Gallic mythology, though not as the name of a historical person (cf. CGH index p. 519); and 'Minocynus' resembled the Irish sea god Manannan, son of Lir, later adopted into Welsh literature as Manawydan.

416.4 COROTICUS: Muirchu 28, *musicam artem audivit a quodam cantare, quod de solio regali transiret* cf. p. 219 above; the poet 'blasphemed' or 'satirised' the king, foretelling his end. To be effective, he is more likely to have sung in British than in Irish.

416.4 MAELGWN: Gildas 34, 6, cf. p. 415 above.

416.4 NENNIUS: 62, cf. **Q**.

417.1 OLDEST POEMS: see **M** and **T**. Most of the early poems survive in a few major medieval collections. Texts, not always accurately transcribed, were published by W.F.Skene FAB, with translations that outdo all other publications of bad verse in the English language. Most of the main MSS were published in transcript or facsimile by J.G.Evans 70 years ago, and several of the main poems have been edited by Sir Ifor Williams, with notes and introduction in modern Welsh, and by A.O.H.Jarman. Only the *Gododdin* has been accurately but literally translated in full, by Kenneth Jackson, but selections have appeared in most anthologies and histories of Welsh literature, cf. Works Cited, Sources, below.

417.3 DINOGAD: CA 88 (lines 1101 ff.), translated Parry HWL 22.

419.2 MAXIMUS' WIFE: Maximus first came to Britain in 367–368; his son was a child in 383, cf. PLRE 1, Victor 14, and is shown on coin portraits of 384 to 388 as a boy of 16 to 18. In 388 Maximus' daughters were apparently still unmarried, Ambrose *Ep.* 40, 32. He may have met and married his wife in Britain; her name is not known; several fourth-century empresses were named Helena.

420.2 ISIDORE: *Etymologiae* 9, 102, *Britones quidam Latine nominatos suspicantur eo quod bruti sunt*; cf. Heiric *vita Germani* 3, 246–247, *Britannia, brutis Barbara quo feritet gens ultro moribus omnis.*

420.2 CUANU: cf. **E**; ' "Britus son of Silvius son of Ascanius . . . Aeneas the father of Ascanius, ancestor of Britan the odious". Thus our noble senior Guanach deduced the genealogy of the British from the Chronicles of the Romans', Irish Nennius (*Lebor Bretnach*) 6, translated into Latin, Zimmer, *Nennius Interpretatus*, MGH AA 13 p. 152. 'Guanach' is a mis-spelling of Cuana (cf. MGH p. 141), who probably died c. 640, cf. **E**.

420.3 LOEGRIUS: cf. e.g. the 14th century pleas to the Pope, printed in Skene CPS, especially pp. 222, 243–247.

420.5 WELSH LITERATURE: surveyed by T.Parry and H.I.Bell: anthologies and translations, in OBWV, by Gwyn Williams, Conran, Bell, Graves, E.D.Jones and others include medieval and modern verse, cf. CSW 103 ff., and Works Cited, 1.

421.3 ENGLISH LITERATURE: see especially Works Cited, 1.

421.3 AETHELBERT: Attenborough LEEK, cf. Bede HE 2, 5.

421.4 CAEDMON: Bede HE 4, 24. The curious modern notion that he was a 'cowherd', of 'humble' origin, rests on inexact reading of Bede's words, cf. **E** and p. 314 above.

421.4 CAEDMON'S VERSES: cf. Plummer *Bede* 2, 248–258 and subsequent literature; in the 19th century his name was read after verses inscribed on the Ruthwell Cross, in Dumfriesshire; cf. Sweet OET 125, etc.; the reading is doubted.

421.5 ENGLISH . . . LATIN: see especially Manitius *Lateinsichen Literatur* and Laistner *Thought and Letters.*

421.5 BEOWULF, WIDSITH: cf. **T**.

421.5 SAXON CHRONICLE: see **T**.

421.5 MONASTIC . . . RECORDS: Wilfred at Selsey, in the early 680s, was able to look up the day of Oswald's death in the 'books in which the burial of the dead were recorded' (Bede HE 4, 14). Selsey kept an up-to-date Martyrology, and is likely to have matched it with an annalistic record. The probable form is an entry in an Easter Table *Occisio Osuualdi nonis Aug*, under the year 642, transcribed into a copy of a Martyrology under the 5th day of August.

422.2 IRISH LITERATURE: see especially Dillon and Chadwick *Celtic Realms* 239 ff.; Schoepperle, *Tristan*, and Works Cited, I.

422.2 ROMAN WRITERS: especially Posidonius, most fully reported by Diodorus 5, 31; Caesar *de Bello Gallico*, especially 6, 13; Strabo 4, 4, 4; Ammian 15, 9, 8 citing Timagenes, where *euhages* misreads Greek *ouates*. The texts are summarised in N.K.Chadwick *The Druids* xiii ff.; cf. T.Kendrick *The Druids*; cf. A.Ll.Owen *The Famous Druids* 15 ff.; PIRA 60 C, 1959–60; cf. Jackson OIT, especially 39, ff.; etc.

422.3 FILID: the principal text is the Preface to the List of Tales in the Book of Leinster 189 b (24,915 ff.; 4,835), translated O'Curry 583 ff.

422.3 SECULAR SCHOOLS: cf. *Book of Aichill*, preface, cf. O'Curry 512, translated 50–51.

422.4 OGAM: cf. **O**; O'Curry 464 ff., Jackson LHEB 151 ff., where however the description of the staves as 'short', the 4th-century date, and the suggested origin among Irish colonists in Britain do not accommodate all the evidence. The script does not distinguish 'pagans' from 'Christians', Jackson LHEB 176, note I. Varying sizes of sticks are envisaged in different tales. Some of them were long staffs cut from the trunks of small apple or yew trees (O'Curry 473, 475); others, as Patrick's 'wooden tablets', evidently Christian texts in Ogam characters, looked like swords (Book of Armagh 8 b 2, VT 300–301, with note), while others were much smaller. For the so-called 'Pictish Ogams', see p. 191.1 above.

422.4 CENNFAELAD: cf. **E**, and **G** INE.

423.2 REMOTE PAST: cf. p. 147 above.

423.2 WINDOW . . . IRON AGE: Kenneth Jackson OIT.

423.2 ANCIENT STORY: S.H.O'Grady, *Silva Gadaelica*, vol. I (text), 2 (translation), contains a considerable collection, principally of tales set in the period of Finn or of the Historical Cycle; P.W.Joyce, *Old Celtic Romances*, translates a number of mythological tales, and some of the late extravagant and tediuos *Imrama* (Voyages), that contrast with the more matter-of-fact Latin versions, as the Irish-language Saints' Lives compare with their Latin originals. The *Tain Bo Cualgne* (Cattle Raid of Cooley), of the Heroic Age, has been several times edited with translation. There are several translations of smaller sections of the literature; K.Meyer and others have translated a number of poems; cf. also M.Dillon and N.K.Chadwick, *The Celtic Realms*, 227 ff., 244 ff., and Kenneth Jackson, *The International Popular Tale*.

423.4 MACFIRBIS: O'Curry 122, reproduced CS, introduction p. xix.

423.4 LITERARY FORMS: cf. e.g. Carney *Medieval Irish Lyrics*.

424.2 MILKING A BULL: Adomnan, 2, 17, in a partially rationalised version.

424.2 FECHIN OF FORE: *vita* 9 (VSH 2, 79) *Res miranda atque novitate inusitata. . . . Hoc enim possibile fuit illi solo qui produxit mel de petra, oleumque de saxo durissimo.*

424.3 SENAN: *vita* 20 (Sal. 748–749), lines 673–711. Translation loses some of the wit of the original, which is reinforced by solemn rhyme and alliteration. The fourth verse here cited, lines 683–684 reads

Nam, interruptis precibus, egre ferebat monachus
ablucione parvuli sanctum liquorem pollui

The tenth verse, lines 697–700 reads

Metitur quoque baculo que sit maris altitudo
volens tantum procedere ut premineret pectore
Huic inde, inquam, anxio ista erat intencio
Ut non intraret alcius quam demonstraret baculus

426.2 ATTRACTA: *vita* 12, Colgan ASH 280, *taediosus factus est tibi Dominus Deus tuus.*

426.2 ADOMNAN: Irish Life, extract printed with translation, Skene CPS 408.

427.2 GEOFFREY: see **T.**

427.3 GEOFFREY'S ... FANCY: in the 12th century deliberate satire need not involve modern rational detachment. In all ages the human mind is capable of believing what it knows to be untrue; and to creative writers of fiction the characters they invent are easily invested with reality. The sharp classical and modern distinction between fiction and fact was alien to the complex psychology of Geoffrey and his age; neither he nor his readers found difficulty in accepting the reality of his inventions, when they had been written down, published to the world, and established in the consciousness of men. There was no contradiction between a conscious jest and a genuine belief in its truth. Geoffrey's academic contemporaries were open to the charge that they could not see the wood for the trees, but Geoffrey's artificial trees made a real wood, a concept of British history fully in accord with the beliefs and aspirations of his own day.

22 **The Economy** (pp. 429–444)

429.1 ANCIENT LAWS: see **J**, and pp. 445, 467 below.

430.2 CURRENCY: see **R.**

430.3 MORE PEOPLE LIVED ... OR ... DIED: neither the size of the population of Roman Britain nor fluctuations thereof have yet been closely studied. Modern estimates have risen from about half a million in 1937 (Colingwood) to about two million in 1968 (Frere), and there is no sign that the estimates have stopped rising. They have however been limited to generalisations about the whole province, and have been hampered by an assumption that it is commendable to strain the evidence to make the figure as small as possible. Avoidable error in either direction is equally undesirable.

Closer estimates will be possible when the archaeological records of a large number of localities have been examined, and interpreted in the light of what is known of Roman population densities elsewhere, and of the earliest statistical record of Britain, the 11th-century Domesday Book.

At present it is only possible to note that in several parts of the country it is difficult to make the minimum Roman population implied by archaeological record as small as the population listed for the same areas in Domesday Book.

In the counties where the population is enumerated, Domesday Book lists a little under 300,000 adult males; the numbers of unlisted wives, children and other relatives are likely to multiply this figure about three to five times, giving a population in the neighbourhood of a million to a million and a half. To these must be added the population of Wales, of the northern counties excluded from the Survey, and various categories of unlisted persons, ploughmen in many regions, the occupants of houses and land entered as such, without numbers of people, and other categories. A substantial addition is needed to assess the mid 11th-century population. King William's devastation of the north is said to have cost 100,000 lives. The figure is patently a guess and doubtless exaggerated, but the casualties were plainly enormous; in Yorkshire the Survey listed 43 persons in one group of 411 manors, whose earlier population was necessarily much greater. Severe but less concentrated devastation is also reported in the Survey in many other parts of the country.

It is therefore probable that the mid 11th century population of the former Roman province was of the order of two to three million. If the thorough study of recorded Roman sites should suggest that the Roman population was normally somewhat greater, then it may argue an overall population of three to four millions.

The available evidence suggests that there were significant movements of population during the later Empire, but does not yet indicate whether the total population increased or decreased. The disasters of the Arthurian period however clearly reduced overall numbers. The urban and industrial population plainly declined; lands were wasted, and emigration and casualties removed people, though losses were doubtless partially offset by the weakening of imperial taxation, formerly a main factor in keeping down the birth rate, and by the immigration of some tens of thousands of English.

These considerations rest on inference rather than information, but the document termed the 'Tribal Hidage' (see **T** and p. 492 below), which iists a little over 200,000 hides in the midlands and the south, suggests the possibility that by the later 7th century population had fallen to a level not greatly in excess of the mid 11th century, when allowance is made for Wales, the north and the south-west. The Scandinavian invasions thereafter doubtless reduced native numbers, but added immigrants.

Until the evidence is more exactly studied, it is possible only to record that between the 4th century and the 11th the population is likely to have fluctuated between the outside limits of about 4,000,000 and about 2,000,000.

430.3 AUSONIUS' GRANDSON: 'Paulinus of Pella', cf. Works Cited, 1.

431.1 GILDAS: ch. 26, 2; see p. 137 above.

431.3 ANIMAL BONES: L.Alcock (*Dinas Powys* 36) tabulates an analysis of animal bones, together with comparable figures from three sites in the Wessex downland (Woodyates, Rotherley and Woodcuts), and from a number of Irish sites. The proportions are

	Dinas Powys	Wessex	Ireland
Cattle	20%	33–39%	70–97%
Sheep	13%	29–40%	1–15%
Pig	61%	2–13%	1–27%
Horse	under 1%	10–26%	1% or less

V.B.Proudfoot (MA 5, 1961, 106) catalogues the presence or absence of animal bones reported in the excavation of some 45 Irish raths, but not the quantities. Cattle were reported at 20 sites, sheep at 8, pigs at 15, horses at 11. The figures in general match Alcock's; horses seem more numerous, for a number of sites each produced horse bones in small numbers. But among the animals named in the Book of Rights tribute lists, sheep are relatively commoner; the figures total 25,220 cattle, 12,340 sheep, 6,410 pigs, in percentages 57%, 28%, and 15%.

432.1 LLANCARFAN AND LLANDAFF: see **T** Gospel Books.

432.1 THREE OR FOUR COWS: 25 times out of 30. The five more expensive values are 10, 14, 14, 25 and 70.

432.1 LANDEILO: the Book of Chad, **T** Gospel Books.

432.1 WESSEX: Laws of Ine 70, 1.

432.1 BOOK OF RIGHTS: tributes summarised on pp. 179 ff. The legend of the *Boruma*, the cattle tribute levied on Leinster (cf. **A** 134 note), gives a payment of equal numbers of cattle and pigs, some texts adding sheep. Cauldrons are required for the king's brewing, but not barley to supply them, nor brewed beer. The lists include cloaks, flitches and beeves, in much smaller quantities than the animals. The texts are late, long after the expansion of arable farming. Legal texts and incidental stories place the same emphasis on cattle.

432.2 MONASTERIES . . . MANY: their size varied. Initial numbers are often small; Winwaloe and Paul Aurelian (with sufficient slaves) began with 12 monks, Samson with 14 monks and 7 *famuli*, Lunaire and Tudwal with 72 monks. In developed houses, Brioc had 168, Gudwal 180, Petroc and Paternus 80. Lasrian of Leighlin with 1,500 and MoChuta with 867 claim unusually large communities. Brendan's numerous monasteries held 3,000 between them. Maedoc took 150 out to harvest. Cadoc, Illtud and Kentigern (at Llanelwy, St. Asaph) are credited with a division between *clerici* and *operarii illiterati*, analogous to that drawn by Cassiodorus in Italy; Illtud and Cadoc maintained the poor, and Cadoc also maintained widows; Cadoc, king as well as abbot, is also assigned a military force, giving totals of 300 to Illtud, 500 to Cadoc, 965 to Kentigern. The traditions that Mocteus of Louth and Ruadan of Lothra, until constrained, maintained clerics who did no agricultural work implies a similar division. These figures are not excessive, though in the nature of the transmission they are liable to inflation in honour of the founding saint. Bede's figure (HE, 2, 2) of over 2,000 in a single monastery of Bangor-on-Dee is exceptionally large. Their hierarchical organisation is matched by Kentigern's '*illos per turmas et conventus dividens*'. The implication of the evidence is that most houses could be numbered in scores or hundreds; their impact was due to their number rather than their individual size.

432.3 DAVID, CARTHACUS; and others. See **E**, under the saints named.

433.2 TOOLS: e.g. the schedule of goods to be divided on divorce, p. 445 below; the price list of 250 items (VC 3, 22, etc) is probably copied from a Wessex list, and concerns the English more than the Welsh, cf. **Q**, **T**.

433.2 WATERMILL: e.g. Carthacus, Ciaran of Clonmacnoise, Eugenius (in Gaul), Fechin and Mo Choemog, Finnian of Moville, Fintan of Dunblesc, Gildas (in Brittany), Ita, Lugid, Gudwal (tidal), Flannan; canalisation, e.g. Fechin, Frigidian (in Italy), Moling. Usually, the nature of the mill is not specified; the donkey mill does not appear; where the power is specified, it is water, occasionally tidal.

433.2 CORN DRYING: Cainnech (Sal.) 35; Ciaran 12, *rota de virgis contexta plena spicis igne supposito*; Finnian (*Lismore* 2629); poem, Mocteus *M.Don.*, *M.Oeng.*, FM 535, also printed Todd *Patrick* 30. Three or four kilns have been excavated in raths (Proudfoot MA 5, 1961, 108 cf. 106), and the corn kiln (*odyn*) is frequently mentioned in Welsh Law (ALW indices).

434.4 ULTAN: the Life is early, written when prayer with arms outstretched was still normal in Ireland.

434.4 NOBLEMAN OF MACHA: *vita Brigit* (Ultan) 61 (TT 534).

435.1 ANOTHER OCCASION: *vita Brigit* (Ultan) 80 (TT 537).

435.2 GERALD: ch. 12 (VSH). 'Gerald' is represented as an Englishman; a number of English followed Colman of Lindisfarne, when he returned to Ireland, to found Mayo, in 664.

435.2 IUGERA: evidently translating Irish *immaire*; cf. a jumbled rehash of the story told in the *vita Gerald*, in the Hymm of Colman, preface, LH 1, 25; 2,12.

435.3 FLANNAN: (of Killaloe) ch. 31 (Sal.).

435.3 ANOTHER TRADITION: *Lebor na hUidre* 128, cited Plummer VSH xcvi 6.

436.3 LAW TRACT: the *Uraicecht Becc*, or 'Small Primer', ALI 5, 1, cf. MacNeill PIRA 36 C, 1923, 255 and *Celtic Ireland* 96 ff., dated by Binchy *Eriu* 18, 1958, 44 ff. to the '8th century or earlier' (p. 48), possibly contemporary with texts of c. 680 (pp. 51–52).

436.4 EXCAVATED RATHS: MA 5, 1961, 94 ff., especially pp. 94, 103 and selected plans p. 100.

436.5 LAW TRACT: ALI 5, 483, cited MacNeill *Celtic Ireland* 167–169.

437.3 STIRRUP: the metal innovation is well dated because it is preserved from numerous dated graves.

437.3 HORSE COLLAR: made of perishable material, and not buried in graves, and therefore less directly evidenced. Various early Slavonic forms are known, but cannot be closely dated; their ultimate origin seems however to be related to that of the stirrup. The evidence is discussed by Lefevre de Noëttes *Attelage*, and others.

437.4 NORICUM: the build of the animal, similar to the medieval Shire horse, is most clearly demonstrated by Roman figurines in Austrian museums, notably at Wels, the Roman Ovilava.

437.4 MONKS . . . SLAVS: cf. Map 29, p. 401, and notes thereto.

437.4 SLAVS . . . SUNDERED: cf. Map 17, p. 277.

438.2 PICTS: cf. **L**.

438.4 ENGLISH: see **S**.

440.2 CHURCHES OF WOOD: e.g. Cadoc and David in Wales, Goueznou in Brittany, Winniocus at Luxeuil in Burgundy (Jonas *Columban* 1, 15; 1, 17), Enda, Flannan of Killaloe, Mo-Choe and many others in Ireland, Finan of Lindisfarne and Aedan at York in Northumbria. Cianan's stone church at Duleek and Ninian's at Whithorn were both regarded as exceptional, the work of foreign craftsmen.

441.2 WINE: in Britain, cf. e.g. Piro, p. 360 above; in Ireland, Muirchu 18, cf. Stokes *Lismore Lives* 316; *vita Ciarani* clonmacnoise 31, cf. *Lismore* 4402.

441.2 COLUMBA: Adomnan 1, 28. *Sulfurea de caelo flamma* that killed 3,000 sounds like a volcano; perhaps Etna, since Vesuvius is not known to have erupted during Columba's lifetime. Reeves' 'Istria' derives from a late martyrologist's guess, cf. **L** Caput Regionis (Kintyre).

441.2 COLUMBAN: Jonas 23 *navis quae Scottorum commercia vexerat*, cf. *vita Winwaloe* 1, 19 *mercatoribus transmarina negotia ausportantibus . . . ad Scotos* (from Brittany).

441.2 PORTH MAWR, PADSTOW: cf. **L**.

441.2 FINNIAN: *vita Finnian Clonard* (Sal.) 4, cf. **E**.

441.3 JOHN THE ALMSGIVER: ch. 9; about AD 600. There is no reason to change the date given in the text.

441.3 VALUE: did not greatly change in many centuries. Over 700 years later, the Book of Ballymote was sold for 140 cows, Kenney 24.

442.1 BOOK OF TEILO: LL xliii, cf. **T** Gospel Books.

442.2 SILVER INGOTS: cf. e.g. H. Willers, *Die roemischen Bronzeeimer von Hemmoor* 291, 'ex offi(cina) Isatis', found at London, Richborough, Coleraine in Ulster, Dierstorf (Minden) in Germany, and elsewhere.

442.4 WEST SAXON LAWS: Ine 25, . . . *ceapie, do thaet beforan gewitnessum*, 'if a trader trade up country, he shall do so before witnesses.'

442.4 KENTISH LAW: . . . *gebycge*, 'if a Kentishman buy goods in London, he shall have reliable men, or the King's reeve to witness'. The law protects the Kentishman against suit for theft; he must prove by witnesses or oath that he had bought the *feoh* with his own *ceape*, or surrender it. Both words commonly mean property in general, and cattle in particular. Ch. 15, demanding surety for the foreign *ciepeman*, implies that traders felt the need of a local patron, for whose protection they presumably paid. The probable context of ch. 16 is that the Kentishman sold cattle in London and bought foreign imports; ch. 15 and the Wessex law appear to envisage a travelling salesman of humble status and dubious honesty, nearer to the 18th-century 'chapman' than to the 'merchant'. These are the only references to traders in the 7th-century laws.

443.2 BOOK OF RIGHTS: p. 432 above.

443.2 HOARDED WEALTH: p. 236 above.

443.2 PENDA: Hostage, Bede HE 3, 24. Distribution, the *Atbret Iudeu* Nennius 65, cf. p. 302 above.

443.3 ENGLISH MONEY: fines, etc. expressed in money values in the laws, may or may not have been paid in cash; cf. **M.**

23 **Welsh and Irish Society** (pp. 445–465)

445.1 LAW: see **J**. The comprehensive collection of *Welsh Laws*, with translation and glossary, is the *Ancient Laws and Institutes of Wales* (AWL), ed. Aneurin Owen, 1841; vol. 1 contains the texts named Venedotian, Demetian and Gwentian Codes (VC, DC, GC); vol. 2 the 'Anomalous Laws' (AL), or 'Cyvreithiau Cymru', and various versions of the 'Laws of Hywel Da', the 'Leges Wallicae' (p. 749) (LW), 'Leges Howelli Boni' (p. 814) (HD), 'Powys Laws' (p. 881), a second 'Leges Howelli Boni', principally concerned with royal rights (p. 893), and the Statute of Rhuddlan (p. 909). A number of other MSS have been published since, usually without translation (cf. **J**), but the laws have not been collated; see CSW 73 ff.; WHR 1963 Special Number; T.P.Ellis *Welsh Tribal Law.*

The comparable comprehensive collection of *Irish Laws* is the *Ancient Laws of Ireland* (ALI). The material is enormous. Among later works, R. Thurneysen and others, *Studies in Early Irish Law* (SEIL) is especially useful. The interaction of Irish and of Roman and Church law is clearest in the *Hibernensis*, cf. Kenney 247, of the early 8th century.

445.1 WELL INHABITED LAND: GC 2, 39, 28.

445.1 COHABITATION: VC 2, 1, 30–31; DC 2, 18, 10 etc.

445.1 BRAKE AND BUSH: VC 2, 1, 33 etc.

445.1 COMES OF AGE: e.g. VC 2, 28, 5 ff.; 2, 30, 3; 5.

445.1 GIRLS' PROPERTY: VC 2, 30, 3; the MS variant 'he wishes' contradicts the rest of the passage, and is clearly wrong.

445.2 VIRGIN BRIDE: e.g. VC 2, 1, 27.

445.2 CHILDREN'S UPBRINGING: e.g. VC 2, 28, 5–8.

445.2 IRISH LAW: cf. the texts cited in SEIL 187 ff.

445.3 DIVORCE: the principal sections of the laws are VC 2, 1; DC 2, 18; GC 2, 29; cf. LW 2, 19; HD 2, 23.

446.3 CHARGE OF IMPOTENCE: VC 2, 1, 66 (cf. 67, variant, 'rape'), discreetly translated into Latin rather than English.

446.4 IRISH . . . DIVORCE: a number of the principal texts are surveyed in SEIL 241 ff.

446.4 HIBERNENSIS: 46, 8–10, Isidore *de Officiis* 2, 20, 12; the text describes and rejects grounds for divorce that were acceptable in Wales and Ireland.

446.4 CHURCH LAW: VC 2, 16, 2.

447.3 INHERITANCE: the principal Welsh texts are VC 2, 12; DC 2, 23; GC 2, 31; cf. AL 9, 26–27, LW 2, 11. Daughters' rights differed in north and south; cf. VC 2, 1, 64, DC 2, 23, 7 and scattered references, cf. AWL indices; the main Irish texts are summarised in SEIL 133 ff.

447.3 CENEDL: see p. 461 below.

447.3 FINE: see especially *Senchus Mor* (ALI 1 p. 261 etc), and MacNeill *Celtic Ireland* 159 ff.

447.4 COMPENSATION: the assumptions of Roman and English law have prompted the notion that a 'blood-feud' must be invented to explain Welsh compensation laws. No evidence supports the assumption, and no word for such a 'feud' exists in Welsh. Germanic law permitted *faida*, legalised enmity, (cf. note 485.2 below) in the exceptional cases when compensation was not paid; in the middle ages, in some Germanic and southern European lands, when customary sanctions broke down, *faida* developed into a chain of violence and counter-violence, that gave rise to the concept of 'blood-feud'. The notion is alien to early Welsh society, and belongs only to a political philosophy which maintains that 'human nature' is mutually destructive unless it is subjected to the authority of an élite.

448.4 RIGDOMNA: cf. MacNeill *Celtic Ireland* 114 ff; the evidence of the Annals and Genealogies argues that practice was more varied and less schematic than MacNeill suggests.

449.4 IRISH SOCIETY: cf. especially the 'Small Primer', p. 436.3 above, and the book of Aichill, cf. **J**.

450.4 DRESS: ALI 2, 146, 10 ff. I am indebted to Professor Binchy for drawing my attention to this passage, which prescribes colours for foster sons, presumably those to which their fathers were entitled. The later texts (e.g. LG 9, 8 (ITS 5,208), cf. Book of Leinster 2035 ff. (ITS 1, 64); FM 3664, cf. 3656; Keating 1, 25 (ITS 2, 123) ascribe their regulations to the mythical Bronze Age kings of the second millennium BC, Eochu Etgudach ('Goodclothes') and Tigernmas; see also the poem LG 96, 2 (ITS, 435).

451.2 SENCHUS FIR nALBAN: CPS 308 ff., see **Q** and p. 180 above.

453.1 PICT INHERITANCE: cf. p. 192 above.

453.2 TRAVELLERS: e.g., among many, Alexander Carmichael, reproduced in Skene CS 3, 378–393, cf. A.N.Palmer, YC 11, 1892, 176 ff., and other accounts.

453.3 CLAN: most of the evidence here discussed is assembled by W.F.Skene in *Celtic Scotland*, especially 3, 303 ff.

454.4 IN BUCHAN: grants inscribed in the Book of Deer.

454.4 MORGAN: see **G** 1 DRL.

455.1 CAMPBELLS: cf. the pedigree printed Skene CS 3, 458.

455.1 LENNOX: cf. the pedigree printed Skene CS 3, 475; **G** IMW; **L** Dergind. The principal adaptations are to turn the Irish Loch Lein into Leamna (Lennox), Maine Munchain into Maine Leamna, and Dergind, p. 158 above, into 'Gergind', equated with Circin or the Mearns.

455.2 SAVAGE AND RUDE: Fordun *Chron.* 2, p. 38, cited Skene CS 3, 307.

455.2 HIGHLAND CLANNA: Wyntoun *Chron.*, ed. 1879, 3, p. 63; *Scotichronicon* 2, p. 420, etc., cited Skene CS 3, 310 ff.

455.2 18th CENTURY OBSERVER: Gartmore MS (1747), cited Skene CS 3, 318.

455.3 DEGENERATE TO . . . COMMON PEOPLE: cf. Sir John Davies' description, in 1607, of the means whereby *tanists* of 'septs' in Ireland 'did spoil and impoverish the people at their pleasure', cited Seebohm EVC 220. In Ireland, as in Scotland, English administrative notions turned local dynasts into 'chiefs' of 'tribes', or 'clans' or 'septs', and rewarded their loyalty to the conqueror by according them the legal right to exploit their own people. In Ireland succession to the 'chieftaincy' normally passed to any member of the *Derb Fine*, elected by show of hands and termed *tanist*, equivalent to the *rigdomna* of the greater dynasties; but in Scotland succession normally passed from father to son.

457.2 EOIN MACNEILL: 'more than any other' Kenney 81; on the clan, Celtic *Ireland*, 1921, 155–156; cf. p. 152, on Joyce's *Social History*, 'from book to book a thousand talkers and writers have said that the social organisation of ancient Ireland in historical times was on a tribal basis, and they have called it the Clan System. Joyce . . . is unable to find a single ancient authority to support it.' Nor has anyone else discovered such evidence. MacNeill protested that the 'cocksure people' who talked of tribes and clans in 1921 constituted a 'formidable body'; they still do. The recent mushrooming of 'clan societies', the 'discovery' of 'clan chiefs', the issue of 'certificates' and the proliferation of new 'tartans' serves modern commercial and political interests; it has no connection with the early history of Scotland, except that its confusion smears the dignity of genuine tradition and record, and tends to make them suspect associates of the current farce.

457.2 SKENE: cf. note 177.1 above.

457.2 TOO LITTLE HEEDED: e.g., among many instances, T.C.Smout *A History of the Scottish People*, 1560–1830, p. 24; 'Celtic society was clearly tribal, based on a real or fancied kinship between every freeman and the head of his tribe. The tribes apparently occupied fairly distinct areas of the country . . . and possessed differing tribal laws', cf. p. 334 'in the early 10th century . . . the Highlands were tribal, in the exact sense that ninteenth century Africa was tribal.'

Published in 1969, nearly 50 years after MacNeill wrote, and 100 years after Skene, this preamble to a history of a later period typifies the 'rubbish' that is still 'imposed' upon otherwise well-informed authors, who have not themselves had occasion to study the evidence.

458.2 SLAVE: the modern word derives from Slavs, prisoners taken by Charlemagne and his successors, who were a mobile marketable commodity, as homeborn agricultural *servi*, serfs, were not, and lacked an appropriate descriptive term.

458.3 CAETH: the laws distinguish different kinds of *caeth*, domestic, agricultural, royal; and differentiate the voluntary *caeth*, a dependent stranger who prefers to give himself to the *uchelwr* rather than to settle as a king's *aillt*, from the purchased *caeth* (e.g. AL 6, 1, 72). The voluntary *caeth* appears to have enjoyed a status not greatly different from the English *hlafaeta*, 'loaf eater', (p. 486 below). Close research into the usage of the texts is likely to reveal more subtle shifts of meaning; but in general *servus* tends to mean *caeth* in legal language, whereas colloquial usage often wrote *servus* for *taeog*. The codes include both legal texts and some texts written in colloquial language, as the 'Privileges of Arvon' (VC 2, 2 etc., cf. **J**) and some of the 'Legal Triads'.

458.4 GILDAS: *Ep.* 3, cf. p. 368 above.

458.4 SAMSON, HERVE, JUSTINIAN: see **E**.

458.4 WESSEX: Ine 74, 1, cf. p. 485.2 below.

458.5 TATHEUS, MALO, WINWALOE: see **E**.

459.3 PLEBES . . . TRIBUS: cf. **N** Tref, and p. 364 above.

459.3 SCHEMATISM: VC 2, 17, 6 ff.; cf. **N** Tref.

459.3 MAINAUR: Book of Teilo (Chad) folio 216, memorandum 6, printed LL xlvii *mainaur Med Diminih*, cf. BBCS 7, 1935, 369, and, for the date, Jackson LHEB 47. The word, superficially similar to *manerium*, manor, was a gift to Norman lawyers, who so translated it.

459.4 AILLT, ALLTUD: cf. **J**.

459.4 VALENTINIAN III: Novella 31, CTh 2, pp. 129–132. It is theoretically possible that up to the late 450s the British government was able to accept and enforce imperial constitutions if it wished, or that Valentinian renewed older laws already in force before 410, and that the Welsh law re-enacts the Roman, but it is more probable that similar causes inspired similar legislation.

460.2 TIR CYVRIV: also called *tir kyllydus*, tax or rent-paying land, cf. especially VC 2, 12, 6 etc. Both king and lord might possess *tir cyvriv*, and on behalf of its *tref* allocate the *tref* land.

460.3 CYLLID: its main constituent was *dawnbwyd*, food render.

460.3 GWESTVA: payable by free *uchelwr*, VC 2, 17, 14–15, but not due from *tir cyvriv*, AL 5, 1, 28; 14, 32, 4 etc. It began as the entertainment of the king's household while on progress; it became a tribute of food, later a tax in money; when commuted to a money payment, *gwestva* was termed *tunc*, cf. 221.2 above.

460.3 CYLCH: cf. ALW indices, 'Progress'.

460.3 PROGRESS: cf. texts cited in *Angles and Britons* 156–157.

460.3 DISPENSING JUSTICE: *vita Gwynlliw* 16 gives a lively account of a dean riding hard through a night of wind and rain to be in time for the hearing of a case at a royal feast in Gwent.

460.3 PAYMENT: exacted by e.g. Maelgwn *vita Cadoci* 69; by 'Arthur', as a compensation fine, *vita* Cadoci 22.

460.3 ANCIENT BREED: white cattle with red ears, in Britain, VC 1, 2, 2, cf. DC 1, 2, 6 and *vita Cadoci* 22 (red in front, white behind), exacted as the kings *saraad*, compensation fine; white with red ears imported into Ireland from Britain, Cormac's *Glossary* 72, *Fir*; encountered in Brittany by Herbot (cf. E); cf. S. Baring-Gould, *A Book of Brittany* 277 (white cows). The breed perhaps survives in modern park cattle, notably the Chillingham herd in Northumberland, (*Eriu* 14, 1946, unnumbered page placed after the first of two pages numbered 169, citing several references in early Irish literature and one from 13th-century Flanders, cf. Whitehead *Cattle* and BBCS 23, 1969, 195). Excavated cattle bones still receive rare and perfunctory examination, and it is therefore not yet possible to say whether or not archaeological evidence for these animals exists, or whether or where they were known in Britain in or before the Roman period.

460.3 FIRE PREVENTION: VC 3, 3, 13 ff. etc.

461.1 TRE'R CEIRI: RCHM Caernarvonshire.

461.1 DINAS POWYS: cf. p. 431 above.

461.2 CANTREF: the principal texts are assembled and discussed in Lloyd HW 1,300 ff. The *cantref* were later subdivided into *cwmwd* (commotes), to which the assembly was transferred.

461.3 CENEDL; cf. ALW indices, 'Kindred', 'Chief of Kindred', 'Caput Gentis', etc. The *cenedl* is frequently named in the codes, but most of the rulings about the *Pencenedl* are in AL.

461.4 LUIDT: Book of Teilo (Chad), folios 141 (memorandum 2) *luidt* and 18 (memorandum 3) *luith*, printed with facsimile LL xliii, xlv; for the date, cf. Jackson LHEB 43–46.

462.1 TEUYTH: *vita Wenefred* 5 *Teuyth . . . interpellans ut sibi fatteret quod de suo patrimonio deliberaret. Ille* (*Cadfan*) *refert 'O vir wenerande, nequaquam mihi vel tibi sortitur. Tamen sequestrare rus a provincie communione ne sibi sit inutile vel mee necessitati. Sed harum quamcumque villarum trium elegeris ad divinum officium tibi libere annuo, si placatus fueris, mihique reliquas relinque.* The place was perhaps Whitford, near Holywell in Flint, *SD 14 78*, the only church in Tegeingl known to have been dedicated to Beuno, cf. Bowen SCSW 83, with figs. 22, 23; cf. Map 24, p. 359 above.

462.4 SURVEYS: large extracts are printed in F. Seebohm, *Tribal System in Wales*, appendices, and discussed pp. 1 ff.

464.1 LLANCARFAN: the grants appended to the Life of Cadoc, cf. **T** Gospel Books. The grants cited are 65; 62; 55; 60; 68. In another, 59, a nobleman 'commended' an estate to his son, with a rent charge to the church.

464.1 LLANDAFF: **T** Gospel Books. Llandaff gives much detail of prices, rentals, extents, that concern its claims. In the one grant that the two have in common (LL 180 = *vita Cadoc* 67) Llandaff reproduces the reasons for the grant more fully, but leaves out many of the details of who made what gift to whom.

464.5 BOOK OF ARMAGH: folios 16 r to 18 v, also printed AB 2, 1883, 213 ff., and VT 334 ff., commonly known as the *Additamenta to Tirechan* 1–16. Sections 8 to 16 are in Irish. The scribe, Ferdomnach, writing in 807, apologised for not translating into Latin passages that he found 'badly written in Irish; not because I am unable to write Latin, but because these accounts are barely intelligible in their original Irish', *finiunt haec pauca per scotticam imperfecte scripta; non quod ego non potuissem romana condere lingua, sed quod vix in sua scoti[c]a hae fabulae agnosci possunt*. Irish that was scarcely intelligible by c. 800 is unlikely to have been much less than a century old; the two datable grants (Cummen, 11; Aed of Sletty, 16) are both late 7th century, and the text transcribed by Feradach was therefore nearly contemporary with the original grants.

464.5 CUMMEN: *add. Tirechan* 11 (VT 340). The genealogies place the chief, Eladach, about 680, (**G** IACF 650 Mael Odur); Colman (of Lindisfarne? **E**) was established at Inis Boffin from 665 to 675.

465.2 FETH: *Add. Tirecham* (VT 338); Drumlease *G 83* in Callraige, Hogan 366, 152.

465.3 FOIRTCHERN: Add. *Tirechan* 4 (VT 336).

465.3 BINEAN: Add. *Tirechan*, 7. (VT 337); the scribe wrote *d[eu]s* for *dedit*; a later hand added *cui dedit* without erasing *d[eu]s*.

24 **English Society** (pp. 466–505)

467.2 LAWS: conveniently collected by Attenborough LEEK, based on ALE and the *Gesetze* of Schmid and Liebermann; extensively discussed by Seebohm TCASL, cf. EVC, TSW, and others: see **J**.

467.2 CHARTERS: the principal collections are BCS and KCD. The charters are comprehensively catalogued by Sawyer, and many are summarised by Finberg ECMW etc., and by Hart; see **C**, and p. 328 above.

467.2 CHARTERS . . . ALTERATIONS: among the commonest changes are the conflation of the witnesses to the original grant and to subsequent confirmations, that creates a superficial appearance of chronological contradiction and ensnares the incautious critic; and the alteration of rights and properties to suit the interest of the copier, with the insertion of words, and of the names of people and titles, places and regions, that belong to the copier's time, but were unknown at the time of the grant. The use of, for example, *Anglia* dates a copy to the 11th century or later, but frequently derives from an original that used a cumbrous old-fashioned term, as 'all the provinces of the English'.

467.2 FORGED . . . GENUINE: the provisional system devised by Finberg, of marking texts by stars, whose number indicates the degree of alteration, is a considerable advance upon the crude categories employed in earlier inexact modern conventions of classification; but is no substitute for precise analysis of what is added to each text.

467.3 GRAVES . . . SOCIAL DIFFERENCE: cf. p. 281 above.

468.2 PLACE NAMES: EPNS, DEPN, EPNE; notes to maps 30 to 36; see **N**.

468.3 ELEMENTS: EPNE (cf. additions and corrections in JEPN I), from which the meanings here given are cited.

468.3 STUDY OF . . . -ING: J.M.Dodgson MA 10, 1966, 1 ff., and *Beitrage zur Namenforschung* (Heidelberg), NF, 2, 1967, 221 ff. and 325 ff.; 3, 1968, 141 ff., on whose work maps 30 and parts of maps 33 and 34 are based. Other maps are adapted from EPNS volumes, and from unpublished material kindly made available.

470.2 ARTOIS: see p. 287 above.

470.4 TUN: EPNE 2, 188 ff. The word already meant a village in the 7th century, *Hlothere* 5. The suggestion in EPNE 2, 190 (5) that many or most began as 'single farms' and later grew into villages is unlikely and unwarranted, and contradicts the archaeological evidence. Later usage, translating *tun* as Latin *villa*, *ham* as *civitas*, contrasts an estate with a community, and does not concern size. See **N.** Relatively few *-tun* names are likely to be earlier than the 7th century.

470.4 TUN . . . SECONDARY COLONISATION: EPNE 2, 191 (9).

472.2 -BOTL: especially EPNE I, 43–44. Its distribution in Europe is limited and localised; A.Bach, *Deutsche Namenkunde*, II 2 map 44, p. 333, para 610 ff., where the Carolingian date suggested is not probable; see Map 17, p. 277.

472.2 -WORTH, -COTE: EPNE 2, 273 ff., especially 274 (3); I, 108 ff.

472.2 -INGTUN: EPNE I, 291 ff., especially 295 (5); *Teottingtun* (Teddington) distinguishes 'Teotta's village' from *Teottingatun*, the 'village of Teotta's people'. It is often impossible to tell the forms apart; but when they can be distinguished, *-ingatun* rarely forms as much as one-fifth of the total, and it is therefore probable that *-ingtun* is normally the form of the great majority; but both forms imply lordship, and also secondary colonisation.

It is however not easy to discover names in any form of *-ingtun* attested before the middle of the 8th century. Their rarity is partly explained by the nature of the record; most such places were too small to figure in the works of Bede, Eddius, or other early writers; and charters commonly grant either royal land or small portions of estates, rather than centres of individual lordship. In some instances however, the name of a settlement is recorded substantially earlier than its *-tun*. *Tun*, though it was the general word for a village in the 7th century, is itself rare in place names of the late 7th and early 8th centuries. Closer study may therefore suggest that 7th century settlements founded by an individual lord with his dependents were at first known by his name, followed by *-inga lond* or the like, but did not acquire their administrative centre and suffix *-tun* until some generations later. Records of *-cote* also begin late.

474.3 KENT: the custom of Kent is lucidly described by Joliffe PFE, emphasising (p. 3) that 'the manors of Kent are more like those of Wales than of Oxford and Berkshire'. The suggestion that Frankish influence on Kentish ornament indicates that the Jutes of Kent and their customs came from the Rhineland (Leeds AASS 126 ff., developed by Joliffe 102 ff.) was made when dates were less understood; Frankish ornament was favoured by the grand-daughters of the first settlers, many of whom came from Jutland (Myres ASP 96, map 7; p. 289 above; see **S**). Third generation ornament has nothing to do with the nationality of the first comers; the nationality of the first settlers is not determined by the fashions that their granddaughters favoured.

474.3 NINE LATHES: excluding Sutton, outside the early borders of Kent.

474.3 WELKECHILDELAND: BBA I, 229, cited Joliffe PFE 27, note 3.

474.3 NINE RAPES: including Ytene, Meonwara and Wight, now in Hampshire.

476.1 WORTHS . . . PENNINES: Heworth, a suburb of York, stands alone in the North Riding; Ravensworth near Richmond is a variant of Ravensford.

476.1 BOTL STRONGHOLDS: Newbottle, etc., by definition secondary, are omitted from Map 35.

476.1 WIDE RANGE OF NAMES: the few that have been examined closely show their potential value; for example, *-wicham* and *-wictun*, derived from Latin *vicus*, are almost entirely confined to the areas of 6th century burials, and are most plentiful where 5th and early 6th century cemeteries are commonest, cf. MA 11, 1967, 87, map. p. 88.

480.1 INTENDS TO DEPART: Ine 64–66.

480.1 CULTIVATED: *gesette* means cultivated and tilled, usually by dependent cultivators, as Seebohm EVC 128, 136 ff., Vinogradoff GM 128, Aston TRHS series 5, 8, 1958, 65; rather than 'sown', as Maitland DBB 238 note 1, Liebermann *Gesetze* (on Ine 64) and others.

480.1 NOBLEMAN: Ine 63.

480.1 UNAUTHORISED EMIGRATION: Ine 39.

480.2 CEORL'S WORTH: Ine 40, 42. Detached words from Ine 42 have been used to suggest the strip cultivation of a later age; in context, they cannot relate thereto, see **Q** and **T**.

482.1 HEBERDEN: BCS 144.

482.1 THURINGIA: *Translatio S. Alexandri* 1.

483.3 SCOTS: cf. p. 451 above.

483.3 WELSH LAW: cf. p. 448 above.

483.3 HIDE: cf. p. 487.2 below.

483.3 ONE TAXPAYER . . . ONE HIDE: cf. e.g. the equation in BCS 144, cf. note 487.2 (HIDE) and p. 499 below.

484.1 ALFRED'S LAWS: 42, 7.

484.3 MANY LAWS: e.g. Alfred 37; Edward 11, 7; Aethelstan II 2; 8; 22, 1; III 4; IV 3; V Preface 1 and 2; 1.

485.2 WEST SAXON . . . WELSHMEN: Ine 74, 1. The law contrasts with *Lex Saxonum* 2, 5, which exposes the *litus* to *faida* without alternative.

485.2 RELATIVES . . . RARELY: e.g. if a killer escaped abroad, the relatives paid half the *leod* (*wergild*), Aethelbert 23; in Wessex, if no paternal kinsmen were discoverable, the maternal relatives paid one third, Alfred 30.

485.2 FAEHDE: the word is the linguistic ancestor of modern 'feud', cf. note 447.4 above, but does not share its meaning of a chain of violence, see Du Cange, *Faida*. Among the Lombards, whose laws are nearest to the English, *faida* is glossed *vindicta mortis*, the simple avenging of death; Ine's *unfaedhe* (e.g. 28, 35, 74) concerns justifiable homicide, and Alfred's equivalent (e.g. 30, 42) is *orwige*.

485.2 RANSOM: it extended beyond physical violence; relatives might ransom a penal slave, Ine 24, 1.

485.3 LORD: see LEEK index.

485.3 NOBLEMAN'S LORD: Ine 50.

485.3 GYLD: see LEEK index, 'Associates', first named in Ine 74, 2. In Alfred 30–31 *gegildan* and relatives pay one third each; the *heafodgemacene* and perhaps the *gedes* of Wihtred 19; 21; 23 may be a Kentish equivalent. Under West Saxon supremacy, from the 9th century, West Saxon legal terminology tended to oust Kentish and other regional terms.

485.3 TOWNS: the urban *frythegyld*, public order guild, of noble and commoner (*eorlisce ge ceorlisce*), Aethelstan VI (*Iudicia Civitatis Lundoniae*, Preamble 1, 1; 6, 3), preceded separate trade guilds.

485.4 GERMANIC CODES: see **J.**

486.2 SAXON LAW: *Lex Saxonum* 44 *qui defunctus non filios sed filias reliquerat, ad eas omnis hereditas pertineat.*

486.2 ANGLIAN LAW: *Lex Anglorum et Werinorum* 27 *ad filiam pecunia et mancipia, terra vero ad proximum paternae generationis*; cf. Bede HA II *quomodo terreni parentes, quem primum partu fuderint, eum principium liberorum suorum cognoscere, et caeteris in partienda sua hereditate praeferendum ducere solent,* with reference to Northumbrian Angles.

486.2 WEST SAXON . . . MOTHER'S KIN: e.g. Alfred 8; 30.

486.3 FRIGMAN: Aethelbert 4, and regularly thereafter.

486.3 LAET: see p. 313.

486.3 LOAF-EATER: *ceorlaes hlafaeta,* valued at only 6s, Aethelbert 25.

486.4 WERGILD: the essential information, contained in the laws of Ine of Wessex and Aethelbert of Kent, both 7th century, is

WELSH OF WESSEX (Ine)		LAET OF KENT (Aethelbert)
theow	50s or 60s (*23, 3*)	
landless man	60s (*32*)	40s third class (*26*)
half-hide man	80s (*32*)	60s second class (*26*)
tax-payer's son	100s (*23, 3*)	—
tax-payer (*gafolgelda*)	120s (*23, 3*) }	80s first class (*26*)
one-hide man	120s (*32*) }	
horswealh	200s (*14*)	—
five-hide man	600s (*24, 2*)	—

ENGLISH OF WESSEX (Ine)

ordinary *weigild*		*fierdwite* fine (51)		compensation for *burgbryc* (45)	
a man (normal)	200s (*34, 1*) }	*cierlisc*	30s	—	
aet twyhundum	200s (*70*) }				
aet syxhundum	600s (*70*)	*gesithcundmon unlandagende*	60s	—	
aet twelfhundum	1200s (*70*) }	*gesithcundmon landagende*	120s	*gesithcundmon landhaebbende*	30s*
Cinges geneat (King's companion)	1200s (*19*) }				
—		—		king's thane	60s
—		—		*ealdormon*	80s
—		—		King and Bishop	120s

* 35s, MS.

ENGLISH OF KENT

Medume leodgeld (ordinary wergild)	100s (Aethelbert 21; Hlothere 3)
eorlcundman	300s (Hlothere 1)

Kentish law does not mention a distinct class of landed noble or royal companion. By the 9th century, the *ceorl*'s violated boundary fence (*edorbryce*) was compensated with 5s; the *syxhyndmon* had a *burg*, whose breach was met by 15s; the *twelfhyndmon*'s compensation was still 30s, but the bishop's and the *ealdormon*'s had fallen to 60s, the archbishop's to 90s; the king still received 120s, (Alfred 40). The basic distinction of *ceorl* and *eorl* lasted well into the middle ages, cf. *Consuetudo West Sexe* 70, 1 *twyhindi, id est villani . . . twelfhindi, id est taini* Liebermann *Gesetze* 1, 462 cf. 458.

Fragments of Mercian and Northumbrian law, preserved in the *Gesetze*, show similar classes and values.

This evidence is discussed at length by Liebermann *Gesetze*, *Seebohm* TCASL, Maitland DBB, Chadwick OEN and SASI, and others.

487.2 HIDE: Bede regularly wrote 'the land of so many families' (e.g. *terra LXXXVII familiarum*, HE 4, 13), or 'possessions of families', or 'of land', or 'of property' (e.g. *possesiones X familiarum, XII possessiones praediorum, XII possessiunculis terrarum*, all in HE 3, 24), described as 'by English measure' (e.g. *mensura iuxta aestimationem Anglorum* HE 2, 9; *quasi familiarum V, iuxta aestimationem Anglorum* HE 3, 4). Bede gives overall figures of 5 families for Iona HE 3, 4; 960 for Anglesey and 300 for Man HE 2, 9; 7,000 for Sussex HE 4, 13; 1,200 for Wight HE 4, 16; 600 for Thanet HE 1, 25; and 5,000 and 7,000 for South and North Mercia HE 3, 24; as well as for numerous individual estates. The figures for Sussex and Mercia agree with those of the 'Tribal Hidage' (p. 493 below), and that for Thanet is proportionate to the total for Kent (15,000); but the assessment of Wight, 600 in the Tribal Hidage, was doubled, evidently after Ceadwalla's conquest, in or about 686. The hide and the individual family remained normally identical into the mid 8th century, since oaths in Ine's law were normally reckoned as of 30, 60 or 120 hides (e.g. 52–54; cf 14; 19; 46), but in Northumbria as of 30, 60 or 120 cultivators (*tributarii* and *manentes*) Dialogue of Egbert (Archbishop of York, c. 750) 1, Oaths are discussed by Chadwick SASI 134 ff.

487.2 TRIBUTARII . . . HIDES: in 725 the Heberden Charter of Nunna of Sussex (p. 499) granted twenty *tributarii* in the Latin text, but twenty hides in the English endorsement, which is probably contemporary.

487.3 UNCIA . . . IUGUM: cf. pp. 459 and 5 above.

487.3 RUSTIC DEIRANS: the nobleman Imma pretended to be a *rusticus* of the supply train, but his Mercian captors observed *ex vultu et habitu et sermonibus eius non erat de paupere vulgo sed de nobilibus* and sold him to a Frisian slaver of London, who allowed him parole to find his ransom, Bede HE 4, 22.

489.1 BENEDICT BISCOP: Bede HA 1.

489.2 BEDE . . . EGBERT: *Epistula ad Egbertum* 10 ff.

491.2 ATTAIN . . . RANK: the texts are discussed by Chadwick SASI 80 ff.

491.4 FOLC GEMOT: Alfred 22; 34; 38, 1. BCS 201.

491.4 REEVE: steward or bailiff, equivalent to the classical Latin *procurator*; the king's reeves, like the emperor's *procuratores*, were officers of importance; the later shire-reeve, or sheriff, was translated *vice-comes*, 'deputy earl', in medieval Latin, whence the modern title 'viscount'.

491.4 EALDORMAN: elder, or senior. The title was restricted to royal princes and great nobles; the *ealdorman* of a region was commonly its greatest magnate, sometimes equivalent to an underking.

492.1 HARROW: BCS 201.

492.1 INE . . . HUNDRED: Ine 54, *on thaere Hyndenne*.

492.1 BARROWS: e.g. Loveden, Lincolnshire; Broadwater, Redbourn (Standard Hill) Hertfordshire; Effingham (Standard Hill), Surrey; Hassocks, Sussex, and many others, see **S**.

492.1 THORSBERG: cf. e.g. the description in *Ant.* 26, 1952, 14.

492.2 LONDONERS: Aethelstan VI 3.

492.3 TRIBAL HIDAGE: BCS 297; Rolls 2 ii 296; see JBAA 40, 1884, 30 and n.s. 35, 1929, 273; EHR 4, 1889, 335; 27, 1912, 625; 40, 1925, 497; NQ 10th series 9, 1908, 384 and 192, 1947, 398 and 423; *Traditio* 5, 1947, 192; TRHS n.s. 14, 1900, 189, etc. See **T**.

493.1 SURREY: see p. 322 above. Surrey and East Kent formed a distinct territory in the 5th and 6th centuries, until annexed by Aethelbert, in or soon after 584, when the East Saxons acquired London and its territory north of the Thames, the future Middlesex, under Aethelbert's suzerainty. On his death, during Redwald's brief supremacy in the 620s, king Taeppa (see p. 323 above), known only from his tomb, appears to have ruled a substantial kingdom north of the Thames, which may have wrested London from the East Saxons for a few years. The name Surrey, southern region, doubtless balanced by a northern region across the Thames, may have been then brought into use. Thereafter the London region was for a while disputed between the West and East Saxons and Kent.

The enduring boundaries were drawn after Wulfhere's conquest, when Surrey was established as a distinct kingdom, whose ruler the copyist of a charter described as *Fritheuualdus provinciae Surrianorum subregulus Wlfarii Mercianorum regis* (BCS 34). Its northern boundary was sealed by the grant of almost all the Thames bank from Chertsey to Bermondsey to monasteries, and the London region on the opposite bank then or soon after became the *provincia* of Middlesex, though no *subregulus* is there attested. The Tribal Hidage lists the separate names of the small peoples who were organised into these two *provinciae*, in spellings that later copyists grossly corrupted, which have not yet been examined by philologists; but it did not know the names or existence of the future Surrey and Middlesex, and it is therefore probable that the original text was drawn up before Wulfhere's reorganisation created them.

493.2 DOMESDAY . . . PERSONS: adult males are numbered. Since some men were unwed brothers, the number of families was necessarily a little smaller, perhaps nearer to 200,000.

493.3 HUNDREDS . . . MET MONTHLY: cf., e.g. Edgar I 1; Edward II 8.

494.2 SHIRES: the word means a 'sheared' portion of a whole, and is rendered in Latin by *comitatus*, in English 'county', the territory of a *comes*, used to translate English 'earl'. The shires and counties had differing origins. The earliest were the five, or six, constituent kingdoms of Wessex (pp. 324–325 above), some of which were termed shires while still ruled by kings. Outside Wessex, the imperial arrogance of Offa abolished the monarchies of the old kingdoms of the south-east, to the distress of Alcuin (p. 331 above), and restricted their rulers to the humbler style of *dux* or *comes*. In the 9th century, Egbert and his sons for a while themselves exercised the title of king of East Anglia or Kent, but the title 'king' lapsed in the course of the Scandinavian wars. East Anglia reverted to its two original 5th and 6th century constituents, the North and South Folk. The old south-eastern kingdoms retained their identity as counties, and as such were included under the generalised heading of 'shires', but, since they were not 'sheared' portions of a whole the suffix 'shire' was not and is not appended to the former kingdoms or *provinciae* of Sussex, Kent or Surrey, Middlesex or Essex, Norfolk or Suffolk.

In the east midlands, the tenth century Danes organised the Hundreds, in their language *wapentakes*, military districts, into army areas grouped round fortresses or boroughs. The West Saxon kings of the English applied their own word shire to these regions, and extended it to the west midlands, English Mercia. North of the Trent, the former Mercian territory south of the

Ribble remained part of Cheshire until the 12th century, while the Pennines, north of Danish Derbyshire, and all the English northwest, were grouped with the Danish kingdom of York in the huge county of Yorkshire. The old name of Northumbria or Northumberland was restricted to the former Bernicia, and the military border bishopric of Durham became a separate county. Cumberland retained its old name, 'the Welsh land', on its annexation by the English in 1092; Lancashire and Westmorland are creations of the 12th century.

The king's officer, or reeve, in each shire or county was termed shire-reeve, or sheriff, in principle not hereditary. The English term *eorl*, 'earl', originally the general word for nobleman, was influenced by its Scandinavian equivalent *jarl*, used for the head of an army or army district, a midland shire, and was commonly used of hereditary rulers. In the 11th century it was chiefly used of the rulers of former kingdoms, Mercia or Wessex, but from the 12th century onward earls, in Latin *comites*, were increasingly appointed to individual counties, and in time *dux*, duke, came into use as the title of a superior earl, at first for royal princes.

496.3 OSRIC . . . BAPTISED: Bede HE 4, 13.

497.1 BATH: BCS 43, dated 6 November 676.

497.1 GLOUCESTER: BCS 60; Finberg ECWM 158. *Oba* (huba), meaning *numerus mancipiorum, praedium*; and *sule* (sola), a measure, see Du Cange.

497.1 VICARIUM: Cartulary of Landevennec para. 45, cf. 46, 17 etc. The word renders the ecclesiastical and colloquial *plebs, plou-* etc.

498.3 ALDHELM: see pp. 415 and 496 above and E.

498.3 PAGHAM: BCS 50, see John *Land Tenure* 8 and Finberg *Lucerna* 149.

499.1 NUNNA: BCS 144, see p. 482 above. *This is seo Landboc the Nunna cyng gebocade Eadberhte b' into Hugabeorgum xx hida.*

499.1 AETHELRED'S GRANT REVOKED: Evesham Chronicle, cited Finberg ECWM 170.

499.1 TOKI: KCD 805

499.2 CHURCH RIGHT: wording varies, e.g. *ecclesiastica ratio atque regula; monastica ratio* BCS 157; *ecclesiastica* (sic) *ius* BCS 182; *ius episcopalis sedis* BCS 76, etc.

499.2 GRAVER SCANDAL: Bede *Ep. ad Egbertum* 12.

499.2 WITHINGTON: BCS 156.

500.3 KIN RESTRICTION REMOVED: e.g. BCS 77.

500.3 BOOKED TO HIMSELF: BCS 451 *Aethelwulf . . . ruris partem . . . mihi in hereditatem propriam describere iusi; id est me ad habendum . . . et iterum qualicumque prout me placabilis sit aeternaliter relinquendum* 26 December 847.

500.3 INE: BCS 142.

500.3 BEORTRIC: BCS 258.

500.3 KENTISH KING: BCS 496

500.4 ALDHELM: e.g. BCS 108, cf. 109 etc., *Ego Ini . . . rex, cum consilio et decreto . . . Aldhelmi . . . privilegii dignitatem monasteriis confero, ut . . . absque tributum fiscalium negotiorum . . . Deo soli serviant*, without reservation of the public services.

501.1 PUBLIC SERVICES: see p. 492 above.

501.1 LOANLAND: e.g. Alfred *Soliloquies of Augustine*, preface; a man normally cultivates land loaned by his lord until he is granted 'bookland and perpetual possession'.

501.1 ENTAIL: Alfred 41.

501.2 EALDORMAN: Aelfred dux, BCS 558.

501.2 ILLEGITIMATE: so Maitland DBB 246, Stenton ASE 307. The objections of Chadwick SASI 171, note 1, are rightly rejected by John *Land Tenure* 16, note 2.

501.2 FOLK LAND: and Bookland. The problems are discussed, from the point of view of the later middle ages, by Maitland DBB 244 ff.; Pollock and Maitland, *History of English Law* I, 37 ff.; Vinogradoff EHR 8, I, ff.; GM 142 ff., 244 ff.; John *Land Tenure* I ff.; and others.

501.2 REEVE: Edward I, Preface.

501.2 LONDON: *Libertas Londoniensis* 6.

NOTES TO THE MAPS

1 The Shape of Britain: p. 7. Since drift maps are not yet fully available, the surface boundaries are not always known. Attempts at over precise indication are apt to mislead; boundaries are therefore approximate.

2 Roman Britain: p. 47. See the Ordnance Survey *Map of Roman Britain*; for Scotland, cf. maps 11 and 12, pp. 187, 189.

3 Pagan English Settlement 1: p. 59. Period A, AD 430/470. Only dateable sites are shown. Sites marked with a query as uncertain normally represent isolated objects of the period, or sites not yet adequately published, a few possibly not burials.

For details of the sites, see **S**; and, for most of them, Meaney *Gazeteer*. New discoveries and future study are bound to add new sites and to extend the date limits of some of the sites here listed. The list endeavours to date known sites as closely and as fully as possible; and to enable the significance of new knowledge to be noted easily.

The sites are listed, as far as possible, from north to south and from west to east, by counties and within counties. For convenience, the sites shown on all the pagan English settlement maps (3, 6, 18, 21, 22; pp. 59, 107, 285, 297, 305 are here set down together.

New sites in areas previously settled are not listed or mapped in periods B–F. Only the earliest date of each site is given.

	Inhumation		Cremation		Mixed rite	Uncertain rite
	alone	with a little cremation	alone	with a little inhumation		
Large cemeteries	▮	▮·	▬	▬ (with stroke)	✚	
Cemeteries	▯	▯·	▭	▭ (with stroke)	✜	
A few burials	‖		=			//
Single or family burials	|		—			/
Barrow	⌓					

House or houses	Δ
Excavated royal centre	▲
Uncertain date	?
Roman roads	---

Map 3 p. 59 Period A 430/470

YORKSHIRE: ■York, Heworth SE 61 51; ▭York, The Mount SE 59 51; ■Sancton 1 SE 90 40.

LINCOLNSHIRE: ■Kirton-in-Lindsey SE 93 00; ■South Elkington TF 31 88; ▭Lincoln SK 97 71; ■Loveden Hill SK 90 45; ■Ancaster SK 94 43; ■West Keal TF 35 64.

NOTTINGHAMSHIRE: ■Newark SK 79 53.

LEICESTERSHIRE: ■Thurmaston SK 61 08; ▭Leicester SK 57 03.

WARWICKSHIRE: ▮Cestersover SP 52 81.

RUTLAND: ▯Glaston SK 91 00; ▮North Luffenham SK 93 04.

NORTHAMPTONSHIRE: ▮· Nassington TL 07 95; ▙Kettering SP 87 79.

HUNTINGDONSHIRE: ▮Woodston, Peterborough TL 19 98.

NORFOLK: ▬Castle Acre TF 79 15; ▬Pensthorpe TF 95 29; ▬North Elmham TF 98 19; ▭Norwich, Catton TG 22 09; ▭Brundall TG 31 08; ▬Caistor-by-Norwich TG 23 03; ▬Markshall TG 22 03; ▭Shropham TL 98 93; ▬Illington TL 94 89; ΔThetford TL 86 82.

CAMBRIDGESHIRE: ✚Cambridge, St. Johns TL 44 58; ✚Cambridge, Girton TL 42 60; ||Cambridge, Trumpington TL 45 55.

SUFFOLK: ▬Lackford TL 77 71; ▯Ixworth TL 93 70; ||Hoxne TM 18 77.

ESSEX: ΔBulmer TL 83 38; ΔLittle Oakley TM 22 28; ▯Feering, Kelvedon TL 86 19; ||Bradwell, Othona TM 03 08; //Great Stambridge TQ 90 93; Δ ▮Mucking TQ 69 81.

BEDFORDSHIRE: /Harrold TL 95 57; ✚Kempston, Bedford TL 03 47; ✢Sandy TL 18 48; ?Egginton SP 96 25; ?Toddington, Warmark TL 00 28; ✚Luton TL 08 29.

OXFORDSHIRE: ▯Cassington SP 44 11; —Osney SP 50 06; ▮Wheatley SP 60 04; ΔDorchester SU 57 93.

BERKSHIRE: ▮· Frilford SU 43 96; ✚Abingdon SU 49 96; ✚Long Wittenham SU 54 93; ✢Reading SU 74 73; /Sonning SU 75 75.

HAMPSHIRE: ?Portchester SU 62 04; ?Droxford SU 61 18.

MIDDLESEX: ✢Shepperton TQ 06 67; ▯Hanwell TQ 15 79.

SURREY: ΔHam TQ 16 71; ▮Mitcham TQ 27 68; ✢Beddington TQ 30 65; ▮· Croydon TQ 32 65.

KENT: ▮Orpington TQ 46 66; ▮· Riseley TQ 56 67; ▮Milton, Sittingbourne TQ 90 64; ▮Faversham TR 01 61; ▯Canterbury TR 14 57; ▮Bekesbourne, Cowslip TR 20 55; ▮Howletts TR 20 56; ▮Sarre TR 26 66; ▮Buttsole, Eastry TR 31 54; |Deal TR 37 52; ▮Dover TR 30 43.

Map 6 p. 107 Period B 460/500

NORTHUMBERLAND: ?Howick NU 23 16; ||Corbridge NY 98 64.

LANCASHIRE: ?Crossmoor SD 44 38; ▭Ribchester SD 65 35; —Manchester SJ 84 99.

YORKSHIRE: ||Cowlam SE 96 66; |Rudstone TA 09 67; ΔElmswell TA 00 57; ▯Driffield TA 04 57; ▯Sancton II SE 90 40.

LINCOLNSHIRE: ▯South Ferriby SE 99 22; ||Flixborough TA 88 13; ▯Fonaby TA 11 03; //Cleethorpes TA 29 08; /Hatton TF 18 76; ▯Carlton Scroop SK 93 45; ▯· Caythorpe SK 96 49; ▮Sleaford TF 06 45; ▭Baston TF 11 13.

NOTTINGHAMSHIRE: ▬Kingston-on-Soar SK 50 27; ▭Sutton Bonnington SK 51 24; ▯Holme Pierrepoint SK 62 39; ||Cotgrave SK 63 35; ▮Willoughby-on-the-Wolds SK 64 25.

LEICESTERSHIRE: ✚Saxby SK 81 19; ▯Glen Parva SP 56 98; ▯Wigston Magna SP 60 97.

RUTLAND: Δ ▮Empingham SK 94 07; ✢Great Casterton SK 99 08.

NORTHAMPTONSHIRE: /Helpstone TF 10 06; /Little Weldon SP 92 89; ✢Newton-le-Willows SP 83 88; ✢Rothwell SP 81 81; ▯Islip SP 98 79; /Cranford SP 94 77; —Addington SP 96 75; ✢Barton Seagrave SP 88 77; ✚Brixworth SP 74 72; ▭Pitsford SP 74 68; ▯Welton SP 57 66; ▯Holdenby SP 69 67; ▯Duston SP 72 60; /Milton SP 73 55; ▯· Marston St. Lawrence SP 54 43.

HUNTINGDONSHIRE: ?Godmanchester TL 25 70; —Somersham TL 36 77; //Eynesbury TL 18 59.

NORFOLK: =Snettisham TF 58 34; =Walsingham Abbey TF 93 36; ▭Wolterton TG 14 32; ⌂North Runcton TF 64 15; /Thuxton TG 03 07; ▭Norwich, Drayton TG 18 13; ▬Rushford (Brettenham) TL 93 83.

CAMBRIDGESHIRE: ?Arrington (Wimpole) TL 33 50; ▯Barrington A TL 37 49; ▮Barrington B TL 38 39; ▮- Haslingfield TL 41 52; ✚Little Wilbraham TL 56 57.

SUFFOLK: ▯Exning TL 62 65; ▯Undley TL 69 81; ▮Holywell Row TL 71 76; ▮Lakenheath TL 73 82; ▯Icklingham TL 77 72; Δ▮West Stow TL 79 71; =Ingham (Culford) TL 85 73; ▯Bury St. Edmunds TL 84 65; ▬Eye TM 15 74; |Coddenham TM 13 54; ▬Snape TM 40 59; |Ufford TM 29 52; //Waldringfield TM 28 44.

ESSEX: ✚Great Chesterford TL 50 43; —Ashdon TL 57 43; /Heybridge TL 85 08; =Colchester TL 99 25.

HERTFORDSHIRE: /Royston TL 35 40; ΔStevenage TL 25 21; /Hertford TL 33 13; ?Ware TL 35 14.

BUCKINGHAMSHIRE: ?Bishopstone SP 79 11.

OXFORDSHIRE: ?Hornton SP 39 45; -▯Souldern SP 51 31; ▯Ewelme SU 64 92; /Oxford SP 50 06.

BERKSHIRE: ΔSutton Courtenay SU 48 94; ▯Hanwell SU 48 88; ▯Blewburton SU 54 86; ▯- Wallingford SU 60 89; ▮East Shefford SU 38 74.

HAMPSHIRE: ?Micheldever SU 50 39; ✚Worthy Park SU 50 32; ▮Droxford SU 61 18; ΔPortchester SU 62 04; ?Alton SU 71 38.

SUSSEX: ▮High Down, Ferring TQ 09 04; ▯Lewes, Saxonbury TQ 40 09; ▯Lewes, Malling TQ 42 11; ▯Selmeston TQ 51 07; ▮- Bishopstone TQ 47 02; ▮Alfriston TQ 51 03.

SURREY: ▯- Guildown SU 98 48.

KENT: ✛Northfleet TQ 62 73; ✛Hollingbourne TQ 82 54; ✚Westbere TR 19 61; ▮Bifrons TR 18 55; ▯Wingham TR 24 56; ▯Lyminge TR 16 40; ▯Lympne TR 10 35.

Map 18 p. 285 Periods C 490/530; D1 510/540; D2 530/560

One dot indicates period **D1**, two dots period **D2**.

NORTHUMBERLAND: D2 ||..Benwell NZ 21 64.

DURHAM: C/D ?Castle Eden NZ 42 38.

CUMBERLAND: D 1/2 |..Birdoswald NY 61 66.

WESTMORLAND: D1 /.Brough NY 79 14.

YORKSHIRE: C ✛Saltburn (Marske) NZ 65 20; D1 | Kingthorpe SE 83 85; C ΔWykeham SE 96 86; C | Ganton Wold TA 00 76; C ▯Hornsea TA 20 48.

DERBYSHIRE: C ▬King's Newton SK 34 26; D1 ⌂Swarkeston SK 36 29.

LEICESTERSHIRE: C/D /Loughborough SK 53 19; C ▯Rothley Temple SK 56 12.

WARWICKSHIRE: C ✚Baginton SP 34 74; C ?Long Itchington SP 41 65; C ▯Warwick, Longbridge SP 29 65; C ✚Stratford-on-Avon SP 21 54; C ✚Bidford-on-Avon SP 09 51 D1 ▯Stretton-on-the-Fosse SP 22 38.

WORCESTERSHIRE: D1 ▮.Beckford SP 98 36; D1 ▯.Broadway SP 11 37.

GLOUCESTERSHIRE: D1 ▯.Bishop's Cleeve SO 95 27; D1? ▯-.Hampnett SO 10 15; D1 (?C) ▮.Fairford SP 14 01; D1? ||.Chavenage ST 87 96; D1 ▯.Kemble 1 ST 99 98; D1? |.Minety SU 01 91.

OXFORDSHIRE: D I [].Broughton Poggs SP 22 04; D I [].Filkins SP 23 04; C ▲ Brighthampton SP 38 03.

WILTSHIRE: D I/2 ▮..Harnham Hill SU 13 28; D I/2 ▮..Petersfinger SU 16 29;

HAMPSHIRE: D I? /.Stockbridge SU 37 35; C/D I ▮Chessell Down, IoW SZ 39 85.

Map 21 p. 297 Periods D3 550/590; E 570/610

NORTHUMBERLAND: ||Galewood NT 95 32; /Lowick NU 01 39; []▲Old Yeavering NT 92 30; /Wooler NT 99 28; /Newham NU 16 29.

DURHAM: /Lanchester NZ 16 47; []Darlington NZ 28 15.

YORKS: ||Catterick SE 22 98; /Fridaythorpe SE 87 59; []Sewerby TA 20 69; []△Nafferton TA 06 58.

STAFFORDSHIRE: ▭Yoxall SK 14 19; []Wichnor SK 19 15.

DERBYSHIRE: |Duffield SK 36 44.

NOTTINGHAMSHIRE: /Tuxford SK 73 71.

LEICESTERSHIRE: /High Cross, Wibtoft SP 47 88; []Market Harborough SP 73 87; |Medbourne SP 80 93; []Caves Inn, Shawell (Tripontium) SP 53 79.

NORTHAMPTONSHIRE: /Naseby SP 68 78; |Clipston SP 71 81; []· Desborough I SP 80 83; []Desborough II SP 80 84; |Loddington SP 81 78; ||Thorpe Malsor SP 83 78; ||Cransley SP 83 77; []Badby SP 56 59; []Newnham, Daventry SP 59 59; ||Norton (Bannaventa) SP 61 63; ||Daventry SP 58 62; /Northampton II SP 77 61; []· Northampton III SP 77 60; |Northampton IV SP 75 61; |– Irchester SP 92 66; /Aynho SP 52 32.

WARWICKSHIRE: —Brinklow SP 43 79; /Clifton-on-Dunsmore SP 54 76; |Napton-on-the-Hill SP 45 61; |Arrow, Ragley Park SP 07 55; |Aston Cantlow SP 13 59.

WORCESTERSHIRE: []Upton Snodsbury SO 94 54; ||Evesham SP 04 43.

GLOUCESTERSHIRE: |Kempsford SU 15 97.

OXFORDSHIRE: []Lower Heyford SP 48 24; ||Burford SP 24 12; []Minster Lovell SP 31 11; []Standlake SP 38 04.

BUCKINGHAMSHIRE: /Buckingham SP 68 36; ||Tickford SP 88 43; []Newport Pagnell SP 88 44; /Oving SP 78 21; |Ashendon SP 70 14; /Winchendon SP 75 15; []Stone I SP 77 12; |Stone II SP 78 12; /Aylesbury SP 83 14; []Dinton SP 76 11; []Bishopstone SP 79 11; []· Kinsey SP 73 07; /Bledlow SP 77 01; ||Ellesborough SP 84 07; |High Wycombe SU 89 91; |High Wycombe SU 90 91; ||Hedsor SU 81 86.

BEDFORDSHIRE: |Farndish SP 92 63; △Felmersham SP 99 57; /Moggerhanger TL 14 48; /Shefford TL 13 38; /Langford TL 18 40; /Clifton TL 17 39; ||Pegsdon TL 12 31.

HUNTINGDONSHIRE: /Hemingford Grey TL 29 70.

HERTFORDSHIRE: |Ashwell TL 29 38; /Kings Walden TL 14 23.

MIDDLESEX: ||Northolt TQ 14 84; / /London TQ 33 81.

ESSEX: /Hockley TQ 84 93; /West Bergholt TL 96 28; /Dovercourt TL 24 31; /Dagenham TQ 49 84; ▮Rainham TQ 55 84; ⌓Clacton TM 17 16.

SOMERSET: ||Huish Episcopi ST 43 27; /Pitney ST 44 28; ||Ilchester ST 52 23; []Queen Camel ST 59 25; /Ham Hill ST 48 17.

WILTSHIRE: []Purton SU 10 87; []Wanborough SU 22 82; []Bassett Down SU 11 80; /Barbury Castle SU 15 76; /Preshute, Temple Down SU 13 72; []Mildenhall SU 21

69; ||East Grafton SU 29 60; /Wilton SU 09 31; ▯Winterbourne Gunner SU 18 35; /Winterslow SU 23 34.

BERKSHIRE: /Coleshill SU 23 94; /Ashdown SU 29 83; ⌓Lambourn SU 32 82; |East Garston SU 35 77; |Lockinge Park SU 42 87; ⌓Cuckhamsley SU 45 85; ⌓East Ilsley SU 50 81; ⌓Lowbury SU 54 83; ⌓Cookham, Cock Marsh SU 88 87; ||Cookham SU 88 85.

HAMPSHIRE: /Silchester SU 64 62; ▯Shalcombe Down SZ 39 85; ▯- Bowcombe Down SZ 46 87; ||Arreton Down SZ 53 87.

SUSSEX: /Chichester SZ 88 05; ▮Ocklynge TQ 59 00; ▯Eastbourne TV 60 99.

SURREY: ∆Farnham SU 84 46; |Banstead TQ 24 60; /Limpsfield TQ 42 53.

KENT: /West Wickham TQ 39 65; /Belmont Park, Throwley TQ 98 56.

Map 22 p. 305 Period F: 7th Century

NORTHUMBERLAND: ||Hepple NY 98 00; ||Great Tosson NU 02 00; /Sweethope NY 95 81; ⌓Capheaton NZ 01 79; |Barrasford NY 91 73; |Tynemouth NZ 37 69.

CUMBERLAND: ⌓near Carlisle NY 43 52; /Moresby NX 98 21.

DURHAM: /Hurbeck, Lanchester NZ 13 48; |East Boldon NZ 36 61; |Cornforth NZ 31 32.

YORKSHIRE: |Richmond NZ 17 02; |Ingleton SD 70 73; /Brough-by-Bainbridge SD 93 90; ||Ripon SE 31 73; |Burton Leonard SE 34 66; |Occaney, Aldborough SE 35 62; ⌓Hawnby SE 52 89; |Lilla Howe SE 88 98; ||Robin Hoods Bay NZ 94 05; |Hambleton Moor SE 55 80; ||Yearsley SE 58 74; |Appleton SE 73 71; ∆York Castle SE 60 51; /York SE 60 52; ▯Aclam Wold SE 79 61; ▮Uncleby SE 82 59; ▯Painsthorpe Wold SE 82 58; ||North Newbold SE 90 36; /Cave Castle SE 92 28; ||Everthorpe SE 90 31; /Brough-on-Humber SE 93 26; /Beverley TA 03 39; /Leven TA 11 46; ||Burton Pidsea TA 25 31; /Holderness TA 3 2; |Womersley, Pontefract SE 53 19; |North Elmsall SE 47 12.

LANCASHIRE: /Stalmine Moss SD 39 45; ⌓Wigan SD 56 05.

STAFFORDSHIRE: ▭Stretton SK 25 26; |Barlaston SJ 89 38; /Forsbrook SJ 95 41; ⌓Caulden SK 07 48; |Calton SK 10 50; |Musden (Ilam) SK 11 50; |Musden (Ilam) SK 11 50; |Castern (Ilam) SK 12 52; |Steep Lowe SK 12 56; ||Tamworth SK 21 04; |Wetton SK 11 54; /Throwley SK 11 53.

DERBYSHIRE: ⌓Cow Law SK 10 72; ⌓Hurdlow SK 11 66; ⌓Grindlow SK 20 67; /Youlgreave SK 20 64; ⌓Brundcliff, Hartington SK 13 60; ⌓Cold Eaton SK 14 56; ⌓Benty Grange SK 14 64; |Alsop SK 16 55; ⌓Newhaven House SK 16 60; ⌓White Lowe SK 22 59; ⌓Standlow SK 15 53; /Galley Low SK 21 56; ⌓Tissington SK 15 52; ⌓Wigber Low SK 20 51; ⌓Wyaston SK 19 42; /Borrowash SK 41 34.

NOTTINGHAMSHIRE: /Nottingham I SK 56 39; /Nottingham II SK 56 39; ⌓Oxton SK 63 51; /Winkburn SK 71 60.

LEICESTERSHIRE: |Stoke Golding SP 39 97; /Hinckley SP 42 94.

WARWICKSHIRE: /Alcester SP 08 57; ||Walton SP 28 52; ||Compton Verney SP 31 52; ||Lighthorne SP 33 55; /Burton Dassett SP 38 53, ▯- Long Compton (Rollright) SP 29 30.

NORTHAMPTONSHIRE: ||Hardingstone SP 73 57.

WORCESTERSHIRE: ||Wyre Piddle SO 96 47; /Bricklehampton SO 98 41; |Littlehampton SP 03 42.

GLOUCESTERSHIRE: ▯Ebrington SP 18 40; ||Oddington SP 21 25; ▯- Blockley SP 18 36 ||Leckhampton SO 94 18; ||Withington SP 01 18; ΔSalmonsbury SP 17 20; | Stratton, Cirencester SP 01 04; ||Cirencester SP 02 02; /Sea Mills, Bristol ST 55 78.

OXFORDSHIRE: ▯Lyneham SP 29 21; ▯ΔChadlington SP 33 21; /Spelsbury SP 35 21; | Great Tew SP 39 29; ⌓Asthall SP 28 10; Δ▯Wilcote SP 37 13; ||North Leigh SP 38 14; /Bampton SP 32 03; | Yelford SP 36 04.

BUCKINGHAMSHIRE: ⌓Taplow SU 90 82.

HERTFORDSHIRE: /Hitchin TL 17 29; //Ippollits TL 19 27; ||Redbourn TL 11 12; ▯Wheathampstead TL 17 14; /Hemel Hempstead, Boxmoor TL 03 05; ▯Verulamium TL 13 07; ||Furneaux Pelham TL 44 26; /Waltham Cross TQ 37 99.

ESSEX: ⌓Broomfield TL 71 09; /Forest Gate TL 41 86; ▯Prittlewell TQ 87 87; ||Great Wakering TQ 95 87; /Asheldam TL 97 01; ▮Saffron Walden TL 53 38; ||Wendens Ambo TL 51 36; /Sturmer TL 69 43.

SOMERSET: ΔWorle Hall ST 36 64; ▯Saltford ST 68 68; ▮Camerton ST 68 57; ||Buckland Denham ST 74 50; | Evercreech ST 64 38; /Shapwick ST 42 38; ||Taunton ST 23 25.

DORSET: ⌓Hardown Hill SY 40 94; | Maiden Castle SY 67 88; /Milton Abbas ST 80 01; ⌓Woodyates SU 03 19; /Wor SU 01 17; | Oakley Down SU 02 17.

WILTS: | Roundaway Down SU 00 64; ΔWestbury ST 88 50; ||Battlesbury ST 89 45; ||Tilshead Lodge SU 02 47; | Shrewton SU 06 43; ⌓Rodmead Down ST 81 36; ||Sherrington ST 96 39; ⌓Ford SU 17 33; ▯Winkelbury ST 95 21; | Ansty, Swallowcliffe ST 96 27; /Bishopstone SU 07 26.

HANTS: | Basingstoke SU 62 51; | Brown Candover SU 58 39; | Preston Candover SU 60 40; | Preshaw SU 58 24; ▯Southampton SU 43 13; /Boscombe Chine SZ 11 91; ||Christchurch SZ 16 93.

SUSSEX: ΔMedmerry SZ 83 94; /Pagham SZ 88 97; | Arundel TQ 02 06; ||Burpham TQ 05 09; ||Blackpatch, Patching TQ 09 08; ||Clapham TQ 08 09; /Thakeham TQ 12 18; ▭Hassocks TQ 29 15; | Kemp Town, Brighton TQ 32 04; —South Moulscombe TQ 32 06.

SURREY: ▯Hawkshill, Fetcham TQ 15 55; ▯Farthingdown TQ 29 58.

KENT: ||Wrotham TQ 61 59; ||Wrotham TQ 61 59; ▯Snodland TQ 69 62; ||Aylesford TQ 72 58; ▯Maidstone TQ 73 56; ||Harrietsham TQ 87 53; ||Lenham TQ 90 52; | Westwell TQ 99 47; ||Ashford TR 01 42; ||Wye TR 07 46; ||Crundale TR 06 49; ▯Smeath TR 07 39.

4 The British in Gaul: p. 89. cf. notes 90.3, 90.5 above: and Doble *Saints in Normandy*. Only the registers of Rouen have been systematically examined; further research is likely to detect more dedications between the estuaries of the Seine and the Rhine. In the diocese of Amiens some well-known foundations, as St. Winwaloe's Abbey at Montreuil-sur-mer, honoured British saints, but systematic evidence is not yet available. Clusters of such dedications suggest the likelihood of a 6th century population of British ancestry; isolated sites do not.

Some sites may owe their names to the evacuation of relics by refugees from Scandinavian and other raiders; but present evidence does not clearly show whether houses without previous British connections took British names because they received such relics, or whether the refugees migrated to houses with which they already had links.

Places named Breteuil may have the same origin as those named Bretteville, cf. note 90.3 above.

5 The War Zone: p. 101.

AMBROS-PLACE NAMES (see p. 100).

HEREFORDSHIRE Amberley *SO 54 47* DPNE 9
WORCESTERSHIRE Ombersley *SO 84 63*; Ambresdene and Ambresmedwe in Freckenham EPNS 268
GLOUCESTERSHIRE Amberley *SO 85 01* EPNS 95
OXFORDSHIRE Ambrosden *SP 60 19* EPNS 161
WILTSHIRE Amesbury *SU 16 41* EPNS 359
SUSSEX Ambersham *SU 91 20* EPNS 97; Amberley *TQ 02 13* EPNS 146 Amberstone *TQ 59 11* EPNS 435
ESSEX Ambersury Banks *TL 43 00* EPNS 22, in Epping Forest; Amberden *TL 56 30* EPNS 523, near Debden; Amberley *TL 67 24* EPNS 632, in Stebbing; Amberland *TQ 36 91* Folly Lane, Walthamstow; Amberland, Roydon *TL 41 09*; Emberdon, Matching *TL 53 13*; Ambyrmede, Wickham Bishops *TL 84 13* EPNS 106
KENT Amsbury, Hunton *TQ 73 51* PNK 161

The cluster of *Amber-* names in Derbyshire derive from the river Amber; Amersham, Bucks., and names in *Amble-*, *Ample-* etc. have a different origin. Further *Amber-* names may come to light when Hampshire, Berkshire and other southern and south-western counties are surveyed by EPNS.

MASSACRE AND BATTLE SITES (references in Meaney, *Gazeteer*)
The sites are marked on the map with the symbol X unless otherwise indicated.

WILTSHIRE Heytesbury *ST 92 42*; Knook *ST 95 44*; Roche Court Down *SU 25 35*; Old Sarum* *SU 14 32*; Alvediston [1] (Ebbesbourne Wake) *ST 96 25*
BERKSHIRE, Uffington Castle (White Horse Hill) *SU 30 86*; Wallingford† *SO 61 89* (Hull and Reading Museums); Cookham† *SU 90 85* cf. *Ant. Jl.* 1, 1921, 316; *Arch.* 69, 1919, 13 [11-12]. etc.
SURREY, Battersea† *TQ 26 76*, etc. (London Museum, BM)
BEDFORDSHIRE, Dunstable, Five Knolls* *TL 05 10*; Puddlehill[1] *TL 00 23*
CAMBRIDGESHIRE. Bran Ditch *TL 40 43*; Fleam Ditch *TL 57 54* (approximate); War Ditches, Cherry Hinton *TL 48 55*

**many, but not all, of the burials at Dunstable, Five Knolls, and perhaps also at Old Sarum, may be gallows burials of a later date.*
[1]*single burial, fatal bone wounds.*
†*concentrations of weapons in the Thames.*
Many single burials with shield and spear or sword without sign of 6*th century ornament may also be battle casualties. They are most numerous in the same region.*

6 Pagan English Settlement 2: p. 107. **Period B 460/500.** See Notes to map 3 above.

7 The Demetian Campaign' p. 128
1 *-cnwc* and *moydir* (Irish *bothar*) names; after Melville Richards JRSAI 90, 1960 133 ff.; Lochlann 2, 1962, 129.
2 The words *cil-*, *rath*, etc. do not imply that the places and sites were built or founded by Irishmen; they do imply that Irish words were in use locally when the names were given.
3 The military sites are

IN THE BRYCHAN DOCUMENTS

1 *Garth Matrun* . . . Talgarth . . . *SO 15 33*
2 *Llan Maes* . . . near Brecon . . . *SO 03 28*
3 *Lan Semin* . . . Glasnevin . . . *SN 73 28*
4 *Methrum* . . . Meidrim . . . *SN 28 21*
5 *Porth Mawr* . . . Whitesands Bay . . . *SM 73 27*

NOT NAMED IN TEXTS

6 Caer Farchell . . . *SM 79 27*
7 Llan Marchell . . . *SO 14 42*

IN THE VITA CADOCI

Prologue

8 *Bochriu Carn* . . . Fochriw . . . *SO 10 05*
9 *Altgundliu* . . . ?Wentloog Castle? *ST 25 03*
(*palacium Gundlei*)

ch. 22

10 *Tref Redinauc* . . . Tredunnock-on-Usk *ST 37 94*

For the identification of the places, see **P** Theodoric.

8 Partition: p. 135. See Maps 6 and 13, pp. 107 and 209.

9 Fifth Century Ireland: p. 153.

1 ROYAL CENTRES

(Those starred were probably not in use in the 5th century, but were venerated as ancient national centres)

All Ireland . . . Tara (Meath)
Northern Ui Neill . . . Ailech
Dal Riada . . . Muirbolc
Dal Araide . . . Rath Mor
Dal Fiatach . . . Dun Leithglaisse
Airgialla
. . . Airthir, Ui Bresail . . . Emain*
. . . Ui Crimthann . . . Clogher
Meath
. . . Brega . . . Duleen
. . . Tethba . . . Uisnech* (anciently in Connacht)
Connacht . . . Cruachu*
Leinster
. . . North (Ui Dunlaing) . . . Almu*
. . . South (Ui Cennselach, Ui Bairrche) . . . Dinn Rig*
Munster . . . Cashel

2 MONASTERIES

The name of the founder is given, with the date of his death, as entered in the Annals or indicated in the Lives, with the modern county and grid reference.

Cianan of Duleek 491 Meath *O 06*
Mo-Choe of Nendrum 498 Down *J 56*
Enda of Aran early 6th? Galway *L 80*
Senan of Inis Cathy (Scattery Island) early 6th? Clare *Q 95*

Darerca of Killevy 516 Armagh *J 02*
Boecius of Monasterboice 521 Louth *O 08*
Abban of Moyarney early 6th Wexford *S 72*
Brigit of Kildare 525 *N 71*
Mocteus of Louth 533 *H 20*
Faencha and a few other names are recorded. It is likely that several other small houses were founded, especially for women, few of which retained later importance.

3 EPISCOPAL CENTRES (to 540, before the development of large scale monasticism). The name of the bishop is given, with the date of death, as entered in the Annals, or indicated by the Lives, the modern county and grid reference, and the ancient territory.
Patrick of Saul, Ulaid (Dal Fiatach), Downpatrick, Down *J 54* and Airgialla (Airthir, Ui Bressail) Armagh *H 84*, 459
Fiacc of Sletty, South Leinster (Ui Bairrche), Leix *S 77*, late 5th
Mael of Ardagh, Tethba, Longford *N 16*, 486
Mac Caille of Croghan, Ui Failge, Offaly *N 43*, 492
Mac Cuilin of Lusk, Brega, Dublin *O 25*, 496
Foirtchernn of Trim, Brega, Meath *N 75*, late 5th
Ibar of Wexford, South Leinster, *T 02*, Ui Cennselach, 499
Declan of Ardmore, Munster (Dessi), Waterford *X 17*, early 6th?
Cerpan of Tara, Brega, Meath *N 95*, 505
Mac Cairthinn of Clogher, Airgialla (Ui Crimthann), Tyrone *H 55*, 505
Bronn of Cuil Irra (Killaspugbrone), Connacht (Ui Fiachrach Aidni), Sligo *G 63*, 508
Mac Nissi Aengus of Connor, Dal Araide, Antrim *J 19*, 509
Erc of Slane, Brega, Meath *N 97*, 512
Cairnech of Drumleen, Northern Ui Neill (Tir Eogain), Donegal *C 20*, and Duleen, Brega, *N 77*, early 6th
Conlaed of Kildare, North Leinster (Ui Dunlaing), *N 71*, 516
Ciaran of Saigir, Ossory, Offaly *N 10*, c. 520
Beoaid of Ardcarn, Connacht (Brefni), Roscommon *G 80*, 522
Ailbe of Emly, Munster, Tipperary *R 73*, 528

Some of the five bishops in Brega were bishops of different Ui Neill High Kings; others may have succeeded each other. The Lives freely accord the title bishop to other saints, in some cases perhaps with justification. There is no sign that bishops' sees were yet fixed to a single centre in each kingdom.

11 The Picts: p. 187.
Place names see especially K.H.Jackson in Wainwright PP, and Watson CPNS.
Memorial Stones cf. note 194.1 above. Half a dozen stones south of the Forth do not make the Lothians Pictish; nor do an equal number in the north-east make Caithness Pictish. Various archaeological objects are ascribed to the Picts because they are found in the same area; but are open to misinterpretation if the north-west is treated as Pictish.

12 The Picts and their Neighbours: p. 189. The most comprehensive mapping of the sites is in IANB. Most of the forts are pre-Roman. Whether those situated to north and south of the Roman Antonine Wall differ significantly from each other can only be established by systematic enquiry.

14 Brittany: p. 255
GRID Squares are designated between lines of longitude (letters) and latitude (figures),

as marked on the Michelin 1 km to 2 cm map. Letter squares run from A (= 8°40′ to 8°20′) to Y (= 3°60′ to 3°40′) longitude; figure squares from 0 (= 54°20′ to 54°00′) to 9 (= 52°60′ to 52°40′) latitude. The letters and figures are marked in the borders of the map. Each square is designated by a letter (reading downwards) and figure (reading across) as Brest, E 3.

SITES shown on the map by a number are

1 Avranches V 1
2 Bangor-en-Belle-Ile L 9
3 Ile Brehat M 0
4 Ile de Batz G 1
5 Dinan R 2
6 Douarnenez E 4
7 Cap Frehel Q 1
8 Guingamp L 2
9 St. Gildas-de-Rhuys N 8
10 Granville U 0
11 Huelgoat I 3
12 St. Lunaire R 1
13 Laval Y 4
14 Landerneau F 2
15 Landevennec F 3
16 Landivisiau G 2
17 St. Malo R 1
18 Mont St. Michel U 1
19 St. Meen Q 4
20 St. Nazaire Q 9
21 Ile d'Ouessant (Ushant) A 2
22 Ploudalmazeau D 2
23 Ploermel P 5
24 Pointe de Penmarc E 6
25 Pontivy M 4
26 Quiberon L 8
27 Quimperlé J 6
28 Redon R 7
29 Pointe du Raz C 5
30 Tréguier L 0
31 Trégastel-Plage J 0
32 Primel-Trégastel H 1
33 Ile Tristan E 4

15 The Homeland of the English: p. 263. See especially Genrich *Formenkreise* map 10, and Brøndsted *Danmarks Oldtid* figs. 176 and 246.

16 English Migration in Europe: p. 275. The material has not been surveyed, and the sites shown here are therefore incomplete; see especially the collection in Weimar Museum (examples in *Alt Thüringen* 1, 1953/4, 258, fig. 2), and Svoboda *Bohemia in the Migration Period*, passim. The burials are recognised as Anglian or Saxon at Weimar, but elsewhere are sometimes catalogued and labelled as 'Lower Elbe', or 'Iron Age' in general.

17 Pressures on the Continental English: p. 277.
Germanic place names, see Bach *Deutsche Namenkunde* 2, maps 44–45, pp. 333–334, cf. p. 588.
Slavonic place names are taken from a modern map at 1: 400,000, ignoring those that plainly have a modern origin, as Terezin.

1 Modern German names in *-au* may either transliterate Slavonic *-ow*, or else preserve Frankish *-au*, 'island' or isolated settlement, equivalent to Old English *-eg*, which is normally *-ey* in the endings of modern English place names. Only detailed research can distinguish Slavonic from Germanic *-au*. Slavonic *-ow* names can therefore be recognised on a modern map only when they have not been transliterated into German, and are therefore here omitted, since a significant list should include many *-au* names.

2 Some places to the west of the Slavonic border bear German words for Slav, as Windisch, and indicate that Slavonic settlement penetrated somewhat deeper into western Germany at some time.

18 Pagan English Settlement 3: p. 285. Periods C 490/530; D 1 510/540; D 2 530/560. See Notes to map 3 above.

19 The English in Northern Gaul: A *Artois and Flanders* p. 288. The names are given as spelt on *Carte Michelin* 1 cm to 2 km., sheet 51; many of the differences reflect only modern dialect variations. The origin of names in *-egem*, which extend farther eastward, and are there numerous, is not clear.
B *Normandy* p. 289. Two distinct settlements appear to meet and overlap to the west of Caen.

20 The English Conquest of the South: p. 295. Applied saucer brooches with a design of a Maltese Cross enclosing four outlined faces are most numerous among the Eslingas and at Kempston; a variant, similarly punched, with Six Faces, has a similar distribution. One group of Great Squareheaded brooches, classified B 6 by Leeds, and described by him as a 'striking individual group . . . the only group . . . (with) . . . a border of masks on the headplate as its distinctive feature' (Leeds *Corpus* 62) has a border of similar faces, freestanding, and is similarly distributed; three other Great Squareheaded brooches, classified by Leeds in different groups, have the same distinctive headplate border.

APPLIED SAUCER BROOCHES

with *Maltese cross* design

CAMBRIDGESHIRE	Barrington A, *TL 37 49*, 5 burials, Ashmolean Museum.
	Barrington B, *TL 37 48*, with a girdle hanger, Cambridge Museum (CASP 5, pl. iv).
	Haslingfield, *TL 41 52*, 2 burials, Ashmolean Museum (DSB 178 pl. xxvii 1).
	Linton, grave 72, *TL 56 47*, with wristclasp and squareheaded brooch, Cambridge Museum.
	Odsey (Ashwell Station), *TL* **29 38**, ACR 254, Cambridge Museum.
SUFFOLK	Lakenheath, *TL 73 82*, with Great Squarehead A 3 (14), Cambridge Museum.
HERTFORDSHIRE	King's Walden, *TL 14 22*, St. Alban's Museum.
	Ashwell, 'near the station', see Odsey, Cambridgeshire.
BEDFORDSHIRE	Kempston, *TL 03 47*, 5 burials, British Museum; BB 275 pl. xlvii and 341 pl. lxviii a.
BERKSHIRE	Frilford, *SU 43 96*, 2 burials, Ashmolean Museum.
	East Shefford, *SU 38 74* (derivative), British Museum.
NORTHAMPTONSHIRE	Kettering, *SP 87 97* (fragment), Northampton Museum.

with *Six Face* design

BEDFORDSHIRE	Kempston, *TL 03 47*, British Museum.
	Luton, *TL 08 22* (fragment), Luton Museum, and (derivative) *Ant. Jl.* 8, 1928, 180, pl. xxviii 1.
BERKSHIRE	Reading, *SU 74 73*, DSB 170 pl. xxvi 1; BB 315 pl. lviii 5.
GLOUCESTERSHIRE	Fairford, *SP 14 01*, 2 burials, DSB 164 fig. 5; 165 fig. 6.
NORTHAMPTONSHIRE	Nassington, grave 6, *TL 07 95*, with wrist clasp, *Ant. Jl.* 24, 1944, 106, pl. xxiii a (0).

GREAT SQUAREHEADED BROOCHES

Leeds *Corpus* type B 6, nos. 95–100, found at *Luton*, Beds., *TL 08 22*; *Market Overton*, Rutland, *SK 92 18*; *Fairford*, Gloucs., *SP 14 01*; *Mitcham*, Surrey, *TQ 27 68*; *Abingdon*, Berks., *SU 49 96*; *Haslingfield*, Cambs., *TL 41 52*. *Hornton*, Oxon., *SP 39 45*; *Marston*

St. Lawrence, Northants. *SP 54 43*; and *Coleshill*, Berks., *SU 23 94*. The other Square-headed brooches with similar borders are A 2, 9 *Linton Heath*, Cambs., *TL 58 48*; A 2, 10 *Tuddenham*, Suffolk, *TL 74 70*; and A 3, 27 *Orwell* (*Barrington A*), Cambs., *TL 37 49*. The concentration of finds in the Eslinga territory south-west of Cambridge suggests that this territory was Cutha's starting point and homeland.

PLACES named from Cutha (references in the appropriate EPNS county volumes). 'Lost' place names, no longer in use, are italicised.

BUCKINGHAMSHIRE	Cuddington *SP 74 12*.
OXFORDSHIRE	*Cudan hlaewe*, Cuxham, Watlington *SU 67 96*.
	Cudendone, Watlington *SU 68 95*.
	Cuddesdon *SP 59 04*.
	Cutslow, North Oxford *SP 51 11*.
GLOUCESTERSHIRE	Cudnall, Charlton Kings, Cheltenham *SO 97 21*.
WILTSHIRE	Cutteridge, North Bradley, Bradford *ST 87 56*.
SURREY	Cuddington *TQ 26 65*.
	Cudworth *TQ 28 42*.
KENT	Cudham *TQ 45 59*.
SUSSEX	*Cudnor*, Westham, Pevensey *TQ 64 04*.
	Cudlow, Climping, Bognor *SU 99 03*.

Cudanhlaewe and Cutslow in Oxfordshire suggest the burial mounds of two separate persons, both called Cutha, perhaps Cuthwulf and Cuthwine.

Further names may be recognised when the EPNS surveys of Hampshire, Berkshire and Kent are published.

A few *Cutha* names are found outside the area of this map, in Devonshire and West Somerset, in Worcester, Shropshire and Cheshire, and in the Pennines.

The Cutha names in Wessex are located on the left, Oxfordshire, bank of the Thames; as are the places that Cutha captured in 571. They suggest that Cutha's West Saxon kingdom lay east of the Thames, leaving the older Middle Thames territory west of the river, in Berkshire, to Ceawlin.

-*TUNS* taken in 571

Limbury (Luton), Beds., *TL 07 24*.
Aylesbury, Bucks., *SP 82 14*.
Benson, Oxon., *SU 62 91*.
Eynsham, Oxon. *SP 43 09*.

21 Pagan English Settlement 4: p. 297. Periods D 3 550/590 and E 570/610. See Notes to Map 3.

22 Pagan English Settlement 5: p. 305. Period F, 7th century. See Notes to Map 3. A number of sites here shown, that may only be described as 'late', might alternatively be shown on map 21.

23 The Seventh Century Kingdoms: p. 319. Many boundaries were ill-defined and short-lived. The immediate political allegiance of north-western England, and of Surrey and the London region, was variable and uncertain. The stronger kings of the West Saxons were sometimes able to assert authority over Kent and the South Saxons, and in Surrey. Their western border is shown as it was in the earlier 7th century; by the end of the century they had subdued all or most of Devon and of eastern Somerset. The Mercians at times exercised direct authority in north-western Wessex. The Northumbrians ruled

Carlisle and Galloway, but their authority did not endure; the extent of Northumbrian authority in northern Lancashire is also uncertain. London remained under the effective control of the Mercian kings; when and in what respect it was also subject to the East Saxon kingdom is uncertain.

24 Monks in Wales: p. 359. See especially Bowen SCSW.

25 Monks in Cornwall: p. 362. See especially Doble *Saints of Cornwall* and *LBS*, under the relevant names; cf. **D, E** and **L.**

26 Monks in the North: p. 371. Dedications to Columba, Kentigern, Ninian are listed in Reeves' *Adomnan* 289 ff., cf. 462; Forbes *Kalendars* 306; 372; 423 ff.; MacKinlay ACDS 2, 42 ff.; 180 ff.; 24 ff.; Arnold-Foster SCD 2, 144; 231; 223 ff. Many chantries, altars, and monastic and episcopal dependencies founded during the Middle Ages, listed by MacKinlay, are not here mapped; all however are located in the same districts as the ancient dedications, and most are immediately adjacent thereto.

27 Monks in Ireland: p. 373.

The modern county and grid reference, the name of the founder and date of foundation, as entered in the Annals or indicated in the Lives, are given. Seventh century foundations are placed in brackets. Fifth century dates are in bold type. See **E** under the saints named.

Aghaboe Leix *S 38* Cainnech c. 550.
Aran Galway *L 80* Enda (c.**470**).
Ardstraw Tyrone *H 38* Eugenius c. 530.
Armagh *H 84* Patrick (c. **450**).

(Balla) Mayo *M 28* Mo-Chua 619
Bangor Down *J 58* Comgall 558.
Begerin Wexford *T 02*, various saints, early 6th.
Birr Offaly *N 00* Brendan c. 550.

Clogher Tyrone *H 55* Mac Nissi Aengus (c. **490**).
Clonard Meath *N 64* Finnian c. 540.
Clonenagh Leix *S 39* Fintan c. 560.
Clones Monaghan *H 52* Tigernach c. 530.
Clonfert Galway *M 92* Brendan 561.
Clonmacnoise Offaly *N 02* Ciaran 547.
Coleraine Derry *C 38* bishop Cairpre c. 540.

Derry *C 41* Columba of Iona c. 545.
Devenish Fermanagh *H 24* Lasrian (Mo-Laisse) c. 540.
Dromore Down *J 25* Colman c. 540.
Duleek Meath *N 77* Cianan (c. **470**).
Durrow Offaly *N 33* Columba of Iona c. 555.

Ferns Wexford *T 05* Aedan (Maedoc) c. 585.
(Fore) West Meath *N 57* Fechin c. 640.

Kells Meath *N 77* Columba of Iona c. 560?
Kildare *N 71* Brigit (c. **490**).
Killabban Leix *S 68* Abban c. 500.
(Killala) Mayo *G 13* Cellach c. 630?

(Leighlin) Carlow *S 66* Lasrian (Mo-Laisse) c. 635.
(Lismore) Waterford *X 09* Carthacus 638.
Lothra (Lorra) Tipperary *M 90* Ruadan c. 555.
Lough Ree (Saints' Island) Galway *M 61*, various saints, mid 6th.
Louth *H 90* Mocteus (c. **495**).

(Mayo) *M 27* Colman of Lindisfarne 664.
Monasterboice Louth *O 08* Boecius (c. **480**).
Moville Down *J 57* Finnian c. 560.

Nendrum Down *J 56* Mo-Choe (c. **470**).

Rahan Offaly *N 22* Carthacus c. 580.
Raphoe Donegal *C 20* Columba of Iona c. 560.
(Roscrea) Tipperary *S 18* Cronan c. 610.

Saigir (Sierkieran) Offaly *N 10* Ciaran (c. **470**).
Sletty Leix *S 77* (late **5th**).
Swords Dublin *O 14* Columba of Iona c. 555.

(Taghmon) Wexford *S 91* Fintan Munnu c. 615.
Terryglass Tipperary *R 89* Columba of Terryglass c. 545.
Tory Island Donegal *B 84* Columba of Iona c. 560?

28 Monks in the English Kingdoms: p. 393.
Houses founded by IRISHMEN (those starred were, as far as is known, short-lived, and of limited influence): Lindisfarne, Hanbury, Burgh Castle,* Malmesbury, Abingdon, Bosham.* ANGLO-IRISH houses, founded by the immediate pupils of Aedan of Lindisfarne and others; Tyninghame, Coldingham, Melrose, Coquet Island, Gateshead, Ebchester, Hartlepool, Gilling, Whitby, Lastingham, Barrow, Bradwell, Tilbury. ENGLISH foundations: Jarrow, Wearmouth, Beverley, Bardney, Partney, Wenlock, Pershore, Fladbury, Evesham, Bredon, Crowland, Peterborough, Oundle, Ely, Gloucester, Bath, Bradford-on-Avon, Chertsey, Bermondsey, Barking. BRITISH AND ROMAN origin: St. Albans, Glastonbury. POSSIBLY OF BRITISH origin; Carlisle, Dacre, Burton, Repton, Dunwich. NORTH ITALIAN CHURCHES: Brixworth, Wing. (Wenden's Ambo, Saffron Walden, Essex, may be as early.)

DEDICATIONS

to *David*: Holme Bridge, Airmyn, Yorkshire; Farnsfield and Holme, Nottinghamshire; Wettenhall, Cheshire; Caldecote, Warwickshire; Newbold-on-Stour, Worcestershire; Moreton-in-the-Marsh, Gloucestershire; Barton, Somerset; Exeter. Dewsbury *SE* 25 22 (the *burh* of Dewi, or David, EPNS WRY 2, 184), whose church, dedicated to All Saints, was evidently rededicated by the English, may also have originated as a foundation in honour of David.
to *Gulval*: (Finstall) Worcestershire.
to *Melor*: Amesbury, Wiltshire.
to *Samson*: York; Cressage, Shropshire; Colesbourne, Gloucestershire; Cricklade, Wiltshire; Milton Abbas, Dorset; Norwich?
to *Cyngar* (Docco): Congresbury and Banwell, Somerset.
to *Winwaloe*: Norwich; Wereham (and Downham Market) Norfolk; Cockenach, Nuthamstead, Hertfordshire, cf. 314.3 note above.

See Arnold-Foster SCD and Baring-Gould LBS under these saints, and **D** and **E**.

29 Monks Abroad: p. 401. See **E** index; Kenney 486 ff.; Jedin *Atlas*, especially map 25.

The question marks draw attention to the 8th and early 9th century Christianity of the Greater Moravian empire, where the impact of Virgilius of Salzburg and of other offshoots of the work of Boniface, Permin and their successors, is difficult to assess. The architecture of many churches suggests an Anglo-Irish origin. The material is comprehensively surveyed by V.Richter in *Magna Moravia* 121–360, with plans of nearly 500 churches, and an immense bibliography; the argument is however obscured by rigid word play and an unreal antithesis between the terms 'iroschottisch', 'angelsaechsisch', 'Carolingian', 'Bavarian', 'Benedictine' etc.; cf. the short discussion and views summarised by Hruby *Staré Mesto* 177–178. Influence from the second generation of the Anglo-Irish foundations in German lands was considerable, whatever the labels applied to them. The artificial term 'iroschottisch' mistakes both the national and religious realities of the monks in central Europe, cf. n. 403.4.

30-36 English Colonisation 1-7: pp. 469 ff. Maps 30, 33 and 34 are based, with permission, on those of J.M.Dodgson MA 10, 1966, 7 ff., and on map 21 above. Maps 31–36 make use of additional material, published and unpublished, collected by EPNS.

31 Central Bedfordshire: p. 471. For the cemeteries see *Beds. Arch. Jl.* 1, 1962, 63 ff. The *-inga(s)* names are Wooton Pillinge *TL 009 405*; Worthy End *TL 038 339*; Lidlington *SP 991 388*; Kitchen End *TL 074 332*; EPNS Beds. 87; 150; 77; 161.

32 Settlement by . . . Individuals: p. 473. The *-ingtun* symbol is an approximate indicator. It is at present possible to distinguish between *-ingtun*, *-ingatun*, and *-ingastun* only in a few counties; and early evidence is wanting for many names. It has not yet been possible to distinguish systematically the places with these terminations that begin with a personal name from those prefixed by a geographical, folk or other name.

Where information is available, a considerable majority of the places with these endings appear to derive from *-ingtun* prefixed by a personal name, implying a colony planted by a great man, accompanied by followers and dependents. The proportion of personal *-ingtuns* among the various forms of the ending seems to increase towards the west country. The symbols on the map are not therefore strictly comparable with those for *-worth* and *-cote*; they do not indicate a recorded number of individual settlements, but a category of names within which such settlements are likely to be numerous. Closer local study is likely to give a more accurate view of the proportions in different districts of settlements by substantial independent freemen, by dependent cottagers, and by lords.

33, 34 Kent etc.: Essex etc.: pp. 476, 477. Places called Sheepcote and Saltcote are omitted.

35 The North and West: p. 478. Based on EPNE maps 3, 4 and 8, corrected by separate county volumes, and by other information when available. The names Newbottle, etc., are omitted, since by definition they do not belong to the earliest phase of settlement in their region.

36 -Botl . . . in the South: p. 479. Based on EPNE map 8 and other information, when available; the names Newbottle etc. are included to show their relationship to other *-botl* names.

INDEX

Italic figures refer to the notes.

An asterisk (*) indicates a note on the name or word concerned.

The letters f (*filius*) and m (*mac* or *map*) mean 'son of'; f. means 'following'.

Bold letters, as **A**, refer to the sections of *Arthurian Sources* (p. 519 above).

Modern conventions on the spelling of names vary, and are often arbitrary; thus, Aethelbert or Ethelbert are nowadays equally familiar, Athelbert unfamiliar, but Athelstan prevails over Ethelstan or Aethelstan. The most recognisable form is normally used. Irish names are normally given in plain English spelling.